History 111

Out of Many

A History of the American People

CUSTOM EDITION FOR UNIVERSITY OF CINCINNATI

John Mack Faragher
Mari Jo Buhle
Daniel Czitrom
Susan H. Armitage

Taken From:

Out of Many: A History of the American People, Fifth Edition
by John Mack Faragher, Mari Jo Buhle, Daniel Czitrom, Susan H. Armitage

Learning Solutions

New York   Boston   San Francisco
London   Toronto   Sydney   Tokyo   Singapore   Madrid
Mexico City   Munich   Paris   Cape Town   Hong Kong   Montreal

Cover Art: Courtesy of Photodisc/Getty Images and Comstock

Taken from:

Out of Many: A History of the American People, Fifth Edition
by John Mack Faragher, Mari Jo Buhle, Daniel Czitrom, Susan H. Armitage
Copyright © 2009, 2006, 2005, 2003, 2000 by Pearson Education, Inc.
Published by Prentice Hall
Upper Saddle River, New Jersey 07458

Printed in the United States of America

2 3 4 5 6 7 8 9 10   V011   14 13 12 11 10 09

2009300166

WH

www.pearsonhighered.com

ISBN 10: 0-558-38219-3
ISBN 13: 978-0-558-38219-3

13

14

17

RECONSTRUCTION, 1863–1877   432

Seeing History

Interpreting the Past

18

CONQUEST AND SURVIVAL, 1860–1900   464

Seeing History

19

PRODUCTION AND CONSUMPTION IN THE GILDED AGE, 1865–1900   498

20

DEMOCRACY AND EMPIRE, 1870–1900   524

21

URBAN AMERICA AND THE PROGRESSIVE ERA, 1900–1917 556

22

A GLOBAL POWER, 1901–1920 590

23

THE TWENTIES, 1920–1929   622

Seeing History

Interpreting the Past

MAPS

Denotes Interactive Map Exploration

CHARTS, GRAPHS & TABLES

Seeing History

Interpreting the Past

American Communities

OVERVIEW TABLES

Out of Many: A History of the American People, fifth edition, offers a distinctive and timely approach to American history, highlighting the experiences of diverse communities of Americans in the unfolding story of our country. The stories of these communities offer a way of examining the complex historical forces shaping people's lives at various moments in our past. The debates and conflicts surrounding the most momentous issues in our national life—independence, emerging democracy, slavery, westward settlement, imperial expansion, economic depression, war, technological change—were largely worked out in the context of local communities. Through communities we focus on the persistent tensions between everyday life and those larger decisions and events that continually reshape the circumstances of local life.

Each chapter opens with a description of a representative community. Some of these portraits feature American communities struggling with one another: African slaves and English masters on the rice plantations of colonial Georgia, or *Tejanos* and Americans during the Texas war of independence. Other chapters feature portraits of communities facing social change: the feminists of Seneca Falls, New York, in 1848, or the African Americans of Montgomery, Alabama, in 1955. As the story unfolds we find communities growing to include ever larger groups of Americans: the soldiers from every colony who forged the Continental Army into a patriotic national force at Valley Forge during the American Revolution, or the moviegoers who aspired to a collective dream of material prosperity and upward mobility during the 1920s.

Out of Many is also the only American history text with a truly continental perspective. With community vignettes from New England to the South, the Midwest to the far West, we encourage students to appreciate the great expanse of our nation. For example, a vignette of seventeenth-century Santa Fé, New Mexico, illustrates the founding of the first European settlements in the New World. We present territorial expansion into the American West from the viewpoint of the Mandan villagers of the upper Missouri River of North Dakota. A continental perspective drives home to students that American history has never been the preserve of any particular region.

Out of Many includes extensive coverage of our diverse heritage. Our country is appropriately known as "a nation of immigrants," and the history of immigration to America, from the seventeenth to the twenty-first centuries, is fully integrated into the text. There is sustained and close attention to our place in the world, with special emphasis on our relations with the nations of the Western Hemisphere, especially our near neighbors, Canada and Mexico.

In these ways *Out of Many* breaks new ground, but without compromising its coverage of the traditional turning points that we believe are critically important to an understanding of the American past. *Out of Many* also looks back in a new and comprehensive way—from the vantage point of the beginning of a new century and the end of the Cold War—at the salient events of the last fifty years and their impact on American communities. The community focus of *Out of Many* weaves the stories of the people and the nation into a single compelling narrative.

Out of Many, fifth edition, is completely updated with the most recent scholarship on the history of America and the United States. All the chapters have been extensively reviewed, revised, and rewritten. The final chapter details the tumultuous events of the new century, including a completely new section on the "war on terror," and concluding with the national election of 2004. Throughout the book the text and graphics are presented in a stunning new design. Moreover, this edition incorporates two important new features designed to bring history vividly alive for students: *Interpreting the Past*, featuring primary sources on a controversial provocative historical issue and *Seeing History*, carefully chosen images that show how visual sources can illuminate their understanding of American history.

SPECIAL FEATURES

With each edition of *Out of Many, Teaching and Learning Classroom Edition*, we have sought to strengthen its unique integration of the best of traditional American history with its innovative community-based focus and strong continental perspective and engage students through special features that encourage their exploration of the questions that historians seek to answer about the past. This new version is no exception. A wealth of special features and pedagogical aids reinforces our narrative and motivates students desire to understand and appreciate America's history. The special walkthrough on pages xxiii–xlii highlights these features.

COMMUNITY AND DIVERSITY

This special introductory essay begins students' journey into the narrative history that unfolds in *Out of Many*. The essay acquaints students with the major themes of the book and provides them with a framework for understanding American History. (pp. xliii–xlv)

SUPPLEMENTARY MATERIAL

Out of Many is supported by an extensive supplements package for instructors and students that gives flexibility to the process of teaching and learning. A full description of the supplements available with the text is provided on page xlii.

ACKNOWLEDGMENTS

In the years it has taken to bring *Out of Many* from idea to reality and to improve it in successive editions, we have often been reminded that although writing history sometimes feels like isolated work, it actually involves a collective effort. We want to thank the dozens of people whose efforts have made the publication of this book possible.

We wish to thank our many friends at Prentice Hall for their efforts in creating the fifth edition of *Out of Many*: Yolanda de Rooy, President; Charlyce Jones Owen, Publisher; Jeannine Cilotta and James Miller, Development Editors; Rochelle Diogenes, Editor-in-Chief, Development Sue Westmoreland, Executive Marketing Manager; Brandy Dawson, Director of Marketing; Mayda Bosco, Media Editor; Denise Brown, Production Liaison; Mary Carnis, Managing Editor; Blair Brown, Cover Designer; Fiorella Mari, Production Editor; and Donna Mulder, Copyeditor. We also thank John Reisbord for his editorial contributions to the fifth edition.

Although we share joint responsibility for the entire book, the chapters were individually authored: John Mack Faragher wrote chapters 1–8; Susan Armitage wrote chapters 9–16; Mari Jo Buhle wrote chapters 18–20, 25–26, 29; and Daniel Czitrom wrote chapters 17, 21–24, 27–28. (For this edition Buhle and Czitrom co-authored Chapters 30–31.)

Each of us depended on a great deal of support and assistance with the research and writing that went into this book. We want to thank: Kathryn Abbott, Nan Boyd, Krista Comer, Jennifer Cote, Crista DeLuzio, Keith Edgerton, Carol Frost, Jesse Hoffnung Garskof, Pailin Gaither, Jane Gerhard, Todd Gernes, Mark Krasovic, Melani McAlister, Cristi, Rebecca McKenna, and Mitchell, J. C. Mutchler, Keith Peterson, Alan Pinkham, Tricia Rose, Gina Rourke, Jessica Shubow, Gordon P. Utz Jr., Maura Young, Teresa Bill, Gill Frank, and Naoko Shibusawa.

Our families and close friends have been supportive and ever so patient over the many years we have devoted to this project. But we want especially to thank Paul Buhle, Meryl Fingrutd, Bob Greene, and Michele Hoffnung.

John Mack Faragher John Mack Faragher is Arthur Unobskey Professor of American History and director of the Howard R. Lamar Center for the Study of Frontiers and Borders at Yale University. Born in Arizona and raised in southern California, he received his B.A. at the University of California, Riverside, and his Ph.D. at Yale University. He is the author of *Women and Men on the Overland Trail* (1979), *Sugar Creek: Life on the Illinois Prairie* (1986), *Daniel Boone: The Life and Legend of an American Pioneer* (1992), *The American West: A New Interpretive History* (2000), and *A Great and Noble Scheme: The Tragic Story of the Expulsion of the French Acadians from their American Homeland* (2005).

Daniel Czitrom Daniel Czitrom is Professor of History at Mount Holyoke College. Born and raised in New York City, he received his B.A. from the State University of New York at Binghamton and his M.A. and Ph.D. from the University of Wisconsin, Madison. He is the author of *Media and the American Mind: From Morse to McLuhan* (1982), which won the First Books Award of the American Historical Association and has been translated into Spanish and Chinese. He is co-author of *Rediscovering Jacob Riis: Exposure Journalism and Photography in Turn of the Century New York* (2007). He has served as a historical consultant and featured on-camera commentator for several documentary film projects, including the PBS productions *New York: A Documentary Film; American Photography: A Century of Images*; and *The Great Transatlantic Cable*. He currently serves on the Executive Board of the Organization of American Historians.

Mari Jo Buhle Mari Jo Buhle is William R. Kenan Jr. University Professor and Professor of American Civilization and History at Brown University, specializing in American women's history. She received her B.A. from the University of Illinois, Urbana–Champaign, and her Ph.D. from the University of Wisconsin, Madison. She is the author of *Women and American Socialism, 1870–1920* (1981) and *Feminism and Its Discontents: A Century of Struggle with Psychoanalysis* (1998). She is also coeditor of *Encyclopedia of the American Left*, second edition (1998). Professor Buhle held a fellowship (1991–1996) from the John D. and Catherine T. MacArthur Foundation.

Susan H. Armitage Susan H. Armitage is Claudius O. and Mary R. Johnson Distinguished Professor of History at Washington State University. She earned her Ph.D. from the London School of Economics and Political Science. Among her many publications on western women's history are three coedited books, *The Women's West* (1987), *So Much To Be Done: Women on the Mining and Ranching Frontier* (1991), and *Writing the Range: Race, Class, and Culture in the Women's West* (1997). She currently serves as an editor of a series of books on women and American history for the University of Illinois Press.

Out of Many

Dear Reader,

Out of Many grew out of our years of experience teaching the American history survey course. When we were young professors, the old narrative of strict political history was in the process of being supplemented with a new narrative of social history. But the two remained mostly unconnected. New textbooks sequestered these two narratives in separate chapters. Isn't there a way, we wondered, to write a new, unified narrative of American history, in which political and social history might be combined? This was the inspiration behind *Out of Many*, one of the most successful American history textbooks of this generation. Organized around the theme of American communities, the text offers a single, engaging narrative of American social, economic, and political history.

We began working on this book twenty years ago. It has been a long and rewarding journey. We are proud to have been the first American history college text to put the diversity of America's peoples at the center of our historical experience. Our narrative weaves the distinct experiences and voices of northerners, southerners, and westerners, of African Americans, Latinos, and immigrants, of women and men, throughout each chapter. Coming ourselves from different backgrounds and from different regions of the country, we developed a continental approach to the American past, demonstrating how each region has been closely linked to the broader currents of global development. It is our hope that *Out of Many* will best help students understand the history that has produced the increasingly complex America of the twenty-first century.

*O*ut *of* Many, you experience America's history...

Out of Many provides truly integrated coverage of American social and political history. The authors weave the everyday stories of individuals and communities and the major events of the nation's political history into a single compelling narrative that both enlightens and inspires students. This integrated approach to history offers students the best possible insight into the American experience.

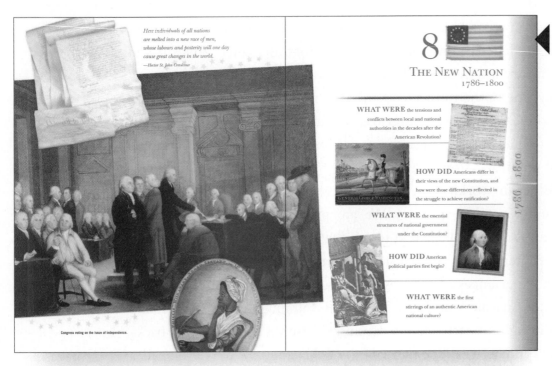

Here individuals of all nations are melted into a new race of men, whose labours and posterity will one day cause great changes in the world.
—Hector St. John Crèvecœur

Congress voting on the issue of independence.

8
THE NEW NATION
1786–1800

WHAT WERE the tensions and conflicts between local and national authorities in the decades after the American Revolution?

GENERAL GEORGE WASHINGTON

HOW DID Americans differ in their views of the new Constitution, and how were those differences reflected in the struggle to achieve ratification?

WHAT WERE the essential structures of national government under the Constitution?

HOW DID American political parties first begin?

WHAT WERE the first stirrings of an authentic American national culture?

1786   1800

The TLC Edition of *Out of Many* offers **an engaging visual presentation** to pique—and retain—student interest. The text is packed with **stunning visuals** including chapter openers that highlight key events in the chapter. **Chapter opening questions** provide an overview and guide to the important concepts students need to learn.

The TLC Edition of *Out of Many* includes **a variety of pedagogical tools** to help students organize and reinforce their learning.

AMERICAN COMMUNITIES
Expansion Touches Mandan Villages on the Upper Missouri

IN MID-OCTOBER 1804, NEWS ARRIVED AT THE MANDAN VILLAGES, prominently situated on bluffs overlooking the upper Missouri River, that an American military party led by Meriwether Lewis and William Clark was coming up the river. The principal chiefs, hoping for expanded trade and support against their enemies the Sioux, welcomed these first American visitors. As the expedition's three boats and forty-three men approached the village, Clark wrote, "great numbers on both sides flocked down to the bank to view us." That evening, the Mandans welcomed the Americans with an enthusiastic dance and gifts of food.

Lewis and Clark had been sent by President Thomas Jefferson to survey the Louisiana Purchase and to find an overland route to the Pacific Ocean. They were also instructed to inform the Indians that they now owed loyalty—and trade—to the American government. Meeting with the village chiefs, the Americans off-----

ies, the party reached the Pacific Ocean at the mouth of the Columbia River, where they spent the winter. Overdue and feared lost, they returned in triumph to St. Louis in September 1806. Before long the Americans had established Fort Clark at the Mandan villages, giving American traders a base for challenging British dominance of the western fur trade. The permanent American presence brought increased contact, and with it much more disease. In 1837, a terrible smallpox epidemic carried away the vast majority of the Mandans, reducing the population to fewer than 150. Four Bears, a Mandan chief who had been a child at the time of the Lewis and Clark visit, spoke these last words to the remnants of his people:

"I have loved the whites," he declared. "I have lived with them ever since I was a boy." But in return for the kindness of the Mandans, the Americans had brought this plague. "I do not fear death, my friends," he said, "but to die with my face rotten, that even the wolves will shrink with horror at seeing me, and ...ay to themselves, that is Four Bears, the friend of the whites. ...have deceived me," he pronounced with his last breath. ...always considered as brothers turned ...

Out of Many is among the first texts to focus on the many ethnic and multicultural communities that have played a vital role in the evolution of the United States. Each chapter begins with an *American Community* feature that shows how the events discussed in the chapter affected a particular community. These snapshots of life add up to a well-rounded understanding of the American story.

Creating Celebrity

Seeing History

A common definition for "celebrity" is one who is famous for being famous. Although politics, the arts, science, and the military have produced famous people for centuries, the celebrity is a twentieth-century phenomenon, one closely linked to the emergence of modern forms of mass media. In the 1920s Hollywood's "star system," along with tabloid newspapers and the new profession of public relations, created the modern celebrity. Film producers were at first wary of identifying screen actors by name, but they soon discovered that promoting popular leading actors would boost the box office for their movies. The use of "close-ups" in movies and the fact that screen images were literally larger than life distinguished the images of film actors from, say, stage performers or opera singers.

WHAT VISUAL themes strike you as most powerful in the accompanying images? How do they compare to celebrity images of today? Why do you think male stars such as Valentino and Fairbanks were so often portrayed as exotic foreigners?

Fans identified with their favorites in contradictory ways. Stars like Charlie Chaplin and Mary Pickford were like royalty. Audiences were also curious about the stars' private lives. Film studios took advantage of this curiosity by carefully controlling the public i... ...s releases, planted stories in newspapers, and ca... ...arances. By the 1920s film stars were essenti... ...uiring enormous capital investment. ∎

New ***Seeing History*** features offer in-depth analysis of an image or series of images from a particular historical period. These visually engaging features help students to understand how various individuals and events have been depicted throughout American history and underscore the important role images and illustrations play in understanding and interpreting the past.

New to the Fifth Edition, ***Interpreting the Past*** features provide documents and images on a key event or topic to help students see how historians understand and interpret the past. A critical thinking question provides students with the opportunity to analyze how these historical records illuminate this event or topic.

Realities of Freedom

The Freedmen's Bureau established in 1865 by Congress provided freedmen with clothing, temporary shelter, food, and series of freedmen's schools across the South. Southern response was to fall into the use of terror to deter blacks from becoming economically independent using the agencies of groups like the Ku Klux Klan. Sharecropping, tenant farming, and peonage were insidious economic arrangements that placed whites and blacks in a form of economic slavery to large land holders in the South of the post-Civil War era.

The story of African Americans after the end of slavery is complex and varied. Some blacks attempted to seek out better places to establish their new lives while others remained in the security of the only home they had known as slaves. ∎

FOLLOWING EMANCIPATION, what economic and social opportunities existed for African Americans in the United States? How did these opportunities change the lives of freedmen after the official end to slavery?

AN ACT TO ESTABLISH A BUREAU FOR THE RELIEF OF FREEDMEN AND REFUGEES, 1865

BE IT enacted, That there is hereby established in the War Department, to continue during the present war of rebellion, and for one year thereafter, a bureau of refugees, freedmen, and abandoned lands, to which shall be committed, as hereinafter provided, the supervision and management of all abandoned lands, and the control of all subjects relating to refugees and freedmen from rebel states, or from any district of country within the territory embraced in the operations of the army, under such rules and regulations as may be prescribed by the head of the bureau and approved by the President. The said bureau shall be under the management and control of a commissioner to be appointed by the President, by and with the advice and consent of the Senate...∎

African-American family working together in the cotton fields.

WHEN WE WORKED ON SHARES, WE COULDN'T MAKE NOTHING

AFTER SLAVERY we had to get in before night too. If you didn't, Ku Klux would drive you in. They would come and visit you anyway.... When he got you good and scared he would drive on away. They would whip you if they would catch you out in the night time...

I've forgot who it is that that told us that we was free. Somebody come and told us we're free now. I done forgot who it was.

After freedom, we worked on shares a while. Then we rented. When we worked on shares, we couldn't make nothing, just overalls and something to eat. Half went to the other man and you would destroy your half if you weren't careful. A man that didn't know how to count would always lose. He might lose anyhow. They didn't give no itemized statement. No, you just had to take their word. They never give you no details. They just say you owe so much. No matter how good account you kept, you had to go by their account and now, Brother, I'm tellin' you the truth about this. It's been that way for a long time. You had to take the white man's work on note, and everything. Anything you

A Share croppers and their families were evicted from the plantation they were working after being convicted of engaging in a conspiracy to retain their homes. This picture was taken just after the evictions before the families were moved into a tent colony.

wanted, you could git if you were a good hand. You could git anything you wanted as long as you worked. If you didn't make no money, that's all right; they would advance you more. But you better not leave him, you better not try to leave and get caught. They'd keep you in debt. . . . Anything that kept you a slave because he was always right and you were always wrong. . . . ∎

SHARE CROPPER CONTRACT, 1882

To every one appling to rent land upon shares, the following conditions must be read, and agreed to.

To every 30 or 35 acres, I agree to furnish the team, plow, and farming implements, except cotton planters, and I do not agree to furnish a cart to every cropper. The croppers are to have half of the cotton, corn and fodder (and peas and pumpkins and potatoes if any are planted...

Croppers are to have no part or interest in the cotton seed raised from the crop planted and worked by them. No vine crops of any description, that is, no watermelons, muskmelons,...squashes or anything of that kind, except peas and pumpkins, and potatoes, are to be planted in the cotton or corn. All must work under my direction. All plantation work to be done by the croppers....

For every mule or horse furnished by me there must be 1000 sized rails...hauled, and the fence repaired as far as they will go, the fence to be torn down and put up from the bottom if I so direct. All croppers to haul rails and work on fence whenever I may order. Rails to be split when I may say. . . .

Each cropper must keep in good repair all bridges in his crop or over ditches that he has to clean out and when a bridge needs repairing that is outside of all their crops... then any one that I call on must repair it....

No cropper to work off the plantation when there is any work to be done on the land he has rented, or when his work is needed by me or other croppers. Trees to be cut down on Orchard, House field & Evanson fences, leaving such as I may designate. . . . . ∎

Interpreting the Past

Out *of* Many, you experience America's history...

Out of Many's Teaching and Learning Classroom (TLC) Edition offers an engaging visual design and numerous tools that help students learn and review the material.

---

depressed Northeast to boost the region's population (see Map 30.2).

The Sunbelt witnessed a dramatic turnaround in demographic and economic trends. Southern cities reversed the century-long trend of out-migration among African Americans. The Southwest and West changed yet more dramatically. California became the nation's most populous state; Texas moved to third, behind New York. Former farms and deserts were turned almost overnight into huge metropolitan areas ringed by new automobile-dependent suburbs. Phoenix grew from 664,000 in 1960 to 1,509,000 in 1980, Las Vegas from 127,000 to 463,000.

Much Sunbelt wealth tended to be temporary or sharply cyclical, producing a boom-and-bust economy. Income was also distributed unevenly. Older Hispanic populations made only modest gains, while recent Mexican immigrants and Indian peoples suffered from a combination of low wages and poor public services. The Sunbelt states directed their tax and federal dollars to strengthening police forces, building roads or sanitation systems for the expanding suburbs, and creating budget surpluses.

The "Snowbelt" (or "Rustbelt") states, longtime centers of voting strength for the Democratic Party, meanwhile suffered severe population losses accompanying the sharp decline of industry.

New York City offered a spectacular example of decline. A fiscal crisis in 1975 forced Democratic Mayor Abraham Beame to choose between wage freezes for public employees and devastating cuts and layoffs. Eventually, with the municipal government teetering on the brink of bankruptcy, he chose both. In response to cutbacks in mass transit and the deterioration of municipal services, a large sector of the m...

THE ENDANGERED ENVIRONMENT

The environmental downside of the post–World War II economy... painfully evident. Cutting across nearly all population... concern for the environment reached into conservative ar... South with warnings of the dangers of toxic wastes, the de... and the ruin of fishing ind... ...matic in Love Canal, ne... ...cer and h...

WHAT MAJOR groups made up the Southern Republicans?

myhistorylab
Review Summary

Union League Republican party organizations in Northern cities that became an important organizing device among freedmen in Southern cities after 1865.

Carpetbaggers Northern transplants to the South, many of whom were Union soldiers who stayed in the South after the war.

...regi... ican political activ... out the South.

Begun during the war... club, the Union League now be... Union League chapters brought together... Freedmen's Bureau agents to demand the vote and... tion against African Americans. It brought out African American voters, instructed freedmen in the rights and duties of citizenship, and promoted Republican candidates. Not surprisingly, newly enfranchised freedmen voted Republican and formed the core of the Republican Party in the South. For most ordinary African Americans, politics was inseparable from economic issues, especially the land question. Grassroots political organizations frequently intervened in local disputes with planters over the terms of labor contracts. African American political groups closely followed the congressional debates over Reconstruction policy and agitated for land confiscation and distribution. Perhaps most important, politics was the only arena where black and white Southerners might engage each other on an equal basis.

SOUTHERN POLITICS AND SOCIETY

By the summer of 1868, when the South had returned to the Union, the majority of Republicans believed the task of Reconstruction to be finished. Ultimately, they put their faith in a political solution to the problems facing the vanquished South. Most Republican congressmen were moderates, conceiving Reconstruction in limited terms. They rejected radical calls for confiscation and redistribution of land, as well as permanent military rule of the South. The Reconstruction Acts of 1867 and 1868 laid out the requirements for the readmission of southern states, along with the procedures for forming and electing new governments.

Yet over the next decade, the political structure created in the southern states proved too restricted and fragile to sustain itself. To most southern whites, the active participation of African Americans in politics seemed extremely dangerous. Federal troops were needed to protect Republican governments and their supporters from violent opposition. Congressional action to monitor southern elections and protect black voting rights became routine. Despite initial successes, southern Republicanism proved an unstable coalition of often conflicting elements, unable to sustain effective power for very long. By 1877, Democrats had regained political control of all the former Confederate states.

SOUTHERN REPUBLICANS

Three major groups composed the fledgling Republican coalition in the postwar South. African American voters made up a large majority of southern Republicans throughout the Reconstruction era. Yet African Americans outnumbered whites in only three southern states; Republicans would have to attract white support to win elections and sustain power.

A second group consisted of white Northerners, derisively called "**carpetbaggers**" by native white Southerners. Most were veterans of the Union army who stayed in the South after the war. Others included Freedmen's Bureau agents and businessmen who had invested capital in cotton plantations and other enterprises. Although they made up a tiny percentage of the population, carpetbaggers played

---

Critical thinking questions from the chapter opener are repeated in the margins at each major section of the chapter to promote critical reading. **Quick reviews** help students review selected topics as they go through the chapter.

A **running glossary** provides definitions for key terms and concepts, which are then listed at the end of the chapter for review.

...through an engaging learner-centered format.

OVERVIEW | Currents of Progressivism

	Key Figures	Issues
Local Communities	Jane Addams, Lillian Wald, Florence Kelley, Frederic C. Howe, Samuel Jones	• Improving health, education, welfare in urban immigrant neighborhoods • Child labor, eight-hour day • Celebrating immigrant cultures • Reforming urban politics • Municipal ownership/regulation of utilities
State	Robert M. La Follette, Hiram Johnson, Al Smith	• Limiting power of railroads, other corporations • Improving civil service • Direct democracy • Applying academic scholarship to human needs
National	James K. Vardaman, Hoke Smith, Theodore Roosevelt, Woodrow Wilson	• Disfranchisement of African Americans • Trust-busting • Conservation and western development • National regulation of corporate and financial excesses • Reform of national banking
Intellectual/Cultural	Jacob Riis, Lincoln Steffens, Ida Tarbell, Upton Sinclair, S. S. McClure	• Muckraking
	John Dewey, Louis Brandeis, Edwin A. Ross	• Education reform • Sociological jurisprudence • Empowering "ethical elite"

myhistorylab

Overview: *Currents of Progressivism*

She offered Henry Street as a meeting place to the National Negro Conference in 1909, out of which emerged the National Association for the Advancement of Colored People.

Social reformer Florence Kelley helped direct the support of the settl... behind groundbreaking state and federal lab...

Overview tables help students review key points of complex topics and issues. References to the **Myhistorylab** website and the **Primary Source CDROM** are included in the margins throughout the chapters to alert students to documents, activities, and additional content related to topics in the chapters.

Map Explorations are selected maps that can be explored interactively on the Web and MyHistoryLab. **Critical thinking questions** help to strengthen map analysis skills and geographic literacy.

---

depressed Northeast to boost the region's population (see Map 30.2).

The Sunbelt witnessed a dramatic turnaround in demographic and economic trends. Southern cities reversed the century-long trend of out-migration among African Americans. The Southwest and West changed yet more dramatically. California became the nation's most populous state; Texas moved to third, behind New York. Former farms and deserts were turned almost overnight into huge metropolitan areas ringed by new automobile-dependent suburbs. Phoenix grew from 664,000 in 1960 to 1,509,000 in 1980, Las Vegas from 127,000 to 463,000.

Much Sunbelt wealth tended to be temporary or sharply cyclical, producing a boom-and-bust economy. Income was also distributed unevenly. Older Hispanic populations made only modest gains, while recent Mexican immigrants and Indian peoples suffered from a combination of low wages and poor public services. The Sunbelt states directed their tax and federal dollars to strengthening police forces, building roads or sanitation systems for the expanding suburbs, and creating budget surpluses.

The "Snowbelt" (or "Rustbelt") states, longtime centers of voting strength for the Democratic Party, meanwhile suffered severe population losses accompanying the sharp decline of industry.

New York City offered a spectacular example of decline. A fiscal crisis in 1975 forced Democratic Mayor Abraham Beame to choose between wage freezes for public employees and devastating cuts and layoffs. Eventually, with the municipal government teetering on the brink of bankruptcy, he chose both. In respon... ...backs in mass transit and the deteriorati... ...r of the middle class fled.

MAP EXPLORATION

To explore an interactive version of this map, go to http://www.prenhall.com/faraghertlc/map30.2

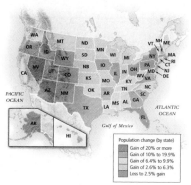

Population change (by state)
Gain of 20% or more
Gain of 10% to 19.9%
Gain of 6.4% to 9.9%
Gain of 2.6% to 6.3%
Loss to 2.5% gain

MAP 30.2
Population Shifts, 1970–80 Industrial decline in the Northeast coincided with an economic boom in the Sunbelt, encouraging millions of Americans to head for warmer climates and better jobs.

HOW WERE the changes in population between 1970 and 1980 reflected in the American economy?

Out of Many, you experience America's history...

Every new copy of *Out of Many* includes the *Primary Source: Documents in U.S. History* CD-ROM. This versatile resource offers 400 primary source documents—in accessible PDF format—and over 350 images and maps. It also provides a number of features that help students work with documents, including headnotes, focus questions, highlighting and note-taking tools, and a glossary of terms for certain documents.

Primary Source
Documents in U.S. History

View Tutorial | Help | Exit

| Chapter | Theme | Author | Timeline | Recent Documents |

▶ Chapter 1: A CONTINENT OF VILLAGES TO 1500

▶ Chapter 2: WHEN WORLDS COLLIDE 1492-1590

▶ Chapter 3: PLANTING COLONIES IN NORTH AMERICA 1588-1701

▶ Chapter 4: SLAVERY AND EMPIRE 1441-1770

▶ Chapter 5: THE CULTURES OF COLONIAL NORTH AMERICA 1700-1780

▶ Chapter 6: FROM EMPIRE TO INDEPENDENCE 1750-1776

▶ Chapter 7: THE AMERICAN REVOLUTION 1776-1786

▶ Chapter 8: THE NEW NATION 1786-1800

▶ Chapter 9: AN AGRARIAN REPUBLIC 1790-1824

▶ Chapter 10: THE SOUTH AND SLAVERY 1790s-1850s

▶ Chapter 11: THE GROWTH OF DEMOCRACY 1824-1840

▶ Chapter 12: INDUSTRY AND THE NORTH 1790s-1840s

▶ Chapter 13: COMING TO TERMS WITH THE NEW AGE 1820s-1850s

▶ Chapter 14: THE TERRITORIAL EXPANSION OF THE UNITED STATES 1830s-1850s

An **easy navigation function** allows students to search for documents by chapter, theme, author, or timeline.

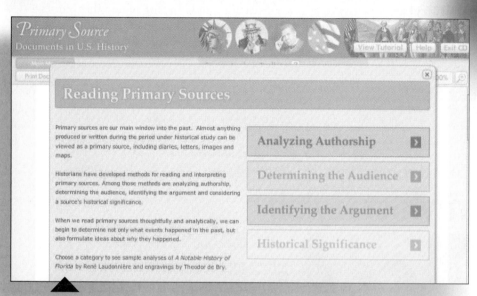

An **interactive tutorial** offers strategies for reading, analyzing, and writing about various types of documents.

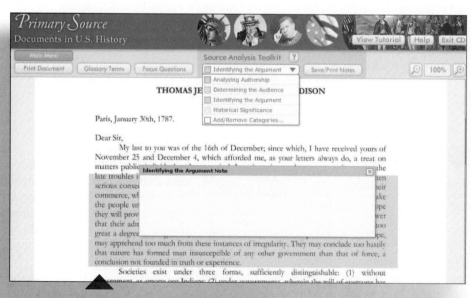

An accessible *Source Analysis Toolkit* helps students easily utilize reading, analyzing, and writing tools.

Out of Many, you experience America's history...

MyHistoryLab is an easy to use online teaching and learning system that provides helpful tools to both students and instructors. In addition to numerous instructor and student resources, it includes a complete e-book version of *Out of Many*, making an interactive online text available to students.

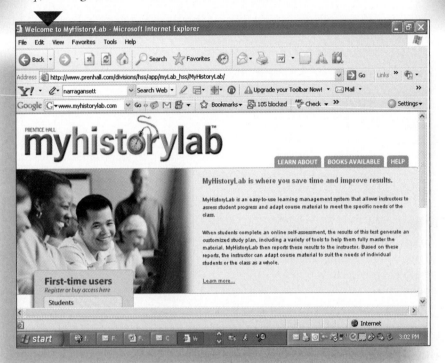

For students

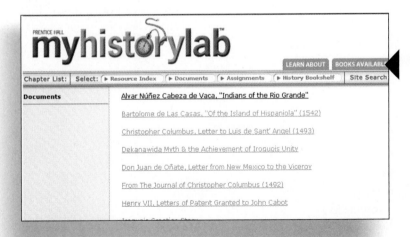

MyHistoryLab is packed with **readings that expand upon the material** found in the text. These include over 300 primary source documents with questions for analysis as well as classic works such as Thomas Paine's *Common Sense*.

...with online resources available through MyHistoryLab.

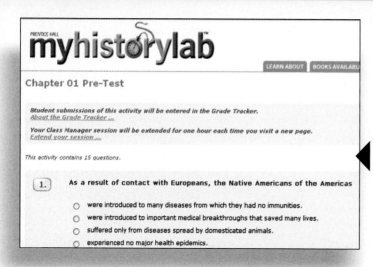

MyHistoryLab offers students various **review and assessment tools** in one convenient on-line platform. Self-study quizzes with targeted feedback help students assess their progress. A study guide, PowerPoint™ presentations, and key terms flashcards help students master the material in preparation for exams.

MyHistoryLab interactive activities and exercises let students explore materials from the text in an engaging fashion. MyHistoryLab brings U.S. history to life via *Exploring America* interactive learning activities, map explorations, animation, and audio and video clips.

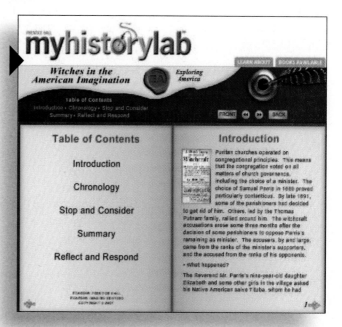

For instructors

MyHistoryLab is a one-stop collection of instructional material for teaching from *Out of Many*, including the instructor's manual, the test item file, images, maps, charts, and graphs from the text, video and audio clips, and PowerPoint™ lecture presentations. In addition, MyHistoryLab provides instructor access to all student resources.

For more information, contact your local Pearson sales representative or visit www.myhistorylab.com and click Prentice Hall.

_O_ut of Many, you experience America's history…

…with tools for instructors and students.

Prentice Hall is proud to offer a number of supplementary resources that help students and instructors get the most from _Out of Many_.

For students

- A robust **Study Guide** provides practice tests, essay questions, chronologies, an expanded map skills section, and _Interpreting the Past_ activities for each chapter.
  For **Volume I**: 978-0-13-602836-9
  For **Volume II**: 978-0-13-602835-2

- A full-color **Atlas of United States History** offers maps and charts depicting crucial times and events in U.S. History. An index lists historically important places, areas, events, and geographical features.
  978-0-13-603349-3

- **VangoNotes** downloadable audio study guides are ideal for both concept review and exam preparation. The content includes _Big Ideas_ overviews, practice tests, audio flashcards of key terms, and _Rapid Review_ quick drill sessions.
  www.vangonotes.com

- The print version of **Primary Source: Documents in U.S. History** presents a collection of more than 300 primary source documents that directly relate to the themes and content of the text.
  For **Volumes I**: 978-0-13-605198-5
  For **Volume II**: 978-0-13-605199-2

For instructors

- The **Instructor's Resource Manual** contains everything instructors need for developing and preparing lecture presentations, including chapter outlines and overviews, lecture topics, discussion questions, and information about audio-visual resources. It also includes a new section on teaching American history.
  ISBN: 978-0-13-606049-9

- An **Instructor's Resource CD-ROM** includes all of the instructor supplements, multimedia resources, images, and art from the text.
  ISBN: 978-0-13-606052-9

- The **Test Item File** contains more than 3,000 multiple-choice, identification, matching, and essay questions.
  ISBN: 978-0-13-606051-2

- **Test Generator**—a computerized test management program available for Windows and Macintosh environments—allows instructors to design their own exams by selecting items from the Test Item File. Instructors may download the Test Gen from the Pearson Instructor Resource Center.
  www.prenhall.com/irc

- The **Transparencies Set** offers over 150 full-color transparency acetates of all the maps, charts, and graphs in the text for easy classroom presentation.
  978-0-13-602839-0

- A customized **Retrieving the American Past reader** may be created to accompany _Out of Many_. Instructors can select from a database of 300 primary source documents on key topics in American history to create a reader ideally suited to their course.
  http://www.pearsoncustom.com/database/rtap.html

- The two-volume **American Stories: Biographies in United States History, Third Edition** presents sixty-two biographies of key figures in American history with introductions, pre-reading questions, suggested readings, and a special prologue about the role of biography in the study of American history.
  For **Volumes I**: 978-0-13-182654-0
  For **Volume II**: 978-0-13-182653-3

- The Prentice Hall **Package a Penguin program** provides instructors an opportunity to receive significant discounts on Penguin American history titles when ordered with _Out of Many_.

One of the most characteristic features of our country is its astounding variety. The American people include the descendants of native Indians, colonial Europeans of British, French, and Spanish background, Africans, and migrants from virtually every country and continent. Indeed, at the beginning of the new century the United States is absorbing a flood of immigrants from Latin America and Asia that rivals the great tide of people from eastern and southern Europe one hundred years before. The struggle to meld a single nation out of our many far-flung communities is what much of American history is all about. That is the story told in this book.

Every human society is made up of communities. A community is a set of relationships linking men, women, and their families to a coherent social whole that is more than the sum of its parts. In a community people develop the capacity for unified action. In a community people learn, often through trial and error, how to transform and adapt to their environment. The sentiment that binds the members of a community together is the mother of group consciousness and ethnic identity. In the making of history, communities are far more important than even the greatest of leaders, for the community is the institution most capable of passing a distinctive historical tradition to future generations.

Communities bind people together in multiple ways. They can be as small as local neighborhoods, in which people maintain face-to-face relations, or as large as the nation itself. This book examines American history from the perspective of community life—an ever-widening frame that has included larger and larger groups of Americans.

Networks of kinship and friendship, and connections across generations and among families, establish the bonds essential to community life. Shared feelings about values and history establish the basis for common identity. In communities, people find the power to act collectively in their own interest. But American communities frequently took shape as a result of serious conflicts among groups, and within communities there was often significant fighting among competing groups or classes. Thus the term *community*, as we use it here, includes conflict and discord as well as harmony and agreement.

For decades Americans have complained about the "loss of community." But community has not disappeared—it has been continuously reinvented. Until the late eighteenth century, community was defined

Harvey Dinnerstein, *Underground, Together* 1996, oil on canvas, 90" × 107".

Photograph courtesy of Gerold Wunderlich & Co., New York, NY.

primarily by space and local geography. But in the nineteenth century communities were reshaped by new and powerful historical forces such as the marketplace, industrialization, the corporation, mass immigration, mass media, and the growth of the nation-state. In the twentieth century, Americans struggled to balance commitments to multiple communities. These were defined not simply by local spatial arrangements, but by categories as varied as race and ethnicity, occupation, political affiliation, and consumer preference. The "American Communities" vignettes that open each chapter reflect these transformations.

The title for our book was suggested by the Latin phrase selected by John Adams, Benjamin Franklin, and Thomas Jefferson for the Great Seal of the United States: *E Pluribus Unum*—"Out of Many Comes Unity." These men understood that unity could not be imposed by a powerful central authority but had to develop out of mutual respect among Americans of different backgrounds. The revolutionary leadership expressed the hope that such respect could grow on the basis of a remarkable proposition: "We hold these truths to be self-evident, that all men are created equal; that they are endowed by their Creator with certain unalienable rights; that among these are life, liberty, and the pursuit of happiness." The national government of the United States would preserve local and state authority but would guarantee individual rights. The nation would be strengthened by guarantees of difference.

"Out of Many" comes strength. That is the promise of America and the premise of this book. The underlying dialectic of American history, we believe, is that as a people we must locate our national unity in the celebration of the differences that exist among us; these differences can be our strength, as long as we affirm the promise of the Declaration. Protecting the "right to be different," in other words, is absolutely fundamental to the continued existence of democracy, and that right is best protected by the existence of strong and vital communities. We are bound together as a nation by the ideal of local and cultural differences protected by our common commitment to the values of the American Revolution.

Our history demonstrates that the promise has always been problematic. Centrifugal forces have been powerful in the American past, and at times the country seemed about to fracture into its component parts. Our transformation from a collection of groups and regions into a nation was marked by painful and often violent struggles.

Our most influential leaders have also sometimes suffered a crisis of faith in the American project of "liberty

Thomas Satterwhite Noble, *Last Sale of Slaves on the Courthouse Steps*, 1860, oil on canvas, Missouri Historical Society.

and justice for all." Thomas Jefferson not only believed in the inferiority of African Americans but feared that immigrants from outside the Anglo-American tradition might "warp and bias" the development of the nation "and render it a heterogeneous, incoherent, distracted mass." We have not always lived up to the American promise and there is a dark side to our history. It took the bloodiest war in American history to secure the human rights of African Americans, and the struggle for full equality for all our citizens has yet to be won.

The process by which diverse communities have come to share a set of common American values is one of the most fundamental aspects of our history. It did not occur, however, because of compulsory Americanization programs, but because of free public education, popular participation in democratic politics, and the impact of popular culture. Contemporary America does have a common culture: We share a commitment to freedom of thought and expression, we join in the aspirations to own our own homes and send our children to

college, we laugh at the same television programs or video clips on You Tube.

To a degree that too few Americans appreciate, this common culture resulted from a complicated process of mutual discovery that took place when different ethnic and regional groups encountered one another.

The American educator John Dewey recognized this diversity early in the last century. "The genuine American, the typical American, is himself a hyphenated character," he declared, "international and interracial in his make-up." It was up to all Americans, Dewey argued, "is to see to it that the hyphen connects instead of separates." We, the authors of *Out of Many*, endorse Dewey's perspective. "Creation comes from the impact of diversity," the American philosopher Horace Kallen wrote about the same time. We also endorse Kallen's vision of the American promise: "A democracy of nationalities, cooperating voluntarily and autonomously through common institutions, . . . a multiplicity in a unity, an orchestration of mankind." And now, let the music begin.

Out of Many

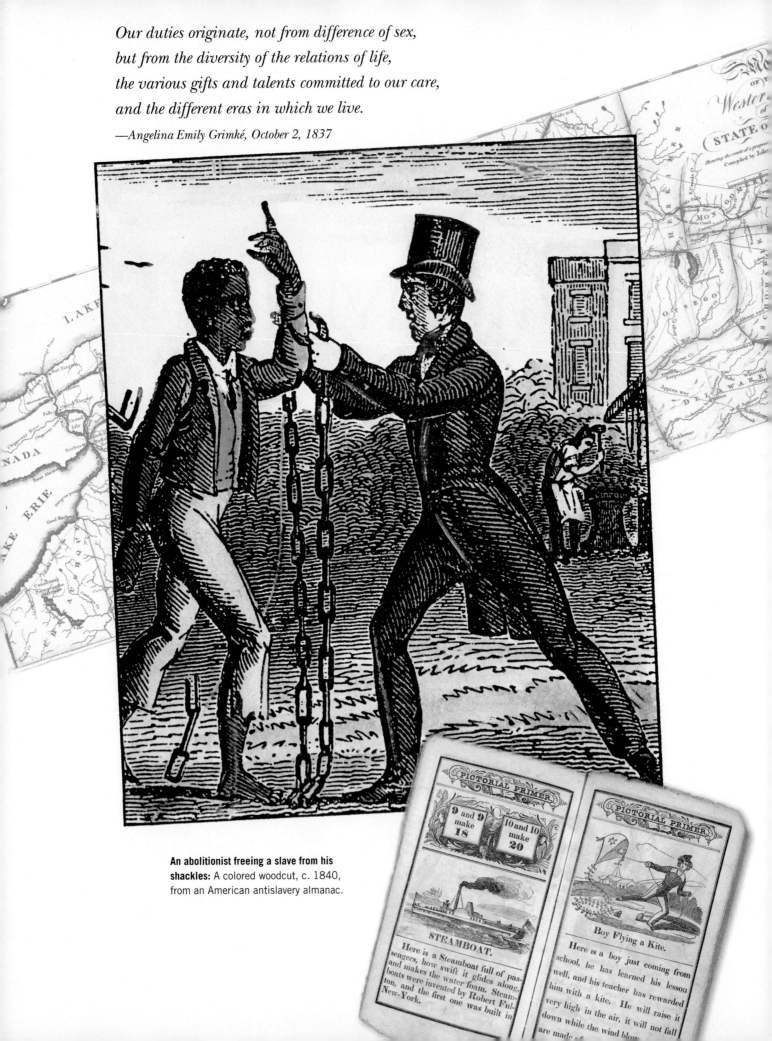

Our duties originate, not from difference of sex,
but from the diversity of the relations of life,
the various gifts and talents committed to our care,
and the different eras in which we live.
—*Angelina Emily Grimké, October 2, 1837*

An abolitionist freeing a slave from his shackles: A colored woodcut, c. 1840, from an American antislavery almanac.

13

MEETING THE CHALLENGES OF THE NEW AGE
IMMIGRATION, URBANIZATION, SOCIAL REFORM
1820s–1850s

WHO MIGRATED to America in the first half of the nineteenth century?

WHO WERE the major proponents of the labor movement?

WHAT ROLE did women play in the development of American education?

WHO WERE the abolitionists and what were their racial attitudes?

WHAT CONNECTIONS were there between the women's rights movement and previous movements for social reform?

AMERICAN COMMUNITIES

Women Reformers of Seneca Falls Respond to the Market Revolution

IN THE SUMMER OF 1848, CHARLOTTE WOODWARD, A NINETEEN-YEAR-old glove maker who did outwork in her rural home, saw a small advertisement in an upstate New York newspaper announcing a "convention to discuss the social, civil, and religious condition and rights of woman," to be held at Seneca Falls on July 19 and 20. Woodward persuaded six friends to join her in the forty-mile journey to the convention. "At first we travelled quite alone," she recalled. "But before we had gone many miles we came on other wagon-loads of women, bound in the same direction. As we reached different crossroads we saw wagons coming from every part of the country, and long before we reached Seneca Falls we were a procession."

To the surprise of the convention organizers, almost 300 people—men as well as women—attended the two-day meeting, which focused on the **Declaration of Sentiments**, a petition for women's rights modeled on the Declaration of Independence. "We hold these truths to be self-evident," it announced: "That all men and women are created equal." As the Declaration of Independence detailed the oppressions King George III had imposed on the colonists, the Declaration of Sentiments detailed, in a series of resolutions, the oppressions men had imposed on women.

The struggle for women's rights was only one of many reform movements that emerged in the United States in the wake of the economic and social disruptions of the market revolution that deeply affected regions like Seneca Falls. Swamped by newcomers (among them a growing number of poor Irish Catholics), the inhabitants of Seneca Falls struggled to maintain a sense of community. They formed volunteer organizations of all kinds—religious, civic, social, educational, and recreational. And they became active participants in reform movements seeking to counteract the effects of industrialization, rapid growth, and the influx of newcomers.

Many reformers belonged to liberal religious groups with wide social perspectives. Perhaps a third of those attending the women's rights convention, for example, were members of the Wesleyan Methodist Society of Seneca Falls, which had broken with the national Methodist organization because it would not take a strong stand against slavery. Another quarter were Progressive Quakers of the nearby town of Waterloo, who had broken with their national organization for the same reason.

The idea for the women's rights convention emerged during a meeting in early July 1848 between Lucretia Mott, a Philadelphia Quaker and the nation's best-known woman reformer, and Elizabeth Cady Stanton of Seneca Falls, wife of a well-known antislavery orator. Stanton first met Mott in 1840 at the World AntiSlavery Conference in London. In 1848, Stanton renewed her acquaintance with Mott and, in this context of friendship and shared concern for reform, the two began planning the convention.

But what of Charlotte Woodward, a local farm girl, unaware of the national reform community? Why was she there? In this age of hopefulness and change, she wanted a better life for herself. She was motivated, she said, by "all the hours that I sat and sewed gloves for a miserable pittance, which, after it was earned, could never be mine." By law and custom, her father, as head of the household, was entitled to her wages. "I wanted to work," she explained, "but I wanted to choose my task and I wanted to collect my wages." The reforming women of Seneca Falls, grouped together on behalf of social improvement, had found in the first women's rights convention a way to speak for the needs of working women such as Charlotte Woodward.

Seneca Falls

All over the North, in communities like Seneca Falls as well as in cities like New York, Americans gathered together in reform organizations to try to solve the problems that the market revolution posed for work, family life, personal and social values, and urban growth. Through these organizations, local women and men became participants in wider communities of social concern, but in spite of their best efforts, they were rarely able to settle the issues that had brought them together. The aspirations of some, among them women, free blacks, and immigrants, clashed with the social control agendas of other groups. In this fervent atmosphere of reform, many problems were raised but few were resolved.

Declaration of Sentiments The resolutions passed at the Seneca Falls Convention in 1848 calling for full female equality, including the right to vote.

IMMIGRATION AND THE CITY

Although the market revolution affected all aspects of American life, nowhere was its impact so noticeable as in the cities. And it was primarily in cities that the startlingly large number of new immigrants clustered.

THE GROWTH OF CITIES

The market revolution dramatically increased the size of America's cities, with the great seaports leading the way. The proportion of America's population living in cities increased from only 7 percent in 1820 to almost 20 percent in 1860, a rate of growth greater than at any other time in the country's history. The nation's five largest cities in 1850 were the same as in 1800, with one exception. New York, Philadelphia, Baltimore, and Boston still topped the list, but New Orleans had edged out Charleston. The rate of urban growth was extraordinary. All four Atlantic seaports grew at least 25 percent each decade between 1800 and 1860, and often much more. New York, which grew from 60,000 in 1800 to 202,600 in 1830 and to more than 1 million in 1860, emerged as the nation's most populous city, its largest port, and its financial center.

Philadelphia, which had been the nation's largest city in 1800, was half the size of New York in 1850. Nevertheless, its growth was substantial—from 70,000 in 1800 to 389,000 in 1850 and to 565,529 in 1860. Philadelphia became as much an industrial as a commercial city.

Another result of the market revolution was the appearance of "instant" cities at critical points on the new transportation network. Utica, New York, once a frontier trading post, was transformed by the opening of the Erie Canal into a commercial and manufacturing center. Chicago, on the shores of Lake Michigan, was transformed by the coming of the railroad into a major junction for water and rail transport. The city, which emerged as a fur trading center around Fort Dearborn, an army post built in 1803, had become, by the 1850s, a hub of trade boasting grain storage facilities, slaughterhouses, and warehouses of all kinds. Farm implement manufacturers such as Cyrus McCormick built manufacturing plants there to serve the needs of midwestern farmers. By 1860 Chicago had a population of over 100,000, making it the nation's eighth largest city (see Table 13.1).

WHO MIGRATED to America in the first half of the nineteenth century?

myhistorylab
Review Summary

QUICK REVIEW

"Instant" Cities

- Utica, New York transformed by opening of Erie Canal.
- Railroad made growth of Chicago possible.
- Chicago's population reached 100,000 in 1860.

TABLE 13.1

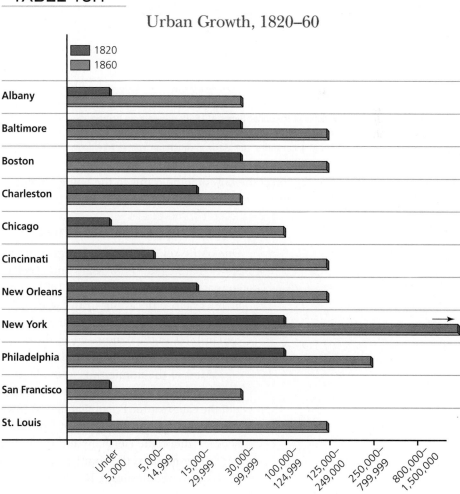

Urban Growth, 1820–60

MAP 13.1

Distribution of Foreign-Born Residents of the United States in 1860   The ethnic composition of the American population was increased by Irish and German immigration in the 1840s and 1850s, Chinese attraction to the California gold rush, Mormon recruitment of Scottish and English followers to Utah, and the reclassification of Mexicans after the Mexican-American War as foreigners in what had been their own lands.

HOW DID events in Europe affect the flow of immigrants to the United States in the 1840s and 1850s?

PATTERNS OF IMMIGRATION

One of the key aspects of urban growth was a surge in immigration to the United States that began in the 1820s and accelerated dramatically after 1830. From an annual figure of about 20,000 in 1831, immigration ballooned to a record 430,000 in 1854 before declining in the years prior to the Civil War. The proportion of immigrants in the population jumped from 1.6 percent in the 1820s to 11.2 percent in 1860. In the nation's cities, the proportion was vastly larger: by 1860, nearly half of New York's population (48 percent) was foreign-born (see Map 13.1).

Most of the immigrants to the United States during this period came from Ireland and Germany. Political unrest and poor economic conditions in Germany and the catastrophic Potato Famine of 1845–49 in Ireland were responsible for an enormous surge in immigration from those countries between 1845 and 1854. Between them, the Germans and the Irish represented the largest influx of non-English immigrants the country had known. They were also the poorest: most of the Irish arrived destitute. In addition, most of the Irish and half of the Germans were Catholics, an unwelcome novelty that provoked a nativist backlash among some Protestant Americans, including many leaders of national reform movements (see Chapter 15).

It would be a mistake, however, to think that immigration was unwelcome to everyone. Industries needed willing workers, and western states, among them Wisconsin, Iowa, and Minnesota, actively advertised in Europe for settlers. Many of the changes in industry and transportation that accompanied the market revolution would have been impossible without immigrants.

Few immigrants found life in the United States pleasant or easy. In addition to the psychological difficulties of leaving a home and familiar ways behind, most immigrants endured harsh living and working conditions. America's cities were unprepared for the social problems posed by large numbers of immigrants.

IRISH IMMIGRATION

The first major immigrant wave to test American cities was caused by the catastrophic Irish Potato Famine of 1845–49. Throughout Ireland, many native Irish subsisted on small landholdings and a diet of potatoes while working as laborers on British-owned farms. Young people who knew they could not hope to own land in Ireland had long looked to America for better opportunities. But in 1845, Ireland's green fields of potato plants turned black with blight. The British government could not cope with the scale of the disaster. The Irish had two choices: starve or leave. One million people died, and another 1.5 million emigrated, the majority to the United States. Starving, diseased, and destitute, hundreds of thousands (250,000 in 1851 alone) disembarked in the East Coast ports of New York, Philadelphia, Boston, and Baltimore. Lacking the money to go inland and begin farming, they remained in the cities. Crowded together in miserable housing, desperate for work at any wages, foreign in their religion and pastimes, tenaciously nationalistic and bitterly anti-British, they created ethnic enclaves of a kind new to American cities.

The largest numbers of Irish came to New York, which managed to absorb them. But Boston, a much smaller and more homogeneous city, was overwhelmed by the Irish influx. By 1850, a quarter of Boston's population was Irish, most of them recent immigrants. Boston, the home of Puritanism and the center of American intellectualism, did not welcome illiterate Irish Catholic peasants. All over the city, in places of business and in homes normally eager for domestic servants, the signs went up: "No Irish Need Apply."

GERMAN IMMIGRATION

Germans, like the Irish, had a long history of emigration to America. The nineteenth-century immigration of Germans began somewhat later and more slowly than that of the Irish, but by 1854 it had surpassed the Irish influx. The typical German immigrant was a small farmer or artisan dislodged by the same market forces at work in America: the industrialization of production and consolidation, and the commercialization of farming. There was also a small group of middle-class liberal intellectuals who left the German states (Germany was not yet a unified nation) after 1848 when attempts at revolution had failed.

German migrants were not as poor as the Irish, and they could afford to move out of the East Coast seaports to other locations. Many settled in Pittsburgh, Cincinnati, St. Louis, and Milwaukee and on farms in Ohio, Indiana, Missouri, and Texas. In Texas, the nucleus of a German community began with a Mexican land grant in the 1830s. Few Germans settled either in northeastern cities or in the South.

German agricultural communities took a distinctive form that fostered cultural continuity. Immigrants formed predominantly German towns by clustering, or taking up adjoining land. A small cluster could support German churches, German-language schools, and German customs and thereby attract other Germans, some directly from Europe and some from other parts of the United States.

IMAGE KEY

for pages 322–323

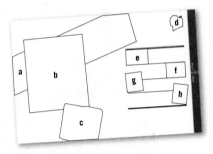

a. A map of western New York State in 1811 including the proposed Erie Canal route, the Finger Lakes, Lake Ontario, and Lake Erie.

b. An abolitionist freeing a slave from his shackles: colored woodcut, c. 1840, from an American antislavery almanac.

c. Pages from an *American Pictorial Primer*, c. 1845.

d. A Cotton gin used to separate cotton from its seeds, stems, etc.

e. New York's most notorious slum, Five Points, is illustrated in this 1859 lithograph.

f. The seal of the General Society of Mechanics and Tradesman.

g. Dorothea Dix, a crusader for mental health reforms.

h. Frederick Douglass (1817?–1895), a portrait attributed to E. Hammond.

Wright's Grove, shown here in an 1868 illustration, was the popular picnic grounds and beer garden for the large German community on Chicago's North Side. Establishments such as this horrified American temperance advocates, who warned about the dangerous foreign notion of mixing alcohol with family fun.

THE CHINESE IN CALIFORNIA

Another area attracting immigrants in the early nineteenth century was Gold Rush California, which drew, among others, numbers of Chinese (see Chapter 14). The Chinese who came to California worked in the mines, mostly as independent prospectors. Other miners disliked their industriousness and their clannishness. By the mid-1860s, Chinese workers made up 90 percent of the laborers building the Central Pacific Railroad, replacing more expensive white laborers and sowing the seeds of the long-lasting hostility of American workers toward Chinese. In the meantime, however, San Francisco's Chinatown, the oldest Chinese ethnic enclave in America, became a well-established, thriving community and a refuge in times of anti-Chinese violence.

ETHNIC NEIGHBORHOODS

Ethnic neighborhoods were not limited to the Chinese. Almost all new immigrants preferred to live in neighborhoods where they could find not only family ties and familiar ways but also community support as they learned how to survive in new surroundings. Isolated partly by their religious beliefs, Irish immigrants created their own communities in Boston and New York, their major destinations. They raised the money to erect Catholic churches with Irish priests. They established parochial schools with Irish nuns as teachers and sent their children to them in preference to the openly anti-Catholic public schools. They formed mutual aid societies based on kinship or town of origin in Ireland. Men and women formed religious and social clubs, lodges, and brotherhoods and their female auxiliaries. Irishmen manned fire and militia companies as well. This dense network of associations served the same purpose that social welfare organizations do today: providing help in time of need and offering companionship in a hostile environment.

Germans who settled in urban areas also built their own ethnic enclaves—"Little Germanies"—in which they sought to duplicate the rich cultural life of their homeland. Like the Irish, the Germans formed church societies, mutual benefit societies, and fire and militia companies to provide mutual support. Partly because their communities were more prosperous than those of the Irish, the Germans also formed a network of leisure organizations: singing societies, debating and political clubs, concert halls like New York's Beethoven Hall, theaters, *turnvereins* (gymnastics associations), and beer gardens. They published German-language newspapers as well.

URBAN PROBLEMS

I t was within the new urban environment, with its stimulating and frightening confusion of rapid growth, occupational and ethnic change, and economic competition, that new American political and social forms began to emerge.

NEW LIVING PATTERNS IN THE CITIES

The preindustrial cities of eighteenth-century America had been small and compact "walking cities," in which people, rich and poor, lived near their work in a dense, small-scale housing pattern that fostered neighborliness and the mingling of social classes. The growth caused by immigration changed the character of urban life by sharpening class differences.

Even though per capita income in America is estimated to have doubled between 1800 and 1850, the gap between rich and poor was glaringly apparent in the nation's cities. Differences in income affected every aspect of urban life. Very poor families, including almost all new immigrants, performed unskilled labor in jobs where the future was uncertain at best, lived in cheap rented housing, moved frequently, and depended on more than one income to survive. Artisans and skilled workers with incomes of $500 or more could live adequately, though often in cramped quarters that also served as their shops. A middle-class family with an income of more than $1,000 a year could live comfortably in a house of four to six rooms complete with carpeting, wallpaper, and good furniture. The very rich built mansions and large town houses and staffed them with many servants. In the summer, they left the cities for country estates or homes at seaside resorts such as Newport, Rhode Island, which attracted wealthy families from all over the country.

Early nineteenth-century cities lacked municipal water supplies, sewers, and garbage collection. Every American city suffered epidemics of sanitation-related diseases such as yellow fever, cholera, and typhus. Philadelphia's yellow fever epidemic of 1793 caused 4,000 deaths and stopped all business with the outside world for more than a month. Major cholera epidemics ravaged New York in 1832 and 1849, and New Orleans suffered repeated episodes of cholera and yellow fever.

WHO WERE the major proponents of the labor movement?

Review Summary

Yet the cities were slow to take action. Mostly, this was due to poor understanding of the links between sanitation and disease, but expense was also a factor. Garbage collection remained a private service, and cities charged property owners for the costs of sewers, water mains, and street paving. Poorer areas of the cities could not afford the costs. When disease struck, wealthier people simply left the cities, leaving the poor to suffer.

Lack of municipal services encouraged residential segregation. Richer people clustered in neighborhoods that had the new amenities. By the 1850s, the middle class began to escape cities completely by moving to the new "streetcar suburbs," named for the new mode of urban transportation that connected these nearby areas to the city itself.

As the middle class left the city, the poor clustered in bad neighborhoods that became known as slums. The worst New York slum in the nineteenth century was Five Points, a stone's throw from City Hall. There, immigrants, free black people, and criminals were crammed into rundown buildings known in the slang of the time as "rookeries." Notorious gangs of thieves and pickpockets with names such as the Plug Uglies and the Shirt Tails dominated the district. Starvation and murder were commonplace.

THE FIVE POINTS IN 1859
Crossing of Baxter [late Orange] Park [late Cross] & Worth [late Anthony] Sts.

The Five Points neighborhood in lower Manhattan illustrates the segregated housing patterns that emerged as New York City experienced rapid growth. Immigrants, free African Americans, the poor, and criminals were crowded together in New York's most notorious slum, while wealthier people moved to more prosperous neighborhoods.

With the influx of European immigrants after 1830, middle-class Americans increasingly saw slums as the home of strange and foreign people, who deserved less than American-born citizens did. In this way, residential patterns came to embody larger issues of class and citizenship. Even disease itself was blamed on immigrants. As banker John Pintard reasoned in 1832, the cholera epidemic must be God's judgment on "the lower classes of intemperate dissolute and filthy people huddled together like swine in their polluted habitations."

ETHNICITY IN URBAN POPULAR CULTURE

Immigrants to American cities contributed to a new urban popular culture, with New York, the largest city, leading the way. In the period 1820–60, New York experienced the replacement of artisanal labor by wagework, two serious depressions (1837–43 and 1857), and a vast influx of immigrant labor (see Figure 13.1). In response to these pressures, working-class amusements became rougher and rowdier.

Irish immigrants, in particular, faced not only employment discrimination but also persistent cultural denigration. It was common for newspapers of the time to caricature the Irish as monkeys, similar to the way cartoonists portrayed African Americans. The Irish response, which was to insist on their "whiteness," played itself out in urban popular culture in violence and mockery.

Theaters, which had been frequented by men of all social classes, provided another setting for violence. Few women, except for the prostitutes who met their customers in the third tier of the balcony, attended.

By the 1830s, middle-class and upper-class men withdrew to more respectable theaters to which they could bring their wives and daughters, and workers found new amusements in theaters such as the Lafayette Circus, which featured dancing girls and horseback riders as well as theatrical acts (see Seeing History).

The new working-class culture flourished especially on the Bowery, a New York City street filled with workshops, small factories, shops with cheap goods, dance halls, theaters, ice cream parlors, and oyster bars. Here working-class youth, the "Bowery b'hoys" (slang pronunciation of "boys") and "gals," found Saturday night amusement and provided it for themselves with outrageous clothing and behavior. The deliberately provocative way they dressed was, in effect, a way of thumbing their noses at the more respectable classes.

THE LABOR MOVEMENT AND URBAN POLITICS

By the 1830s, the status of artisans and independent craftsmen in the nation's cities had deteriorated. Members of urban workers' associations, increasingly angry over their declining status in the economic and social order, became active defenders of working-class interests in their cities.

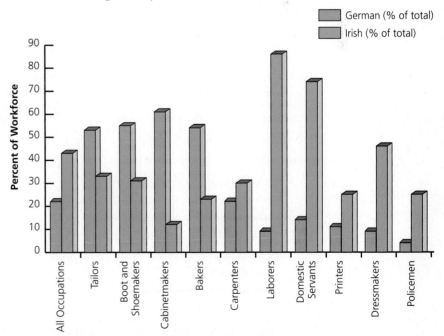

Figure 13.1 Participation of Irish and German Immigrants in the New York City Workforce for Selected Occupations, 1855
This chart shows the impact of the new immigrants on the New York's workforce, and the dramatic difference between groups. German workers predominate in the skilled trades, while the Irish are clustered in low-skilled, low paying occupations.

Robert Ernst, *Immigrant Life in New York City 1825–1863* (Syracuse: Syracuse University Press, 1994).

Thomas "Daddy" Rice, Blackface Minstrel, Dances Jim Crow

In 1832, a young white man in blackface appeared at a variety show at the Bowery Theater where he sang and danced the following:

First, on de heel tap,
Den on the toe
Every time I wheel about
I jump Jim Crow.
Wheel about and turn about
En do j's so
And every time I wheel about,
I jump Jim Crow.

This performance was so wildly popular that Thomas Rice had to repeat it twenty times before the audience would let him go. In this way, the cruel stereotype of the slow-witted slave, Jim Crow, entered American popular culture and Rice himself became one of the best-known blackface minstrels. He was far from alone, for blackface minstrel shows were among the most popular American entertainments. A full evening's performance by a company of minstrels (all white men with faces blackened by cork) consisted of songs,

wisecracks, parodies of politicians and other notable figures, comedy scenes of plantation life, dancing, and music. Minstrel shows were a favorite American entertainment for the rest of the nineteenth century.

WHAT EXPLAINS its appeal to white audiences and what does it tell us about popular stereotypes of blacks?

When it first appeared, in the popular culture of the 1830s and 1840s, blackface minstrelsy was a clear indicator of how the issue of slavery permeated all aspects of American life in both the North and South. ■

IRISH EMIGRANT.

Patrick, (just landing.) "By my Sowl, you're black, old fellow! How long have ye bin here?"

Nigger, (imitatng the brogue.) "Jist three months, my honey!"

Pat. "By the powers, I'll go back to Tipperary in a jiffy! I'd not be so black as that fur all the whiskey in Roscrea!"

This cartoon encounter between a newly arrived Irishman and an African American expresses the fear of many immigrants that they would be treated like blacks and denied the privileges of whiteness.

Between 1833 and 1837, a wave of strikes in New York City cut the remaining ties between master craftsmen and the journeymen who worked for them. In 1833, journeymen carpenters struck for higher wages. Workers in fifteen other trades came to their support, and within a month the strike was won. The same year, representatives from nine different craft groups formed the General Trades Union (GTU) of New York. By 1834, similar groups had sprung up in over a dozen cities. In 1834 also, representatives of several local GTUs met in Baltimore and organized the National Trades Union (NTU). In its founding statement the NTU criticized the "unjustifiable distribution of the wealth of society in the hands of a few individuals," which had created for working people "a humiliating, servile dependency, incompatible with . . . natural equality."

Naturally, employers disagreed with the NTU's criticism of the economic system. In Cincinnati and elsewhere, employers prevailed upon police to arrest strikers even when no violence had occurred. In another case, New York employers took striking journeymen tailors to court in 1836. Judge Ogden Edwards pronounced the strikers guilty of conspiracy and declared unions un-American. The GTU responded with a mass rally at which Judge Edwards was burned in effigy.

A year later, stunned by the effects of the Panic of 1837, the GTU collapsed. The founding of these general unions, a visible sign of a class-based community of interest among workers, is generally considered to mark the beginning of the American labor movement. However, the early unions included only white men in skilled trades, who made up only a small percentage of all workers. The majority of workers—men in unskilled occupations, all free African Americans, and all women—were excluded.

Although workers were unable to create strong unions or stable political parties that spoke for their economic interests, they were a vital factor in urban politics. As America's cities experienced unprecedented growth, the electorate mushroomed. In New York, for example, the number of voters grew from 20,000 in 1825 to 88,900 in 1855. Furthermore, by 1855 half of the voters were foreign-born. Because immigrants clustered in neighborhoods, their impact on politics could be concentrated and manipulated. In New York, for example, the Irish-dominated districts quickly became Democratic Party strongholds. Germans, who were less active politically than the Irish, nevertheless voted heavily for the new Republican Party in the 1850s. Between them, these two new blocs of immigrant voters destroyed the Whig Party that had controlled New York politics before the immigrants arrived.

In New York City, the **Tammany Society**, begun in the 1780s as a fraternal organization of artisans, slowly evolved into the key organization of the new mass politics. Tammany, which was affiliated with the national Democratic Party, reached voters by using many of the techniques of mass appeal made popular earlier by craft organizations—parades, rallies, popular songs, and party newspapers.

CIVIC ORDER

The challenges to middle-class respectability posed by new immigrants and unruly workers were fostered and publicized by the immensely popular "penny papers," which began publication in 1833, and by the rapidly growing number of political papers. This exuberant urban popular culture was unquestionably a part of the same new democratic political spirit that led to the great upsurge in political participation discussed in Chapter 11.

In New York, the prosperous classes were increasingly frightened by the urban poor and by working-class rowdyism. New York City's tradition of New Year's Eve "frolics," in which laborers, apprentices, and other members of the lower classes paraded through the streets playing drums, trumpets, whistles, and other noisemakers, was an example. By 1828, the revelry had been taken over by gangs of young workers from the lower classes, 4,000 strong, who marched through the city, overturning carts, breaking windows, obstructing traffic, and harassing middle-class citizens. In the following year, the city government banned the traditional New Year's Eve parade.

In colonial days, civic disturbances had been handled informally: members of the city watch asked onlookers for whatever assistance was necessary to keep the peace. New York City's first response in the 1820s and 1830s to increasing civic disorder was to hire more city watchmen and to augment them with constables and marshals. When riots occurred, the militia were called, and deaths were increasingly common as they forcibly restrained mobs. Finally, in 1845, the city created a permanent police force with a mandate to keep the poor in order. Southern cities, because of fear of slave disorder, had police forces much earlier.

But even with police forces in place, the pressures of rapid urbanization, immigration, and the market revolution proved to be too much for America's cities. Beginning in the 1830s, a series of urban riots broke out against the two poorest urban groups: Catholics and free black people. As if their miserable living conditions were not enough, Irish immigrants were met with virulent anti-Catholicism.

Tammany Society A fraternal organization of artisans begun in the 1780s that evolved into a key organization of the new mass politics in New York City.

By 1855, half the voters in New York City were foreign-born. This 1858 engraving of an Irish bar in the Five Points area appeared in the influential *Harper's Weekly*. It expressed the temperance reformers' dislike of immigrants and their drinking habits and the dismay of political reformers that immigrant saloons and taverns were such effective organizing centers for urban political machines.

In 1834, rioters burned an Ursuline convent in Charlestown, Massachusetts; in 1844, a Philadelphia mob attacked priests and nuns and vandalized Catholic churches; in 1854, a mob destroyed an Irish neighborhood in Lawrence, Massachusetts. Often the Irish replied in kind—for example, in an 1806 riot in New York, when they counterattacked a mob that disrupted their Christmas Eve mass in a Catholic church on Augustus Street. But the most common targets of urban violence were free African Americans.

FREE AFRICAN AMERICANS IN THE CITIES

By 1860, there were nearly half a million free African Americans in the United States, constituting about 11 percent of the country's total black population. More than half of all free African Americans lived in the North, mostly in cities, where they competed with immigrants and native-born poor white people for jobs as day laborers and domestic servants. Philadelphia and New York had the largest black communities. There were much smaller but still significant black communities in the New England cities of Boston, Providence, and New Haven and in Ohio cities like Cincinnati.

Free African Americans in northern cities faced residential segregation, pervasive job discrimination, segregated public schools, and severe limitations on their civil rights. In addition to these legal restrictions, there were matters of custom: African Americans of all economic classes endured daily affronts, such as exclusion from public concerts, lectures, and libraries, and segregation or exclusion from public transportation. For example, in Massachusetts—which had the reputation

This appealing portrait of a musician, *The Bone Player*, evokes the prevalent stereotype of African Americans as innately musical, but it also clearly portrays a man who is proud of his talent.

William Sidney Morris (American, 1807–1868), "The Bone Player," 1856. Oil on canvas, 91.76 × 73.98 cm (36 1/8 × 29 1/8 in.). Courtesy, Museum of Fine Arts, Boston. Bequest of Martha C. Karolik for the M. and M. Karolik Collection of American Paintings. 48.46 Reproduced with permission. Photograph © 2006 Museum of Fine Arts, Boston. All Rights Reserved.

of being more hospitable to black people than any other northern state—the famed African American abolitionist Frederick Douglass was denied admission to a zoo on Boston Common, a public lecture and revival meeting, a restaurant, and a public omnibus, all within the space of a few days.

In common with Irish and German immigrants, African Americans created defenses against the hostile larger society by building their own community structures. They formed associations for aiding the poorest members of the community, for self-improvement, and for socializing. Tired of being insulted by the white press, African American communities supported their own newspapers. The major community organization was the black Baptist or African Methodist Episcopal (AME) church.

Employment prospects for black men deteriorated from 1820 to 1850. Those who had held jobs as skilled artisans were forced from their positions, and their sons denied apprenticeships, by white mechanics and craftsmen who were themselves suffering from the effects of the market revolution. Limited to day labor, African Americans found themselves in direct competition with the new immigrants, especially the Irish, for jobs. On the waterfront, black men lost their jobs as carters and longshoremen to the Irish. One of the few occupations to remain open to them was that of seaman. More than 20 percent of all American sailors in 1850 were black. Mothers, wives, and daughters worked as domestic servants (in competition with Irishwomen), washerwomen, and seamstresses.

Free African Americans remained committed to their enslaved brethren in the South. In New York, for example, black communities rioted four times—in 1801, 1819, 1826, and 1832—against slave catchers taking escaped slaves back to slavery. But even more frequently, free African Americans were themselves targets of urban violence. Philadelphia, "the City of Brotherly Love," was repeatedly rocked by antiblack riots in the period between 1820 and 1859.

SOCIAL REFORM MOVEMENTS

The passion for reform that had become such an important part of the new middle-class thinking was focused on the problems of the nation's cities. As the opening of this chapter describes, the earliest response to the dislocations caused by the market revolution was community based and voluntary. Middle-class people tried to deal with social changes in their communities by joining organizations devoted to reforms. The reform message was vastly amplified by inventions such as the steam printing press, which made it possible to publish reform literature in great volume. Soon there were national networks of reform groups.

RELIGION, REFORM, AND SOCIAL CONTROL

Evangelical religion was fundamental to social reform. Men and women who had been converted to the enthusiastic new faith assumed personal responsibility for making changes in their own lives. Personal reform quickly led to social reform. Religious converts were encouraged in their social activism by such leading revivalists as Charles G. Finney, who preached a doctrine of "perfectionism," claiming it

WHAT ROLE did women play in the development of American education?

myhistorylab
Review Summary

11–4
Charles Finney, *What a Revival of Religion Is* (1835)

was possible for all Christians to personally understand and live by God's will and thereby become "as perfect as God." This new religious feeling evoked by Finney was intensely hopeful: members of evangelistic religions really did expect to convert the world and create the perfect moral and religious community on earth.

Much of America was swept by this reform-minded religious fervor, and it was the new middle class that set the agenda. Reform efforts arose from the recognition that the traditional methods of small-scale local relief were no longer adequate. Reformers realized that large cities had to make large-scale provisions for social misfits and that institutional rather than private efforts were needed. This thinking was especially true of the institutional reform movements that began in the 1830s, such as the push for insane asylums. At this time, of course, the federal government provided no such relief.

A second characteristic of the reform movements was a belief in the basic goodness of human nature. All reformers believed that the condition of the unfortunate—the poor, the insane, the criminal—would improve in a wholesome environment. Prison reform carried this sentiment to the extreme. On the theory that bad social influences were largely responsible for crime, some "model" prisons completely isolated prisoners from one another, making them eat, sleep, work, and do required Bible reading in their own cells. The failure of these prisons to achieve dramatic changes for the better in their inmates (a number of isolated prisoners went mad, and some committed suicide) or to reduce crime was one of the first indications that reform was not a simple task.

A third characteristic of the reform movements was their moralistic dogmatism. Reformers were certain they knew what was right and were determined to see their improvements enacted. It was a short step from developing individual self-discipline to imposing discipline on others. The reforms that were proposed thus took the form of social controls. Lazy, sinful, intemperate, or unfit members of society were to be reformed for their own good, whether they wanted to be or not. This attitude was bound to cause controversy; by no means did all Americans share the reformers' beliefs, nor did those for whom it was intended always take kindly to being the targets of the reformers' concern.

Indeed, some aspects of the social reform movements were harmful. The evangelical Protestantism of the reformers promoted a dangerous hostility to Catholic immigrants from Ireland and Germany that, as noted earlier, repeatedly led to urban riots. The temperance movement, in particular, targeted immigrants for their free drinking habits. Seeking uniformity of behavior rather than tolerance, the reformers thus helped to promote the virulent nativism that infected American politics between 1840 and 1860 (see Chapter 15).

Regional and national reform organizations quickly grew from local projects to deal with social problems such as drinking, prostitution, mental illness, and crime. In 1828, for example, Congregationalist minister Lyman Beecher joined other ministers in forming a General Union for Promoting the Observance of the Christian Sabbath; the aim was to prevent business on Sundays. To achieve its goals, the General Union adopted the same methods used by political parties: lobbying, petition drives, fundraising, and special publications.

In effect, Beecher and similar reformers engaged in political action but remained aloof from direct electoral politics, stressing their religious mission. In any case, sabbatarianism was controversial. Workingmen (who usually worked six days a week) were angered when the General Union forced the Sunday closure of their favorite taverns and were quick to vote against the Whigs, the party perceived to be most sympathetic to reform thinking. But in many new western cities, **sabbatarianism** divided the business class itself. In Rochester, a city created by the Erie Canal,

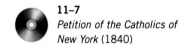

11–7
Petition of the Catholics of New York (1840)

Sabbatarianism   Reform movement that aimed to prevent business on Sundays.

businessmen who wished to observe Sunday only in religious ways were completely unable to stop the traffic of passenger and freight boats owned by other business-men. Other reforms likewise muddied the distinction between political and social activity. It is not surprising that women, who were barred from electoral politics but not from moral and social activism, were major supporters of reform.

EDUCATION AND WOMEN TEACHERS

11–11
Horace Mann, *Report No. 12 of the Massachusetts School Board* (1848)

Women became deeply involved in reform movements through their churches. It was they who did most of the fundraising for the home missionary societies that were beginning to send the evangelical message worldwide—at first by ministers alone, later by married couples. Nearly every church had a maternal association, where mothers gathered to discuss ways to raise their children as true Christians. These asso-ciations reflected a new and more positive definition of childhood. The Puritans had believed that children were born sinful and that their wills had to be broken before they could become godly. Early schools reflected these beliefs: teaching was by rote, and punishment was harsh and physical. Educational reformers, however, tended to believe that children were born innocent and needed gentle nurturing and encour-agement if they were to flourish. At home, mothers began to play the central role in child rearing. Outside the home, women helped spread the new public education pio-neered by Horace Mann, secretary of the Massachusetts State Board of Education.

Although literacy had long been valued, especially in New England, schooling since colonial times had been a private enterprise and a personal expense. In 1827, Massachusetts pioneered compulsory education by legislating that public schools be supported by public taxes. Soon schooling for white children between the ages of five and nineteen was common, although, especially in rural schools, the term might be only a month or so long. Uniformity in curriculum and teacher training, and the grading of classes by ability—measures pioneered by Horace Mann in the 1830s—quickly caught on in other states. In the North and West (the South lagged far behind), more and more children went to school, and more and more teachers, usu-ally young single women, were hired to teach them.

The spread of public education created the first real career opportunity for women. By 1850, women were dominant in primary school teaching, which had come to be regarded as an acceptable occupation for educated young women dur-ing the few years between their own schooling and marriage. For some women, teaching was a great adventure; they enthusiastically volunteered to be "school-marms" on the distant western frontiers of Wisconsin and Iowa. Still others thought globally. The young women who attended Mary Lyon's Mount Holyoke Female Seminary in Massachusetts, founded in 1837, hoped to be missionary teachers in dis-tant lands. For others, a few years of teaching was quite enough. Low pay (half of what male schoolteachers earned) and strict community supervision (women teach-ers had to board with families in the community) were probably sufficient to make almost any marriage proposal look appealing.

TEMPERANCE

Reformers believed not only that children could be molded but also that adults could change. The largest reform organization of the period, the **American Society for the Promotion of Temperance**, founded in 1826, boasted more than 200,000 members by the mid-1830s. Dominated by evangelicals, local chapters used revival methods—lurid **temperance** tracts detailing the evils of alcohol, large prayer and song meetings, and heavy group pressure—to encourage young men to stand up, confess their bad habits, and "take the pledge" not to drink. Here again, women played an important role (see Figure 13.2).

QUICK REVIEW

Women and Reform

♦ Women often became involved in reform through their churches.

♦ Maternal associations focused on raising of children as true Christians.

♦ Women helped spread public education of children.

American Society for the Promotion of Temperance Largest reform organization of its time dedicated to ending the sale and consumption of alcoholic beverages.

Temperance Reform movement originating in the 1820s that sought to eliminate the consumption of alcohol.

Excessive drinking was a national problem, and it appears to have been mostly a masculine one, for respectable women did not drink in public. Men drank hard cider and liquor—whiskey, rum—in abundance. Traditionally, drinking had been a basic part of men's working lives. It concluded occasions as formal as the signing of a contract and accompanied such informal activities as card games. Drink was a staple offering at political speeches, rallies, and elections. In the old artisanal workshops, drinking had been a customary pastime. Much of the drinking was well within the bounds of sociability, but the widespread use must have encouraged drunkenness.

There were many reasons to support temperance. Heavy-drinking men hurt their families economically by spending their wages on drink. Women had no recourse: the laws of the time gave men complete financial control of the household, and divorce was difficult as well as socially unacceptable. Excessive drinking also led to violence and crime, both within the family and in the larger society.

But there were other reasons. The new middle class, preoccupied with respectability, morality, and efficiency, found the old easygoing drinking ways unacceptable. Temperance became a social and political issue. Whigs, who embraced the new morality, favored it; Democrats, who in northern cities consisted increasingly of immigrant workers, were opposed. Both German and Irish immigrants valued the social drinking that occurred in beer gardens and saloons and were hostile to temperance reform.

The Panic of 1837 affected the temperance movement. Whereas most temperance crusaders in the 1820s had been members of the middle class, the long depression of 1837–43 prompted artisans and skilled workers to give up or at least cut down substantially on drinking. Forming associations known as Washington Temperance Societies, these workers spread the word that temperance was the workingman's best chance to survive economically and to maintain his independence. Their wives, gathered together in Martha Washington Societies, were frequently even more committed to temperance than their husbands.

By the mid-1840s, alcohol consumption had been more than halved, to about the level of today. Concern over drinking would remain constant throughout the nineteenth century and into the twentieth.

MORAL REFORM, ASYLUMS, AND PRISONS

Alcohol was not the only "social evil" that reform groups attacked. Another was prostitution, which was common in the nation's port cities. The customary approach of evangelical reformers was to "rescue" prostitutes, offering them the salvation of religion, prayer, and temporary shelter. The success rate was not very high. As an alternative to prostitution, reformers usually offered domestic work, a low-paying and restrictive occupation that many women scorned. Nevertheless, campaigns against prostitution, generally organized by women, continued throughout the nineteenth century.

One of the earliest and most effective antiprostitution groups was the **Female Moral Reform Society**. Founded by evangelical women in New York in 1834 (the first president was Lydia Finney), it boasted 555 affiliates throughout the country by 1840. The societies quickly realized that prostitution was not as much a moral as an economic issue and moved to organize charity and work for poor women and orphans. They also took direct action against the patrons of prostitutes by printing their names in local papers and then successfully lobbied the New York state legislature for criminal penalties against the male clients as well as the women themselves.

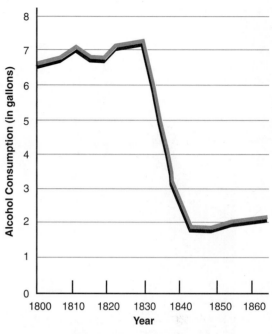

Figure 13.2 Per Capita Consumption of Alcohol, 1800–60
The underlying cause of the dramatic fall in alcohol consumption during the 1830s was the changing nature of work brought about by the market revolution. Contributing factors were the shock of the Panic of 1837 and the untiring efforts of temperance reformers.

W. J. Rorabaugh, *The Alcoholic Republic: An American Tradition* (New York: Oxford University Press, 1979).

11–2
Lyman Beecher, *Six Sermons on Intemperance* (1828)

11–5
Temperance and the Washingtonians (1836)

Female Moral Reform Society
Antiprostitution group founded by evangelical women in New York in 1834.

This Currier and Ives lithograph, *The Drunkard's Progress*, dramatically conveys the message that the first glass leads the drinker inevitably to alcoholism and finally to the grave, while his wife and child (shown under the arch) suffer.

Another dramatic example of reform was the asylum movement, spearheaded by the evangelist Dorothea Dix. In 1843, Dix horrified the Massachusetts state legislature with the results of her several years of study of the conditions to which insane women were subjected. She described in lurid detail how the women were incarcerated with ordinary criminals, locked up in "cages, closets, stalls, pens! Chained, naked, beaten with rods, and lashed into obedience!" Dix's efforts led to the establishment of a state asylum for the insane in Massachusetts and to similar institutions in other states.

Other reformers were active in related causes, such as prison reform and the establishment of orphanages, homes of refuge, and hospitals. Model penitentiaries were built in Auburn and Ossining (known as "Sing Sing"), New York, and in Philadelphia and Pittsburgh. Characterized by strict order and discipline, these prisons were supposed to reform rather than simply incarcerate their inmates, but their regimes of silence and isolation caused despair more often than rehabilitation.

UTOPIANISM AND MORMONISM

Amid all the political activism and reform fervor of the 1830s, a few people chose to escape into utopian communities and new religions. The upstate New York area along the Erie Canal was the seedbed for this movement, just as it was for evangelical revivals and reform movements like the **Seneca Falls convention**. The area was so notable for its reform enthusiasm that it has been called "the Burned-Over District," a reference to the waves of reform that swept through like forest fires (see Map 13.2).

Seneca Falls convention   The first convention for women's equality in legal rights, held in upstate New York in 1848.

⸙ MAP EXPLORATION

To explore an interactive version of this map, go to **http://www.prenhall.com/faraghertic/map13.2**

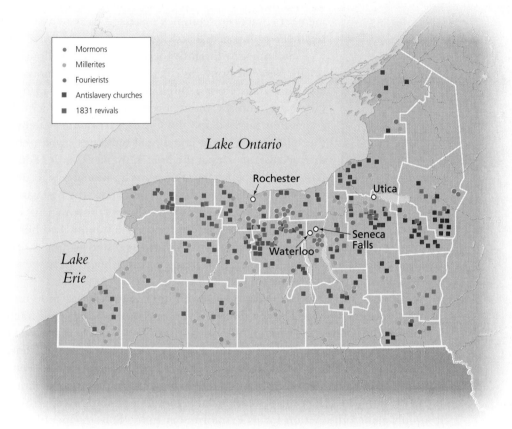

MAP 13.2

Reform Movements in the Burned-Over District   The so-called Burned-Over District, the region of New York State most changed by the opening of the Erie Canal, was a seedbed of religious and reform movements. The Mormon Church originated there and utopian groups and sects like the Millerites and the Fourierists thrived. Charles G. Finney held some of his most successful evangelical revivals in the district. Antislavery feeling was common in the region, and the women's rights movement began at Seneca Falls.

Whitney Cross, *The Burned-Over District* (1950; reprint, New York: Hippocrene Books, 1981).

WHY WERE the many religious revivals and reform movements in the Burned-Over District in the 1830s and 1840s strongest in this region of the country?

Apocalyptic religions tend to spring up in places experiencing rapid social change. The Erie Canal region, which experienced the full impact of the market revolution in the early nineteenth century, was such a place. A second catalyst is hard times, and the prolonged depression that began with the Panic of 1837 led some people to embrace a belief in imminent catastrophe.

The **Shakers**, founded by "Mother" Ann Lee in 1774, were the oldest utopian group. An offshoot of the Quakers, the Shakers espoused a radical social philosophy that called for the abolition of the traditional family in favor of a family of brothers and sisters joined in equal fellowship. Despite its insistence on celibacy, the Shaker movement grew between 1820 and 1830, eventually reaching twenty settlements in eight states with a total membership of 6,000. The Shakers' simple and highly structured lifestyle, their isolation from the changing world, and their belief in equality drew new followers, especially among women. In contrast, another

 11–12
John Humphrey Noyes, *Speech to the Convention of Perfectionists* (1845) and *Bible Communism* (1849)

Shakers   The followers of Mother Ann Lee, who preached a religion of strict celibacy and communal living.

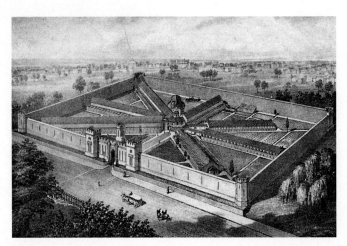

Begun in 1822, the castle-like Eastern State Penitentiary in Philadelphia was intended as a model of rational prison reform. Replacing the crowded mass imprisonment of the past, prisoners were held in isolation from other inmates in separate cells. But instead of the expected repentance and reform, isolation bred despair and attempts at suicide.

The Library Company of Philadelphia.

10–1
Joseph Smith, *The Beginnings of Mormorism* (1823)

14–2
Harriet Beecher Stowe, *Uncle Tom's Cabin* (1852)

Mormonism   The doctrines based on the Book of Mormon, taught by Joseph Smith and the succeeding prophets and leaders of the Church.

WHO WERE the abolitionists and what were their racial attitudes?

myhistorylab
Review Summary

utopian community, the Oneida Community, became notorious for its sexual freedom. Founded by John Humphrey Noyes in 1848, the Oneida community, like the Shaker community, viewed itself as one family. But rather than celibacy, members practiced "complex marriage," a system of highly regulated group sexual activity.

Still other forthrightly socialist communities flourished briefly. New Harmony, Indiana, founded by the famous Scottish industrialist Robert Owen in 1825, was to be a manufacturing community without poverty and unemployment. The community survived only three years. Faring little better were the "phalanxes," huge communal buildings structured on the socialist theories of the French thinker Charles Fourier. Based on his belief that there was a rational way to divide work, Fourier suggested, for example, that children would make the best garbage collectors because they didn't mind dirt! The rapid failure of these socialist communities was due largely to inadequate planning and organization. Another reason may have been, as author Louisa May Alcott suggested in her satirical reminiscence, *Transcendental Wild Oats*, that the women were left to do all the work while the men philosophized.

The most successful of the nineteenth-century communitarian movements was also a product of the Burned-Over District. In 1830, a young man named Joseph Smith founded the Church of Jesus Christ of Latter-Day Saints, based on the teachings of the Book of Mormon, which he claimed to have received from an angel in a vision. Initially **Mormonism**, as the new religion became known, seemed little different from the many other new religious groups and utopian communities of the time. But under the benevolent authority of its patriarch, Joseph Smith, it rapidly gained distinction for its extraordinary unity. Close cooperation and hard work made the Mormon community successful, attracting both new followers and the animosity of neighbors.

The Mormons were harassed in New York and driven west to Ohio and then Missouri. Finally they seemed to find an ideal home in Nauvoo, Illinois, where in 1839 they built a model community, achieving almost complete self-government and isolation from non-Mormon neighbors. But in 1844, dissension within the community over Joseph Smith's new doctrine of polygamy (marriage between one man and more than one woman simultaneously) gave outsiders a chance to intervene. Smith and his brother were arrested peacefully but were killed by a mob from which their jailers failed to protect them. The beleaguered Mormon community decided to move beyond reach of harm. Led by Brigham Young, the Mormons migrated in 1846 to the Great Salt Lake in present-day Utah. Their hopes of isolation were dashed, however, by the California Gold Rush of 1849. (See Chapter 14)

ANTISLAVERY AND ABOLITIONISM

The antislavery feeling that was to play such an important role in the politics of the 1840s and 1850s also had its roots in the religious reform movements that began in the 1820s and 1830s. Three groups—free African Americans, Quakers, and militant white reformers—worked to bring an end to slavery, but each in different ways. Their efforts eventually turned a minor reform movement into the dominant political issue of the day.

THE AMERICAN COLONIZATION SOCIETY

The first national attempt to "solve" the problem of slavery was a plan for gradual emancipation of slaves (with compensation to their owners) and their resettlement in Africa. This plan was the work of the **American Colonization Society**, formed in 1817 by northern religious reformers (Quakers prominent among them) and a number of southern slave owners, most from the Upper South and the border states (Kentuckian Henry Clay was a supporter). The American Colonization Society was remarkably ineffective; by 1830, it had managed to send only 1,400 black people to a colony in Liberia, West Africa. Critics pointed out that more slaves were born in a week than the society sent back to Africa in a year.

AFRICAN AMERICANS AGAINST SLAVERY

For free African Americans, the freedom of other black people had always been a goal, but in order to achieve change, they needed white allies. Most free African Americans rejected the efforts of the American Colonization Society, insisting instead on a commitment to the immediate end of slavery and the equal treatment of black people in America. "We are natives of this country," an African American minister in New York pointed out. Then he added bitterly, "We only ask that we be treated as well as foreigners." By 1830, there were at least fifty African American abolitionist societies in the North. The first African American newspaper, founded in 1827 by John Russwurm and Samuel Cornish, announced its antislavery position in its title, *Freedom's Journal.*

In 1829, David Walker, a free African American in Boston, wrote a widely distributed pamphlet, *Appeal to the Colored Citizens of the World*, that encouraged slave rebellion. "We must and shall be free . . . in spite of you," Walker warned whites. "And woe, woe will be it to you if we have to obtain our freedom by fighting." White Southerners blamed pamphlets such as these and the militant articles of African American journalists for stirring up trouble among southern slaves and, in particular, for Nat Turner's revolt in 1831.

ABOLITIONISTS

The third and best-known group of antislavery reformers was headed by William Lloyd Garrison. In 1831, Garrison broke with the gradualist persuaders of the American Colonization Society and began publishing his own paper, the *Liberator.* Garrison's approach was to mount a sweeping crusade condemning slavery as sinful and demanding its immediate abolition. In reality, Garrison did not expect that all slaves would be freed immediately, but he did want and expect everyone to acknowledge the immorality of slavery. On the other hand, Garrison took the truly radical step of demanding full social equality for African Americans, referring to them individually as "a man and a brother" and "a woman and a sister."

Garrison's moral vehemence radicalized northern antislavery religious groups. Theodore Weld, an evangelical minister, joined Garrison in 1833 in forming the American Anti-Slavery Society. The following year, Weld encouraged a group of students at Lane Theological Seminary in Cincinnati to form an antislavery society. When the seminary's president, Lyman Beecher, sought to suppress it, the students moved en masse to Oberlin College in northern Ohio, where they were joined by revivalist Charles Finney, who became president of the college. Oberlin soon became known as the most liberal college in the country, not only for its antislavery stance but for its acceptance of African American students and of women students as well.

The style of abolitionist writings and speeches was similar to the oratorical style of the religious revivalists. Northern abolitionists believed that a full description of the evils of slavery would force southern slave owners to confront their wrongdoing

American Colonization Society Organization founded in 1817 by antislavery reformers, that called for gradual emancipation and the removal of freed blacks to Africa.

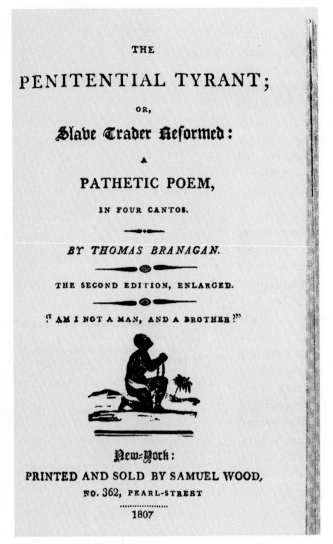

THE

PENITENTIAL TYRANT;

OR,

Slave Trader Reformed:

A

PATHETIC POEM,

IN FOUR CANTOS.

BY THOMAS BRANAGAN.

THE SECOND EDITION, ENLARGED.

"AM I NOT A MAN, AND A BROTHER?"

New-York:

PRINTED AND SOLD BY SAMUEL WOOD,

NO. 362, PEARL-STREET

1807

The different dates on these two widely used antislavery images are important. The title page of Thomas Branagan's 1807 book includes an already commonly used image at the time of a male slave. The engraving of a chained female slave was made by Patrick Reason, a black artist, in 1835. The accompanying message saying "Am I Not a Woman and a Sister?" spoke particularly to white female abolitionists in the North, who were just becoming active in antislavery movements in the 1830s.

and lead to a true act of repentance—freeing their slaves. They were confrontational, denunciatory, and personal in their message, much like the evangelical preachers. Southerners, however, regarded abolitionist attacks as libelous and abusive.

Abolitionists adopted another tactic of revivalists and temperance workers when, to enhance their powers of persuasion, they began to publish great numbers of antislavery tracts. In 1835 alone, they mailed more than a million pieces of antislavery literature to southern states. This tactic also drew a backlash: southern legislatures banned abolitionist literature, encouraged the harassment and abuse of anyone distributing it, and looked the other way when (as in South Carolina) proslavery mobs seized and burned it. Most serious, the majority of southern states reacted by toughening laws concerning emancipation, freedom of movement, and all aspects of slave behavior. Hoping to prevent the spread of the abolitionist message, most southern states reinforced laws making it a crime to teach a slave how to read. Ironically, then, the immediate impact of abolitionism in the South was to stifle dissent and make the lives of slaves harder.

Even in the North, controversy over abolitionism was common. Some places were prone to anti-abolitionist violence. The Ohio Valley, settled largely by Southerners, was one such place, as were northern cities experiencing the strains of rapid growth, such as Philadelphia. Immigrant Irish, who found themselves pitted against free black people for jobs, were often violently anti-abolitionist. William Lloyd Garrison was stoned, dragged through the streets, and on one occasion almost hanged by a Boston mob. In a three-day New York riot of 1834, abolitionist Arthur Tappan's home and store were sacked at the same time that black churches and homes were damaged and free blacks attacked. In 1837, antislavery editor Elijah P. Lovejoy of Alton, Illinois, was killed and his press destroyed.

ABOLITIONISM AND POLITICS

Abolitionism began as a social movement but soon intersected with sectional interests and became a national political issue. In the 1830s, massive abolitionist petition drives gathered a total of nearly 700,000 petitions requesting the abolition of slavery and the slave trade in the District of Columbia but were rebuffed by Congress. At southern insistence and with President Andrew Jackson's approval, Congress passed a "gag rule" in 1836 that prohibited discussion of antislavery petitions.

In 1837, white abolitionist Elijah P. Lovejoy had placed the press he used to print his antislavery newspaper in an Alton, Illinois, warehouse in order to protect the press against a mob. This contemporary woodcut depicts the mob's attack on the warehouse. Lovejoy died defending it.

Many Northerners viewed the gag rule and censorship of the mails, which Southerners saw as necessary defenses against abolitionist frenzy, as alarming threats to free speech. First among them was Massachusetts representative John Quincy Adams, the only former president ever to serve in Congress after leaving the executive branch. Adams so publicly and persistently denounced the gag rule as a violation of the constitutional right to petition that it was repealed in 1844. Less well-known Northerners, like the thousands of women who canvassed their neighborhoods with petitions, made personal commitments to abolitionism that they did not intend to abandon.

Although abolitionist groups raised the nation's emotional temperature, they failed to achieve the moral unity they had hoped for, and they began to splinter. Frederick Douglass and William Lloyd Garrison parted ways when Douglass, refusing to be limited to a simple recital of his life as a slave, began to make specific suggestions for improvements in the lives of free African Americans.

Douglass and other free African Americans worked under persistent discrimination, even from antislavery whites; some of the latter refused to hire black people or to meet with them as equals. While many white reformers eagerly pressed for civil equality for African Americans, they did not accept the idea of social equality. On the other hand, black and white "stations" worked closely in the risky enterprise of passing fugitive slaves north over the famous Underground Railroad, as the various routes by which slaves made their way to freedom were called. Contrary to abolitionist legend, however, it was free African Americans, rather than white people, who played the major part in helping the fugitives.

In 1840, the abolitionist movement formally split. The majority moved toward party politics (which Garrison abhorred), founding the **Liberty Party** and choosing James G. Birney (whom Theodore Weld had converted to abolitionism) as their presidential candidate. Thus, the abolitionist movement, which began as an effort at moral reform, took its first major step into politics, and this step in turn led to the formation of the Republican Party in the 1850s and to the Civil War. (See Chapter 15)

For one particular group of antislavery reformers, the abolitionist movement opened up new possibilities for action. Through their participation in antislavery activity, some women came to a vivid realization of the social constraints on their activism.

Liberty Party   The first antislavery political party, formed in 1840.

WHAT CONNECTIONS were there between the women's rights movement and previous movements for social reform?

myhistorylab
Review Summary

myhistorylab
Exploring America: *Angelina Grimké*

11–0
Declaration of Sentiments and Resolutions, Woman's Rights Convention, Seneca Falls, New York (1848)

11–13
Sojourner Truth, *Address to the Woman's Rights Convention, Akron, Ohio* (1851)

THE WOMEN'S RIGHTS MOVEMENT

American women, without the vote or a role in party politics, found a field of activity in social reform movements. There was scarcely a reform movement in which women were not actively involved. The majority of women did not participate in these activities, for they were fully occupied with housekeeping and child rearing (families with five children were the average). A few women—mostly members of the new middle class, who could afford servants—had the time and energy to look beyond their immediate tasks. Touched by the religious revival, these women enthusiastically joined reform movements. Led thereby to challenge social restrictions, some, such as the Grimké sisters, found that their commitment carried them beyond the limits of what was considered acceptable activity for women.

THE GRIMKÉ SISTERS

Sarah and Angelina Grimké, members of a prominent South Carolina slaveholding family, rejected slavery out of religious conviction and moved north to join a Quaker community near Philadelphia. In the 1830s, these two sisters found themselves drawn into the growing antislavery agitation in the North. Because they knew about slavery firsthand, they were in great demand as speakers. At first they spoke to "parlor meetings" of women only, as was considered proper. But interested men kept sneaking into the talks, and soon the sisters found themselves speaking to mixed gatherings. The meetings got larger and larger, and the sisters became the first female public speakers in America.

The Grimké sisters were criticized for speaking because they were women. A letter from a group of ministers cited the Bible in reprimanding the sisters for stepping out of "woman's proper sphere" of silence and subordination. Sarah Grimké answered the ministers in her 1838 *Letters on the Equality of the Sexes and the Condition of Women*, claiming that "men and women were CREATED EQUAL. . . . Whatever is right for a man to do, is right for woman."

Not all female assertiveness was as dramatic as Sarah Grimké's, but women in the antislavery movement found it a constant struggle to be heard. Some solved the problem of male dominance by forming their own groups, like the Philadelphia Female Anti-Slavery Society. In the antislavery movement and other reform groups as well, men accorded women a secondary role, even when—as was frequently the case—women constituted a majority of the members.

WOMEN'S RIGHTS

The Seneca Falls Convention of 1848, the first women's rights convention in American history, was an outgrowth of almost twenty years of female activity in social reform. As described in the chapter opener, the long agenda of rights was drawn directly from the discrimination many women had experienced in social reform groups. Every year after 1848, women gathered to hold women's rights conventions and to work for political, legal, and social equality. Over the years, in response to persistent lobbying, states passed property laws more favorable to women, and altered divorce laws to allow women to retain custody of children. Teaching positions in higher education opened up to women, as did jobs in some other occupations, and women gained the vote in some states, beginning with Wyoming Territory in 1869. In 1920, seventy-two years after universal woman suffrage was first proposed at Seneca Falls, a woman's right to vote was at last guaranteed in the Nineteenth Amendment to the Constitution.

Historians have only recently realized how much the reform movements of this "Age of the Common Man" were due to the efforts of the "common woman." Women played a vital role in all the social movements of the day. In doing so, they implicitly

A CONVENTION OF HEMMERS AND STITCHERS HELD AT LYNN, FEB. 28, FOR ADOPTING A LIST OF PRICES; MRS. E. HALL, PRESIDING.—(See page 284.)

Women's gatherings, like the first women's rights convention in Seneca Falls in 1848, and this meeting of strikers in Lynn in 1860, were indicators of widespread female activism.

challenged the popular notion of separate spheres for men and women—the public world for him, home and family for her. The separate spheres argument, although it heaped praise on women for their allegedly superior moral qualities, was meant to exclude them from political life. The reforms discussed in this chapter show clearly that women reformers believed they had a right and a duty to propose solutions for the moral and social problems of the day. Empowered by their own religious beliefs and activism, the Seneca Falls reformers spoke for all American women when they demanded an end to the unfair restrictions they suffered as women.

CONCLUSION

Beginning in the 1820s, the market revolution changed the size and social order of America's preindustrial cities and towns. Immigration, dramatically rapid population growth, and changes in working life and class structure created a host of new urban problems ranging from sanitation to civic order. These changes occurred so rapidly that they seemed overwhelming. Former face-to-face methods of social control no longer worked. To fill the gap, new kinds of associations—the political party, the religious crusade, the reform cause, the union movement—sprang up. These associations were new manifestations of the deep human desire for social connection, for continuity, and—especially in the growing cities—for social order. A striking aspect of these associations was the uncompromising nature of the attitudes and beliefs on which they were based. Most groups were formed of like-minded people who wanted to impose their will on others. Such intolerance boded ill for the future. If political parties, religious bodies, and reform groups were to splinter along sectional lines (as happened in the 1850s), political compromise would be very difficult. In the meantime, however, Americans came to terms with the market revolution by engaging in a passion for improvement. As a perceptive foreign observer, Francis Grund noted, "Americans love their country not as it is but as it will be."

CHRONOLOGY

1817 American Colonization Society founded

1820s Shaker colonies grow

1825 New Harmony founded, fails three years later

1826 American Society for the Promotion of Temperance founded

1827 Workingmen's Party founded in Philadelphia

Freedom's Journal begins publication

Public school movement begins in Massachusetts

1829 David Walker's *Appeal to the Colored Citizens of the World* is published

1830 Joseph Smith founds Church of Jesus Christ of Latter-Day Saints (Mormon Church)

Charles G. Finney's revivals in Rochester

1831 William Lloyd Garrison begins publishing antislavery newspaper, the *Liberator*

1832 Immigration begins to increase

1833 American Anti-Slavery Society founded by William Lloyd Garrison and Theodore Weld

1834 First Female Moral Reform Society founded in New York

National Trades Union formed

1836 Congress passes "gag rule" to prevent discussion of antislavery petitions

1837 Antislavery editor Elijah P. Lovejoy killed

Angelina Grimké addresses Massachusetts legislature

Sarah Grimké writes *Letters on the Equality of the Sexes and the Condition of Women*

Panic begins seven-year depression

1839 Theodore Weld publishes *American Slavery As It Is*

1840s New York and Boston complete public water systems

1840 Liberty Party founded

1843 Millerites await the end of the world

Dorothea Dix spearheads asylum reform movement

1844 Mormon leader Joseph Smith killed by mob

1845 New York creates city police force

Beginning of Irish Potato Famine and mass Irish immigration into the United States

1846 Mormons begin migration to the Great Salt Lake

1848 Women's Rights Convention at Seneca Falls

John Noyes founds Oneida Community

REVIEW QUESTIONS

1. What impact did the new immigration of the 1840s and 1850s have on American cities?
2. Why did urbanization produce so many problems?
3. What motivated the social reformers of the period? Were they benevolent helpers or dictatorial social controllers? Study several reform causes and discuss similarities and differences among them.
4. Abolitionism differed little from other reforms in its tactics, but the effects of antislavery activism were politically explosive. Why was this so?
5. Women were active members of almost every reform group. What reasons might women have given for their unusual degree of participation?

KEY TERMS

American Colonization Society (p. 343)
American Society for the Promotion of Temperance (p. 338)
Declaration of Sentiments (p. 324)
Female Moral Reform Society (p. 339)
Liberty Party (p. 345)

Mormonism (p. 342)
Sabbatarianism (p. 337)
Seneca Falls convention (p. 340)
Shakers (p. 341)
Tammany Society (p. 334)
Temperance (p. 338)

myhistorylab
Flashcard Review

RECOMMENDED READING

Tyler Anbinder, *Five Points* (2001). A social history of New York's most notorious slum.

Paul Boyer, *Urban Masses and the Moral Order in America, 1820–1920* (1978). Interprets reform as an effort to reestablish the moral order of the preindustrial community.

Kathleen Neils Conzen, *Immigrant Milwaukee, 1836–1860: Accommodation and Community in a Frontier City* (1976). Milwaukee rapidly became the most German city in the nation. This book explains how and why.

David Grimsted, *American Mobbing, 1828–1865: Toward Civil War* (1998). A national perspective on mob violence, North and South, including political violence.

James Oliver Horton and Lois E. Horton, *In Hope of Liberty: Culture, Community and Protest Among Northern Free Blacks, 1700–1860* (1997). A fine portrait that adds the perspective of change over time to earlier studies.

Mary Kelley, *Learning to Stand and Speak: Women, Education, and Public Life in America's Republic* (2006). The centrality of education to women's growing role in civic life.

Bruce Laurie, *Beyond Garrison: Antislavery and Social Reform* (2005). Focus on reformers in Massachusetts shows how antislavery and other social reforms were interconnected.

Steven Mintz, *Moralists and Modernizers: America's Pre–Civil War Reformers* (1995). A brief but inclusive study of reforms and reformers.

David Roediger, *The Wages of Whiteness* (1991). Explores the links between artisanal republicanism, labor organization, and white racism.

Mary Ryan, *Civic Wars: Democracy and Public Life in the American City During the Nineteenth Century* (1997). A study of New York, New Orleans, and San Francisco that argues that urban popular culture was "meeting-place democracy" in action.

Deborah Van Broekhoven, *The Devotion of These Women: Rhode Island in the Antislavery Network* (2002). Shows how informal women's activities sustained antislavery protest at the local level.

For study resources for this chapter, go to **www.myhistorylab.com** and choose *Out of Many, Teaching and Learning Classroom Edition.* You will find a wealth of study and review material for this chapter, including pretests and posttests, customized study plan, key-term review flash cards, interactive map and document activities, and documents for analysis.

*They immigrate constantly, hardly no one
to prevent them, and take possession of
the location that best suits them without either
asking leave or going through any formality
other than that of building their homes.*

—José Maria Sánchez

Albert Bierstadt (1830–1902), "The Oregon Trail" (oil on canvas).

Private Collection/Bridgeman Art Library International Ltd., New York

Butler Institute of American Art, Youngstown, OH, USA/Gift of Joseph G. Butler III
1946/Bridgeman Art Library.

14

THE TERRITORIAL EXPANSION OF THE UNITED STATES
1830s–1850s

WHAT ROLE did the federal government play in the exploration of the West?

WHAT WERE the major differences between the Oregon, Texas, and California frontiers?

WHAT WERE the most important consequences of the Mexican-American War?

WHAT KINDS of people participated in the California Gold Rush?

WHAT KEY factors explain the outcome of the election of 1848?

AMERICAN COMMUNITIES

Texans and Tejanos "Remember the Alamo!"

FOR THIRTEEN DAYS IN FEBRUARY AND MARCH 1836, A FORCE OF 187 Texans held the mission fortress known as the Alamo against a siege by 5,000 Mexican troops under General Antonio López de Santa Anna, president of Mexico. Santa Anna had come north to subdue rebellious Texas, the northernmost part of the Mexican province of Coahuila y Tejas, and to place it under central authority. On March 6 he ordered a final assault, and in brutal fighting that claimed over 1,500 Mexican lives, his army took the mission. All the defenders were killed, including Commander William Travis and the well-known frontiersmen Jim Bowie and Davy Crockett. It was a crushing defeat for the Texans. But the cry "Remember the Alamo!" rallied their remaining forces, which, less than two months later, routed the Mexican army and forced Santa Anna to grant Texas independence from Mexico. Today, the Alamo is one of the most cherished historic sites in the United States.

But memory is selective: within a generation of the uprising, few remembered that many Tejanos, Spanish-speaking people born in Texas, had joined with American settlers fighting for Texas independence.

The Tejano community, descended from eighteenth-century Spanish and Mexican settlers, included wealthy rancheros who raised cattle on the shortgrass prairies of southern Texas, as well as the cowboys known as *vaqueros* and the *peónes*, or poor tenant farmers. The Tejano elite, enthusiastic about American plans for the economic development of Texas, welcomed the American immigrants. Many Americans married into elite Tejano families, who hoped that by thus assimilating and sharing power with the Americans, they could not only maintain but also strengthen their community.

The Mexican state, however, was politically and socially unstable during these first years after its successful revolt against Spain in 1821. When, in 1828, the conservative centralists came to power in Mexico City and decided the Americans had too much influence in Texas, many Tejanos rose up with the Americans in opposition. In 1832, the Tejano elite of San Antonio and many prominent rancheros favored provincial autonomy and a strong role for the Americans.

As Santa Anna's army approached from the south, the wealthy ranchero Juan Nepomuceno Seguín recruited a company of Tejano volunteers and joined the American force inside the walls of the Alamo. In April, Seguín led a regiment of Tejanos in the decisive battle of San Jacinto that won independence for Texas.

Pleased with independence, Tejanos played an important political role in the new Republic of Texas at first. The liberal Lorenzo de Zavala was chosen vice president, and Seguín became the mayor of San Antonio. But soon things began to change. Illustrating a recurring pattern in the American occupation of new lands—a striking shift in the relations between different cultures in frontier areas. Most commonly, in the initial stage newcomers blended with native Peoples, creating a "frontier of inclusion." The first hunters, trappers, and traders on every American frontier—west of the Appalachians, in the Southwest, and in the Far West—married into the local community and tried to learn native ways. Outnumbered American settlers—initially invited in by Mexicans and Tejanos—developed an anti-Mexican passion, regarding all Spanish speakers as their Mexican enemies rather than their Tejano allies. Tejanos were attacked and forced from their homes; some of their villages were burned to the ground. "On the pretext that they were Mexicans," Seguín wrote, Americans treated Tejanos "worse than brutes. . . . My countrymen ran to me for protection against the assaults or exactions of these adventurers." But even in his capacity as mayor, Seguín could do little, and in 1842, he and his family, like hundreds of other Tejano families, fled south to Mexico in fear for their lives.

Spanish-speaking communities in Texas, and later in New Mexico and California, like the communities of Indians throughout the West, became conquered peoples. "White folks and Mexicans were never made to live together," a Texas woman told a traveler a few years after the revolution. "The Mexicans had no business here," she said, and the Americans might "just have to get together and drive them all out of the country." The descendants of the first European settlers of the American Southwest had become foreigners in the land their people had lived in for two centuries.

San Antonio

EXPLORING THE WEST

There seemed to be no stopping the expansion of the American people. By 1840, they had occupied all of the land east of the Mississippi River and had organized all of it (except for Florida and Wisconsin) into states. The speed and success of this expansion were a source of deep national pride that whetted appetites for further expansion. Many Americans looked eagerly westward to the vast unsettled reaches of the Louisiana Purchase: to Texas, Santa Fé, to trade with Mexico, and even to the Far West, where New England sea captains had been trading for furs since the 1780s. By 1848, the United States had gained all of these coveted western lands. This chapter examines the way the United States became a continental nation, forming many frontier communities in the process. Exploring the vast continent of North America and gaining an understanding of its geography took several centuries and the efforts of many people.

THE FUR TRADE

The fur trade, which flourished from the 1670s to the 1840s, was an important spur to exploration on the North American continent. In the 1670s, the British Hudson's Bay Company and its French Canadian rival, Montreal's North West Company, began exploring beyond the Great Lakes in the Canadian West in search of beaver pelts. Indeed, Alexander Mackenzie of the North West Company reached the Pacific Ocean in 1793, becoming the first European to make a transcontinental crossing of North America. Traders and trappers for both companies depended on the goodwill and cooperation of the native peoples of the region. From the marriages of European men with native women arose a distinctive mixed-race group, the "métis" (French for "mixed").

WHAT ROLE did the federal government play in the exploration of the West?

myhistorylab
Review Summary

IMAGE KEY
for pages 350–351

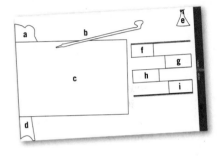

a. A tanned buffalo skin.
b. A long wooden pipe of the Mandan tribe.
c. Albert Bierstadt (1830–1902), "The Oregon Trail."
d. Cactus with a large pink flower.
e. A model of a Plains Indian tepee.
f. John Gast's "American Progress," c. 1872, depicting America heading westward.
g. "The Interior of Fort Laramie," 1858–1860, by Alfred Jacob Miller.
h. "General Winfield Scott at the Siege of Vera Cruz, March 1847" by Nathaniel Currier.
i. A drawing of an 1855 San Francisco gambling saloon.

The artist Alfred Jacob Miller, a careful observer of the western fur trade, shows a mountain man and his Indian wife in his 1837 *Bourgeois Walker and His Wife*. Walker and his wife worked together to trap and prepare beaver pelts for market, as did other European men and their Indian wives.

Alfred Jacob Miller, "Bourgeois Walker and His Wife," 1837. Watercolor. 37.1940.78. The Walters Art Museum, Baltimore.

Most American trappers, like the British and French before them, sought accommodation and friendship with Indian peoples: nearly half of them contracted long-lasting marriages with Indian women, who not only helped in the trapping and curing of furs but also acted as vital diplomatic links between the white and Indian worlds. One legendary trapper adapted so well that he became a Crow chief: the African American Jim Beckwourth, who married a Crow woman and was accepted into her tribe.

For all its adventure, the American fur trade was short-lived. By the 1840s, the population of beaver in western streams was virtually destroyed, and the day of the mountain man was over. But with daring journeys like that of Jedediah Smith, the first American to enter California over the Sierra Nevada Mountains, the mountain men had helped forge a clear picture of western geography. Soon permanent settlers would follow the trails they had blazed.

GOVERNMENT-SPONSORED EXPLORATION

Following the lead of fur trade explorers like Alexander Mackenzie, David Thompson and others', the federal government played a major role in the exploration and development of the U.S. West. The exploratory and scientific aspects of the Lewis and Clark expedition in 1804–06 set a precedent for many government-financed quasi-military expeditions. In 1806 and 1807, Lieutenant Zebulon Pike led an expedition to the Rocky Mountains in Colorado. Major Stephen Long's exploration and mapping of the Great Plains in the years 1819–20 was part of a show of force meant to frighten British fur trappers out of the West. Then, in 1843 and 1844, another military explorer, John C. Frémont, mapped the overland trails to Oregon and California. In the 1850s, the Pacific Railroad surveys explored possible transcontinental railroad routes (see Map 14.1).

In the wake of the pathfinders came hundreds of government geologists and botanists as well as the surveyors who mapped and plotted the West for settlement according to the Land Ordinance of 1785. The basic pattern of land survey and sale established by these measures (see Chapter 7) was followed all the way to the Pacific Ocean. The federal government sold the western public lands at low prices. The federal government also shouldered the expense of Indian removal by making long-term commitments to compensate the Indian people themselves and supporting the forts and soldiers whose task was to maintain peace between settlers and Indian peoples in newly opened areas.

EXPANSION AND INDIAN POLICY

While American artists were painting the way of life of western Indian peoples, eastern Indian tribes were being removed from their homelands to Indian Territory (present-day Oklahoma, Kansas, and Nebraska), a region west of Arkansas, Missouri, and Iowa on the eastern edge of the Great Plains, widely regarded as unfarmable and popularly known as the Great American Desert.

Encroachment on Indian Territory was not long in coming (see Map 14.2). The territory was crossed by the **Santa Fé Trail**, established in 1821; in the 1840s, the northern part was crossed by the heavily traveled Overland Trails to California, Oregon, and the Mormon community in Utah. In 1854, the government abolished the northern half of Indian Territory, establishing the Kansas and Nebraska Territories in its place and opening them to immediate white settlement. The tribes of the area—the Potawatomis, Wyandots, Kickapoos, Sauks, Foxes, Delawares, Shawnees, Kaskaskias, Peorias, Piankashaws, Weas, Miamis, Omahas, Otos, and Missouris—signed treaties accepting either vastly reduced reservations or allotments. Those who accepted allotments—sections of private land—

Santa Fé Trail The 900-mile trail opened by American merchants for trading purposes following Mexico's liberalization of the formerly restrictive trading policies of Spain.

MAP EXPLORATION

To explore an interactive version of this map, go to **http://www.prenhall.com/faraghertlc/map14.1**

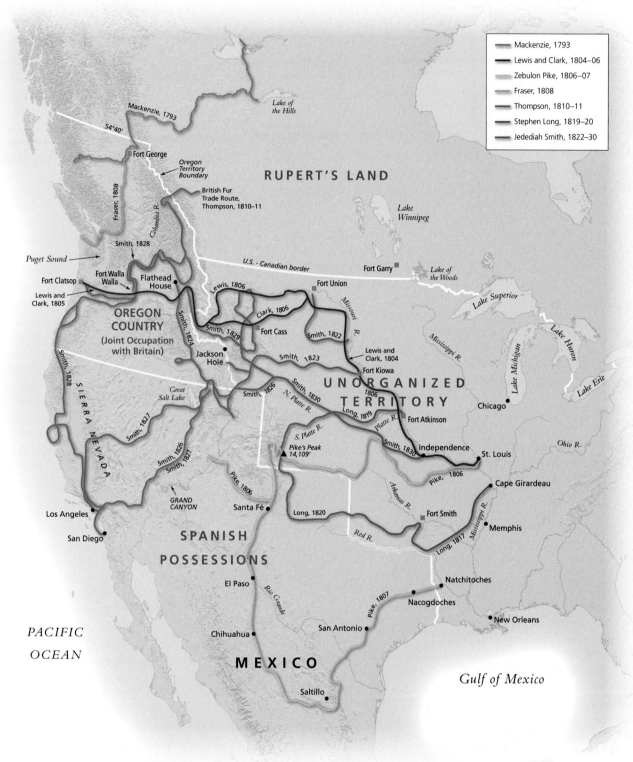

Legend:
- Mackenzie, 1793
- Lewis and Clark, 1804–06
- Zebulon Pike, 1806–07
- Fraser, 1808
- Thompson, 1810–11
- Stephen Long, 1819–20
- Jedediah Smith, 1822–30

MAP 14.1

Exploration of the Continent, 1804–30 Members of British fur trading companies like Alexander Mackenzie and David Thompson led the way. Lewis and Clark's "voyage of discovery" of 1804–06 was the first of many U.S. government-sponsored western military expeditions. Lieutenant Zebulon Pike crossed the Great Plains in 1806, followed by Major Stephen Long in 1819–20. Meanwhile, American fur trappers, among them the much-traveled Jedediah Smith, became well acquainted with the Far West as they hunted beaver for their pelts.

WHAT ROLE did the routes taken by major expeditions westward between 1804 and 1830 play in shaping United States policy in the West?

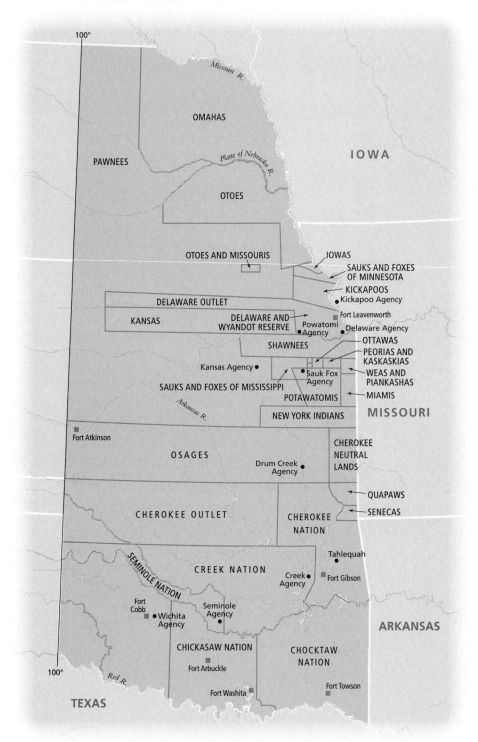

MAP 14.2

Indian Territory Before the Kansas-Nebraska Act of 1854   Indian Territory lay west of Arkansas, Missouri, and Iowa and east of Mexican Territory. Most of the Indian peoples who lived there in the 1830s and the 1840s had been "removed" from east of the Mississippi River. The southern part (now Oklahoma) was inhabited by peoples from the Old Southwest: the Cherokees, Chickasaws, Choctaws, Creeks, and Seminoles. North of that (in what is now Kansas and Nebraska) lived peoples who had been removed from the Old Northwest. All these Indian peoples had trouble adjusting not only to a new climate and a new way of life but also to the close proximity of some Indian tribes who were their traditional enemies.

DISCUSS THE effect of the Kansas-Nebraska Act on Indian tribes and territories.

often sold them, under pressure, to white people. Thus, many of the Indian people who had hoped for independence and escape from white pressures in Indian Territory lost both their autonomy and their tribal identity.

The people in the southern part of Indian Territory, in what is now Oklahoma, fared somewhat better. Those members of the southern tribes—the Cherokees, Chickasaws, Choctaws, Creeks, and Seminoles—who had survived the trauma of forcible removal from the Southeast in the 1830s, quickly created impressive new communities. Until after the Civil War, these southern tribes were able to withstand outside pressures and remain the self-governing communities that treaties had assured them they would be.

THE POLITICS OF EXPANSION

America's rapid expansion had many consequences, but perhaps the most significant was that it reinforced Americans' sense of themselves as pioneering people. Ever since the time of Daniel Boone, venturing into the wilderness has held a special place in the American imagination and been seen almost as a right.

MANIFEST DESTINY, AN EXPANSIONIST IDEOLOGY

How did Americans justify their restless expansionism? After all, the United States was already a very large country with much undeveloped land. In 1845, newspaperman John O'Sullivan provided such a justification. It was, he wrote, "our **manifest destiny** to overspread the continent allotted by Providence for the free development of our yearly multiplying millions." Sullivan argued that Americans had a God-given right to bring the benefits of American democracy to other, more backward peoples—meaning Mexicans and Indians—by force, if necessary. The notion of manifest destiny summed up the powerful combination of pride in what America had achieved and missionary zeal and racist attitudes toward other peoples that lay behind the thinking of many expansionists. Americans were proud of their rapid development: the surge in population, the remarkable canals and railroads, the grand scale of the American enterprise. Why shouldn't America be even bigger?

Expansionism was deeply tied to national politics. O'Sullivan, whose "manifest destiny" became the expansionist watchword, was not a neutral observer: he was the editor of the *Democratic Review*, a party newspaper. Most Democrats were wholehearted supporters of expansion, whereas many Whigs (especially in the North) opposed it. Whigs welcomed most of the changes brought by industrialization but advocated strong government policies that would guide growth and development within the country's existing boundaries. They feared (correctly, as it turned out) that expansion would raise the contentious issue of the extension of slavery to new territories.

On the other hand, many Democrats feared the industrialization that the Whigs welcomed. Where the Whigs saw economic progress, Democrats saw economic depression, uncontrolled urban growth, and growing social unrest. For many Democrats, the answer to the nation's social ills was to continue to follow Thomas Jefferson's vision of establishing agriculture in the new territories in order to counterbalance industrialization. Another factor in the political struggle over expansion in the 1840s was that many Democrats were Southerners, for whom the continual expansion of cotton-growing lands was a matter of social faith as well as economic necessity.

MAP 14.3

The Overland Trails, 1840 All the great trails west started at the Missouri River. The Oregon, California, and Mormon Trails followed the Platte River into Wyoming, crossed South Pass, and divided in western Wyoming. The much harsher Santa Fé Trail stretched 900 miles southwest across the Great Plains. All of the trails crossed Indian Territory and, to greater or lesser extent, Mexican possessions as well.

WHAT DANGERS did settlers face as they followed the overland trails?

These were politicians' reasons. The average farmer moved west for many other reasons: land hunger, national pride, plain and simple curiosity, and a sense of adventure.

THE OVERLAND TRAILS

The 2,000-mile trip on the Overland Trails from the banks of the Missouri River to Oregon and California usually took seven months, sometimes more. Travel was slow, dangerous, tedious, and exhausting. Yet despite the risks, settlers streamed west: 5,000 to Oregon by 1845 and about 3,000 to California by 1848 (before the discovery of gold) (see Map 14.3).

Pioneers had many motives for making the trip. Glowing reports from Oregon's Willamette Valley, for example, seemed to promise economic opportunity and healthy surroundings, an alluring combination to farmers in the malaria-prone Midwest who had been hard hit by the Panic of 1837. But rational motives do not tell the whole story. Many men were motivated by a sense of adventure, by a desire to experience the unknown.

12–3
Across the Plains with Catherine Sager Pringle (1844)

17–2
Lydia Allen Rudd, Diary of Westward Travel (1852)

This painting by William Henry Jackson shows the wagon of westward migrants waiting at Council Bluffs, Iowa, to cross the Missouri River on the ferry established by the Mormons. At the height of the migration this was a major bottleneck: some people waited as long as ten days for their turn to cross.

Few pioneers traveled alone, partly because they feared Indian attack (which was rare) but largely because they needed help fording rivers or crossing mountains with heavy wagons. Most Oregon pioneers traveled with their families but usually also joined a larger group, forming a "train." In the earliest years, when the route was still uncertain, trains hired "pilots," generally former fur trappers.

Wagon trains started westward as soon as the prairies were green (thus ensuring feed for the livestock). The daily routine was quickly established. Men took care of the moving equipment and the animals, while the women cooked and kept track of the children. Slowly, at a rate of about fifteen miles a day, the wagon trains moved west. In addition to tedium and exhaustion, wagon trains were beset by such trail hazards as illness and accident. Danger from Indian attack, which all pioneers feared, was actually very small. It appears that unprovoked white attacks on Indians were more common than the reverse.

In contrast, cholera killed at least a thousand people a year in 1849 and in the early 1850s, when it was common along sections of the trail along the Platte River. Drownings were not uncommon, nor were accidental ax wounds or shootings, and children sometimes fell out of wagons and were run over. The members of the wagon train community provided support for survivors: men helped widows drive their wagons onward, women nursed and tended babies whose mothers were dead, and at least one parentless family, the seven Sager children, were brought to Oregon in safety.

By 1860, almost 300,000 people had traveled the Overland Trails to Oregon or California. Ruts from the wagon wheels can be seen in a number of places along the route even today. In 1869, the completion of the transcontinental railroad marked the end of the wagon train era (see Figure 14.1).

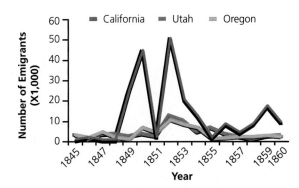

Figure 14.1 Overland Emigration to Oregon, California, and Utah, 1840–60

Before 1849, the westward migration consisted primarily of family groups going to Oregon or Utah. The discovery of gold in California dramatically changed the migration: through 1854, most migrants were single men "rushing" to California, which remained the favored destination up until 1860. Over the twenty-year period from 1840 to 1860, the Overland Trails were transformed from difficult and dangerous routes to well-marked and well-served thoroughfares.

John Unruh Jr., *The Plains Across* (Champaign-Urbana: University of Illinois Press, 1979), pp. 119–20.

OREGON

The American settlement of Oregon provides a capsule example of the stages of frontier development. The first contacts between the region's Indian peoples and Europeans were commercial. Spanish, British, Russian, and American ships traded for sea otter skins from the 1780s to about 1810. Subsequently, land-based groups scoured the region for beaver skins as well. In this first "frontier of inclusion" there were frequent contacts, many of them sexual, between Indians and Europeans.

Both Great Britain and the United States claimed the Oregon Country by right of discovery, but in the Convention of 1818, the two nations agreed to occupy it jointly, postponing a final decision on its disposition. In reality, the British clearly dominated the region. In 1824, the Hudson's Bay Company consolidated Britain's position by establishing a major fur trading post at Fort Vancouver, on the banks of the Columbia River. Like all fur-trading ventures, the post exemplified the racial mixing of a "frontier of inclusion." Fort Vancouver housed a polyglot population of eastern Indians (Delawares and Iroquois), local Chinook Indians, French and métis from Canada, British traders, and Hawaiians. But the effect of the fur trade on native tribes in Oregon was catastrophic; suffering the fate of all Indian peoples after their initial contact with Europeans, they were decimated by European diseases.

The first permanent European settlers in Oregon were retired fur trappers and their Indian wives and families. The next to arrive were Protestant and Catholic. None of these missionaries was very successful. Epidemics had taken the lives of many of the region's peoples, and those who were left were disinclined to give up their nomadic life and settle down as the missionaries wanted them to do.

Finally, in the 1840s, came the Midwest farmers who would make up the majority of Oregon's permanent settlers, carried on the wave of enthusiasm known as "Oregon fever" and lured by free land and patriotism. By 1845, Oregon boasted 5,000 American settlers, most of them living in the Willamette Valley and laying claim to lands to which they had as yet no legal right. Their arrival signaled Oregon's transition away from a "frontier of inclusion."

In June 1846, Britain and the United States concluded a treaty establishing the 49th parallel as the U.S.–Canada border but leaving the island of Vancouver in British hands. The British then quietly wound up their declining fur trade in the region. In 1849, the Hudson's Bay Company closed Fort Vancouver and moved its operations to Victoria, thus ending the Pacific Northwest's largely successful experience with joint occupancy. Oregon's Donation Land Claim Act of 1850 codified the practice of giving 320 acres to each white male age eighteen or over and 640 acres to each married couple to settle in the territory (African Americans, Hawaiians, and American Indians were excluded).

The white settlers realized that they had to forge strong community bonds if they hoped to survive on their distant frontier. Cooperation and mutual aid were the rule. Until well into the 1850s, residents organized yearly parties that traveled back along the last stretches of the **Oregon Trail** to help straggling parties making their way to the territory. Kinship networks were strong and vital: many pioneers came to join family who had migrated before them. Food sharing and mutual labor were essential in the early years when crop and livestock loss to weather or natural predators was common. Help, even to total strangers, was customary in times of illness or death.

Relations with the small and unthreatening disease-thinned local Indian tribes were generally peaceful until 1847, when Cayuse Indians killed the missionaries Marcus and Narcissa Whitman. Their deaths triggered a series of "wars" against the remaining native people. A "frontier of exclusion" had been achieved.

Oregon Trail Overland trail of more than two thousand miles that carried American settlers from the Midwest to new settlements in Oregon, California, and Utah.

This view of Fort Vancouver on the Columbia River shows established agriculture and thriving commerce, indicated by the large sailing ship on the river, which is probably the Hudson's Bay Company yearly supply ship from England. It was a scene like this that led Narcissa Whitman to call Fort Vancouver "the New York of the Pacific."

Nonetheless, the process by which Oregon became part of the United States (it was admitted as a state in 1859) was relatively peaceful, especially when compared with American expansion into the Spanish provinces of New Mexico and Texas.

THE SANTA FÉ TRADE

Commerce with Santa Fé, first settled by colonists from Mexico in 1609, and the center of the Spanish frontier province of New Mexico, had long been desired by American traders. But Spain had forcefully resisted American penetration.

When Mexico gained its independence from Spain in 1821, this exclusionary policy changed. American traders were now welcome in Santa Fé, but the trip over the legendary Santa Fé Trail from Independence, Missouri, was a forbidding 900 miles of arid plains, deserts, and mountains. The number of people venturing west in the trading caravans increased yearly because the profits were so great. By the 1840s, a few hundred American trappers and traders (called *extranjeros*, or "foreigners") lived permanently in New Mexico. In Santa Fé, some American merchants married daughters of important local families, suggesting the start of the inclusive stage of frontier contact.

Tejanos   Persons of Spanish or Mexican descent born in Texas.

Settlements and trading posts soon grew up along the long Santa Fé Trail. One of the most famous was Bent's Fort, on the Arkansas River in what is now eastern Colorado, which did a brisk trade in beaver skins and buffalo robes. Like most trading posts, it had a multiethnic population. This racially and economically mixed existence was characteristic of all early trading frontiers, but another western frontier, the American agricultural settlement in Texas, was different from the start.

MEXICAN TEXAS

In 1821, when Mexico gained its independence from Spain, there were 2,240 Tejano (Spanish-speaking) residents of Texas. As was customary throughout New Spain, communities were organized around three centers: missions and *presidios* (forts), which formed the nuclei of towns, and the large cattle-raising ranchos on which rural living depended. As elsewhere in New Spain, society was divided into two classes: the *ricos* (rich), who claimed Spanish descent, and the mixed-blood *pobres* (poor). Most **Tejanos** were neither ricos nor vaqueros but small farmers or common laborers who led hardscrabble frontier lives. But all Tejanos, rich and poor, faced the constant threat of raids by Comanche Indians.

Legendary warriors, the Comanches raided the small Texas settlements at will and even struck deep into Mexico itself. The nomadic Comanches followed the immense buffalo herds on which they depended for food and clothing. Their relentless raids on the Texas settlements rose from a determination to hold onto this rich buffalo territory, for the buffalo provided all that they wanted. They had no interest in being converted by mission priests or incorporated into mixed-race trading communities.

AMERICANS IN TEXAS

In 1821, seeking to increase the strength of its buffer zone between the heart of Mexico and the marauding Comanches, the Mexican government granted Moses Austin of Missouri an area of 18,000 square miles within the territory of Texas. Moses died shortly thereafter, and the grant was taken up by his son Stephen F. Austin, who became the first American empresario (land agent). From the beginning, the American settlement of Texas differed markedly from that of other frontiers. Elsewhere, Americans frequently settled on land to which Indian peoples still held title, or, as in the case of Oregon, they occupied lands to which other

Painted by George Catlin in about 1834, this scene, *Commanche Village Life*, shows how the everyday life of the Comanches was tied to buffalo. The women in the foreground are scraping buffalo hide, and buffalo meat can be seen drying on racks. The men and boys may be planning their next buffalo hunt.

countries also made claim. In contrast, the Texas settlement was fully legal: Austin and other **empresarios** owned their lands as a result of formal contracts with the Mexican government.

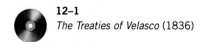

12–1
The Treaties of Velasco (1836)

Insisting that "no frontiersman who has no other occupation than that of hunter will be received—no drunkard, no gambler, no profane swearer, no idler," Austin chose instead prosperous southern slave owners eager to expand the lands devoted to cotton. Soon Americans (including African American slaves, to whose presence the Mexican government turned a blind eye) outnumbered Tejanos by nearly two to one.

The Austin settlement of 1821 was followed by others, twenty-six in all, concentrating in the fertile river bottoms of eastern Texas (along the Sabine River) and south central Texas (the Brazos and the Colorado Rivers). These large settlements were highly organized farming enterprises whose principal crop was cotton, grown by African American slave labor and sold in the international market.

Austin's colonists and those who settled later were predominantly Southerners who viewed Texas as a natural extension of the cotton frontier in Mississippi and Louisiana. These settlers created "**enclaves**" (self-contained communities) that had little contact with Tejanos or Indian peoples. In fact, although they lived in Mexican territory, most Americans never bothered to learn Spanish. Yet, because of the nature of agreements made by the empresarios, the Americans could not set up local American-style governments like the one created by settlers in Oregon. Like the immigrants who flooded into East Coast cities (see Chapter 13), the Americans in Texas were immigrants to another country—but one to which they did not intend to adapt.

For a brief period, Texas was big enough to hold three communities: Comanche, Tejano, and American. Each group would fight to hold its land: the Comanches, their rich hunting grounds; the Mexicans, their towns and ranchos; and the newcomers, the Americans, their rich land grants.

The balance among the three communities in Texas was broken in 1828, when centrists gained control of the government in Mexico City and, in a dramatic shift of policy, decided to exercise firm control over the northern province. As the Mexican government restricted American immigration, outlawed slavery, levied customs duties and taxes, and planned other measures, Americans seethed and talked of rebellion. Bolstering their cause were as many as 20,000 additional Americans, many of them openly expansionist, who flooded into Texas after 1830.

Many of the post-1830 immigrants were vehemently anti-Mexican. Statements of racial superiority were commonplace, and even Stephen Austin wrote in 1836 that he saw the Texas conflict as one of barbarism on the part of "a mongrel Spanish-Indian and negro race, against civilization and the Anglo-American race."

Between 1830 and 1836, in spite of the mediation efforts of Austin, the mood on both the Mexican and the American-Texan sides became more belligerent. In the fall of 1835, war finally broke out, and a volunteer American and Tejano army assembled. After the disastrous defeat at the **Alamo** described in the chapter opener, Mexican general and president Antonio López de Santa Anna led his army in pursuit of the remaining army of American and Tejano volunteers commanded by General Sam Houston.

On April 21, 1836, at the San Jacinto River in eastern Texas, Santa Anna thought he had Houston trapped at last. Confident of victory against the exhausted Texans, Santa Anna's army rested in the afternoon, failing even to post sentries. Although Houston advised against it, Houston's men voted to attack immediately rather than wait till the next morning. Shouting "Remember the Alamo!" for the first time, the Texans completely surprised their opponents and won an overwhelming victory. On May 14, 1836, Santa Anna signed a treaty fixing the southern boundary of the newly independent Republic of Texas at the Rio Grande. The

Empresarios Agents who received a land grant from the Spanish or Mexican government in return for organizing settlements.

Enclave Self-contained community.

Alamo Franciscan mission at San Antonio, Texas that was the site in 1836 of a siege and massacre of Texans by Mexican troops.

MAP 14.4

Texas: From Mexican Province to U.S. State In the space of twenty years, Texas changed shape three times. Initially part of the Mexican province of Coahuila y Tejas, it became the Republic of Texas in 1836, following the Texas Revolt, and was annexed to the United States in that form in 1845. Finally, in the Compromise of 1850 following the Mexican-American War, it took its present shape.

WHO SUPPORTED the formation of the Republic of Texas? What were the forces that resulted in eventual statehood?

Mexican Congress, however, repudiated the treaty and refused to recognize Texan independence (see Map 14.4).

THE REPUBLIC OF TEXAS

The Republic of Texas was unexpectedly rebuffed in another quarter as well. The U.S. Congress refused to grant it statehood when, in 1837, Texas applied for admission to the Union. Petitions opposing the admission of a fourteenth slave state (there were then thirteen free states) poured into Congress. Congressman (and former president) John Quincy Adams of Massachusetts led the opposition to the admission of Texas. Congress debated and ultimately dropped the Texas application.

The unresolved conflict with Mexico put heavy stress on American–Tejano relations. As before, ambitious Anglos married into the Tejano elite, which made it easier for those Tejano families to adjust to the changes in law and commerce that the Americans quickly enacted. But following a temporary recapture of San Antonio by Mexican forces in 1842, positions hardened. Many more of the Tejano elite fled to Mexico, and Americans discussed banishing or imprisoning all Tejanos until the border issue was settled. This was, of course, impossible. Culturally, San Antonio remained a Mexican city long after the Americans had declared independence.

American control over the other Texas residents, the Indians, was also slow in coming. The Comanches still rode the high plains of northern and western Texas. West of the Rio Grande, equally fierce Apache bands were in control. Both groups soon learned to distrust American promises to stay out of their territory, and they did not hesitate to raid settlements and to kill trespassers. Not until after the Civil War and major campaigns by the U.S. Army were these fierce Indian tribes conquered.

Texans continued to press for annexation to the United States, while at the same time seeking recognition and support from Great Britain. The idea of an independent and expansionist republic on its southern border that might gain the support of America's traditional enemy alarmed many Americans. Annexation thus became an urgent matter of national politics. This issue also added to the troubles of a governing Whig Party that was already deeply divided by the policies of John Tyler, who had become president by default when William Harrison died in office (see Chapter 11). Tyler raised the issue of annexation in 1844, hoping thereby to ensure his reelection, but the strategy backfired. Presenting the annexation treaty to Congress, Secretary of State John Calhoun awakened sectional fears by connecting Texas with the urgent need of southern slave owners to extend slavery.

In a storm of antislavery protest, Whigs rejected the treaty proposed by their own president and ejected Tyler himself from the party. In his place, they chose Henry Clay, the party's longtime standard-bearer, as their presidential candidate. Clay took a noncommittal stance on Texas, favoring annexation, but only if Mexico approved. Since Mexico's emphatic disapproval was well known, Clay's position was widely interpreted as a politician's effort not to alienate voters on either side of the fence.

In contrast, in the Democratic Party, wholehearted and outspoken expansionists seized control. The Democrats nominated their first "dark horse" candidate, James K. Polk of Tennessee. Democrats enthusiastically endorsed Polk's platform, which called for "the re-occupation of Oregon and the re-annexation of Texas at the earliest practicable period."

Polk won the 1844 election by a narrow margin. The 1844 election was widely interpreted as a mandate for expansion. Thereupon, John Tyler, in one of his last actions as president, pushed through Congress a joint resolution (which did not require the two-thirds approval by the Senate necessary for treaties) for the annexation of Texas. When Texas entered the Union in December 1845, it was the twenty-eighth state and the fifteenth slave state.

THE MEXICAN-AMERICAN WAR

James K. Polk lived up to his campaign promises. In 1846, he peacefully added Oregon south of the 49th parallel to the United States; in 1848, following the **Mexican-American War**, he acquired Mexico's northern provinces of California and New Mexico as well. Thus, with the annexation of Texas, the United States, in the short space of three years, had added 1.5 million square miles of territory, an increase of nearly 70 percent. Polk was indeed the "manifest destiny" president.

ORIGINS OF THE WAR

In the spring of 1846, just as the controversy over Oregon was drawing to a peaceful conclusion, tensions with Mexico grew more serious. Because the United States supported the Texas claim of all land north of the Rio Grande, it became embroiled

WHAT WERE the most important consequences of the Mexican-American War?

Review Summary

Mexican-American War   War fought between Mexico and the United States between 1846 and 1848 over control of territory in southwest North America.

in a border dispute with Mexico. In June 1845, Polk sent General Zachary Taylor to Texas, and by October a force of 3,500 Americans were on the Nueces River with orders to defend Texas in the event of a Mexican invasion.

Polk had something bigger than border protection in mind. He coveted the continent clear to the Pacific Ocean. At the same time that he sent Taylor to Texas, Polk secretly instructed the Pacific naval squadron to seize the California ports if Mexico declared war. He also wrote the American consul in Monterey, Thomas Larkin, that a peaceful takeover of California by its residents—Spanish Mexicans and Americans alike—would not be unwelcome.

In April 1846, a brief skirmish between American and Mexican soldiers broke out in the disputed zone. Polk seized on the event, sending a war message to Congress: "Mexico has passed the boundary of the United States, has invaded our territory and shed American blood upon American soil. . . . War exists, and, notwithstanding all our efforts to avoid it, exists by the act of Mexico herself." This claim of President Polk's was, of course, contrary to fact. On May 13, 1846, Congress declared war on Mexico (see Map 14.5).

MR. POLK'S WAR

From the beginning, the Mexican-American War was politically divisive. Whig critics in Congress, among them a gawky young congressman from Illinois named Abraham Lincoln, questioned Polk's account of the border incident. They accused the president of misleading Congress and of maneuvering the country into an unnecessary war. As the Mexican-American War dragged on and casualties and costs mounted, opposition increased, especially among northern antislavery Whigs. Many Northerners asked why Polk had been willing to settle for only a part of Oregon but was so eager to pursue a war for slave territory. Thus, expansionist dreams served to fuel sectional antagonisms.

Whigs termed the war with Mexico "Mr. Polk's War," but the charge was not just a Whig jibe. Although he lacked a military background, Polk assumed the overall planning of the war's strategy. By his personal attention to the coordination of civilian political goals and military requirements, Polk gave a new and expanded definition to the

QUICK REVIEW

War with Mexico

* Polk sought a war that would give United States control of California.

* Mexico fought hard but could not match American military.

* Treaty of Guadalupe Hidalgo (1848): Mexico gave up claim to Texas north of Rio Grande, Alta California, and New Mexico.

General Winfield Scott's amphibious attack on the Mexican coastal city of Veracruz in March 1847 was greeted with wide popular acclaim in the United States. It was the first successful amphibious attack in U.S. military history. Popular interest in the battles of the Mexican-American War was fed by illustrations such as this in newspapers and magazines.

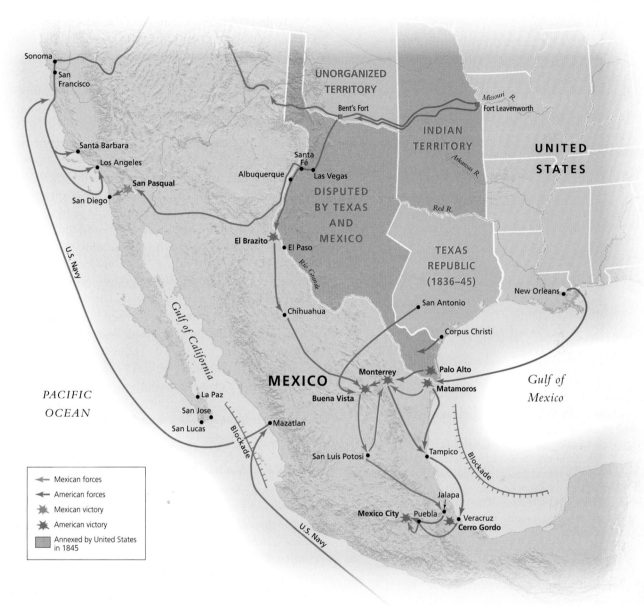

MAP 14.5

The Mexican-American War, 1846–48   The Mexican-American War began with an advance by U.S. forces into the disputed area between the Nueces River and the Rio Grande in Texas. The war's major battles were fought by General Zachary Taylor in northern Mexico and General Winfield Scott in Veracruz and Mexico City. Meanwhile Colonel Stephen Kearny secured New Mexico and, with the help of the U.S. Navy and John C. Frémont's troops, California.

WHY WAS the United States more successful than Mexico in achieving its goals?

role of the president as commander in chief during wartime. By the end of 1846, the northern provinces that Polk had coveted were secured, but contrary to his expectations, Mexico refused to negotiate. In March 1847, General Winfield Scott launched an amphibious attack on the coastal city of Veracruz and rapidly captured it. Americans celebrated these twin victories joyously, but they were to be the last easy victories of the war. It took Scott six months of brutal fighting against stubborn Mexican resistance on the battlefield and harassing guerrilla raids to force his way to Mexico City. American troops reacted bitterly to their high casualty rates, retaliating against Mexican citizens with acts of murder, robbery, and rape. In September, Scott took Mexico City, and Mexican resistance came to an end.

CANADA

Treaty Line

OREGON
TERRITORY
(1846)

UNORGANIZED
TERRITORY

MINNESOTA
TERRITORY
(1849)

MEXICAN
CESSION
(1848)

INDIAN
TERRITORY

GADSDEN
PURCHASE
(1853)

TEXAS
ANNEXATION
(1845)

*PACIFIC
OCEAN*

MEXICO

*Gulf of
Mexico*

MAP 14.6
Territory Added, 1845–53 James K. Polk was elected president in 1844 on an expansionist platform. He lived up to most of his campaign rhetoric by gaining the Oregon Country (to the 49th parallel) peacefully from the British, Texas by the presidential action of his predecessor John Tyler, and present-day California, Arizona, Nevada, Utah, New Mexico, and part of Colorado by war with Mexico. In the short space of three years, the size of the United States grew by 70 percent. In 1853, the Gadsden Purchase added another 30,000 square miles.

WHAT CHALLENGES did the United States face as it absorbed substantial new territories?

12–5
Thomas Corwin, *Against the Mexican War* (1847)

WHAT KINDS of people participated in the California Gold Rush?

myhistorylab

Review Summary

Californios Californians of Spanish descent.

With the American army went a special envoy, Nicholas Trist, who delivered Polk's terms for peace. In the Treaty of Guadalupe Hidalgo, signed February 2, 1848, Mexico ceded its northern provinces of California and New Mexico (which included present-day Arizona, Utah, Nevada, and part of Colorado) and accepted the Rio Grande as the boundary of Texas. The United States agreed to pay Mexico $15 million and assume about $2 million in individual claims against that nation.

When Trist returned to Washington with the treaty, however, Polk was furious. He had actually recalled Trist after Scott's sweeping victory, intending to send a new envoy with greater demands, but Trist had ignored the recall order. "All Mexico!" had become the phrase widely used by those in favor of further expansion, Polk among them. But two very different groups opposed further expansion. The first group, composed of northern Whigs. The second group was composed of Southerners who realized that Mexicans could not be kept as conquered people but would have to be offered territorial government as Louisiana had been offered in 1804. Bowing to these political protests, Polk reluctantly accepted the treaty. A later addition, the $10 million Gadsden Purchase of parts of present-day New Mexico and Arizona, added another 30,000 square miles to the United States in 1853 (see Map 14.6).

THE PRESS AND POPULAR WAR ENTHUSIASM

The Mexican-American War was the first war in which regular, on-the-scene reporting by representatives of the press caught the mass of ordinary citizens up in the war's daily events. Thanks to the recently invented telegraph, newspapers could get the latest news from their reporters, who were among the world's first war correspondents. The "penny press," with more than a decade's experience of reporting urban crime and scandals, was quick to realize that the public's appetite for sensational war news was apparently insatiable. For the first time in American history, accounts by journalists, and not the opinions of politicians, became the major shapers of popular attitudes toward a war. From beginning to end, news of the war stirred unprecedented popular excitement (see Seeing History).

Exciting, sobering, and terrible, war news had a deep hold on the popular imagination. It was a lesson newspaper publishers never forgot.

CALIFORNIA AND THE GOLD RUSH

In the early 1840s, California was inhabited by many seminomadic Indian tribes whose people numbered approximately 50,000. There were also some 7,000 **Californios**, descendants of the Spanish-Mexican pioneers who had begun to settle in 1769. Even American annexation at the end of the Mexican-American War changed little for the handful of Americans on this remote frontier. But then came the gold rush of 1849, which changed California permanently.

War News from Mexico

The unprecedented immediacy of the news reporting from the battlefields of the Mexican-American War, transmitted for the first time by telegraph, is captured in this painting by the American artist Richard Caton Woodville, painted in 1848 (the year the war ended). Woodville was one of a number of genre painters who enlivened their depictions of everyday life and ordinary people by focusing on political debates or dramatic moments like the one shown here.

Almost every aspect of this painting is political commentary. The central figure in the painting is standing on the porch of the American Hotel reading the latest war news to the crowd of men gathered around him from a cheap "penny paper" full of sensational stories, war news, and lithographs of battle scenes from the war. Although the audience seems deeply engaged, the range of expressions reminds the viewer that the war was very divisive, with many antislavery Northerners in outright opposition. The placement of the African American man at a lower level on the step is a clear statement of his exclusion from political participation. Don't overlook the woman leaning out of the window on the right side of the painting. She too is excluded from politics but is obviously just as interested and concerned as the men. Woodville's inclusion of the black child in a white smock seems to be an ambiguous statement about the impact of the Mexican-American War on slavery. ∎

ARE YOU surprised at the extent of political commentary in this painting? Are paintings an appropriate media for political opinion?

Richard Caton Woodville, "War News from Mexico," Oil on canvas. Manovgian Foundation on loan to the National Gallery of Art, Washington, DC. © Board of Trustees, National Gallery of Art, Washington.

RUSSIAN–CALIFORNIOS TRADE

The first outsiders to penetrate the isolation of Spanish California were not Americans but Russians. A mutually beneficial barter of California food for iron tools and woven cloth from Russia was established in 1806. This arrangement became even brisker after the Russians settled Fort Ross (near present-day Mendocino) in 1812 and led in time to regular trade with Mission San Rafael and Mission Sonoma. That the Russians in Alaska, so far from their own capital, were better supplied with manufactured goods than the Californios is an index of the latter's isolation.

When Mexico became independent in 1821, the California trade was thrown open to ships of all nations. Nevertheless, Californios continued their special relationship with the Russians, exempting them from the taxes and inspections that they required of Americans. However, agricultural productivity declined after 1832, when the Mexican government ordered the secularization of the California missions, and the Russians regretfully turned to the rich farms of the Hudson's Bay Company in the Pacific Northwest for their food supply. In 1841, they sold Fort Ross, and the Russian–Californio connection came to an end.

EARLY AMERICAN SETTLEMENT

It was Johann Augustus Sutter, a Swiss who had settled in California in 1839, becoming a Mexican citizen, who served as a focal point for American settlement in the 1840s. In the 1840s, Sutter offered valuable support to the handful of American overlanders who chose California over Oregon, the destination preferred by most pioneers. Most of these Americans, keenly aware that they were interlopers in Mexican territory, settled near Sutter in California's Central Valley, away from the Californios clustered along the coast.

The 1840s' immigrants made no effort to intermarry with the Californios or to conform to Spanish ways. They were bent on taking over the territory. In June 1846, these Americans banded together at Sonoma in the Bear Flag Revolt (so called because their flag bore a bear emblem), declaring independence from Mexico. The American takeover of California was not confirmed until the Treaty of Guadalupe Hidalgo in 1848.

GOLD!

In January 1848, carpenter James Marshall noticed small flakes of gold in the millrace at Sutter's Mill (present-day Coloma). Soon he and all the rest of John Sutter's employees were panning for gold in California's streams. But not until the autumn of 1848 did the East Coast hear the first rumors about the discovery of gold in California. The spirit of excitement and adventure so recently aroused by the Mexican-American War was now directed toward California, the new El Dorado. Thousands left farms and jobs and headed west, by land and by sea, to make their fortune. Later known as "forty-niners" for the year the gold rush began in earnest, these people came from all parts of the United States—and indeed, from all over the world. They transformed what had been a quiet ranching paradise into a teeming and tumultuous community in search of wealth in California's rivers and streams.

Eighty percent of the forty-niners were Americans. The second largest group of migrants was from nearby Mexico and the western coast of Latin America (13 percent). The remainder came from Europe and Asia (see Figure 14.2).

The presence of Chinese miners surprised many Americans. Several hundred Chinese arrived in California in 1849 and 1850, and in 1852 more than 20,000 landed in San Francisco hoping to share in the wealth of "Gum Sam"

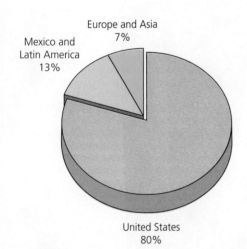

Europe and Asia
7%

Mexico and
Latin America
13%

United States
80%

Figure 14.2 Where the Forty-Niners Came From
Americans drawn to the California gold rush of 1849 encountered a more diverse population than most had previously known. Nearly as novel to them as the 20 percent from foreign countries was the regional variety from within the United States itself.

This drawing of the bar of a gambling saloon in San Francisco in 1855 shows the effects of the gold rush on California. Men from all parts of the world are gathered at this elegant bar in the large cosmopolitan city of San Francisco, which had been only a small trading post before gold was discovered in 1849.

Frank Marryat, "The Bar of a Gambling Saloon," published 1855. Lithograph. Collection of the New-York Historical Society, New York City.

(Golden Mountain). Most came, like the Americans, as temporary sojourners, intending to return home as soon as they made some money. Again, like most of the American miners, the majority of Chinese were men who left their wives at home. The distinctive appearance of the Chinese, added to the threat of economic competition that they posed, quickly aroused American hostility. A special tax was imposed on foreign miners in 1852, and in the 1870s, Chinese immigration was sharply curtailed.

In 1849, as the gold rush began in earnest, San Francisco, the major entry port and supply point, sprang to life. From a settlement of 1,000 in 1848, it grew

Chinese first came to California in 1849 attracted by the gold rush. Frequently, however, they were forced off their claims by intolerant whites. Rather than enjoy an equal chance in the goldfields, they were often forced to work as servants or in other menial occupations.

QUICK REVIEW

Discovery of Gold

♦ Gold discovered at Sutter's Mill in 1848.
♦ Most forty-niners were Americans.
♦ Gold rush led rapid growth of San Francisco.

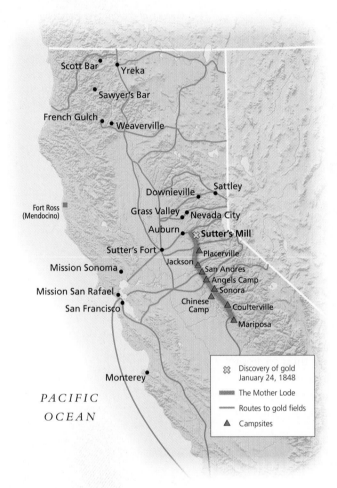

MAP 14.7

California in the Gold Rush   This map shows the major gold camps along the mother lode in the western foothills of the Sierra Nevada Mountains. Gold seekers reached the camps by crossing the Sierra Nevada near Placerville on the Overland Trail or by sea via San Francisco. The main area of Spanish-Mexican settlement, the coastal region between Monterey and Los Angeles, was remote from the goldfields.

Warren A. Beck and Ynez D. Haase, *Historical Atlas of California* (Norman: University of Oklahoma Press, 1974), map 50.

WHAT WAS life like in the California gold camps during the gold rush?

myhistõrylab

Exploring America:
The Unwelcome Mat

17–1
Edward Gould Buffum, *Six Months in the Gold Mines* (1850)

to a city of 35,000 in 1850. This surge suggested that the real money to be made in California was not in panning for gold but in feeding, clothing, housing, provisioning, and entertaining the miners. The white population of California jumped from an estimated pre–gold rush figure of 11,000 to more than 100,000 by 1852. California was admitted into the Union as a state in 1850.

MINING CAMPS

As had occurred in San Francisco, most mining camps boomed almost instantly to life, but unlike San Francisco, they were empty again within a few years. Most miners lived in tents or hovels, unwilling to take time from mining to build themselves decent quarters. They cooked monotonous meals of beans, bread, and bacon or, if they had money, bought meals at expensive restaurants and boardinghouses. They led a cheerless, uncomfortable, and unhealthy existence, especially during the long, rainy winter months, with few distractions apart from the saloon, the gambling hall, and the prostitute's bed (see Map 14.7).

Most miners were young, unmarried, and unsuccessful. Only a small percentage ever struck it rich in California. Gold deposits that were accessible with pick and shovel were soon exhausted, and the deeper deposits required capital and machinery. Increasingly, those who stayed on in California had to give up the status of independent miners and become wage earners for large mining concerns.

Every mining community had its saloonkeepers, gamblers, prostitutes, merchants, and restauranteurs. Like the miners themselves, these people were transients, always ready to pick up and move at the word of a new gold strike. The majority of women in the early mining camps were prostitutes. Most of the other women were hardworking wives of miners, and in this predominantly male society, they made good money doing domestic work by keeping boardinghouses, cooking, and doing laundry.

Partly because few people put any effort into building communities violence was endemic in mining areas, and much of it was racial. Discrimination, especially against Chinese, Mexicans, and African Americans, was common.

By the mid-1850s, the immediate effects of the gold rush had passed. California had a booming population, a thriving agriculture, and a corporate mining industry. The gold rush also left California with a population that was larger, more affluent, and (in urban San Francisco) more culturally sophisticated than that in other newly settled territories. And it was significantly more multicultural than the rest of the nation, for many of the Chinese and Mexicans, as well as immigrants from many European countries, remained in California after the gold rush subsided. But the gold rush left some permanent scars, and not just on the foothills landscape: the virtual extermination of the California Indian peoples, the dispossession of many Californios who were legally deprived of their land grants, and the growth of racial animosity toward the Chinese in particular.

THE POLITICS OF MANIFEST DESTINY

In three short years, from 1845 to 1848, the territory of the United States grew an incredible 70 percent, and a continental nation took shape. This expansion, pushed by economic desires and feelings of American cultural superiority, led directly to the emergence of the divisive issue of slavery as the dominant issue in national politics.

THE WILMOT PROVISO

In 1846, almost all the northern members of the Whig Party opposed Democratic president James Polk's belligerent expansionism on antislavery grounds. Northern Whigs correctly feared that expansion would reopen the issue of slavery in the territories. But the outpouring of popular enthusiasm for the Mexican-American War convinced most Whig congressmen that they needed to vote military appropriations for the war in spite of their misgivings.

Ironically, it was not the Whigs but a freshman Democratic congressman from Pennsylvania, David Wilmot, who opened the door to sectional controversy over expansion. In August 1846, only a few short months after the beginning of the Mexican-American War, Wilmot proposed, in an amendment to a military appropriations bill, that slavery be banned in all the territories acquired from Mexico. In the debate and voting that followed, something new and ominous occurred: southern Whigs joined southern Democrats to vote against the measure, while Northerners of both parties supported it. Sectional interest had triumphed over party loyalty.

The **Wilmot Proviso** was so controversial that it was deleted from the necessary military appropriations bills during the Mexican-American War. But in 1848, following the Treaty of Guadalupe Hidalgo, the question of the expansion of slavery could no longer be avoided or postponed. Antislavery advocates from the North argued with proslavery Southerners in a debate that was much more prolonged and bitter than in the Missouri Crisis debate of 1819. The Wilmot Proviso posed a fundamental challenge to both parties. Neither the Democrats nor the Whigs could

WHAT KEY factors explain the outcome of the election of 1848?

myhistorylab
Review Summary

myhistorylab
Overview: *Expansion Causes the First Splits in the Second American Party System*

Wilmot Proviso   The amendment offered by Pennsylvania Democrat David Wilmot in 1846 which stipulated that "as an express and fundamental condition to the acquisition of any territory from the Republic of Mexico ... neither slavery nor involuntary servitude shall ever exist in any part of said territory."

OVERVIEW | Expansion Causes the First Splits in the Second American Party System

1844	Whigs reject President John Tyler's move to annex Texas and expel him from the Whig Party.
	Southern Democrats choose expansionist James K. Polk as their presidential candidate, passing over Martin Van Buren, who is against expansion.
	Liberty Party runs abolitionist James Birney for president, attracting northern antislavery Whigs.
1846	The Wilmot Proviso, proposing to ban slavery in the territories that might be gained in the Mexican-American War, splits both parties: southern Whigs and Democrats oppose the measure; northern Whigs and Democrats support it.
1848	The new Free-Soil Party runs northern Democrat Martin Van Buren for president, gaining 10 percent of the vote from abolitionists, antislavery Whigs, and some northern Democrats. This strong showing by a third party causes Democrat Lewis Cass to lose the electoral votes of New York and Pennsylvania, allowing the Whig Zachary Taylor to win.

In 1848, the Whigs nominated a hero of the Mexican-American War, General Zachary Taylor, who ran on his military exploits. In this campaign poster, every letter of Taylor's name is decorated with scenes from the recent war, which had seized the popular imagination in a way no previous conflict had done.

QUICK REVIEW

Slavery and the Election of 1848

◆ Democratic candidate Lewis Cass argued that territorial residents should decide issue of slavery.

◆ Whig nominee Zachary Taylor remained silent on slavery issue.

◆ Taylor's election gave country first president from Lower South.

Liberty Party The first antislavery political party, formed in 1840.

Popular sovereignty A solution to the slavery crisis suggested by Michigan senator Lewis Cass by which territorial residents, not Congress, would decide slavery's fate.

take a strong stand on the amendment because neither party could get its northern and southern wings to agree.

THE FREE-SOIL MOVEMENT

Why did David Wilmot propose this controversial measure? Wilmot, a northern Democrat, was propelled not by ideology but by the pressure of practical politics. The dramatic rise of the **Liberty Party**, founded in 1840 by abolitionists, threatened to take votes away from both the Whig and the Democratic parties.

The Liberty Party took an uncompromising stance against slavery. The party proposed to prohibit the admission of slave states to the Union, end slavery in the District of Columbia, and abolish the interstate slave trade that was vital to the expansion of cotton growing into the Old Southwest. Liberty Party doctrine was too uncompromising for the mass of northern voters, who immediately realized that the southern states would leave the Union before accepting it. Still, many Northerners opposed slavery. From this sentiment, the Free-Soil Party was born.

The free-soil argument was a calculated adjustment of abolitionist principles to practical politics. It shifted the focus from the question of the morality of slavery to the ways in which slavery posed a threat to northern expansion. The free-soil doctrine thus established a direct link between expansion, which most Americans supported, and sectional politics.

Free-soilers were willing to allow slavery to continue in the existing slave states because they supported the Union, not because they approved of slavery. They were unwilling, however, to allow the extension of slavery to new and unorganized territory. If the South were successful in extending slavery, they argued, northern farmers who moved west would find themselves competing at an economic disadvantage with large planters using slave labor. Free-soilers also insisted that the northern values of freedom and individualism would be destroyed if the slave-based southern labor system were allowed to spread.

Many free-soilers really meant "anti-black" when they said "antislavery." They proposed to ban all African American people from the new territories, Most Northerners were unwilling to consider social equality for African Americans, free or slave. Banning all black people from the western territories seemed a simple solution.

THE ELECTION OF 1848

A swirl of emotions—pride, expansionism, sectionalism, abolitionism, free-soil sentiment—surrounded the election of 1848. Lewis Cass of Michigan, the Democratic nominee for president (Polk, in poor health, declined to run for a second term), proposed to apply the doctrine of popular sovereignty to the crucial slave–free issue. **Popular sovereignty** was based on the accepted constitutional principle that decisions about slavery should be made at the state rather than the national level. In reality, popular sovereignty was an admission of the national failure to resolve sectional differences.

For their part, the Whigs passed over perennial candidate Henry Clay and turned to a war hero, General Zachary Taylor. Taylor, a Louisiana slaveholder, refused to take a position on the Wilmot Proviso, allowing both northern and southern voters to hope that he agreed with them.

The deliberate vagueness of the two major candidates displeased many northern voters. An uneasy mixture of disaffected Democrats (among them David Wilmot) and Whigs joined former Liberty Party voters to support the candidate

CHRONOLOGY

1609	First Spanish settlement in New Mexico
1670s	British and French Canadians begin fur trade in western Canada
1716	First Spanish settlements in Texas
1769	First Spanish settlement in California
1780s	New England ships begin sea otter trade in Pacific Northwest
1793	Alexander Mackenzie of the North West Company reaches the Pacific Ocean
1803	Louisiana Purchase
1804–06	Lewis and Clark expedition
1806	Russian–Californio trade begins
1806–07	Zebulon Pike's expedition across the Great Plains to the Rocky Mountains
1819–20	Stephen Long's expedition across the Great Plains
1821	Hudson's Bay Company gains dominance of western fur trade
	Mexico seizes independence from Spain
	Santa Fé Trail opens, soon protected by U.S. military
	Stephen F. Austin becomes first American empresario in Texas
1824	First fur rendezvous sponsored by Rocky Mountain Fur Company
	Hudson's Bay Company establishes Fort Vancouver in Oregon Country
1830	Indian Removal Act moves eastern Indians to Indian Territory
1833–34	Prince Maximilian and Karl Bodmer visit Plains Indians
1834	Jason Lee establishes first mission in Oregon Country
1835	Texas revolts against Mexico
1836	Battles of the Alamo and San Jacinto
	Republic of Texas formed
1843–44	John C. Frémont maps trails to Oregon and California
1844	Democrat James K. Polk elected president on an expansionist platform
1845	Texas annexed to the United States as a slave state
	John O'Sullivan coins the phrase "manifest destiny"
1846	Oregon question settled peacefully with Britain
	Mexican-American War begins
	Bear Flag Revolt in California
	Wilmot Proviso
1847	Cayuse War begins in Oregon
	Americans win battles of Buena Vista, Veracruz, and Mexico City
1848	Treaty of Guadalupe Hidalgo
	Free-Soil Party captures 10 percent of the popular vote in the North
	General Zachary Taylor, a Whig, elected president
1849	California gold rush

of the Free-Soil Party, former president Martin Van Buren. In the end, Van Buren garnered 10 percent of the vote (all in the North). The vote for the Free-Soil Party cost Cass the electoral votes of New York and Pennsylvania, and General Zachary Taylor won the election with only 47 percent of the popular vote. This was the second election after 1840 that the Whigs had won by running a war hero who could duck hard questions by claiming to be above politics. Uncannily, history was to repeat itself: Taylor, like William Henry Harrison, died before his term was completed, and the chance he offered to maintain national unity—if ever it existed—was lost.

CONCLUSION

I n the decade of the 1840s, westward expansion took many forms, from relatively peaceful settlement in Oregon, to war with Mexico over Texas, to the overwhelming numbers of gold rushers who changed California forever. Most of these frontiers—in Oregon, New Mexico, and California—began as frontiers of

inclusion, in which small numbers of Americans were eager for trade, accommodation, and intermarriage with the original inhabitants. Texas, with its agricultural enclaves, was the exception to this pattern. Yet on every frontier, as the number of American settlers increased, so did the sentiment for exclusion, so that by 1850, whatever their origins, the far-flung American continental settlements were more similar than different, and the success of manifest destiny seemed overwhelming.

The amazing expansion achieved by the Mexican-American War—America's manifest destiny—made the United States a continental nation but stirred up the issue that was to tear it apart. Sectional rivalries and fears now dominated every aspect of politics. Expansion, once a force for unity, now divided the nation into Northerners and Southerners, who could not agree on the community they shared—the federal Union.

REVIEW QUESTIONS

1. Define and discuss the concept of manifest destiny.

2. Trace the different ways in which the frontiers in Oregon, Texas, and California moved from frontiers of inclusion to frontiers of exclusion.

3. Take different sides (Whig and Democrat) and debate the issues raised by the Mexican-American War.

4. The California gold rush was an unprecedented scramble for riches. What were its effects on its participants, on California, and on the nation as a whole?

5. Referring to Chapter 13, compare the positions of the Liberty Party and the Free-Soil Party. Examine the factors that made the free-soil doctrine politically so acceptable and abolitionism so controversial.

KEY TERMS

myhistorylab

Flashcard Review

Alamo (p. 363)
Californios (p. 368)
Empresarios (p. 363)
Enclave (p. 363)
Liberty Party (p. 374)
Manifest destiny (p. 357)

Mexican-American War (p. 365)
Oregon Trail (p. 360)
Popular sovereignty (p. 374)
Santa Fé Trail (p. 354)
Tejanos (p. 362)
Wilmot Proviso (p. 373)

RECOMMENDED READING

Sucheng Chan, *This Bittersweet Soil: The Chinese in California Agriculture 1860–1910* (1987). The Chinese in California after the gold rush.

John Mack Faragher, *Women and Men on the Overland Trail* (1979). One of the first books to consider the experience of women on the journey west.

Paul Foos, *A Short, Offhand, Killing Affair: Soldiers and Social Conflict During the Mexican-American War* (2002). The lives and attitudes of ordinary American soldiers.

Robert W. Johannsen, *To the Halls of the Montezumas: The Mexican War in the American Imagination* (1985). A lively book that explores the impact of the Mexican-American War on public opinion.

Susan Johnson, *Roaring Camp: The Social World of the California Gold Rush* (2000). A beautifully written study of the varieties of mining camp experience.

Paul D. Lack, *The Texas Revolutionary Experience: A Political and Social History, 1835–1836* (1992). A political and social history that stresses the chaotic and discordant nature of the Texas Revolt.

Andrés Reséndez, *Changing National Identities at the Frontier: Texas and New Mexico, 1800–1850* (2004). The choices faced by Latinos, American Indians, and Anglos.

Randy Roberts and James S. Olson, *A Line in the Sand: The Alamo in Blood and Memory* (2001). How the battle became a symbol.

Malcolm Rohrbough, *Days of Gold: The California Gold Rush and the American Nation* (1997). A lively history that emphasizes the effects of this "great American epic" on the national self-image.

David J. Weber, *The Mexican Frontier, 1821–1846: The American Southwest under Mexico* (1982). A fine study of the history of the Southwest before American conquest by a leading borderlands historian.

myhistorylab™
Where it's a good time to connect to the past!

For study resources for this chapter, go to **www.myhistorylab.com** and choose *Out of Many, Teaching and Learning Classroom Edition.* You will find a wealth of study and review material for this chapter, including pretests and posttests, customized study plan, key-term review flash cards, interactive map and document activities, and documents for analysis.

This horror, this nightmare abomination!
Can it be in my country! It lies like lead on
my heart, it shadows my life with sorrow . . .
— Harriet Beecher Stowe, December 16, 1852

Republican night-time parade.

15

THE COMING CRISIS
THE 1850s

WHY DID people in the North and the South tend to see the issue of slavery differently?

WHAT WAS the intent of the Compromise of 1850?

WHAT EXPLAINS the end of the Second American Party System and the rise of the Republican Party?

WHAT WAS the outcome of the *Dred Scott* decision?

WHY DID the South secede following the Republican Party victory in the election of 1860?

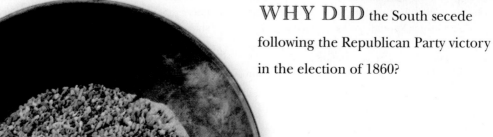

AMERICAN COMMUNITIES
Illinois Communities Debate Slavery

"THE PRAIRIES ARE ON FIRE," ANNOUNCED THE *NEW YORK EVENING POST* correspondent who covered the debates. "It is astonishing how deep an interest in politics these people take." The reason was clear: by 1858, the American nation was in political crisis. The decade-long effort to solve the problem of the future of slavery had failed. For most of this time, Washington politicians trying to build broad national parties with policies acceptable to voters in both the North and the South had done their best not to talk about slavery. That the **Lincoln–Douglas debates** were devoted to one issue alone—slavery and the future of the Union—showed how serious matters had become.

Democratic Senator Stephen A. Douglas of Illinois and his Republican challenger, Springfield lawyer Abraham Lincoln, presented their views in three hours of closely reasoned argument. But they did not speak alone. Cheers, boos, groans, and shouted questions from active, engaged listeners punctuated all seven of the now famous confrontations between the two men. Thus, the Lincoln–Douglas debates were community events in which Illinois citizens—who, as did Americans everywhere, held varying political beliefs—took part.

Stephen Douglas was the leading Democratic contender for the 1860 presidential nomination, but before he could mount a campaign for national office, he had first to win reelection to the Illinois seat he had held in the U.S. Senate for twelve years. His vote against allowing slavery in Kansas had alienated him from the strong southern wing of his own party and had put him in direct conflict with its top leader, President James Buchanan. Because the crisis of the Union was so severe and Douglas's role so pivotal, his reelection campaign clearly previewed the 1860 presidential election.

Lincoln had represented Illinois in the House of Representatives in the 1840s but had lost political support in 1848 because he had opposed the Mexican-American War. Developing a prosperous Springfield law practice, he had been an influential member of the Illinois Republican Party since its founding in 1856. Lincoln was radicalized by the issue of the extension of slavery. Even though his wife's family were Kentucky slave owners, Lincoln's commitment to freedom and his resistance to the spread of slavery had now become absolute: for him, freedom and the Union were inseparable.

The first of the seven debates, held in Ottawa, in northern Illinois, on Saturday, August 21, 1858, showed not only the seriousness but also the exuberance of the democratic politics of the time. By early morning, the town was jammed with people. The clouds of dust raised by carriages driving to Ottawa, one observer complained, turned the town into "a vast smoke house." By one o'clock, the town square was filled to overflowing, and the debate enthralled an estimated 12,000 people. Ottawa in northern Illinois, was pro-Republican, and the audience heckled Douglas unmercifully. But as the debates moved south in the state, where Democrats predominated, the tables were turned, and Lincoln sometimes had to plead for a chance to be heard.

Although Douglas won the 1858 senatorial election in Illinois, the acclaim that Lincoln gained in the famous debates helped establish the Republicans' claim to be the only party capable of stopping the spread of slavery and made Lincoln himself a strong contender for the Republican presidential nomination in 1860. But the true winners of the Lincoln–Douglas debates were the people of Illinois who gathered peacefully to discuss the most serious issue of their time. The young German immigrant Carl Schurz, who attended the Quincy debate, was deeply impressed by its democratic character. He noted, "There was no end of cheering and shouting and jostling on the streets of Quincy that day. But in spite of the excitement created by the political contest, the crowds remained very good-natured, and the occasional jibes flung from one side to the other were uniformly received with a laugh."

The Lincoln–Douglas debates are famous for their demonstration of the widespread public belief in commonality and community to resolve disagreements. Unfortunately, differences that could be resolved through conversation and friendship in the local community were less easy to resolve at the national level. In the highly charged and highly public political atmosphere of Congress, politicians struggled in vain to find compromises to hold the national community together.

Illinois

Lincoln-Douglas debates Series of debates in the 1858 Illinois senatorial campaign during which Douglas and Lincoln staked out their differing opinions on the issue of slavery.

AMERICA IN 1850

The America of 1850 was a very different nation from the republic of 1800. Geographic expansion, population increase, economic development, and the changes wrought by the market revolution had transformed the struggling new nation. Economically, culturally, and politically Americans had forged a strong sense of national identity.

EXPANSION AND GROWTH

America was now a much larger nation than it had been in 1800. Through war and diplomacy, the country had grown to continental dimensions, more than tripling in size from 890,000 to 3 million square miles. Its population had increased enormously from 5.3 million in 1800 to more than 23 million, 4 million of whom were African American slaves and 2 million new immigrants, largely from Germany and Ireland. Comprising just sixteen states in 1800, America in 1850 had thirty-one states, and more than half of the population lived west of the Appalachians. America's cities had undergone the most rapid half century of growth they were ever to experience (see Map 15.1).

America was also much richer: it is estimated that real per capita income doubled between 1800 and 1850 Southern cotton was no longer the major influence on the domestic economy. The growth of manufacturing in the Northeast and the rapid opening up of rich farmlands in the Midwest had serious domestic implications. As the South's share of responsibility for economic growth waned, so did its political importance—at least in the eyes of many Northerners. Thus, the very success of the United States both in geographic expansion and in economic development served to undermine the role of the South in national politics and to hasten the day of open conflict between the slave South and the free-labor North and Midwest.

POLITICS, CULTURE, AND NATIONAL IDENTITY

Pride in democracy was one unifying theme in a growing sense of national identity and the new middle-class values, institutions, and culture that supported it. Since the turn of the century, American writers had struggled to find distinctive American themes, and these efforts bore fruit in the 1850s in the burst of creative activity termed the "American Renaissance." Newspapers, magazines, and communication improvements of all kinds created a national audience for the American scholars and writers who emerged during this decade.

During the American Renaissance, American writers pioneered new literary forms. Nathaniel Hawthorne, in works like "Young Goodman Brown" (1835), raised the short story to a distinctive American literary form. Poets like Walt Whitman and Emily Dickinson experimented with unrhymed and "off-rhyme" verse. Henry David Thoreau published *Walden* in 1854. A pastoral celebration of his life at Walden Pond, in Concord, Massachusetts, the essay was also a searching meditation on the cost to the individual of the loss of contact with nature that was a consequence of the market revolution.

Indeed, although the midcentury popular mood was one of self-congratulation, most of the writers of the American Renaissance were social critics. In *The Scarlet Letter* (1850) and *The House of the Seven Gables* (1851), Nathaniel Hawthorne brilliantly exposed the repressive and hypocritical aspects of Puritan New England in the colonial period and the often impossible moral choices faced by individuals. Hawthorne's friend Herman Melville, in his great work *Moby Dick* (1851), used the story of Captain Ahab's obsessive search for the white whale to write a profound study of the nature of good and evil and a critique of American society in the 1850s. The strongest social critique, however, was Frederick Douglass's starkly simple autobiography, *Narrative of the Life of Frederick Douglass* (1845), which told of his brutal life as a slave.

WHY DID people in the North and the South tend to see the issue of slavery differently?

myhistorylab
Review Summary

IMAGE KEY
for pages 378–379

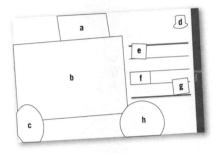

a. Dred Scott and his family, c. 1857.
b. Republican night-time parade.
c. A portrait photo of John Brown (1800–1859).
d. An old fashioned black stovepipe hat with a narrow brim like the one worn by Abe Lincoln.
e. A poster of *Uncle Tom's Cabin* with an illustration of a slave woman standing in the doorway of a log cabin. The copy describes various editions of the book for sale.
f. Robert Marshall Root's painting of the Lincoln-Douglas debate.
g. A contemporary colored engraving of the inside of the Armory at Harper's Ferry, Virginia, where John Brown and his men were trapped by the fire of the U.S. Marines under the command of Col. Robert E. Lee, October 18, 1859.
h. Gold ore and gravel in a shallow pan like those used by '49ers.

MAP EXPLORATION

To explore an interactive version of this map, go to **http://www.prenhall.com/faraghertlc/map15.1**

People per square mile
- More than 6
- 2 to 6
- Fewer than 2

MAP 15.1
U.S. Population and Settlement, 1850 By 1850, the United States was a continental nation. Its people, whom Thomas Jefferson had once thought would not reach the Mississippi River for forty generations, had not only passed the river but also leapfrogged to the West Coast. In comparison to the America of 1800 (see Map 9.1 on p. 210), the growth was astounding.

WHAT WERE the reasons behind these growth patterns?

14–2
Harriet Beecher Stowe, *Uncle Tom's Cabin* (1852)

The most successful American novel of the mid-nineteenth century was also about the great issue of the day—slavery. In writing *Uncle Tom's Cabin*, Harriet Beecher Stowe combined the literary style of the popular women's domestic novels of the time (discussed in Chapter 12) with vivid details of slavery culled from firsthand accounts by northern abolitionists and escaped slaves. Published in 1851, it was a runaway best seller. More than 300,000 copies were sold in the first year, and within ten years, the book had sold more than 2 million copies, becoming the all-time American best seller in proportion to population. Turned into a play that remained popular throughout the nineteenth century, *Uncle Tom's Cabin* reached an even wider audience. *Uncle Tom's Cabin* was more than a heart-tugging story: it was a call to action. In 1863, when Harriet Beecher Stowe was introduced to Abraham Lincoln, the president is said to have remarked, "So you're the little woman who wrote the book that made this great war!"

CRACKS IN NATIONAL UNITY

Stowe's novel clearly spoke to the growing concern of the American people. The year 1850 opened to the most serious political crisis the United States had ever known. The issue raised by the 1846 Wilmot Proviso—whether slavery should be extended to the new territories—could no longer be ignored (see Chapter 14). Furthermore, California, made rich and populous by the gold rush, applied for statehood in 1850, thereby reopening the issue of the balance between slave and free states.

THE COMPROMISE OF 1850

The **Compromise of 1850** was actually five separate bills embodying three separate compromises.

First, California was admitted as a free state, but the status of the remaining former Mexican possessions was left to be decided by **popular sovereignty** (a vote of the territory's inhabitants) when they applied for statehood. The result was, for the time being, fifteen slave states and sixteen free states. Second, Texas (a slave state) was required to cede land to New Mexico Territory (free or slave status undecided). Finally, the slave trade, but not slavery itself, was ended in the District of Columbia, but a stronger fugitive slave law, to be enforced in all states, was enacted (see Map 15.2).

Jubilation and relief greeted the news that compromise had been achieved, but analysis of the votes on the five bills that made up the compromise revealed no consistent majority. The sectional splits within each party that had existed before the compromise remained. Antislavery northern Whigs and proslavery southern Democrats, each the larger wing of their party, were the least willing to compromise.

POLITICAL PARTIES SPLIT OVER SLAVERY

The Second American Party System, forged in the great controversies of Andrew Jackson's presidency (see Chapter 11), was a national party system. At a time when the ordinary person still had very strong sectional loyalties, the mass political party created a national community of like-minded voters. Yet, by the election of 1848, sectional interests were eroding the political "glue" in both parties. Although each party still appeared united, sectional fissures ran deep.

Political splits were preceded by divisions in other social institutions. Disagreements about slavery had already split the country's great religious organizations into northern and southern groups: the Presbyterians in 1837, the Methodists in 1844, and the Baptists in 1845. Theodore Weld, the abolitionist leader, saw these splits as inevitable: "Events . . . have for years been silently but without a moment's pause, settling the basis of two great parties, the nucleus of one slavery, of the other, freedom."

CONGRESSIONAL DIVISIONS

But was freedom national and slavery sectional, or was it the other way around? In the midst of the debate that preceded the Compromise of 1850, President Zachary Taylor died. A bluff military man, Taylor had been prepared to follow Andrew Jackson's precedent during the Nullification Crisis of 1832 and simply demand that southern dissidents compromise. Vice President Millard Fillmore, who assumed the presidency, was a much weaker man who did not seize the opportunity for presidential action.

This poster advertises *Uncle Tom's Cabin*, the best-selling novel by Harriet Beecher Stowe. The poignant story of long-suffering African American slaves had an immense impact on northern popular opinion, swaying it decisively against slavery. In that respect, the poster's boast, "The Greatest Book of the Age," was correct.

WHAT WAS the intent of the Compromise of 1850?

myhistorylab
Review Summary

Compromise of 1850   The four-step compromise which admitted California as a free state, allowed the residents of the New Mexico and Utah territories to decide the slavery issue for themselves, ended the slave trade in the District of Columbia, and passed a new fugitive slave law to enforce the constitutional provision stating that a slave escaping into a free state shall be delivered back to the owner.

Popular sovereignty   A solution to the slavery crisis suggested by Michigan senator Lewis Cass by which territorial residents, not Congress, would decide slavery's fate.

OVERVIEW | The Great Sectional Compromises

1820	Missouri Compromise	Admits Missouri to the Union as a slave state and Maine as a free state; prohibits slavery in the rest of the Louisiana Purchase Territory north of 36°30'.
		Territory Covered: The entire territory of the Louisiana Purchase, exclusive of the state of Louisiana, which had been admitted to the Union in 1812.
1850	Compromise of 1850	Admits California to the Union as a free state, settles the borders of Texas (a slave state); sets no conditions concerning slavery for the rest of the territory acquired from Mexico. Enacts national Fugitive Slave Law.
		Territory Covered: The territory that had been part of Mexico before the end of the Mexican-American War and the Treaty of Guadalupe Hidalgo (1848): part of Texas, California, Utah Territory (now Utah, Nevada, and part of Colorado), and New Mexico Territory (now New Mexico and Arizona).

myhistory lab

Overview: *The Great Sectional Compromises*

14–7
Hinton Rowan Helper, *A White Southerner Speaks Out Against Slavery* (1857)

14–4
John C. Calhoun, *A Dying Statesman Speaks Out Against the Compromise of 1850*

And southerners, personified by John C. Calhoun, were unwilling to compromise. Calhoun, who had uncompromisingly spoken for the slave South since the Nullification Crisis in 1828 (see Chapter 11) insisted that the states rights' doctrine was necessary to protect the legitimate rights of a minority in a democratic system governed by majority rule. Now in 1850 Calhoun broadened his argument to insist that Congress did not have a constitutional right to prohibit slavery in the territories. The territories, he said, were the common property of all the states, North and South, and slave owners had a constitutional right to the protection of their property wherever they moved. Calhon's position on the territories quickly became southern dogma: anything less than full access to the territories was unconstitutional. As Congressman Robert Toombs of Georgia put the case in 1850, the choice was stark: "Give us our just rights and we are ready to stand by the Union. Refuse [them] and for one, I will strike for independence."

Calhoun's failing health served to make his ultimatum all the more ominous. He brought an aura of death with him as he sat on the Senate floor for the last time, listening to the speech that he was too ill to read for himself. He died less than a month later, still insisting on the right of the South to secede if necessary, to preserve its way of life.

The southern threat to secede confirmed for many Northerners the warnings of antislavery leaders that they were endangered by a menacing "slave power." Liberty Party leader James Birney, in a speech in 1844, was the first to add this phrase to the nation's political vocabulary. "The slave power," Birney explained, was a group of aristocratic slave owners who not only dominated the political and social life of the South but conspired to control the federal government as well, posing a danger to free speech and free institutions throughout the nation.

Birney's warning about the "slave power" in 1844 had seemed merely the overheated rhetoric of an extremist group of abolitionists. But the defensive southern political strategies of the 1850s convinced an increasing number of northern voters that "the slave power" did in fact exist. The long-standing proslavery strategy of maintaining supremacy in the Senate by having at least as many slave as free states admitted to the Union (a plan that required slavery expansion) now looked like a conspiracy by sectional interests to control national politics. In northern eyes, the South became a demonic monolith that threatened the national government.

TWO COMMUNITIES, TWO PERSPECTIVES

Ironically, it was their common commitment to expansion that made the argument between Northerners and Southerners so irreconcilable. Basically, both North and South believed in manifest destiny, but each on its own terms.

MAP 15.2

The Compromise of 1850 The Compromise of 1850, messier and more awkward than the Missouri Compromise of 1820, reflected heightened sectional tensions. California was admitted as a free state, the borders of Texas were settled, and the status of the rest of the former Mexican territory was left to be decided later by popular sovereignty. No consistent majority voted for the five separate bills that made up the compromise.

WHAT GROUPS opposed the Compromise of 1850? Why?

Similarly, both North and South used the language of basic rights and liberties in the debate over expansion. But free-soilers were speaking of personal liberty, whereas Southerners meant their right to own a particular kind of property (slaves) and to maintain a way of life based on the possession of that property. In defending its own rights, each side had taken measures that infringed on the rights of the other.

By 1850, North and South had created fixed stereotypes of the other. To antislavery Northerners, the South was an economic backwater dominated by a small slave-owning aristocracy that lived off the profits of forced labor and deprived poor whites of their democratic rights and the fruits of honest work. The slave system was not only immoral but also a drag on the entire nation, for, in the words of Senator William Seward of New York, it subverted the "intelligence, vigor and energy" that were essential for national growth. In contrast, the dynamic and enterprising commercial North boasted a free-labor ideology that offered economic opportunity to the common man and ensured his democratic rights.

Things looked very different through southern eyes. Far from being economically backward, the South, through its export of cotton, was, according to Southerners, the great engine of national economic growth from which the North benefited. Slavery was not only a blessing to an inferior race but also the cornerstone of democracy, for it ensured the freedom and independence of all white men without entailing the bitter class divisions that marked the North. Slave owners accused northern manufacturers of hypocrisy for practicing "wage slavery" without the paternal benevolence they claimed to bestow on their slaves.

In 1850, the three men who had long represented America's three major regions attempted to resolve the political crisis brought on by the application of California for statehood. Henry Clay is speaking; John C. Calhoun stands second from right; and Daniel Webster is seated at the left, with his head in his hand. Both Clay and Webster were ill, and Calhoun died before the Compromise of 1850 was arranged by a younger group of politicians led by Stephen A. Douglas.

13–5
De Bow's Review, *"The Stability of the Union,"* (1850)

myhistorylab

Exploring America: *Anthony Burns*

Fugitive Slave Law Part of the Compromise of 1850 that required the authorities in the North to assist Southern slave catchers and return runaway slaves to their owners.

By the early 1850s, these vastly different visions of the North and the South—the result of many years of political controversy—had become fixed, and the chances of national reconciliation increasingly slim.

In the country as a whole, the feeling was that the Compromise of 1850 had solved the question of slavery in the territories. The *Philadelphia Pennsylvanian* was confident that "peace and tranquillity" had been ensured, and the *Louisville Journal* said that a weight seemed to have been lifted from the heart of America. But many Southerners felt that their only real gain in the contested compromise was the Fugitive Slave Law, which quickly turned out to be an inflammatory measure.

THE FUGITIVE SLAVE LAW

From the early days of their movement, northern abolitionists had urged slaves to escape, promising assistance and support when they reached the North. Some free African Americans had given far more than verbal support, and most escaped slaves found their most reliable help within northern free black communities. Northerners had long been appalled by professional slave catchers, who zealously seized African Americans in the North and took them south into slavery again. Most abhorrent in northern eyes was that captured black people were at the mercy of slave catchers because they had no legal right to defend themselves. In more than one case, a free African American was captured in his own community and helplessly shipped into slavery.

As a result of stories like this, nine northern states passed personal liberty laws between 1842 and 1850, serving notice that they would not cooperate with federal recapture efforts. These laws enraged Southerners, who had long been convinced that all Northerners, not just abolitionists, were actively hindering efforts to reclaim their escaped slaves. At issue were two distinct definitions of "rights": Northerners were upset at the denial of legal and personal rights to escaped slaves.

The **Fugitive Slave Law**, enacted in 1850, dramatically increased the power of slave owners to capture escaped slaves. The full authority of the federal government now supported slave owners, and although fugitives were guaranteed a hearing before a federal commissioner, they were not allowed to testify on their own behalf. Furthermore, the new law imposed federal penalties on citizens who protected or assisted fugitives or who did not cooperate in their return. A number of free northern blacks, estimated at 30,000 to 40,000, emigrated to Canada to avoid the possibility of capture.

In Boston, the center of the American abolitionist movement, reaction to the Fugitive Slave Law was fierce. In the most famous Boston case, a biracial group of armed abolitionists led by Unitarian clergyman Thomas Wentworth Higginson stormed the federal courthouse in 1854 in an attempt to save escaped slave Anthony Burns. The rescue effort failed, and a federal deputy marshal was killed. President Pierce sent marines, cavalry, and artillery to Boston to reinforce the guard over Burns and ordered a federal ship to be ready to deliver the fugitive back into slavery. When the effort by defense lawyers to argue for Burns's freedom failed, Bostonians raised money to buy his freedom. But the U.S. attorney, ordered by the president to enforce the Fugitive Slave Law in all circumstances, blocked the purchase. The case was lost, and Burns was marched to the docks through streets lined with sorrowing abolitionists. Buildings were shrouded in black and draped with American flags hanging upside down, while bells tolled as if for a funeral.

In this volatile atmosphere, escaped African Americans wrote and lectured bravely on behalf of freedom. Frederick Douglass, the most famous and eloquent of the fugitive slaves, spoke out fearlessly in support of armed resistance. Openly active in the underground network that helped slaves reach safety in Canada, Douglass himself had been constantly in danger of capture until his friends bought his freedom in 1847. Harriet Jacobs, who escaped to the North after seven years in hiding in the South, wrote bitterly in her *Incidents in the Life of a Slave Girl* (1861) that "I was, in fact, a slave in New York, as subject to slave laws as I had been in a slave state . . . I had been chased during half my life, and it seemed as if the chase was never to end." Threatened by owners who came north for her, Jacobs was forced into hiding while northern white friends arranged her purchase. "A gentleman near me said, 'It's true; I have seen the bill of sale.' 'The bill of sale!' Those words struck me like a blow. So I was sold at last! A human being sold in the free city of New York!"

The Fugitive Slave Law made slavery national and forced northern communities to confront the full meaning of slavery. Although most people were still unwilling to grant social equality to the free African Americans who lived in the northern states, more and more had come to believe that the institution of slavery was wrong. The strong northern reaction against the Fugitive Slave Law also had consequences in the South. Northern protests against the Fugitive Slave Law bred suspicion in the South and encouraged secessionist thinking. These new currents of public opinion were reflected in the election of 1852.

13–7
George Fitzhugh, *"The Blessings of Slavery"* (1857)

13–6
Benjamin Drew, *Narratives of Escaped Slaves* (1855)

14–5
Frederick Douglass, *Independence Day Speech* (1852)

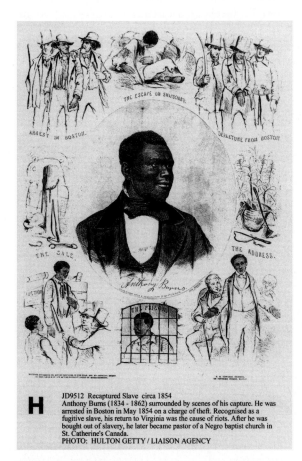

H JD9512 Recaptured Slave circa 1854
Anthony Burns (1834 - 1862) surrounded by scenes of his capture. He was arrested in Boston in May 1854 on a charge of theft. Recognised as a fugitive slave, his return to Virginia was the cause of riots. After he was bought out of slavery, he later became pastor of a Negro baptist church in St. Catherine's Canada.
PHOTO: HULTON GETTY / LIAISON AGENCY

Escaped slave Anthony Burns, shown here surrounded by scenes of his capture in 1854, was the cause of Boston's greatest protest against the Fugitive Slave Law. The injustice of his trial and shipment back to the South converted many Bostonians to the antislavery cause.

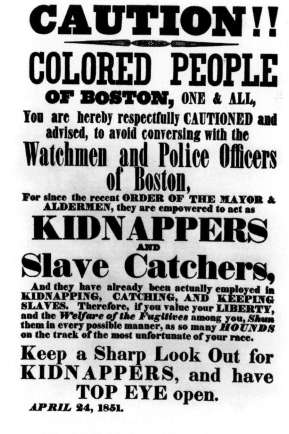

CAUTION!!
COLORED PEOPLE
OF BOSTON, ONE & ALL,
You are hereby respectfully CAUTIONED and advised, to avoid conversing with the
Watchmen and Police Officers
of Boston,
For since the recent ORDER OF THE MAYOR & ALDERMEN, they are empowered to act as
KIDNAPPERS
AND
Slave Catchers,
And they have already been actually employed in KIDNAPPING, CATCHING, AND KEEPING SLAVES. Therefore, if you value your LIBERTY, and the *Welfare of the Fugitives* among you, *Shun* them in every possible manner, as so many *HOUNDS* on the track of the most unfortunate of your race.
Keep a Sharp Look Out for
KIDNAPPERS, and have
TOP EYE open.
APRIL 24, 1851.

This handbill warning free African Americans of danger circulated in Boston following the first of the infamous recaptures under the Fugitive Slave Law, that of Thomas Sims in 1851.

THE ELECTION OF 1852

The first sign of the weakening of the national party system in 1852 was the difficulty both parties experienced at their nominating conventions. After fifty-two
ballots General Winfield Scott (a military hero like two of the party's previous
three candidates), rather than the sitting President Fillmore, was nominated. Many
southern Whigs were permanently alienated by the choice; although Whigs were
still elected to Congress from the South, their loyalty to the national party was
strained to the breaking point.

The Democrats had a wider variety of candidates. Lewis Cass, Stephen Douglas, and James Buchanan competed for forty-nine ballots, each strong enough to
block the others but not strong enough to win. Finally, the party turned to Franklin
Pierce of New Hampshire, who was thought to have southern sympathies. Uniting
on a platform pledging "faithful execution" of all parts of the Compromise of
1850, including the Fugitive Slave Law, Democrats polled well in the South and in
the North. Most Democrats who had voted for the Free-Soil Party in 1848 voted
for Pierce. So, in record numbers, did immigrant Irish and German voters, who
were eligible for citizenship after three years' residence. The strong immigrant
vote for Pierce was a sign of the strength of Democratic Party organizations in
northern cities. Pierce easily won the 1852 election, 254 electoral votes to 42.

"YOUNG AMERICA": THE POLITICS OF EXPANSION

Pierce entered the White House in 1853 on a wave of good feeling. This goodwill
was soon strained by Pierce's support for the expansionist adventures of the "Young
America" movement.

The "Young America" movement began as a group of writers and politicians
in the New York Democratic Party who believed in the democratic and nationalistic promise of "manifest destiny." By the 1850s, however, their lofty goals had
shrunk to a desire to conquer Central America and Cuba. During the Pierce
administration, several private "filibusters" (from the Spanish *filibustero*, meaning
an "adventurer" or "pirate") invaded Caribbean and Central American countries,
usually with the declared intention of extending slave territory.

The Pierce administration, not directly involved in the filibustering, *was* deeply
involved in an effort to obtain Cuba. In 1854, Pierce authorized his minister to Spain,
Pierre Soulé, to try to force the unwilling Spanish to sell Cuba for $130 million. Soulé
met in Ostend, Belgium, with the American ministers to France and England, John
Mason and James Buchanan, to compose the offer. At first appealing to Spain to recognize the deep affinities between the Cubans and American Southerners that made
them "one people with one destiny," the document went on to threaten to "wrest"
Cuba from Spain if necessary. This amazing document, which became known as the
Ostend Manifesto, was supposed to be secret but was soon leaked to the press. Deeply
embarrassed, the Pierce administration was forced to repudiate it.

In another expansionist gesture in another direction, President Franklin
Pierce dispatched Commodore Matthew Perry across the Pacific to Japan, a nation
famous for its insularity and hostility to outsiders. The mission resulted in 1854 in
a commercial treaty that opened Japan to American trade.

Overall, however, the complicity between the Pierce administration and
proslavery expansionists was foolhardy and lost it the northern goodwill with
which it had begun. The sectional crisis that preceded the Compromise of 1850
had made obvious the danger of reopening the territorial issue. Ironically, it was
not the Young America expansionists but the prime mover of the Compromise
of 1850, Stephen A. Douglas, who reignited the sectional struggle over slavery
expansion.

THE CRISIS OF THE NATIONAL PARTY SYSTEM

In 1854, Douglas introduced the **Kansas-Nebraska Act**, proposing to open those lands that had been the northern part of Indian Territory to American settlers under the principle of popular sovereignty. He thereby reopened the question of slavery in the territories. Douglas knew he was taking a political risk, but he believed he could satisfy both his expansionist aims and his presidential ambitions. He was wrong: he pushed the national party system into crisis, first killing the Whigs and then destroying the Democrats.

THE KANSAS-NEBRASKA ACT

In a stunning example of the expansionist pressures generated by the market revolution, Stephen Douglas introduced the Kansas-Nebraska Act to further the construction of a transcontinental railroad across what was still considered the "Great American Desert" to California. Douglas wanted the rail line to terminate in Chicago, in his own state of Illinois, rather than in the rival St. Louis, but for that to happen, the land west of Iowa and Missouri had to be organized into territories (the first step toward statehood). To get Congress to agree to the organization of the territories, however, Douglas needed the votes of southern Democrats, who were unwilling to support him unless the territories were open to slavery (see Map 15.3).

The Kansas-Nebraska bill passed, but it badly strained the major political parties. Southern Whigs voted with southern Democrats in favor of the measure; northern Whigs rejected it absolutely, creating an irreconcilable split that left Whigs unable to field a presidential candidate in 1856. The damage to the Democratic Party was almost as great. In the congressional elections of 1854, northern Democrats lost two-thirds of their seats (a drop from ninety-one to twenty-five), giving the southern Democrats (who were solidly in favor of slavery extension) the dominant voice both in Congress and within the party.

Douglas had committed one of the greatest miscalculations in American political history. A storm of protest arose throughout the North. Douglas, who confidently

WHAT EXPLAINS the end of the Second American Party System and the rise of the Republican Party?

myhistorylab
Review Summary

Kansas-Nebraska Act   Law passed in 1854 creating the Kansas and Nebraska Territories but leaving the question of slavery open to residents, thereby repealing the Missouri Compromise.

A Japanese painting shows Commodore Matthew Perry landing in Japan in 1853. The commercial treaty Perry signed with the Japanese government, which opened a formerly closed country to American trade, was viewed in the United States as another fruit of manifest destiny.

"The Landing of Commodore Perry in Japan in 1853." (Detail) Japanese, Edo period, 19th century. Handscroll; ink and color on paper, 10 7/8 × 211 1/8 in. (27.6 × 536.3 cm). Museum of Fine Arts, Boston. William Sturgis Bigelow Collection, RES.11.6054. Photograph © 2006 Museum of Fine Arts, Boston.

This engraving shows "Border Ruffians" from Missouri lining up to vote for slavery in the Kickapoo, Kansas Territory, election of 1855. The widespread practice of illegal voting and of open violence earned Kansas the dreadful nickname of "Bleeding Kansas."

QUICK REVIEW

The Kansas-Nebraska Act

◆ Passed in 1854.

◆ Made the status of slavery in new territories subject to the principal of popular sovereignty.

◆ Act aroused storm of protest in the North.

14–6
Kansas Begins to Bleed
(1856)

---

believed that "the people of the North will sustain the measure when they come to understand it," found himself shouted down more than once at public rallies when he tried to explain the bill.

The Kansas-Nebraska bill shifted a crucial sector of northern opinion: the wealthy merchants, bankers, and manufacturers, called the "Cotton Whigs," who had economic ties with southern slave owners and had always disapproved of abolitionist activity. Convinced that the bill would encourage antislavery feeling in the North, Cotton Whigs urged southern politicians to vote against it, only to be ignored. Passage of the Kansas-Nebraska Act convinced many northern Whigs that compromise with the South was impossible.

In Kansas in 1854, hasty treaties were concluded with the Indian tribes who owned the land. Some, such as the Kickapoos, Shawnees, Sauks, and Foxes, agreed to relocate to small reservations. Others, like the Delawares, Weas, and Iowas, agreed to sell their lands to whites. Once the treaties were signed, both proslavery and antislavery white settlers began to pour in, and the battle was on.

"BLEEDING KANSAS"

The first to claim land in Kansas were residents of nearby Missouri, itself a slave state. Missourians took up land claims, established proslavery strongholds such as the towns of Leavenworth, Kickapoo, and Atchison, and repeatedly and blatantly swamped Kansas elections with Missouri votes. In 1855, in the second of several notoriously fraudulent elections, 6,307 ballots were cast in a territory that had fewer than 3,000 eligible voters. Most of the proslavery votes were cast by "border ruffians," as they proudly called themselves, from Missouri.

Northerners quickly responded. The first party of New Englanders arrived in the summer of 1854 and established the free-soil town of Lawrence, named for former "Cotton Whig" Amos Lawrence, who financed them. More than a thousand others had joined them by the following summer. Many northern migrants were Free-Soilers, and many were religious reformers as well. The contrast of values between them and the border ruffians was almost total.

Kansas soon became a bloody battleground as the two factions struggled to secure the mandate of "popular sovereignty." Free-Soilers in Lawrence received shipments of heavy crates, innocuously marked "BOOKS" but actually containing Sharps repeating rifles, sent by eastern supporters. For their part, the border ruffians called for reinforcements.

In the summer of 1856, these lethal preparations exploded into open warfare. First, proslavery forces burned and looted the town of Lawrence. In retaliation, a grim old man named John Brown led his sons in a raid on the proslavery settlers of Pottawatomie Creek, killing five unarmed people. A wave of violence ensued. Armed bands roamed the countryside, and burnings and killings became commonplace.

The rest of the nation watched in horror as the residents of Kansas slaughtered each other in the pursuit of sectional goals. Americans' pride in their nation's great achievements was threatened by the endless violence in one small part—but a part that increasingly seemed to represent the divisions of the whole.

THE POLITICS OF NATIVISM

The violence in Kansas was echoed by increasing violence in the nation's cities. Serious violence marred the elections of 1854 and 1856 in New York. In New Orleans, anger over corrupt elections caused a self-appointed vigilance committee to erect barricades in Jackson Square in the heart of the city, where they skirmished for five

MAP 15.3

The Kansas-Nebraska Act, 1854   The Kansas-Nebraska Act, proposed by Steven A. Douglas in 1854, opened the central and northern Great Plains to settlement. The act had two major faults: it robbed Indian peoples of half the territory guaranteed to them by treaty and, because it repealed the Missouri Compromise line, it opened up the lands to warring proslavery and antislavery factions.

WHY DID the act provoke such a passionate response from antislavery activists?

days with an opposing force composed largely of Catholics and immigrants. In Chicago, riots started in 1855, when the mayor attempted to close the saloons on Sunday. German workingmen joined by Irishmen and Swedes paraded in protest and were met by 200 men of the National Guard, militia, and special police. The ensuing "Lager Beer Riots" ended with the imposition of martial law on the entire city.

This urban violence, like that in Kansas, was caused by the breakdown of the two-party system. The breakup of the Whig Party left a political vacuum that was filled by one of the strongest bursts of nativism, or anti-immigrant feeling, in American history, and by the rapid growth of the new American Party, which formed in 1850 to give political expression to nativism. The new party was in part a reaction to the Democratic Party's success in capturing the support of the rapidly growing population of mostly Catholic foreign-born voters. Irish immigrants in particular voted Democratic, both in reaction to Whig hostility (as in Boston) and because of their own antiblack prejudices.

The reformist and individualistic attitudes of many Whigs inclined them toward nativism. Many Whigs disapproved of the new immigrants because they were poor, Catholic, and often disdainful of the temperance movement. Moreover nativist Whigs held immigration to be solely responsible for the increases in crime and the rising cost of relief for the poor that accompanied the astoundingly rapid urban growth of the 1830s and 1840s (see Chapter 13).

myhistorylab

Exploring America: *The Unwelcome Mat*

	Electoral Vote (%)	Popular Vote (%)
JAMES BUCHANAN (Democrat)	174 (59)	1,832,955 (45)
John C. Frémont (Republican)	114 (39)	1,339,932 (33)
Millard Fillmore (American)	8 (3)	871,731 (22)

MAP 15.4

The Election of 1856 Because three parties contested the 1856 election, Democrat James Buchanan was a minority president. Although Buchanan alone had national support, Republican John Frémont won most of the free states, and Millard Fillmore of the American Party gained 40 percent of the vote in most of the slave states.

WHAT GROUPS constituted Buchanan's political base?

This nighttime meeting of supporters of the Know-Nothing Party in New York City was dramatically spotlighted by a new device borrowed from the theater, an incandescent calcium light, popularly called a limelight.

Nativism drew former Whigs, especially young men in white-collar and skilled blue-collar occupations, to the new American Party. At the core of the party were several secret fraternal societies open only to native-born Protestants. When questioned about their beliefs, party members maintained secrecy by answering, "I know nothing"—hence, the popular name for American Party members, the **Know-Nothings**.

Know-Nothings scored startling victories in northern state elections in 1854, winning control of the legislature in Massachusetts and polling 40 percent of the vote in Pennsylvania. But in the 1850s, no party could ignore slavery, and in 1855, the American Party split into northern (antislavery) and southern (proslavery) wings. Soon after this split, many people who had voted for the Know-Nothings shifted their support to another new party, one that combined many characteristics of the Whigs with a westward-looking, expansionist, free-soil policy. This was the **Republican Party**, founded in 1854.

THE REPUBLICAN PARTY AND THE ELECTION OF 1856

Many constituencies found room in the new Republican Party. Its supporters included many former northern Whigs who opposed slavery absolutely, many Free-Soil Party supporters who opposed the expansion of slavery but were willing to tolerate it in the South, and many northern reformers concerned about temperance and Catholicism. The Republicans also attracted the economic core of the old Whig Party—the merchants and industrialists who wanted a strong national government to promote economic growth by supporting a protective tariff, transportation improvements, and cheap land for western farmers.

The immediate question facing the nation in 1856 was which new party, the Know-Nothings or the Republicans, would emerge the stronger. But the more important question was whether the Democratic Party could hold together. The two strongest contenders for the Democratic nomination were President Pierce and Stephen A. Douglas. Douglas had proposed the Kansas-Nebraska Act and Pierce had actively supported it. But it was precisely their support of this act that made Northerners oppose both of them. The Kansas-Nebraska Act's divisive effect on the Democratic Party now became clear: no one who had voted on the bill, either for or against, could satisfy both wings of the party. A compromise candidate was found in James Buchanan of Pennsylvania, the "northern man with southern principles." Luckily for him, he had been ambassador to Great Britain at the time of the Kansas-Nebraska Act and, thus, had not had to commit himself.

The election of 1856 appeared to be a three-way contest that pitted Buchanan against explorer John C. Frémont of the Republican Party and the American (Know-Nothing) Party's candidate, former president Millard Fillmore (see Map 15.4). In fact, the election was two separate contests, one in the North and one in the South. The northern race was between Buchanan and Frémont, the southern

Brooks Beats Sumner

In a violent episode on the floor of the U.S. Senate in 1856, Senator Charles Sumner of Massachusetts suffered permanent injury in a vicious attack by Congressman Preston Brooks of South Carolina. Trapped at his desk, Sumner was helpless as Brooks beat him so hard with his cane that it broke. A few days earlier, Sumner had given an insulting antislavery speech. Using the abusive, accusatory style favored by abolitionists, he had singled out for ridicule Senator Andrew Butler of South Carolina, charging him with choosing "the harlot, slavery" as his mistress. Senator Butler was Preston Brooks's uncle; in Brooks's mind, he was simply avenging an intolerable affront to his uncle's honor.

So far had the behavioral codes of North and South diverged that each man found his own action perfectly justifiable and the action of the other outrageous. Their attitudes were mirrored in their respective sections. Protest rallies were held in most northern cities; Sumner himself received sympathy letters from hundreds of strangers, all expressing indignation, as one writer put it, over "the most foul, most damnable and dastardly attack," and sympathetic illustrations like this one appeared in northern papers. In contrast, southern newspapers almost unanimously supported Brooks, regarding it as a well-deserved whipping for an intolerable insult. A group of Charleston merchants even bought Brooks a new cane inscribed: "Hit him again." ■

WHAT WOULD a southern version of this episode look like? Which version is "true"?

SOUTHERN CHIVALRY — ARGUMENT versus CLUB'S.

Know-Nothings Name given to the antiimmigrant party formed from the wreckage of the Whig Party and some disaffected Northern democrats in 1854.

Republican Party Party that emerged in the 1850s in the aftermath of the bitter controversy over the Kansas-Nebraska Act, consisting of former Whigs, some Northern Democrats, and many Know-Nothings.

WHAT WAS the outcome of the *Dred Scott* decision?

myhistorylab
Review Summary

one between Buchanan and Fillmore. Buchanan won the election with only 45 percent of the popular vote, because he was the only national candidate. But the Republicans, after studying the election returns, claimed "victorious defeat," for they realized that in 1860, the addition of just two more northern states to their total would mean victory. Furthermore, the Republican Party had clearly defeated the American Party in the battle to win designation as a major party. These were grounds for great optimism—and great concern—for the Republican Party was a sectional, rather than a national, party; it drew almost all its support from the North. Southerners viewed its very existence as an attack on their vital interests. Thus, the rapid rise of the Republicans posed a growing threat to national unity.

THE DIFFERENCES DEEPEN

Although James Buchanan firmly believed that he alone could hold together a nation so split by hatred and violence, his self-confidence outran his abilities. He was so deeply indebted to the strong southern wing of the Democratic Party that he could not take the impartial actions necessary to heal "**Bleeding Kansas**." And his support for a momentous pro-southern decision by the Supreme Court further aggravated sectional differences.

THE *DRED SCOTT* DECISION

In *Dred Scott* v. *Sandford*, decided on March 6, 1857, two days after James Buchanan was sworn in, a southern-dominated Supreme Court attempted—and failed—to solve the political controversy over slavery. Dred Scott had been a slave all his life. His owner, army surgeon John Emerson, had taken Scott on his military assignments during the 1830s to Illinois (a free state) and Wisconsin Territory (a free territory, north of the Missouri Compromise line). During that time, Scott married another slave, Harriet, and their daughter Eliza was born in free territory. Emerson and the Scotts then returned to Missouri (a slave state) and there, in 1846, Dred Scott sued for his freedom and that of his wife and his daughter born in Wisconsin Territory (who as women had no legal standing of their own) on the grounds that residence in free lands had made them free. It took eleven years for the case to reach the Supreme Court, and by then its importance was obvious to everyone.

Declaring the Missouri Compromise unconstitutional Chief Justice Roger B. Taney asserted that the federal government had no right to interfere with the free movement of property throughout the territories. He then dismissed the *Dred Scott* case on the grounds that only citizens could bring suits before federal courts and that black people—slave or free—were not citizens. With this bold judicial intervention into the most heated issue of the day, Taney intended to settle the controversy over the expansion of slavery once and for all. Instead, he inflamed the conflict.

The five southern members of the Supreme Court concurred in Taney's decision, as did one Northerner, Robert C. Grier. Historians have found that President-elect Buchanan had pressured Grier, a fellow Pennsylvanian, to support the majority. Two of the three other Northerners vigorously dissented, and the last voiced other objections. This was clearly a sectional decision, and the response to it was sectional. Southerners expressed great satisfaction and strong support for the Court.

Northerners disagreed. Many were so troubled by the ***Dred Scott* decision** that, for the first time, they found themselves seriously questioning the power of the Supreme Court to establish the "law of the land." The

These sympathetic portraits of Harriet and Dred Scott and their daughters in 1857 helped to shape the northern reaction to the Supreme Court's decision that denied the Scotts' claim to freedom. The infamous *Dred Scott* decision was intended to resolve the issue of slavery expansion but instead heightened angry feelings in both North and South.

New York legislature passed a resolution declaring that the Supreme Court had lost the confidence and respect of the people of that state and another resolution refusing to allow slavery within its borders "in any form or under any pretense, or for any time, however short."

14–8
Dred Scott v. Sandford (1857)

THE LECOMPTON CONSTITUTION

In Kansas, the doctrine of popular sovereignty led to continuing civil strife and the political travesty of two territorial governments. The first election of officers to a territorial government in 1855 produced a lopsided proslavery outcome that was clearly the result of illegal voting by Missouri border ruffians. Free-Soilers protested by forming their own government, giving Kansas both a proslavery territorial legislature in Lecompton and a Free-Soil government in Topeka.

Free-Soil voters boycotted a June 1857 election of representatives to a convention called to write a constitution for the territory once it reached statehood. As a result, the convention had a proslavery majority that wrote the proslavery **Lecompton constitution** and then applied to Congress for admission to the Union under its terms. In the meantime, in October, Free-Soil voters had participated in relatively honest elections for the territorial legislature, elections that returned a clear Free-Soil majority. Nevertheless, Buchanan, in the single most disastrous mistake of his administration, endorsed the proslavery constitution, because he feared the loss of the support of southern Democrats. It seemed that Kansas would enter the Union as a sixteenth slave state, making the number of slave and free states equal.

Unexpected congressional opposition came from none other than Stephen Douglas, author of the legislation that had begun the Kansas troubles in 1854. Now, in 1857, in what was surely the bravest step of his political career, Douglas opposed the Lecompton constitution on the grounds that it violated the principle of popular sovereignty. He insisted that the Lecompton constitution must be voted on by Kansas voters in honest elections. Defying James Buchanan, the president of his own party, Douglas voted with the majority in Congress in April 1858 to refuse admission to Kansas under the Lecompton constitution. In a new referendum, the people of Kansas also rejected the Lecompton constitution, 11,300 to 1,788. Kansas was finally admitted as a free state in January 1861.

THE PANIC OF 1857

Adding to the growing political tensions was the short, but sharp, depression of 1857 and 1858. Technology played a part. In August 1857, the failure of an Ohio investment house—the kind of event that had formerly taken weeks to be widely known—was the subject of a news story flashed immediately over telegraph wires to Wall Street and other financial markets. A wave of panic selling ensued, leading to business failures and slowdowns that threw thousands out of work. The major cause of the panic was a sharp, but temporary, downturn in agricultural exports to Britain, and recovery was well under way by early 1859.

Because it affected cotton exports less than northern exports, the **Panic of 1857** was less harmful to the South than to the North. Southerners took this as proof of the superiority of their economic system to the free-labor system of the North.

It seemed that all matters of political discussion were being drawn into the sectional dispute. The next step toward disunion was an act of violence perpetrated by the grim abolitionist from Kansas, John Brown.

JOHN BROWN'S RAID

In the heated political mood of the late 1850s, some improbable people became heroes. None was more improbable than John Brown, the self-appointed avenger who had slaughtered unarmed proslavery men in Kansas in 1856. In 1859, Brown

QUICK REVIEW

The *Dred Scott* Decision

♦ 1857 attempt by Supreme Court to solve the political controversy over slavery.

♦ Court ruled that slaves were property and government could not restrain free movement of property.

♦ Decision invalidated the Missouri Compromise.

Bleeding Kansas   Violence between pro- and antislavery forces in Kansas Territory after the passage of the Kansas-Nebraska Act in 1854.

***Dred Scott* decision**   Supreme Court ruling, in a lawsuit brought by Dred Scott, a slave demanding his freedom based on his residence in a free state, that slaves could not be U.S. citizens and that Congress had no jurisdiction over slavery in the territories.

Lecompton constitution   Proslavery draft written in 1857 by Kansas territorial delegates elected under questionable circumstances; it was rejected by two governors, supported by President Buchanan, and decisively defeated by Congress.

Panic of 1857   Banking crisis that caused a credit crunch in the North; it was less severe in the South, where high cotton prices spurred a quick recovery.

OVERVIEW | Political Parties Split and Realign

Whig Party	Ran its last presidential candidate in 1852. The candidate, General Winfield Scott, alienated many southern Whigs, and the party was so split it could not field a candidate in 1856.
Democratic Party	Remained a national party through 1856, but Buchanan's actions as president made southern domination of the party so clear that many northern Democrats were alienated. Stephen Douglas, running as a northern Democrat in 1860, won 29 percent of the popular vote; John Breckinridge, running as a southern Democrat, won 18 percent.
Liberty Party	Antislavery party; ran James G. Birney for president in 1844. He won 62,000 votes, largely from northern antislavery Whigs.
Free-Soil Party	Ran Martin Van Buren, former Democratic president, in 1848. Gained 10 percent of the popular vote, largely from Whigs but also from some northern Democrats.
American (Know-Nothing) Party	Nativist party made striking gains in 1854 congressional elections, attracting both northern and southern Whigs. In 1856, its presidential candidate, Millard Fillmore, won 21 percent of the popular vote.
Republican Party	Founded in 1854. Attracted many northern Whigs and northern Democrats. Presidential candidate John C. Frémont won 33 percent of the popular vote in 1856; in 1860, Abraham Lincoln won 40 percent and was elected in a four-way race.

myhistorylab

Overview: *Political Parties Split and Realign*

proposed a wild scheme to raid the South and start a general slave uprising. He believed that discontent among southern slaves was so great that such an uprising needed only a spark to get going. On October 16, 1859, Brown led a group of twenty-two white and African American men against the arsenal. In less than a day, the raid was over. Eight of Brown's men (including two of his sons) were dead, no slaves had joined the fight, and Brown himself was captured. Moving quickly to prevent a lynching by local mobs, the state of Virginia tried and convicted Brown (while he was still weak from the wounds of battle) of treason, murder, and fomenting insurrection.

Brown's death by hanging on December 2, 1859, was marked throughout northern communities with public rites of mourning not seen since the death of George Washington. Church bells tolled, buildings were draped in black, ministers preached sermons, prayer meetings were held, abolitionists issued eulogies. Naturally, not all Northerners supported Brown's action. But many people, while rejecting Brown's raid, increasingly supported the antislavery cause that he represented.

Brown's raid shocked the South because it aroused the fear of slave rebellion. Southerners believed that northern abolitionists were provoking slave revolts, a suspicion apparently confirmed when documents captured at Harpers Ferry revealed that Brown had the financial support of half a dozen members of the northern elite.

Even more shocking to Southerners than the raid itself was the extent of northern mourning for Brown's death. Although the Republican Party disavowed Brown's actions, Southerners simply did not believe the party's statements. Senator Robert Toombs of Georgia warned that the South would "never permit this Federal government to pass into the traitorous hands of the Black Republican party." Talk of secession as the only possible response became common throughout the South.

THE SOUTH SECEDES

WHY DID the South secede following the Republican Party victory in the election of 1860?

By 1860, sectional differences had caused one national party, the Whigs, to collapse. The second national party, the Democrats, stood on the brink of dissolution. Not only the politicians but also ordinary people in both the North and the South were coming to believe there was no way to avoid what in 1858 William Seward (once a Whig, now a Republican) had called an "irrepressible conflict."

myhistorylab

Review Summary

THE ELECTION OF 1860

The split of the Democratic Party into northern and southern wings that had occurred during President Buchanan's tenure became official at the Democratic nominating conventions in 1860. The party convened first in Charleston, South Carolina. Although Stephen Douglas had the support of the plurality of delegates, he did not have the two-thirds majority necessary for nomination. As the price of their support, Southerners insisted that Douglas support a federal slave code—a guarantee that slavery would be protected in the territories. Douglas could not agree without violating his own belief in popular sovereignty and losing his northern support.

After ten days, the convention ended where it had begun: deadlocked. Northern supporters of Douglas were angry and bitter: "I never heard Abolitionists talk more uncharitably and rancorously of the people of the South than the Douglas men," one reporter wrote. "They say they do not care a damn where the South goes."

In June, the Democrats met again in Baltimore. The Douglasites, recognizing the need for a united party, were eager to compromise wherever they could, but most southern Democrats were not. More than a third of the delegates bolted. Later, holding a convention of their own, they nominated Buchanan's vice president, John C. Breckinridge of Kentucky. The remaining two-thirds of the Democrats nominated Douglas, but everyone knew that a Republican victory was inevitable. To make matters worse, some southern Whigs joined with some border-state nativists to form the **Constitutional Union Party**, which nominated John Bell of Tennessee.

Republican strategy was built on the lessons of the 1856 "victorious defeat." The Republicans planned to carry all the states Frémont had won, plus Pennsylvania, Illinois, and Indiana. The two leading Republican contenders were Senator William H. Seward of New York and Abraham Lincoln of Illinois. Seward, the party's best-known figure, had enemies among party moderates, who thought he was too radical, and among nativists with whom he had clashed in the New York Whig Party. Lincoln, on the other hand, appeared new, impressive, more moderate than Seward, and certain to carry Illinois. Lincoln won the nomination on the third ballot.

The election of 1860 presented voters with one of the clearest choices in American history. On the key issue of slavery, Breckinridge supported its extension to the territories; Lincoln stood firmly for its exclusion. Douglas attempted to hold the middle ground with his principle of popular sovereignty; Bell vaguely favored compromise as well. Although they spoke clearly against the extension of slavery, Republicans sought to dispel their radical abolitionist image. The Republican platform condemned John Brown's raid as "the gravest of crimes," repeatedly denied that Republicans favored the social equality of black people, and strenuously affirmed that they sought to preserve the Union. In reality, Republicans simply did not believe the South would secede if Lincoln won.

The only candidate who spoke urgently and openly about the impending threat of secession was Douglas. Breaking with convention, Douglas campaigned personally, in both the North and, bravely, in the hostile South. Realizing his own chances for election were slight, he told his private secretary, "Mr. Lincoln is the next President. We must try to save the Union. I will go South."

In accordance with tradition, Lincoln did not campaign for himself, but many other Republicans spoke for him. The Republicans did not campaign in the South; Breckinridge did not campaign in the North. Each side was, therefore, free to believe the worst about the other.

The mood in the Deep South was close to mass hysteria. Rumors of slave revolts swept the region, and vigilance committees sprang up to counter the

In a contemporary engraving, John Brown and his followers are shown trapped inside the armory at Harpers Ferry in October 1859. Captured, tried, and executed, Brown was regarded as a martyr in the North and a terrorist in the South.

Constitutional Union Party   National party formed in 1860, mainly by former Whigs, that emphasized allegiance to the Union and strict enforcement of all national legislation.

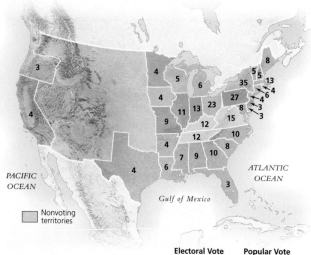

	Electoral Vote (%)	Popular Vote (%)
ABRAHAM LINCOLN (Republican)	180 (59)	1,865,593 (40)
John C. Breckinridge (Southern Democrat)	72 (24)	848,356 (18)
John Bell (Constitutional Union)	39 (13)	592,906 (13)
Stephen A. Douglas (Northern Democrat)	12 (4)	1,382,713 (29)
States that Republicans lost in 1856, won in 1860		

MAP 15.5

The Election of 1860 The election of 1860 was a sectional election. Lincoln won no votes in the South, Breckinridge none in the North. The contest in the North was between Lincoln and Douglas, and although Lincoln swept the electoral vote, Douglas's popular vote was uncomfortably close. The large number of northern Democratic voters opposed to Lincoln was a source of political trouble for him during the Civil War.

WHAT DO the results of the election of 1860 tell us about support for Lincoln in the North on the eve of the Civil War?

supposed threat. In the South Carolina up-country, the question of secession dominated races for the state legislature. Candidates such as A. S. Wallace of York, who advocated "patriotic forbearance" if Lincoln won, were soundly defeated. The very passion and excitement of the election campaign moved Southerners toward extremism.

The election of 1860 produced the second highest voter turnout in U.S. history. The election turned out to be two regional contests: Breckinridge versus Bell in the South, Lincoln versus Douglas in the North. Lincoln won all eighteen of the free states (he split New Jersey with Douglas) and almost 40 percent of the popular vote. Douglas carried only Missouri but gained nearly 30 percent of the popular vote. Lincoln's electoral vote total was overwhelming: 180 to a combined 123 for the other three candidates. But although Lincoln had won 54 percent of the vote in the northern states, his name had not even appeared on the ballot in ten southern states. The true winner of the 1860 election was sectionalism (see Map 15.5).

THE SOUTH LEAVES THE UNION

The results of the election shocked Southerners. They were humiliated and frightened by the prospect of becoming a permanent minority in a political system dominated by a party pledged to the elimination of slavery. In southern eyes, the Republican triumph meant they would become unequal partners in the federal enterprise, their way of life (the slave system) existing on borrowed time. Mary Boykin Chesnut, member of a well-connected South Carolina family, confided to her diary, "The die is cast—no more vain regrets— sad forebodings are useless. The stake is life or death."

The governors of South Carolina, Alabama, and Mississippi, each of whom had committed his state to secession if Lincoln were elected, immediately issued calls for special state conventions. At the same time, calls went out to southern communities to form vigilance committees and volunteer militia companies. Cooperationists (the term used for those opposed to immediate secession) were either intimidated into silence or simply left behind by the speed of events.

On December 20, 1860, a state convention in South Carolina, accompanied by all the hoopla and excitement of bands, fireworks displays, and huge rallies, voted unanimously to secede from the Union. In the weeks that followed, conventions in six other southern states (Mississippi, Florida, Alabama, Georgia, Louisiana, and Texas) followed suit, with the support, on average, of 80 percent of their delegates. There was genuine division of opinion in the Deep South, especially in Georgia and Alabama, along customary up-country–low-country lines. Yeoman farmers who did not own slaves and workers in the cities of the South were most likely to favor compromise with the North. But secessionists constantly reminded both groups that the Republican victory would lead to the emancipation of the slaves and the end of white privilege. And all Southerners, most of whom were deeply loyal to their state and region, believed that Northerners threatened their way of life. Throughout the South, secession occurred because Southerners no longer believed they had a choice.

In every state that seceded, the joyous scenes of South Carolina were repeated as the decisiveness of action replaced the long years of anxiety and tension. People danced in the streets, most believing the North had no choice but to accept secession peacefully. They ignored the fact that eight other slave states—Delaware, Maryland, Kentucky, Missouri, Virginia, North Carolina, Tennessee, and Arkansas—had not acted, though the latter four states did secede after war broke out (see Map 15.6). Just as Republicans had miscalculated in thinking southern threats a mere bluff, so secessionists now miscalculated in believing they would be able to leave the Union in peace.

THE NORTH'S POLITICAL OPTIONS

What should the North do? Buchanan, indecisive as always, did nothing. The decision thus rested with Abraham Lincoln, even before he officially became president. One possibility was compromise, and many proposals were suggested, ranging from full adoption of the Breckinridge campaign platform to reinstatement of the Missouri Compromise line. Lincoln cautiously refused them all, making it clear that he would not compromise on the extension of slavery, which was the South's key demand. He hoped, by appearing firm but moderate, to discourage additional southern states from seceding, while giving pro-Union Southerners time to organize. He succeeded in his first aim but not in the second. Lincoln and most of the Republican Party had seriously overestimated the strength of pro-Union sentiment in the South.

A second possibility, suggested by Horace Greeley of the *New York Tribune*, was to let the seven seceding states "go in peace." This is what many secessionists expected, but too many Northerners—including Lincoln himself—believed in the Union for this to happen. As Lincoln said, what was at stake was "the necessity of proving that popular government is not an absurdity. We must settle this question now, whether in a free government the minority have the right to break up the government whenever they choose."

The third possibility was force, and this was the crux of the dilemma. Although he believed their action was wrong, Lincoln was loath to go to war to force the seceding states back into the Union. On the other hand, he refused to give up federal powers over military forts and customs posts in the South. These were precisely the powers the seceding states had to command if they were to function as an independent nation. A confrontation was bound to come.

ESTABLISHMENT OF THE CONFEDERACY

In February, delegates from the seven seceding states met in Montgomery, Alabama, and created the **Confederate States of America**. They wrote a constitution that was identical to the Constitution of the United States, with a few crucial exceptions: it strongly supported states' rights and made the abolition of slavery practically impossible. These two clauses did much to define the Confederate enterprise. L. W. Spratt of South Carolina confessed as much in 1859: "We stand committed to the South, but we stand more vitally committed to the cause of slavery. It is, indeed, to be doubted whether the South [has] any cause apart from the institution which affects her."

The Montgomery convention chose Jefferson Davis of Mississippi as president and Alexander Stephens of Georgia as vice president of the new nation. Both men were known as moderates. The choice of moderates was deliberate, for the strategy of the new Confederate state was to argue that secession was a normal, responsible, and expectable course of action, and nothing for the North to get upset about. This was the theme that President Jefferson Davis of the Confederate States of America struck in his Inaugural Address, delivered to a crowd of 10,000 from the steps of the State Capitol at Montgomery, Alabama, on February 18, 1861. Secession was a legal and peaceful step that, Davis said, quoting from the Declaration of Independence, "illustrates the American idea that governments rest on the consent

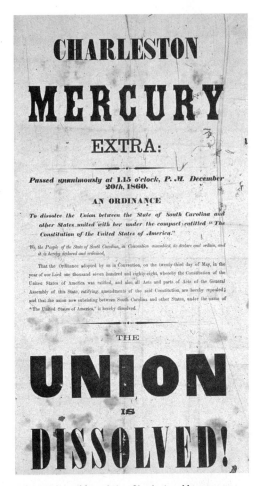

CHARLESTON MERCURY

EXTRA:

Passed unanimously at 1.15 o'clock, P. M. December 20th, 1860.

AN ORDINANCE

To dissolve the Union between the State of South Carolina and other States united with her under the compact entitled "The Constitution of the United States of America."

We, the People of the State of South Carolina, in Convention assembled, do declare and ordain, and it is hereby declared and ordained,

That the Ordinance adopted by us in Convention on the twenty-third day of May, in the year of our Lord one thousand seven hundred and eighty-eight, whereby the Constitution of the United States of America was ratified, and also, all Acts and parts of Acts of the General Assembly of this State, ratifying amendments of the said Constitution, are hereby repealed; and that the union now subsisting between South Carolina and other States, under the name of "The United States of America," is hereby dissolved.

THE

UNION
IS
DISSOLVED!

This special edition of the *Charleston Mercury* was issued on December 20, 1860, the day South Carolina voted to secede from the Union.

14–9
Abraham Lincoln, *A House Divided* (1858)

Confederate States of America
Nation proclaimed in Montgomery, Alabama, in February 1861, after the seven states of the Lower South seceded from the United States.

OVERVIEW | The Irrepressible Conflict

1776	Declaration of Independence	Thomas Jefferson's denunciation of slavery deleted from the final version.
1787	Northwest Ordinance	Slavery prohibited in the Northwest Territory (north of the Ohio River).
1787	Constitution	Slavery unmentioned but acknowledged in Article I, Section 2, counting three-fifths of all African Americans, slave and free, in a state's population; and in Article I, Section 9, which barred Congress from prohibiting the international slave trade for twenty years.
1803	Louisiana Purchase	Louisiana admitted as a slave state in 1812; no decision about the rest of Louisiana Purchase.
1820	Missouri Compromise	Missouri admitted as a slave state, but slavery prohibited in Louisiana Purchase north of 36°30'.
1846	Wilmot Proviso	Proposal to prohibit slavery in territory that might be gained in Mexican-American War causes splits in national parties.
1850	Compromise of 1850	California admitted as free state; Texas (already admitted in 1845) is a slave state; the rest of Mexican Cession to be decided by popular sovereignty. Ends the slave trade in the District of Columbia, but a stronger Fugitive Slave Law, leading to a number of violent recaptures, arouses northern antislavery opinion.
1854	Kansas-Nebraska Act	At the urging of Stephen A. Douglas, Congress opens Kansas and Nebraska Territories for settlement under popular sovereignty. Open warfare between proslavery and antislavery factions breaks out in Kansas.
1857	Lecompton Constitution	President James Buchanan's decision to admit Kansas to the Union with a proslavery constitution is defeated in Congress.
1857	Dred Scott Decision	The Supreme Court's denial of Dred Scott's case for freedom is welcomed in the South, condemned in the North.
1859	John Brown's Raid and Execution	Northern support for John Brown shocks the South.
1860	Democratic Party Nominating Conventions	The Democrats are unable to agree on a candidate; two candidates, one northern (Stephen A. Douglas) and one southern (John C. Breckinridge) split the party and the vote, thus allowing Republican Abraham Lincoln to win.

myhistorylab

Overview: *The Irrepressible Conflict*

QUICK REVIEW

Northern Response to Secession

- Buchanan did nothing in response to secession.
- Lincoln refused calls to compromise on the question of slavery.
- Lincoln also rejected proposals to let the seven seceding states leave the Union.

of the governed . . . and that it is the right of the people to alter or abolish them at will whenever they become destructive of the ends for which they were established."

LINCOLN'S INAUGURATION

The country as a whole waited to see what Abraham Lincoln would do, which at first appeared to be very little. In Springfield, Lincoln refused to issue public statements before his inaugural for fear of making a delicate situation worse. Similarly, during a twelve-day whistle-stopping railroad trip east from Springfield, he was careful to say nothing controversial. Eastern intellectuals, already suspicious of a mere "prairie lawyer," were not impressed. These signs of moderation and caution did not appeal to an American public with a penchant for electing military heroes. Americans wanted leadership and action.

Lincoln continued, however, to offer nonbelligerent firmness and moderation. And at the end of his Inaugural Address on March 4, 1861, as he stood ringed by federal troops called out in case of a Confederate attack, the new president offered unexpected eloquence:

> I am loath to close. We are not enemies, but friends. We must not be enemies. Though passion may have strained, it must not break our bonds of affection. The mystic chords of memory, stretching from every battlefield, and patriot grave, to every living heart and hearthstone, all over this broad land, will yet swell the chorus of the Union, when again touched, as surely they will be, by the better angels of our nature.

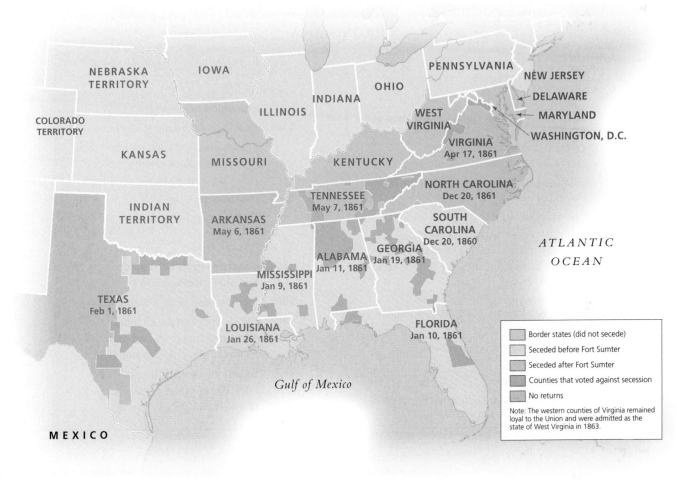

MAP 15.6
The South Secedes The southern states that would constitute the Confederacy seceded in two stages. The states of the Lower South seceded before Lincoln took office. Arkansas and three states of the Upper South—Virginia, North Carolina, and Tennessee—waited until after the South fired on Fort Sumter. And four border slave states—Delaware, Maryland, Kentucky, and Missouri—chose not to secede. Every southern state (except South Carolina) was divided on the issue of secession, generally along up-country–low-country lines. In Virginia, this division was so extreme that West Virginia split off to become a separate nonslave state admitted to the Union in 1863.

WHY WERE some states quicker to secede than others?

CONCLUSION

Americans had much to boast about in 1850. Their nation was vastly larger, richer, and more powerful than it had been in 1800. But the issue of slavery was slowly dividing the North and the South, two communities with similar origins and many common bonds. The following decade was marked by frantic efforts at political compromise, beginning with the Compromise of 1850, continuing with the Kansas-Nebraska Act of 1854, and culminating in the Supreme Court's 1859 decision in the *Dred Scott* case. Increasingly, the ordinary people of the two regions demanded resolution of the crisis. The two great parties of the Second American Party System, the Democrats and the Whigs, unable to find a solution, were destroyed. Two new sectional parties—the Republican Party and a southern party devoted to the defense of slavery—fought the 1860 election, but Southerners refused to accept the national verdict. Politics had failed: the issue of slavery was irreconcilable. The only remaining recourse was war. But although Americans were divided, they were still one people. That made the war, when it came, all the more terrible.

CHRONOLOGY

1820	Missouri Compromise
1828–32	Nullification Crisis
1846	Wilmot Proviso
1848	Treaty of Guadalupe Hidalgo ends Mexican-American War
	Zachary Taylor elected president
	Free-Soil Party formed
1849	California and Utah seek admission to the Union as free states
1850	Compromise of 1850
	California admitted as a free state
	American (Know-Nothing) Party formed
	Zachary Taylor dies; Millard Fillmore becomes president
1851	North reacts to Fugitive Slave Law
	Harriet Beecher Stowe's *Uncle Tom's Cabin* published
1852	Franklin Pierce elected president
1854	Ostend Manifesto
	Kansas-Nebraska Act
	Treaties with Indians in northern part of Indian Territory renegotiated

	Republican Party formed as Whig Party dissolves
1855	William Walker leads his first filibustering expedition to Nicaragua
1856	Burning and looting of Lawrence, Kansas
	John Brown leads Pottawatomie massacre
	Attack on Senator Charles Sumner
	James Buchanan elected president
1857	*Dred Scott* decision
	President Buchanan accepts proslavery Lecompton constitution in Kansas
	Panic of 1857
1858	Congress rejects Lecompton constitution
	Lincoln–Douglas debates
1859	John Brown's raid on Harpers Ferry
1860	Four parties run presidential candidates
	Abraham Lincoln elected president
	South Carolina secedes from Union
1861	Six other Deep South states secede
	Confederate States of America formed
	Lincoln takes office

REVIEW QUESTIONS

1. What aspects of the remarkable economic development of the United States in the first half of the nineteenth century contributed to the sectional crisis of the 1850s?

2. How might the violent efforts by abolitionists to free escaped slaves who had been recaptured and the federal armed enforcement of the Fugitive Slave Law have been viewed differently by northern merchants (the so-called Cotton Whigs), Irish immigrants, and abolitionists?

3. Consider the course of events in "Bloody Kansas" from Douglas's Kansas-Nebraska Act to the congressional rejection of the Lecompton constitution. Were these events the inevitable result of the political impasse in Washington, or could other decisions have been made that would have changed the outcome?

4. The nativism of the 1850s that surfaced so strongly in the Know-Nothing Party was eclipsed by the crisis over slavery. But nativist sentiment has been a recurring theme in American politics. Discuss why it was strong in the 1850s and why it has emerged periodically since then.

5. Evaluate the character and actions of John Brown. Was he the hero proclaimed by northern supporters or the terrorist condemned by the South?

6. Imagine that you lived in Illinois, home state to both Douglas and Lincoln, in 1860. How would you have voted in the presidential election, and why?

KEY TERMS

Bleeding Kansas (p. 395)
Compromise of 1850 (p. 383)
Confederate States of America (p. 399)
Constitutional Union Party (p. 397)
Dred Scott **decision** (p. 395)
Fugitive Slave Law (p. 386)

Kansas-Nebraska Act (p. 389)
Know-Nothings (p. 394)
Lecompton constitution (p. 395)
Lincoln-Douglas debates (p. 380)
Panic of 1857 (p. 395)
Popular sovereignty (p. 383)
Republican Party (p. 394)

myhistorylab
Flashcard Review

RECOMMENDED READING

William L. Barney, *The Secessionist Impulse: Alabama and Mississippi in 1860* (1974). Covers the election of 1860 and the subsequent conventions that led to secession.

Nicole Etcheson, *Bleeding Kansas: Contested Liberty in the Civil War Era* (2004). A look at the Kansas issue from the perspective of white settlers.

Don E. Fehrenbacher, *The* Dred Scott *Case: Its Significance in American Law and Politics* (1978). A major study by the leading historian on this controversial decision.

Eric Foner, *Free Soil, Free Labor, Free Men: The Ideology of the Republican Party before the Civil War* (1970). One of the first studies to focus on the free labor ideology of the North and its importance in the political disputes of the 1850s.

William A. Link, *Roots of Secession: Slavery and Politics in Antebellum Virginia* (2003). Draws connections between the changing circumstances of slavery and politics in the 1850s.

Robert E. May, *Manifest Destiny's Underworld: Filibustering in Antebellum America* (2002). A study of the activities and attitudes toward the adventurers.

David S. Reynolds, *John Brown, Abolitionist* (2005). Argues that Brown's extremism became the Civil War norm.

Kenneth M. Stampp, *America in 1857: A Nation on the Brink* (1990). A study of the "crucial" year by a leading southern historian.

John Stauffer, *The Black Hearts of Men: Radical Abolitionists and the Transformation of Race* (2001). Argues that radical abolitionists rejected the gender and racial conventions of their day.

myhistorylab
Where it's a good time to connect to the past!

For study resources for this chapter, go to **www.myhistorylab.com** and choose *Out of Many, Teaching and Learning Classroom Edition.* You will find a wealth of study and review material for this chapter, including pretests and posttests, customized study plan, key-term review flash cards, interactive map and document activities, and documents for analysis.

*If it is necessary that I should
fall on the battle-field
for my Country I am ready.*
—Sullivan Ballou

Awaiting combat, 1861: Union Soldiers from New York relax
at camp awaiting orders to move to the front. The young men
show great confidence and determination for their coming
engagements, though one fellow to the left of the tent,
perhaps a teenager far from home, seems to long for something
as he stares beyond the camera. Note also the young
African American with a broom sitting apart from the soldiers.

16

THE CIVIL WAR
1861–1865

WHAT ADVANTAGES did the North possess at the outset of the Civil War?

HOW DID the power of the federal government expand as the war progressed?

WHAT SUCCESSES did the South enjoy in the early years of the war and how were they achieved?

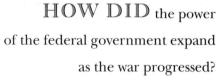

HOW DID the end of slavery affect the war efforts of the North and South?

WHAT IMPACT did the war have on northern political, economic, and social life? and on the same aspects of southern life?

HOW DID Grant and Sherman turn the tide of the war?

AMERICAN COMMUNITIES

Mother Bickerdyke Connects Northern Communities to Their Boys at War

IN MAY 1861, THE REVEREND EDWARD BEECHER INTERRUPTED HIS customary Sunday service at Brick Congregational Church in Galesburg, Illinois, to read a disturbing letter to the congregation. Two months earlier, Galesburg had proudly sent 500 of its young men off to join the Union army. They had not yet been in battle. Yet, the letter reported, an alarming number were dying of diseases caused by inadequate food, medical care, and sanitation at the crowded military camp in Cairo, Illinois. Most army doctors were surgeons trained to operate and amputate on the battlefield. The letter writer, appalled by the squalor and misery he saw around him, complained of abuses by the army. The Union army, however, was overwhelmed with the task of readying recruits for battle and had made few provisions for their health when they were not in combat.

The shocked and grieving members of Beecher's congregation quickly decided to send not only supplies but also one of their number to inspect the conditions at the Cairo camp and to take action. In spite of warnings that army regulations excluded women from encampments, the congregation voted to send their most qualified member, Mary Ann Bickerdyke, a middle-aged widow who made her living as a "botanic physician."

"Mother" Bickerdyke, as she was called, let nothing stand in the way of helping her "boys." When she arrived in Cairo, she immediately set to work cleaning the hospital tents and the soldiers themselves, and finding and cooking nourishing food for them. The hospital director, who resented her interference, ordered her to leave, but she blandly continued her work. When he reported her to the commanding officer, General Benjamin Prentiss, she quickly convinced the general to let her stay.

A plain spoken, hardworking woman, totally unfazed by rank or tender masculine egos, Mother Bickerdyke single-mindedly devoted herself to what she called "the Lord's work." Once, when an indignant officer's wife complained about Bickerdyke's rudeness, General William Tecumseh Sherman joked, "You've picked the one person around here who outranks me. If you want to lodge a complaint against her, you'll have to take it to President Lincoln."

Other communities all over the North rallied to make up for the Army's shortcomings with supplies and assistance. By their actions, Mother Bickerdyke and others like her exposed the War Department's inability to meet the needs of the nation's first mass army. The efforts of women on the local level quickly took on national dimensions. The Women's Central Association of Relief (WCAR) eventually had 7,000 chapters throughout the North. Its volunteers raised funds, made and collected food, clothes, medicine, bandages, and more than 250,000 quilts and comforters, and sent them to army camps and hospitals. All told, association chapters supplied an estimated $15 million worth of goods to the Union troops.

In June 1861, responding to requests by officials of the WCAR for formal recognition of the organization, President Abraham Lincoln created the United States Sanitary Commission and gave it the power to investigate and advise the Medical Bureau.

Although at first she worked independently and remained suspicious of all organizations (and even of many other relief workers), in 1862 Mother Bickerdyke was persuaded to become an official agent of "the Sanitary," as it was known. The advantage to her was access to the commission's warehouses and the ability to order from them precisely what she needed. The advantage to the Sanitary was that Mother Bickerdyke was an unequaled fundraiser. With the help of Bickerdyke's blunt appeals, the Sanitary raised $50 million for the Union war effort.

The Civil War was a national tragedy, ripping apart the political fabric of the country and causing more casualties than any other war in the nation's history. The death toll of approximately 620,000 exceeded the number of dead in all the other wars from the Revolution through the Vietnam War. Yet in another sense, it was a community triumph. Local communities directly supported and sustained their soldiers on a massive scale in unprecedented ways. As national unity failed, the strength of local communities, symbolized by Mother Bickerdyke, endured.

Illinois

COMMUNITIES MOBILIZE FOR WAR

A neutral observer in March 1861 might have seen ominous similarities. Two nations—the United States of America (shorn of seven states in the Deep South) and the Confederate States of America—each blamed the other for the breakup of the Union. Two new presidents—Abraham Lincoln and Jefferson Davis—each faced the challenging task of building and maintaining national unity. Two regions—North and South—scorned each other and boasted of their own superiority. But the most important similarity was not yet apparent: both sides were unprepared for the ordeal that lay ahead.

FORT SUMTER: THE WAR BEGINS

Fort Sumter, a federal military installation, sat on a granite island at the entrance to Charleston harbor. So long as it remained in Union hands, Charleston, the center of secessionist sentiment, would be immobilized. Thus, it was hardly surprising that Fort Sumter would provide President Lincoln with his first crisis.

With the fort dangerously low on supplies, Lincoln had to decide whether to abandon it or risk the fight that might ensue if he ordered it resupplied. On April 6, 1861, Lincoln took cautious and careful action, notifying the governor of South Carolina that he was sending a relief force to the fort carrying only food and no military supplies. Now the decision rested with Jefferson Davis. On April 10, he ordered General P. G. T. Beauregard to demand the surrender of Fort Sumter and to attack it if the garrison did not comply. On April 12, Beauregard opened fire. Two days later, the defenders surrendered.

Even before the attack on Fort Sumter, the Confederate Congress had authorized a volunteer army of 100,000 men to serve for twelve months. Men flocked to enlist, and their communities sent them off in ceremonies featuring bands, bonfires, and belligerent oratory.

The "thunderclap of Sumter" startled the North into an angry response. The apathy and uncertainty that had prevailed since Lincoln's election disappeared, to be replaced by strong feelings of patriotism. On April 15, Lincoln issued a proclamation calling for 75,000 state militiamen to serve in the federal army for ninety days. Enlistment offices were swamped with so many enthusiastic volunteers that men were sent home. Free African Americans, among the most eager to serve, were turned away: this was not yet a war for or by black people.

WHAT ADVANTAGES did the North possess at the outset of the Civil War?

myhistorylab
Review Summary

15-1
Jefferson Davis, *Address to the Provisional Congress of the Confederate States of America* (1861)

15-2
Alexander Hamilton Stephens, *The "Cornerstone Speech"* (1861)

15-4
Why They Fought (1861)

This Currier and Ives lithograph shows the opening moment of the Civil War. On April 12, 1861, Confederate General P.G.T. Beauregard ordered the shelling of Fort Sumter in Charleston harbor. Two days later, Union Major Robert Anderson surrendered, and mobilization began for what turned out to be the most devastating war in American history.

IMAGE KEY

for pages 404–405

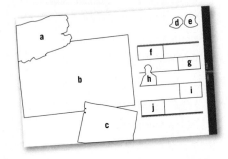

a. A federal flag that flew over Fort Sumter.

b. A photo of engineers of the 8th New York State Militia, 1861.

c. The battle flag of the Second Battalion Hilliard's Alabama Legion. This flag was pierced 83 times during the charge up Snod Grass Hill at Chickamauga, Georgia.

d. The gray cap of a Confederate soldier from the American Civil War.

e. A blue Union soldier's hat with a bugle emblem embroidered on the front.

f. The opening moment of the Civil War, April 12, 1861, at Fort Sumter in Charleston harbor.

g. A painting by William C. Washington, *Jackson Entering the City of Winchester*, shows General "Stonewall" Jackson saving the Virginia town from Union capture in 1862.

h. Robert E. Lee (1807–1870), commander-in-chief of the Confederate armies during the Civil War.

i. American President Abraham Lincoln presents the Emancipation Proclamation to grateful black slaves and white peasants in a political cartoon about education, freedom, and equality.

j. A black family runs through a vacant lot while being chased by white hooligans during the 1863 race riots in New York City.

The mobilization in Chester, Pennsylvania, was typical of the northern response to the outbreak of war. As volunteers marched off to Washington (the gathering place for the Union army), companies of home guards were organized by the men who remained behind. Within a month, the women of Chester had organized a countywide system of war relief. Such relief organizations, some formally organized, some informal, emerged in every community, North and South, that sent soldiers off to the Civil War. These organizations not only played a vital role in supplying the troops, but they also maintained the human, local link on which so many soldiers depended. In this sense, every American community accompanied its young men to war.

THE BORDER STATES

The first secession, between December 20, 1860, and February 1, 1861, had taken seven Deep South states out of the Union. Now, in April, the firing on Fort Sumter and Lincoln's call for state militias forced the other southern states to take sides. Courted—and pressured—by both North and South, four states of the Upper South (Virginia, Arkansas, Tennessee, and North Carolina) joined the original seven in April and May 1861. Virginia's secession tipped the other three toward the Confederacy. The capital of the Confederacy was now moved to Richmond.

Still undecided was the loyalty of the northernmost tier of slave-owning states: Missouri, Kentucky, Maryland, and Delaware. Each controlled vital strategic assets. Missouri not only bordered the Mississippi River but also controlled the routes to the west. Kentucky controlled the Ohio River. The main railroad link with the West ran through Maryland and the hill region of western Virginia. Delaware controlled access to Philadelphia. Finally, were Maryland to secede, the nation's capital would be completely surrounded by Confederate territory.

Delaware was loyal to the Union (less than 2 percent of its population were slaves), but Maryland's loyalty was divided, as an ugly incident on April 19 showed. When the Sixth Massachusetts Regiment marched through Baltimore, a hostile crowd of 10,000 southern sympathizers, carrying Confederate flags, pelted the troops with bricks, paving stones, and bullets. Finally, in desperation, the troops fired on the crowd, killing twelve people and wounding others. In retaliation, southern sympathizers burned the railroad bridges to the North and destroyed the telegraph line to Washington, cutting off communication between the capital and the rest of the Union for six days.

Lincoln's response was swift and stern. He stationed Union troops along Maryland's crucial railroads, declared martial law in Baltimore, and arrested the suspected ringleaders of the pro-Confederate mob and held them without trial. The arrests in Maryland were the first of a number of violations of basic civil rights during the war, all of which the president justified on the basis of national security.

An even bloodier division occurred in Missouri, where old foes from "Bleeding Kansas" faced off. The proslavery governor and most of the legislature fled to Arkansas, where they declared a Confederate state government in exile, while Unionists remained in control in St. Louis. Consequently, Missouri was plagued by guerrilla battles throughout the war. In Kentucky, division took the form of a huge illegal trade with the Confederacy through neighboring Tennessee.

That Delaware, Maryland, Missouri, and Kentucky chose to stay in the Union was a severe blow to the Confederacy. Among them, the four states could have added 45 percent to the white population and military manpower of the Confederacy and 80 percent to its manufacturing capacity.

THE BATTLE OF BULL RUN

Once sides had been chosen and the initial flush of enthusiasm had passed, the nature of the war, and the mistaken notions about it, soon became clear. The event that shattered the illusions was the First Battle of Bull Run, at Bull Run Creek near Manassas in Virginia in July 1861. Confident of a quick victory, a Union army of 35,000 men marched south. The troops were accompanied not only by journalists but also by a crowd of politicians and sightseers. At first the Union troops held their ground against the 25,000 Confederate troops. But when 2,300 fresh Confederate troops arrived as reinforcements, the untrained northern troops broke ranks in an uncontrolled retreat that swept up the frightened sightseers as well.

THE RELATIVE STRENGTHS OF NORTH AND SOUTH

Bull Run was sobering—and prophetic. The Civil War was the most lethal military conflict in American history, leaving a legacy of devastation on the battlefield and desolation at home. It claimed the lives of nearly 620,000 soldiers, more than the First and Second World Wars combined. One out of every four soldiers who fought in the war never returned home.

Overall, in terms of both population and productive capacity, the Union seemed to have a commanding edge over the Confederacy. The North had two and a half times the South's population and enjoyed an even greater advantage in industrial capacity (nine times that of the South). These advantages were ultimately to prove decisive: by the end of the war, the Union had managed to field and equip more than 2 million soldiers as compared to the Confederacy's 800,000. The Confederacy's problems of supply, however, were due mostly to a poor railroad system. But in the short term, the South had important assets to counter the advantage of the North (see Figure 16.1).

The first was the nature of the struggle. For the South, this was a defensive war, in which the basic principle of the defense of home and community united almost all white citizens, regardless of their views about slavery. The North would have to invade the South and then control it against guerrilla opposition in order to win.

Second, the military disparity was less extreme than it appeared. Although the North had manpower, its troops were mostly untrained. Moreover, the South appeared to have an advantage in military leaders, the most notable of which was Robert E. Lee.

Finally, it was widely believed that slavery would work to the South's advantage, for slaves could continue to do the vital plantation work while their masters

15–3
Mary Boykin Chesnut,
A Confederate Lady's Diary
(1861)

15–5
*A Confederate General
Assesses First Bull Run*
(1861)

QUICK REVIEW

The First Battle of Bull Run

◆ July 1861: Beauregard (Confederacy) and McDowell (Union) meet at Manassas.

◆ Confederate troops repulse a strong Union attack.

◆ Battle foreshadowed war to come.

QUICK REVIEW

Northern Advantages

◆ Two and a half times the South's population.

◆ North controlled much of nation's industrial capacity.

◆ Could field a much larger army.

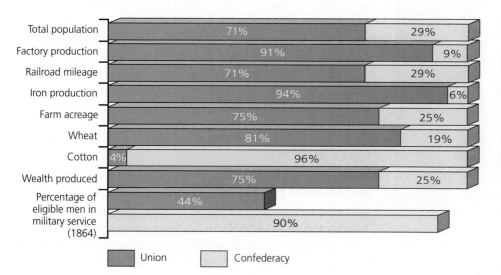

	Union	Confederacy
Total population	71%	29%
Factory production	91%	9%
Railroad mileage	71%	29%
Iron production	94%	6%
Farm acreage	75%	25%
Wheat	81%	19%
Cotton	4%	96%
Wealth produced	75%	25%
Percentage of eligible men in military service (1864)	44%	90%

Figure 16.1
As this chart shows, the North far surpassed the South in the resources necessary to support a large, long war. Initially, however, these strengths made little difference in a struggle that began as a traditional war of maneuver in which the South held the defensive advantage. Only slowly did the Civil War become a modern war in which all the resources of society, including the property and lives of civilians, were mobilized for battle.

The Times Atlas of World History (Maplewood, New Jersey: Hammond, 1978).

went off to war. But above all, the South had the weapon of cotton. Because of the crucial role of cotton in industrialization, Southerners were confident that the British and French need for southern cotton would soon bring those countries to recognize the Confederacy as a separate nation.

THE GOVERNMENTS ORGANIZE FOR WAR

HOW DID the power of the federal government expand as the war progressed?

myhistorylab
Review Summary

The Civil War forced the federal government to assume powers unimaginable just a few years before. Abraham Lincoln took as his primary task leading and unifying the nation in his role as commander in chief. He found the challenge almost insurmountable. Jefferson Davis's challenge was even greater. He had to create a Confederate nation out of a loose grouping of eleven states, each believing strongly in states' rights. Yet in the Confederacy, as in the Union, the conduct of the war required central direction.

LINCOLN TAKES CHARGE

Lincoln's first task as president was to assert control over his own cabinet. Because he had few national contacts outside the Republican Party, Lincoln chose to staff his cabinet with other Republicans, including, most unusually, several who had been his rivals for the presidential nomination. That the Republican Party was a not-quite-jelled mix of former Whigs, abolitionists, moderate Free-Soilers, and even some prowar Democrats made Lincoln's task as party leader much more difficult than it might otherwise have been.

After the fall of Fort Sumter, military necessity prompted Lincoln to call up the state militias, order a naval blockade of the South, and vastly expand the military budget. Breaking with precedent, he took these actions without congressional sanction because Congress was not in session. Military necessity—the need to hold the border states—likewise prompted other early actions, such as the suspension of habeas corpus and the acceptance of Kentucky's ambiguous neutrality. The president also repudiated an unauthorized declaration issued by General John C. Frémont, military commander in Missouri, in August 1861 that would have freed Missouri's slaves. Lincoln feared that such an action would lead to the secession of Kentucky and Maryland.

Lincoln was the first president to act as commander in chief in both a practical and a symbolic way. He actively directed military policy, because he realized that a civil war presented problems different from those of a foreign war of conquest. Lincoln wanted above all to persuade the South to rejoin the Union, and his every military order was dictated by the hope of eventual reconciliation—hence, his caution and his acute sense of the role of public opinion. At the same time, he presided over a vast expansion of the powers of the federal government.

EXPANDING THE POWER OF THE FEDERAL GOVERNMENT

The greatest expansion in government power during the war was in the War Department, which by early 1862 was faced with the unprecedented challenge of feeding, clothing, and arming 700,000 Union soldiers. Initially, the government relied on the individual states to equip and supply their vastly expanded militias. But the size of the Union army and the complexity of fully

This photograph, taken a month before his inauguration, shows Lincoln looking presidential. It was clearly intended to reassure a public still doubtful about his abilities.

supplying it demanded constant efforts at all levels—government, state, and community—throughout the war. Thus, in the matter of procurement and supply, as in mobilization, the battlefront was related to the home front on a scale that Americans had not previously experienced.

The need for money for the vast war effort was pressing. Treasury Secretary Salmon P. Chase worked closely with Congress to develop ways to finance the war. With the help of Philadelphia financier Jay Cooke, the Treasury used patriotic appeals to sell war bonds to ordinary people in amounts as small as $50. By the war's end, the United States had borrowed $2.6 billion for the war effort, the first example in American history of the mass financing of war.

Most radical of all was Chase's decision to print and distribute Treasury notes (paper money). Until then, the money in circulation had been a mixture of coins and state bank notes issued by 1,500 different state banks. The **Legal Tender Act** of February 1862 created a national currency. In 1863, Congress passed the **National Bank Act**, which prohibited state banks from issuing their own notes and forced them to apply for federal charters. The switch to a national currency was widely recognized as a major step toward centralization of economic power in the hands of the federal government.

Although the outbreak of war overshadowed everything else, the Republican Party in Congress was determined to fulfill its campaign pledge of a comprehensive program of economic development. Republicans quickly passed the **Morrill Tariff Act** (1861). In 1862 and 1864, Congress created two federally chartered corporations to build a transcontinental railroad thus fulfilling the dreams of the many expansionists who believed America's economic future lay in trade with Asia across the Pacific Ocean. The **Homestead Act** (1862) gave 160 acres of public land to any citizen who agreed to live on the land for five years, improve it by building a house and cultivating some of the land, and pay a small fee. The **Morrill Land Grant Act** (1862) gave states public land that would allow them to finance land-grant colleges offering education to ordinary citizens in practical skills such as agriculture, engineering, and military science. Coupled with this act, the establishment of a federal Department of Agriculture in 1862 gave American farmers a big push toward modern commercial agriculture.

The enactment of the Republican program increased the role of the federal government in national life. Although many of the executive war powers lapsed when the battles ended, the accumulation of strength by the federal government was never reversed.

DIPLOMATIC OBJECTIVES

To Secretary of State William Seward fell the job of making sure that Britain and France did not extend diplomatic recognition to the Confederacy. Although Southerners had been certain that King Cotton would gain them European support, they were wrong. British public opinion would not countenance the recognition of a new nation based on slavery. British cotton manufacturers found economic alternatives to southern cotton. In spite of Union protests, however, both Britain and France did allow Confederate vessels to use their ports, and British shipyards sold six ships to the Confederacy. But in 1863, when the Confederacy commissioned Britain's Laird shipyard to build two ironclad ships, the Union threatened war, and the British government made sure that the Laird ironclads were never delivered.

JEFFERSON DAVIS TRIES TO UNIFY THE CONFEDERACY

Although Jefferson Davis had held national cabinet rank (as secretary of war under President Franklin Pierce), had experience as an administrator, and was a former military man, he was unable to hold the Confederacy together.

Legal Tender Act Act creating a national currency in February 1862.

National Bank Act Act prohibiting state banks from issuing their own notes and forcing them to apply for federal charters.

Morrill Tariff Act Act that raised tariffs to more than double their prewar rate.

Homestead Act Law passed by Congress in May 1862 providing homesteads with 160 acres of free land in exchange for improving the land within five years of the grant.

Morrill Land Grant Act Law passed by Congress in July 1862 awarding proceeds from the sale of public lands to the states for the establishment of agricultural and mechanical colleges.

15–6
Charles Harvey Brewster, *Three Letters from the Civil War Front* (1862)

Davis's first cabinet of six men, appointed in February 1861, included a representative from each of the states of the first secession except Mississippi, which was represented by Davis himself. This careful attention to the equality of the states pointed to the fundamental problem Davis was unable to overcome. A shared belief in states' rights—that is, in their own autonomy—was a poor basis on which to build a unified nation. Although Davis saw the need for unity, he was unable to impose it. Soon his style of leadership—micromanagement—angered his generals, alienated cabinet members, and gave southern governors reason to resist his orders. After the first flush of patriotism had passed, the Confederacy never lived up to its hope of becoming a unified nation.

CONTRADICTIONS OF SOUTHERN NATIONALISM

The failure of "cotton diplomacy" was a crushing blow. White Southerners were stunned that Britain and France would not recognize their claim to independence. Well into 1863, the South hoped that a decisive battlefield victory would change the minds of cautious Europeans.

Perhaps the greatest southern failure was in the area of finances. At first, the Confederate government tried to raise money from the states, but governors refused to impose new taxes. By the time uniform taxes were levied in 1863, it was too late. Heavy borrowing and the printing of great sums of paper money produced runaway inflation (a ruinous rate of 9,000 percent by 1865, compared with 80 percent in the North). Inflation, in turn, caused incalculable damage to morale and prospects for unity.

After the initial surge of volunteers, enlistment in the military fell off, as it did in the North also. In April 1862, the Confederate Congress passed the first draft law in American history, and the Union Congress followed suit in March 1863. The southern law declared that all able-bodied men between eighteen and thirty-five were eligible for three years of military service. Purchase of substitutes was allowed, as in the North. The most disliked part of the draft law was a provision exempting one white man on each plantation with twenty or more slaves. This provision not only seemed to disprove the earlier claim that slavery freed white men to fight, but also it aroused class resentments.

In the early days of the war, Jefferson Davis successfully mobilized feelings of regional identity and patriotism. Many Southerners felt part of a beleaguered region that had been forced to resist northern tyranny. But most felt loyalty to their own state and local communities, not to a Confederate nation. The strong belief in states' rights and aristocratic privilege undermined the Confederate cause. Some southern governors resisted potentially unifying actions such as moving militias outside their home states. Broader measures, such as general taxation, were widely evaded by rich and poor alike.

The inequitable draft was only one of many things that convinced the ordinary people of the South that this was a war for privileged slave owners, not for them. With its leaders and

This painting by William C. Washington, *Jackson Entering the City of Winchester*, shows the dashing Confederate General "Stonewall" Jackson saving the Virginia town from Union capture in 1862. Jackson and other Confederate generals evoked fierce loyalty to the Confederacy. Unfortunately, by the time this victory was commemorated, Jackson himself was dead from wounds caused by friendly fire at the Battle of Chancellorsville in May of 1863.

William Washington, "Stonewall Jackson Entering the City of Winchester, Virginia." Oil painting. Valentine Museum Library, Richmond, Virginia.

The contrast between the hope and valor of these young southern volunteer soldiers, photographed shortly before the First Battle of Bull Run, and the later advertisements for substitutes (at right), is marked. Southern exemptions for slave owners and lavish payment for substitutes increasingly bred resentment among the ordinary people of the South.

(above) Cook Collection. Valentine Museum Library/Richmond History Center.

SUBSTITUTE NOTICES.

WANTED—A SUBSTITUTE for a conscript, to serve during the war. Any good man over the age of 35 years, not a resident of Virginia, or a foreigner, may hear of a good situation by calling at Mr. GEORGE BAGBY'S office, Shockoe Slip, to-day, between the hours of 9 and 11 A. M.   [jy 9—1t*]   A COUNTRYMAN.

WANTED—Two SUBSTITUTES—one for artillery, the other for infantry or cavalry service. Also, to sell, a trained, thoroughbred cavalry HORSE.   Apply to   DR. BROOCKS, Corner Main and 12th streets, or to   T. T. BROOCKS,
jy 9—3t*   Petersburg, Va.

WANTED—Immediately, a SUBSTITUTE. A man over 35 years old, or under 18, can get a good price by making immediate application to Room No. 50, Monument Hotel, or by addressing "J. W.," through Richmond P. O.   jy 9—1t*

WANTED—A SUBSTITUTE, to go into the 24th North Carolina State troops, for which a liberal price will be paid. Apply to me at Dispatch office this evening at 4 o'clock P. M.
jy 9—1t*   R. R. MOORE.

WANTED—A SUBSTITUTE, to go in a first-rate Georgia company of infantry, under the heroic Jackson. A gentleman whose health is impaired, will give a fair price for a substitute. Apply immediately at ROOM, No. 13, Post-Office Department, third story, between the hours of 10 and 3 o'clock.   jy 9—6t*

WANTED—Two SUBSTITUTES for the war. A good bonus will be given. None need apply except those exempt from Conscript. Apply to-day at   GEORGE I. HERRING'S,
jy 9—1t*   Grocery store, No. 56 Main st.

citizens fearing (perhaps correctly) that centralization would destroy what was distinctively southern, the Confederacy was unable to mobilize the resources—financial, human, and otherwise—that might have prevented its destruction by northern armies.

THE FIGHTING THROUGH 1862

Just as political decisions were often driven by military necessity, the basic northern and southern military strategies were affected by political considerations as much as by military ones. The initial policy of limited war, thought to be the best route to ultimate reconciliation, ran into difficulties because of the public's impatience for victories. But victories, as the mounting slaughter made clear, were not easy to achieve.

THE WAR IN NORTHERN VIRGINIA

The initial northern strategy, dubbed by critics the Anaconda Plan (after the constrictor snake), envisaged slowly squeezing the South with a blockade at sea and on the Mississippi River. The plan avoided invasion and conquest in the hope that a strained South would recognize the inevitability of defeat and thus surrender. Lincoln accepted the basics of the plan, but public clamor for a fight pushed him to agree to the disastrous Battle of Bull Run and then to a major buildup of Union troops in northern Virginia under General George B. McClellan (see Map 16.1).

WHAT SUCCESSES did the South enjoy in the early years of the war and how were they achieved?

myhistorylab
Review Summary

MAP EXPLORATION

To explore an interactive version of this map, go to **http://www.prenhall.com/faraghertlc/map16.1**

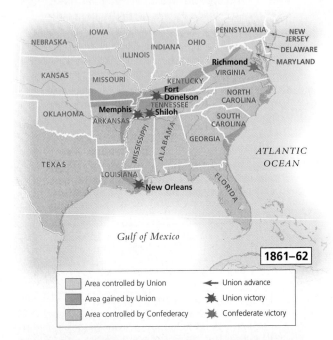

☐ Area controlled by Union	← Union advance
☐ Area gained by Union	✹ Union victory
☐ Area controlled by Confederacy	✹ Confederate victory

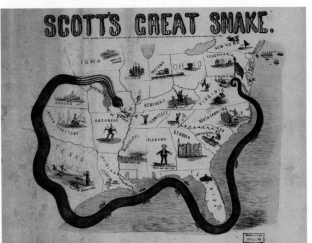

MAP 16.1
Overall Strategy of the Civil War   The initial northern strategy for subduing the South, the so-called Anaconda Plan (see cartoon above), entailed strangling it by a blockade at sea and obtaining control of the Mississippi River. But at the end of 1862, it was clear that the South's defensive strategy could only be broken by the invasion of southern territory. In 1864, Sherman's "March to the Sea" and Grant's hammering tactics in northern Virginia brought the war home to the South. Lee's surrender to Grant at Appomattox Courthouse on April 9, 1865, ended the bloodiest war in the nation's history.

HOW DID the military strategies of the North and the South reflect each side's larger goals?

In March 1862, after almost a year spent drilling the raw Union recruits and after repeated exhortations by an impatient Lincoln, McClellan committed 120,000 troops to what became known as the **Peninsular campaign**. The objective was to capture Richmond, the Confederate capital. Inching up the James Peninsula, he tried to avoid battle, hoping his overwhelming numbers would convince the South to surrender. In a series of battles known as the Seven Days, Robert E. Lee boldly counterattacked, repeatedly catching McClellan off guard. Taking heavy losses as well as inflicting them, Lee drove McClellan back. In August, Lee routed another Union army, commanded by General John Pope, at the Second Battle of Bull Rull (Second Manassas).

THE CIVIL WAR, 1861–1865   **CHAPTER 16**   **415**

Lincoln, alarmed at the threat to Washington and disappointed by McClellan's inaction, ordered him to abandon the Peninsular campaign and return to the capital.

Jefferson Davis, like Abraham Lincoln, was an active commander in chief. And like Lincoln, he responded to a public that clamored for more action than a strictly defensive war entailed. After the Seven Days victories, Davis supported a Confederate march into Maryland. At the same time, he issued a proclamation urging the people of Maryland to make a separate peace. But in the brutal battle of Antietam on September 17, 1862, which claimed more than 5,000 dead and 19,000 wounded, McClellan's army checked Lee's advance. Lee retreated to Virginia, inflicting terrible losses on northern troops at Fredericksburg when they again made a thrust toward Richmond in December 1862. The war in northern Virginia was stalemated: neither side was strong enough to win, but each was too strong to be defeated (see Map 16.2).

SHILOH AND THE WAR FOR THE MISSISSIPPI

Although most public attention was focused on the fighting in Virginia, battles in Tennessee and along the Mississippi River proved to be the key to eventual Union victory. In February 1862, General Ulysses S. Grant captured Fort Henry and Fort Donelson, on the Tennessee and Cumberland Rivers, establishing Union control of much of Tennessee and forcing Confederate troops to retreat into northern Mississippi.

Moving south with 28,000 men, Grant met a 40,000-man Confederate force at Shiloh Church in April 1862. Seriously outnumbered on the first day, Grant's forces were reinforced by the arrival of 35,000 troops. After two days of bitter and bloody fighting in the rain, the Confederates withdrew. The losses on both sides were enormous: the North lost 3,000 men, the South 11,000. Nevertheless, Union forces kept moving, capturing Memphis in June and beginning a campaign to eventually capture Vicksburg. Grant and other Union generals faced strong Confederate resistance, and progress was slow. Earlier that year, naval forces under Admiral David Farragut had captured New Orleans and then continued up the Mississippi River. By the end of 1862, it was clearly only a matter of time before the entire river would be in Union hands. Arkansas, Louisiana, and Texas would then be cut off from the rest of the Confederacy (see Map 16.3).

THE WAR IN THE TRANS–MISSISSIPPI WEST

Although only one western state, Texas, seceded from the Union, the Civil War was fought in small ways in many parts of the West. A Confederate force led by General Henry H. Sibley occupied Santa Fé and Albuquerque early in 1862 without resistance, thus posing a serious threat to the entire Southwest. Confederate hopes were dashed,

MAP 16.2

Major Battles in the East, 1861–62   Northern Virginia was the most crucial and the most constant theater of battle. The prizes were the two opposing capitals, Washington and Richmond, only 70 miles apart. By the summer of 1862, George B. McClellan, famously cautious, had achieved only stalemate in the Peninsular campaign. He did, however, turn back Robert E. Lee at Antietam in September.

WHAT WAS the Anaconda Plan? Why did it fail?

Peninsular campaign Union offensive led by McClellan with the objective of capturing Richmond.

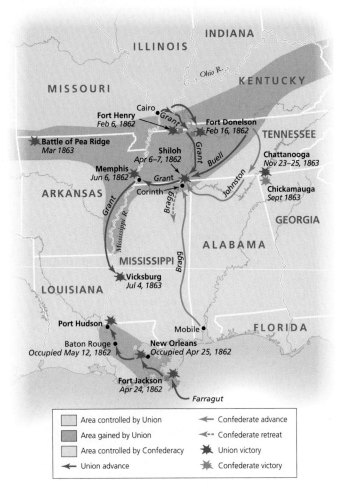

MAP 16.3

Major Battles in the Interior, 1862–63 Ulysses S. Grant waged a mobile war, winning at Fort Henry and Fort Donelson in Tennessee in February 1862, at Shiloh in April, and capturing Memphis in June. He then laid siege to Vicksburg, as Admiral David Farragut captured New Orleans and began to advance up the Mississippi River.

WHAT ROLE did Indians Play in the Fighting in the West?

however, by a ragtag group of 950 miners and adventurers organized into the first Colorado Volunteer Infantry Regiment. After an epic march of 400 miles from Denver, which was completed in thirteen days despite snow and high winds, the Colorado militia stopped the unsuspecting Confederate troops in the Battle of Glorieta Pass on March 26–28, 1862. This dashing action, coupled with the efforts of California militias to safeguard Arizona and Utah from seizure by Confederate sympathizers, secured the Far West for the Union.

Another civil war took place in Indian Territory, south of Kansas. The southern Indian tribes who had been removed there from the Old Southwest in the 1830s included many who were still bitter over the horrors of their removal by federal troops, and they sympathized with the Confederacy. The Confederacy actively sought Indian support by offering Indian people representation in the Confederate Congress. Consequently, many Indians fought for the South. Union victories at Pea Ridge (in northwestern Arkansas) in 1862 and near Fort Gibson (in Indian Territory) in 1863 secured the area for the Union but did little to stop dissension among the Indian groups themselves. After the Civil War, the victorious federal government used the tribes' wartime support for the Confederacy as a justification for demanding further land cessions.

Elsewhere in the West, other groups of Indians found themselves caught up in the wider war. An uprising by the Santee Sioux in Minnesota occurred in August 1862, just as McClellan conceded defeat in the Peninsular campaign in Virginia. Alarmed whites, certain that the uprising was a Confederate plot, ignored legitimate Sioux grievances and responded in kind to Sioux ferocity. In little more than a month, 500 to 800 white settlers and an even greater number of Sioux were killed. Thirty-eight Indians were hanged in a mass execution in Mankato on December 26, 1862, and subsequently all Sioux were expelled from Minnesota. In 1863, U.S. Army Colonel Kit Carson invaded Navajo country in Arizona in retaliation for Indian raids on U.S. troops. Eight thousand Navajos were forced on the brutal "Long Walk" to Bosque Redondo on the Pecos River in New Mexico, where they were held prisoner until a treaty between the United States and the Navajos was signed in 1868.

THE NAVAL WAR

The Union's naval blockade of the South, intended to cut off commerce between the Confederacy and the rest of the world, was initially unsuccessful. The U.S. Navy had only thirty-three ships with which to blockade 189 ports along 3,500 miles of coastline. Beginning in 1863, however, as the Union navy became larger, the blockade began to take effect. As a result, fewer and fewer supplies reached the South.

North and South also engaged in a brief duel featuring the revolutionary new technology of ironcladding. The Confederacy refitted a scuttled Union vessel, the *Merrimac*, with iron plating and renamed it the *Virginia*. On March 8, 1862, the *Virginia* steamed out of Norfolk harbor to challenge the Union blockade. The iron plating protected the *Virginia* from the fire of the Union ships, which found themselves defenseless against its ram and its powerful guns. Two Union ships went down, and the blockade seemed about to be broken. But the North had an experimental ironclad of its own, the *Monitor*, which was waiting for the *Virginia* when it emerged from port on March 9. The historic duel between these first two ironclads was inconclusive. But this brief duel prefigured the naval and land battles of the world wars of the twentieth century as much as did the massing of huge armies on the battlefield.

For the Union, the most successful naval operation in the first two years of the war was not the blockade but the seizing of exposed coastal areas. The Sea Islands of South Carolina were taken, as were some of the North Carolina islands and Fort Pulaski, which commanded the harbor of Savannah, Georgia. Most damaging to the South was the capture of New Orleans.

THE BLACK RESPONSE

The capture of Port Royal in the South Carolina Sea Islands in 1861 was important for another reason. Whites fled at the Union advance, but 10,000 slaves greeted the troops with jubilation and shouts of gratitude. Union troops had unwittingly freed these slaves in advance of any official Union policy on the status of slaves in captured territory.

Early in the war, an irate Southerner who saw three of his slaves disappear behind Union lines at Fortress Monroe, Virginia, demanded the return of his property, citing the Fugitive Slave Law. The Union commander, Benjamin Butler, replied that the Fugitive Slave Law no longer applied and that the escaped slaves were "contraband of war." Two days later, eight runaway slaves appeared; the next day, fifty-nine black men and women arrived at the fort. Union commanders had found an effective way to rob the South of its basic workforce. The "contrabands," as they were known, were put to work building fortifications and doing other useful work in northern camps.

THE DEATH OF SLAVERY

As Union troops drove deeper into the South, the black response grew. When Union General William Tecumseh Sherman marched his army through Georgia in 1864, 18,000 slaves—entire families, people of all ages—flocked to the Union lines. By the war's end, nearly a million black people, fully a quarter of all the slaves in the South, had "voted with their feet" for the Union. The overwhelming response of black slaves to the Union advance changed the nature of the war. As increasing numbers of slaves flocked to Union lines, the conclusion that the South refused to face was unmistakable: the southern war to defend the slave system did not have the support of the slaves themselves. Any northern policy that ignored the issue of slavery and the wishes of the slaves themselves was unrealistic.

THE POLITICS OF EMANCIPATION

In 1862, as the issue of slavery loomed ever larger, Abraham Lincoln, acutely aware of divided northern opinion, inched his way toward a declaration of emancipation. Lincoln was correct to be worried about opinion in the North. Before the war, within the Republican Party, only a small group of abolitionists had favored freeing the slaves. There was also the question of what would become of slaves who were freed. Northern Democrats effectively played on racial fears in the 1862 congressional elections, warning that freed slaves would pour into northern cities and take jobs from white laborers.

QUICK REVIEW

The War at Sea

◆ Union naval blockade strengthened over time.

◆ Confederate ships had limited success running the blockade.

◆ Restriction of trade hurt the Southern cause.

HOW DID the end of slavery affect the war efforts of the North and South?

Review Summary

Nevertheless, the necessities of war demanded that Lincoln adopt a policy to end slavery. Even as Radical Republicans chafed at Lincoln's slow pace, he was edging toward a new position. Following the Union victory at Antietam in September 1862, Lincoln issued a preliminary decree: unless the rebellious states returned to the Union by January 1, 1863, he would declare their slaves "forever free." Although Lincoln did not expect the Confederate States to surrender because of his proclamation, the decree increased the pressure on the South by directly linking the slave system to the war effort.

On January 1, 1863, Lincoln duly issued the final **Emancipation Proclamation**, which turned out to be less than sweeping. The proclamation freed the slaves in the areas of rebellion—the areas the Union did not control—but specifically exempted slaves in the border states and in former Confederate areas conquered by the Union. Lincoln's purpose was to meet the abolitionist demand for a war against slavery while not losing the support of conservatives, especially in the border states.

One group greeted the Emancipation Proclamation with open celebration. On New Year's Day, hundreds of African Americans gathered outside the White House and cheered the president. Free African Americans predicted that the news would encourage southern slaves either to flee to Union lines or refuse to work for their masters. Both of these things were already happening as African Americans seized on wartime changes to reshape white–black relations in the South. In one sense, then, the Emancipation Proclamation simply gave a name to a process already in motion.

Abolitionists set about moving Lincoln beyond his careful stance in the Emancipation Proclamation. Reformers such as Elizabeth Cady Stanton and Susan B. Anthony lobbied and petitioned for a constitutional amendment outlawing slavery. Congress, at Lincoln's urging, approved and sent to the states a statement banning slavery throughout the United States. Quickly ratified by the Union states in 1865, the statement became the **Thirteenth Amendment** to the Constitution. (The southern states, being in a state of rebellion, could not vote.) Lincoln's firm support for this amendment is a good indicator of his true feelings about slavery when he was freed of the kinds of military and political considerations necessarily taken into account in the Emancipation Proclamation.

BLACK FIGHTING MEN

As part of the Emancipation Proclamation, Lincoln gave his support for the first time to the recruitment of black soldiers. Early in the war, eager black volunteers had been bitterly disappointed at being turned away. Many, like Robert Fitzgerald, a free African American from Pennsylvania, found other ways to serve the Union cause. Fitzgerald first drove a wagon and mule for the Quartermaster Corps, and later, in spite of persistent seasickness, he served in the Union navy. After the Emancipation Proclamation, however, Fitzgerald was able to do what he had wanted to do all along: be a soldier. He enlisted in the Fifth Massachusetts Cavalry, a regiment that, like all the units in which black soldiers served, was 100 percent African American but commanded by white officers (see Seeing History).

In Fitzgerald's company of eighty-three men, half came from slave states and had run away to enlist. Other regiments had volunteers from Africa. The proportion of volunteers from the loyal border states (where slavery was still legal) was upwards of 25 percent—a lethal blow to the slave system in those states.

Black volunteers, eager and willing to fight, made up 10 percent of the Union army. Nearly 200,000 African Americans (one out of every five black males in the nation) served in the Union army or navy. A fifth of them—37,000—died defending their own freedom and the Union.

Emancipation Proclamation Decree announced by President Abraham Lincoln in September 1862 and formally issued on January 1, 1863, freeing slaves in all Confederate states still in rebellion.

Thirteenth Amendment Constitutional amendment ratified in 1865 that freed all slaves throughout the United States.

Come and Join Us Brothers

This is a recruitment poster for the Massachusetts 54th Infantry regiment, one of the first official black regiments in the U.S. Army. Organized in March 1863, the 600-man unit led the charge against Fort Wagner, South Carolina, in July, resulting in 116 deaths, including that of the white commanding officer, Colonel Robert Gould Shaw, and many casualties. The bravery of the recruits at Fort Wagner and in other battles changed the minds of many Union officers, who had previously disparaged the fighting abilities of African Americans.

COMPARE THE portraits of the men in this recruiting poster with the caricatures of African Americans shown in Chapter 13. What has changed? Frederick Douglass said, "Once let the black man get upon his person the brass letters, U.S., let him get an eagle on his button and a musket on his shoulder and bullets in his pocket," Douglass continued, and "there is no power on earth that can deny that he has earned the right to citizenship." Was Douglass right?

A general belief in African American inferiority was rampant in the North, but the army service of black men made a dent in white racism. Massachusetts enacted the first law forbidding discrimination against African Americans in public facilities. Some major cities, among them San Francisco, Cincinnati, Cleveland, and New York, desegregated their streetcars. Some states—Ohio, California, Illinois—repealed statutes that had barred black people from testifying in court or serving on juries. ∎

Seeing History

COME AND JOIN US BROTHERS.

PUBLISHED BY THE SUPERVISORY COMMITTEE FOR RECRUITING COLORED REGIMENTS
1210 CHESTNUT ST. PHILADELPHIA.

E. Sachse and Company, "The Shackle Broken by the Genius of Freedom", Baltimore, Md.; 1874, Chicago Historical Society.

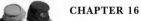

myhistorylab

Exploring America: *Fort Pillow*

15–8
James Henry Gooding, *Letter to President Lincoln* (1863)

WHAT IMPACT did the war have on northern political, economic, and social life? and on the same aspects of southern life?

myhistorylab

Review Summary

15–12
Susie King Taylor, *Reminiscences of an Army Laundress* (1902)

Military service was something no black man could take lightly. African American soldiers faced prejudice within the army and had to prove themselves in battle. Moreover, the Confederates hated and feared African American troops and threatened to treat any captured black soldier as an escaped slave subject to execution. In 1864, Confederate soldiers massacred 262 black soldiers at Fort Pillow, Tennessee, after they had surrendered. Although large-scale episodes such as this were rare (especially after President Lincoln threatened retaliation), smaller ones were not.

Another extraordinary part of the story of the African American soldiers was their reception by black people in the South, who were overjoyed at the sight of armed black men, many of them former slaves themselves, wearing the uniform of the Union army. As his regiment entered Wilmington, North Carolina, one soldier wrote, "Men and women, old and young, were running throughout the streets, shouting and praising God. We could then truly see what we have been fighting for."

African American soldiers were not treated equally by the Union army. They were segregated in camp, given the worst jobs, and paid less than white soldiers ($10 a month rather than $13). Although they might not be able to do much about the other kinds of discrimination, the men of the Fifty-fourth Massachusetts found an unusual way to protest their unequal pay: they refused to accept it, preferring to serve the army for free until it decided to treat them as free men. The protest was effective; in June 1864, the War Department equalized the wages of black and white soldiers.

THE FRONT LINES AND THE HOME FRONT

Civil War soldiers wrote millions of letters home, more proportionately than in any American war. Their letters and the ones they received in return were links between the front lines and the home front, between the soldiers and their home communities. They are a testament to the patriotism of both Union and Confederate troops, for the story they tell is frequently one of slaughter and horror.

THE TOLL OF WAR

In spite of early hopes for what one might call a "brotherly" war, one that avoided excessive brutality, Civil War battles were appallingly deadly (see Figure 16.2). One reason was technology: improved weapons, particularly modern rifles, had much greater range and accuracy than the muskets they replaced.

Civil War generals, however, were slow to adjust to this new reality. Almost all Union and Confederate generals remained committed to the conventional military doctrine of massed infantry offensives. Part of this strategy had been to "soften up" a defensive line with artillery before an infantry assault, but now the range of the new rifles made artillery itself vulnerable to attack. As a result, generals relied less on "softening up" than on immense numbers of infantrymen, hoping that enough of them would survive the withering rifle fire to overwhelm the enemy line.

Medical ignorance was another factor in the casualty rate. Because the use of antiseptic procedures was in its infancy, men often died because minor wounds became infected. Disease was an even more frequent killer, taking twice as many men as were lost in battle.

Both North and South were completely unprepared to handle the supply and health needs of their large armies. Nor were the combatants prepared to deal with masses of war prisoners, as the shocking example of the Confederate prison camp at Andersonville in northern Georgia demonstrated. Andersonville was an open stockade with no shade or shelter, erected early in 1864 to hold 10,000 northern prisoners. But by midsummer, it held 33,000.

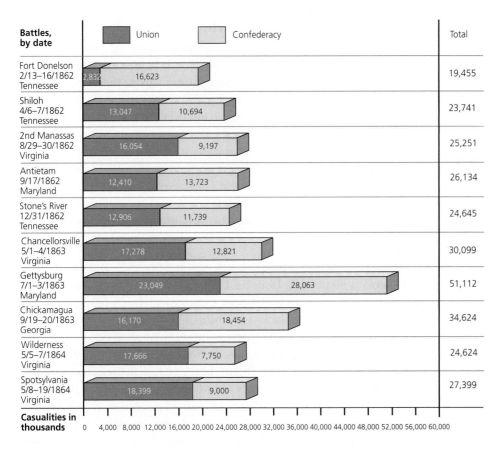

Battles, by date	Union	Confederacy	Total
Fort Donelson 2/13–16/1862 Tennessee	2,832	16,623	19,455
Shiloh 4/6–7/1862 Tennessee	13,047	10,694	23,741
2nd Manassas 8/29–30/1862 Virginia	16,054	9,197	25,251
Antietam 9/17/1862 Maryland	12,410	13,723	26,134
Stone's River 12/31/1862 Tennessee	12,906	11,739	24,645
Chancellorsville 5/1–4/1863 Virginia	17,278	12,821	30,099
Gettysburg 7/1–3/1863 Maryland	23,049	28,063	51,112
Chickamagua 9/19–20/1863 Georgia	16,170	18,454	34,624
Wilderness 5/5–7/1864 Virginia	17,666	7,750	24,624
Spotsylvania 5/8–19/1864 Virginia	18,399	9,000	27,399

Casualities in thousands   0   4,000 8,000 12,000 16,000 20,000 24,000 28,000 32,000 36,000 40,000 44,000 48,000 52,000 56,000 60,000

Figure 16.2 The Casualties Mount Up
This chart of the ten costliest battles of the Civil War shows the relentless toll of casualties (killed, wounded, missing, captured) on both the Union and Confederate sides.

ARMY NURSES

There was an urgent need for skilled nurses to care for wounded and convalescent soldiers. Under the pressure of wartime necessity, and over the objections of most army doctors, women became army nurses. Hospital nursing, previously considered a job only disreputable women would undertake, now became a suitable vocation for middle-class women. By the war's end more than 3,000 northern women had worked as paid army nurses and many more as volunteers.

Southern women were also active in nursing and otherwise aiding soldiers, though the South never boasted a single large-scale organization like the Sanitary Commission. As in the North, middle-class women at first faced strong resistance from army doctors and even their own families, who believed that a field hospital was "no place for a refined lady." Kate Cumming of Mobile, who nursed in Corinth, Mississippi, after the Battle of Shiloh, faced down such reproofs, though she confided to her diary that nursing wounded men was very difficult: "Nothing that I had ever heard or read had given me the faintest idea of the horrors witnessed here." She and her companion nurses persisted and became an important part of the Confederate medical services. For southern women, who had been much less active in the public life of their communities than their northern reforming sisters, this Civil War activity marked an important break with prewar tradition.

15–7
Clara Barton, *Medical Life at the Battlefield* (1862)

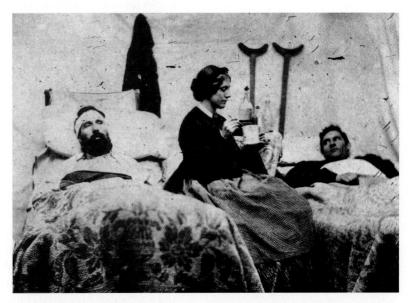

Nurse Ann Bell shown preparing medicine for a wounded soldier. Prompted by the medical crisis of the war, women such as Bell and "Mother" Bickerdyke actively participated in the war effort as nurses.

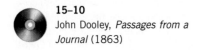

15–10
John Dooley, *Passages from a Journal* (1863)

THE LIFE OF THE COMMON SOLDIER

The conditions experienced by the eager young volunteers of the Union and Confederate armies included massive, terrifying, and bloody battles, apparently unending, with no sign of victory in sight. Soldiers suffered from the uncertainty of supply, which left troops, especially in the South, without uniforms, tents, and sometimes even food. They endured long marches over muddy, rutted roads while carrying packs weighing fifty or sixty pounds. Disease was rampant in their dirty, verminous, and unsanitary camps, and hospitals were so dreadful that more men left them dead than alive. As a result, desertion was common: an estimated one of every nine Confederate soldiers and one of every seven Union soldiers deserted. Unauthorized absence was another problem. At Antietam, Robert E. Lee estimated that unauthorized absence reduced his strength by a third to a half.

WARTIME POLITICS

In the earliest days of the war, Northerners had joined together in support of the war effort. Democrat Stephen A. Douglas, Lincoln's defeated rival, paid a visit to the White House to offer Lincoln his support, then traveled home to Illinois, where he addressed a huge rally of Democrats in Chicago: "There can be no neutrals in this war, only patriots—or traitors!" Within a month, Douglas was dead at age forty-eight. By 1862, Democrats had split into two factions: the War Democrats and the Peace Democrats, derogatorily called "**Copperheads**" (from the poisonous snake).

Despite the split in the party in 1860 and the secession of the South, the Democratic Party remained a powerful force in northern politics. It had received 44 percent of the popular vote in the North in the 1860 election, and its united opposition to the emancipation of slaves explains much of Lincoln's equivocal action on this issue.

The leader of the Copperheads, Clement Vallandigham, a former Ohio congressman, advocated an armistice and a negotiated peace that would "look only to the welfare, peace and safety of the white race, without reference to the effect that settlement may have on the African." Western Democrats, he threatened, might form their own union with the South, excluding New England with its radical abolitionists and high-tariff industrialists. Indeed, in the fall and winter of 1862–63 rumors swirled that the Northwest was ready to secede. Lincoln could not afford to take these threats and rumors lightly. In 1862, Lincoln proclaimed that all people who discouraged enlistments in the army or otherwise engaged in disloyal practices would be subject to martial law. More than 13,000 people, most of them deserters and war profiteers, were arrested, tried in military courts, and imprisoned. Some, however, were convicted in military courts on charges of "declaring sympathy for the enemy." Lincoln rejected all protests, claiming that his arbitrary actions were necessary for national security.

Lincoln also faced challenges from the radical faction of his own party. As the war continued, the Radicals gained strength: it was they who pushed for emancipation in the early days of the war and for harsh treatment of the defeated South after it ended. The most troublesome Radical was Salmon P. Chase, who in December 1862 caused a cabinet crisis when he encouraged Senate Republicans to complain that Secretary of State William Seward was "lukewarm" in his support for emancipation. This Radical challenge was a portent of the party's difficulties after the war, which Lincoln did not live to see—or prevent.

ECONOMIC AND SOCIAL STRAINS ON THE NORTH

Wartime needs caused a surge in northern economic growth, but the gains were unequally distributed. Early in the war, some industries suffered: textile manufacturers could not get cotton, and shoe factories that had made cheap shoes for

Copperheads A term Republicans applied to Northern war dissenters and those suspected of aiding the Confederate cause during the Civil War.

slaves were without a market. But other industries boomed—boot making, ship-building, and the manufacture of woolen goods such as blankets and uniforms, to give just three examples. Coal mining expanded, as did ironmaking, especially the manufacture of iron rails for railroads. Agricultural goods were in great demand, promoting further mechanization of farming. Women, left to tend the family farm while the men went to war, found that with mechanized equipment, they could manage the demanding task of harvesting.

Meeting wartime needs enriched some people honestly, but speculators and profiteers also flourished, as they have in every war. By the end of the war, government contracts had exceeded $1 billion. Not all of this business was free from corruption. New wealth was evident in every northern city.

For most people, however, the war brought the day-to-day hardship of inflation. During the four years of the war, the North suffered an inflation rate of 80 percent, or nearly 15 percent a year. Wages rose only half as much as prices, and workers responded by joining unions and striking. Manufacturers, bitterly opposed to unions, freely hired strikebreakers (many of whom were African Americans, women, or immigrants) and formed organizations of their own to prevent further unionization and to blacklist union organizers. Thus, both capital and labor moved far beyond the small, localized confrontations of the early industrial period. The formation of large-scale organizations, fostered by wartime demand, laid the groundwork for the national battle between workers and manufacturers that would dominate the last part of the nineteenth century.

Another major source of social tension was conscription. The Union introduced a draft in March 1863. Especially unpopular was a provision in the draft law that allowed the hiring of substitutes or the payment of a commutation fee of $300. Substitutes were mostly recent immigrants who had not yet filed for citizenship and were thus not yet eligible to be drafted. It is estimated that immigrants (some of whom were citizens) made up 20 percent of the Union army.

As practiced in the local communities, conscription was indeed often marred by favoritism and prejudice. Local officials called up many more poor than rich men and selected a higher proportion of immigrants than nonimmigrants. In reality, however, only 7 percent of all men called to serve actually did so. About 25 percent hired a substitute, another 45 percent were exempted for "cause" (usually health reasons), and another 20 to 25 percent simply failed to report to the community draft office. Nevertheless, by 1863, many northern urban workers believed that the slogan "a rich man's war but a poor man's fight," though coined in the South, applied to them as well.

The New York City Draft Riots

In the spring of 1863, there were protests against the draft throughout the North. Riots and disturbances broke out in many cities, and several federal enrollment officers were killed. The greatest trouble occurred in New York City between July 13 and July 16, 1863, where a wave of working-class looting, fighting, and lynching claimed the lives of 105 people, many of them African American. The rioting, the worst up to that time in American history, was quelled only when five units of the U.S. Army were rushed from the battlefield at Gettysburg, where they had been fighting Confederates the week before.

The riots had several causes. Anger at the draft and racial prejudice were what most contemporaries saw. From a historical perspective, however, the riots were at least as much about the urban growth and tensions described in Chapter 13. The Civil War made urban problems worse and heightened the visible contrast between the lives of the rich and those of the poor. These tensions exploded, but were not solved, during those hot days in the summer of 1863.

QUICK REVIEW

Sources of Social and Economic Tension in the North

- Uneven economic growth.
- Runaway inflation.
- Conscription.

15–11
A Firsthand Account of the New York Draft Riots (1863)

QUICK REVIEW

The Draft Riots

♦ 1863: Congress passed national conscription law.

♦ New York, July 1863: looting, fighting, and lynching claim lives of 105 people.

♦ Racial and class antagonisms fueled riot.

Ironically, African American men, a favorite target of the rioters' anger, were a major force in easing the national crisis over the draft. Though they had been barred from service until 1863, in the later stages of the war African American volunteers filled much of the manpower gap that the controversial draft was meant to address.

THE FAILURE OF SOUTHERN NATIONALISM

The war brought even greater changes to the South. As in the North, war needs led to expansion and centralization of government control over the economy. The expansion of government brought sudden urbanization, a new experience for the predominantly rural South. The population of Richmond, the Confederate capital, almost tripled, in large part because the Confederate bureaucracy grew to 70,000 people. Because of the need for military manpower, a good part of the Confederate bureaucracy consisted of women, who were referred to as "government girls." All of this—government control, urban growth, women in the paid workforce—was new to Southerners, and not all of it was welcomed.

Even more than in the North, the voracious need for soldiers fostered class antagonisms. When small yeoman farmers went off to war, their wives and families struggled to farm on their own, without the help of mechanization, which they could not afford, and without the help of slaves, which they had never owned. But wealthy men could be exempted from the draft if they had more than twenty slaves. Furthermore, many upper-class Southerners—at least 50,000—avoided military service by paying liberally ($5,000 and more) for substitutes. Worst of all was the starvation. The North's blockade and the breakdown of the South's transportation system restricted the availability of food in the South, and these problems were vastly magnified by runaway inflation. Prices in the South rose by an unbelievable 9,000 percent from 1861 to 1865. Speculation and hoarding by the rich made matters even worse. In the spring of 1863, food riots broke out in four Georgia cities (Atlanta among them) and in North Carolina. In Richmond, more than a thousand people, mostly women, broke into bakeries and snatched loaves of bread, crying "Bread! Bread! Our children are starving while the rich roll in wealth!"

Increasingly, the ordinary people of the South, preoccupied with staying alive, refused to pay taxes, to provide food, or to serve in the army. Soldiers were drawn home by the desperation of their families as well as by the discouraging course of the war. By January 1865, the desertion rate had climbed to 8 percent a month.

At the same time, the life of the southern ruling class was irrevocably altered by the changing nature of slavery. By the end of the war, one-quarter of all slaves had fled to the Union lines, and those who remained often stood in a different relationship to their owners. As white masters and overseers left to join the army, white women were left behind on the plantation to cope with shortages, grow crops, and manage the labor of slaves. Lacking the patriarchal authority of their husbands, white women found that white–black relationships shifted, sometimes drastically (as when slaves fled) and sometimes more subtly. Slaves increasingly made their own decisions about when and how they would work. One black woman, implored by her mistress not to reveal the location of a trunk of money and silver plate when the invading Yankees arrived, looked her in the eye and said, "Mistress, I can't lie over that; you bought that silver plate when you sold my three children."

Peace movements in the South were motivated by a confused mixture of realism, war weariness, and the animosity of those who supported states' rights and opposed Jefferson Davis. The anti-Davis faction was led by his own vice president, Alexander Stephens, who early in 1864 suggested a negotiated peace. Peace sentiment was especially strong in North Carolina, where more than a hundred public meetings in support of negotiations were held in the summer of 1863. Davis would have none of it, and he commanded enough votes in the Confederate Congress to enforce his will and to suggest that peace sentiment was traitorous.

THE TIDE TURNS

As Lincoln's timing of the Emancipation Proclamation showed, by 1863 the nature of the war was changing. The proclamation freeing the slaves struck directly at the southern home front and the civilian workforce. That same year, the nature of the battlefield war changed as well. The Civil War became the first total war.

THE TURNING POINT OF 1863

In the summer of 1863, the moment finally arrived when the North could begin to hope for victory. But for the Union army, the year opened with stalemate in the East and slow and costly progress in the West. For the South, 1863 represented its highest hopes for military success and for diplomatic recognition by Britain or France.

Attempting to break the stalemate in northern Virginia, General Joseph "Fighting Joe" Hooker and a Union army of 130,000 men attacked a Confederate army half that size at Chancellorsville in May. In response, Robert E. Lee daringly divided his forces, sending General Thomas "Stonewall" Jackson and 30,000 men on a day-long flanking movement that caught the Union troops by surprise. Chancellorsville was a great Confederate victory; there were 17,000 Union losses. However, Confederate losses were also great: 13,000 men, representing more than 20 percent of Lee's army.

Though weakened, Lee moved to the attack. In June, in his second and most dangerous single thrust into Union territory, he moved north into Maryland and Pennsylvania. His purpose was as much political as military: he hoped that a great Confederate victory would lead Britain and France to intervene in the war and demand a negotiated peace. The ensuing Battle of Gettysburg, July 1–3, 1863, was another horrible slaughter.

Lee retreated from the field, leaving more than one-third of his army behind—28,000 men killed, wounded, or missing. Union general George Meade elected not to pursue with his battered Union army (see Map 16.4).

The next day, July 4, 1863, Ulysses S. Grant took Vicksburg, Mississippi, after a costly siege. The combined news of Gettysburg and Vicksburg dissuaded Britain and France from recognizing the Confederacy and checked the northern peace movement. It also tightened the North's grip on the South, for the Union now controlled the entire Mississippi River. In November, Generals Grant and Sherman broke the Confederate hold on Chattanooga, Tennessee, thereby opening the way to Atlanta.

HOW DID Grant and Sherman turn the tide of the war?

myhistorylab
Review Summary

MAP EXPLORATION
To explore an interactive version of this map, go to
http://www.prenhall.com/faraghertlc/map16.4

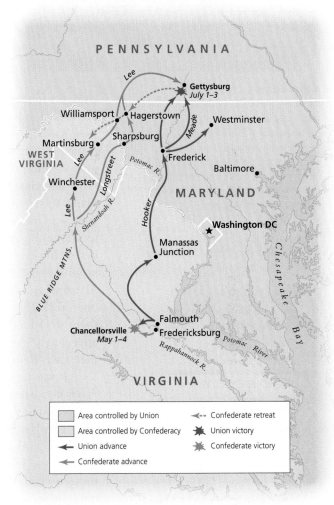

MAP 16.4
The Turning Point, 1863 In June, Lee boldly struck north into Maryland and Pennsylvania, hoping for a victory that would cause Britain and France to demand a negotiated peace on Confederate terms. Instead, he lost the hard-fought battle of Gettysburg, July 1–3. The very next day, Grant's long siege of Vicksburg succeeded. These two great Fourth of July victories turned the tide in favor of the Union. The Confederates never again mounted a major offensive. Total Union control of the Mississippi now exposed the Lower South to attack.

WHAT WAS Lee hoping to achieve with his campaign northward and why was his defeat at Gettysburg the war's turning point?

A **black man** is lynched during the New York City Draft Riots in July 1863. Free black people and their institutions were major victims of the worst rioting in American history until then. The riots were more than a protest against the draft; they were also an outburst of frustration over urban problems that had been festering for decades.

15–9
Abraham Lincoln, *Gettysburg Address* (1863)

15–13
General William Tecumseh Sherman on War (1864)

QUICK REVIEW

Grant's Strategy

♦ Better coordination of Union effort and the application of steady pressure.

♦ The waging of nonstop warfare.

♦ Grant's plan worked in the long run, but at a high cost.

GRANT AND SHERMAN

In March 1864, President Lincoln called Grant east and appointed him general-in-chief of all the Union forces. Grant devised a plan of strangulation and annihilation. While he took on Lee in northern Virginia, he sent General William Tecumseh Sherman to defeat Confederate general Joe Johnston's Army of Tennessee, which was defending the approach to Atlanta. Both Grant and Sherman exemplified the new kind of warfare. They aimed to inflict maximum damage on the fabric of southern life, hoping that the South would choose to surrender rather than face total destruction. This decision to broaden the war so that it directly affected civilians was new in American military history and prefigured the total wars of the twentieth century.

In northern Virginia, Grant pursued a policy of destroying civilian supplies. He said he "regarded it as humane to both sides to protect the persons of those found at their homes, but to consume everything that could be used to support or supply armies." One of those supports was slaves. Grant welcomed fleeing slaves to Union lines and encouraged army efforts to put them to work or enlist them as soldiers.

The most famous example of the new strategy of total war was General Sherman's 1864 march through Georgia. Sherman captured Atlanta on September 2, 1864, and the rest of Georgia now lay open to him. In November, Sherman set out to march the 285 miles to the coastal city of Savannah, living off the land and destroying everything in his path. His military purpose was to tighten the noose around Robert E. Lee's army in northern Virginia by cutting off Mississippi, Alabama, and Georgia from the rest of the Confederacy. But his second purpose, openly stated, was to "make war so terrible" to the people of the South, to "make them so sick of war that generations would pass away before they would again appeal to it." Accordingly, he told his men to seize, burn, or destroy everything in their path (but, significantly, not to harm civilians).

It was estimated that Sherman's army did $100 million worth of damage. "They say no living thing is found in Sherman's track," Mary Boykin Chesnut wrote, "only chimneys, like telegraph poles, to carry the news of [his] attack backwards."

Terrifying to white southern civilians, Sherman was initially hostile to black Southerners as well. In the interests of speed and efficiency, his army turned away many of the 18,000 slaves who flocked to it in Georgia, causing a number to be recaptured and reenslaved. This callous action caused such a scandal in Washington that Secretary of War Edwin Stanton arranged a special meeting in Georgia with Sherman and twenty African American ministers who spoke for the freed slaves. This meeting in itself was extraordinary: no one had ever before asked slaves what they wanted. Equally extraordinary was Sherman's response in Special Field Order 15, issued in January 1865: he set aside more than 400,000 acres of Confederate land to be given to the freed slaves in forty-acre parcels. This was war of a kind that white Southerners had never imagined.

THE 1864 ELECTION

The war complicated the 1864 presidential election. Lincoln was renominated during a period when the war was going badly. Opposed by the Radicals, who thought he was too conciliatory toward the South, and by Republican conservatives, who disapproved of the Emancipation Proclamation, Lincoln had little support within his own party.

In contrast, the Democrats had an appealing candidate: General George McClellan, a war hero (always a favorite with American voters) who was known to be sympathetic to the South. Democrats played shamelessly on the racist fears of the urban working class, accusing Republicans of being "negro-lovers" and warning that racial mixing lay ahead.

A deeply depressed Lincoln fully expected to lose the election. "I am going to be beaten," he told an army officer in August 1864, "and unless some great change takes place badly beaten." A great change did take place: Sherman captured Atlanta on September 2. Lincoln won the election with 55 percent of the popular vote. The vote probably saved the Republican Party from extinction. Ordinary people and war-weary soldiers had voted to continue a difficult and divisive conflict. The election was important evidence of northern support for Lincoln's policy of unconditional surrender for the South. There would be no negotiated peace; the war would continue.

NEARING THE END

As Sherman devastated the lower South, Grant was locked in struggle with Lee in northern Virginia. Grant did not favor subtle strategies. He bluntly said, "The art of war is simple enough. Find out where your enemy is. Get at him as soon as you can. Strike at him as hard as you can, and keep moving on." Following this plan, Grant eventually hammered Lee into submission but at enormous cost. Lee inflicted heavy losses on the Union army in a succession of bloody encounters in the spring and summer of 1864: almost 18,000 at the battle of the Wilderness, more than 8,000 at Spotsylvania, and 12,000 at Cold Harbor. At Cold Harbor, Union troops wrote their names and addresses on scraps of paper and pinned them to their backs, so certain were they of being killed or wounded in battle.

Grim and terrible as Grant's strategy was, it proved effective. Rather than pulling back after his failed assaults, he kept moving South, finally settling in for a prolonged siege of Lee's forces at Petersburg. The North's great advantage in population finally began to tell. There were more Union soldiers to replace those lost in battle, but there were no more white Confederates (see Map 16.5).

In desperation, the South turned to what had hitherto been unthinkable: arming slaves to serve as soldiers in the Confederate army. But—and this was the bitter irony—the African American soldiers and their families would have to be promised freedom or they would desert to the Union at the first chance they had. The Confederate Congress balked at first. As one member said, the idea was "revolting to Southern sentiment, Southern pride, and Southern honor." Another candidly admitted, "If slaves make good soldiers our whole theory of slavery is wrong." Finally, on March 13, the Confederate Congress authorized a draft of black soldiers—without mentioning freedom.

This striking photograph by Thomas C. Roche shows a dead Confederate soldier, killed at Petersburg on April 3, 1865, only six days before the surrender at Appomattox. The new medium of photography conveyed the horror of the war with a gruesome reality to the American public.

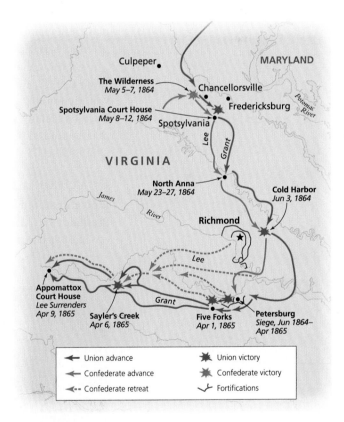

MAP 16.5

The Final Battles in Virginia, 1864–65   In the war's final phase early in 1865, Sherman closed one arm of a pincers by marching north from Savannah, while Grant attacked Lee's last defensive positions in Petersburg and Richmond. Lee retreated from them on April 2 and surrendered at Appomattox Court House on April 9, 1865.

WHAT DESPERATE measures did the South resort to as the war came to an end?

By the spring of 1865, public support for the war simply disintegrated in the South. Starvation, inflation, dissension, and the prospect of military defeat were too much. In February, Jefferson Davis sent his vice president, Alexander Stephens, to negotiate terms at a peace conference at Hampton Roads. Lincoln would not countenance anything less than full surrender, although he did offer gradual emancipation with compensation for slave owners. Davis, however, insisted on southern independence at all costs. Consequently, the Hampton Roads conference failed and southern resistance faded away. In March 1865, Mary Boykin Chesnut recorded in her diary: "I am sure our army is silently dispersing. Men are going the wrong way all the time. They slip by now with no songs nor shouts. They have given the thing up."

APPOMATTOX

In the spring of 1865, Lee and his remaining troops, outnumbered two to one, still held Petersburg and Richmond. Starving, short of ammunition, and losing men in battle or to desertion every day, Lee retreated from Petersburg on April 2. The Confederate government fled Richmond, stripping and burning the city. Seven days later, Lee and his 25,000 troops surrendered to Grant at Appomattox Court House. Grant treated Lee with great respect and set a historic precedent by giving the Confederate troops parole. This meant they could not subsequently be prosecuted for treason. Grant then sent the starving army on its way with three days' rations for every man. Jefferson Davis, who had hoped to set up a new government in Texas, was captured in Georgia on May 10. The war was finally over.

Sensing that the war was near its end, Abraham Lincoln visited Grant's troops when Lee withdrew from Petersburg on April 2. Thus it was that Lincoln came to visit Richmond, and to sit briefly in Jefferson Davis's presidential office, soon after Davis had left it. As Lincoln walked the streets of the burned and pillaged city, black people poured out to see him and surround him, shouting "Glory to God! Glory! Glory! Glory!"

DEATH OF A PRESIDENT

Lincoln had only the briefest time to savor the victory. On the night of April 14, President and Mrs. Lincoln went to Ford's Theater in Washington. There Lincoln was shot at point-blank range by John Wilkes Booth, a Confederate sympathizer.

The 55th Massachusetts Colored Regiment is shown entering Charleston, February 21, 1865, greeted by happy crowds of African Americans. For white Charlestonians, the sight of victorious black troops in the cockpit of the Confederacy must have been devastating.

Harper's Weekly, March 18, 1865. Courtesy of William C. Hine.

CHRONOLOGY

1861   March: Morrill Tariff Act

April: Fort Sumter falls; war begins

April: Mobilization begins

April–May: Virginia, Arkansas, Tennessee, and North Carolina secede

June: United States Sanitary Commission established

July: First Battle of Bull Run

December: French troops arrive in Mexico, followed by British and Spanish forces in January

1862   February: Legal Tender Act

February: Battles of Fort Henry and Fort Donelson

March: Battle of Pea Ridge

March: Battle of the *Monitor* and the *Merrimack* (renamed the *Virginia*)

March–August: George B. McClellan's Peninsular campaign

March: Battle of Glorieta Pass

April: Battle of Shiloh

April: Confederate Conscription Act

April: David Farragut captures New Orleans

May: *El Cinqo de Mayo:* Mexican troops repel French invaders

May: Homestead Act

June–July: Seven Days Battles

July: Pacific Railway Act

July: Morrill Land Grant Act

August: Santee Sioux Uprising, Minnesota

September: Battle of Antietam

December: Battle of Fredericksburg

1863   January: Emancipation Proclamation

February: National Bank Act

March: Draft introduced in the North

March: Colonel Kit Carson sends 8,000 Navajos on the "Long Walk" to Bosque Redondo, New Mexico Territory

April: Richmond bread riot

May: Battle of Chancellorsville

June: French occupy Mexico City

July: Battle of Gettysburg

July: Surrender of Vicksburg

July: New York City Draft Riots

November: Battle of Chattanooga

November: Union troops capture Brownsville, Texas

1864   March: Ulysses S. Grant becomes general-in-chief of Union forces

April: Fort Pillow massacre

May: Battle of the Wilderness

May: Battle of Spotsylvania

June: Battle of Cold Harbor

June: Maximilian becomes Emperor of Mexico

September: Atlanta falls

October: St. Albans incident

November: Abraham Lincoln reelected president

November–December: William Tecumseh Sherman's march to the sea

1865   April: Richmond falls

April: Robert E. Lee surrenders at Appomattox

April: Lincoln assassinated

December: Thirteenth Amendment to the Constitution becomes law

He died the next day. After a week of observances in Washington, Lincoln's coffin was loaded on a funeral train that slowly carried him back to Springfield. All along the railroad route, day and night, in small towns and large, people gathered to see the train pass and to pay their last respects. At that moment, the Washington community and the larger Union community were one and the same.

The nation as a whole was left with Lincoln's vision for the coming peace, expressed in the unforgettable words of his Second Inaugural Address:

> With malice toward none, with charity for all, with firmness in the right as God gives us to see the right, let us strive on to finish the work we are in, to bind up the nation's wounds, to care for him who shall have borne the battle and for his widow and his orphan, to do all which may achieve and cherish a just and lasting peace among ourselves and with all nations.

CONCLUSION

In 1865, a divided people were forcibly reunited by battle. Their nation, the United States of America, had been permanently changed by civil war. Devastating losses among the young men of the country—the greatest such losses the nation was ever to suffer—would affect not only their families but also all of postwar society. Politically, the deepest irony of the Civil War was that only by fighting it had America become completely a nation. For it was the war that broke down local isolation. Ordinary citizens in local communities, North and South, developed a national perspective as they sent their sons and brothers to be soldiers, their daughters to be nurses and teachers. Then, too, the federal government, vastly strengthened by wartime necessity, reached the lives of ordinary citizens more than ever before. The question now was whether this strengthened but divided national community, forged in battle, could create a just peace.

REVIEW QUESTIONS

1. At the outset of the Civil War, what were the relative advantages of the North and the South, and how did they affect the final outcome?

2. In the absence of the southern Democrats, in the early 1860s, the new Republican Congress was able to pass a number of party measures with little opposition. What do these measures tell you about the historical roots of the Republican Party? More generally, how do you think we should view legislation passed in the absence of the customary opposition, debate, and compromise?

3. The greatest problem facing Jefferson Davis and the Confederacy was the need to develop a true feeling of nationalism. Can the failure of this effort be blamed on Davis's weakness as a leader alone, or are there other causes?

4. In what ways can it be said that the actions of African Americans, both slave and free, came to determine the course of the Civil War?

5. Wars always have unexpected consequences. List some of those consequences both for soldiers and for civilians in the North and in the South.

6. Today Abraham Lincoln is considered one of our greatest presidents, but he did not enjoy such approval at the time. List and evaluate some of the contemporary criticisms of Lincoln.

KEY TERMS

myhistorylab

Flashcard Review

Copperheads (p. 422)
Emancipation Proclamation (p. 418)
Homestead Act (p. 411)
Legal Tender Act (p. 411)
Morrill Land Grant Act (p. 411)

Morrill Tariff Act (p. 411)
National Bank Act (p. 411)
Peninsular campaign (p. 415)
Thirteenth Amendment (p. 418)

RECOMMENDED READING

Edward Ayers, *In the Presence of Mine Enemies: War in the Heart of America, 1859–1863* (2003). A study of two counties, one Confederate, one Union, in the war.

Paul A. Cimbala and Randall M. Miller, *Union Soldiers and the Northern Home Front: Wartime Experiences, Postwar Adjustments* (2002). The effects of the Civil War on ordinary people.

Paul Escott, *After Secession: Jefferson Davis and the Failure of Confederate Nationalism* (1978). A thoughtful study of Davis's record as president of the Confederacy.

Drew Gilpin Faust, *Mothers of Invention: Women of the Slaveholding South in the American Civil War* (1996). A major study that considers the importance of gender at the white South's "moment of truth."

James M. Mc Pherson, *Battle Cry of Freedom: The Civil War Era* (1988). An acclaimed, highly readable synthesis of much scholarship on the war.

—, *The Atlas of the Civil War* (1994). Detailed battle diagrams with clear descriptions.

Pauli Murray, *Proud Shoes: The Story of an American Family* (1956). Murray tells the proud story of her African American family and her grandfather, Robert Fitzgerald.

Nina Silbar, *Daughters of the Union: Northern Women Fight the Civil War* (2005). Argues that women found a new sense of self and citizenship in wartime.

Keith P. Wilson, *Campfires of Freedom: The Camp Life of Black Soliders During the Civil War* (2002). Camp life examined to show the soldiers' personal transition from slavery to freedom.

The war passed from words to stones which the white children began to hurl at the colored. Several colored children were hurt and, as they had not resented the rock throwing . . . , the white children became more aggressive and abusive.

— T. Thomas Fortune, *from* Norfolk Journal and Guide, *1866*

Women and children escaping slavery.

Theo. Kaufmann, "On to Liberty," 1867, Oil on canvas. The Metropolitan Museum of Art. Gift of Erving and Joyce Wolf, 1982 (1982.443.3) Photograph © 1982 The Metropolitan Museum of Art.

17

RECONSTRUCTION
1863–1877

WHAT WERE the competing political plans for reconstructing the defeated Confederacy?

WHAT WERE the most important changes in the lives of African Americans in the years immediately following the war?

WHAT MAJOR groups made up the Southern Republicans?

WHAT PRECIPITATED the electoral crisis of 1876?

AMERICAN COMMUNITIES

Hale County, Alabama: From Slavery to Freedom in a Black Belt Community

ON A BRIGHT SATURDAY MORNING IN MAY 1867, 4,000 FORMER SLAVES streamed into the town of Greensboro to hear speeches from two delegates to a recent freedmen's convention in Mobile and to find out about the political status of black people under the Reconstruction Act just passed by Congress. Tensions mounted in the days following this unprecedented gathering, as military authorities began supervising voter registration for elections to the upcoming constitutional convention that would rewrite the laws of Alabama. On June 13, John Orrick, a local white, confronted Alex Webb, a politically active freedman, on the streets of Greensboro and shot Webb dead. Hundreds of armed and angry freedmen formed a posse to search for Orrick but failed to find him. Galvanized by Webb's murder, 500 local freedmen formed a chapter of the Union League, the Republican Party's organizational arm in the South. The chapter functioned as both a militia company and a forum to agitate for political rights.

West-central Alabama had emerged as a fertile center of cotton production just two decades before the Civil War. There African Americans, as throughout the South's black belt, constituted more than three-quarters of the population. With the arrival of federal troops in the spring of 1865, African Americans in Hale County, like their counterparts elsewhere, began to challenge the traditional organization of plantation labor.

Above all, freed people wanted more autonomy. Overseers and owners grudgingly allowed them to work the land "in families," letting them choose their own supervisors and find their own provisions. The result was a shift from the gang labor characteristic of the antebellum period, in which large groups of slaves worked under the harsh and constant supervision of white overseers, to the sharecropping system, in which African American families worked small plots of land in exchange for a small share of the crop. This shift represented less of a victory for newly freed African Americans than a defeat for plantation owners, who resented even the limited economic independence it forced them to concede to their black workforce.

Local African Americans also organized politically. In 1866, Congress had passed the Civil Rights Act and sent the Fourteenth Amendment to the Constitution to the states for ratification; both promised full citizenship rights to former slaves. Hale County freedmen joined the Republican Party and local Union League chapters. They used their new political power to press for better labor contracts, demand greater autonomy for the black workforce, and agitate for the more radical goal of land confiscation and redistribution. "The colored people are very anxious to get land of their own to live upon independently; and they want money to buy stock to make crops," reported one black Union League organizer. "The only way to get these necessaries is to give our votes to the [Republican] party." Two Hale County former slaves, Brister Reese and James K. Green, won election to the Alabama state legislature in 1869.

It was not long before these economic and political gains prompted a white counterattack. In the spring of 1868, the Ku Klux Klan came to Hale County. Disguised in white sheets, armed with guns and whips, and making nighttime raids on horseback, Klansmen flogged, beat, and murdered freed people. They intimidated voters and silenced political activists. Planters used Klan terror to dissuade former slaves from leaving plantations or organizing for higher wages.

With the passage of the Ku Klux Klan Act in 1871, the federal government cracked down on the Klan, breaking its power temporarily in parts of the former Confederacy. But no serious effort was made to stop Klan terror in the west Alabama black belt, and planters there succeeded in reestablishing much of their social and political control.

The events in Hale County illustrate the struggles that beset communities throughout the South during the Reconstruction era after the Civil War. The destruction of slavery and the Confederacy forced African Americans and white people to renegotiate their old roles. These community battles both shaped and were shaped by the victorious and newly expansive federal government in Washington. But the new arrangements of both political power sharing and the organization of labor had to be worked out within local communities. In the end, Reconstruction was only partially successful. Not until the "Second Reconstruction" of the twentieth-century civil rights movement would the descendants of Hale County's African Americans begin to enjoy the full fruits of freedom—and even then not without challenge.

Greensboro

THE POLITICS OF RECONSTRUCTION

Although President Abraham Lincoln insisted early on that the purpose of the war was to preserve the Union, by 1863 it had evolved as well into a struggle for African American liberation. Indeed, the political, economic, and moral issues posed by slavery were the root cause of the Civil War, and the war ultimately destroyed slavery, although not racism, once and for all.

The Civil War also settled the Constitutional crisis provoked by the secession of the Confederacy and its justification in appeals to states' rights. The old notion of the United States as a voluntary union of sovereign states gave way to the new reality of a single nation, in which the federal government took precedence over the individual states. The key historical developments of the Reconstruction era revolved around precisely how the newly strengthened national government would define its relationship with the defeated Confederate states and the 4 million newly freed slaves.

THE DEFEATED SOUTH

The white South paid an extremely high price for secession, war, and defeat. In addition to the battlefield casualties, the Confederate states sustained deep material and psychological wounds. Much of the best agricultural land lay waste. Many towns and cities were in ruins. By 1865, the South's most precious commodities, cotton and African American slaves, no longer were measures of wealth and prestige.

Emancipation proved the most bitter pill for white Southerners to swallow, especially the planter elite. Conquered and degraded, and in their view robbed of their slave property, white people responded by regarding African Americans, more than ever, as inferior to themselves. In the antebellum South, white skin had defined a social bond that transcended economic class. It gave even the lowliest poor white a badge of superiority over even the most skilled slave or prosperous free African American. Emancipation, however, forced white people to redefine their world. The specter of political power and social equality for African Americans made racial order the consuming passion of most white Southerners during the Reconstruction years. In fact, racism can be seen as one of the major forces driving Reconstruction and, ultimately, undermining it.

WHAT WERE the competing political plans for reconstructing the defeated Confederacy?

myhistorylab
Review Summary

16–2
Carl Schurz, *Report on the Condition of the South* (1865)

16–9
The Nation, *"The State of the South"* (1872)

"Decorating the Graves of Rebel Soldiers," *Harper's Weekly,* August 17, 1867. After the Civil War, both Southerners and Northerners created public mourning ceremonies honoring fallen soldiers. Women led the memorial movement in the South that, by establishing cemeteries and erecting monuments, offered the first cultural expression of the Confederate tradition. This engraving depicts citizens of Richmond, Virginia, decorating thousands of Confederate graves with flowers at the Hollywood Memorial Cemetery on the James River. A local women's group raised enough funds to transfer over 16,000 Confederate dead from northern cemeteries for reburial in Richmond.

Photography pioneer Timothy O'Sullivan took this portrait of a multi-generational African American family on the J. J. Smith plantation in Beaufort, South Carolina, in 1862. Many white plantation owners in the area had fled, allowing slaves like these to begin an early transition to freedom before the end of the Civil War.

16–1
"Address from the Colored Citizens of Norfolk, Virginia, to the People of the United States" (1865)

Radical Republicans   A shifting group of Republican congressmen, usually a substantial minority, who favored the abolition of slavery from the beginning of the Civil War and later advocated harsh treatment of the defeated South.

Field Order 15   Order by General William T. Sherman in January 1865 to set aside abandoned land along the southern Atlantic coast for forty-acre grants to freedmen; rescinded by President Andrew Johnson later that year.

ABRAHAM LINCOLN'S PLAN

By late 1863, Union military victories had convinced President Lincoln of the need to fashion a plan for the reconstruction of the South (see Chapter 16). Lincoln based his reconstruction program on bringing the seceded states back into the Union as quickly as possible. His Proclamation of Amnesty and Reconstruction of December 1863 offered "full pardon" and the restoration of property, not including slaves, to white Southerners willing to swear an oath of allegiance to the United States and its laws, including the Emancipation Proclamation. Prominent Confederate military and civil leaders were excluded from Lincoln's offer, though he indicated that he would freely pardon them.

The president also proposed that when the number of any Confederate state's voters who took the oath of allegiance reached 10 percent of the number who had voted in the election of 1860, this group could establish a state government that Lincoln would recognize as legitimate. Fundamental to this Ten Percent Plan was acceptance by the reconstructed governments of the abolition of slavery. Lincoln's plan was designed less as a blueprint for reconstruction than as a way to shorten the war and gain white people's support for emancipation.

Lincoln's amnesty proclamation angered those Republicans—known as **Radical Republicans**—who advocated not only equal rights for the freedmen but also a tougher stance toward the white South. In July 1864, Senator Benjamin F. Wade of Ohio and Congressman Henry W. Davis of Maryland, both Radicals, proposed a harsher alternative to the Ten Percent Plan. The Wade–Davis bill required 50 percent of a seceding state's white male citizens to take a loyalty oath before elections could be held for a convention to rewrite the state's constitution. Lincoln wanted to weaken the Confederacy by creating new state governments that could win broad support from southern white people. The Wade–Davis bill threatened his efforts to build political consensus within the southern states. Lincoln, therefore, pocket-vetoed the bill by refusing to sign it within ten days of the adjournment of Congress.

As Union armies occupied parts of the South, commanders improvised a variety of arrangements involving confiscated plantations and the African American labor force. For example, in 1862 General Benjamin F. Butler began a policy of transforming slaves on Louisiana sugar plantations into wage laborers under the close supervision of occupying federal troops.

In January 1865, General William T. Sherman issued Special **Field Order 15**, setting aside the Sea Islands off the Georgia coast and a portion of the South Carolina low-country rice fields for the exclusive settlement of freed people. Each family would receive forty acres of land and the loan of mules from the army. By the summer of 1865 some 40,000 freed people, eager to take advantage of the general's order, had been settled on 400,000 acres of "Sherman land."

Conflicts within the Republican Party prevented the development of a systematic land distribution program. Still, Lincoln and the Republican Congress supported other measures to aid the emancipated slaves. In March 1865 Congress established the **Freedmen's Bureau**. Along with providing food, clothing, and fuel to destitute former slaves, the bureau was charged with supervising and managing "all the abandoned lands in the South and the control of all subjects relating to refugees and freedmen." The act that established the bureau also stated that forty acres of abandoned or confiscated land could be leased to freed slaves or white Unionists, who would have an option to purchase after three years.

On the evening of April 14, 1865, while attending the theater in Washington, President Lincoln was shot by John Wilkes Booth and died of his wounds several hours later. At the time of his assassination, Lincoln's reconstruction policy remained unsettled and incomplete. In its broad outlines the president's plans had seemed to favor a speedy restoration of the southern states to the Union and a minimum of federal intervention in their affairs. But with his death the specifics of postwar Reconstruction had to be hammered out by a new president, Andrew Johnson of Tennessee, a man whose personality, political background, and racist leanings put him at odds with the Republican-controlled Congress.

ANDREW JOHNSON AND PRESIDENTIAL RECONSTRUCTION

Throughout his career, Andrew Johnson had championed yeoman farmers and viewed the South's plantation aristocrats with contempt. He was the only southern member of the U.S. Senate to remain loyal to the Union, and he held the planter elite responsible for secession and defeat. In 1862, Lincoln appointed Johnson to the difficult post of military governor of Tennessee. There he successfully began wartime Reconstruction and cultivated Unionist support in the mountainous eastern districts of that state.

In 1864, the Republicans, in an appeal to northern and border state "**War Democrats**," nominated Johnson for vice president. But despite Johnson's success in Tennessee and in the 1864 campaign, many Radical Republicans distrusted him. In the immediate aftermath of Lincoln's murder, however, Johnson appeared to side with those Radical Republicans who sought to treat the South as a conquered province. But support for Johnson quickly faded as the new president's policies unfolded. Johnson defined Reconstruction as the province of the executive, not the legislative branch, and he planned to restore the Union as quickly as possible. He blamed individual Southerners—the planter elite—rather than entire states for leading the South down the disastrous road to secession. In line with this philosophy, Johnson outlined mild terms for reentry to the Union.

In the spring of 1865, Johnson granted amnesty and pardon, including restoration of property rights except slaves, to all Confederates who pledged loyalty to the Union and support for emancipation. Fourteen classes of Southerners, mostly major Confederate officials and wealthy landowners, were excluded. But these men could apply individually for presidential pardons. (During his tenure Johnson pardoned roughly 90 percent of those who applied.) Significantly, Johnson instituted this plan while Congress was not in session.

By the fall of 1865, ten of the eleven Confederate states claimed to have met Johnson's requirements to reenter the Union. But a serious division within the federal government was taking shape, for the Congress was not about to allow the president free rein in determining the conditions of southern readmission. Johnson's open sympathy for his fellow white Southerners, his antiblack bias, and his determination to control the course of Reconstruction placed him on a collision course with the powerful Radical wing of the Republican Party.

FREE LABOR AND THE RADICAL REPUBLICAN VISION

Most Radicals were men whose careers had been shaped by the slavery controversy. One of the most effective rhetorical weapons used against slavery and its

IMAGE KEY

for pages 432–433

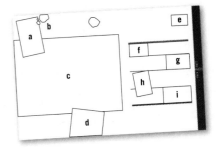

a. A young African American boy with new clothes and a book provided by the Freedmen's Bureau.

b. Rocks and stones like those used to hurl at slaves.

c. Women and children escaping slavery.

d. Two members of the Ku Klux Klan holding guns and wearing hoods and long robes, pictured in *Harper's Weekly*.

e. Pages 44 and 45 from the New England primer show the religious content of the work.

f. The dead at Gettysburg were strewn across the battlefield.

g. Freedmen (freed black slaves) vote in 1867 while standing in line. The Stars and Stripes hang overhead.

h. Three white men decry the Reconstruction Acts of Congress as "usurpations and unconstitutional, revolutionary, and void" while clasping hands above the fallen body of a black man.

i. The "tramp" became a symbol of the misery caused by industrial depression as seen in this *Harper's Weekly* illustration, "The Tramp," September 2, 1876.

Freedmen's Bureau Agency established by Congress in March 1865 to provide social, educational, and economic services, advice, and protection to former slaves and destitute whites; lasted seven years.

War Democrats Those from the North and the border states who broke with the Democratic Party and supported the Abraham Lincoln's military policies during the Civil War.

QUICK REVIEW

Johnson's Reconstruction Plan

♦ Johnson extended pardons to Southerners who swore an oath of allegiance.

♦ He restored property rights to Southerners who swore an oath of allegiance.

♦ His plan had nothing to say about the voting and civil rights of former slaves.

Black codes   Laws passed by states and municipalities denying many rights of citizenship to free black people before the Civil War.

Civil Rights Bill   1866 act that gave full citizenship to African Americans.

16–3
Clinton B. Fisk, *Plain Counsels for Freedmen* (1865)

16–4
Mississippi Black Codes (1865)

16–7
The Fourteenth Amendment (1868)

"Office of the Freedmen's Bureau, Memphis, Tennessee," *Harper's Weekly*, June 2, 1866. Established by Congress in 1865, the Freedmen's Bureau provided economic, educational, and legal assistance to former slaves in the post–Civil War years. Bureau agents were often called on to settle disputes between black and white Southerners over wages, labor contracts, political rights, and violence. Although most southern whites only grudgingly acknowledged the bureau's legitimacy, freed people gained important legal and psychological support through testimony at public hearings like this one.

spread had been the ideal of a society based upon free labor. The model of free individuals, competing equally in the labor market and enjoying equal political rights, formed the core of this worldview.

Radicals now looked to reconstruct southern society along these same lines, backed by the power of the national government. They argued that once free labor, universal education, and equal rights were implanted in the South, that region would be able to share in the North's material wealth, progress, and social mobility. In the Radicals' view, the power of the federal government would be central to the remaking of southern society, especially in guaranteeing civil rights and suffrage for freedmen.

Northern Republicans were especially outraged by the stringent "**black codes**" passed by South Carolina, Mississippi, Louisiana, and other states. These were designed to restrict the freedom of the black labor force and keep freed people as close to slave status as possible. Laborers who left their jobs before contracts expired would forfeit wages already earned and be subject to arrest by any white citizen. Vagrancy, very broadly defined, was punishable by fines and involuntary plantation labor. Apprenticeship clauses obliged black children to work without pay for employers. Some states attempted to bar African Americans from land ownership. Other laws specifically denied African Americans equality with white people in civil rights, excluding them from juries and prohibiting interracial marriages.

The Radicals, although not a majority of their party, were joined by moderate Republicans as growing numbers of Northerners grew suspicious of white southern intransigence and the denial of political rights to freedmen. When the Thirty-ninth Congress convened in December 1865, the large Republican majority prevented the seating of the white Southerners elected to Congress under President Johnson's provisional state governments.

In the spring of 1866, Congress passed two important bills designed to aid African Americans. The landmark **Civil Rights Bill**, which bestowed full citizenship on African Americans, overturned the 1857 *Dred Scott* decision and the black codes. It defined all persons born in the United States (except Indian peoples) as national citizens, and it enumerated various rights, including the rights to make and enforce contracts, to sue, to give evidence, and to buy and sell property. Under this bill,

African Americans acquired "full and equal benefit of all laws and proceedings for the security of person and property as is enjoyed by white citizens."

Congress also voted to enlarge the scope of the Freedmen's Bureau, empowering it to build schools and pay teachers, and also to establish courts to prosecute those charged with depriving African Americans of their civil rights. The bureau achieved important, if limited, success in aiding African Americans. Bureau-run schools helped lay the foundation for southern public education. The bureau's network of courts allowed freed people to bring suits against white people in disputes involving violence, nonpayment of wages, or unfair division of crops. The very existence of courts hearing public testimony by African Americans provided an important psychological challenge to traditional notions of white racial domination.

An angry President Johnson vetoed both of these bills. But Johnson's intemperate attacks on the Radicals—he damned them as traitors unwilling to restore the Union—united moderate and Radical Republicans and they succeeded in overriding the vetoes. Congressional Republicans, led by the Radical faction, were now unified in challenging the president's power to direct Reconstruction and in using national authority to define and protect the rights of citizens.

In June 1866, fearful that the Civil Rights Act might be declared unconstitutional, and eager to settle the basis for the seating of southern representatives, Congress passed the Fourteenth Amendment. The amendment defined national citizenship to include former slaves and prohibited the states from violating the privileges of citizens without due process of law. It also empowered Congress to reduce the representation of any state that denied the suffrage to males over twenty-one. Republicans adopted the Fourteenth Amendment as their platform for the 1866 congressional elections and suggested that southern states would have to ratify it as a condition of readmission.

For their part, the Republicans skillfully portrayed Johnson and northern Democrats as disloyal and white Southerners as unregenerate. Republicans began an effective campaign tradition known as "waving the bloody shirt"—reminding northern voters of the hundreds of thousands of Yankee soldiers left dead or maimed by the war. In the November 1866 elections, the Republicans increased their majority in both the House and the Senate and gained control of all the northern states. The stage was now set for a battle between the president and Congress. Was it to be Johnson's "restoration" or **Congressional Reconstruction**?

CONGRESSIONAL RECONSTRUCTION AND THE IMPEACHMENT CRISIS

In March 1867, Congress passed the **First Reconstruction Act** over Johnson's veto. This act divided the South into five military districts subject to martial law. To achieve restoration, southern states were first required to call new constitutional conventions, elected by universal manhood suffrage. Once these states had drafted new constitutions, guaranteed African American voting rights, and ratified the Fourteenth Amendment, they were eligible for readmission to the Union. Supplementary legislation, also passed over the president's veto, invalidated the provisional governments established by Johnson, empowered the military to administer voter registration, and required an oath of loyalty to the United States (see Map 17.1).

Congress also passed several laws aimed at limiting Johnson's power. One of these, the **Tenure of Office Act**, stipulated that any officeholder appointed by the president with the Senate's advice and consent could not be removed until the Senate had approved a successor. In August 1867, with Congress

Congressional Reconstruction   Name given to the period 1867–1870 when the Republican-dominated Congress controlled Reconstruction-era policy.

First Reconstruction Act   1877 act that divided the South into five military districts subject to martial law.

Tenure of Office Act   Act stipulating that any officeholder appointed by the president with the Senate's advice and consent could not be removed until the Senate had approved a successor.

QUICK REVIEW

Key Components of the Radical Agenda

- Free labor.
- Universal education.
- Equal rights.

QUICK REVIEW

The Tenure of Office Act and Johnson's Impeachment

- Act prohibited the president from removing certain officeholders without the Senate's approval of a successor.
- Johnson deliberately violated the act in February 1868.
- Johnson escaped impeachment by one vote.

MAP EXPLORATION

To explore an interactive version of this map, go to
http://www.prenhall.com/faraghertlc/map17.1

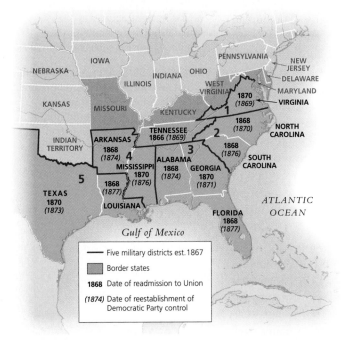

MAP 17.1
Reconstruction of the South, 1866–77   Dates for the readmission of former Confederate states to the Union and the return of Democrats to power varied according to the specific political situations in those states.

WHAT WERE the competing plans for reconstructing the Southern states?

adjourned, Johnson suspended Stanton and appointed General Ulysses S. Grant interim secretary of war. This move enabled the president to remove generals in the field that he judged to be too radical and replace them with men who were sympathetic to his own views. It also served as a challenge to the Tenure of Office Act. In January 1868, when the Senate overruled Stanton's suspension, Grant broke openly with Johnson and vacated the office. Stanton resumed his position and barricaded himself in his office when Johnson attempted to remove him once again.

Outraged by Johnson's relentless obstructionism, and seizing upon his violation of the Tenure of Office Act as a pretext, moderate and Radical Republicans in the House of Representatives again joined forces and voted to impeach the president by a vote of 126 to 47 on February 24, 1868, charging him with eleven counts of high crimes and misdemeanors. To ensure the support of moderate Republicans, the articles of impeachment focused on violations of the Tenure of Office Act.

An influential group of moderate Senate Republicans feared the damage a conviction might do to the constitutional separation of powers. They also worried about the political and economic policies that might be pursued by Benjamin Wade, the president pro tem of the Senate and a leader of the Radical Republicans, who, because there was no vice president, would succeed to the presidency if Johnson were removed from office. Behind the scenes during his Senate trial, Johnson agreed to abide by the Reconstruction Acts. In May, the Senate

The Fifteenth Amendment, ratified in 1870, stipulated that the right to vote could not be denied "on account of race, color, or previous condition of servitude." This illustration expressed the optimism and hopes of African Americans generated by this consitutional landmark aimed at protecting black political rights. Note the various political figures (Abraham Lincoln, John Brown, Frederick Douglass) and movements (abolitionism, black education) invoked here, providing a sense of how the amendment ended a long historical struggle.

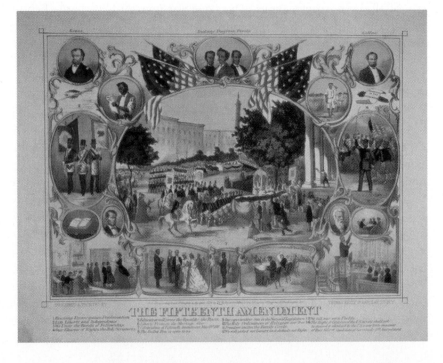

voted 35 for conviction, 19 for acquittal—one vote shy of the two-thirds necessary for removal from office. Johnson's narrow acquittal established the precedent that only criminal actions by a president—not political disagreements—warranted removal from office.

THE ELECTION OF 1868

By the summer of 1868, seven former Confederate states (Alabama, Arkansas, Florida, Louisiana, North Carolina, South Carolina, and Tennessee) had ratified the revised constitutions, elected Republican governments, and ratified the Fourteenth Amendment. They had thereby earned readmission to the Union. In 1868 Republicans nominated Ulysses S. Grant, the North's foremost military hero, as their nominee for President. Grant enjoyed tremendous popularity after the war, especially when he broke with Johnson. Totally lacking in political experience, Grant admitted, after receiving the nomination, that he had been forced into it in spite of himself.

Significantly, at the very moment that the South was being forced to enfranchise former slaves as a prerequisite for readmission to the Union, the Republicans rejected a campaign plank endorsing black suffrage in the North. State referendums calling for black suffrage failed in eight northern states between 1865 and 1868, succeeding only in Iowa and Minnesota. The Democrats, determined to reverse Congressional Reconstruction, nominated Horatio Seymour, former governor of New York and a longtime foe of emancipation and supporter of states' rights.

The **Ku Klux Klan** emerged as a potent instrument of terror (see the opening of this chapter). In Louisiana, Arkansas, Georgia, and South Carolina, the Klan threatened, whipped, and murdered black and white Republicans to prevent them from voting. This terrorism enabled the Democrats to carry Georgia and Louisiana, but it ultimately cost the Democrats votes in the North. In the final tally, Grant carried twenty-six of the thirty-four states for an electoral college victory of 214 to 80. Significantly, more than 500,000 African American voters cast their ballots for Grant, demonstrating their overwhelming support for the Republican Party. The Republicans also retained large majorities in both houses of Congress.

In February 1869, Congress passed the **Fifteenth Amendment**, providing that "the right of citizens of the United States to vote shall not be denied or abridged on account of race, color, or previous condition of servitude." To enhance the chances of ratification, Congress required the four remaining unreconstructed states—Mississippi, Georgia, Texas, and Virginia—to ratify both the Fourteenth and Fifteenth Amendments before readmission. They did so and rejoined the Union in early 1870. The Fifteenth Amendment was ratified in February 1870. In the narrow sense of simply readmitting the former Confederate states to the Union, Reconstruction was complete.

WOMAN SUFFRAGE AND RECONSTRUCTION

Many women's rights advocates had long been active in the abolitionist movement. The Fourteenth and Fifteenth Amendments, which granted citizenship and the vote to freedmen, both inspired and frustrated these activists. Insisting that the causes of the African American vote and the women's vote were linked, Elizabeth Cady Stanton, Susan B. Anthony, and Lucy Stone founded the American Equal Rights Association in 1866. The group launched a series of lobbying and petition campaigns to remove racial and sexual restrictions on voting from state constitutions. Throughout the nation, the old abolitionist organizations and the Republican Party

Ku Klux Klan Perhaps the most prominent of the vigilante groups that terrorized black people in the South during Reconstruction era, founded by the Confederate veterans in 1866.

Fifteenth Amendment Passed by Congress in 1869, guaranteed the right of American men to vote, regardless of race.

16–8
Albion W. Tourgee, *Letter on Ku Klux Klan Activities* (1870)

Susan B. Anthony (1820–1906) and Elizabeth Cady Stanton (1815–1902), the two most influential leaders of the woman suffrage movement. As founders of the militant National Woman Suffrage Association, Stanton and Anthony established an independent woman suffrage movement with a broader spectrum of goals for women's rights and drew millions of women into public life during the late nineteenth century.

OVERVIEW | Reconstruction Amendments to the Constitution, 1865–1870

Amendment and Date Passed by Congress	Main Provisions	Ratification Process (3/4 of all States Including Ex-Confederate States Required)
13 (January 1865)	• Prohibited slavery in the United States	December 1865 (27 states, including 8 southern states)
14 (June 1866)	• Conferred national citizenship on all persons born or naturalized in the United States • Reduced state representation in Congress proportionally for any state disfranchising male citizens • Denied former Confederates the right to hold state or national office • Repudiated Confederate debt	July 1868 (after Congress made ratification a prerequisite for readmission of ex-Confederate states to the Union)
15 (February 1869)	• Prohibited denial of suffrage because of race, color, or previous condition of servitude	March 1870 (ratification required for readmission of Virginia, Texas, Mississippi, and Georgia)

myhistorylab

Overview: *Reconstruction Amendments to the Constitution, 1865–1870*

16–10
Susan B. Anthony and the "New Departure" for Women (1873)

WHAT WERE the most important changes in the lives of African Americans in the years immediately following the war?

myhistorylab

Review Summary

emphasized passage of the Fourteenth and Fifteenth Amendments and withdrew funds and support from the cause of woman suffrage. Disagreements over these amendments divided suffragists for decades and by 1869 woman suffragists had split into two competing organizations: the moderate American Woman Suffrage Association (AWSA), which sought the support of men, and the more radical all-female National Woman Suffrage Association (NWSA).

Although women did not win the vote in this period, they did establish an independent suffrage movement that eventually drew millions of women into political life. The NWSA in particular demonstrated that self-government and democratic participation in the public sphere were crucial for women's emancipation. The failure of woman suffrage after the Civil War was less a result of factional fighting than of the larger defeat of Radical Reconstruction and the ideal of expanded citizenship.

THE MEANING OF FREEDOM

For nearly 4 million slaves, freedom arrived in various ways in different parts of the South. In many areas, slavery had collapsed long before Lee's surrender at Appomattox. In regions far removed from the presence of federal troops, African Americans did not learn of slavery's end until the spring of 1865. But regardless of specific regional circumstances, the meaning of "freedom" would be contested for years to come. The deep desire for independence from white control formed the underlying aspiration of newly freed slaves. For their part, most southern white people sought to restrict the boundaries of that independence.

MOVING ABOUT

The first impulse of many emancipated slaves was to test their freedom. The simplest, most obvious way to do this involved leaving home. Throughout the summer and fall of 1865, observers in the South noted enormous numbers of freed

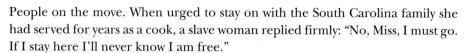

People on the move. When urged to stay on with the South Carolina family she had served for years as a cook, a slave woman replied firmly: "No, Miss, I must go. If I stay here I'll never know I am free."

Yet many who left their old neighborhoods returned soon afterward to seek work in the general vicinity or even on the plantation they had left. Many wanted to separate themselves from former owners, but not from familial ties and friendships. Others moved away altogether, seeking jobs in nearby towns and cities. Many former slaves left predominantly white counties, where they felt more vulnerable and isolated, for new lives in the relative comfort of predominantly black communities. In most southern states, there was a significant population shift toward black belt plantation counties and towns after the war. Many African Americans, attracted by schools, churches, and fraternal societies as well as the army, preferred the city.

Disgruntled planters had difficulty accepting African American independence. The deference and humility white people expected from African Americans could no longer be taken for granted. Indeed, many freed people went out of their way to reject the old subservience. Moving about freely was one way of doing this, as was refusing to tip one's hat to white people, ignoring former masters or mistresses in the streets, and refusing to step aside on sidewalks.

THE AFRICAN AMERICAN FAMILY

Emancipation allowed freed people to strengthen family ties. For many former slaves, freedom meant the opportunity to find long-lost family members. To track down these relatives, freed people trekked to faraway places, put ads in newspapers, sought the help of Freedmen's Bureau agents, and questioned anyone who might have information about loved ones. Many thousands of family reunions, each with its own story, took place after the war. One North Carolina slave, who had seen his parents separated by sale, recalled many years later what for him had been the most significant aspect of freedom. "I has got thirteen great-gran' chilluns an' I know whar dey ever'one am. In slavery times dey'd have been on de block long time ago." Thousands of African American couples who had lived together under slavery streamed to military and civilian authorities and demanded to be legally married. By 1870, the two-parent household was the norm for a large majority of African Americans.

Emancipation brought changes to gender roles within the African American family as well. By serving in the Union army, African American men played a more direct role than women in the fight for freedom. In the political sphere, black men could now serve on juries, vote, and hold office; black women, like their white counterparts, could not. Freedmen's Bureau agents designated the husband as household head and established lower wage scales for women laborers.

African American men asserted their male authority, denied under slavery, by insisting their wives work at home instead of in the fields. African American women generally wanted to devote more time than they had under slavery to caring for their children and to performing such domestic chores as cooking, sewing, gardening, and laundering. Yet African American women continued to work outside the home, engaging in seasonal field labor for wages or working a family's rented plot. The key difference from slave times was that African American families themselves, not white masters and overseers, decided when and where women and children worked.

AFRICAN AMERICAN CHURCHES AND SCHOOLS

The creation of separate African American churches proved the most lasting and important element of the energetic institution building that went on in post-emancipation years. Before the Civil War, southern Protestant churches had

An overflow congregation crowds into Richmond's First African Baptist Church in 1874. Despite their poverty, freed people struggled to save money, buy land, and erect new buildings as they organized hundreds of new black churches during Reconstruction. As the most important African American institution outside the family, the black church, in addition to tending to spiritual needs, played a key role in the educational and political life of the community.

relegated slaves and free African Americans to second-class membership. Black worshipers were required to sit in the back during services, they were denied any role in church governance, and they were excluded from Sunday schools. Even in larger cities, where all-black congregations sometimes built their own churches, the law required white pastors.

In communities around the South, African Americans now pooled their resources to buy land and build their own churches. Churches became the center not only for religious life but also for many other activities that defined the African American community: schools, picnics, festivals, and political meetings. The church became the first social institution fully controlled by African Americans. In nearly every community, ministers, respected for their speaking and organizational skills, were among the most influential leaders. By 1877, the great majority of black Southerners had withdrawn from white-dominated churches.

The rapid spread of schools reflected African Americans' thirst for self-improvement. Southern states had prohibited education for slaves. But many free black people managed to attend school, and a few slaves had been able to educate themselves. Still, over 90 percent of the South's adult African American population was illiterate in 1860. Access to education thus became a central part of the meaning of freedom. Freedmen's Bureau agents repeatedly expressed amazement at the number of makeshift classrooms organized by African Americans in rural areas.

African American communities received important educational aid from outside organizations. By 1869, the Freedmen's Bureau was supervising nearly 3,000 schools serving over 150,000 students throughout the South. Over half of the roughly 3,300 teachers in these schools were African Americans, many of whom had been free before the Civil War. Other teachers included dedicated northern white women, volunteers sponsored by the American Missionary Association (AMA). The bureau and the AMA also assisted in the founding of several black colleges, including Tougaloo, Hampton, and Fisk, designed to train black teachers. Black self-help proved crucial to the education effort. Throughout the South in 1865 and 1866, African Americans raised money to build schoolhouses, buy supplies, and pay teachers. Black artisans donated labor for construction, and black families offered room and board to teachers.

LAND AND LABOR AFTER SLAVERY

Most newly emancipated African Americans aspired to quit the plantations and to make new lives for themselves. Some freed people did find jobs in railroad building, mining, ranching, or construction work. Others raised subsistence crops and tended vegetable gardens as squatters. White planters, however, tried to retain African Americans as permanent agricultural laborers. Restricting the employment of former slaves was an important goal of the black codes.

The majority of African Americans hoped to become self-sufficient farmers. Many former slaves believed they were entitled to the land they had worked throughout their lives. This perception was not merely a wishful fantasy. Frequent reference in the Congress and the press to the question of land distribution made the idea of "forty acres and a mule" not just a pipe dream but a matter of serious public debate. But by 1866, the federal government had already pulled back from the various wartime experiments involving the breaking up of large plantations and the leasing of small plots to individual families. President Johnson directed General Oliver O. Howard of the Freedmen's Bureau to evict tens of thousands of freed people settled on confiscated and abandoned land in southeastern Virginia, southern Louisiana, and the Georgia and South Carolina low country.

In communities throughout the South, freed people and their former masters negotiated new arrangements for organizing agricultural labor (see Map 17.2). By the late 1860s, **sharecropping** and tenant farming had emerged as the dominant form of working the land. Sharecropping represented a compromise between planters and former slaves. Under sharecropping arrangements that were usually very detailed, individual families contracted with landowners to be responsible for a specific plot. Large plantations were thus broken into family-sized farms. Generally, sharecropper families received one-third of the year's crop if the owner furnished implements, seed, and draft animals or one-half if they provided their own supplies. African Americans preferred sharecropping to gang labor, as it allowed families to set their own hours and tasks and offered freedom from white supervision and control. For planters, the system stabilized the workforce by requiring sharecroppers to remain until the harvest and to employ all family members. It also offered a way around the chronic shortage of cash and credit that plagued the postwar South. Freed people did not aspire to sharecropping. Owning land outright or tenant farming (renting land) were both more desirable. But though black sharecroppers clearly enjoyed more autonomy than in the past, the vast majority never achieved economic independence or land ownership. They remained a largely subordinate agricultural labor force.

THE ORIGINS OF AFRICAN AMERICAN POLITICS

Inclusion, rather than separation, was the objective of early African American political activity. The greatest political activity by African Americans occurred in areas occupied by Union forces during the war. In 1865 and 1866, African Americans throughout the South organized scores of mass meetings, parades, and petitions that demanded civil equality and the right to vote. In the cities, the growing web of churches and fraternal societies helped bolster early efforts at political organization.

Hundreds of African American delegates, selected by local meetings or churches, attended statewide political conventions held

16–5
James C. Beecher, *Report on Land Reform in the South Carolina Islands* (1865, 1866)

16–11
James T. Rapier, *Testimony Before U.S. Senate Regarding the Agricultural Labor Force in the South* (1880)

A Sharecrop Contract (1882)

Sharecropping Labor system that evolved during and after Reconstruction whereby landowners furnished laborers with a house, farm animals, and tools and advanced credit in exchange for a share of the laborers' crop.

"The First Vote," *Harper's Weekly*, November 16, 1867, reflected the optimism felt by much of the northern public as former slaves began to vote for the first time. The caption noted that freedmen went to the ballot box "not with expressions of exultation or of defiance of their old masters and present opponents depicted on their countenances, but looking serious and solemn and determined."

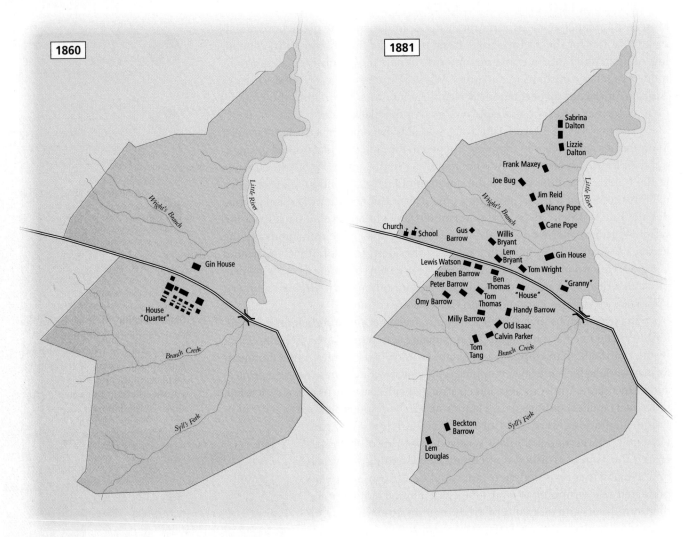

MAP 17.2
The Barrow Plantation, Oglethorpe County, Georgia, 1860 and 1881 (approx. 2,000 acres) These two maps, based on drawings from *Scribner's Monthly*, April 1881, show some of the changes brought by emancipation. In 1860, the plantation's entire black population lived in the communal slave quarters, right next to the white master's house. In 1881, black sharecropper and tenant families lived on individual plots, spread out across the land. The former slaves had also built their own school and church.

WHAT CHANGES in the lives of Black Southerners are reflected in the two maps of the Barrow Plantation?

throughout the South in 1865 and 1866. Previously free African Americans, as well as black ministers, artisans, and veterans of the Union army, tended to dominate these proceedings, setting a pattern that would hold throughout Reconstruction. Convention debates sometimes reflected the tensions within African American communities, such as friction between poorer former slaves and better-off free black people, or between lighter- and darker-skinned African Americans. But most of these state gatherings concentrated on passing resolutions on issues that united all African Americans. The central concerns were suffrage and equality before the law.

The passage of the First Reconstruction Act in 1867 encouraged even more political activity among African Americans. The military started registering the South's electorate, ultimately enrolling approximately 735,000 black and 635,000 white voters in the ten unreconstructed states. Five states—Alabama, Florida, Louisiana, Mississippi, and South Carolina—had black electoral majorities. Four-fifths of the

Changing Images of Reconstruction

After the Civil War, northern journalists and illustrators went south to describe Reconstruction in action. They took a keen interest in how the newly freed slaves were reshaping local and national politics. A drawing by *Harper's Weekly* illustrator William L. Sheppard titled "Electioneering in the South" clearly approved of the freedmen's exercise of their new citizenship rights. "Does any man seriously

HOW DOES the portrayal of the larger African American community in "Electioneering in the South" reflect the political point being made? What do the caricatures in "The Ignorant Vote" suggest about Reconstruction era ideas about the meaning of "whiteness"?

doubt," the caption asked, "whether it is better for this vast population to be sinking deeper and deeper in ignorance and servility, or rising into general intelligence and self-respect? They can not be pariahs; they can not be peons; they must be slaves or citizens."

Thomas Nast was the nation's best-known political cartoonist during the 1860s and 1870s. During the Civil War he strongly supported the Union cause and the aspirations of the newly freed slaves. But by 1876, like many Northerners originally sympathetic to guaranteeing blacks full political and civil rights, Nast had turned away from the early ideals of Reconstruction. Nast used grotesque racial caricature to depict southern African Americans and northern Irish

immigrants as undeserving of the right to vote. The aftermath of the disputed 1876 presidential election included charges of widespread vote fraud from both Republicans and Democrats. Nast's view—published in *Harper's Weekly* in December 1876, while the election's outcome was still in doubt—reflected concerns among many middle-class Northerners that the nation's political system was tainted by the manipulation of "ignorant" voters in both the South and the North. ∎

registered black voters cast ballots in these elections. Much of this new African American political activism was channeled through local **Union League** chapters throughout the South.

Begun during the war as a northern, largely white middle-class patriotic club, the Union League now became the political voice of the former slaves. Union League chapters brought together local African Americans, soldiers, and Freedmen's Bureau agents to demand the vote and an end to legal discrimination against African Americans. It brought out African American voters, instructed freedmen in the rights and duties of citizenship, and promoted Republican candidates. Not surprisingly, newly enfranchised freedmen voted Republican and formed the core of the Republican Party in the South. For most ordinary African Americans, politics was inseparable from economic issues, especially the land question. Grassroots political organizations frequently intervened in local disputes with planters over the terms of labor contracts. African American political groups closely followed the congressional debates over Reconstruction policy and agitated for land confiscation and distribution. Perhaps most important, politics was the only arena where black and white Southerners might engage each other on an equal basis.

SOUTHERN POLITICS AND SOCIETY

By the summer of 1868, when the South had returned to the Union, the majority of Republicans believed the task of Reconstruction to be finished. Ultimately, they put their faith in a political solution to the problems facing the vanquished South. Most Republican congressmen were moderates, conceiving Reconstruction in limited terms. They rejected radical calls for confiscation and redistribution of land, as well as permanent military rule of the South. The Reconstruction Acts of 1867 and 1868 laid out the requirements for the readmission of southern states, along with the procedures for forming and electing new governments.

Yet over the next decade, the political structure created in the southern states proved too restricted and fragile to sustain itself. To most southern whites, the active participation of African Americans in politics seemed extremely dangerous. Federal troops were needed to protect Republican governments and their supporters from violent opposition. Congressional action to monitor southern elections and protect black voting rights became routine. Despite initial successes, southern Republicanism proved an unstable coalition of often conflicting elements, unable to sustain effective power for very long. By 1877, Democrats had regained political control of all the former Confederate states.

SOUTHERN REPUBLICANS

Three major groups composed the fledgling Republican coalition in the postwar South. African American voters made up a large majority of southern Republicans throughout the Reconstruction era. Yet African Americans outnumbered whites in only three southern states; Republicans would have to attract white support to win elections and sustain power.

A second group consisted of white Northerners, derisively called "**carpetbaggers**" by native white Southerners. Most were veterans of the Union army who stayed in the South after the war. Others included Freedmen's Bureau agents and businessmen who had invested capital in cotton plantations and other enterprises. Although they made up a tiny percentage of the population, carpetbaggers played

Union League Republican party organizations in Northern cities that became an important organizing device among freedmen in Southern cities after 1865.

Carpetbaggers Northern transplants to the South, many of whom were Union soldiers who stayed in the South after the war.

a disproportionately large role in southern politics. They won a large share of Reconstruction offices, particularly in Florida, South Carolina, and Louisiana and in areas with large African American constituencies.

The third major group of southern Republicans were the native whites pejoratively termed "**scalawags**." They had even more diverse backgrounds and motives than the northern-born Republicans. Some were prominent prewar Whigs who saw the Republican Party as their best chance to regain political influence. Others viewed the party as an agent of modernization and economic expansion. Loyalists during the war and traditional enemies of the planter elite (most were small farmers), these white Southerners looked to the Republican Party for help in settling old scores and relief from debt and wartime devastation.

Southern Republicanism also reflected prewar political divisions. Its influence was greatest in those regions that had long resisted the political and economic power of the plantation elite. Yet few white Southerners identified with the political and economic aspirations of African Americans. Moderate elements more concerned with maintaining white control of the party, and encouraging economic investment in the region, outnumbered and defeated "confiscation radicals" who focused on obtaining land for African Americans.

QUICK REVIEW

Southern Republicans

- African American voters.
- White Northerners called "carpetbaggers" by white Southerners.
- Native whites pejoratively termed "scalawags."

Scalawags Southern whites, mainly small landowning farmers and well-off merchants and planters, who supported the Southern Republican party during Reconstruction.

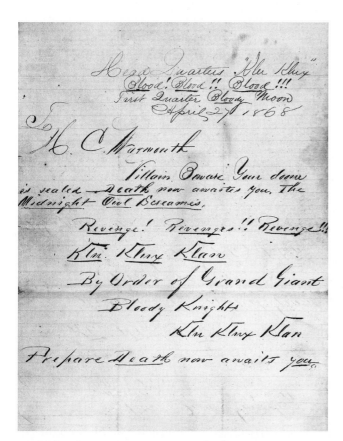

The Ku Klux Klan emerged as a potent political and social force during Reconstruction, terrorizing freed people and their white allies. An 1868 Klan warning threatens Louisiana governor Henry C. Warmoth with death. Warmoth, an Illinois-born "carpetbagger," was the state's first Republican governor. Two Alabama Klansmen, photographed in 1868, wear white hoods to hide their identities.

myhistorylab

Exploring America: *Did Reconstruction Work for the Freed People?*

RECONSTRUCTING THE STATES: A MIXED RECORD

With the old Confederate leaders barred from political participation, and with carpetbaggers and newly enfranchised African Americans representing many of the plantation districts, Republicans managed to dominate the ten southern constitutional conventions from 1867 to 1869. Most of these conventions produced constitutions that expanded democracy and the public role of the state. The new documents guaranteed the political and civil rights of African Americans, and they abolished property qualifications for officeholding and jury service as well as imprisonment for debt. They created the first state-funded systems of education in the South to be administered by state commissioners. The new constitutions also mandated establishment of orphanages, penitentiaries, and homes for the insane. In 1868, only three years after the end of the war, Republicans came to power in most of the southern states. By 1869, new constitutions had been ratified in all the old Confederate states.

Republican governments in the South faced a continual crisis of legitimacy that limited their ability to legislate change. They had to balance reform against the need to gain acceptance, especially by white Southerners. Their achievements were thus mixed. In the realm of race relations there was a clear thrust toward equal rights and against discrimination. Republican legislatures followed up the federal Civil Rights Act of 1866 with various antidiscrimination clauses in new constitutions and laws prescribing harsh penalties for civil rights violations.

Segregation, though, became the norm in public school systems. African American leaders often accepted segregation because they feared that insistence on integrated education would jeopardize funding for the new school systems. Segregation in railroad cars and other public places was more objectionable. By the early 1870s, as black influence and assertiveness grew, laws guaranteeing equal access to transportation and public accommodation were passed in many states. By and large, though, such civil rights laws were difficult to enforce in local communities.

In economic matters, Republican governments failed to fulfill African Americans' hopes of obtaining land. Few former slaves possessed the cash to buy land in the open market, and they looked to the state for help. Republicans tried to weaken the plantation system and promote black ownership by raising taxes on land. Yet even when state governments seized land for nonpayment of taxes, the property was never used to help create black homesteads.

Republican leaders envisioned promoting northern-style capitalist development—factories, large towns, and diversified agriculture—through state aid. Much Republican state lawmaking was devoted to encouraging railroad construction. But in spite of all the new laws, it proved impossible to attract significant amounts of northern and European investment capital. The obsession with railroads withdrew resources from education and other programs. As in the North, it also opened the doors to widespread corruption and bribery of public officials. Railroad failures eroded public confidence in the Republicans' ability to govern.

WHITE RESISTANCE AND "REDEMPTION"

The emergence of a Republican Party in the reconstructed South brought two parties, but not a two-party system, to the region. The opponents of Reconstruction, the Democrats, refused to acknowledge Republicans' right to participate in southern political life. Republicans were split between those who urged conciliation in an effort to gain white acceptance and those who emphasized consolidating the party under the protection of the military.

From its founding in 1868 through the early 1870s, the Ku Klux Klan fought an ongoing terrorist campaign against Reconstruction governments and local leaders. Just as the institution of slavery had depended on violence and the threat of violence, the Klan acted as a kind of guerrilla military force in the service of the Democratic Party, the planter class, and all those who sought the restoration of white supremacy. It employed a wide array of terror tactics: destroying ballot boxes, issuing death threats, the beating and murdering of politically active blacks and their white allies. Freedmen and their allies sometimes resisted the Klan. In Hale County, Alabama, Union Leaguers set up a warning system using buglers to signal the activities of Klan raiders. But violence and intimidation decimated Union League leadership in the countryside by 1869.

In October 1870, after Republicans carried Laurens County in South Carolina, bands of white people drove 150 African Americans from their homes and murdered thirteen white and black Republican activists. In March 1871, three African Americans were arrested in Meridian, Mississippi, for giving "incendiary" speeches. At their court hearing, Klansmen killed two of the defendants and the Republican judge, and thirty more African Americans were murdered in a day of rioting. The single bloodiest episode of Reconstruction era violence took place in Colfax, Louisiana, on Easter Sunday 1873. Nearly 100 African Americans were murdered after they failed to hold a besieged courthouse during a contested election.

Southern Republicans looked to Washington for help. In 1870 and 1871, Congress passed three Enforcement Acts designed to counter racial terrorism. These declared that interference with voting was a federal offense. The acts provided for federal supervision of voting and authorized the president to send the army and to suspend the writ of habeas corpus in districts declared to be in a state of insurrection. The most sweeping measure was the Ku Klux Klan Act of April 1871, which made the violent infringement of civil and political rights a federal crime punishable by the national government. By the election of 1872, the federal government's intervention had helped break the Klan and restore a semblance of law and order.

The Civil Rights Act of 1875 outlawed racial discrimination in theaters, hotels, railroads, and other public places. But the law proved more an assertion of principle than a direct federal intervention in southern affairs. Enforcement required African Americans to take their cases to the federal courts, a costly and time-consuming procedure.

As wartime idealism faded, northern Republicans became less inclined toward direct intervention in southern affairs. They had enough trouble retaining political control in the North. In 1874, the Democrats gained a majority in the House of Representatives for the first time since 1856. Key northern states also began to fall to the Democrats. Northern Republicans slowly abandoned the freedmen and their white allies in the South. Southern Democrats were also able to exploit a deepening fiscal crisis by blaming Republicans for excessive extension of public credit and the sharp increase in tax rates.

Gradually, conservative Democrats "redeemed" one state after another. Virginia and Tennessee led the way in 1869, North Carolina in 1870, Georgia in 1871, Texas in 1873, and Alabama and Arkansas in 1874. In Mississippi, white conservatives employed violence and intimidation to wrest control in 1875 and "redeemed" the state the following year. Republican infighting in Louisiana in 1873 and 1874 led to a series of contested election results, including bloody clashes between black militia and armed whites, and finally to "redemption" by the Democrats in 1877.

Several Supreme Court rulings involving the Fourteenth and Fifteenth Amendments effectively constrained federal protection of African American civil rights. In

Slaughterhouse cases Group of cases resulting in one sweeping decision by the U.S. Supreme Court in 1873 that contradicted the intent of the Fourteenth Amendment by decreeing that most citizenship rights remained under state, not federal, control.

the so-called **Slaughterhouse cases** of 1873, the Court issued its first ruling on the Fourteenth Amendment. The cases involved a Louisiana charter that gave a New Orleans meatpacking company a monopoly over the city's butchering business on the grounds of protecting public health. A rival group of butchers had sued, claiming the law violated the Fourteenth Amendment, which prohibited states from depriving any person of life, liberty, or property without due process of law. The Court held that the Fourteenth Amendment protected only the former slaves, not butchers, and that it protected only national citizenship rights, not the regulatory powers of states. It separated national citizenship from state citizenship and declared that most of the rights that Americans enjoyed on a daily basis—freedom of speech, fair trials, the right to sit on juries, protection from unreasonable searches, and the right to vote—were under the control of state law. The ruling in effect denied the original intent of the Fourteenth Amendment—to protect against state infringement of national citizenship rights as spelled out in the Bill of Rights.

Three other decisions curtailed federal protection of black civil rights. In *United States* v. *Reese* (1876) and *United States* v. *Cruikshank* (1876), the Court restricted congressional power to enforce the Ku Klux Klan Act. Future prosecution would depend on the states rather than on federal authorities. In these rulings, the Court held that the Fourteenth Amendment extended the federal power to protect civil rights only in cases involving discrimination by states; discrimination by individuals or groups was not covered. The Court also ruled that the Fifteenth Amendment did not guarantee a citizen's right to vote; it only barred certain specific grounds for denying suffrage—"race, color, or previous condition of servitude." This interpretation opened the door for southern states to disenfranchise African Americans for allegedly nonracial reasons. States back under Democratic control began to limit African American voting by passing laws restricting voter eligibility through poll taxes and property requirements.

Finally, in the 1883 Civil Rights Cases decision, the Court declared the Civil Rights Act of 1875 unconstitutional, holding that the Fourteenth Amendment gave Congress the power to outlaw discrimination by states but not by private individuals. The majority opinion held that black people must no longer "be the special favorite of the laws." Together, these Supreme Court decisions marked the end of federal attempts to protect African American rights until well into the next century.

KING COTTON: SHARECROPPERS, TENANTS, AND THE SOUTHERN ENVIRONMENT

The Republicans' vision of a "New South" remade along the lines of the northern economy failed to materialize. In the post–Civil War years, "King Cotton" expanded its realm, as greater numbers of small white farmers found themselves forced to switch from subsistence crops to growing cotton for the market (see Map 17.3).

A chronic shortage of capital and banking institutions made local merchants and planters the sole source of credit. They advanced loans and supplies to small owners, tenant farmers, and sharecroppers in exchange for a lien, or claim, on the year's cotton crop. At the end of the year, sharecroppers and tenants found themselves deep in debt to stores for seed, supplies, and clothing. The spread of the "crop lien" system as the South's main form of agricultural credit forced more and more farmers into cotton growing.

As the "crop lien" system spread, and as more and more farmers turned to cotton growing as the only way to obtain credit, expanding production depressed cotton prices. Competition from new cotton centers in the world market, such as Egypt and India, accelerated the downward spiral. As cotton prices declined, per

---

QUICK REVIEW

The End of Federal Intervention: Key Supreme Court Cases

- Slaughterhouse cases (1873).
- *United States* v. *Reese* (1876).
- *United States* v. *Cruikshank* (1876).
- Civil Rights Cases (1883).

MAP EXPLORATION

To explore an interactive version of this map, go to **http://www.prenhall.com/faraghertlc/map17.3**

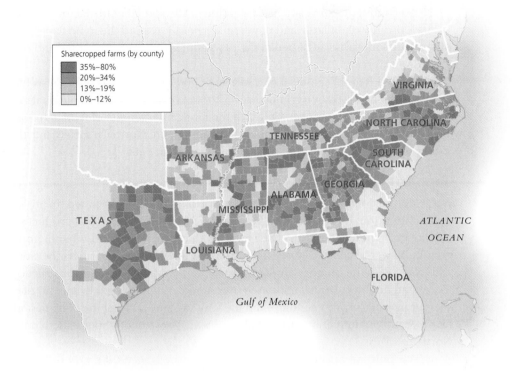

MAP 17.3

Southern Sharecropping and the Cotton Belt, 1880   The economic depression of the 1870s forced increasing numbers of southern farmers, both white and black, into sharecropping arrangements. Sharecropping was most pervasive in the cotton belt regions of South Carolina, Georgia, Alabama, Mississippi, and eastern Texas.

HOW DID this new form of labor affect the lives of former slaves?

capita wealth in the South fell steadily, equaling only one-third that of the East, Midwest, or West by the 1890s. Small farmers caught up in a vicious cycle of low cotton prices, debt, and dwindling food crops found their old ideal of independence sacrificed to the cruel logic of the cotton market.

To obtain precious credit, most southern farmers, both black and white, found themselves forced to produce cotton for market and, thus, became enmeshed in the debt-ridden crop lien system. In traditional cotton producing areas, especially the black belt, landless farmers growing cotton had replaced slaves growing cotton. In the up-country and newer areas of cultivation, cotton-dominated commercial agriculture, with landless tenants and sharecroppers as the main workforce, had replaced the more diversified subsistence economy of the antebellum era. By 1900, over roughly half of the South's 2,620,000 farms were operated by tenants, who rented land, or sharecroppers, who pledged a portion of the crop to owners in exchange for some combination of work animals, seed, and tools. Over one-third of the white farmers and nearly three-quarters of the African American farmers in the cotton states were tenants or sharecroppers. Large parts of the southern landscape would remain defined by this system well into the twentieth century: small farms operated by families who did not own their land, mired in desperate poverty and debt.

RECONSTRUCTING THE NORTH

WHAT PRECIPITATED the

electoral crisis of 1876?

myhistorylab

Review Summary

The triumph of the North brought with it fundamental changes in the economy, labor relations, and politics. The spread of the factory system, the growth of large and powerful corporations, and the rapid expansion of capitalist enterprise all hastened the development of a large unskilled and routinized workforce.

The old Republican ideal of a society bound by a harmony of interests had become overshadowed by a grimmer reality of class conflict. A violent national railroad strike in 1877 was broken only with the direct intervention of federal troops. That conflict struck many Americans as a turning point. Northern society, like the society of the South, appeared more hierarchical than equal.

THE AGE OF CAPITAL

In the decade following Appomattox, the North's economy continued the industrial boom begun during the Civil War. By 1873, America's industrial production had grown 75 percent over the 1865 level. By that time, too, the number of nonagricultural workers in the North had surpassed the number of farmers. Between 1860 and 1880, the number of wage earners in manufacturing and construction more than doubled, from 2 million to over 4 million. Only Great Britain boasted a larger manufacturing economy than the United States. During the same period, nearly 3 million immigrants arrived in America, almost all of whom settled in the North and West.

The railroad business both symbolized and advanced the new industrial order. Shortly before the Civil War, enthusiasm mounted for a transcontinental line. Private companies took on the huge and expensive job of construction, but the federal government funded the project, providing the largest subsidy in American history. The Pacific Railway Act of 1862 granted the Union Pacific and the

Chinese immigrants, like these section gang workers, provided labor and skills critical to the successful completion of the first transcontinental railroad. This photo was taken in Promontory Point, Utah Territory, in 1869.

Central Pacific rights to a broad swath of land extending from Omaha, Nebraska, to Sacramento, California. An 1864 act bestowed a subsidy of $15,000 per mile of track laid over smooth plains country and varying larger amounts up to $48,000 per mile in the foothills and mountains of the Far West. The Union Pacific employed gangs of Irish American and African American workers to lay track heading west from Omaha.

Meanwhile the Central Pacific, pushing east from California, had a tougher time finding workers, and began recruiting thousands of men from China. Some 12,000 Chinese laborers (about 90 percent of the workforce) bore the brunt of the difficult conditions in the Sierra Nevada where blizzards, landslides, and steep rock faces took an awful toll. But after completion of the transcontinental line threw thousands of Chinese railroad workers onto the California labor market, these workers faced a virulent tide of anti-Chinese agitation among western politicians and labor unions. In 1882, Congress passed the Chinese Exclusion Act, suspending any further Chinese immigration for ten years.

Railroad corporations became America's first big businesses. Railroads required huge outlays of investment capital, and their growth increased the economic power of banks and investment houses centered in Wall Street. Bankers often gained seats on the boards of directors of railroad companies, and their access to capital sometimes gave them the real control of the corporations. By the early 1870s the Pennsylvania Railroad was the nation's largest single company with more than 20,000 employees. A new breed of aggressive entrepreneur sought to ease cutthroat competition by absorbing smaller companies and forming "pools" that set rates and divided the market.

Some of the nation's most prominent politicians routinely accepted railroad largesse. Republican senator William M. Stewart of Nevada, a member of the Committee on Pacific Railroads, received a gift of 50,000 acres of land from the Central Pacific for his services. The worst scandal of the Grant administration grew out of corruption involving railroad promotion. When the scandal broke in 1872, it politically ruined Vice President Schuyler Colfax and led to the censure of two congressmen.

Other industries also boomed in this period, especially those engaged in extracting minerals and processing natural resources. Railroad growth stimulated expansion in the production of coal, iron, stone, and lumber, and these also received significant government aid. For example, under the National Mineral Act of 1866, mining companies received millions of acres of free public land. Oil refining enjoyed a huge expansion in the 1860s and 1870s. As with railroads, an early period of fierce competition soon gave way to concentration.

LIBERAL REPUBLICANS AND THE ELECTION OF 1872

With the rapid growth of large-scale, capital-intensive enterprises, Republicans increasingly identified with the interests of business rather than the rights of freedmen or the antebellum ideology of "free labor." State Republican parties now organized themselves around the spoils of federal patronage rather than grand causes such as preserving the Union or ending slavery. Republicans had no monopoly on political scandal. In 1871 New York City newspapers reported the shocking story of how Democratic Party boss William M. Tweed and his friends had systematically stolen tens of millions from the city treasury. But to many, the scandal represented only the most extreme case of the routine corruption that now plagued American political life.

"The Tramp," *Harper's* *Weekly*, September 2, 1876. The depression that began in 1873 forced many thousands of unemployed workers to go "on the tramp" in search of jobs. Men wandered from town to town, walking or riding railroad cars, desperate for a chance to work for wages or simply for room and board. The "tramp" became a powerful symbol of the misery caused by industrial depression and, as in this drawing, an image that evoked fear and nervousness among the nation's middle class.

By the end of President Grant's first term, a large number of disaffected Republicans sought an alternative. The **Liberal Republicans**, as they called themselves, emphasized the doctrines of classical economics. They called for a return to limited government, arguing that bribery, scandal, and high taxes all flowed from excessive state interference in the economy.

Liberal Republicans were also suspicious of expanding democracy. They believed that politics ought to be the province of "the best men"—educated and well-to-do men like themselves, devoted to the "science of government." They proposed civil service reform as the best way to break the hold of party machines on patronage.

Although most Liberal Republicans had enthusiastically supported abolition, the Union cause, and equal rights for freedmen, they now opposed continued federal intervention in the South. The national government had done all it could for the former slaves; they must now take care of themselves. In the spring of 1872 a diverse collection of Liberal Republicans nominated Horace Greeley to run for president. A longtime foe of the Democratic Party, Greeley nonetheless won that party's presidential nomination as well. All Americans, Greeley urged, must put the Civil War behind them and "clasp hands across the bloody chasm."

Grant easily defeated Greeley, carrying every state in the North and winning 56 percent of the popular vote. But the 1872 election accelerated the trend toward federal abandonment of African American citizenship rights. The Liberal Republicans quickly faded as an organized political force. But their ideas helped define a growing conservative consciousness among the northern public. Their agenda included retreat from the ideal of racial justice, hostility toward trade unions, suspicion of immigrant and working-class political power, celebration of competitive individualism, and opposition to government intervention in economic affairs.

THE DEPRESSION OF 1873

In the fall of 1873 the postwar boom came to an abrupt halt as a severe financial panic triggered a deep economic depression. The collapse resulted from commercial overexpansion, especially speculative investing in the nation's rail-

Liberal Republicans Disaffected Republicans that emphasized the doctrines of classical economics.

road system. By 1876 half the nation's railroads had defaulted on their bonds. Over the next two years more than 100 banks folded and 18,000 businesses shut their doors. The depression that began in 1873 lasted sixty-five months—the longest economic contraction in the nation's history until then.

The human toll was enormous. As factories began to close across the nation, the unemployment rate soared to about 15 percent. In many cities the jobless rate was much higher. The Pennsylvania Bureau of Labor Statistics noted that never before had "so many of the working classes, skilled and unskilled, been moving from place to place seeking employment that was not to be had." Farmers were also hard hit by the depression. Agricultural output continued to grow, but prices and land values fell sharply.

Mass meetings of workers in New York and other cities issued calls to government officials to create jobs through public works. But these appeals were rejected. Indeed, many business leaders and political figures denounced even meager efforts at charity. They saw the depression as a natural, if painful, part of the business cycle, one that would allow only the strongest enterprises (and workers) to survive.

The depression of the 1870s prompted workers and farmers to question the old free-labor ideology that celebrated a harmony of interests in northern society. More people voiced anger at and distrust of large corporations that exercised great economic power from outside their communities.

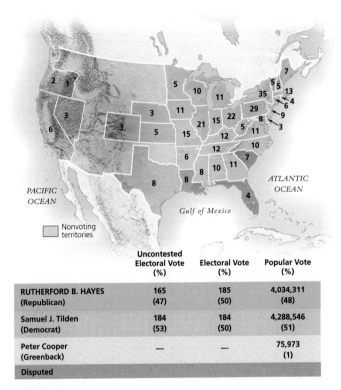

	Uncontested Electoral Vote (%)	Electoral Vote (%)	Popular Vote (%)
RUTHERFORD B. HAYES (Republican)	165 (47)	185 (50)	4,034,311 (48)
Samuel J. Tilden (Democrat)	184 (53)	184 (50)	4,288,546 (51)
Peter Cooper (Greenback)	—	—	75,973 (1)
Disputed			

MAP 17.4
The Election of 1876   The presidential election of 1876 left the nation without a clear-cut winner.

WHAT LED to the electoral crisis of 1876?

THE ELECTORAL CRISIS OF 1876

With the economy mired in depression, Democrats looked forward to capturing the White House in 1876. Democrats nominated Governor Samuel J. Tilden of New York, who brought impeccable reform credentials to his candidacy. In 1871 he had helped expose and prosecute the "Tweed Ring" in New York City. As governor he had toppled the "Canal Ring," a graft-ridden scheme involving inflated contracts for repairs on the Erie Canal. In their platform, the Democrats linked the issue of corruption to an attack on Reconstruction policies.

Republican nominee Rutherford B. Hayes, governor of Ohio, also sought the high ground. As a lawyer in Cincinnati he had defended runaway slaves. Later he had distinguished himself as a general in the Union army. Hayes promised, if elected, to support an efficient civil service system, to vigorously prosecute officials who betrayed the public trust, and to introduce a system of free universal education.

On an election day marred by widespread vote fraud and violent intimidation, Tilden received 250,000 more popular votes than Hayes. But Republicans refused to concede victory, challenging the vote totals in the electoral college. Tilden garnered 184 uncontested electoral votes, one shy of the majority required to win, while Hayes received 165 (see Map 17.4). The problem centered on twenty disputed votes from Florida, Louisiana, South Carolina, and Oregon.

The crisis was unprecedented. In January 1877 Congress moved to settle the deadlock, establishing an Electoral Commission composed of five senators, five representatives, and five Supreme Court justices; eight were Republicans and seven

QUICK REVIEW

The Depression of 1873

◆ End of postwar boom brought depression.

◆ Collapse resulted from commercial overexpansion.

◆ Longest economic contraction in the nation's history until then.

CHRONOLOGY

1865	Freedmen's Bureau established
	Abraham Lincoln assassinated
	Andrew Johnson begins Presidential Reconstruction
	Black codes begin to be enacted in southern states
	Thirteenth Amendment ratified
1866	Civil Rights Act passed
	Congress approves Fourteenth Amendment
	Ku Klux Klan founded
1867	Reconstruction Acts, passed over President Johnson's veto, begin Congressional Reconstruction
	Tenure of Office Act
	Southern states call constitutional conventions
1868	President Johnson impeached by the House but acquitted in Senate trial
	Fourteenth Amendment ratified
	Most Southern states readmitted to the Union
	Ulysses S. Grant elected president
1869	Congress approves Fifteenth Amendment
	Union Pacific and Central Pacific tracks meet at Promontory Point in Utah Territory

	Suffragists split into National Woman Suffrage Association and American Woman Suffrage Association
1870	Fifteenth Amendment ratified
1871	Ku Klux Klan Act passed
	"Tweed Ring" in New York City exposed
1872	Liberal Republicans break with Grant and Radicals, nominate Horace Greeley for president
	Crédit Mobilier scandal
	Grant reelected president
1873	Financial panic and beginning of economic depression
	Slaughterhouse cases
1874	Democrats gain control of House for first time since 1856
1875	Civil Rights Act
1876	Disputed election between Samuel Tilden and Rutherford B. Hayes
1877	Electoral Commission elects Hayes president
	President Hayes dispatches federal troops to break Great Railroad Strike and withdraws last remaining federal troops from the South

were Democrats. The commission voted along strict partisan lines to award all the contested electoral votes to Hayes. Outraged by this decision, Democratic congressmen threatened a filibuster to block Hayes's inauguration. Violence and stalemate were avoided when Democrats and Republicans struck a compromise in February. In return for Hayes's ascendance to the presidency, the Republicans promised to appropriate more money for southern internal improvements, to appoint a Southerner to Hayes's cabinet, and to pursue a policy of noninterference ("home rule") in southern affairs.

Shortly after assuming office, Hayes ordered removal of the remaining federal troops in Louisiana and South Carolina. Without this military presence to sustain them, the Republican governors of those two states quickly lost power to Democrats. "Home rule" meant Republican abandonment of freed people, Radicals, carpetbaggers, and scalawags. It also effectively nullified the Fourteenth and Fifteenth Amendments and the Civil Rights Act of 1866. The **Compromise of 1877** completed repudiation of the idea, born during the Civil War and pursued during Congressional Reconstruction, of a powerful federal government protecting the rights of all American citizens.

Compromise of 1877 The Congressional settling of the 1876 election which installed Republican Rutherford B. Hayes in the White House and gave Democrats control of all state governments in the South.

CONCLUSION

Reconstruction succeeded in the limited political sense of reuniting a nation torn apart by the Civil War. The Radical Republican vision, emphasizing racial justice, equal civil and political rights guaranteed by the Fourteenth and Fifteenth Amendments, and a new southern economy organized around independent small farmers, never enjoyed the support of the majority of its party or the northern public. By 1877, the political force of these ideals was spent and the national retreat from them nearly complete.

The end of Reconstruction left the way open for the return of white domination in the South. The freed people's political and civil equality proved only temporary. It would take a "Second Reconstruction," the civil rights movement of the next century, to establish full black citizenship rights once and for all. Yet the newly autonomous black family, along with black-controlled churches, schools, and other social institutions, provided the foundations for the modern African American community. If the federal government was not yet fully committed to protecting equal rights in local communities, the Reconstruction era at least pointed to how that goal might be achieved. Even as the federal government retreated from the defense of equal rights for black people, it took a more aggressive stance as the protector of business interests. In the aftermath of Reconstruction, the struggle between capital and labor had clearly replaced "the southern question" as the number one political issue of the day.

REVIEW QUESTIONS

1. How did various visions of a "reconstructed" South differ? How did these visions reflect the old political and social divisions that had led to the Civil War?

2. What key changes did emancipation make in the political and economic status of African Americans? Discuss the expansion of citizenship rights in the post–Civil War years. To what extent did women share in the gains made by African Americans?

3. What role did such institutions as the family, the church, the schools, and the political parties play in the African American transition to freedom?

4. How did white Southerners attempt to limit the freedom of former slaves? How did these efforts succeed, and how did they fail?

5. Evaluate the achievements and failures of Reconstruction governments in the southern states.

6. What were the crucial economic changes occurring in the North and South during the Reconstruction era?

KEY TERMS

Black codes (p. 438)
Carpetbaggers (p. 448)
Civil Rights Bill (p. 438)
Congressional Reconstruction (p. 439)
Compromise of 1877 (p. 458)
Field Order 15 (p. 436)
Fifteenth Amendment (p. 441)
First Reconstruction Act (p. 439)
Freedmen's Bureau (p. 437)

Ku Klux Klan (p. 441)
Liberal Republicans (p. 456)
Radical Republicans (p. 436)
Scalawags (p. 449)
Sharecropping (p. 445)
Slaughterhouse cases (p. 452)
Tenure of Office Act (p. 439)
Union League (p. 448)
War Democrats (p. 437)

RECOMMENDED READING

David W. Blight, *Race and Reunion: The Civil War in American Memory* (2001). An elegantly written and deeply researched inquiry into how Americans "remembered" the Civil War in the half century after Appomattox, arguing that sectional reconciliation came at the cost of racial division.

Thomas J. Brown, ed., *Reconstructions: New Perspectives on the Postbellum United States* (2006). A wide-ranging collection of essays that explores Reconstruction from a broadly national perspective, including economic, political, and cultural impacts.

Jane Dailey, *Before Jim Crow: The Politics of Race in Postemancipation Virginia* (2000). A fine study that focuses on the tension between the drive to establish white supremacy and the struggle for biracial coalitions in post–Civil War Virginia politics.

Laura F. Edwards, *Gendered Strife & Confusion: The Political Culture of Reconstruction* (1997). An ambitious analysis of how gender ideologies played a key role in shaping the party politics and social relations of the Reconstruction era south.

Michael W. Fitzgerald, *The Union League Movement in the Deep South* (1989). Uses the Union League as a lens through which to examine race relations and the close connections between politics and economic change in the post–Civil War South.

Eric Foner, *Forever Free: The Story of Emancipation and Reconstruction* (2005). An excellent brief one-volume overview that condenses Foner's more comprehensive work on Reconstruction. It also includes several striking "visual essays" by Joshua Brown, documenting the changes in visual representations of African Americans in popular media of the era.

Eric Foner, *Reconstruction: America's Unfinished Revolution, 1863–1877* (1988). The most comprehensive and thoroughly researched overview of the Reconstruction era.

Steven Hahn, *A Nation Under Our Feet: Black Political Struggles in the Rural South from Slavery to the Great Migration* (2003). This Pulitzer Prize–winning history includes excellent chapters detailing the political activism of recently freed slaves and the violent resistance they encountered throughout the rural South.

Elizabeth Regosin, *Freedom's Promise: Ex-Slave Families and Citizenship in the Age of Emancipation* (2002). A thoughtful analysis of how freedmen and freedwomen asserted familial relationships as a means to claiming citizenship rights after emancipation, based on research into federal pension applications made by dependent survivors of Civil War soldiers.

Scott Reynolds Nelson, *Iron Confederacies: Southern Railways, Klan Violence, and Reconstruction* (1999). Pathbreaking analysis of how conservative southern and northern business interests rebuilt the South's railroad system and also achieved enormous political power within individual states.

Heather Cox Richardson, *West From Appomattox: The Reconstruction of America After the Civil War* (2007). A new interpretation of the era that both emphasizes post–Civil War change in the nation's West and large cities and locates the origins of current political divisions in the Reconstruction period.

For study resources for this chapter, go to **www.myhistorylab.com** and choose *Out of Many, Teaching and Learning Classroom Edition*. You will find a wealth of study and review material for this chapter, including pretests and posttests, customized study plan, key-term review flash cards, interactive map and document activities, and documents for analysis.

Realities of Freedom

The Freedmen's Bureau established in 1865 by Congress provided freedmen with clothing, temporary shelter, food, and series of freedmen's schools across the South. Southern response was to fall into the use of terror to deter blacks from becoming economically independent using the agencies of groups like the Ku Klux Klan. Sharecropping, tenant farming, and peonage were insidious economic arrangements that placed whites and blacks in a form of economic slavery to large land holders in the South of the post-Civil War era.

The story of African Americans after the end of slavery is complex and varied. Some blacks attempted to seek out better places to establish their new lives while others remained in the security of the only home they had known as slaves.■

FOLLOWING EMANCIPATION, what economic and social opportunities existed for African Americans in the United States? How did these opportunities change the lives of freedmen after the official end to slavery?

African-American family working together in the cotton fields.

AN ACT TO ESTABLISH A BUREAU FOR THE RELIEF OF FREEDMEN AND REFUGEES, 1865

BE IT enacted, That there is hereby established in the War Department, to continue during the present war of rebellion, and for one year thereafter, a bureau of refugees, freedmen, and abandoned lands, to which shall be committed, as hereinafter provided, the supervision and management of all abandoned lands, and the control of all subjects relating to refugees and freedmen from rebel states, or from any district of country within the territory embraced in the operations of the army, under such rules and regulations as may be prescribed by the head of the bureau and approved by the President. The said bureau shall be under the management and control of a commissioner to be appointed by the President, by and with the advice and consent of the Senate. . .■

When We Worked on Shares, We Couldn't Make Nothing

AFTER SLAVERY we had to get in before night too. If you didn't, Ku Klux would drive you in. They would come and visit you anyway. . . . When he got you good and scared he would drive on away. They would whip you if they would catch you out in the night time. . . .

I've forgot who it is that that told us that we was free. Somebody come and told us we're free now. I done forgot who it was.

After freedom, we worked on shares a while. Then we rented. When we worked on shares, we couldn't make nothing, just overalls and something to eat. Half went to the other man and you would destroy your half if you weren't careful. A man that didn't know how to count would always lose. He might lose anyhow. They didn't give no itemized statement. No, you just had to take their word. They never give you no details. They just say you owe so much. No matter how good account you kept, you had to go by their account and now, Brother, I'm tellin' you the truth about this. It's been that way for a long time. You had to take the white man's work on note, and everything. Anything you wanted, you could git if you were a good hand. You could git anything you wanted as long as you worked. If you didn't make no money, that's all right; they would advance you more. But

Share croppers and their families were evicted from the plantation they were working after being convicted of engaging in a conspiracy to retain their homes. This picture was taken just after the evictions before the families were moved into a tent colony.

you better not leave him, you better not try to leave and get caught. They'd keep you in debt. They were sharp. Christmas come, you could take up twenty dollar, in somethin' to eat and much as you wanted in whiskey. You could buy a gallon of whiskey. . . . Anything that kept you a slave because he was always right and you were always wrong it there was difference. If there was an argument, he would get mad and there would be a shooting take place. . . .■

Share Cropper Contract, 1882

TO EVERY one applying to rent land upon shares, the following conditions must be read, and agreed to.

To every 30 or 35 acres, I agree to furnish the team, plow, and farming implements, except cotton planters, and I do not agree to furnish a cart to every cropper. The croppers are to have half of the cotton, corn and fodder (and peas and pumpkins and potatoes if any are planted. . .

Croppers are to have no part or interest in the cotton seed raised from the crop planted and worked by them. No vine crops of any description, that is, no watermelons, muskmelons,...squashes or anything of that kind, except peas and pumpkins, and potatoes, are to be planted in the cotton or corn. All must work under my direction. All plantation work to be done by the croppers. . . .

For every mule or horse furnished by me there must be 1000 good sized rails...hauled, and the fence repaired as far as they will go, the fence to be torn down and put up from the bottom if I so direct. All croppers to haul rails and work on fence whenever I may order. Rails to be split when I may say. . . .

Each cropper must keep in good repair all bridges in his crop or over ditches that he has to clean out and when a bridge needs repairing that is outside of all their crops, then any one that I call on must repair it. . . .

No cropper to work off the plantation when there is any work to be done on the land he has rented, or when his work is needed by me or other croppers. Trees to be cut down on Orchard, House field & Evanson fences, leaving such as I may designate. . . .■

*The two locomotives then moved up until they
touched each other, . . .and at one p.m.,
under an almost cloudless sky, and in
the presence of about one thousand one hundred
people, the completion of the greatest railroad
on earth was announced.*

—*Andrew J. Russel, from* Frank Leslie's Illustrated Railroad,
June 5, 1869

**This engraving, showing passengers shooting buffalo from a train
crossing the plains,** suggests the often casual approach
Americans took toward the Western Environment. The destruction
of the buffalo herds, for both profit and "sport," also destroyed
the basis of the Plains Indians' economy and culture.

18

CONQUEST AND SURVIVAL
THE TRANS–MISSISSIPPI WEST, 1860–1900

WHAT WAS the impact of U.S. western expansion on Indian Society?

HOW DID the mining industry develop in the United States?

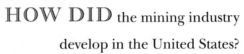

WHAT WAS life like for a cowboy in the late nineteenth century?

WHO TOOK advantage of the Homestead Act?

HOW DID agribusiness differ from more traditional forms of farming?

WHAT PLACE did the West hold in the national imagination?

WHAT KIND of Indian society did reformers envision?

AMERICAN COMMUNITIES
The Oklahoma Land Rush

DECADES AFTER THE EVENT, COWBOY EVAN G. BARNARD VIVIDLY recalled the preparations made by settlers when Oklahoma territorial officials announced the biggest "land rush" in American history. "Thousands of people gathered along the border. . . . As the day for the race drew near, the settlers practiced running their horses and driving carts." Finally, the morning of April 22, 1889, arrived. Like many others, Barnard displayed his guns prominently on his hips, determined to discourage competitors from claiming the 160 acres of prime land that he intended to grab for himself.

Evan Barnard's story was one strand in the larger tale of the destruction and creation of communities in the trans–Mississippi West. In the 1830s, the federal government designated what was to become the state of Oklahoma as Indian Territory, reserved for the Five Civilized Tribes (Cherokees, Chickasaws, Choctaws, Creeks, and Seminoles) who had been forcibly removed from their eastern lands. All five tribes had reestablished themselves as sovereign republics in Indian Territory. The Cherokees and Choctaws became prosperous cotton growers. The Creeks managed large herds of hogs and cattle, and the Chickasaws grazed not only cattle but also sheep and goats on their open fields. The Five Tribes also ran sawmills, gristmills, and cotton gins. Indian merchants were soon dealing with other tribespeople as well as licensed white traders and even contracting with the federal government.

The Civil War, however, took a heavy toll on their success. Some tribes, slaveholders themselves, sided with the Confederacy; others with the Union. When the war ended, more than 10,000 people—nearly one-fifth of the population of Indian Territory—had died. To make matters worse, new treaties required the Five Civilized Tribes to cede the entire western half of the territory, including the former northern Indian territory of Nebraska and Kansas, for the resettlement of tribes from other regions.

Western Oklahoma thereby became home to thousands of newly displaced peoples, including the Pawnees, Peorias, Ottawas, Wyandots, and Miamis. Many small tribes readily took to farming and rebuilt their communities. But the nomadic, buffalo-hunting Kiowas, Cheyennes, Comanches, and Arapahoes did not settle so peacefully. They continued to traverse the plains until the U.S. Army finally forced them onto reservations.

Eventually, more than 80,000 tribespeople were living on twenty-one separate reservations in western Oklahoma, all governed by agents appointed by the federal government.

The opening of the unassigned far western district of Oklahoma (No Man's Land) however, signaled the impending end of Indian sovereignty. Many non-Indians saw this almost 2-million-acre strip as a Promised Land, perfect for dividing into thousands of small farms. Meanwhile, the railroads, seeing the potential for lucrative commerce, put constant pressure on the federal government to open No Man's Land for settlement. In 1889, the U.S. Congress finally gave in.

Cowboy Barnard was just one of thousands to pour into No Man's Land on April 22, 1889. In a little over two months, after 6,000 homestead claims had been filed, the first sod houses appeared, sheltering growing communities of non-Indian farmers, ranchers, and other entrepreneurs. Some Indian leaders petitioned the federal government for the right to resettle on new land distant from white settlers, but nothing came from their efforts.

Dramatic as it was, the land rush of 1889 was only one in a series of events that soon dispossessed Oklahoma's Indians of their remaining lands. First, the federal government broke up the estates held collectively by various tribes in western Oklahoma, assigning to individuals the standard 160-acre allotment and allowing non-Indian homesteaders to claim the rest. Then, in 1898, Congress passed the Curtis Act, which abolished tribal jurisdiction over all Indian Territory.

By this time, in 1907, tribespeople were outnumbered in Oklahoma by ten to one. By this time also, nearly one-quarter of the entire population of the United States lived west of the Mississippi River. Hundreds of new communities, supported primarily by cattle ranching, agriculture, mining, or other industries, had not only grown with the emerging national economy but also helped to shape it in the process. The newcomers had displaced communities that had formed centuries earlier. They also drastically transformed the physical landscape. Through their activities and the support of Easterners, the United States realized an ambition that John L. O'Sullivan had described in 1845 as the nation's "manifest destiny to overspread the continent" and remake it in a new image.

Indian Territory (Oklahoma)

INDIAN PEOPLES UNDER SIEGE

The Indians living west of the Mississippi River keenly felt the pressure of the gradual incorporation of the West into the American nation. California became a state in 1850, Oregon in 1859. Congress consolidated the national domain in the next decades by granting territorial status to Utah, New Mexico, Washington, Dakota, Colorado, Nevada, Arizona, Idaho, Montana, and Wyoming. The purchase of Alaska in 1867 added an area twice the size of Texas.

A series of events brought large numbers of white settlers into these new states and territories: the discovery of gold in California in 1848, the opening of western lands to homesteaders in 1862, and the completion of the transcontinental railroad in 1869. With competition for the land and its resources escalating into violent skirmishes and small wars, federal officials became determined to end tribal rule and bring Indians into the American mainstream.

INDIAN TERRITORY

Before the European colonists reached the New World, various Indian tribes had occupied western lands for more than 20,000 years. Invasion by the English, Spanish, and other Europeans brought disease, religious conversion, and new patterns of commerce. But geographic isolation still gave many tribes a margin of survival unknown in the East. At the close of the Civil War, approximately 360,000 Indian peoples still lived in the trans–Mississippi West, the majority of them in the Great Plains (see Map 18.1).

The surviving tribes adapted to changing conditions. The Plains Indians learned to ride the horses and shoot the guns introduced by Spanish and British traders. The Pawnees migrated farther westward to evade encroaching non-Indian settlers, while the Sioux and the Comanches fought neighboring tribes to gain control of large stretches of the Great Plains. The southwestern Hopis and Zunis,

WHAT WAS the impact of U.S. western expansion on Indian Society?

Review Summary

17–6
Congressional Report on Indian Affairs (1887)

IMAGE KEY

for pages 464–465

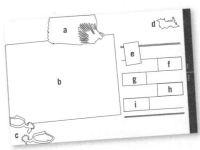

a. A feather fan carried by Yuchi dancers.
b. Passengers and the train crew shooting buffalo on the line of the Kansas-Pacific Railroad in this colored line engraving of 1871.
c. Confederate cavalry spurs from the American Civil War.
d. An old fashioned steam locomotive engine.
e. Wooly Head's wife and child.
f. A Chinese mine worker steadies a water cannon in a shallow riverbed in Idaho with a fellow laborer standing nearby.
g. Buffalo Bill Cody from an 1899 poster for his "Wild West Show."
h. Nebraska homesteaders in 1886.
i. Thirty-three horse team harvester, cutting, threshing, and sacking wheat, c. 1902.

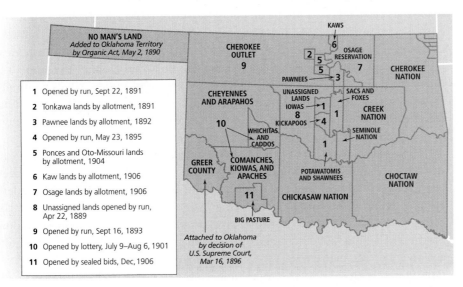

MAP 18.1
Oklahoma Territory   Land openings to settlers came at different times, making new land available through various means.

From *Historical Atlas of Oklahoma*, 3rd edition, by John W. Morris, Charles R. Goins, and Edwin C. McReynolds. Copyright © 1965, 1976, 1986 by the University of Oklahoma Press, Norman. Reprinted by permission of the publisher. All rights reserved.

WHAT WAS the impact of the land rush on Indian settlements?

conquered earlier by the Spanish, continued to trade with the Mexicans who lived near them. Some tribes took dramatic steps toward accommodation with white ways. Even before they were uprooted and moved across the Mississippi River, the Cherokees had learned English, converted to Christianity, established a constitutional republic, and become a nation of farmers.

Legally, the federal government had long regarded Indian tribes as autonomous nations residing within American boundaries and had negotiated numerous treaties with them over land rights and commerce. But pressured by land-hungry whites, several states had violated these federal treaties so often that the U.S. Congress passed the Indian Removal Act of 1830 (see Chapter 10), which provided funds to relocate all eastern tribes by force if necessary. The Cherokees challenged this legislation, and the Supreme Court ruled in their favor in *Cherokee Nation* v. *Georgia* (1831). Ignoring the Court's decision, President Andrew Jackson, known as a hardened Indian fighter, forced many tribes to cede their land and remove to Indian Territory. But soon, the onslaught of white settlers, railroad entrepreneurs, and prospectors rushing for gold pressured tribes to cede millions of their acres to the United States. As demand for resources and land accelerated, the entire plan for a permanent Indian Territory fell apart.

THE RESERVATION POLICY AND THE SLAUGHTER OF THE BUFFALO

As early as the 1840s, highly placed officials had outlined a plan to subdue the intensifying rivalry over natural resources and land. Under the terms of their proposal, individual tribes would agree to live within clearly defined zones—reservations. In exchange, the Bureau of Indian Affairs would provide guidance, while U.S. military forces ensured protection. By the end of the 1850s, eight western reservations had been established where Indian peoples were induced to speak English, take up farming, and convert to Christianity (see Map 18.2).

Those tribes that moved to reservations often found federal policies inadequate to their needs. The Medicine Lodge Treaty of 1867 assigned reservations in existing Indian Territory to Comanches, Plains (Kiowa) Apaches, Kiowas, Cheyennes, and Arapahoes, bringing these tribes together with Sioux, Shoshones, and Bannocks. All told, more than 100,000 people found themselves competing intensely for survival. Corrupt officials of the Bureau of Indian Affairs routinely diverted funds for their own use and reduced food supplies, a policy promoting malnutrition, demoralization, and desperation. Meanwhile, white prospectors and miners continued to flood the Dakota Territory.

The mass slaughter of the buffalo brought this crisis to a peak. In earlier eras, vast herds of buffalo had literally darkened the western horizon. As gunpowder and the railroad moved west, the number of buffalo fell rapidly. Non-Indian traders avidly sought fur for coats, hide for leather, bones for fertilizer, and heads for trophies. New rifles, like the .50 caliber Sharps, could kill at 600 feet; one sharpshooter bragged of killing 3,000 buffalo. Army commanders encouraged the slaughter, accurately predicting that starvation would break tribal resistance to the reservation system. With their food sources practically destroyed, diseases such as smallpox and cholera (brought by fur traders) sweeping through their villages, and their way of life undermined, many Great Plains tribes, including many Sioux, concluded that they could only fight or die.

THE INDIAN WARS

In 1864, large-scale war erupted. Having decided to terminate all treaties with tribes in eastern Colorado, territorial governor John Evans encouraged a group of white civilians, the Colorado Volunteers, to stage raids through Cheyenne camp-grounds. Seeking protection, Chief Black Kettle brought a band of 800 Cheyennes to a U.S. fort and received orders to set up camp at Sand Creek. Feeling secure in this arrangement, Black Kettle sent out most of his young warriors to hunt. Several weeks later, on November 29, 1864, the Colorado Volunteers and soldiers attacked. While Black Kettle held up a U.S. flag and a white truce banner, a disorderly group of 700 men, many of them drunk, slaughtered 105 Cheyenne women and children and 28 men. They mutilated the corpses and took scalps back to Denver to exhibit as trophies. Months after the **Sand Creek Massacre**, bands of Cheyennes, Sioux, and Arapahoes were still retaliating, burning civilian outposts and sometimes killing whole families.

The Sioux played the most dramatic roles in the Indian Wars. In 1851, believing the U.S. government would recognize their own rights of conquest over other Indian tribes, the Sioux relinquished large tracts of land as a demonstration of good faith. But within a decade, a mass invasion of miners and the construction of military forts along the Bozeman Trail in Wyoming, the Sioux's principal buffalo range, threw the tribe's future into doubt. During the **Great Sioux War** of 1865–67, the Oglala Sioux warrior Red Cloud fought the U.S. Army to a stalemate and forced the government to abandon its forts, which the Sioux then burned to the ground. The Treaty of Fort Laramie, signed in 1868, restored only a temporary peace to the region.

The **Treaty of Fort Laramie** granted the Sioux the right to occupy the Black Hills, or Paha Sapa, their sacred land, "as long as the grass shall grow," but the discovery of gold soon undermined this guarantee. White prospectors hurriedly invaded the territory. Directed to quash rumors of fabulous deposits of the precious metal, Lieutenant Colonel George Armstrong Custer organized a surveying expedition to the Black Hills during the summer of 1874, but, contrary to plan, the Civil War hero described rich veins of ore that could be cheaply extracted. The U.S. Congress then pushed to purchase the territory for Americans. To protect their land, thousands of Sioux, Cheyenne, and Arapaho warriors moved into war camps during the summer of 1876 and prepared for battle (see Map 18.2).

After several months of skirmishes between the U.S. Army and Indian warriors, Lieutenant Colonel Custer decided to rush ahead to a site in Montana that was known to white soldiers as Little Bighorn and to Lakotas as Greasy Grass. This foolhardy move offered the allied Cheyenne and Sioux warriors a perfect opportunity to cut off Custer's logistical and military support. On June 25, 1876, Custer and his troops were wiped out by one of the largest Indian contingents ever assembled, an estimated 2,000 to 4,000 warriors.

"Custer's Last Stand" gave Indian-haters the emotional ammunition to whip up public excitement. The U.S. Army tracked down the disbanded Indian contingents one by one and forced them to surrender. In February 1877, Sioux leadership in the Indian Wars ended.

Among the last to hold out against the reservation system were the Apaches in the Southwest. Most Apache bands had abided by the Medicine Lodge Treaty of 1867, but in 1874, some of the Apache bands, unable to tolerate the harsh conditions on the reservation, returned to their old ways of seizing territory and stealing cattle.

Pursued by the U.S. Army, the Apaches earned a reputation as intrepid warriors. Brilliant strategists like Geronimo and skilled horse-riding braves became legendary for lightning-swift raids against the white outposts in the rugged Arizona terrain. In 1874–75, the Kiowas and the Comanches, both powerful tribes, joined the Apaches in one of the bloodiest conflicts of the era, the Red

myhistorylab
Exploring America: *Dakota Sioux Conflict*

Sand Creek Massacre   The near annihilation in 1864 of Black Kettle's Cheyenne band by Colorado troops under Colonel John Chivington's orders to "kill and scalp all, big and little."

Great Sioux War   From 1865 to 1867 the Oglala Sioux warrior Red Cloud waged war against the U.S. Army, forcing the U.S. to abandon its forts built on land relinquished to the government by the Sioux.

Treaty of Fort Laramie   The treaty acknowledging U.S. defeat in the Great Sioux War in 1868 and supposedly guaranteeing the Sioux perpetual land and hunting rights in South Dakota, Wyoming, and Montana.

MAP EXPLORATION
To explore an interactive version of this map, go to **http://www.prenhall.com/faraghertlc/map18.2**

MAP 18.2

Major Indian Battles and Indian Reservations, 1860–1900 As commercial routes and white populations passed through and occupied Indian lands, warfare inevitably erupted. The displacement of Indians to reservations opened access by farmers, ranchers, and investors to natural resources and to markets.

WHY WERE the Indians forcibly removed to reservations?

River War. The U.S. Army ultimately prevailed, although less by military might than by denying Indians access to food. Small-scale warfare sputtered on until September 1886, when Geronimo, his band reduced to only thirty people, finally surrendered, thereby ending the Indian Wars.

THE NEZ PERCÉ

For generations, the Nez Percé had regarded themselves as good friends to white traders and settlers. Living in the plateau where Idaho, Washington, and Oregon now meet, they had saved the Lewis and Clark expedition from starvation in 1803.

The Oglala Sioux spiritual leader, Chief Red Cloud, in an 1868 photograph. Here he is seen with (l. to r.) Red Dog, Little Wound, interpreter John Bridgeman (standing), (Red Cloud), American Horse, and Red Shirt. He ventured to Washington with this delegation to discuss with President Ulysses S. Grant the various provisions of the peace treaty, just signed, to end the violent conflict over the Bozeman Trail.

But the discovery of gold on Nez Percé territory in 1860 changed their relations with whites for the worse. Pressed by prospectors and mining companies, government officials demanded, in the treaty of 1863, that the Nez Percé cede 6 million acres, nine-tenths of their land, at less than ten cents per acre. Some of the Nez Percé leaders agreed to the terms of the treaty, which had been fraudulently signed on behalf of the entire tribe, but others refused. At first, federal officials listened to Nez Percé complaints against the treaty and decided to allow them to remain on their land. But responding to pressure from settlers and politicians, they almost immediately reversed their decision, ordering the Nez Percé, including Chief Joseph and his followers, to sell their land and to move onto a reservation.

Intending to comply, Chief Joseph's band set out from the Wallowa Valley with their livestock and all the possessions they could carry. Along the way, some young members of another Indian band traveling with them rode away from camp to avenge the death of one of their own by killing several white settlers. Hoping to explain the situation, a Nez Percé truce team approached U.S. troops. The troops opened fire, and the Indian riders fired back, killing one-third of the soldiers. Brilliantly outmaneuvering vengeful U.S. troops sent to intercept them, the 750 Nez Percé retreated for some 1,400 miles into Montana and Wyoming through mountains and prairies and across the Bitterroot Range. U.S. troops finally trapped the Nez Percé in the Bear Paw Mountains of northern Montana, just thirty miles from the Canadian border. Suffering from hunger and cold, they surrendered.

Promised they would be returned to Oregon, the Nez Percé were sent instead to disease-ridden bottomland near Fort Leavenworth in Kansas, and then to Oklahoma. Arguing for the right of his people to return to their Oregon reservation, Joseph spoke eloquently, through an interpreter, to Congress in 1879: "Treat all men alike. Give them all the same law. Give them all an even chance to live and grow. All men were made by the same Great Spirit Chief." The last remnant of

Joseph's band were deported under guard to a non–Nez Percé reservation in Washington, where Chief Joseph died in 1904 "of a broken heart," and where his descendants continue to live in exile to this day.

THE INTERNAL EMPIRE

HOW DID the mining industry develop in the United States?

myhistorylab
Review Summary

Determined to make their fortunes, be it from copper in Arizona, wheat in Montana, or oranges in California, numerous adventurers traveled west. As a group, they carried out the largest migration and greatest commercial expansion in American history.

But the settlers themselves also became the subjects of a huge "internal empire" whose financial, political, and industrial centers of power remained in the East. Only a small number of settlers actually struck it rich. Meanwhile, older populations—Indian peoples, Hispanic peoples, and more recently settled communities like the Mormons—struggled to create places for themselves in this new expansionist order.

MINING TOWNS

The discovery of gold in California in 1848 attracted fortune seekers from as far away as Chile and China; just ten years later, approximately 35,000 Chinese men were working in western mines. Meanwhile, prospecting parties overran the territories, setting a pattern for intermittent rushes for gold, silver, and copper that extended from the Colorado mountains to the Arizona deserts, from California to Oregon and Washington, and from Alaska to the Black Hills of South Dakota. Mining camps and boomtowns soon dotted what had once been thinly

Kiowa Preparing for a War Expedition, ca. 1887. This sketch on paper was made by an Indian artist, Silverhorn, who had himself taken part in the final revolt of the Kiowas in 1874. He later became a medicine man and then served as a private in the U.S. Cavalry at Fort Sill, Oklahoma Territory.

Silverhorn (Native American), "Kiowa Preparing for a War Expedition." From "Sketchbook," 1887. Graphite, ink and crayon on paper. Collection of the McNay Art Museum, Gift of Mrs. Terrell Bartlett.

settled regions and speeded the urban development of the West. Mining soon brought the West into a vast global market for capital, commodities, and labor (see Map 18.3).

 MAP EXPLORATION

To explore an interactive version of this map, go to **http://www.prenhall.com/faraghertlc/map18.3**

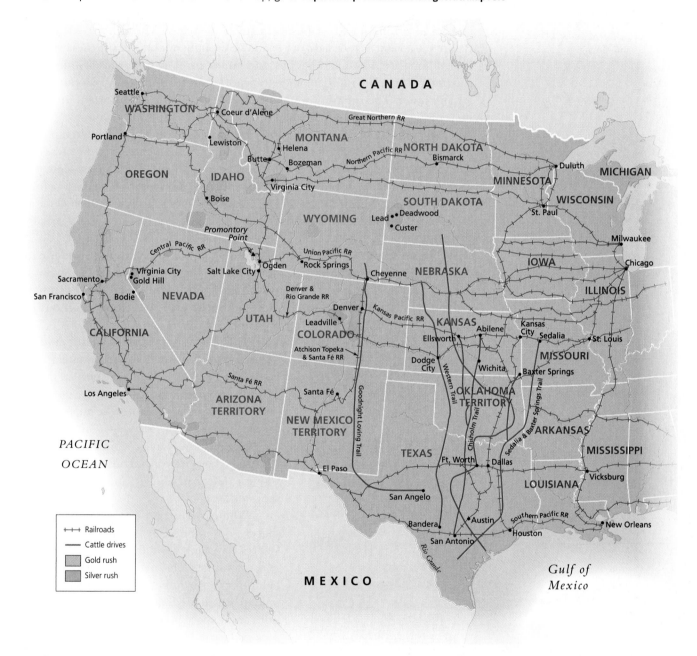

MAP 18.3

Railroad Routes, Cattle Trails, Gold and Silver Rushes, 1860–1900   By the end of the nineteenth century, the vast region of the West was crosscut by hundreds of lines of transportation and communication. The trade in precious metals and in cattle helped build a population almost constantly on the move, following the rushes for gold or the herds of cattle.

Encyclopedia of American Social History.

HOW DID the growth of railroads and mining impact the environment and the lives of native peoples?

Caminetti Act 1893 act giving the state the power to regulate the mines.

The mining industry quickly grew from its treasure-hunt origins into a grand corporate enterprise. The most successful mine owners bought out the smaller claims and built an entire industry around their stakes. They purchased the latest in extractive technology. They gained access to timber to fortify their underground structures and water to feed the hydraulic pumps that washed down mountains. They built smelters to refine the crude ore into ingots and often financed railroads to transport the product to distant markets.

The mining corporations laid the basis for a new economy as well as an interim government and established many of the region's first white settlements. Before the advent of railroads, ore had to be brought out of, and supplies brought into, mining areas by boats, wagons, and mules traveling hundreds of miles over rough territory. The railroad made transportation of supplies and products easier and faster. The shipping trade meanwhile grew into an important industry of its own, employing thousands of merchants, peddlers, and sailors.

The many boomtowns, known as "Helldorados," flourished, if only temporarily, as ethnically diverse communities. Men outnumbered women by as much as ten to one, and very few lived with families or stayed very long. The Chinese men, the sojourners who hoped to find riches in the "Gold Mountain" of America before returning home, clustered together and created their own institutions such as social clubs, temples, and fraternal societies known as tongs. The town center was usually the saloon.

The western labor movement began in these camps, partly as a response to dangerous working conditions. Miners began to organize in the 1860s, demanding good pay for dangerous and life-shortening work. By the end of the century, they had established the strongest unions in the West.

The unions fought hard, but they did so exclusively for the benefit of white workers. The native-born and the Irish and Cornish immigrants (from Cornwall, England) far outnumbered other groups before the turn of the century, when Italians, Slavs, and Greeks began to replace them. Labor unions eventually admitted these new immigrants but refused Chinese, Mexican, Indian, and African American workers.

When prices and ore production fell sharply, not even unions could stop the owners from shutting down the mines and leaving ghost towns in their wake. Often they also left behind an environmental disaster. Hydraulic mining, which used water cannons to blast hillsides and expose gold deposits, drove tons of rock and earth into the rivers and canyons. By the late 1860s, California's rivers were clogged, producing floods that wiped out towns and farms. In 1893, Congress finally passed the **Caminetti Act**, giving the state the power to regulate the mines. Underground mining continued unregulated, using up whole forests for timbers and filling the air with dangerous, sulfurous smoke.

William Henry Jackson (1843–1942) was the first person to photograph the Yellowstone region in Wyoming Territory. Documenting the Grand Tetons, including the magnificent waterfalls and geysers, his images caught the public's attention and likewise helped to convince Congress to create the Yellowstone National Park in 1872. Jackson then joined up with the U.S. Geological Survey to photograph various sites in the Rocky Mountains. Here he captures "John, the Cook" baking slapjacks in a mining camp in 1874.

MORMON SETTLEMENTS

Led by their new prophet, Brigham Young, the Mormons migrated in 1846–47 from the Midwest to the Great Salt Lake Basin to form an independent theocratic state called Deseret and to affirm the sanctity of plural marriage, or polygamy. By 1870, more than 87,000 Mormons lived in Utah Territory, creating relatively sizable communities complemented by satellite villages joined to communal farmlands and a common pasture. Eventually, nearly 500 Mormon communities spread from Oregon to Idaho to northern Mexico (see Map 18.4).

As territorial rule tightened, the Mormons saw their unique way of life once again threatened. The Supreme Court finally ruled against polygamy in the 1879 case of *United States* v. *Reynolds,* which granted the freedom of belief but not the freedom of practice. In 1882, Congress passed the **Edmunds Act,** which effectively disenfranchised those who believed in or practiced polygamy and threatened them with fines and imprisonment. Equally devastating was the **Edmunds-Tucker Act,** passed five years later, which destroyed the temporal power of the Mormon Church by confiscating all assets over $50,000 and establishing a federal commission to oversee all elections in the territory. By the early 1890s, Mormon leaders officially renounced the practice of plural marriage.

The "celestial" law of plural marriage had been central to the Mormons' messianic mission. Forced to give up the right to the practice, they gave up many other aspects of their distinctive communal life, including the common ownership of land. By the time Utah became a state in 1896, Mormon communities resembled in some ways the society that the original settlers had sought to escape. Nevertheless, they combined their religious cohesion with leadership in the expanding regional economy to become a major political force in the West.

MEXICAN BORDERLAND COMMUNITIES

The Treaty of Guadalupe Hidalgo, which ended the Mexican-American War in 1848, allowed the Hispanic people north of the Rio Grande to choose between immigrating to Mexico or staying in what was now the United States. But the new Mexican-American border, one of the longest unguarded boundaries in the world, did not sever communities that had been connected for centuries. What gradually emerged was an economically and socially interdependent zone, the Anglo-Hispanic borderlands linking the United States and Mexico.

Although under the treaty all Hispanics were formally guaranteed citizenship and the "free enjoyment of their liberty and property," local Anglos (as the Mexicans called white Americans) often violated these provisions and, through fraud or coercion, took control of the land. The Sante Fe Ring, a group of lawyers, politicians, and land speculators, stole millions of acres from the public domain and grabbed over 80 percent of the Mexicano landholdings in New Mexico alone.

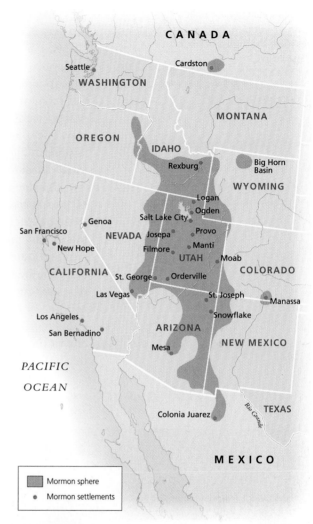

MAP 18.4

Mormon Cultural Diffusion, ca. 1883   Mormon settlements permeated many sparsely populated sections of Idaho, Nevada, Arizona, Wyoming, Colorado, and New Mexico. Built with church backing and the strong commitment of community members, they survived and even prospered in adverse climates.

Mormon Cultural Diffusion, ca. 1883, Donald W. Meinig, "The Geography of the American West, 1847–1964" from *The Annals of the Association of American Geographers* 55, no. 2, June 1965.

WHY WERE many western parks and national Forests established before eastern ones?

Edmunds Act   1882 act that effectively disenfranchised those who believed in or practiced polygamy and threatened them with fines and imprisonment.

Edmunds-Tucker Act   1887 act which destroyed the temporal power of the Mormon Church by confiscating all assets over $50,000 and establishing a federal commission to oversee all elections in the Utah territory.

Hispanic-American Alliance
Organization formed to protect and fight for the rights of Spanish Americans.

For a time, Arizona and New Mexico seemed to hold out hope for a mutually beneficial interaction between Mexicanos and Anglos. A prosperous class of Hispanic landowners, with long-standing ties to Anglos through marriage, had established itself in cities like Albuquerque and Tucson, old Spanish towns that had been founded in the seventeenth and eighteenth centuries. These Mexican elites, well integrated into the emerging national economy, continued to wield political power as ranchers, landlords, and real estate developers until the end of the century. They secured passage of bills for education in their regions and often served as superintendents of local schools. Several prominent merchants became territorial delegates to Congress.

But the majority of Mexicans who had lived in the mountains and deserts of the Southwest for well over two centuries were less prepared for these changes. With the Anglos came land closures as well as commercial expansion, prompted by railroad, mining, and timber industries. Many poor families found themselves crowded onto plots too small for subsistence farming. Many turned to seasonal labor on the new Anglo-owned commercial farms, where they became the first of many generations of poorly paid migratory workers. Other Mexicanos adapted by taking jobs on the railroad or in the mines. Meanwhile, their wives and daughters moved to the new towns and cities in such numbers that by the end of the century, Mexicanos had become a predominantly urban population, dependent on wages for survival.

Women were quickly drawn into the expanding network of market and wage relations. They tried to make ends meet by selling produce from their backyard gardens; more often they worked as seamstresses or laundresses. Formerly at the center of a communal society, Mexicanas found themselves with fewer options in the cash economy. What wages they could now earn fell below even the low sums paid to their husbands, and women lost status within both the family and community.

Occasionally, Mexicanos organized to reverse these trends or at least to limit the damage done to their communities. In the 1880s, Las Gorras Blancas, a band of agrarian rebels in New Mexico, destroyed railroad ties and farm machinery and posted demands for justice on fences of the new Anglo farms and ranches. In 1890, Las Gorras turned from social banditry to political organization, forming *El Partido del Pueblo Unido* (The People's Party). Organized along similar lines, *El Alianzo Hispano-Americano* (The **Hispanic-American Alliance**) was formed "to protect and fight for the rights of Spanish Americans" through political

Mexican Americans in San Antonio continued to conduct their traditional market bazaar well after the incorporation of this region into the United States. Forced off the land and excluded from the better-paying jobs in the emerging regional economy, many Mexicanos, and especially women, sought to sell the products of their own handiwork for cash or for bartered food and clothing.

Thomas Allen, "Market Plaza," 1878–1879. Oil on canvas, 26 × 39 1/2. Witte Museum, San Antonio, Texas.

action. *Mutualistes* (mutual aid societies) provided sickness and death benefits to Mexican families.

Despite many pressures, Mexicanos preserved much of their cultural heritage. Many persisted in older ways simply because they had few choices. In addition, the influx of new immigrants from Mexico helped to reinforce traditional cultural norms. Beginning in the late 1870s, the modernizing policies of Porfirio Diaz, the president of Mexico from 1876 to 1911, brought deteriorating living conditions to the masses of poor people and prompted a migration northward that accelerated through the first decades of the twentieth century. These newcomers revitalized old customs and rituals associated with family and religion. Spanish language and Spanish place names continued to distinguish the Southwest.

THE OPEN RANGE

The slaughter of the buffalo made way for the cattle industry, one of the most profitable businesses in the West. Texas longhorns, introduced by the Spanish, numbered over 5 million at the close of the Civil War and represented a potentially plentiful supply of beef for eastern consumers. In the spring of 1866, entrepreneurs such as Joseph G. McCoy began to build a spectacular cattle market in the eastern part of Kansas, where the Kansas Pacific Railroad provided crucial transportation links to slaughtering and packing houses and commercial distributors in Kansas City, St. Louis, and Chicago.

THE LONG DRIVES

The great cattle drives depended on the cowboy, a seasonal or migrant worker. After the Civil War, cowboys rounded up herds of Texas cattle and drove them as much as 1,500 miles north to grazing ranches or to the stockyards where they were readied for shipping by rail to eastern markets. In return for his labor, the cowboy received at the best of times about $30 per month. Wages were usually paid in one lump sum at the end of a drive, a policy that encouraged cowboys to spend their money quickly and recklessly in the booming cattle towns. In the 1880s, when wages began to fall along with the price of beef, cowboys fought back by stealing cattle or by forming unions. Aided by the legendary camaraderie fostered in the otherwise desolate conditions of the long drive, cowboys, along with miners, were among the first western workers to organize against employers.

Like other parts of the West, the cattle range was ethnically diverse. Between one-fifth and one-third of all workers were Indian, Mexican, or African American. Indian cowboys worked mainly on the northern plains and in Indian Territory; the *vaqueros*, who had previously worked on the Mexican cattle *haciendas*, or huge estates, predominated in South Texas and California. African American cowboys worked primarily in Texas, where the range cattle industry was founded (see Seeing History).

Like the vaqueros, African American cowboys were highly skilled managers of cattle. Unlike Mexicans, they earned wages comparable to those paid to Anglos and, especially during the early years, worked in integrated drover parties. By the 1880s, as the center of the cattle industry shifted to the more settled regions around the northern ranches, African Americans were forced out, and they turned to other kinds of work.

WHAT WAS life like for a cowboy in the late nineteenth century?

Review Summary

17–3
Horace Greeley, *An Overland Journey* (1860)

17–4
Joseph G. McCoy, *Historic Sketches of the Cattle Trade of the West and Southwest* (1874)

Very few women participated in the long drives. Most women stayed back at the ranch. Occasionally, a husband and wife worked as partners, sharing even the labor of wrangling cattle, and following her husband's death, a woman might take over altogether. The majority of wives attended to domestic chores, caring for children and maintaining the household. Their daughters, however, often tagged along after their fathers and learned to love outdoor work. They were soon riding astride, "clothespin style," roping calves, branding cattle or cutting their ears to mark them, and castrating bulls. But not until 1901 did a woman dare to enter an official rodeo contest.

THE SPORTING LIFE

In cattle towns as well as mining camps, saloons, gambling establishments, and dance halls were regular features on the horizon. Although prostitution was illegal in most towns, the laws were rarely enforced until the end of the century, when reformers led campaigns to shut down the red-light districts.

Like the cowboys who bought their services, most prostitutes were unmarried and in their teens or twenties. Often fed up with underpaid jobs in dressmaking or domestic service, they found few alternatives to prostitution in the cattle towns, where the cost of food and lodging was notoriously high. Still, earnings in prostitution were slim, except during the cattle-shipping season when young men outnumbered women by as much as three to one. Injury or even death from violent clients, addiction to narcotics such as cocaine or morphine, and venereal disease were workaday dangers.

FRONTIER VIOLENCE AND RANGE WARS

The combination of prostitution, gambling, and drinking discouraged the formation of stable communities. Personal violence was notoriously commonplace on the streets and in the barrooms of cattle towns and mining camps populated mainly by young, single men. Many western towns such as Wichita outlawed the carrying of handguns, but enforcement usually lagged. Local specialty shops and mail-order catalogues continued to sell weapons with little regulation.

After the Civil War, violent crime, assault, and robbery rose sharply throughout the United States. In the West, the most prevalent crimes were horse theft and cattle rustling, which peaked during the height of the open range period and then fell back by the 1890s.

The "range wars" of the 1870s produced violent conflicts. By this time, both farmers and sheepherders were encroaching on the fields where cattle had once grazed freely. Sheep chew grass down to its roots, making it practically impossible to raise cattle on land they have grazed. Farmers meanwhile set about building fences to protect their domestic livestock and property. Great cattle barons fought back against farmers by ordering cowboys to cut the new barbed-wire fences.

The cattle barons helped to bring about their own demise, but they did not go down quietly. Eager for greater profits, and often backed by foreign capital, they overstocked their herds, and eventually the cattle began to deplete the

As early as 1879, the local newspaper described Leadville, Colorado, as a town that never sleeps: "The dancing houses and liquoring shops are never shut . . . . The streets are full of drunken carousers taking the town." This photograph of a typical saloon was taken shortly before the silver mining town reached its peak, with a population topping 60,000 in 1893. That year, the repeal of the Sherman Silver Act forced thousands of out-of-work miners to search for jobs elsewhere in the West.

The Legendary Cowboy: Nat Love, Deadwood Dick

Nat Love was born a slave in 1854 and spent his childhood on a plantation in Tennessee. In 1907 he published a short autobiography, *The Life and Adventures of Nat Love, Better Known in the Cattle Country as "Deadwood Dick,"* recounting his "unusually adventurous" life during the decades after emancipation. He worked as a cowboy, a ranch hand, an Indian fighter, and a rodeo performer. His most famous episode occurred in the boomtown of Deadwood, South Dakota, where in 1876 he won a cowboy tournament. It began with a roping contest, in which Love roped, saddled, and mounted a mustang in just nine minutes, winning the almost unbelievably large prize of $200. In the second part of this competition, a shooting contest, Love once again came out on top, hitting the bull's-eye in ten out of twelve shots. He boasted that the miners and gamblers who had gathered for the tournament were so awed that they called him "Deadwood Dick," a name he proudly claimed until his death in 1921.

That name became familiar to the many readers of Edward Wheeler's *Deadwood Dick* dime novels, and at least five of Love's contemporaries claimed to be that character. Wheeler published the first installment in this popular series in 1877 as *Deadwood Dick, the Prince of the Road, or, The Black Rider of the Black Hills.* It is said that Love's autobiography reads like a dime novel, packed with adventures that no historian has yet been able to authenticate.

The photograph illustrating Love's popular autobiography captures the standard image of the cowboy of the legendary Wild West—the chaps, firearm, and ammunition in the cartridge belt circling his waist, the tack on the floor (saddle, harness, rope), and the assertive body language. But in Love's case, the cowboy is a black man. ■

HOW DOES Nat Love fit into the legendary Wild West? How readily would you expect nineteenth-century readers of the *Deadwood Dick* dime novels to accept the hero's identity as a black man?

How does Nat Love's identity as an African American line up with the image of the heroic cowboy in modern American popular culture?

limited supply of grass. Finally, during 1885–87, a combination of summer drought and winter blizzards killed 90 percent of the cattle in the northern Plains. Many ranchers went bankrupt. Along the way, they often took out their grievances against the former cowboys who had gathered small herds for themselves. They charged these small ranchers with cattle rustling, taking them to court or, in some cases, rounding up lynching parties.

FARMING COMMUNITIES ON THE PLAINS

The vision of a huge fertile garden extending from the Appalachians to the Pacific Ocean had inspired Americans since the early days of the republic. But the first explorers who actually traveled through the Great Plains quashed this dream. "The Great Desert" was the name they gave to the region stretching west from Kansas and Nebraska, north to Montana and the Dakotas, and south again to Oklahoma and Texas. It took massive improvements in both transportation and farm technology—as well as unrelenting advertising and promotional campaigns—to open the Great Plains to widescale agriculture.

THE HOMESTEAD ACT

The **Homestead Act of 1862** offered the first incentive to prospective white farmers. This act granted a quarter section (160 acres) of the public domain free to any settler who lived on the land for at least five years and improved it; or a settler could buy the land for $1.25 per acre after only six months' residence. Restricting its provisions to household heads, the Homestead Act encouraged adventurous and hardworking unmarried women to file between 5 and 15 percent of the claims.

Homesteaders achieved their greatest success in the central and upper Midwest, where the soil was rich and weather relatively moderate. But those settlers lured to the Great Plains by descriptions of land "carpeted with soft grass—a sylvan paradise" found themselves locked in a fierce struggle with the harsh climate and arid soil.

Rather than filing a homestead claim with the federal government, most settlers acquired their land outright. State governments and land companies usually held the most valuable land near transportation and markets, and the majority of farmers were willing to pay a hefty price for those benefits. The big-time land speculators did even better, plucking choice locations at bargain prices and selling high. And the railroads, which received land grants from the federal government, did best, selling off the holdings near their routes at top dollar.

POPULATING THE PLAINS

The rapid settlement of the West could not have taken place without the railroad. Although the Homestead Act offered prospective farmers free land, it was the railroad that promoted settlement, brought people to their new homes, and carried crops and cattle to eastern markets. The railroads, therefore, wielded tremendous economic and political power.

Along with providing transportation links between the East and the West and potential markets as distant as Russia and China, the western railroads directly encouraged settlement. Unlike the railroads built before the Civil War, which followed the path of villages and towns, the western lines preceded settlement. Bringing people west became their top priority, and the railroad companies conducted aggressive promotional and marketing campaigns. Agents enticed Easterners and Europeans alike with long-term loans and free transportation by rail to distant

---

WHO TOOK advantage of the Homestead Act?

Review Summary

17–15
Homestead Act of 1862
(1874)

QUICK REVIEW

The Homestead Act

◆ 1862 Act granted 160 acres to any settler who lived on land for five years and improved it.

◆ Achieved greatest success in the central and upper Midwest.

◆ Most settlers acquired their land outright, rather than filing a homestead claim.

Homestead Act of 1862 1862 act which granted a quarter section (160 acres) of the public domain free to any settler who lived on the land for at least five years and improved it.

points in the West. The Santa Fe Railroad sent agent C. B. Schmidt to Germany, where he managed to entice nearly 60,000 Germans to settle along the rail line. The railroads also sponsored land companies to sell parcels of their own huge allotments from the federal government. The National Land Company, founded in Chicago in 1869, alone organized sixteen colonies of mainly European immigrants in parts of Kansas and Colorado.

More than 2 million Europeans, many recruited by professional promoters, settled the Great Plains between 1870 and 1900. Some districts in Minnesota seemed to be virtual colonies of Sweden; others housed the largest number of Finns in the New World. Nebraska, whose population as early as 1870 was 25 percent foreign-born, concentrated Germans, Swedes, Danes, and Czechs. But Germans outnumbered all other immigrants by far. A smaller portion of European immigrants reached Kansas, still fewer the territories to the south where Indian and Hispanic peoples and African Americans remained the major ethnic populations.

In 1887, Lizzie Chrisman filed the first homestead claim on Lieban Creek in Custer County, Nebraska. Joined by her three sisters, she is shown here standing in front of her sod cabin. "Soddies," as these small houses were called, were constructed of stacked layers of cut prairie turf, which were eventually fortified by a thick network of roots. The roofs, often supported by timber, were usually covered with more sod, straw, and small branches.

Having traveled the huge distance with kin or members of their Old World villages, immigrants tended to form tight-knit communities on the Great Plains. Many married only within their own group. For example, only 3 percent of Norwegian men married women of a different ethnic background. Like many Mexicanos in the Southwest, several immigrant groups retained their languages well into the twentieth century, usually by sponsoring parochial school systems and publishing their own newspapers. A few groups closed their communities to outsiders. The Poles who migrated to central Nebraska in the 1880s, for example, formed an exclusive settlement; and the German Hutterites, who disavowed private property, lived in seclusion as much as possible in the Bon Homme colony of South Dakota, established in 1874.

Among the native-born settlers of the Great Plains, the largest number had migrated from states bordering the Mississippi River. Settling as individual families rather than as whole communities, they faced an exceptionally solitary life on the Great Plains. To stave off isolation, homesteaders sometimes built their homes on the adjoining corners of their homestead plots. Still, the prospect of doing better, which brought most homesteaders to the Great Plains in the first place, caused many families to keep seeking greener pastures. Mobility was so high that between one-third and one-half of all households pulled up stakes within a decade.

Communities eventually flourished in prosperous towns like Grand Island, Nebraska; Coffeyville, Kansas; and Fargo, North Dakota, that served the larger agricultural region. Built alongside the railroad, they grew into commercial centers, home to banking, medical, legal, and retail services. Town life fostered a special intimacy. But closeness did not necessarily promote social equality or even friendship. A social hierarchy based on education (for the handful of doctors and lawyers) and, more important, investment property (held mainly by railroad agents and bankers) governed relationships between individuals and families. Reinforced by family ties and religious and ethnic differences, this hierarchy often persisted across generations.

WORK, DAWN TO DUSK

Most farm families survived, and prospered if they could, through hard work, often from dawn to dusk. Men's activities in the fields tended to be seasonal, with heavy work during planting and harvest. At other times, their labor centered on construction or repair of buildings and on taking care of livestock. Women's activities were usually far more routine, week in and week out: cooking and canning of seasonal fruit and vegetables, washing, ironing, churning cream for butter, and keeping chickens for their eggs. Women tended to the young children, and they might occasionally take in boarders, usually young men working temporarily in railroad construction.

Milking the cows, hauling water, and running errands to neighboring farms could be done by the children, once they had reached the age of nine or so. The "one-room school," where all grades learned together, taught the basics of literacy and arithmetic that a future farmer or commercial employee would require.

The harsh climate and unyielding soil nevertheless forced all but the most reclusive families to seek out friends and neighbors. Neighbors might agree to work together haying, harvesting, and threshing grain. A well-to-do farmer might "rent" his threshing machine in exchange for a small cash fee and, for instance, three days' labor. His wife might barter her garden produce for her neighbor's bread and milk or for help during childbirth or disability. Women often combined work and leisure in quilting bees and sewing circles, where they made friends while sharing scraps of material and technical information. Whole communities turned out for special events, such as the seasonal husking bees and apple bees, which were organized mainly by women.

Much of this informal barter, however, resulted from lack of cash rather than from a lasting desire to cooperate. When annual harvests were bountiful, even the farm woman's practice of bartering goods with neighbors and local merchants—butter and eggs in return for yard goods or seed—diminished sharply, replaced by cash transactions.

For many farmers, the soil simply would not yield a livelihood, and they often owed more money than they took in. Start-up costs, including the purchase of land and equipment, put many farmers deep in debt to local creditors. Some lost their land altogether. By the turn of the century, more than one-third of all farmers in the United States were tenants on someone else's land.

The Garden of Eden was not to be found on the prairies or on the plains, no matter how hard the average farm family worked. Again and again, foreclosures wiped out the small landowner through dips in commodity prices, bad decisions, natural disasters, or illness. The swift growth of rural population soon ended. Although writers and orators alike continued to celebrate the family farm as the source of virtue and economic well-being, the hard reality of big money and political power told a far different story.

HOW DID agribusiness differ from more traditional forms of farming?

Review Summary

THE WORLD'S BREADBASKET

During the second half of the nineteenth century, commercial farms employed the most intensive and extensive methods of agricultural production in the world. Hardworking farmers brought huge numbers of acres under cultivation, while new technologies allowed them to achieve unprecedented levels of efficiency in the planting and harvesting of crops. As a result, farming became increasingly tied to international trade, and modern capitalism soon ruled western agriculture, as it did the mining and cattle industries.

NEW PRODUCTION TECHNOLOGIES

Only after the trees had been cleared and grasslands cut free of roots could the soil be prepared for planting. But as farmers on the Great Plains knew so well, the sod west of the Mississippi did not yield readily to cultivation and often broke the cast-iron plows typically used by eastern farmers. Farther west, some farmers resorted to drills to plant seeds for crops such as wheat and oats. Even in the best locations, where loamy, fertile ground had built up over centuries into eight or more inches of decayed vegetation, the preliminary breaking, or "busting," of the sod required hard labor.

This **"thirty-three** horse team harvester" was photographed at the turn of the century in Walla Walla, Washington. Binding the grain into sheaves before it could hit the ground, the "harvester" cut, threshed, and sacked wheat in one single motion.

Agricultural productivity depended as much on new technology as on the farmers' hard labor. In 1837, John Deere had designed his famous "singing plow," which easily turned prairie grasses under and turned up even highly compacted soils. Around the same time, Cyrus McCormick's reaper began to be used for cutting grain; by the 1850s, his factories were turning out reapers in mass quantities. The harvester, invented in the 1870s, drew the cut stalks upward to a platform where two men could bind them into sheaves; by the 1880s, an automatic knotter tied them together. Drastically reducing the number of people traditionally required for this work, the harvester increased the pace many times over. The introduction of mechanized corn planters and mowing or raking machines for hay all but completed the technological arsenal (see Table 18.1). The improvements allowed an average farmer to produce up to ten times more than was possible with the old implements.

Scientific study of soil, grain, and climate conditions was another factor in the record output. Beginning in the mid-nineteenth century, federal and state

QUICK REVIEW

Changes in Farming

- Increased emphasis on production for exchange.
- International demand for wheat supported wheat farming in U.S.
- New technology encouraged the consolidation of land into large farms.

TABLE 18.1

Hand v. Machine Labor on the Farm, ca. 1880

Crop	Time Worked		Labor Cost	
	Hand	**Machine**	**Hand**	**Machine**
Wheat	61 hours	3 hours	$3.55	$0.66
Corn	39 hours	15 hours	3.62	1.51
Oats	66 hours	7 hours	3.73	1.07
Loose Hay	21 hours	4 hours	1.75	0.42
Baled Hay	35 hours	12 hours	3.06	1.29

governments added inducements to the growing body of expertise, scientific information, and hands-on advice. Through the **Morrill Act of 1862**, "land-grant" colleges acquired space for campuses in return for promising to institute agricultural programs. The Department of Agriculture, which attained cabinet-level status in 1889, and the Weather Bureau (transferred from the War Department in 1891) also made considerable contributions to farmers' knowledge. The federal Hatch Act of 1887, which created a series of state experimental stations, provided for basic agricultural research, especially in the areas of soil minerals and plant growth. Many states added their own agricultural stations, usually connected with state colleges and universities.

Nature nevertheless often reigned over technological innovation and seemed in places to take revenge against these early successes. West of the 98th meridian—a north–south line extending through western Oklahoma, central Kansas and Nebraska, and eastern Dakota—perennial dryness due to an annual rainfall of less than 20 inches constantly threatened to turn soil into dust and to break plows on the hardened ground. Summer heat burned out crops and ignited grass fires. Mountains of winter snows turned rivers into spring torrents that flooded fields; heavy fall rains washed crops away. Even good weather invited worms and flying insects to infest the crops. During the 1870s, grasshoppers in clouds a mile long ate everything organic, including tree bark and clothes.

After the Civil War, the veteran John Wesley Powell set off to explore much of the trans–Mississippi West and soon concluded that the shortage of water would remain a huge problem unless settlers worked together to plan irrigation projects. His *Report on the Lands of the Arid Region,* published in 1878, advised prospective farmers to settle near watersheds and to construct, where necessary, dams and canals. Congress ignored his suggestions, fearing that such planning would inhibit free enterprise.

PRODUCING FOR THE GLOBAL MARKET

Farming changed in important ways during the last third of the nineteenth century. Although the family remained the primary source of labor, farmers tended to put more emphasis on production for exchange rather than for home use. They continued to plant vegetable gardens and often kept fowl or livestock for the family's consumption but raised crops mainly for a market that stretched across the world.

The new machines and expanding market did not necessarily guarantee success. Land, draft animals, and equipment remained very expensive, and start-up costs could keep a family in debt for decades. A year of good returns often preceded a year of financial disaster. Weather conditions, international markets, and railroad and steamship shipping prices all proved equally unpredictable and heartless.

The new technology and scientific expertise favored the large, well-capitalized farmer over the small one. The majority of farmers with fewer resources expanded at more modest rates. Between 1880 and 1900, average farm size in the seven leading grain-growing states increased from 64.4 acres to more than 100 acres.

CALIFORNIA AGRIBUSINESS

The trend toward bonanza farming reached an apex in California, where farming as a business surpassed farming as a way of life. Bankers, railroad magnates, and other Anglos made rich by the gold rush took possession of the best farming land in the state. They introduced the latest technologies, built dams and canals, and invested huge amounts of capital, setting the pattern for the state's prosperous agribusiness.

Morrill Act of 1862 Act by which "land-grant" colleges acquired space for campuses in return for promising to institute agricultural programs.

This painting by the British-born artist Thomas Hill (1829–1908) depicts workers tending strawberry fields in the great agricultural valley of northern California. Chinese field hands, such as the two men shown here, supplied not only cheap labor but also invaluable knowledge of specialized fruit and vegetable crops.

Thomas Hill, "Irrigating at Strawberry Farm, Santa Clara," 1888. Courtesy of the Bancroft Library, University of California, Berkeley.

Farms of nearly 500 acres dominated the California landscape in 1870; by the turn of the century, two-thirds of the state's arable land was in 1,000-acre farms.

By 1900, California had become the model for American agribusiness—not the home of self-sufficient homesteaders but the showcase of heavily capitalized farm factories that employed a huge tenant and migrant workforce, including many Chinese. After the mines gave out and work on the transcontinental railroad ended, thousands of Chinese helped to bring new lands under cultivation. Chinese tenant farmers specialized in labor-intensive crops, such as vegetables and fruits, and peddled their crops door-to-door or sold them in roadside stands. Others worked in packing and preserving in all the major agricultural regions of the state. However, the Chinese, like the majority of field hands, rarely rose to the ranks of agricultural entrepreneurs. By the turn of the century, amid intense legislative battles over land and irrigation rights, it was clear that the rich and powerful dominated California agribusiness.

THE TOLL ON THE ENVIRONMENT

Viewing the land as a resource to command, the new inhabitants often looked past the existing flora and fauna toward a landscape remade strictly for commercial purposes. The changes they produced in some areas were nearly as cataclysmic as those that occurred during the Ice Age.

Farmers "improved" the land by introducing exotic plants and animals—that is, biological colonies indigenous to other regions and continents. Farmers also unintentionally introduced new varieties of weeds, insect pests, and rats. Surviving portions of older grasslands and meadows eventually could be found only alongside railroad tracks, in graveyards, or inside national parks.

Numerous species disappeared altogether or suffered drastic reduction. The grizzly bear, for example, an animal exclusive to the West, could once be found in large numbers from the Great Plains to California and throughout much of Alaska; by the early decades of the twentieth century, one nature writer estimated that only 800 survived, mostly in Yellowstone National Park. At the same time, the number of wolves declined from perhaps as many as 2 million to just 200,000. By the mid-1880s, no more than 5,000 buffalo survived in the entire United States.

The slaughter of the buffalo had a dramatic impact, not only on the fate of the species, but also on the grasslands of the Great Plains. Overall, the biological diversity of the region had been drastically reduced. Having killed off the giant herds, ranchers and farmers quickly shifted to cattle and sheep production. Unlike the roaming buffalo, these livestock did not range widely and soon devoured the native grasses down to their roots. With the ground cover destroyed, the soil eroded and became barren. By the end of the century, huge dust storms swept across the plains.

Large-scale commercial agriculture also took a heavy toll on inland waters. Before white settlement, rainfall had drained naturally into lakes and underground aquifers, and watering spots were abundant throughout the Great Plains. Farmers mechanically rerouted and dammed water to irrigate their crops, causing many bodies of water to disappear and the water table to drop significantly. In the 1870s, successful ranchers in California pressed for ever greater supplies of water and contracted Chinese work gangs to build the largest irrigation canal in the West. In 1887, the state of California formed irrigation districts, securing bond issues for the construction of canals, and other western states followed. But by the 1890s, irrigation had seemed to reach its limit without federal support. The Newlands or **National Reclamation Act** of 1902 added 1 million acres of irrigated land, and state irrigation districts added more than 10 million acres. Expensive to taxpayers, and ultimately benefiting corporate farmers rather than small landowners, these projects further diverted water and totally transformed the landscape.

Although western state politicians and federal officials debated water rights for decades, they rarely considered the impact of water policies on the environment. Lake Tulare in California's Central Valley, for example, had occupied up to 760 square miles. After farmers began to irrigate their land by tapping the rivers that fed Tulare, the lake shrank dramatically, covering a mere 36 square miles by the early twentieth century. Finally the lake, which had supported rich aquatic and avian life for thousands of years, disappeared entirely. The land left behind, now wholly dependent on irrigation, grew so alkaline in spots that it could no longer be used for agricultural purposes.

The need to maintain the water supply indirectly led to the creation of national forests and the Forest Service. Western farmers supported the **General Land Revision Act of 1891**, which gave the president the power to establish forest reserves to protect watersheds against the threats posed by lumbering, overgrazing, and forest fires. In the years that followed, President Benjamin Harrison established fifteen forest reserves exceeding 16 million acres, and President Grover Cleveland added more than 21 million acres. But only in 1897 did the secretary of the interior finally gain the authority to regulate the use of these reserves.

The **Forest Management Act** of 1897 and the National Reclamation Act of 1902 set the federal government on the path of large-scale regulatory activities. The Forest Service was established in 1905, and in 1907, forest reserves were transferred from the Department of the Interior to the Department of Agriculture. The federal government would now play an even larger role in economic development of the West, dealing mainly with corporate farmers and ranchers eager for improvements.

National Reclamation Act 1902 act which added 1 million acres of irrigated land to the United States.

General Land Revision Act of 1891 Act which gave the president the power to establish forest reserves to protect watersheds against the threats posed by lumbering, overgrazing, and forest fires.

Forest Management Act 1897 act which, along with the National Reclamation Act, set the federal government on the path of large-scale regulatory activities.

THE WESTERN LANDSCAPE

Throughout the nineteenth century, many Americans viewed western expansion as the nation's "manifest destiny," and just as many marveled at the region's natural and cultural wonders. The public east of the Mississippi craved stories about the West and visual images of its sweeping vistas. Artists and photographers built their reputations on what they saw and imagined. Scholars, from geologists and botanists to historians and anthropologists, toured the trans–Mississippi West in pursuit of new data. The region and its peoples came to represent what was both unique and magnificent about the American landscape.

NATURE'S MAJESTY

Moved by such evidence, reports of the West's natural beauty, the federal government began to set aside huge tracts of land as nature reserves. In 1864, Congress passed the Yosemite Act, which placed the spectacular cliffs and giant sequoias under the management of the State of California. Meanwhile, explorers returned to the East awestruck by the varied terrain of the Rocky Mountains, the largest mountain chain in North America, and described huge sky-high lakes, boiling mud, and spectacular waterfalls. In 1872, Congress named Yellowstone the first national park. Yosemite and Sequoia in California, Crater Lake in Oregon, Mount Rainier in Washington, and Glacier in Montana all became national parks between 1890 and 1910 (see Map 18.5).

Landscape painters, particularly the group that became known as the Rocky Mountain School, also piqued the public's interest in western scenery. In the 1860s, German-born Albert Bierstadt's "earthscapes"—huge canvases with exacting details of animals and plants—thrilled viewers and sold for tens of thousands of dollars.

Albert Bierstadt became one of the first artists to capture on enormous canvases the vastness and rugged terrain of western mountains and wilderness. Many other artists joined Bierstadt to form the Rocky Mountain School. In time, the camera largely replaced the paintbrush, and most Americans formed an image of these majestic peaks from postcards and magazine illustrations.

WHAT PLACE did the West hold in the national imagination?

myhistorylab
Review Summary

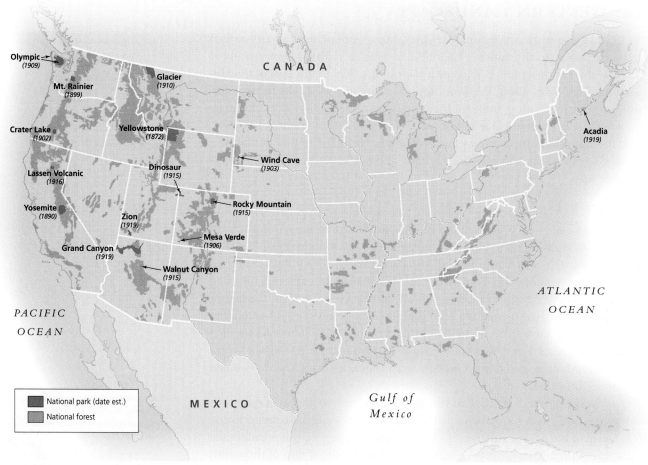

MAP 18.5

The Establishment of National Parks and Forests   The setting aside of land for national parks saved large districts of the West from early commercial development and industrial degradation, setting a precedent for the later establishment of additional parks in economically marginal, but scenic, territory. The West, home to the vast majority of park space, became a principal site of tourism by the end of the nineteenth century.

WHAT IF any factors in the West provided a more conducive environment in which the Mormons could flourish?

THE LEGENDARY WILD WEST

By the end of the century, many Americans, rich and poor alike, imagined the West as a land of promise and opportunity and, above all, of excitement and adventure. Future president Theodore Roosevelt helped to promote this view. Soon after his election to the New York State Assembly in 1882, Roosevelt was horrified to see himself lampooned in the newspapers as a dandy and a weakling. A year later, after buying a ranch in North Dakota, he began to reconstruct his public image. He wrote three books recounting his adventures in the West, claiming that they had instilled in him not only personal bravery and "hardihood" but also self-reliance. The West, Roosevelt insisted, meant "vigorous manhood."

The first "westerns," the "dime novels" that sold in the 1860s in editions of 50,000 or more, reflected these myths. Edward Zane Carroll Judson's *Buffalo Bill, the King of the Border Men,* first published in 1869, spawned hundreds of other novels, thousands of stories, and an entire magazine devoted to Buffalo Bill.

The former Pony Express rider, army scout, and famed buffalo hunter William F. Cody hit upon the idea of an extravaganza that would bring the legendary West to those who could never experience it in person. "Buffalo Bill" Cody made sharpshooter Annie Oakley a star performer. Entrancing crowds with her stunning accuracy with pistol or rifle, Oakley shot dimes in midair and cigarettes from her husband's mouth. Cody also hired Sioux Indians and hundreds of cowboys to perform in mock stagecoach robberies and battles.

Cody's Wild West Show attracted masses of fairgoers at the World's Columbian Exposition, the spectacular celebration of the 400th anniversary of Columbus's landing in the New World held in Chicago in 1893. Less well attended but nonetheless significant was the annual meeting of the American Historical Association, the leading professional society of historians, and the presentation of an essay that one historian has deemed "the single most influential piece of writing in the history of American history."

At this meeting, Frederick Jackson Turner, a young historian at the University of Wisconsin, read a paper that, like Cody's Wild West Show, celebrated the West. "The Significance of the Frontier in American History" made a compelling argument that the continuous westward movement of settlement allowed Americans to develop new standards for democracy. Turner reasoned that each generation, in its move westward, mastered the "primitive conditions" and thereby developed a distinctive American character.

What became known as the "frontier thesis" also sounded a warning bell. The 1890 federal census revealed that the "free land" had been depleted, prompting Turner to conclude that the "closing" of the frontier marked the end of the formative period of American history. The "frontier thesis" lived on, although most historians no longer consider the frontier as the key to all American history. Many have pointed out that the concept of "the frontier" has meaning only to Euro-Americans and not to the tribal people who had occupied this land for centuries. Nevertheless, many of Turner's contemporaries found in his thesis the rationale for seeking new "frontiers" through overseas expansion.

THE "AMERICAN PRIMITIVE"

New technologies of graphic reproduction encouraged painters and photographers to provide new images of the West, authentic as well as fabricated. A young German American artist, Charles Schreyvogel, saw Buffalo Bill's tent show in Buffalo and decided to make the West his life's work. His canvases depicted Indian warriors and U.S. cavalry fighting furiously but without blood and gore. Charles Russell, a genuine cowboy, painted the life he knew but also indulged in imaginary scenarios, producing paintings of buffalo hunts and first encounters between Indian peoples and white explorers.

Frederic Remington, the most famous of all the western artists, left Yale Art School to visit Montana in 1881, became a Kansas sheepherder and tavern owner, and then returned to painting. Inspired by newspaper stories of the army's campaign against the Apaches, he made himself into a war correspondent and captured vivid scenes of battle in his sketches. Painstakingly accurate in physical details, especially of horses, his paintings celebrated the "winning of the West" from the Indian peoples.

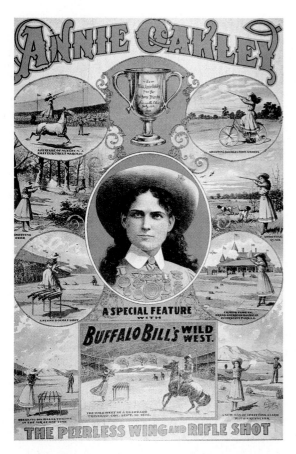

Born Phoebe Ann Moses in 1860, Annie Oakley was a star attraction in Buffalo Bill's Wild West show. Dubbed "Little Sure Shot" by Chief Sitting Bull, Oakley traveled with Cody's show for seventeen years. This poster from 1901 advertises her sharp-shooting talents.

Photographers often produced highly nuanced portraits of Indian peoples. Dozens of early photographers from the Bureau of American Ethnology captured the gaze of noble tribespeople or showed them hard at work digging clams or grinding corn. President Theodore Roosevelt praised Edward Sheriff Curtis for vividly conveying tribal virtue.

Painters and photographers led the way for scholarly research on the various Indian societies. The early ethnographer and pioneer of fieldwork in anthropology Lewis Henry Morgan devoted his life to the study of Indian family or kinship patterns, mostly of eastern tribes such as the Iroquois, who adopted him into their Hawk Clan. In 1851, he published *League of the Ho-de-no-sau-nee, or Iroquois*, considered the first scientific account of an Indian tribe.

One of the most influential interpreters of the cultures of living tribespeople was the pioneering ethnographer Alice Cunningham Fletcher. In 1879, Fletcher met Susette (Bright Eyes) La Flesche of the Omaha tribe, who was on a speaking tour to gain support for her people, primarily to prevent their removal from tribal lands. Fletcher, then forty-two years old, accompanied La Flesche to Nebraska, telling the Omahas that she had come "to learn, if you will let me, something about your tribal organization, social customs, tribal rites, traditions and songs. Also to see if I can help you in any way." After transcribing hundreds of songs, Fletcher became well known as an expert on Omaha music. She also promoted assimilation through the allotment of individual claims to 160-acre homesteads, eked out of tribal lands, and helped to draft the model legislation that was enacted by Congress as the **Omaha Act of 1882**. In 1885, Fletcher produced for the U.S. Senate a report titled *Indian Education and Civilization*, one of the first general statements on the status of Indian peoples. As a founder of the American Anthropological Society and president of the American Folklore Society, she encouraged further study of Indian societies.

THE TRANSFORMATION OF INDIAN SOCIETIES

In 1871, the U.S. government formally ended the treaty system, eclipsing without completely abolishing the sovereignty of Indian nations. Still, the tribes persisted. Using a mixture of survival strategies from farming and trade to the leasing of reservation lands, they both adapted to changing conditions and maintained old traditions.

REFORM POLICY AND POLITICS

By 1880, many Indian tribes had been forcibly resettled on reservations, but very few had adapted to white ways. For decades, reformers, mainly from the Protestant churches, had lobbied Congress for a program of salvation through assimilation, and they looked to the Board of Indian Commissioners, created in 1869, to carry out this mission. The board often succeeded in mediating conflicts among the various tribes crowded onto reservations but made far less headway in converting them to Christianity or transforming them into prosperous farming communities.

The majority of Indian peoples lived in poverty and misery, deprived of their traditional means of survival and, more often than not, subjected to fraud by corrupt government officials and private suppliers. Reformers who observed

---

WHAT KIND of Indian society did reformers envision?

myhistorylab
Review Summary

17–5
Helen Hunt Jackson, from
A Century of Dishonor (1881)

Omaha Act of 1882 Act which allowed the establishment of individual title to tribal lands.

OVERVIEW | Major Indian Treaties and Legislation of the Late Nineteenth Century

1863	Nez Percé Treaty	Signed illegally on behalf of the entire tribe, in which the Nez Percé abandoned 6 million acres of land in return for a small reservation in northeastern Oregon. Led to Nez Percé wars, which ended in 1877 with the surrender of Chief Joseph.
1867	Medicine Lodge Treaty	Assigned reservations in existing Indian Territory to Comanches, Plains (Kiowa), Apaches, Kiowas, Cheyennes, and Arapahoes, bringing these tribes together with Sioux, Shoshones, Bannocks, and Navajos.
1868	Treaty of Fort Laramie	Successfully ended Red Cloud's war by evacuating federal troops from Sioux Territory along the Bozeman Trail; additionally granted Sioux ownership of the western half of South Dakota and rights to use Powder River country in Wyoming and Montana.
1871		Congress declares end to treaty system.
1887	Dawes Severalty Act	Divided communal tribal land, granting the right to petition for citizenship to those Indians who accepted the individual land allotment of 160 acres. Successfully undermined sovereignty.

these conditions firsthand nevertheless remained unshaken in their belief that tribespeople must be raised out of the darkness of ignorance into the light of civilization. Some conceded, however, that the reservation system might not be the best means to this end.

Unlike most Americans, who saw the conquest of the West as a means to national glory, some reformers were genuinely outraged by the government's continuous violation of treaty obligations and the military enforcement of the reservation policy. One of the most influential was Helen Hunt Jackson, a noted poet and author of children's stories. In 1879, Jackson had attended a lecture in Hartford, Connecticut, by a chief of the Ponca tribe whose destitute people had been forced from their Dakota homeland.

Jackson threw herself into the Indian Rights Association, an offshoot of the Women's National Indian Association (WNIA), which had been formed in 1874 to rally public support for a program of assimilation. The two organizations helped to place Protestant missionaries in the West to work to eradicate tribal customs as well as to convert Indian peoples to Christianity. By 1882, the WNIA had gathered 100,000 signatures on petitions urging Congress to phase out the reservation system, to establish universal education for Indian children, and to award title to 160 acres to any Indian individual willing to work the land.

The **Dawes Severalty Act**, passed by Congress in 1887, incorporated many of these measures and established federal Indian policy for decades to come. The act allowed the president to distribute land, not to tribes, but to individuals legally "severed" from their tribes. The commissioner of Indian affairs rendered the popular interpretation that "tribal relations should be broken up, socialism destroyed and the family and autonomy of the individual substituted. The allotment of land in severalty, the establishment of local courts and police, the development of a personal sense of independence and the universal adoption of the English language are means to this end."

myhistorylab

Overview: *Major Indian Treaties and Legislation of the Late Nineteenth Century*

Dawes Severalty Act   An 1887 law terminating tribal ownership of land and allotting some parcels of land to individual Indians with the remainder opened for white settlement.

Those individuals who accepted the land allotment of 160 acres and agreed to allow the government to sell unallotted tribal lands (with some funds set aside for education) could petition to become citizens of the United States. A little over a decade after its enactment, many reformers believed that the Dawes Act had resolved the basis of the "Indian problem." Hollow Horn Bear, a Sioux chief, offered a different opinion, judging the Dawes Act to be "only another trick of the whites."

The Dawes Act successfully undermined tribal sovereignty but offered little compensation. Indian religions and sacred ceremonies were banned, the telling of legends and myths forbidden, and shaman and medicine men imprisoned or exiled for continuing their traditional practices. "Indian schools" forbade Indian languages, clothing styles, and even hair fashions.

These and other measures did little to integrate Indians into white society. Treated as savages, Indian children fled most white schools. Nor did adults receive much encouragement to become property holders. Government agencies allotted them inferior farmland, inadequate tools, and little training for agricultural self-sufficiency. Seeing scant advantage in assimilating, only a minority of adults dropped their tribal religion for Christianity or their communal ways for the accumulation of private property. Within the next forty years, the Indian peoples lost 60 percent of the reservation land remaining in 1887 and 66 percent of the land allotted to them as homesteaders. The tenets of the Dawes Act were not reversed until 1934. In that year, Congress passed the Indian Reorganization Act, which affirmed the integrity of Indian cultural institutions and returned some land to tribal ownership (see Chapter 24).

THE GHOST DANCE

After the passage of the Dawes Severalty Act, one more cycle of rebellion remained for the Sioux. In 1888, the Paiute prophet Wovoka, ill with scarlet fever, had a vision during a total eclipse of the sun. In his vision, the Creator told him that if the Indian peoples learned to love each other, they would be granted a special place in the afterlife. The Creator also gave him the Ghost Dance, which the prophet performed for others and soon spread throughout the tribe. The Sioux came to believe that when the day of judgment came, all Indian peoples who had ever lived would return to their lost world and white peoples would vanish from the earth.

Many white settlers and federal officials feared the Ghost Dancers, even though belief in a sudden divine judgment was common among Christians and Jews. Before the Civil War, Protestant groups such as the Millerites, who had renounced personal property and prepared themselves for the millennium, were tolerated by other Americans. But after decades of Indian warfare, white Americans took the Ghost Dance as a warning of tribal retribution rather than a religious ceremony. As thousands of Sioux danced to exhaustion, local whites intolerantly demanded the practice be stopped. The U.S. Seventh Cavalry, led in part by survivors of the Battle of Little Bighorn, rushed to the Pine Ridge Reservation, and a group of the Sioux led by Big Foot, now fearing

The celebrated artist Frederic Remington (1861–1909) produced this sketch of Oglala Sioux at the Pine Ridge Indian Reservation in South Dakota. Published in the popular magazine *Harper's Weekly*, Remington's depiction of the ghost dance of 1890 showed dancers in vividly patterned robes and shirts, some decorated with stars symbolizing the coming of a new age for the Indians.

Ogallala Sioux performing the Ghost Dance at the Pine Ridge Indian Agency, South Dakota. Illustration by Frederic Remington, 1890. The Granger Collection.

mass murder, moved into hiding in the Bad Lands of South Dakota. After a skirmish, the great leader Sitting Bull and his young son lay dead.

The Seventh Cavalry pursued the Sioux Ghost Dancers and 300 undernourished Sioux, freezing and without horses, to Wounded Knee Creek on the Pine Ridge Reservation. There, on December 29, 1890, while the peace-seeking Big Foot, who had personally raised a white flag of surrender, lay dying of pneumonia, they were surrounded by soldiers armed with automatic guns. The U.S. troops expected the Sioux to surrender their few remaining weapons, but an accidental gunshot from one deaf brave who misunderstood the command caused panic on both sides.

Within minutes, 200 Sioux had been cut down and dozens of soldiers wounded, mostly by their own cross fire. For two hours soldiers continued to shoot at anything that moved—mostly women and children straggling away. Many of the injured froze to death in the snow; others were transported in open wagons and finally laid out on beds of hay under Christmas decorations at the Pine Ridge Episcopal church. The massacre, which took place almost exactly 400 years after Columbus "discovered" the New World for Christian civilization, seemed to mark the final conquest of the continent's indigenous peoples.

ENDURANCE AND REJUVENATION

The most tenacious tribes were those occupying land rejected by white settlers or those distant from their new communities. Still, not even an insular, peaceful agricultural existence on semiarid, treeless terrain necessarily provided protection. Nor did a total willingness to peacefully accept white offers prevent attack.

The Pimas of Arizona, for instance, had a well-developed agricultural system adapted to a scarce supply of water, and they rarely warred with other tribes. After the arrival of white settlers, they integrated Christian symbolism into their religion, learned to speak English, and even fought with the U.S. cavalry against the Apaches. Still, the Pimas saw their lands stolen, their precious waterways diverted, and their families impoverished.

The similarly peaceful Yana tribes of California, hunters and gatherers rather than farmers, were even less fortunate. Suffering enslavement, prostitution, and multiple new diseases from white settlers, they faced near extinction within a generation. One Yana tribe, the Yahi, chose simply to disappear. For more than a decade, they lived in caves and avoided all contact with white settlers.

A majority of tribes, especially smaller ones, sooner or later reached numbers too low to maintain their collective existence. Intermarriage, although widely condemned by the white community, drew many young people outside their Indian communities. Some tribal leaders also deliberately chose a path toward assimilation. The Quapaws, for example, formally disbanded in the aftermath of the Dawes Severalty Act. The minority that managed to prosper in white society as tradespeople or farmers abandoned their language, religious customs, and traditional ways of life.

For those tribes who remained on reservations, the aggressively assimilationist policies of the Office of Indian Affairs (OIA) challenged their traditional ways. The Southern Ute, for example, at one time hunted, fished, and gathered throughout a huge region spanning the Rocky Mountains and the Great Basin. In 1848, they began to sign a series of treaties in accord with the reservation policy of the U.S. government. Twenty years later their territory had been reduced to approximately one-quarter of Colorado Territory, and in 1873, they had further relinquished about one-quarter of this land. After the passage of the Dawes Act, the U.S. government, pressured by white settlers, gave the tribe two choices: they could break up their communal land holdings and accept the 160 acres granted to the male heads of families, or they could maintain their tribal status and move to a reservation in Utah.

17–7
Tragedy at Wounded Knee (1890)

17–8
Benjamin Harrison, Report on Wounded Knee Massacre and the Decrease in Indian Land Acreage (1891)

The Utes divided over the issue, but a considerable number chose to live on reservations under the administration of the OIA.

Under the terms of the Dawes Act, Southern Ute men and women endured continuous challenges to their egalitarian practices. The OIA assumed, for example, that Ute men would represent the tribe in all official matters, a policy that forced Ute women to petition the U.S. government to recognize their rights and concerns. Similarly, Ute women struggled to hold on to their roles as producers within the subsistence family economy against the efforts of the OIA agents to train them for homemaking alone.

A small minority of tribes, grown skillful in adapting to dramatically changing circumstances, managed to persist and even grow. Never numbering more than a few thousand people, during the late eighteenth century the Cheyennes had found themselves caught geographically between aggressive tribes in the Great Lakes region and had migrated into the Missouri area, where they split into small village-sized communities. By the mid-nineteenth century, they had become expert horse traders on the Great Plains.

The Navajos experienced an extraordinary renewal, largely because they built a life in territory considered worthless by whites. Having migrated to the Southwest from the northwestern part of the continent perhaps 700 years ago, the Diné ("the People"), as they called themselves, had already survived earlier invasions by the Spanish. In 1863, they had been conquered again through the cooperation of hostile tribes led by the famous Colonel Kit Carson. Their crops burned, their fruit trees destroyed, 8,000 Navajo were forced in the 300-mile "Long Walk" to the desolate Bosque Redondo reservation, where they nearly starved. Four years later, the Indian Bureau allowed the severely reduced tribe to return to a fraction of its former lands.

By 1880, the Navajos' population had returned to nearly what it had been before their conquest by white Americans. Quickly depleting the deer and antelope on their hemmed-in reservation, they had to rely on sheep alone as a food reserve during years of bad crops. With their wool rugs and blankets much in demand in the East, the Navajos increasingly turned to crafts, eventually including silver jewelry as well as weaving, to survive. Although living on the economic margin, they persevered to become the largest Indian nation in the United States.

The nearby Hopis, like the Navajos, survived by stubbornly clinging to lands unwanted by white settlers, and by adapting to drastically changing conditions. The Hopis' highly developed theological beliefs, peaceful social system, sand paintings, and kachina dolls interested many educated and influential whites. The resulting publicity helped them gather the public supporters and financial resources needed to fend off further threats to their reservations.

Fortunate northwestern tribes remained relatively isolated from white settlers until the early twentieth century, although they had begun trading with white visitors centuries earlier. Northwestern peoples relied largely on salmon and other resources of the region's rivers and bays. In potlatch ceremonies, leaders redistributed tribal wealth and maintained their personal status and the status of their tribe by giving lavish gifts to invited guests. Northwestern peoples also made intricate wood carvings, including commemorative "totem" poles that recorded their history and identified their regional status. Northwestern peoples maintained their cultural integrity in part through connections with kin in Canada, as did southern tribes with kin in Mexico. In Canada and Mexico, native populations suffered less pressure from new populations and retained more tribal authority than in the United States.

QUICK REVIEW

Adaptation

- Cheyenne became expert horse traders.

- Navajos turned to crafts for survival.

- Interest of influential whites helped Hopis fend off threats.

CHRONOLOGY

1848	Treaty of Guadalupe Hidalgo
1853	Gadsden Purchase
1862	Homestead Act makes free land available
	Morrill Act authorizes "land-grant" colleges
1865–67	Great Sioux War
1866	Texas cattle drives begin
1867	Medicine Lodge Treaty established reservation system
	Alaska purchased
1869	Board of Indian Commissioners created
	Buffalo Bill, the King of the Border Men sets off "Wild West" publishing craze
1870s	Grasshopper attacks on the Great Plains
1872	Yellowstone National Park created
1873	Timber Culture Act
1874–75	Sioux battles in Black Hills of Dakotas
	Red River War

1876	Custer's Last Stand
1877	Defeat of the Nez Percé
1878	John Wesley Powell published *Report on the Lands of the Arid Region*
1881	Helen Hunt Jackson, *A Century of Dishonor*
1882	Edmunds Act outlaws polygamy
1885–87	Droughts and severe winters cause the collapse of the cattle boom
1887	Dawes Severalty Act
1890	Sioux Ghost Dance movement
	Massacre of Lakota Sioux at Wounded Knee
	Census Bureau announces the end of the frontier line
1893	Frederick Jackson Turner presents his "frontier thesis"
1897	Forest Management Act gives the federal government authority over forest reserves

Indian nations approached their nadir as the nineteenth century came to a close. The descendants of the great pre-Columbian civilizations had been conquered by foreigners, their population reduced to fewer than 250,000. Under the pressure of assimilation, the remaining tribespeople became known to non-Indians as "the vanishing Americans." It would take several generations before Indian sovereignty experienced a resurgence.

CONCLUSION

The West, rich in natural resources, soon served the nation in supplying ore and timber for its expanding industries and agricultural products for the growing urban populations. Envisioning the West as a cornucopia whose boundless treasures would offer themselves to the willing pioneer, most of the new residents failed to calculate the odds against their making a prosperous livelihood as miners, farmers, or petty merchants. Nor could they appreciate the long-term consequences of the violence they brought with them from the battlefields of the Civil War to the far reaches of the West.

The new settlers adapted their political and legal systems, as well as many of their economic and cultural institutions, to western circumstances. Ironically though, even after statehood, they would still be only distant representatives of an empire whose financial, political, and industrial centers remained in the Northeast. They were often frustrated by their isolation and enraged at the federal regulations that governed them and at the eastern investors and lawyers who seemed poised on all sides to rob them of the fruits of their labor. Embittered Westerners, along with Southerners, would form the core of a nationwide discontent that would soon threaten to uproot the American political system.

REVIEW QUESTIONS

1. Discuss the role of federal legislation in accelerating and shaping the course of westward expansion.

2. How did the incorporation of western territories into the United States affect Indian nations such as the Sioux or the Nez Percé? Discuss the causes and consequences of the Indian Wars. Discuss the significance of reservation policy and the Dawes Severalty Act for tribal life.

3. What were some of the major technological advances in mining and in agriculture that promoted the development of the western economy?

4. Describe the unique features of Mexicano communities in the Southwest before and after the mass immigration of Anglos. How did changes in the economy affect the patterns of labor and the status of women in these communities?

5. What role did the Homestead Act play in western expansion? How did farm families on the Great Plains divide chores among their members? What factors determined the likelihood of economic success or failure?

6. Describe the responses of artists, naturalists, and conservationists to the western landscape. How did their photographs, paintings, and stories shape perceptions of the West in the East?

myhistorylab

Flashcard Review

KEY TERMS

Caminetti Act (p. 474)

Dawes Severalty Act (p. 491)

Edmunds Act (p. 475)

Edmunds-Tucker Act (p. 475)

Forest Management Act (p. 486)

General Land Revision Act of 1891 (p. 486)

Great Sioux War (p. 469)

Hispanic-American Alliance (p. 476)

Homestead Act of 1862 (p. 480)

Morrill Act of 1862 (p. 484)

National Reclamation Act (p. 486)

Omaha Act of 1882 (p. 490)

Sand Creek Massacre (p. 469)

Treaty of Fort Laramie (p. 469)

RECOMMENDED READING

Jon Gjerde, *The Minds of the West: Ethnocultural Evolution in the Rural Middle West, 1830–1917* (1997). A combination cultural and economic history that weighs the importance of ethnicity in the shaping of American identities in the farming regions of the Middle West. Gjerde pays close attention to the religious institutions and systems of belief of European immigrants as the basis of community formation.

Robert V. Hine and John Mack Faragher, *The American West: A New Interpretive History* (2000). A sweeping, amply illustrated survey of western history with reference to recent scholarship. The authors emphasize Native Americans and include rich material on ethnicity, the environment, and the role of women.

John C. Hudson, *Making the Corn Belt: A Geographical History of Middle-Western Agriculture* (1994). An ecologically oriented study of corn growing that traces its development from Indians to Southerners moving westward.

Andrew C. Isenberg, *The Destruction of the Bison: An Environmental History, 1750–1920* (2000). A rich study of the forces behind the near-extinction of the bison, with special attention to the interplay among Indians, Euroamericans, and the environment of the Great Plains. Isenberg constructs a narrative that is as much cultural as economic in framing the problem.

Karl Jacoby, *Crimes Against Nature: Squatters, Poachers, Thieves, and the Hidden History of American Conservation* (2001). A complex analysis of the origins of national parks in the Adirondacks, Yellowstone, and the Grand Canyon. Rather than focusing on the individuals and groups that led the conservation of vast public lands, Jacoby switches perspective to focus on those who were dispossessed by the process.

Elizabeth Jameson and Susan Armitage, eds., *Writing the Range* (1997). A collection of essays on women in the West that presents an inclusive historical narrative based on the experiences of women of differing backgrounds, races, and ethnic groups.

Valerie Sherer Mathes and Richard Lowitt, *The Standing Bear Controversy: Prelude to Indian Reform* (2003). A fascinating account of the Ponca chief's efforts to bring attention to the injustices surrounding the forced removal of the Poncas from their tribal lands.

Katherine M. B. Osburn, *Southern Ute Women: Autonomy and Assimilation on the Reservation, 1887–1934* (1998). Presents a careful analysis of the impact of the Dawes Act on the role and status of women among the Southern Ute. Osburn acknowledges the changes brought by the Office of Indian Affairs programs on the reservations but emphasizes the resistance of the Ute and the retention of old ways.

Glenda Riley, *Building and Breaking Families in the American West* (1996). Essays covering the variety of cultures in the American West, organized topically to highlight courtship, marriage and intermarriage, and separation and divorce.

Thomas E. Sheridan, *Los Tucsonenses: The Mexican Community in Tucson, 1854–1941* (1986). A highly readable account of Mexican American communities in the Southwest. Sheridan shows how a midcentury accommodation of Anglos and Mexicanos faded with the absorption of the region into the national economy and with the steady displacement of the Mexicano community from its agricultural landholdings.

Louis S. Warren, *Buffalo Bill's America: William Cody and the Wild West Show* (2005). Deals with many of the legends Cody created about himself and his performers and relates his celebrity at the turn of the twentieth century to continuing forms of mass entertainment.

Liping Zhu, *A Chinaman's Chance: The Chinese on the Rocky Mountain Mining Frontier* (1997). Studies the mining communities of Chinese in the Boise Basin of Idaho. Zhu emphasizes the success the Chinese enjoyed not only as miners but also as merchants in the face of discriminatory practices and laws.

Here we had been taken to a lonely place;
. . . our things were taken away, our friends
separated from us; a man came to inspect us,
as if to ascertain our full value . . .
—*Mary Antin, from* The Promised Land

Noted urban photographer Lewis Hines captures the cramped working conditions
and child labor in this late nineteenth-century canning factory. Women and children
provided a cheap and efficient work force for labor-intensive industries.

19

PRODUCTION AND CONSUMPTION IN THE GILDED AGE

1865–1900

WHAT WAS the effect of the expansion in the production of both capital goods and consumer goods?

WHAT WERE the sources of the new labor being recruited for factory work in Gilded Age America?

HOW DID the development of Southern industry affect the lives of African Americans living in the South?

WHAT CONTRIBUTED to the growing population of American cities?

WHAT ACCOUNTS for the rise of a consumer society and how did various groups participate in its development?

WHAT ROLE did public spaces play in late nineteenth-century popular culture?

AMERICAN COMMUNITIES
Haymarket Square, Chicago, May 4, 1886

As Rain approached the City, approximately 1,500 People gathered for a mass meeting in Haymarket Square to protest the brutality of the previous day, when Chicago police killed four strikers at the fiercely antiunion McCormick Reaper Works. The crowd listened peacefully as several speakers denounced the violence. Around 10:00 P.M., when the winds picked up, most headed for home, including the city's longtime mayor, Democrat Carter Harrison. According to newspaper reports, the crowd quickly dwindled to only 600 people. The final speaker, stone hauler Samuel Fielden, jumped up on the hay wagon that served as a make-shift stage and concluded on an ominous note. He warned that "war has been declared on us" and advised the crowd "to get hold of anything that will help you to resist the onslaught of the enemy and the usurper."

Within minutes, a column of 176 police marched down the street, pushing what remained of the crowd onto the wooden sidewalks and commanding them to disperse. Then, according to the city's leading newspaper, the *Tribune*, "something like a miniature rocket suddenly rose out of the crowd on the east sidewalk." The bomb exploded "with terrific force, shaking buildings on the street and creating havoc among the police." One policeman died immediately, provoking others to open fire into the scattering crowd. At the end of just a few minutes of chaos, seven policemen had received mortal wounds and as many as sixty more were injured, many in their own cross fire. Several civilians were killed, and dozens were injured.

Those who attended the rally were mainly disgruntled workers, recent immigrants from central and eastern Europe who had come to Chicago to take advantage of the city's growing industries. They were determined to establish unions and a workday shorter than the customary ten or twelve hours.

Since early in the year, an eight-hour campaign had been sweeping the nation, with its center in Chicago. Workers and sympathetic consumers alike boycotted brands of beer, tobacco, bread, and other products made in longer-hour shops.

With more than wages at stake, workers were joining unions and striking so often that the era became known as the "Great Upheaval." Their leaders responded to this upsurge by calling for a general strike across all industries on May 1, 1886.

A community of radical workers who had emigrated from Germany and settled in Chicago's near North Side made up the most militant contingent of the movement. They called themselves "revolutionary socialists," seeking a government of working people in place of politicians and corporate power. Writing in the *Arbeiter-Zeitung* (*Workers' Newspaper*), the local German-language newspaper, editor August Spies greeted May 1, hailed as "Emancipation Day," calling: "Workmen, let your watchword be: No compromise! Cowards to the Rear! Men to the front!"

On May Day, Spies renewed the cry of "eight for ten" and helped to lead the spectacular parade of 80,000 men, women, and children up Michigan Avenue, Chicago's main street. A Saturday, the day passed peacefully. However, when the workweek resumed on Monday, May 3, the deadly confrontation of strikers and police at the McCormick Reaper Works set the stage for virtual class warfare.

Feelings of animosity on all sides intensified. In the days following the tragedy at Haymarket Square, Chicago police arrested hundreds of working people, rounded up known leaders, and searched their homes and detained them without warrants. Meanwhile, newspapers denounced them as "enemy forces" and the "scum" of Europe. Sentiment swung sharply against immigrants. Many prominent citizens called for a ban on "foreign savages who might come to America with their dynamite bombs and anarchic purposes."

Ultimately, eight men were charged with incitement to murder. In the most celebrated trial of the nineteenth century, a jury of middle-class men pronounced all eight guilty despite the lack of evidence linking the defendants to the bombing. Three of the eight had not even been at Haymarket Square on the evening of May 4. The judge sentenced them to death by hanging.

By the final decades of the nineteenth century, the nation's eyes were fixed on Chicago because the city was marking the steps being taken by the nation as a whole. If class differences sharpened and led to violence, the rise in living standards provided a different, more appealing focus. The city with the most technologically advanced industries in the world seemed to be leading the way—but to what?

Chicago

THE RISE OF INDUSTRY, THE TRIUMPH OF BUSINESS

At the time of the Civil War, the typical American business firm was a small enterprise, owned and managed by a single family, and producing goods for a local or regional market. By the turn of the century, businesses depending on large-scale investments had organized as corporations and grown to unforeseen size. These mammoth firms could afford to mass-produce goods for national and even international markets. At the helm stood unimaginably wealthy men, powerful representatives of a new national business community, who led in the transformation of the United States from a rural to an urban industrial nation.

MECHANIZATION TAKES COMMAND

The second industrial revolution (1871–1914) proceeded at a pace that was not only unprecedented but also previously unimaginable. In 1865, the annual production of goods was estimated at $2 billion; by 1900, it stood at $13 billion, transforming the United States from fourth to first in the world in terms of productivity. American industry had outstripped its European rivals, Germany and Great Britain, and manufactured one-third of the world's goods.

A major force behind economic growth was the completion of the most extensive transportation network in the world. As the nation's first big business and recipient of generous government subsidies, railroads linked cities in every state and served as a nationwide distributor of goods. Freight trains carried the bountiful natural resources, such as iron, coal, and minerals that supplied the raw materials for industry, as well as food and other commodities for the growing urban populations (see Map 19.1).

No factor was more important in promoting economic growth than the application of new technologies to increase the productivity of labor and the volume of goods. Machines, factory managers, and workers together created a system of continuous production by which more could be made—and faster—than anywhere else on earth. Higher productivity depended not only on machinery and technology but also on economies of scale and speed, reorganization of factory labor and business management, and the unparalleled growth of a market for goods of all kinds.

New systems of mass production replaced wasteful and often chaotic practices and speeded up the delivery of finished goods. Within a generation, continuous production—the assembly line—became standard in most areas of manufacturing, revolutionizing the making of furniture, cloth, grain products, soap, and canned goods; the refining, distilling, and processing of animal and vegetable fats; and eventually, the manufacture of automobiles.

EXPANDING THE MARKET FOR GOODS

To distribute the growing volume of goods and to create a dependable market, businesses demanded new techniques of merchandising on a national and, in some cases, international scale. For generations, legions of sellers, or "drummers," had worked their routes, pushing goods, especially hardware and patent medicines, to individual buyers and local retail stores. After the Civil War, the appearance of mail-order houses, which accompanied the consolidation of the railroad lines and the expansion of the postal system, helped to get new products to consumers.

Growing directly out of these services, the successful Chicago-based mail-order houses drew rural and urban consumers into a common marketplace. Sears,

---

WHAT WAS the effect of the expansion in the production of both capital goods and consumer goods?

myhistorylab
Review Summary

IMAGE KEY

for pages 498–499

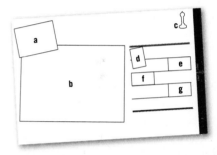

a. A classroom at work in the Chinese Public Primary School in Chinatown, San Francisco, with a Caucasian teacher.

b. A crowd of children at work in a nineteenth-century canning factory. The children sit on overturned baskets while poring over their work under the gaze of an adult male supervisor in their midst.

c. A replica of the first light bulb.

d. Joseph Keppler's *The Two Philanthropists*, caricatures magnates Jay Gould and Cornelius Vanderbilt. The cartoon was published February, 1888 in *Puck* magazine.

e. The Sixth Maryland Militia in Baltimore fires into a hostile crowd of laborers chucking rocks during the Great Railroad Strike of 1877.

f. Humorous drawing of Thomas Edison's laboratories in Menlo Park, New Jersey, around 1880.

g. Fashionable people crowded the Boardwalk in Atlantic City each Easter Sunday to see and be seen in the early twentieth century.

 18–13
Frederick Winslow Taylor, *Scientific Management* (1919)

⟨ MAP EXPLORATION

To explore an interactive version of this map, go to **http://www.prenhall.com/faraghertlc/map19.1**

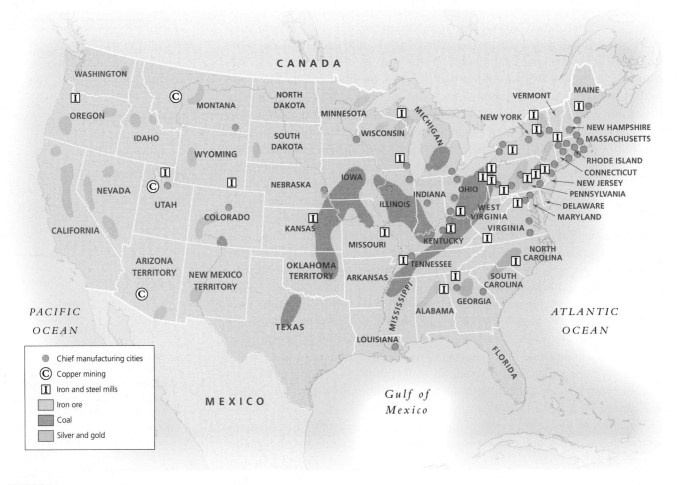

MAP 19.1

Patterns of Industry, 1900 Industrial manufacturing concentrated in the Northeast and Midwest, whereas the raw materials for production came mostly from other parts of the nation.

WHY DID industrial patterns differ from region to region?

Roebuck and Company and Montgomery Ward offered an enormous variety of goods, from shoes to buggies to gasoline stoves and cream separators. The mail-order catalogue also returned to rural folks the fruits of their own labor, now processed and packaged for easy use. In turn, the purchases made by farm families through the Sears catalogue sent cash flowing into Chicago.

The chain store achieved similar economies of scale. By 1900, a half-dozen grocery chains had sprung up. Other chains selling drugs, costume jewelry, shoes, cigars, and furniture soon appeared, offering a greater selection of goods and lower prices than the small, independent stores.

Opening shortly after the Civil War, department stores began to take up much of the business formerly enjoyed by specialty shops, offering a spectrum of services that included restaurants, rest rooms, ticket agencies, nurseries, reading rooms, and post offices. Elegantly appointed with imported carpets, sweeping marble staircases, and crystal chandeliers, the department store raised retailing to new heights.

Advertising lured customers to the department stores, the chains, and the independent neighborhood stores. The advertising revolution began in 1869, when Francis Wayland Ayer founded the earliest advertising agency. Ayer's managed the accounts of such companies as Montgomery Ward, Wanamaker's Department Store, Singer Sewing Machines, and the National Biscuit Company. With the help of this new sales tool, gross revenues of retailers raced upward from $8 million in 1860 to $102 million in 1900.

INTEGRATION, COMBINATION, AND MERGER

The business community aspired to exercise greater control of the economy and to enlarge the commercial empire. From the source of raw materials to the organization of production, from the conditions of labor to the climate of public opinion, business leaders acted shrewdly. Economic cycles alternating between rapid growth and sharp decline also promoted the rise of big business. Major economic setbacks in 1873 and 1893 wiped out weaker competitors, allowing the strongest firms to rebound swiftly and to expand their sales and scale of operation during the recovery period.

Businesses grew in two distinct, if overlapping, ways. Through *vertical integration* a firm gained control of production at every step of the way—from raw materials through processing to the transporting and merchandising of the finished items. In 1899, the United Fruit Company began to build a network of wholesale houses in the United States, and within two years it had opened distribution centers in twenty-one major cities. Eventually, it controlled an elaborate system of Central American plantations and temperature-controlled shipping and storage facilities for its highly perishable bananas.

The second means of growth, *horizontal combination*, entailed gaining control of the market for a single product. The most famous case was the Standard Oil Company, founded by John D. Rockefeller in 1870. Operating out of Cleveland in a highly competitive but lucrative field, Rockefeller first secured preferential rates from railroads eager to ensure a steady supply of oil. He then convinced or coerced other local oil operators to sell their stock to him. The Standard Oil Trust, established in 1882, controlled over 90 percent of the nation's oil-refining industry (see Seeing History).

In 1890, Congress passed the Sherman Antitrust Act to restore competition by encouraging small business and outlawing "every . . . combination . . . in restraint of trade or commerce." Ironically, the courts interpreted the law in ways that inhibited the organization of trade unions and actually helped the consolidation of business. More than 2,600 firms vanished between 1898 and 1902 alone.

THE GOSPEL OF WEALTH

Ninety percent of the nation's business leaders were Protestant, and the majority attended church services regularly. They attributed their personal achievement to hard work and perseverance and made these the principal tenets of a new faith that imbued the pursuit of wealth with old-time religious zeal.

One version of this "**gospel of wealth**" justified the ruthless behavior of the entrepreneurs who accumulated unprecedented wealth and power through shady deals and conspiracies. Speculator Jay Gould, known in the popular press as the

The Marshall Field building constructed in Chicago's Loop between 1893 and 1915 came to occupy an entire block to reign as the world's largest department store. In addition to all kinds of fine goods, the retail store offered a host of personal amenities, such as lunch and tea rooms, travel agencies, hair salons, and even personal shoppers. The photograph here features its 6,000 square foot mosaic dome, which was surfaced with 1.6 million pieces of iridescent Tiffany art glass.

 18–2
Henry George, *Progress and Poverty* (1879)

Vertical integration The consolidation of numerous production functions, from the extraction of the raw materials to the distribution and marketing of the finished products, under the direction of one firm.

Horizontal combination The merger of competitors in the same industry.

Gospel of wealth Thesis that hard work and perseverance lead to wealth, implying that poverty is a character flaw.

"Worst Man in the World," wrung his fortune, it was widely believed, from the labor of others. He rose quickly from his modest origins through a series of unsavory financial maneuvers. At his death, one obituary described Jay Gould as "an incarnation of cupidity and sordidness," whose life symbolized "idolatrous homage [to] the golden calf."

Andrew Carnegie—the "Richest Man in the World"—offered a strikingly different model. Carnegie built an empire in steel. A genius at vertical integration, he undercut his competitors by using the latest technology and designing his own system of cost analysis. By 1900, Carnegie managed the most efficient steel mills in the world, which accounted for one-third of the nation's output. When he sold out to J. P. Morgan's new United States Steel Corporation in 1901, his personal share of the proceeds came to $225 million.

Carnegie was well known as a civic leader. From one point of view, he was a factory despot who underpaid his employees and ruthlessly managed their working conditions. But to the patrons of the public libraries, art museums, concert halls, colleges, and universities that he funded, Carnegie appeared to be the single greatest philanthropist of the age. Late in his life, he outlined his personal philosophy in a popular essay, *The Gospel of Wealth* (1889), explaining that "there is no genuine, praiseworthy success in life if you are not honest, truthful, and fair-dealing." By the time he died, he had given away his massive personal fortune.

Whether following the rough road of Gould or the smooth path of Carnegie, the business community worked together to fashion the new conservative ideology of social Darwinism, which purportedly explained, and justified, why some Americans grew rich while others remained poor. Grafted on the biological theory of evolution propounded by the famed British naturalist Charles Darwin, social Darwinism raised the principle of the "survival of the fittest" as an ideal for modern society. In 1883, the Yale professor William Graham Sumner published an essay entitled *What Social Classes Owe to Each Other*, wherein he argued that to tamper with the "natural" order by establishing welfare programs to help the poor or redistributing wealth in any way would be hazardous to society.

LABOR IN THE AGE OF BIG BUSINESS

Like the gospel of wealth, the "gospel of work" affirmed the dignity of hard work, the virtue of thrift, and the importance of individual initiative. But unlike business leaders, the philosophers of American working people did not believe in riches as the proof of work well done or in the lust for power as the driving force of progress. On the contrary, they contended that honesty and competence should be the badge of all morally responsible citizens.

Behind the "gospel of work" stood the reality of the rising industrial order, especially its new systems of production that were, in turn, enabled by new technologies. The impact of the new order on the lives of working people would be nothing less than revolutionary. Increasingly, Americans made their livelihoods by producing, not for their own subsistence, but exclusively for the market, and they earned wages in return for their labor. Big business thus found its mirror image in the labor movement spawned by the consolidation of the wage system.

THE WAGE SYSTEM

The accelerating growth of industry, especially the steady mechanization of production, dramatically changed employer–employee relations and created new categories of workers. Both in turn fostered competition among workers and created conditions often hazardous to health. In many occupations—meat processing,

WHAT WERE the sources of the new labor being recruited for factory work in Gilded Age America?

myhistorylab
Review Summary

The Standard Oil Company

John D. Rockefeller, who formed the Standard Oil Company in 1870, sought to control all aspects of the industry, from the transportation of crude oil to the marketing and distribution of the final products.

Rockefeller's best-known critic was Ida Tarbell. In 1904 she published *The History of the Standard Oil Company*, first in serial form in the popular *McClure's Magazine* and later as a book. Tarbell's muckraking exposé attracted a great deal of attention. But even more popular were political cartoons depicting Rockefeller's stranglehold on the entire oil industry.

WHAT DOES this cartoon tell us about Rockefeller's reputation at the turn of the twentieth century? What does it suggest about Americans' feelings about the trusts?

Puck magazine, which had been founded in 1871 by Joseph Keppler, an immigrant from Austria, held up Rockefeller and his company to ridicule. This cartoon, published in *Puck* in 1904, shows Standard Oil as a sinister octopus, wrapping its arms around the White House and Congress as well as workers and even the denizens of Wall Street. In 1911, in response to an antitrust suit, the Supreme Court ordered the company to break up. The modern corporations Exxon, Mobil, Chevron, Amoco, and Sohio (some of which have recently merged) all descended from Rockefeller's Standard Oil.

This engraving of steel manufacturing at Andrew Carnegie's plant in 1886 features a Bessemer Converter, which converts molten pig iron into steel. The process was named after Sir Henry Bessemer of Sheffield, England, who first patented the process in 1855.

clothing and textile manufacturing, cigar making, and mining, for example—immigrants from Europe and Asia predominated by the end of the century.

For most craft workers, the new system destroyed long-standing practices and chipped away at their customary autonomy. Managers now constantly supervised workers, set the pace of production and rate of payment, and introduced new, faster machinery that made many skills obsolete. In the woodworking trades, highly skilled cabinetmakers, who for generations had brought their own tools to the factory, were largely replaced with "green hands"—immigrants, including many women—who with only minimal training and close supervision could operate new woodworking machines at cheaper rates of pay.

Not all trades conformed to this pattern. The garment industry, for example, grew at a very fast pace in New York, Boston, Chicago, Philadelphia, Cleveland, and St. Louis but retained older systems of labor along with the new. The highly mechanized factories employed hundreds of thousands of young immigrant women, while the outwork system, established well before the Civil War, contracted ever-larger numbers of families to work in their homes on sewing machines or by hand.

Industrial expansion also offered new opportunities for women to work outside the home, and many young women fled the family farm for the factory. African American and immigrant women found employment in trades least affected by technological advances, such as domestic service. In contrast, English-speaking white women moved into the better-paying clerical and sales positions in the rapidly expanding business sector. After the typewriter and telephone came into widespread use in the 1890s, the number of women employed in office work rose even faster. At the turn of the century, 8.6 million women worked outside their homes—nearly triple the number in 1870.

By contrast, African American men found themselves excluded from many fields. In Cleveland, for example, the number of black carpenters declined after 1870, just as the volume of construction was rapidly increasing. African American men were also systematically driven from restaurant service and barred from newer trades such as boilermaking, plumbing, electrical work, and paperhanging, which European immigrants secured for themselves.

Discriminatory or exclusionary practices fell hardest on workers recruited earlier from China. A potent and racist anti-Chinese movement organized to protest "cheap" Chinese labor and to demand a halt to Chinese immigration. By the 1870s white rioters were insistently calling for deportation measures and razing Chinese neighborhoods. In 1882, Congress passed the **Chinese Exclusion Act**, which restricted Chinese immigration by barring laborers, limited the civil rights of resident Chinese, and forbade their naturalization.

myhist&rylab

Exploring America: *French Canadian Controversy*

19–1
Memorial of the Chinese Six Companies to U.S. Grant, President of the United States (1876)

Chinese Exclusion Act Act which suspended Chinese immigration, limited the civil rights of resident Chinese, and forbade their naturalization.

For even the best-placed wage earners, the new work-place could be unhealthy, even dangerous. Factory owners often failed to mark high-voltage wires, locked fire doors, and allowed the emission of toxic fumes. Moreover, machines ran faster in American factories than anywhere else in the world, and workers who could not keep up or suffered serious injury found themselves without a job.

Even under less hazardous conditions, workers complained about the tedium of performing repetitive tasks for many hours each day. Although federal employees had been granted the eight-hour day in 1868, most workers still toiled upward of ten to twelve hours. "Life in a factory," one textile operative grumbled, "is perhaps, with the exception of prison life, the most monotonous life a human being can live." Nor could glamour be found in the work of saleswomen in the elegant department stores. Clerks could not sit down, despite workdays as long as sixteen hours in the busy season, or hold "unnecessary conversations" with customers or other clerks.

Moreover, steady employment was rare. Between 1866 and 1897, fourteen years of prosperity stood against seventeen years of hard times. The major depressions of 1873–79 and 1893–97 were the worst in the nation's history up to that time. Three "minor" recessions (1866–67, 1883–85, and 1890–91) did not seem insignificant to the millions who lost their jobs.

THE KNIGHTS OF LABOR

The Noble and Holy Order of the **Knights of Labor**, founded by a group of Philadelphia garment cutters in 1869, grew to become the largest labor organization in the nineteenth century. The order sought to bring together wage earners, regardless of skill. The Knights endorsed a variety of reform measures—the restriction of child labor, a graduated income tax, more land set aside for homesteading, the abolition of contract labor, and monetary reform—to offset the power of the industrialists. They believed that the "producing classes," once freed from the grip of corporate monopoly and the curses of ignorance and alcohol, would transform the United States into a genuinely democratic society.

The Knights sought to overturn the wage system and, as an alternative, they promoted producers' cooperatives. In these factories, workers collectively made all decisions on prices charged for goods and shared all the profits. Local assemblies launched thousands of small co-ops. The Knights also ran small cooperative cigar shops and grocery stores, often housed in their own assembly buildings. Successful for a time, most cooperatives could not compete against the heavily capitalized enterprises and ultimately failed.

For women, the Knights of Labor created a special department within the organization "to investigate the abuses to which our sex is subjected by unscrupulous employers, to agitate the principles which our Order teaches of equal pay for equal work and the abolition of child labor." At the 1886 convention, delegates approved this plan. With perhaps 65,000 women members at its peak, the Knights ran daycare centers and occasionally even set up cooperative kitchens to reduce the drudgery of cooking.

E PLURIBUS UNUM (EXCEPT THE CHINESE).

Thomas Nast (1840–1902), the most famous political cartoonist of the late nineteenth century, used his art to comment on pressing political issues, such as the plight of former slaves during Reconstruction, the evils of machine politics, and the rivalry between the national political parties. His drawings were made into wood engravings that were then printed in newspapers and popular magazines. In this cartoon, published in *Harper's Weekly*, April 1, 1882, Nast shows America welcoming all immigrants except Chinese.

Knights of Labor   Labor union founded in 1869 that included skilled and unskilled workers irrespective of race or gender.

The Knights reached their peak during the great campaign for a shorter workday. The organization grew from a few thousand in 1880 to nearly three-quarters of a million six years later. The Knights welcomed workers usually excluded by other unions. Nearly 3,000 women formed their own "ladies assemblies" or joined mixed locals. The Knights also organized African American workers—20,000 to 30,000 nationally—mainly in separate assemblies within the organization. Chinese workers, however, were barred from membership.

The Haymarket affair in Chicago, where the Knights were headquartered, virtually crushed the organization. Local employers' associations successfully pooled funds to rid their factories of troublesome organizers and announced that companies would no longer bargain with unions. The wage system had triumphed.

THE AMERICAN FEDERATION OF LABOR

The events of 1886 also signaled the rise of a very different kind of organization, the **American Federation of Labor (AFL)**. Unlike the Knights, the AFL accepted the wage system. Following a strategy of "pure and simple unionism," the AFL sought recognition of its union status to bargain with employers for better working conditions, higher wages, and shorter hours. In return, it offered compliant firms the benefit of amenable day-to-day relations with the most highly skilled wage earners. Only if companies refused to bargain in good faith would union members resort to strikes.

The new federation rapidly pushed ahead of the rival Knights by organizing craft workers. AFL president Samuel Gompers disregarded unskilled workers, racial minorities, and immigrants, believing they were impossible to organize and even unworthy of membership. He also believed in the "family wage," a wage paid to a male household head that would keep women and children comfortable

American Federation of Labor (AFL)
Union formed in 1886 that organized skilled workers along craft lines and emphasized a few workplace issues rather than a broad social program.

At the 1886 General Assembly of the Knights of Labor, which met in Richmond, Virginia, sixteen women attended as delegates. Elizabeth Rodgers, the first woman in Chicago to join the Knights and the first woman to serve as a master workman in a district assembly, attended with her two-week-old daughter. The convention established a Department of Women's Work and appointed Leonora M. Barry, a hosiery worker, as general investigator.

within the confines of domesticity. Women, Gompers insisted, did not belong in the factory, where they would serve only to lower wages.

Rank-and-file AFL members did not always share Gompers's opinions, and they often revived some of the best qualities of the Knights of Labor. They provided support to strikers, gathered votes for pro-labor political candidates, sponsored social activities, and published their own weekly newspapers.

Although the AFL represented only a small minority of working Americans—about 10 percent at the end of the century—local unions often played important roles in their communities. They may not have been able to slow the steady advance of mass production, which diminished the craft worker's autonomy and eliminated some of the most desirable jobs, but AFL members managed to make their presence felt. Local politicians courted their votes, and Labor Day, first celebrated in the 1880s, became a national holiday in 1894.

THE NEW SOUTH

Physically and financially devastated by the war, the South remained economically stagnant, its per capita wealth only 27 percent of that of the northeastern states. While a few urban centers moved very slowly into the era of modern industry, the countryside receded into greater isolation and poverty. The southern economy in general was held back by dependence on northern finance capital, continued reliance on cotton production, and the legacy of slavery.

AN INTERNAL COLONY

Northern investors secured huge concessions from southern state legislatures, including land, forest, and mineral rights and large tax exemptions. Exploiting the incentives, railroad companies laid more than 22,000 miles of new track, connecting the region to national markets and creating new cities. By 1890, a score of large railroad companies, centered mainly in New York, held more than half of all the track in the South.

Northerners also employed various means to protect their investments from southern competition. By the late 1870s, southern merchants, with help from foreign investors, had begun to run iron factories around Birmingham, Alabama. Southern iron production was soon encroaching on the northeastern market. To stave off this competition, Andrew Carnegie ordered the railroads to charge higher freight fees to Birmingham's iron producers. New York bankers later succeeded in expatriating Birmingham's profits through stock ownership in southern firms. After the turn of the century, U.S. Steel simply bought out the local merchants and took over much of Birmingham's production.

Beyond iron or steel and textiles, southern industry remained largely extractive and, like the South itself, rural. Turpentine and lumbering businesses pushed ever farther into diminishing pine forests, the sawmills and distilleries moving with them. Toward the end of the century, fruit canning and sugar refining flourished. For the most part, southern enterprises mainly produced raw materials for consumption or use in the North, thereby perpetuating the economic imbalance between the sections.

The governing role of capital investments from outside the region reinforced long-standing relationships. Even rapid industrialization—in iron, railroads, and textiles—did not carry the same consequences achieved in the North. Industrialization in the South reinforced, rather than diminished, the region's status as the nation's internal colony.

HOW DID the development of Southern industry affect the lives of African Americans living in the South?

myhistorylab
Review Summary

SOUTHERN LABOR

The advance of southern industry did little to improve the working lives of most African Americans, who made up more than one-third of the region's population. Although the majority continued to work in agriculture, large numbers found jobs in industries such as the railroad. In booming cities like Atlanta, they even gained skilled positions as bricklayers, carpenters, and painters. For the most part, however, African Americans were limited to unskilled, low-paying jobs. Nearly all African American women who earned wages did so as household workers; girls as young as ten worked as domestics or as nurses for white children.

Most trade unions refused membership to black workers. Locals of the all-white carpenters' union maintained a segregation policy so absolute that if too few members were available for a job, the union would send for out-of-town white workers rather than employ local members of the black carpenters' union. In an Atlanta mill in 1897, 1,400 white women operatives went on strike when the company proposed to hire two black spinners.

Wages throughout the South were low for both black and white workers. Southern textile workers' wages were barely half those of New Englanders. Black men earned at or below the poverty line of $300 per year, while black women rarely earned more than $120 and white women about $220 annually. The poorest paid workers were children, the mainstay of southern mill labor.

As industry expanded throughout the nation, so too did the number of children earning wages. This was especially so in the South. Traditions rooted in the agricultural economy reinforced the practice of using the labor of all family members, even the very young. Seasonal labor, such as picking crops or grinding sugarcane, put families on the move, making formal education all but impossible. Not until well into the twentieth century did compulsory school attendance laws effectively restrict child labor in the South.

A system of convict labor also thrived in the South. Bituminous coal mines and public work projects of all kinds, especially in remote areas, employed disciplinary methods and created living and working conditions reminiscent of slavery. African Americans constituted up to 90 percent of the convict workforce.

THE TRANSFORMATION OF PIEDMONT COMMUNITIES

The impact of modern industry was nowhere greater than in the Piedmont, the region extending from southern Virginia and the central Carolinas into northern Alabama and Georgia. After 1870, long-established farms and plantations gave way to railroad tracks, textile factories, numerous mill villages, and a few sizable cities. Once the South's backcountry, the Piedmont now surpassed New England in the production of yarn and cloth to stand first in the world.

Rural poverty and the appeal of a new life encouraged many farm families to strike out for a mill town. Those with the least access to land and credit—mainly widows and their children and single women—were the first to go into the mills. Then families sent their children. Some families worked in the mills on a seasonal basis, between planting and harvesting.

The processing of raw tobacco employed thousands of African American women, who sorted, stripped, stemmed, and hung tobacco leaves as part of the redrying process. After mechanization was introduced, white women took jobs as cigarette rollers, but black women kept the worst, most monotonous jobs in the tobacco factories. The women shown in this photograph are stemming tobacco in a Virginia factory while their white male supervisor oversees their labor.

But as the agricultural crisis deepened, more and more people abandoned the countryside entirely for what they called "public work."

A typical mill community was made up of rows of single-family houses, a small school, several churches, a company-owned store, and the home of the superintendent, who governed everyone's affairs. Millworkers frequently complained that they had no private life at all. A federal report published shortly after the turn of the century concluded that "all the affairs of the village and the conditions of living of all the people are regulated entirely by the mill company. Practically speaking, the company owns everything and controls everything, and to a large extent controls everybody in the mill village."

Mill superintendents also relied on schoolteachers and clergy to set the tone of community life. They hired and paid the salaries of Baptist and Methodist ministers to preach a faith encouraging workers to be thrifty, orderly, temperate, and hardworking. The schools, similarly subsidized by the company, reinforced the lesson of moral and social discipline required of industrial life and encouraged students to follow their parents into the mill. But it was mainly young children between six and eight years old who attended school. When more hands were needed in the mill, superintendents plucked out those youngsters and sent them to join their older brothers and sisters who were already at work.

THE INDUSTRIAL CITY

Before the Civil War, manufacturing had centered in the countryside, in new factory towns such as Lowell, Massachusetts, and Troy, New York. By the end of the nineteenth century, 90 percent of all manufacturing took place in cities. The metropolis stood at the center of the growing industrial economy, a magnet drawing raw material, capital, and labor, and a key distribution point for manufactured goods throughout the nation and worldwide. The industrial city became the home of nearly 20 million immigrants, mainly the so-called "new immigrants" from southern and eastern Europe, who hoped to escape famine, political upheaval, or religious persecution in their homelands or simply make a better life for themselves and their families.

POPULATING THE CITY

The population of cities grew at double the rate of the nation's population as a whole. In 1860, only sixteen cities had more than 50,000 residents. By 1890, one-third of all Americans were city dwellers. Eleven cities claimed more than 250,000 people (see Table 19.1).

TABLE 19.1

A Growing Urban Population

	1870	1880	1890	1900
U.S. population	35,558,000	50,156,000	62,947,000	75,995,000
Urban population	9,902,000	14,130,000	22,106,000	30,160,000
Percent urban	25.7	28.2	35.1	39.7
Percent rural	74.3	71.8	64.9	60.3

Note that during each decade, the U.S. population as a whole grew between 20 and 30 percent. Figures in the table have been rounded to the nearest thousand.

Robert G. Barrows, "Urbanizing America," in Charles W. Calhoun, ed., *The Gilded Age* (Wilmington DE, 1996), 93, 95.

WHAT CONTRIBUTED to the growing population of American cities?

myhistorylab

Review Summary

18–1
Charles Loring Brace, *"The Life of the Street Rats"* (1872)

CHAPTER 19

The nation's largest cities—New York, Chicago, Philadelphia, St. Louis, Boston, and Baltimore—achieved international fame for the size and diversity of their populations. Many of their new residents had migrated from rural communities within the United States. Between 1870 and 1910, an average of nearly 7,000 African Americans moved north each year, hoping to escape the poverty and oppression in the South and to find better-paying jobs. By the end of the century, nearly 80 percent of African Americans in the North lived in urban areas.

Immigrants and their children were the major source of urban population growth in the late nineteenth century. Most of those in the first wave of immigration, before the Civil War, had settled in the countryside. In contrast, in the last half of the nineteenth century, it was the industrial city that drew the so-called new immigrants, who came primarily from eastern and southern Europe. By the turn of the century, Chicago had more Germans than all but a few German cities and more Poles than most Polish cities; New York had more Italians than a handful of the largest Italian cities, and Boston had nearly as many Irish as Dublin. In almost every group except the Irish, men outnumbered women (see Map 19.2).

Like rural migrants, immigrants came to the American city to take advantage of the expanding opportunities for employment. Many intended to work hard, save money, and return to their families in the Old Country. In the 1880s, for example, nearly half of all Italian, Greek, and Serbian men returned to their native lands. Others could not return to their homelands or did not wish to. Jews, for instance, had emigrated to escape persecution in Russia and Russian-dominated Polish and Romanian lands.

Of all groups, Jews had the most experience with urban life. Forbidden to own land in most parts of Europe and boxed into *shtetls* (villages), Jews had also formed thriving urban communities in Vilna, Berlin, London, and Vienna. Many had worked in garment manufacturing, in London's East End, for example, and followed a path to American cities like New York, Rochester, Philadelphia, or Chicago where the needle trades flourished.

Other groups, the majority coming from rural parts of Europe, sought out their kinfolk in American cities, where they could most easily find housing and employment. Bohemians settled largely in Chicago, Pittsburgh, and Cleveland. Still other groups tended toward cities dominated by fishing, shoemaking, or even glassblowing, a craft carried directly from the Old Country. Italians, the most numerous among the new immigrants, settled mainly in northeastern cities, laying railroad track, excavating subways, and erecting buildings.

Resettlement in an American city did not necessarily mark the end of the immigrants' travels. Newcomers, both native-born and immigrant, moved frequently from one neighborhood to another and from one city to another. As manufacturing advanced outward from the city center, working populations followed. American cities experienced a total population turnover three or four times during each decade of the last half of the century.

THE URBAN LANDSCAPE

Faced with a population explosion and an unprecedented building boom, the cities encouraged the creation of many beautiful and useful structures, including commercial offices, sumptuous homes, and efficient public services. At the same time, cities did little to improve the conditions of the majority of the population, who worked in dingy factories and lived in crowded **tenements**. Open space decreased as American cities grew. City officials usually lacked any master plan, save the idea of endless expansion. Factories often occupied the best sites, typically near waterways, where goods could be easily transported and chemical wastes dumped.

QUICK REVIEW

Big Cities

◆ Cities grew at double the rate of the nation as a whole.

◆ Immigrants and their children were the major source of urban population growth.

◆ After the Civil War, most new immigrants settled in cities.

Tenements Four- to six-story residential dwellings, once common in New York, built on tiny lots without regard to providing ventilation or light.

MAP EXPLORATION

To explore an interactive version of this map, go to **http://www.prenhall.com/faraghertlc/map19.2**

MAP 19.2
Population of Foreign Birth by Region, 1880   European immigrants after the Civil War settled primarily in the industrial districts of the northern Midwest and parts of the Northeast. French Canadians continued to settle in Maine, Cubans in Florida, and Mexicans in the Southwest.

Clifford L. Lord and Elizabeth H. Lord, *Lord & Lord Historical Atlas of the United States* (New York: Holt, 1953).

WHY DID immigrants tend to settle in some regions and not in others?

Built after the Civil War, the tenement was designed to maximize the use of space. A typical tenement sat on a lot 25 by 100 feet and rose to five stories. There were four families on each floor, each with three rooms. By 1890, New York's Lower East Side packed more than 700 people per acre into back-to-back buildings, producing one of the highest population densities in the world.

The industrial city established a new style of commercial and civic architecture. Using fireproof materials, expanded foundations, and internal metal construction, the era's talented architects focused on the factory and office building. Concentrating as many offices as possible in the downtown areas, they fashioned hundreds of buildings from steel, sometimes decorating them with elaborate wrought-iron facades. The office building could rise seven, ten, even twenty stories high, and with the invention of the safety elevator, people and goods could easily be moved vertically.

Architects played a key role in the late nineteenth-century City Beautiful movement. Influenced by American wealth and its enhanced role in the global economy, they turned to the monumental or imperial style common in European cities, laying grand concrete boulevards at enormous public cost. New sports amphitheaters spread pride in the city's accomplishments. New schools, courthouses, capitol buildings, hospitals, museums, and huge new art galleries, museums, and concert halls promoted urban excitement as well as cultural uplift. The imperial style also increased congestion and noise, making the city a more desirable place to visit than to live.

Like the railroad, but on a smaller scale, streetcars and elevated railroads changed business dramatically, because they moved traffic of many different kinds—information, people, and goods—faster and farther than before. By 1895, more than 800 communities operated systems of electrically powered cars or trolleys. In 1902, New York opened its subway system, which would grow to become the largest in the nation.

THE CITY AND THE ENVIRONMENT

By making it possible for a great number of workers to live in communities distant from their place of employment, mass transportation allowed the metropolitan region to grow dramatically. By the end of the nineteenth century, suburban trains were bringing nearly 100,000 riders daily into the city of Chicago. Suburbs sprang up outside the major cities, offering many professional workers quiet residential retreats from the city's busy and increasingly polluted downtown.

Electric trolleys eliminated the tons of waste from horsecars that had for decades fouled city streets. But the new rail systems also increased congestion and created new safety hazards for pedestrians. During the 1890s, 600 people were killed each year by Chicago's trains. Elevated trains, designed to avoid these problems, placed entire communities under the shadow of noisy and rickety wooden platforms. Despite many technological advances, the quality of life in the nation's cities did not necessarily improve.

Modern water and sewer systems now constituted a hidden city of pipes and wires, mirroring the growth of the visible city above ground. These advances, which brought indoor plumbing to most homes, did not, however, eradicate serious environmental or health problems. Most cities continued to dump sewage into nearby bodies of water. Moreover, most municipal governments established separate clean-water systems through the use of reservoirs rather than outlawing upriver dumping by factories. Downriver communities began to complain about unendurable stench from the polluted rivers and streams.

The unrestricted burning of coal to fuel the railroads and to heat factories and homes after 1880 greatly intensified urban air pollution. Noise levels continued to rise in the most compacted living and industrial areas. Overcrowded conditions and inadequate sanitary facilities bred tuberculosis, smallpox, and scarlet fever, among other contagious diseases. Children's diseases like whooping cough and measles spread rapidly through poor neighborhoods. Only after the turn of the century, amid an intensive campaign against municipal corruption, did laws and administrative practices address the serious problems of public health (see Chapter 21).

18-10
United States Sanitary Commission, *Sketch of Its Purposes* (1864)

In his watercolor *The Bowery at Night*, painted in 1885, W. Louis Sonntag Jr. shows a New York City scene transformed by electric light. Electricity transformed the city in other ways as well, as seen in the electric streetcars and elevated railroad.

Meanwhile, the distance between the city and the countryside narrowed. Nearby rural lands not destined for private housing or commercial development became sites for water treatment and sewage plants, garbage dumps, and grave-yards—services essential to the city's growing population.

THE RISE OF CONSUMER SOCIETY

The growth of industry and the spread of cities promoted—and depended on—the consumption of mass-produced goods. During the final third of the nineteenth century, the standard of living climbed, although unevenly and erratically. Real wages (pay in relation to the cost of living) rose, fostering improvements in nutrition, clothing, and housing. Meanwhile, prices dropped. More and cheaper products came into the reach of all but the very poor. Food from the farms became more abundant and varied—grains for bread or beer; poultry, pork, and beef; fresh fruits and vegetables from California. Although many Americans continued to acknowledge the moral value of hard work, thrift, and self-sacrifice, the explosion of consumer goods and services promoted sweeping changes in behavior and beliefs, although in vastly and increasingly different ways.

"CONSPICUOUS CONSUMPTION"

Labeled the **"Gilded Age"** by humorist and social critic Mark Twain, the era follow-ing the Civil War favored the growth of a new business class that pursued both money and leisure and formed national networks to consolidate their power. Business lead-ers built diverse stock portfolios and often served simultaneously on the boards of several corporations. Similarly, they intertwined their interests by joining the same religious, charitable, athletic, and professional societies. Their wives and children vaca-tioned together in the sumptuous new seashore and mountain resorts, while they themselves made deals in the exclusive social clubs and on the golf links of subur-ban country clubs. Just as Dun and Bradstreet ranked the leading corporations, the Social Register identified the 500 families that controlled most of the nation's wealth.

According to economist and social critic Thorstein Veblen, the rich had cre-ated a new style of **"conspicuous consumption."** The Chicago mansion of real estate tycoon Potter Palmer, for example, was constructed without exterior door-knobs. Not only could no one enter uninvited, but a visitor's calling card suppos-edly passed through the hands of twenty-seven servants before admittance was allowed. The women who oversaw these elaborate households served as measures of their husbands' status, according to Veblen, by adorning themselves in jewels, furs, and dresses of the latest Paris design.

Toward the end of the century, the wealthy added a dramatic public dimension to the "high life." New York's Waldorf-Astoria hotel, which opened in 1897, incor-porated the grandeur of European royalty but with an important difference. Because rich Americans wanted to be watched, the elegantly appointed corridors and restau-rants were visible to the public through huge windows. The New York rich also estab-lished a unique custom to welcome the New Year: they opened wide the curtains of their Fifth Avenue mansions so that passersby could marvel at the elegant decor.

The wealthy became the leading patrons of the arts as well as the chief pro-curers of art treasures from Europe and Asia. They provided the bulk of funds for the new symphonies, operas, and ballet companies, which soon rivaled those of Continental Europe. Nearly all major museums and art galleries, including the Boston Museum of Fine Arts, the Philadelphia Museum of Art, the Art Institute of Chicago, and the Metropolitan Museum of Art in New York, were founded dur-ing the last decades of the nineteenth century.

WHAT ACCOUNTS for the rise of a consumer society and how did various groups participate in its development?

myhistorylab
Review Summary

 18–3
The Gilded Age (1880)

 18–6
Edward Bellamy, from *Looking Backward* (1888)

Gilded Age Term applied to late nineteenth-century America that refers to the shallow display and worship of wealth characteristic of that period.

Conspicuous consumption Highly visible displays of wealth and consumption.

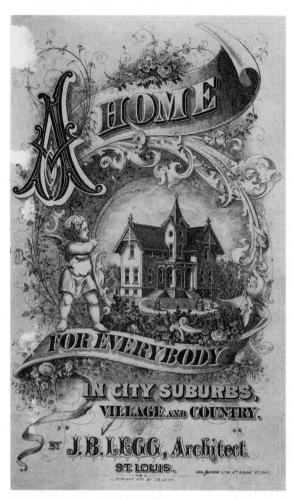

Taken from J. B. Legg's architecture book, this page illustrates the ideal suburban home. His book, published in 1876, was aimed at the prospering middle class.

SELF-IMPROVEMENT AND THE MIDDLE CLASS

A new middle class, very different from its predecessor, formed during the last half of the century. The older middle class comprised the owners or superintendents of small businesses, doctors, lawyers, teachers, and ministers and their families. The new middle class included these professionals but also the growing number of salaried employees—the managers, technicians, clerks, and engineers who worked in the complex web of corporations and government. Long hours of labor earned their families a modest status and sufficient income to live securely in style and comfort.

By the end of the century, many middle-class families were nestled in suburban retreats far from the noise, filth, and dangers of the city. This peaceful domestic setting, with its manicured lawns and well-placed shrubs, afforded both privacy and rejuvenation as well as the separation of business from leisure and the breadwinner from his family for most of the day. Assisted by modern transportation systems, men often traveled one to two hours each day, five or six days a week, to their city offices and back again. Women and children stayed behind.

Middle-class women devoted a large part of their day to care of the home. They frequently employed one or two servants but relied increasingly on the many new appliances to get their work done. Improvements in the kitchen stove, such as the conversion from wood fuel to gas, saved a lot of time. Yet, simultaneously, with the widespread circulation of cookbooks and recipes in newspapers and magazines, as well as the availability of new foods, the preparation of meals became more complex and time-consuming. New devices such as the eggbeater speeded some familiar tasks, but the era's fancy culinary practices offset any gains in saving time. Similarly, the new carpet sweepers surpassed the broom in efficiency, but the fashionable high-napped carpeting demanded more care. Thus, rather than diminishing with technological innovation, household work expanded to fill the time available.

Almost exclusively white, Anglo-Saxon, and Protestant, the new middle class embraced "culture" not for purposes of conspicuous consumption but as a means of self-improvement. Whole families visited the new museums and art galleries. The middle class also provided the bulk of patrons for the new public libraries.

Middle-class families applied the same standards to their leisure activities. What one sporting-goods entrepreneur rightly called the "gospel of exercise" involved men and women in calisthenics and outdoor activities, not so much for pleasure as for physical and mental discipline. Hiking was a favorite among both men and women and required entirely new outfits: for women, loose upper garments and skirts short enough to prevent dragging; for men, rugged outerwear and jaunty hats. Soon men and women began camping out, with almost enough amenities to recreate a middle-class home in the woods.

Leisure became the special province of middle-class childhood. Removed from factories and shops and freed from many domestic chores, children enjoyed creative play and physical activity. The toy market boomed, and lower printing prices helped children's literature flourish. Uplifting classics such as *Little Women* and *Black Beauty* were popular.

LIFE IN THE STREETS

Immigrants often weighed the material abundance they found in the United States against their memories of the Old Country. One could "live better" here, but only by working much harder. Embittered German immigrants called their new land *Malhuerica*, "misfortune"; Jews called it *Ama Reka*, Hebrew for "without soul"; and Slavs referred to it as *Dollaryka*.

Many newcomers, having little choice about their place of residence, concentrated in urban districts marked off by racial or ethnic lines. In San Francisco, city ordinances prevented Chinese from operating laundries in most of the city's neighborhoods, and the city's schools excluded their children. In the 1880s, Chinese San Franciscans, representing 10 percent of the city's population, crowded into a dozen blocks of restaurants, shops, and small factories known as Chinatown. In Los Angeles and San Antonio, Mexicans lived in distinctive barrios. In most cities, African American families were similarly compelled to remain in the dingiest, most crime ridden, and dangerous sections of town.

The working-class home did not necessarily ensure privacy or offer protection from the dangers of the outside world. In the tenements, families often shared their rooms with other families or paying boarders. During the summer heat, adults, children, and boarders alike competed for a sleeping place on the fire escape or roof, and all year round, noise resounded through paper-thin walls.

Whether it was a small cottage or a tenement flat, the working-class home involved women and children in routines of household labor without the aid of new mechanical devices. In addition to cooking and cleaning, women used their cramped domestic space for work that provided a small income. They gathered their children—and their husbands after a hard day's labor—to sew garments, wrap cigars, string beads, or paint vases for a contractor who paid them by the piece. And they cooked and cleaned for the boarders whose rent supplemented the family income.

Despite working people's slim resources, their combined buying power created new and important markets for consumer goods. Often they bought shoddy replicas of products sold to the middle class. Several leading clothing manufacturers specialized in inexpensive ready-to-wear items, usually copied from patterns designed for wealthier consumers but constructed hastily from flimsy materials.

The close quarters of the urban neighborhood allowed immigrants to preserve many Old World customs. In immigrant communities such as Chicago's German North Side, Pittsburgh's Poletown, New York's Lower East Side, or San Francisco's Chinatown, people usually spoke their native language while visiting friends and relatives. No organization was as important as the fraternal society, which sponsored social clubs and provided insurance benefits. Social organizations, known as *huiguan*, were especially important in preserving clan and dialect among the largely male unmarried population of Chinese San Francisco. Immigrants also re-created Old World religious institutions such as the temple, church, or synagogue, or secular institutions such as German family-style saloons or Russian Jewish tearooms. Chinese theaters, in inexpensive daily and nightly performances, presented dramas depicting historical events or explicating moral teachings and thereby preserved much of Chinese native culture. Immigrants also replicated their native cuisine and married, baptized children, and buried their dead according to Old World customs.

The intersection of Orchard and Hester Streets on New York's Lower East Side, photographed ca. 1905. Unlike the middle classes, who worked and played hidden away in offices and private homes, the Jewish lower-class immigrants who lived and worked in this neighborhood spent the greater part of their lives on the streets.

In the cosmopolitan cities, immigrants, by being innovative entrepreneurs as well as the best customers, helped to shape the emerging popular culture. German immigrants, for example, created Tin Pan Alley, the center of the popular music industry. They also became the first promoters of ragtime, which found its way north from Storyville, the red-light district of New Orleans. Created by African American and Creole bands, ragtime captivated those teenage offspring of immigrants who rushed to the new dance halls.

When developers realized that "wholesome fun" for the masses could pay better than upper-class leisure or lower-class vice, in 1895 they decided to transform Coney Island into a magnificent seaside park filled with ingenious amusements such as water slides, mechanized horse races, carousels, roller coasters, and fun houses. On the rides or at the nearby beach, young men and women could easily meet apart from their parents, cast off their inhibitions, and enjoy a hug or kiss. At Coney Island or at Riverview, Chicago's oldest amusement park, located on the city's North Side, millions of working-class people enjoyed cheap thrills that offset the hardships of their working lives.

Cultures in Conflict, Culture in Common

WHAT ROLE did public spaces play in late nineteenth-century popular culture?

myhistorylab
Review Summary

The new commercial entertainments gave Americans from various backgrounds more in common than they would otherwise have had. On New York's Lower East Side, for instance, theater blossomed with dramas that Broadway would adopt years later, while children dreamed of going "uptown" where the popular songs they heard on the streets were transcribed onto sheet music and sold in stores throughout the city. Even so, just as the changes in production fostered conflict in the forms of strikes and workers' protests, so too did the accompanying changes in the daily life of the community. Competing claims to the resources of the new urban, industrial society, such as public schools and urban parks, became more intense as the century moved to a close.

EDUCATION

Business and civic leaders realized that the welfare of society now depended on an educated population, one possessing the skills and knowledge required to keep both industry and government running. In the last three decades of the nineteenth century, the idea of universal free schooling, at least for white children, took hold.

Public high schools, which were rare before the Civil War, increased in number, from 160 in 1870 to 6,000 by the end of the century. In Chicago alone, average daily attendance multiplied sixfold. Despite this spectacular growth, which was concentrated in urban industrial areas, as late as 1890 only 4 percent of children between the ages of fourteen and seventeen were enrolled in school, the majority of them girls planning to become teachers or office workers (See Figure 19.1) Most high schools continued to serve mainly the middle class. The expected benefits of this kind of a high school education rarely outweighed the immediate needs of working-class families who depended on their children's wages.

Higher education also expanded along several lines. Agricultural colleges formed earlier in the century developed into institutes of technology and took their places alongside the prestigious liberal arts colleges. To extend learning to the "industrial classes," Representative Justin Morrill (R., Vermont) sponsored the Morrill Federal Land Grant Act of 1862, which funded a system of state colleges and universities for teaching agriculture and mechanics "without excluding other scientific and classic studies." Still, as the overall number of colleges and universities grew from 563 in 1870 to nearly 1,000 by 1910, only 3 percent of the college-age population took advantage of these new opportunities.

This expansion benefited women, who previously had had little access to higher education. After the Civil War, a number of women's colleges were founded, beginning in 1865 with Vassar, which set the academic standard for the remainder of the century. Smith and Wellesley followed in 1875, Bryn Mawr in 1885. By the end of the century, 125 women's colleges offered a first-rate education comparable to that given to men at Harvard, Yale, or Princeton. Meanwhile, coeducation grew at an even faster rate; by 1890, 47 percent of the nation's colleges and universities admitted women. The proportion of women college students changed dramatically. Women constituted 21 percent of undergraduate enrollments in 1870, 32 percent in 1880, and 40 percent in 1910.

An even greater number of women enrolled in vocational courses. Normal schools, which offered one- or two-year programs for women who planned to become elementary school teachers, developed a collegiate character after the Civil War and had become accredited state teachers' colleges by the end of the century. Other institutions, many founded by middle-class philanthropists, also prepared women for vocations. Founded in 1877, the **Women's Educational and Industrial Union** offered a multitude of classes to Boston's wage-earning women, ranging from elementary French and German to drawing, watercolor, and oil and china paintings; to dressmaking and millinery, stenography and typing; as well as crafts less familiar to women, such as upholstering, cabinetmaking, and carpentry.

The leaders of the business community had also begun to promote manual training for working-class and immigrant boys. Trade unionists often opposed this development, preferring their own methods of apprenticeship to training programs they could not control. But local associations of merchants and manufacturers lobbied hard for "industrial education" and raised funds to supplement the public school budget. By 1895, all elementary and high schools in Chicago offered courses that trained boys for future jobs in industry and business.

The expansion of education did not benefit all Americans or benefit them all in the same way. Because African Americans were often excluded from colleges attended by white students, special colleges were founded shortly after the Civil War. All-black Atlanta and Fisk Universities both soon offered rigorous curricula in the liberal arts. Other institutions, such as Hampton, founded in 1868, specialized in vocational training, mainly in manual trades. Educator Booker T. Washington encouraged African Americans to resist "the craze for Greek and Latin learning" and to strive for practical instruction. In 1881, he founded the Tuskegee Institute in Alabama to provide industrial education and moral uplift. Black colleges, including Tuskegee, trained so many teachers that by the century's end the majority of black schools were staffed by African Americans.

LEISURE AND PUBLIC SPACE

Most large cities set aside open land for leisure-time use by residents. New York's Central Park opened for ice-skating in 1858, providing a model for urban park systems across the United States. These parks were rolling expanses, cut across by

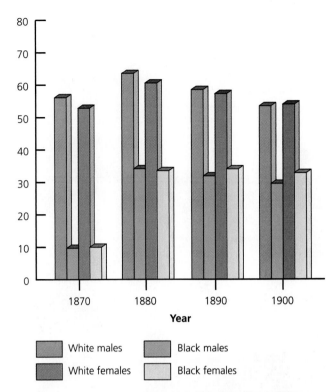

Figure 19.1 School Enrollment of 5- to 19-Year-Olds, 1870–1900
In the final decades of the nineteenth century, elementary and high school enrollments grew across the board but especially so for children of color and for girls.

U.S. Department of Commerce, Bureau of the Census, *Historical Statistics of the United States, Colonial Times to 1970.* U.S. Department of Education, Office of Educational Research and Improvement.

Women's Educational and Industrial Union Boston organization offering classes to wage-earning women.

George Washington Carver (1864–1943), who had been born in slavery, had been invited by Booker T. Washington to direct agricultural research at the Tuskegee Institute in Alabama. A leader in development of agriculture in the New South, Carver promoted crop diversification to rejuvenate soil that was depleted by the continuous planting of cotton and encouraged the cultivation of alternative, high-protein crops such as peanuts and soybeans.

18–4
Richard K. Fox, from *Coney Island Frolics* (1883)

streams and pathways and footbridges and set off by groves of trees, ornamental shrubs, and neat flower gardens. According to the designers' vision, the urban middle class might find here a respite from the stresses of modern life.

The working classes had their own ideas about the use of parks and open land in their communities. Trapped in over-crowded tenements or congested neighborhoods, they wanted space for sports, picnics, and lovers' trysts. Young people openly defied ordinances that prohibited play on the grassy knolls, while their elders routinely voted against municipal bonds that did not include funds for more recreational space. Immigrant ward representatives on the Pittsburgh City Council, for instance, argued that band shells for classical music meant little to their constituents, while spaces suitable for sports meant much.

Toward the end of the century, many park administrators relaxed the rules and expanded the range of permitted activities. By this time, large numbers of the middle class had become sports enthusiasts and pressured municipal governments to turn meadowlands into tennis courts and golfing greens. In the 1890s, bicycling brought many women into the parks. Still, not all city residents enjoyed these facilities. Officials in St. Louis, for example, barred African Americans from the city's grand Forest Park and set aside the smaller Tandy Park for their use. After challenging this policy in court, African Americans won a few concessions, such as the right to picnic at any time in Forest Park and to use the golf course on Monday mornings.

NATIONAL PASTIMES

Toward the end of the century, the younger members of the urban middle class had begun to find common ground in lower-class pastimes, especially ragtime music. Introduced to many Northerners by the African American composer Scott Joplin at the Chicago World's Fair of 1893, "rag" quickly became the staple of entertainment in the new cabarets and nightclubs. Middle-class urban dwellers began to seek out ragtime bands and congregated in nightclubs and even on the rooftops of posh hotels to listen and dance and even to drink.

Vaudeville, the most popular form of commercial entertainment since the 1880s, also bridged middle- and working-class tastes. Drawing on a variety-show tradition of singers, dancers, comedians, jugglers, and acrobats who had entertained Americans since colonial days, "vaude" became a big business that made ethnic and racial stereotypes and the daily frustrations of city life into major topics of amusement.

Sports, however, outdistanced all other commercial entertainments in appealing to all kinds of fans and managing to create a sense of national community. Baseball clubs formed in many cities, and shortly after the Civil War traveling teams with regular schedules made baseball a professional sport. The formation of the National League in 1876 encouraged other spectator sports, but for generations baseball remained the most popular.

Rowdy behavior gave the game a working-class ambience. Team owners, themselves often proprietors of local breweries, counted heavily on beer sales in the parks. Having to contend with hundreds of drunken fans, officials maintained order only with great difficulty. To attract more subdued middle-class fans, the National League raised admission prices, banned the sale of alcohol, and observed Sunday blue laws. Catering to a working-class audience, the American Association kept the price of admission low, sold liquor, and played ball on Sunday.

Baseball, like many other sports, soon became incorporated into the larger business economy. In Chicago, local merchants, such as Marshall Field, supported teams, and by the end of the 1860s there were more than fifty company-sponsored teams playing in the local leagues. By 1870, a Chicago Board of Trade team emerged as the city's first professional club, the White Stockings. Capitalized as a joint stock company, the White Stockings soon succeeded in recruiting a star pitcher from the Boston Red Stockings, Albert Spalding, who eventually became manager and then president of the team.

Spalding tightened the rules of participation in the sport. In 1879, he dictated the "reserve clause," which prevented players from negotiating a better deal and leaving the team that originally signed them. He encouraged his player-manager "Cap" Anson to forbid the White Stockings from playing against any team with an African American member. The firing of Moses "Fleet" Walker, an African American, from the Cincinnati Red Stockings in 1884 marked the first time the color line had been drawn in a major professional sport. Effectively excluded, African Americans organized their own traveling teams. In the 1920s, they formed the Negro Leagues, which produced some of the nation's finest ball players.

Players occasionally organized to regain control over their sport. They frequently complained about low wages and arbitrary rules, and like the Knights of Labor in the 1880s, they formed their own league, the Brotherhood of Professional Base Ball Players, with profits divided between participants and investors. This effort failed, partly because fans would not desert the established leagues, but mostly because successful baseball franchises demanded large quantities of capital. American sports had become big business.

As attendance continued to grow, the enthusiasm for baseball straddled major social divisions, bringing together Americans of many backgrounds, if only on a limited basis. By the end of the century, no section of the daily newspaper drew more readers than the sports pages. Although it interested relatively few women, sports news riveted the attention of men from all social classes. Loyalty to the "home team" helped to create an urban identity, while individual players became national heroes.

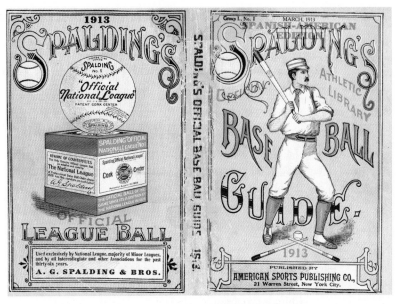

Spalding's Base Ball Guide offered fans nothing less than "the official records of America's national game." The first issue came out in 1877 and by 1889 the publication grew to 180 pages packed with statistics, editorials by players, photographs, and overall assessments of teams in the major and minor leagues.

CONCLUSION

By the end of the nineteenth century, industry and the growing cities had opened a new world for Americans. Fresh from Europe or from the native countryside, ordinary urban dwellers struggled to form communities of fellow newcomers through both work and leisure, in the factory, the neighborhood, the ballpark, and the public school. Meanwhile, their "betters," the wealthy and the new middle class, made and executed the decisions of industry and marketing, established the era's grand civic institutions, and set the tone for high fashion and art. Rich and poor alike shared many aspects of the new order. Yet inequality not only persisted but also increased and prompted new antagonisms.

The Haymarket tragedy highlighted the often strained relationships between Chicago's immigrant working population and civic leaders, precipitating violence, which included the public hanging of four of the eight men brought to trial,

CHRONOLOGY

1862	Morrill Act authorizes "land-grant" colleges
1869	Knights of Labor founded
1870	Standard Oil founded
1873	Financial panic brings severe depression
1876	Baseball's National League founded
	Alexander Graham Bell patents the telephone
1879	Thomas Edison invents the incandescent bulb
	Depression ends
1881	Tuskegee Institute founded
1882	Peak of immigration to the United States (1.2 million) in the nineteenth century
	Chinese Exclusion Act passed
	Standard Oil Trust founded

1883	William Graham Sumner published the social Darwinist classic *What Social Classes Owe to Each Other*
1886	Campaigns for eight-hour workday peak
	Haymarket riot and massacre discredit the Knights of Labor
	American Federation of Labor founded
1889	Andrew Carnegie's *The Gospel of Wealth* recommends honesty and fair dealing
1890	Sherman Antitrust Act passed
1893	Stock market panic precipitates severe depression
1895	Coney Island opens
1901	U.S. Steel Corporation formed

including August Spies. Although the new governor of Illinois, Peter Altgeld, pardoned the three who had their sentences commuted to life in prison, his attempt at amelioration did not signal a shift in the political climate. In the 1890s, hopes for a peaceful reconciliation of these tensions had worn thin, and the lure of overseas empire appeared as one of the few goals that held together a suffering and divided nation.

REVIEW QUESTIONS

1. Discuss the sources of economic growth in the decades after the Civil War. Historians often refer to this period as the era of the "second industrial revolution." Do you agree with this description?

2. Describe the impact of new technologies and new forms of production on the routines of industrial workers. How did these changes affect African American and women workers in particular? What role did trade unions play in this process?

3. Discuss the role of northern capital in the development of the New South. How did the rise of industry affect the lives of rural Southerners? Analyze these changes from the point of view of African Americans.

4. How did urban life change during the Gilded Age? How did economic development affect residential patterns? How did the middle class aspire to live during the Gilded Age? How did their lifestyles compare with those of working-class urbanites?

5. How did the American educational system change to prepare children for their adult roles in the new industrial economy?

6. How did the rise of organized sports and commercial amusements reflect and shape social divisions at the end of the century? Which groups were affected most (or least) by new leisure activities?

KEY TERMS

American Federation of Labor (AFL) (p. 508)

Chinese Exclusion Act (p. 506)

Conspicuous consumption (p. 515)

Gilded Age (p. 515)

Gospel of wealth (p. 503)

Horizontal combination (p. 503)

Knights of Labor (p. 507)

Tenements (p. 512)

Vertical integration (p. 503)

Women's Educational and Industrial Union (p. 519)

myhistorylab
Flashcard Review

RECOMMENDED READING

Sarah Deutsch, *Women and the City: Gender, Space, and Power in Boston, 1870–1940* (2000). A close study of women's struggle to define the shape of the modern city and to ease the oppressive quality of spacial divisions along lines of gender, race, and class. Deutsch illustrates the efforts of women to exert their own principles of "moral geography" in shaping Boston's urban landscape.

Rebecca Edwards, *New Spirits: Americans in the Gilded Age, 1865–1905* (2006). A synthesis of recent scholarship with a thematic arrangement that takes the shape of an engaging essay. Edwards provides regional coverage and links domestic events—political, cultural, and social—to overseas expansion.

James Green, *Death in the Haymarket* (2006). Examines the Haymarket event within the context of changing class relations in Chicago and explores its significance as the first act of bombing for political purposes.

Tera W. Hunter, *To 'Joy My Freedom: Southern Black Women's Lives and Labors after the Civil War* (1997). A careful study of African American working women in the New South city of Atlanta. Hunter covers their various occupations in the modern urban economy without sacrificing attention to their pursuits of pleasure in the emerging world of mass entertainments and leisure.

Susan Strasser, *Satisfaction Guaranteed: The Making of the American Mass Market* (1989). A clear and concise explanation of marketing and distribution during the rise of consumer society. Illustrated with examples of early advertising.

Alan Trachtenberg, *The Incorporation of America: Culture and Society in the Gilded Age*, Twenty-Fifth Anniversary ed. (2007). One of the best and most readable overviews of the post–Civil War era. Trachtenberg devotes great care to describing the rise of the corporation to the defining institution of national life and the reorientation of culture to reflect the new middle classes employed by the corporation.

For study resources for this chapter, go to **www.myhistorylab.com** and choose *Out of Many, Teaching and Learning Classroom Edition.* You will find a wealth of study and review material for this chapter, including pretests and posttests, customized study plan, key-term review flash cards, interactive map and document activities, and documents for analysis.

*Dear Father, In the 5th, 8th, and 19th Wards . . .
the negroes were driven away from the polls, beaten
and wounded . . . No colored votes were polled in
those precincts after twelve o'clock.*
—William Taft, October 22, 1894

Destruction of the battleship Maine in Havana harbor.

20

DEMOCRACY AND EMPIRE
1870–1900

WHAT FACTORS contributed to the growth of government in the late nineteenth century?

HOW AND why did workers and farmers organize to participate in politics during this era?

WHAT CRISES of the 1890s paved the way to political reform?

IN WHAT ways did the election of 1896 represent a turning point in U.S. political history?

HOW DID proponents of imperialism justify colonization?

WHAT CRITIQUES of empire were put forward in the years after the Spanish-American War?

AMERICAN COMMUNITIES
The Annexation of Hawai'i

ON JANUARY 17, 1891, LILI'UOKALANI SUCCEEDED HER BROTHER, KING Kalakaua, to become the queen of Hawai'i. Raised a Christian and fluent in English, the fifty-two-year-old monarch was nevertheless intensely loyal to the Hawaiian people and to their language and customs. This allegiance—and her strong opposition to a movement to annex Hawai'i to the United States—brought her downfall. On January 17, 1893, the queen was deposed in a plot carried out by an American diplomat and his co-conspirators.

This event followed more than a half century of intense economic and diplomatic maneuvering by the United States and other nations. Both American and British missionaries, who had arrived in the 1820s to convert Hawaiians to Christianity, had bought up huge parcels of land, and they and their children—known as the *haole* to native Hawaiians—had grown into a large and powerful community of planters. The missionaries in turn encouraged American businesses to buy into the sugar plantations, and by 1875 U.S. corporations dominated the sugar trade. Within a year Hawaiian sugar was entering the United States duty free. Hawai'i was beginning to appear, in the opinion of Secretary of State James G. Blaine, to be "an outlying district of the state of California," and he pushed for formal annexation.

In 1888 American planters forced on the weak King Kalakaua a new constitution that severely limited his power and established wealth and property qualifications for voting. This so-called Bayonet Constitution, because it implied the use of U.S. arms to implement it, allowed noncitizens, Europeans as well as Americans, to vote but denied the right of suffrage to poor native Hawaiians and the Chinese and Japanese who had come to work in the sugar fields.

In the name of democracy, the haole planters had secured a constitutional government that was closely allied to their economic interests—until King Kalakaua died in 1891. After ascending to the throne, Queen Lili'uokalani struck back. She decided she must empower native Hawaiians and limit the political influence of the haole elite and noncitizens.

The U.S.-led annexation forces first denounced the queen for attempting to abrogate the Bayonet Constitution and then welcomed Blaine's decision to send in U.S. troops to protect American lives and property. With no shots fired or documents signed, Lili'uokalani was deposed and a new provisional government installed. Sanford B. Dole, Honolulu-born son of Protestant missionaries, stepped in as the president of the new provisional government of Hawai'i, now a protectorate of the United States.

Lili'uokalani immediately protested to President Grover Cleveland, explaining that she had yielded "to the superior force of the United States of America" only to avoid a serious armed confrontation and the loss of life. She called on President Cleveland to recognize her authority as "the constitutional sovereign of the Hawaiian Islands" and to reinstate her as queen. After investigating the situation, Cleveland agreed and ordered Lili'uokalani's reinstatement as queen. Ironically, Dole, who had been a major force for annexation, countered by refusing to recognize the right of the U.S. president "to interfere in our domestic affairs." On July 3, 1894, he proclaimed Hawai'i an independent republic, with himself retaining the office of president.

After Lili'uokalani's supporters attempted an unsuccessful military uprising in 1895, the deposed queen was arrested, tried by a military tribunal, and convicted of misprision of treason (having knowledge of treason but not informing the authorities).

President Cleveland later declared privately that he was "ashamed of the whole affair" and stubbornly refused to listen to arguments for annexation. But he was powerless to stop the process before William McKinley succeeded him as president in 1896. Although more than a hundred members of Congress voted against annexation, an improper joint resolution passed to annex Hawai'i. In 1900, at McKinley's urging, Hawai'i became a territory. The people of Hawai'i were never consulted about this momentous change in their national identity.

The path to empire was paved with major changes in government and the party system. As the 1890s culminated in the acquisition of new territories, it also witnessed a decisive realignment of the party system. Voters not only changed affiliations that had been in place since the Civil War but also waged significant challenges to the two-party system at the local, regional, and national levels. While Queen Lili'uokalani was trying to regain control of her government, a mass political movement was forming in the United States to revive the nation's own democratic impulse.

Oahu

TOWARD A NATIONAL GOVERNING CLASS

The basic structure of government changed dramatically in the last quarter of the nineteenth century. Mirroring the fast-growing economy, public administration expanded at all levels—municipal, county, state, and federal—and took on greater responsibility for regulating society, especially market and property relations. Growing numbers of citizens for the first time looked to the government, from the local level upward, for public education, military veterans' pensions, and other social services. The leaders of the business community looked just as eagerly, and with far more influence, for protection of their property and sometimes for personal gain.

Reformers mobilized to rein in corruption and to promote both efficiency and professionalism in the multiplying structures of government. Meanwhile, some notable politicians acted to benefit directly, competing with one another for control of the new mechanisms of power. A lot was at stake.

THE GROWTH OF GOVERNMENT

Before the Civil War, local governments attended mainly to the promotion and regulation of trade and relied on private enterprise to supply vital services such as fire protection and water supplies. Cities gradually introduced professional police and firefighting forces and began to finance expanding school systems, public libraries, roads, and parks, an expansion requiring huge increases in local taxation. State governments grew in tandem, consolidating oversight of banking, transportation systems such as the railroads, and major enterprises such as the construction of dams and canals. By the end of the nineteenth century, city halls and state capitols had become beehives of activity.

At the national level, mobilization for the Civil War and Reconstruction had demanded an unprecedented degree of resources and their coordination, as both revenues and administrative bureaucracy grew quickly. At the end of Reconstruction, various aspects of federal government were trimmed at Congressional order, and the army was reduced to a fraction of its swollen size. Despite these particular reductions, the federal government as a whole continued to expand under the weight of new tasks and responsibilities.

The modern apparatus of departments, bureaus, and cabinets took shape amid this upswing. The Department of the Interior, created in 1849, grew into the largest and most important federal office other than the Post Office. It consisted of some twenty agencies, including the Bureau of Indian Affairs and the U.S. Geological Survey. Through its authority, the federal government was the chief landowner of all the West. The Department of the Treasury, responsible for collecting federal taxes and customs as well as printing money and stamps, quadrupled its own size from 1873 to 1900, to nearly 25,000 employees.

Regulatory agencies sprung up: foremost among them was the **Interstate Commerce Commission (ICC)**. The ICC was created in 1887 to bring order to the growing patchwork of state laws concerning railroads. The five-member commission appointed by the president approved freight and passenger rates set by the railroads. The ICC remained weak in the period, its rate-setting policies usually voided by the Supreme Court. But ICC commissioners could take public testimony on possible violations, examine company records, and generally oversee enforcement of the law. This set a precedent for future regulation of trade as well as for positive government, making rules for business while superseding state laws with federal power—that is, for the intervention of the federal government into the affairs of private enterprise.

WHAT FACTORS contributed to the growth of government in the late nineteenth century?

myhistorylab
Review Summary

IMAGE KEY
for pages 524–525

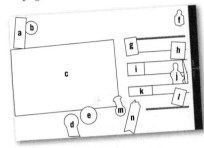

a. 1892 Benjamin Harrison presidential campaign ribbon.
b. Susan B. Anthony medal for the New York State Suffrage Assn. Convention.
c. Destruction of the battleship Maine in Havana harbor.
d,e. Campaign buttons for William McKinley, 1896.
f. A Benjamin Harrison presidential campaign souvenir.
g. Madison Square Garden during the Democratic National Convention of 1888.
h. A poster of Grange artists, from *Kingfisher Reformer*, May 3, 1894.
i. Coxey's Army marching with a band.
j. William Jennings Bryan at the 1896 Democratic Convention.
k. Chinese refugee women studying with a Protestant missionary.
l. An 1898 American magazine cover honoring the U.S.A.'s victory in the Spanish-American War.
m,n. Campaign paraphernalia.

Interstate Commerce Commission (ICC) The 1887 law that expanded federal power over business by prohibiting pooling and discriminatory rates by railroads and establishing the first federal regulatory agency, the Interstate Commerce Commission.

THE MACHINERY OF POLITICS

Only gradually did Republicans and Democrats adapt to the demands of government expansion. The Republican Party continued to run on its Civil War record, pointing to its achievements in reuniting the nation and in passing new reform legislation. Democrats, by contrast, sought to reduce the influence of the federal government, slash expenditures, repeal legislation, and protect states' rights. While Republicans held on to their longtime constituencies, Democrats gathered support from southern white voters and immigrants newly naturalized in the North. But neither party commanded a clear majority of votes until the century drew to a close.

Presidents in the last quarter of the century customarily yielded power to Congress and the state legislatures. Democrats usually held a majority in the House and Republicans a majority in the Senate. With neither party sufficiently strong to govern effectively, Congress passed little legislation before 1890.

One major political issue that separated the two parties was the tariff. Manufacturing regions, especially the Northeast, favored a protective policy, while the southern and western agricultural regions opposed high tariffs as unfair to farmers and ranchers who had to pay the steep fees on imported necessities. Democrats, with a stronghold among southern voters, argued for sharp reductions in the tariff as a way to save the rural economy and to give a boost to workers. Republicans, who represented mainly business interests, raised tariffs to new levels on a wide array of goods during the Civil War and retained high tariffs as long as they held power. Despite the importance of the tariff in setting apart Republicans and Democrats, the two political parties operated essentially as state or local organizations.

By the 1870s partisan politics had become a full-time occupation, with local officials usually running for office every two years. "We work through one campaign," quipped one candidate, "take a bath and start in on the next." Election paraphernalia—leaflets or pamphlets, banners, hats, flags, buttons, inscribed playing cards, or clay pipes featuring a likeness of a candidate's face or the party symbol—became a major expense for both parties. And voters did turn out. During the last quarter of the century, participation in presidential elections peaked at nearly 80 percent of those eligible to vote.

19–10
William T. Riordon, *Plunkitt of Tammany Hall* (1905)

19–13
George Washington Plunkitt, *Honest Graft* (1905)

The rising costs of maintaining local organizations and orchestrating mammoth campaigns drove party leaders to seek ever-larger sources of revenue. Winners often seized and added to the "spoils" of office through an elaborate system of payoffs and patronage. Legislators who supported government subsidies for railroad corporations, for instance, commonly received stock in return and sometimes cash bribes. At the time, few politicians or business leaders regarded these practices as unethical.

At the local level, where a combination of ethnicity, race, and religion determined party loyalty, powerful bosses and political machines dominated both parties. Democrats William Marcy Tweed of New York's powerful political organization, Tammany Hall, and Michael "Hinky Dink" Kenna of Chicago, specialized in giving municipal jobs to loyal voters and holiday food baskets to their families.

A large number of federal jobs, meanwhile, changed hands each time the presidency passed from one party to another. More than 50 percent of all federal jobs were patronage positions, jobs that could be awarded to loyal supporters as part of the "spoils" of the "victor."

Upon taking office, President James Garfield encountered loyal Republicans "lying in wait" for him "like vultures for a wounded bison." His colleagues in Congress were no less besieged. Observers estimated that decisions about patronage filled one-third of their time. Garfield himself served as president

In 1888, Grover Cleveland, with his running mate, Allen G. Thurman, led a spirited campaign for reelection to the presidency. Although he played up his strong record on civil service reform and tariff reduction, Cleveland, an incumbent, lost the election to his Republican challenger, Benjamin Harrison. Cleveland tallied the greatest number of popular votes, but Harrison easily won in the electoral college by a margin of 233 to 168. In this lithograph campaign poster, the Democratic ticket invokes the legacy of Thomas Jefferson and the patriotism of Uncle Sam.

for only four months before being mortally wounded by a disgruntled office seeker, an event that prompted his successor, Chester A. Arthur, to encourage reform of the civil service system.

THE SPOILS SYSTEM AND CIVIL SERVICE REFORM

In January 1883, a bipartisan congressional majority passed the **Pendleton Civil Service Reform Act**. This measure allowed the president to create, with Senate approval, a three-person commission to draw up a set of guidelines for executive and legislative appointments. The commission established a system of standards for various federal jobs and instituted "open, competitive examinations for testing the fitness of applicants for public service." The Pendleton Act also barred political candidates from funding their campaigns by assessing a "tax" on the salaries of holders of party-sponsored government jobs.

Although patronage did not disappear entirely, many departments of the federal government took on a professional character similar to that which doctors, lawyers, and scholars were imposing on their fields through regulatory societies such as the American Medical Association and the American Historical Association. At the same time, the federal judiciary began to act more aggressively to establish the parameters of government. With the Circuit Courts of Appeals Act of 1891, Congress granted the U.S. Supreme Court the right to review all cases at will. Despite these reforms, many observers still viewed government as a sinkhole of self-interest and corruption.

QUICK REVIEW

Civil Service Reform

◆ Reform movement led by Senator George H. Pendleton.

◆ Pendleton Civil Service Reform Act passed in 1883.

◆ Act created commission to reform and professionalize civil service.

Pendleton Civil Service Reform Act
A law of 1883 that reformed the spoils system by prohibiting government workers from making political contributions and creating the Civil Service Commission to oversee their appointment on the basis of merit rather than politics.

FARMERS AND WORKERS ORGANIZE THEIR COMMUNITIES

Farmers and workers began to build regional as well as national organizations to oppose, as a Nebraska newspaper put it, "the wealthy and powerful classes who want the control of government to plunder the people." Over the course of the last quarter of the nineteenth century, they gradually developed a distinctively radical agenda that spoke directly to the increasing power of elected officials and government. By the 1890s, farmers and workers had formed a mass movement that presented the most significant challenge to the two-party system since the Civil War—**Populism**—and pledged themselves to restore the reins of government to "the hands of the people."

THE GRANGE

In 1867, white farmers in the Midwest formed the Patrons of Husbandry for their own "social, intellectual, and moral improvement." Led by Oliver H. Kelley, this fraternal society resembled the secretive Masonic order. In many farming communities, the headquarters of the local chapter, known as the **Grange** (a word for "farm"), became the main social center.

The symbols chosen by Grange artists represented their faith that all social value could be traced to honest labor and most of all to the work of the entire farm family. The hardworking American required only the enlightenment offered by the Grange to build a better community.

HOW AND why did workers and farmers organize to participate in politics during this era?

myhistorylab
Review Summary

Populism   A mass movement of the 1890s formed on the basis of the Southern Farmers' Alliance and other reform organizations.

Grange   The National Grange of the Patrons of Husbandry, a national organization of farm owners formed after the Civil War.

The Granger movement spread rapidly, especially in areas where farmers were experiencing their greatest hardships (see Figure 20.1). Grangers blamed hard times on a band of "thieves in the night"—especially railroads and banks—that charged exorbitant fees for service. They fumed at American manufacturers, such as Cyrus McCormick, who sold farm equipment more cheaply in Europe than in the United States. They raged at the banks that charged high interest rates for the money farmers had to borrow to pay the steep prices for equipment and raw materials.

Grangers mounted their greatest assault on the railroad corporations. By bribing state legislators, railroads enjoyed a highly discriminatory rate policy, commonly charging farmers more to ship their crops short distances than over long hauls. In 1874, several midwestern states responded to pressure and passed a series of so-called **Granger laws** establishing maximum shipping rates. Grangers also complained to their lawmakers about the price-fixing policies of grain wholesalers and operators of grain elevators. In 1873, the Illinois legislature passed a Warehouse Act establishing maximum rates for storing grains. Chicago firms challenged the legality of this measure, but in *Munn* v. *Illinois* (1877), the Supreme Court upheld the law, ruling that states had the power to regulate privately owned businesses like the railroads in the public interest.

Determined to buy less and produce more, Grangers created a vast array of cooperative enterprises for both the purchase of supplies and the marketing of crops. They established local grain elevators, set up retail stores, and even manufactured some of their own farm machinery. Grangers ran banks as well as fraternal life and fire insurance companies.

The deepening depression of the late 1870s wiped out most of these cooperative programs, and Grange membership fell. In the mid-1880s, the Supreme Court overturned most of the key legislation regulating railroads. Despite these setbacks, the Patrons of Husbandry had nonetheless effectively promoted the idea of an activist government with primary responsibility to its producer-citizens. This idea would remain at the heart of farmer-worker protest movements until the end of the century.

THE FARMERS' ALLIANCE

Agrarian unrest did not end with the downward turn of the Grange but instead moved south. In the South, the falling price of cotton underscored the need for action, and farmers readily translated their anger into intense loyalty to the one organization pledged to improve their lot. With more than 500 chapters in Texas alone, and cooperative stores complemented by the cooperative merchandising of crops, the **Southern Farmers' Alliance** became a viable alternative to the capitalist marketplace—if only temporarily.

The Northern Farmers' Alliance took shape in the Great Plains states, drawing on larger organizations in Minnesota, Nebraska, Iowa, Kansas, and the Dakota Territory. During 1886 and 1887, summer drought followed winter blizzards and ice storms, reducing wheat harvests by one-third on the plains. Locusts and cinch bugs ate much of the rest. As if this were not enough, prices for wheat on the world market fell sharply for what little remained.

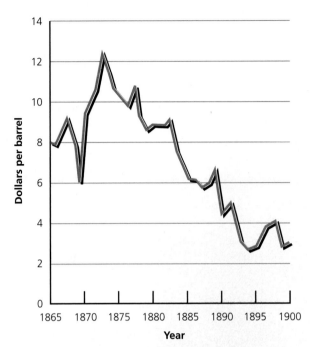

Figure 20.1 Falling Price of Wheat Flour, 1865–1900
The falling price of wheat was often offset by increased productivity, giving farmers a steady, if not higher, income. Nevertheless, in the short term farmers often carried more debt and faced greater risk, both factors in sparking the populists protest by the end of the century.

Granger laws State laws enacted in the Midwest in the 1870s that regulated rates charged by railroads, grain elevator operators, and other middlemen.

Southern Farmers' Alliance The largest of several organizations that formed in the post-Reconstruction South to advance the interests of beleaguered small farmers.

In 1889, the regional organizations joined forces to create the National Farmers' Alliance and Industrial Union. Within a year the combined movement claimed 3 million white members. Excluded from the all-white chapters, the Colored Farmers' Alliance and Cooperative Union organized separately and quickly spread across the South; from its beginnings in Texas and Arkansas it grew to more than a million members.

Grangers had only rarely put up candidates for office. In comparison, the Farmers' Alliance had few reservations about entering electoral races. At the end of the 1880s, regional alliances put up candidates on platforms demanding state ownership of the railroads, a graduated income tax, lower tariffs, restriction of land ownership to citizens, and easier access to money through "the free and unlimited coinage of silver." By 1890, the alliances had won several local and state elections, gained control of the Nebraska legislature, and held the balance of power in Minnesota and South Dakota.

WORKERS SEARCH FOR POWER

Before the end of the century, more than 6 million workers would strike in industries ranging from New England textiles to southern tobacco factories to western mines. Some of the largest strikes were against the corporations targeted by farmers: the railroads. Although most of these strikes ended in failure, they revealed the readiness of workers to spell out their grievances in a direct and dramatic manner. They also suggested how strongly many townspeople, including merchants who depended on workers' wages, would support local strikes and turn them into community uprisings (see Map 20.1).

 MAP EXPLORATION

To explore an interactive version of this map, go to **http://www.prenhall.com/faraghertic/map20.1**

MAP 20.1

Strikes by State, 1880   Most strikes after the Uprising of 1877 could be traced to organized trades, concentrated in the manufacturing districts of the Northeast and Midwest.

Carville Earle, *Geographical Inquiry and American Historical Problems* (Stanford, CA: Stanford University Press, 1992).

WHAT WERE the most important elements of McKinley's campaign platform?

The Great Uprising of 1877, which began as a strike of railroad workers, spread rapidly to communities along the railroad routes. Angry crowds defied the armed militia and the vigilantes hired to disperse them. In Philadelphia, for example, strikers set fire to the downtown, destroying many buildings before federal troops were brought in to stop them. More than a hundred people died before the strike ended, and the railroad corporations suffered a $10 million loss in property.

While the Farmers' Alliance put up candidates in the South and Plains states, workers launched labor parties in dozens of industrial towns and cities. In New York City, popular economist and land reformer Henry George put himself forward in 1886 as candidate for mayor on the United Labor Party ticket. George called on "all honest citizens" to join in independent political action as "the only hope of exposing and breaking up the extortion and speculation by which a standing army of professional politicians corrupt the people whom they plunder."

Tammany Hall delivered many thousands of the ballots cast for George straight into the Hudson River. Nevertheless, George managed to finish a respectable second with 31 percent of the vote. Although his campaign ended in defeat, George had issued a stern warning to the entrenched politicians. Equally important, his impressive showing encouraged labor groups in other cities to form their own parties.

In the late 1880s, labor parties won seats on many city councils and state legislatures. The victories of local labor parties caught the attention of farmers, who began to weigh their prospects for a political alliance with discontented urban workers. For the 1888 presidential election, they formed a coalition to sponsor the Union Labor Party, which ran on a plank of government ownership of the railroads. The new party made no headway against the two-party system, polling little more than 1 percent of the vote. Still, the successes in local communities nurtured hopes for a viable political alliance of the "producing classes," rural as well as urban.

WOMEN BUILD ALLIANCES

Women activists helped build both the labor and agrarian protest movements while campaigning for their own rights as citizens.

The Grangers issued a charter to a local chapter only when women were well represented on its rolls, and in the 1870s, delegates to its conventions routinely gave speeches endorsing woman suffrage and even dress reform. In both the

Great Uprising of 1877
Unsuccessful railroad strike to protest wage cuts and the use of federal troops against strikers; the first nationwide work stoppage in American history.

FRANCES WILLARD   598-10

Frances E. Willard (1839–1898) became a full-time activist for the national Woman's Christian Temperance Union (WCTU) in 1874. From 1879 until her death, she served as president, pushing the organization to expand its interests beyond temperance under the rubric of her "do-everything" policy. Under her leadership, the WCTU established 39 departments promoting a wide array of reform causes ranging from the establishment of free kindergartens to the prohibition of the manufacture of cigarettes.

19–5
The People's Party Platform
(1892)

Woman's Christian Temperance Union (WCTU) Women's organization whose members visited schools to educate children about the evils of alcohol, addressed prisoners, and blanketed men's meetings with literature.

National American Woman Suffrage Association (NAWSA) The organization, formed in 1890, that coordinated the ultimately successful campaign to achieve women's right to vote.

Northern and Southern Farmers' Alliances, women made up perhaps one-quarter of the membership, and several advanced through the ranks to become leading speakers and organizers.

Women in both the Knights of Labor and the Farmers' Alliance found their greatest leader in Frances E. Willard, the most famous woman of the nineteenth century and a shrewd politician in her own right. Willard argued that women, who guarded their families' physical and spiritual welfare, could have only a beneficial impact on the world outside their homes. From 1878 until her death in 1897, she presided over the **Woman's Christian Temperance Union (WCTU)**. By the 1880s, the most militant branches had joined the campaign for an activist government, demanding an overhaul of the prison system, the eradication of prostitution, changes in the age of consent, and even the elimination of the wage system. Willard went so far as to draw up plans for a new system of government whereby all offices, right up to the presidency, would be shared jointly by men and women. By 1890, she had mobilized nearly 200,000 paid members into the largest organization of women in the world.

Willard understood that for women to participate in politics they needed the right to vote. Under her leadership, the WCTU grew into the major force for woman suffrage, far surpassing the American Woman Suffrage Association and the National Woman Suffrage Association. By 1890, when the two rival suffrage associations merged to form the **National American Woman Suffrage Association**, the WCTU had already pushed the heart of the suffrage campaign into the Great Plains states and the West.

POPULISM AND THE PEOPLE'S PARTY

In December 1890, the Farmers' Alliance called a meeting at Ocala, Florida, to press for the creation of a national third party. This was a risky proposition because the Southern Alliance hoped to capture control of the Democratic Party, whereas many farmers in the Plains states voted Republican. In some areas, however, the Farmers' Alliance established its own parties, put up full slates of candidates for local elections, won majorities in state legislatures, and even sent a representative to Congress. Reviewing these successes, delegates at Ocala decided to push ahead and form a national party, and they appealed to other farm, labor, and reform organizations to join them.

In February 1892, 1,300 representatives from the Farmers' Alliance, the Knights of Labor, and the Colored Farmers' Alliance, among others, met in St. Louis under a broad banner that read: "We do not ask for sympathy or pity. We ask for justice." The new People's Party called for government ownership of railroads, banks, and telegraph lines, prohibition of large landholding companies, a graduated income tax, an eight-hour workday, and restriction of immigration. The most ambitious plan called for the national government to build local warehouses—"subtreasuries"—where farmers could store their crops until prices reached acceptable levels. The People's Party convened again in Omaha in July 1892 and nominated James Baird Weaver of Iowa for president and, to please the South, the Confederate veteran James G. Field from Virginia for vice president.

The Populists, as supporters of the People's Party styled themselves, quickly became a major factor in American politics. Although Democrat Grover Cleveland regained the presidency in 1892 (he had previously served from 1885 to

1889), Populists scored a string of local victories. In Idaho, they elected three governors, ten representatives to Congress, and five senators. Despite poor showings among urban workers east of the Mississippi, Populists looked forward to the next round of state elections in 1894. But the great test would come with the presidential election in 1896.

THE CRISIS OF THE 1890S

A series of events in the 1890s shook the confidence of many citizens in the reigning political system. But nothing was more unsettling than the severe economic depression that consumed the nation and lasted for five years. Many feared—while others hoped—that the entire political system would topple.

FINANCIAL COLLAPSE AND DEPRESSION

By the spring of 1893, the nation was drawn into a depression that had been plaguing European nations since the late 1880s. Their market for imported goods, including those manufactured in the United States, sharply contracted. Financial panic in England spread across the Atlantic, as British investors began to sell off their American stocks to obtain funds. Other factors—tight credit, falling agricultural prices, a weak banking system, and overexpansion, especially in railroad construction—all helped to bring about the collapse of the U.S. economy. In May and June a crash in the stock market sent waves of panic splashing over business and financial institutions across the country. Agricultural prices meanwhile continued to plummet until they reached new lows. The business boom of nearly two decades ended, and the entire economy ground to a halt. The new century arrived before prosperity returned.

In many cities, unemployment rates reached 25 percent; Samuel Gompers, head of the American Federation of Labor (AFL), estimated nationwide unemployment at 3 million. Few people starved but millions suffered. Inadequate diets prompted a rise in communicable diseases, such as tuberculosis and pellagra. Unable to buy food, clothes, or household items, families learned to survive with the barest minimum.

WHAT CRISES of the 1890s paved the way to political reform?

myhistorylab
Review Summary

After five weeks the main body of Coxey's Army reached Washington, DC, where on May 1, 1894, the leaders were immediately arrested for trespassing on government property. Fifty years later, on May 1, 1944, the ninety-year-old Coxey finally gave his speech advocating public works programs on the steps of the nation's capitol.

The popular magazine *Harper's Weekly* published this illustration of workers and their families protesting the use of a private security force at the Carnegie Steel Company in Homestead, Pennsylvania, in July 1892.

19–6
The Secret Oath of the American Protective Association (1893)

myhistorylab

Exploring America: *Homestead Strike of 1892*

Coxey's Army A protest march of unemployed workers, led by Populist businessman Jacob Coxey, demanding inflation and a public works program during the depression of the 1890s.

Protective association
Organizations formed by mine owners in response to the formation of labor unions.

As the depression deepened so did demands on the federal government for positive action. Populist Jacob Sechler Coxey decided to gather the masses of unemployed into a huge army and then to march to Washington, DC. Far in advance of the New Deal, Coxey proposed that Congress fund a public work program in order to give jobs to the unemployed. On Easter Sunday, 1894, Coxey left Massillon, Ohio, with several hundred followers. Meanwhile, brigades from across the country joined his "petition in boots." Only 600 men and women reached the nation's capital, where the police first clubbed and then arrested the leaders for trespassing on the grass. **"Coxey's Army"** quickly disbanded but not before voicing the public's expectation of federal responsibility for the welfare of its citizens, especially in times of crisis.

STRIKES: COEUR D'ALENE, HOMESTEAD, AND PULLMAN

Even before the onset of the depression, the conflict between labor and capital had escalated to the brink of civil war. In the 1890s, three major strikes dramatized the extent of collusion between the corporations and government. In each case, state or federal troops were deployed to crush the labor uprising, providing a vivid lesson to workers on the growing role of government in this era.

Wage cuts in the silver and lead mines of northern Idaho led to one of the most bitter conflicts of the decade. To put a brake on organized labor, mine owners had formed a **"protective association,"** and in March 1892, they announced a wage cut throughout the Coeur d'Alene district. After the miners' union refused to accept the cut, the owners locked out all union members and brought in strikebreakers by the trainload. Unionists tried peaceful methods of protest. But after three months of stalemate, they loaded a railcar with explosives and blew up a mine. The governor proclaimed martial law and dispatched a combined state-federal force of about 1,500 troops, who broke the strike. But the miners' union survived, and most members became active in the Populist Party, which at the next session of the Idaho legislature allied with Democrats to cut back all appropriations to the National Guard.

At Homestead, Pennsylvania, members of the Amalgamated Iron, Steel and Tin Workers, the most powerful union of the AFL, had carved out an admirable position for themselves in the Carnegie Steel Company. But, determined to gain control over every stage of production, Carnegie and his chairman, Henry C. Frick, decided not only to lower wages but also to break the union.

In 1892, when Amalgamated's contract expired, Frick announced a drastic wage cut. He also ordered a wooden stockade built around the factory, with grooves for rifles and barbed wire on top. When Homestead's city government—the mayor and police chief were both union members—refused to assign police to disperse the strikers, Frick dispatched a barge carrying a private army armed to the teeth. Gunfire broke out and continued throughout the day. Finally, the governor stepped in and sent the Pennsylvania National Guard, 8,000 strong, to restore order, and Carnegie's factory reopened with strikebreakers doing the work.

After four months, the union was forced to concede a crushing defeat, not only for itself but, in effect, for all steelworkers as well. The Carnegie company reduced its workforce by 25 percent, lengthened the workday, and cut wages 25 percent for those who remained on the job. Within a decade, every major steel company operated without union interference.

Pullman, Illinois, just south of Chicago, had been constructed as a model industrial community. Its creator and proprietor, George M. Pullman, had manufactured luxurious "sleeping cars" for railroads since 1881. He built his company as a self-contained community, with the factory at the center, surrounded by modern cottages, a library, churches, parks, an independent water supply, even its own cemetery, but no saloons. The Pullman Palace Car Company deducted rent, library fees, and grocery bills from each worker's weekly wages.

When times grew hard, the company cut wages by as much as one-half, in some cases down to less than $1 a day. Charges for food and rent remained unchanged. Furthermore, factory supervisors sought to make up for declining profits by driving workers to produce more. In May 1894, after Pullman fired members of a committee that had drawn up a list of grievances, workers voted to strike.

Pullman workers found their champion in Eugene V. Debs, who had recently formed the American Railway Union (ARU). Debs, the architect of the ARU's victory over the Great Northern rail line just one month earlier, advised caution, but delegates to an ARU convention voted to support a nationwide boycott of all Pullman cars. This action soon turned into a sympathy strike by railroad workers across the country.

Compared to the Great Uprising of 1877, the orderly Pullman strike at first produced little violence. ARU officials urged strikers to ignore all provocations and hold their ground peacefully. But Richard C. Olney, a former railroad lawyer, used his current office as attorney general, claiming that the ARU was disrupting mail shipments, to issue a blanket injunction against the strike. On July 4, President Cleveland sent army units to Chicago, over the pro-labor Illinois governor John Peter Altgeld's objections. After a bitter confrontation that left thirteen people dead and more than fifty wounded, the army dispersed the strikers. For the next week, railroad workers in twenty-six other states resisted federal troops, and a dozen more people were killed. On July 17, the strike finally ended when federal marshals arrested Debs and other leaders.

Assailing the arrogance of class privilege that encouraged the government to use brute force against its citizens, Debs concluded that the labor movement could not regain its dignity without seizing the reigns of government. He came out of jail committed to the ideals of socialism, and in 1898 helped to form a political party dedicated to its principles.

THE SOCIAL GOSPEL

"What is socialism?" Debs once asked. "Merely Christianity in action. It recognizes the equality in men." During the 1890s, especially as hard times spread across the nation, a growing number of Protestant and Catholic clergy and lay theologians came close to sharing his perspective, noting a discrepancy between the ideals of Christianity and prevailing attitudes toward the poor.

Social gospel ministers called on the government to be more responsible toward its most impoverished and unprotected citizens. Supporting labor's right to organize and, if necessary, to strike, they petitioned government officials to regulate corporations and place a limit on profits. Women guided the social gospel movement in their communities. In the midst of the depression, women activists were well placed to respond to the plight of the poor and dispossessed. In nearly every sizable city, groups of white women affiliated with various evangelical Protestant sects raised money to establish inexpensive residential hotels for working

IN WHAT ways did the election of 1896 represent a turning point in U.S. political history?

myhistorylab

Review Summary

Sherman Silver Purchase Act   1890 act which directed the Treasury to increase the amount of currency coined from silver mined in the West and also permitted the U.S. government to print paper currency backed by the silver.

women, whose low wages rarely covered the price of safe, comfortable shelter. At the forefront of this movement was the Young Women's Christian Association (YWCA), which by 1900 had more than 600 local chapters. The "Y" sponsored a range of services for needy Christian women, ranging from homes for the elderly and for unmarried mothers to elaborate programs of vocational instruction and physical fitness. Meanwhile, Catholic laywomen and nuns served the poor women of their faith, operating numerous schools, hospitals, and orphanages.

Affiliated principally with the Baptist Church, African American women sponsored dozens of self-help programs and, in addition, emphasized the importance of education to racial uplift. Excluded by the whites-only policy of the YWCA in most localities, they organized their own chapters and branched out to form nurseries, orphanages, hospitals, and nursing homes. In Chicago, for example, African American women established the Phyllis Wheatley Home, which opened in 1908 to provide, in the founders' words, a "Christian influence" for the working women and college students who boarded there.

POLITICS OF REFORM, POLITICS OF ORDER

The severe hardships of the 1890s, following a quarter century of popular unrest and economic uncertainty, led to a crisis in the two-party system. The presidential election of 1896, considered a turning point in American politics, marked both a dramatic realignment of voters and the centrality of economic issues. It also sanctioned the popular call for a stronger government, making the question of control vital to the nation's voters as well as the composition of the electorate. Ultimately, the election of 1896 brought to national office politicians who perceived a clear link between domestic problems and the expansion of markets overseas and were willing to act aggressively to implement this vision.

THE FREE SILVER ISSUE

For generations, reformers had advocated "soft" currency, that is, an increase in the money supply that would loosen credit. During the Civil War the federal government took decisive action, replacing state bank notes with a national paper currency popularly called "greenbacks" (from the color of the bills). Then in 1873 the Coinage Act tightened the money supply by eliminating silver from circulation, prompting farmers who depended on credit to call it "the Crime of '73." This measure actually had little real impact on the economy but opened the door to yet more tinkering.

The **Sherman Silver Purchase Act** of 1890 directed the Treasury to increase the amount of currency coined from silver mined in the West and also permitted the U.S. government to print paper currency backed by silver. In turn Westerners, who stood to benefit most from this reform, agreed to support the McKinley Tariff of 1890 which, by establishing the highest import duties yet on foreign goods, pleased the business community.

Following the crash of 1893, a desperate President Cleveland demanded the repeal of the Sherman Act, insisting that only the gold standard could pull the nation out of depression. By exerting intense pressure on congressional Democrats, Cleveland succeeded in October 1893, but not without ruining his chances for renomination. The midterm elections of 1894 brought the largest shift in congressional power in American history: the Republicans gained 117 seats, while the Democrats lost 113. The "Silver Democrats" of Cleveland's own party vowed revenge and began to look to the Populists, mainly Westerners and farmers who favored "free silver," that is, the unlimited coinage of silver. Republicans confidently began to prepare for the presidential election of 1896, warming to what they called the "battle of the standards."

Free silver Philosophy that the government should expand the money supply by purchasing and coining all the silver offered to it.

POPULISM'S LAST CAMPAIGNS

Populists had been buoyed by the 1894 elections, which delivered to their candidates nearly 1.5 million votes—a gain of 42 percent over their 1892 totals. As Populists prepared for the 1896 presidential campaign, they found themselves at a crossroad: what were they to do with the growing popularity of the Democratic candidate, William Jennings Bryan? A spellbinding orator, Bryan won a congressional seat in 1890. After seizing the Populist slogan "Equal Rights to All, Special Privilege to None," the thirty-six-year-old lawyer from Nebraska became a major contender for president of the United States.

Noting the surging interest in free silver, Bryan became its champion. For two years before the 1896 election, he wooed potential voters in a speaking tour that took him to every state in the nation. Pouring new life into his divided party, Bryan pushed Silver Democrats to the forefront.

At the 1896 party convention, Bryan thrilled delegates with his evocation of agrarian ideals. "Burn down your cities and leave our farms," Bryan preached, "and your cities will spring up again as if by magic; but destroy our farms and the grass will grow in the streets of every city in the country." Bryan carried the Democratic presidential nomination.

The Populists realized that by nominating Bryan the Democrats had stolen their thunder. They also feared that the growing emphasis on currency would overshadow their more important planks calling for government ownership of the nation's railroads and communications systems. As the date of their own convention approached, delegates divided over strategy: they could endorse Bryan and give up their independent status, or they could run an independent campaign and risk splitting the silver vote. In the end, Populists nominated Bryan for president and one of their own, Georgian Tom Watson, for vice president. Most of the state Democratic Party organizations, however, refused to put the "fusion" ticket on the ballot, and Bryan and his Democratic running mate Arthur Sewall simply ignored the Populist campaign.

THE REPUBLICAN TRIUMPH

After Cleveland's blunders, Republicans anticipated an easy victory in 1896, but Bryan's nomination, as party stalwart Mark Hanna warned, "changed everything." Luckily, they had their own handsome, knowledgeable, courteous, and ruthless candidate, Civil War veteran William McKinley.

The Republican campaign in terms of sheer expense and skill of coordination outdid all previous campaigns and established a precedent for future presidential elections. Hanna guided a strategy that raised up to $7 million and outspent Bryan more than ten to one. Fearful that the silver issue would divide their own ranks, Republicans stepped around it while emphasizing the tariff. Delivering a hard-hitting negative campaign, they consistently cast Bryan as a nay-sayer.

This Republican campaign poster of 1896 depicts William McKinley standing on sound money and promising a revival of prosperity. The depression of the 1890s shifted the electorate into the Republican column.

McKinley triumphed in the most important presidential election since Reconstruction. Bryan managed to win 46 percent of the popular vote but failed to carry the Midwest, West Coast, or Upper South (see Map 20.2). Moreover, the free silver campaign rebuffed traditionally Democratic urban voters who feared that soft money would bring higher prices. Many Catholics uncomfortable with Bryan's Protestant moral piety also deserted the Democrats. Finally, neither the reform-minded middle classes nor impoverished blue-collar workers were convinced that Bryan's grand reform vision really included them. The Populist following, disappointed and disillusioned, dwindled away.

Once in office, McKinley strengthened the executive branch and actively promoted a mixture of probusiness and expansionist measures. McKinley's triumph ended the popular challenge to the nation's governing system. With prosperity returning by the end of the century and nationalism rising swiftly, McKinley encouraged Americans to go for "a full dinner pail," the winning Republican slogan of the 1900 presidential campaign. With news of his second triumph, stock prices on Wall Street skyrocketed.

	Electoral Vote (%)	Popular Vote (%)
WILLIAM McKINLEY (Republican)	271 (61)	7,102,246 (51)
William J. Bryan (Democrat)	176 (39)	6,492,559 (47)
Minor parties	—	315,398 (2)

MAP 20.2
Election of 1896 Democratic candidate William Jennings Bryan carried most of rural America but could not overcome Republican William McKinley's stronghold in the populous industrial states.

WHAT WERE the most important elements of McKinley's campaign platform?

18–9
Booker T. Washington, *Atlanta Exposition Address* (1895)

17–10
Plessy v. Ferguson (1896)

Nativism Favoring the interests and culture of native-born inhabitants over those of immigrants.

Jim Crow laws Segregation laws that became widespread in the South during the 1890s.

Segregation A system of racial control that separated the races, initially by custom but increasingly by law during and after Reconstruction.

Plessy v. Ferguson Supreme Court decision holding that Louisiana's railroad segregation law did not violate the Constitution as long as the railroads or the state provided equal accommodations.

NATIVISM AND JIM CROW

Campaign rhetoric aside, McKinley and Bryan had differed only slightly on the major problems facing the nation in the 1890s. Neither Bryan, the reformer, nor McKinley, the prophet of prosperity, addressed the escalation of racism and **nativism** (anti-immigrant feeling) throughout the nation.

Toward the end of the century, many political observers noted, the nation's patriotic fervor took on a strongly nationalistic and antiforeign tone. Striking workers and their employers alike tended to blame "foreigners" for the hard times. Semisecret organizations such as the American Protective Association sprang up to defend American institutions. Fourth of July orators continued to celebrate freedom and liberty but more often boasted about the might and power of their nation.

In the South, local and state governments codified racist ideology by passing discriminatory and segregationist legislation, which became known as **Jim Crow laws**. The phrase, dating from the early decades of the nineteenth century, was made popular by a white minstrel in blackface who used the name "Jim Crow" to demean all African Americans. By the end of the century, "Jim Crow" referred to the customs of **segregation** that were becoming secured by legislation throughout the South. With nine of every ten black Americans living in this region, the significance of this development was sweeping.

To secure their privileges, white Southerners acted directly to impose firm standards of segregation and domination and to forestall any appearance of social equality. State after state in the South enacted new legislation to cover facilities such as restaurants, public transportation, and even drinking fountains.

The United States Supreme Court upheld the new discriminatory legislation. Its decisions in the *Civil Rights Cases* (1883) overturned the Civil Rights Act of 1875; in *Plessy v. Ferguson* (1896), the Court upheld a Louisiana state law formally segregating railroad passenger cars on the basis of the "separate but equal" doctrine. The majority opinion, delivered by Justice Henry Billings Brown, stated that political equality and social equality are distinct: "Legislation is powerless to eradicate racial instincts or to abolish distinctions based on physical differences. If one race be inferior to the other socially, the Constitution of the United States cannot put them on the same plane."

This ruling established the legal rationale for segregation, North as well as South, for the next fifty years. In *Cumming* v. *Richmond County Board of Education* (1899), the Court allowed separate schools for blacks and whites, even where facilities for African American children did not exist. This ruling reverberated in other parts of the country. For example, a year later, in 1900, the New Orleans school board decided to eliminate all schools for black children beyond the fifth grade, reasoning that African Americans needed only minimal education to fit them for menial jobs "to which they are best suited and seem ordained by the proper fitness of things."

Southern states enacted new literacy tests and property qualifications for voting. Loopholes permitted poor whites to vote even under these conditions, except where they threatened the Democratic Party's rule. "**Grandfather clauses**," invented in Louisiana, exempted from all restrictions those who had been entitled to vote on January 1, 1867, together with their sons and grandsons, a measure that effectively enfranchised whites while barring African Americans (see Figure 20.2).

Racial violence escalated. Race riots, which took the lives of hundreds of African Americans, broke out in small towns like Rosewood, Florida, and Phoenix, South Carolina, and in large cities like New Orleans and Tulsa. In November 1898, in Wilmington, North Carolina, where a dozen African Americans had ridden out the last waves of the Populist insurgency to win appointments to minor political offices, a group of white opponents organized to root them out and ultimately staged a violent coup, restoring white rule and forcing black leaders to leave town. "It come so," a black woman explained, "that we in this town is afraid of a white face." As many as 100 African Americans were killed in what came to be known as the Wilmington massacre.

Not only race riots but also thousands of lynchings took place. Between 1882 and the turn of the century, the number of lynchings usually exceeded 100 each year; 1892 produced a record 230 deaths (161 black, 69 white). Mobs often burned or dismembered victims in order to drag out their agony and entertain the crowd of onlookers. Announced in local newspapers, lynchings in the 1890s became public spectacles for entire white families, and railroads sometimes offered special excursion rates for travel to these events.

Antilynching became the one-woman crusade of Ida B. Wells, young editor of a black newspaper in Memphis. Wells launched an international movement against lynching, lecturing across the country and in Europe, demanding an end to the silence about this barbaric crime. Her work also inspired the growth of a black women's club movement. The National Association of Colored Women, founded in 1896, took up the antilynching cause and also fought to protect black women from sexual exploitation by white men.

Few white reformers rallied to defend African Americans. Even the National American Woman Suffrage Association, in an attempt to appease its southern members at its 1899 convention, voted down a resolution condemning racial segregation in public facilities. More than a few Americans had come to believe that their future welfare hinged on white supremacy, not only in their own country but across the globe as well.

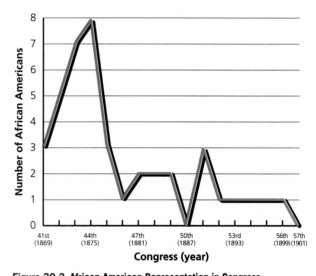

Figure 20.2 African American Representation in Congress, 1867–1900

Black men served in the U.S. Congress from 1870 until 1900. All were Republicans.

QUICK REVIEW

Jim Crow

◆ Neither major party addressed problem of racism and nativism in campaign of 1896.

◆ Local and state governments in the South codified racism in Jim Crow laws.

◆ The Supreme Court upheld the new discriminatory legislation.

 18–8

Ida B. Wells-Barnett, *A Red Record* (1895)

Grandfather clauses   Rules that required potential voters to demonstrate that their grandfathers had been eligible to vote; used in some Southern states after 1890 to limit the black electorate.

HOW DID proponents of imperialism justify colonization?

myhistorylab

Review Summary

THE PATH TO IMPERIALISM

Many Americans attributed the economic crisis of 1893–97 not simply to the collapse of the railroads and banks but also to basic structural problems: an overbuilt economy and an insufficient market for goods. Profits from total sales of manufactured and agricultural products had grown substantially over levels achieved in the 1880s, but output increased even more rapidly. Although the number of millionaires shot up from 500 in 1860 to more than 4,000 in 1892, the majority of Americans did not have enough money to buy a significant portion of what they produced. To find new markets for American goods, many Americans looked abroad.

ALL THE WORLD'S A FAIR

The World's Columbian Exposition, held in Chicago, commemorated the four hundredth anniversary of Columbus's landing and answered Congress's call for "an exhibition of the progress of civilization in the New World." On May Day 1893, less than two months after the nation's economy had collapsed, crowds began to flock to the fair, a complex of more than 400 buildings newly constructed in beaux arts design.

The section known as "The White City" celebrated the achievements of American business in the global economy. Agriculture Hall showcased the production of corn, wheat, and other crops and featured a gigantic globe encircled by samples of American-manufactured farm machinery. Another building housed a model of a canal cut across Nicaragua, suggesting the ease with which American traders might reach Asian markets if transport ships could travel directly from the Caribbean to the Pacific. The symbolism was evident: all eyes were on international trade as a marker of American prowess.

In contrast to the White City was the Midway, a strip nearly a mile long and more than 600 feet wide that offered entertainment. The Midway also offered amusement in the form of "displays" of "uncivilized" people from foreign lands. One enormous sideshow re-created Turkish bazaars and South Sea island huts. There were Javanese carpenters, Dahomean drummers, Egyptian swordsmen, and Hungarian Gypsies, as well as Eskimos, Syrians, Samoans, and Chinese. According to the guidebook, all these peoples had come "from the nightsome North and the splendid South, from the wasty West and the effete East, bringing their manners, customs, dress, religions, legends, amusements, that we might know them better."

By celebrating the brilliance of American industry and simultaneously presenting the "uncivilized" people of the world as a source of exotic entertainment, the planners of the fair delivered a powerful message. Former abolitionist Frederick Douglass, who attended the fair on "Colored People's Day," recognized it immediately. Douglass objected to the stark contrast setting off Anglo-Saxons from people of color, an opposition between "civilization" and "savagery." He and Ida B. Wells also objected to the exclusion of African Americans from representation among the exhibits at the White City. Wells boycotted the special day set aside for African Americans, while Douglass attended, using the occasion to deliver a speech upbraiding white Americans for their racism.

Also speaking at the fair was Frederick Jackson Turner, who read his famous essay about the disappearance of the frontier. Having passed "from the task of filling up the vacant spaces of the continent," the young historian warned, the nation is now "thrown back upon itself." His message was clear: if democracy were to survive, Americans required a new "frontier."

The Chicago World's Fair, which attracted 27 million visitors from all over the world, reassured Turner by marking the coming to age of the United States as a global power and by making a deliberate case for commercial expansion abroad. The exposition also gave material shape to prevalent ideas about the pre-eminence of American civilization as well as the superiority of the Anglo-Saxon race (see Seeing History).

THE "IMPERIALISM OF RIGHTEOUSNESS"

20–1
Josiah Strong, *Our Country* (1885)

Social gospeler Josiah Strong, a Congregational minister who had begun his career hoping to "civilize" the Indians by converting them to Christianity, provided a prescient commentary in 1885. Linking economic and spiritual expansion, he advocated an "imperialism of righteousness." He identified white Americans, who, with "their genius for colonizing," as the best agents for "Christianizing" and "civilizing" the people of Africa and the Pacific and beyond.

The push for overseas expansion coincided with a major wave of religious evangelism and foreign missions. Early in the nineteenth century, Protestant missionaries, hoping to fulfill what they believed to be a divine command to carry God's message to all peoples and to win converts for their church, had focused on North America. As early as the 1820s, however, a few missionaries had traveled to the Sandwich Islands (Hawai'i) in an effort to supplant the indigenous religion with Christianity. After the Civil War, the major evangelical Protestant denominations all sponsored missions directed at foreign lands.

By the 1890s, college campuses blazed with missionary excitement, and the intercollegiate Student Volunteers for Foreign Missions spread rapidly under the slogan "The Evangelicization of the World in This Generation." By the turn of the century, some 23 American Protestant churches had established missions in China, the majority staffed by women.

Young Protestant women rushed to join foreign missionary societies. Since the early part of the nineteenth century, Protestant women had headed "cent" and "mite" societies, which gathered money to support overseas missionaries. By 1820, women were accompanying their minister husbands to distant parts to convert the "heathens" to Christianity. After the Civil War, in tandem with the expansion of higher educational opportunities, unmarried women petitioned church leaders to request their own missionary assignments. By 1900, the various Protestant denominations were supporting forty-one women's missionary boards; several years later more than 3 million women had enrolled in societies to support this work, together surpassing in size all other women's organizations in the United States.

By the end of the nineteenth century, women represented 60 percent of the American missionary force in foreign lands. This photograph shows two Methodist women using "back chairs," a traditional form of transportation, at Mount Omei in Szechwan, China.

Outside the churches, the YMCA and YWCA, which had set up nondenominational missions for the working poor in many American cities, also embarked on a worldwide crusade to reach non-Christians. By the turn of the century, the YWCA had foreign branches in Ceylon (present-day Sri Lanka) and China. After foreign branches multiplied in the next decade, a close observer ironically suggested that the United States had three great occupying forces: the army, the navy, and the "Y." He was not far wrong.

Missionaries played an important role both in generating public interest in foreign lands and in preparing the way for American economic expansion. As Josiah Strong aptly put it, "Commerce follows the missionary."

THE QUEST FOR EMPIRE

20–2
Henry Cabot Lodge,
The Business World vs. the Politicians (1895)

20–3
Albert Beveridge, *The March of the Flag* (1898)

Not only missionaries but also business and political leaders had set their sights on distant lands, which in turn meant new markets. In the 1860s, Secretary of State William Henry Seward, under Abraham Lincoln and then under Andrew Johnson, correctly predicted that foreign trade would play an increasingly important part in the American economy. Between 1870 and 1900, exports more than tripled, from about $400 million to over $1.5 billion, with textiles and agricultural products leading the way. But as European markets for American goods began to contract, business and political leaders, of necessity, looked more eagerly to Asia as well as to lands closer by.

Since the American Revolution, many Americans had regarded all nearby nations as falling naturally within their own territorial realm, destined to be acquired when opportunity allowed. Seward advanced these imperialist principles in 1867 by negotiating the purchase of Alaska. Meanwhile, with European nations launched on their own imperialist missions in Asia and Africa, the United States increasingly viewed the Caribbean as an "American lake" and all of Latin America as a vast potential market for U.S. goods. The crisis of the 1890s transformed this long-standing desire into a perceived economic necessity.

Americans focused their expansionist plans on the Western Hemisphere, determined to dislodge the dominant power, Great Britain. In 1867, when Canada became a self-governing dominion, American diplomats hoped to annex their northern neighbor, believing that Great Britain would gladly accede in order to concentrate its imperial interests in Asia. But Great Britain refused to give up Canada, and the United States backed away. Central and South America proved more accommodating to American designs (see Map 20.3).

Republican stalwart James G. Blaine, secretary of state under presidents Garfield and Harrison, determined to work out a Good Neighbor policy (a phrase coined by Henry Clay in 1820). Bilateral treaties with Mexico, Colombia, the British West Indies, El Salvador, and the Dominican Republic allowed American business to dominate local economies, importing their raw materials at low prices and flooding their local markets with goods manufactured in the United States.

The Good Neighbor policy depended, Blaine knew, on peace and order in the Latin American states. As early as 1875, when revolt shook Venezuela, the Department of State warned European powers not to meddle. If popular uprisings proved too much for local officials, the U.S. Navy would intervene and return American allies to power.

In 1883, wishing to enforce treaties and protect overseas investments, Congress appropriated funds to build up American sea power and in 1884 established the Naval War College in Newport, Rhode Island, to train the officer corps. Beginning with ninety small ships, over one-third of them wooden, the

QUICK REVIEW

The Good Neighbor Policy

- Spearheaded by James G. Blaine, secretary of state under Garfield and Harrison.
- Allowed U.S. to dominate local economies in Central America and the Caribbean.
- U.S. expanded navy to help enforce control of Latin American states.

The White Man's Burden

In 1899, the British poet Rudyard Kipling published "The White Man's Burden" in the American magazine *McClure's* with the subtitle "The United States and the Philippine Islands." Some interpreted the poem as an endorsement of the U.S. imperialist ventures in the Pacific; others read it as a cautionary note warning against taking on colonies. Those who favored expansion embraced the notion of the "white man's burden" as means to justify their position as a noble enterprise, that is, in "uplifting" those people of color who had not yet enjoyed the benefits of "civilization."

The concept even made its way into advertising for soap. In 1789, London soapmaster Andrew Pears began producing a distinctive oval bar of a transparent amber glycerin and marketing it as a luxury item under the name Pears Soap. Barratt's advertising presented Pears Soap as safe and beneficial but suitable only for discerning consumers. Pears Soap promised a smooth, white complexion, underscoring this message by associating dark skins with "uncivilized" people. The advertisement appeared first in 1899 in *McClure's*—the same magazine in which Kipling's poetic exhortation was published.

The first step towards lightening
The White Man's Burden
is through teaching the virtues of cleanliness.
Pears' Soap
is a potent factor in brightening the dark corners of the earth as civilization advances, while amongst the cultured of all nations it holds the highest place—it is the ideal toilet soap.

WHAT DID the readers of *McClure's* magazine understand as "the white man's burden"? How did this responsibility relate to the belief in a hierarchy of races and civilizations expressed in Kipling's poem?

Take up the White Man's burden—
Send forth the best ye breed—
Go bind your sons to exile
To serve your captives' need;
To wait in heavy harness,
On fluttered folk and wild—

Your new-caught, sullen peoples,
Half-devil and half-child.
Take up the White Man's burden—
In patience to abide,
To veil the threat of terror
And check the show of pride... ∎

myhistorylab
Exploring America: *White Man's Burden*

MAP EXPLORATION

To explore an interactive version of this map, go to **http://www.prenhall.com/faraghertlc/map20.3**

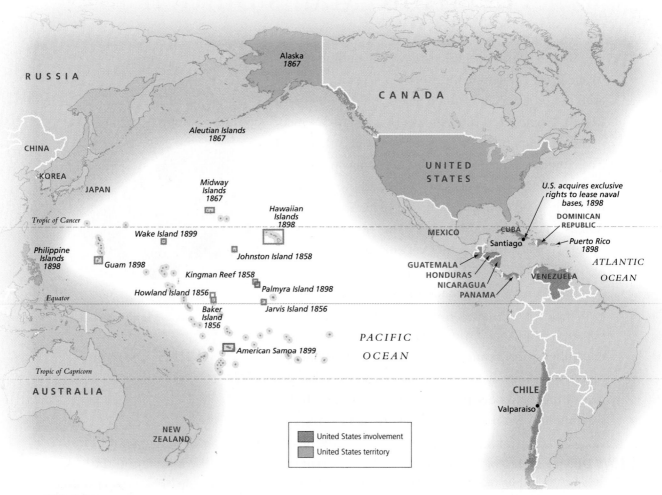

MAP 20.3

The American Domain, ca. 1900   The United States claimed numerous islands in the South Pacific and intervened repeatedly in Latin America to secure its own economic interests.

WHAT FUELED America's expansion overseas?

navy grew quickly to include modern steel fighting ships. The force behind this build-up of the U.S. Navy was Captain Alfred Thayer Mahan, one of the first presidents of the Naval War College.

Mahan achieved international fame for outlining an imperialist strategy based on command of the seas. His book, *The Influence of Sea Power upon History, 1660–1873* (1890), helped to define foreign policy not only for the United States but also for Great Britain, Japan, and Germany by identifying sea power as the key to world dominance. For the United States to achieve global preeminence, he prescribed not only open markets but also the control of colonies out for the annexation of Hawai'i, claiming the United States, with its continental border extending to the Pacific Ocean, was "the proper guardian for this most important position." The Hawaiian archipelago, he insisted, held key strategic value as stepping-stone to Asia and beyond.

ONTO A GLOBAL STAGE

Influenced by Alfred Thayer Mahan, McKinley became an advocate of expansion as a means to make the United States first in international commerce and as a means to implement its humanitarian and democratic goals. He also hoped to achieve these ends peacefully. He was pleased, therefore, to grease the wheels for the annexation of Hawai'i and in June 1898 agreed with representatives from the Republic on a treaty of annexation. Soon, however, McKinley found himself embroiled in a war with Spain that would establish the United States as a strong player in global imperialism (see Map 20.4). By the end of the century, the United States had joined Europe and Japan in the quest for empire and claimed territories spread out from the Caribbean Sea across the Pacific.

A "SPLENDID LITTLE WAR" IN CUBA

Before the Civil War, Southerners pushed for the acquisition of Cuba, a possession of Spain, for the expansion of slavery into its sugar mills, tobacco plantations, and mines. After failing several times to buy the island outright, the United

WHAT CRITIQUES of empire were put forward in the years after the Spanish-American War?

myhistorylab
Review Summary

20–4
The Spanish-American War (1898)

✴ MAP EXPLORATION

To explore an interactive version of this map, go to **http://www.prenhall.com/faraghertlc/map20.4**

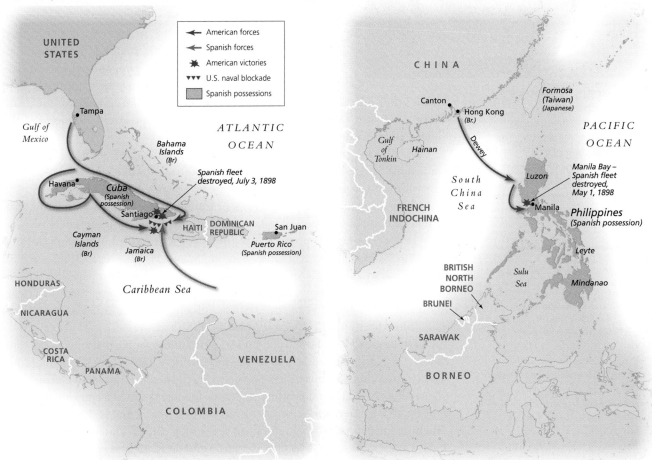

MAP 20.4
The Spanish-American War   In two theaters of action, the United States used its naval power adeptly against a weak foe.

WHAT DID the United States gain from victories in each of these conflicts?

Brought to power with the assistance of American businessmen, Queen Lili'uokalani sought to limit outsider influence. American Marines, Christian missionaries, and sugar planters joined in 1893 to drive her from her throne. A century later, the U.S. government apologized to native Hawaiians for this illegal act.

QUICK REVIEW

Cuba Libre

* At the end of the Spanish-American war, the United States gained effective control over Cuba.

* Platt amendment spelled out Cuban subservience to the United States.

* Terms of the amendment incorporated in the Cuban-American Treaty of 1903.

States settled for the continuation of the status quo and resolved to protect Spain's sovereignty over Cuba against the encroachment of other powers, including Cuba itself.

In the mid-1860s, a movement for independence began in Cuba when Spain, its empire in ruins, began to impose stiff taxes on the island. After a series of defeats, insurgents rallied in the 1890s under the nationalist leadership of José Martí. In May 1895 Spanish troops ambushed and killed Martí, turning him into a martyr and fanning the flames of rebellion. In February 1896 Spain appointed General Valeriano Weyler as governor and gave him full authority to crush the rebellion. Weyler instituted a policy *of reconcentrado,* forcing civilians from the countryside into concentration camps so they could not aid the rebels. Thousands starved or died from the diseases that swept these crowded, dirty camps.

In the United States, the popular press whipped up support for the movement for *Cuba Libre,* circulating sensationalistic and even false stories of the atrocities that Weyler, "the butcher," perpetrated against the insurgents. Newspapers ran stories on mass executions in the "death camps" and featured drawings of emaciated children.

Public sympathy, again whipped up by the press, turned into frenzy on February 15, 1898, when an explosion ripped through the battleship USS *Maine,* stationed in Havana harbor to protect American interests. The newspapers ran banner headlines charging a Spanish conspiracy, although there was no proof. The impatient public, meanwhile, demanded revenge for the death of 266 American sailors. Within days, a new slogan appeared: "Remember the Maine! To Hell with Spain!"

Finally, on April 11, President McKinley asked Congress for a declaration of war against Spain. Yet Congress barely passed the war resolution on April 25, and only with the inclusion of an amendment by Senator Henry Teller (Rep., Colorado) that disclaimed "any disposition or intention to exercise sovereignty, jurisdiction or control over said island, except for the pacification thereof."

Ten weeks later the war was all but over. On land, Lieutenant Colonel Theodore Roosevelt—who boasted of killing Spaniards "like jackrabbits"—led his Rough Riders to victory. On July 3, the main Spanish fleet near Santiago Bay was destroyed; two weeks later Santiago itself surrendered, and the war drew to a close. Roosevelt felt invigorated by the conflict, agreeing with McKinley's Secretary of State John Hay that it had been a "splendid little war."

On August 12, at a small ceremony in McKinley's office marking Spain's surrender, the United States secured Cuba's independence from Spain, but not its own sovereignty. American businesses proceeded to tighten their hold on Cuban sugar plantations, while U.S. military forces oversaw the formation of a constitutional convention that made Cuba a protectorate of the United States. Under the Platt Amendment, sponsored by Republican senator Orville H. Platt of Connecticut in 1901, Cuba was required to provide land for American bases, including a navy base at Guantanomo Bay; to devote national revenues to pay back debts to the United States; to sign no treaty that would be detrimental to American interests; and to acknowledge the right of the United States to intervene at any time to protect its interests in Cuba. After the U.S. withdrawal of troops, the terms of the Platt

Amendment were incorporated into the Cuban-American Treaty of 1903. This treaty, which remained in place until 1934, paved the way for American domination of the island's sugar industry and contributed to anti-American sentiment among Cuban nationalists.

WAR IN THE PHILIPPINES

20–5
William McKinley, *Decision on the Philippines* (1900)

The Philippines, another of Spain's colonies, seemed an especially attractive prospect, its 7,000 islands a natural way station to the markets of mainland Asia. Shortly after Congress declared war on Spain, on May 4, McKinley dispatched 5,000 troops to occupy the Philippines. During the first week of the conflict, the Spanish fleet was demolished in Manila Bay through seven hours of unimpeded target practice. Once the war ended, McKinley refused to sign the armistice unless Spain relinquished all claims to its Pacific islands. When Spain conceded, McKinley quickly drew up plans for colonial administration. He pledged "to educate the Filipinos, and to uplift and civilize and Christianize them." But after centuries of Spanish rule, the majority of islanders—already Christians—were eager to create their own nation.

The Filipino rebels, like the Cubans, at first welcomed American troops and fought with them against Spain. But when the Spanish-American War ended and they perceived that American troops were not preparing to leave, the rebels, led by Emilio Aguinaldo, turned against their former allies and attacked the American base of operations in Manila in February 1899. Predicting a brief skirmish, American commanders seriously underestimated the population's capacity to endure great suffering for the sake of independence.

U.S. troops had provoked this conflict in various ways. Military leaders, the majority veterans of the Indian Wars, commonly described the natives as "gugus," and reported themselves, as one said, as "just itching to get at the niggers." While awaiting action, American soldiers repeatedly insulted or physically abused civilians, raped Filipino women, and otherwise whipped up resentment.

The resulting conflict took the form of modern guerrilla warfare, with brutalities on both sides. By the time the fighting slowed down in 1902, 4,300 American lives had been lost, and one of every five Filipinos had died in battle or from starvation or disease. On some of the Philippine islands, intermittent fighting lasted until 1935.

The conquest of the Philippines, which remained a U.S. colony until 1946, evoked for its defenders the vision of empire. The Philippines joined Hawai'i as yet another stepping-stone for U.S. merchants en route to China. The acquisition of Pacific territories, including Guam, marked the emergence of the United States as a global colonial power.

CRITICS OF EMPIRE

20–8
Mark Twain, *Incident in the Philippines* (1924)

No mass movement formed to forestall U.S. expansion, but distinguished figures like Mark Twain, Andrew Carnegie, William Jennings Bryan, and Harvard philosopher William James voiced their opposition strongly. To protest military action in the Philippines, a small group of prominent Bostonians organized the Anti-Imperialist League.

The *National Labor Standard* expressed its common hope that all those "who believe in the Republic against Empire should join." By 1899, the league claimed a half-million members.

"Uncle Sam Teaches the Art of Self-Government," editorial cartoon, 1898. Expressing a popular sentiment of the time, a newspaper cartoonist shows the rebels as raucous children who constantly fight among themselves and need to be brought into line by Uncle Sam. The Filipino leader, Emilio Aguinaldo, appears as a dunce for failing to learn properly from the teacher. The two major islands where no uprising took place, Puerto Rico and Hawai'i, appear as passive but exotically dressed women, ready to learn their lessons.

Within the press, which overwhelmingly supported the Spanish-American War, the voices of opposition appeared primarily in African American and labor papers. The *Indianapolis Recorder* asked rhetorically in 1899, "Are the tender-hearted expansionists in the United States Congress really actuated by the desire to save the Filipinos from self-destruction or is it the worldly greed for gain?" The *Railroad Telegrapher* similarly commented, "The wonder of it all is that the working people are willing to lose blood and treasure in fighting another man's battle."

Most Americans put aside their doubts and welcomed the new era of imperialism. Untouched by the private tragedies of dead or wounded American soldiers and the mass destruction of civilian society in the Philippines, the vast majority could approve Theodore Roosevelt's defense of armed conflict: "No triumph of peace is quite so great as the supreme triumphs of war."

CONCLUSION

The conflicts marking the last quarter of the nineteenth century that pitted farmers, workers, and the proprietors of small businesses against powerful national interests had offered Americans an important moment of democratic promise. By the end of the century, however, the rural and working-class campaigns to retain a large degree of self-government in their communities had been defeated, their organizations destroyed, their autonomy eroded. The rise

CHRONOLOGY

1867	Grange founded
	Secretary of State Seward negotiates the purchase of Alaska
1874	Granger laws begin to regulate railroad shipping rates
1877	Rutherford B. Hayes elected president.
	Great Uprising of 1877
1879	Henry George publishes *Progress and Poverty*
1881	President James A. Garfield assassinated; Chester A. Arthur becomes president
1882	Chinese Exclusion Act
1883	Pendleton Act passed
1884	Grover Cleveland elected president
1887	Interstate Commerce Act creates the Interstate Commerce Commission
1888	Colored Farmers' Alliance formed
	Benjamin Harrison elected president
1889	National Farmers' Alliance formed
1890	Sherman Silver Purchase Act
	McKinley Tariff enacted
	National American Woman Suffrage Association formed
1892	Populist (People's) Party formed
	Coeur d'Alene miners' strike
	Homestead strike
	Ida B. Wells begins crusade against lynching
1893	Western Federation of Miners formed
	Financial panic and depression
	World's Columbian Exhibition opens in Chicago
1894	"Coxey's Army" marches on Washington, DC
	Pullman strike and boycott
1896	*Plessy* v. *Ferguson* upholds segregation
	William McKinley defeats William Jennings Bryan for president
1897	Dingley Tariff again raises import duties to an all-time high
1898	Eugene V. Debs helps found Social Democratic Party
	Hawai'i is annexed
	Spanish-American War begins
	Anti-Imperialist League formed
	Wilmington, North Carolina, massacre
1899	*Cumming* v. *Richmond County Board of Education* sanctions segregated education
	Guerrilla war begins in the Philippines
1900	Gold Standard Act
	Josiah Strong publishes *Expansion*

of a national governing class and its counterpart, the large bureaucratic state, established new rules of behavior, new sources of prestige, and new rewards for the most successful citizens.

But the nation would eventually pay a steep price for the failure of democratic reform. Regional antagonisms, nativist movements against the foreign-born, and above all deepening racial tensions blighted American society. As the new century opened, progressive reformers moved to correct flaws in government while accepting the framework of a corporate society and its overseas empire. So, too, did the majority of citizens who shared their president's pride in expansion.

William Jennings Bryan made another bid for the presidency in 1900 on a strong anti-imperialist platform and was roundly defeated at the polls. The dream of Queen Lili'uokalani for an independent Hawai'i was likewise crushed, although a century after her overthrow, in 1993 President William Clinton signed a joint congressional resolution apologizing for the "alleged role the United States had played" in deposing her. But in 1900, Americans would find the widening divisions in their own society difficult—if not impossible—to overcome.

REVIEW QUESTIONS

1. Discuss some of the problems accompanying the expansion of government during the late nineteenth century. What role did political parties play in this process? Explain how a prominent reformer such as James Garfield might become a leading "machine" politician.

2. What were the major causes and consequences of the Populist movement of the 1880s and 1890s? Why did the election of 1896 prove so important to the future of American politics?

3. Discuss the role of women in both the Grange and the People's Party. What were their specific goals?

4. Discuss the causes and consequences of the financial crisis of the 1890s. How did various reformers and politicians respond to the event? What kinds of programs did they offer to restore the economy or reduce poverty?

5. How did the exclusion of African Americans affect the outcome of populism? Explain the rise of Jim Crow legislation in the South and discuss its impact on the status of African Americans.

6. Describe American foreign policy during the 1890s. Why did the United States intervene in Cuba and the Philippines? What were some of the leading arguments for and against overseas expansion?

Flashcard Review

KEY TERMS

Coxey's Army (p. 536)

Free silver (p. 539)

Grandfather clauses (p. 541)

Grange (p. 530)

Granger laws (p. 531)

Great Uprising of 1877 (p. 533)

Interstate Commerce Commission (ICC) (p. 527)

Jim Crow laws (p. 540)

National American Woman Suffrage Association (NAWSA) (p. 534)

Nativism (p. 540)

Pendleton Civil Service Reform Act (p. 529)

Plessy v. *Ferguson* (p. 540)

Populism (p. 530)

Protective association (p. 536)

Segregation (p. 540)

Sherman Silver Purchase Act (p. 538)

Southern Farmers' Alliance (p. 531)

Woman's Christian Temperance Union (WCTU) (p. 534)

RECOMMENDED READING

Steven Hahn, *A Nation Under Our Feet: Black Political Struggles in the Rural South from Slavery to the Great Migration* (2003). A sweeping history of African American politics with an eye on its influence in shaping the South and the nation in the last half of the nineteenth century. Hahn emphasizes the emergence of political communities and highlights the 1880s as a period of exceptional assertiveness on the part of southern African Americans.

Evelyn Brooks Higginbotham, *Righteous Discontent: The Women's Movement in the Black Baptist Church, 1880–1920* (1993). Documents the central role of women in shaping the theology and racial uplift programs of the National Baptist Convention, the largest denomination of African Americans at the end of the nineteenth century.

Matthew Frye Jacobson, *Barbarian Virtues: The United States Encounters Foreign Peoples at Home and Abroad, 1876–1917* (2000). Links the histories of immigration and empire-building to examine public discussions about foreign people, especially their "fitness" for self-government. Jacobson casts the search for markets as backdrop for cultural history.

Michael Kazin, *A Godly Hero: The Life of William Jennings Bryan* (2006). Makes a strong case for the relevance of Bryan to the history of American liberalism. Kazin explores the sources of Bryan's popularity among the nation's poor and working classes.

Walter LaFeber, *The New Empire: An Interpretation of American Expansion, 1860–1898* (1963, 1998). The best overview of U.S. imperial involvement in the late nineteenth century. LaFeber shows how overseas commitments grew out of the economic expansionist assumptions of American leaders and expanded continuously, if often chaotically, with the opportunities presented by the crises experienced by the older imperial powers.

Leon F. Litwack, *Trouble in Mind: Black Southerners in the Age of Jim Crow* (1998). An expansive social history of the first generation of African Americans born in freedom and surviving a period of extraordinary violent and repressive race relations in the South. Litwack examines the retrenchment of their political and civil rights but emphasizes their resourcefulness and resistance.

Eric T. L. Love, *Race over Empire and U.S. Imperialism, 1865–1900* (2004). An engaging narrative of expansion in the late nineteenth century and a keen analysis of the policies supporting and opposing annexation of territories and the assimilation of new populations.

Noenoe K. Silva, *Aloha Betrayed: Native Hawaiian Resistance to American Colonialism* (2004). Highlights the active role native Hawaiians played in the face of U.S. annexation pressures. Silva breaks ground by using Hawaiian-languages newspapers and sources.

John Lawrence Tone, *War and Genocide in Cuba, 1895–1898* (2006). Provides a new perspective on the Cuban rebellion from Spain and a careful study of Spanish policy in the hand of General Varleriano Weyler.

William Appleman Williams, *Empire as a Way of Life: An Essay on the Causes and Character of America's Present Predicament* (1982). A lucid general exploration of American views of empire. Williams shows that Americans allowed the idea of empire and, more generally, economic expansion to dominate their concept of democracy, especially in the last half of the nineteenth century.

myhistorylab™
Where it's a good time to connect to the past!

Currency Reform

During the Civil War, farmers in the Midwest had gone deeply into debt to expand their crop production and meet the profitable demand for grain and other crops created by war. During the wild financial swings of booms and busts between 1865 and 1900, farmers again borrowed heavily to meet the demand for grains created by various world events. Farmers frequently had to borrow yearly to obtain the seeds and materials to plant their crops. If crop prices were low at harvest or a crop failure occurred, farmers were in deep financial trouble. Radical variations in international crop prices impacted the farmer's bottom line. Panics or depressions would also drive indebted farmers to the wall resulting in mortgage foreclosures and loss of their farms. Looking for simplistic explanations to complicated problems, farmers decided that the railroads and eastern financial interests were in a conspiracy to reduce them to economic slavery to the industrial East.

EXPLAIN AND describe the powerful political lure of currency reform in American presidential campaigns between 1874 and 1900. Where did various political groups and candidates stand on this issue and to whom did they attempt to appeal?

Simplistic explanations led to simplistic answers and currency reform became the central focus of many farmer political movements. After silver was dropped from the list of authorized coins for the U.S., farmers decided that was the focus of their problems and began demanding the free coinage of silver to create an artificial inflation that would raise crop prices and free them from debt, or so they believed. Currency reform became an emotional issue in politics between 1874 and 1900.■

McKinley stands upon the platform of a gold dollar coin supported by cheering workers, clerks, bankers and industrialists. Shipping and industry thrives behind the President under the banner: "Prosperity at Home, Prestige Abroad."

COINAGE ACT, FEBRUARY 12, 1873

AN ACT revising and amending the Laws relative to the Mints, Assay- offices, and Coinage of the United States.

Called the "Crime of '73" by farmers and Populists, the Coinage Act of 1873 demonetized silver by removing it from the list of dollar coins and relegating it to the minor coinage of the United States. Silver had become too expensive to coin, so the Treasury had ceased minting silver dollars. Demonetizing silver was really simply a housekeeping action by Congress, but farmers considered it a conspiracy mounted by eastern bankers to keep them in peonage to the industrial East. It is this law that launches the issue of free coinage of silver.

SEC. 14. That the gold coins of the United States shall be a One-dollar piece... a quartereagle, or two-and-a-half dollar piece; a three dollar piece; a half-eagle, or five-dollar piece; an eagle, or ten-dollar piece; and a double eagle, or twenty dollar piece... which coins shall be a legal tender in all payments at their nominal value....

SEC. I5. That the silver coins of the United States shall be... a half dollar, or fifty-cent piece, a quarter-dollar, or twenty five-cent piece, a dime, or ten-cent piece;... and said coins shall be a legal tender at their nominal value for any amount not exceeding five dollars in any one payment....

SEC. I7. That no coins, either of gold, silver, or minor coinage, shall hereafter be issued from the mint other than those of the denominations, standards, and weights herein set forth.■

POPULIST PLATFORM, 1892

AUTHORED BY *Ignatius Donnelly, leader in the Grange movement and later with the Populists, this statement of demands along with others was adopted by the Populists at their 1892 convention in Omaha, Nebraska. Populists hoped to democratize the nation's economic system, but they never succeeded in their goal.*

Silver, which has been accepted as coin since the dawn of history, has been demonetized to add to the purchasing power of gold by decreasing the value of all forms of property as well as human labor, and the supply of currency is purposely abridged to fatten usurers, bankrupt enterprise, and enslave industry. A vast conspiracy against mankind has been organized on two continents, and it is rapidly taking possession of the world. If not met and overthrown at once it forebodes terrible social convulsions, the destruction of civilization, or the establishment of an absolute despotism. We demand a national currency, safe, sound, and flexible issued by the general government only, a full legal tender for all debts, public and private…. We demand free and unlimited coinage of silver and gold at the present legal ratio of 16 to 1.■

WILLIAM H. HARVEY, *COIN'S FINANCIAL SCHOOL*, 1893

HARVEY WROTE Coin's Financial School *to explain to farmers the complicated economic issue of bimetallism and the demand for free coinage of silver.*

Hard times are with us; the country is distracted; very few things are marketable at a price above the cost of production; tens of thousands are out of employment; the jails, penitentiaries, workhouses and insane asylums are full… the cry of distress is heard on every hand…

Up to 1873 we were on what was known as a bimetallic basis, but what was in fact a silver basis, with gold as a companion metal enjoying the same privileges as silver, except that silver fixed the unit, and the value of gold was regulated by it. This was bimetallism….

Gold was considered the money of the rich. It was owned, principally by that class of people, and the poor people seldom handled it, and… seldom ever saw any of it….

It is proposed by the bimetallists to remonetize silver, and add it to the quantity of money that is to be used for measuring the value of all other property….

You increase the value of all property by adding to the number of money units in the land. You make it possible for the debtor to pay his debts; business to start anew, and revivify all the industries of the country, which must remain paralyzed so long as silver as well as all other property is measured by a gold standard….

The money lenders in the United States, who own substantially all our money, have a selfish interest in maintaining the gold standard. They, too, will not yield….

With silver remonetized, and gold at a premium, not one-tenth the hardships could result that now afflict us…. The bimetallic standard will make the United States the most prosperous nation on the globe.■

WILLIAM JENNINGS BRYAN, "CROSS OF GOLD SPEECH," OFFICIAL PROCEEDINGS OF THE DEMOCRATIC NATIONAL CONVENTION, CHICAGO, ILLINOIS, JULY 9, 1896.

BRYAN BECAME *the champion of farmers and a candidate for president with this "Cross of Gold" speech, which advocated the free silver position of the earlier Populist movement.*

You come to us and tell us that the great cities are in favor of the gold standard. I tell you that the great cities rest upon these broad and fertile prairies. Burn down your cities and leave our farms, and your cities will spring up again as if by magic. But destroy our farms and the grass will grow in the streets of every city in the country….

If they dare to come out in the open field and defend the gold standard as a good thing, we shall fight them to the uttermost, having behind us the producing masses of the nation and the world. Having behind us the commercial interests and the laboring interests and all the toiling masses, we shall answer their demands for a gold standard by saying to them, you shall not press down upon the brow of labor this crown of thorns. You shall not crucify mankind upon a cross of gold.■

Grant Hamilton, *Judge Magazine*, October 13, 1900 ➤
The cartoonist emphasizes the free silver issue in this cartoon that criticizes Bryan as "worth 53 cents only in free silver."

The women, trudging stoutly along under great difficulties, were able to complete their march only when troops of cavalry from Fort Meyers were rushed into Washington . . . No inauguration has ever produced such scenes . . .

—Washington Post, *March 4, 1913*

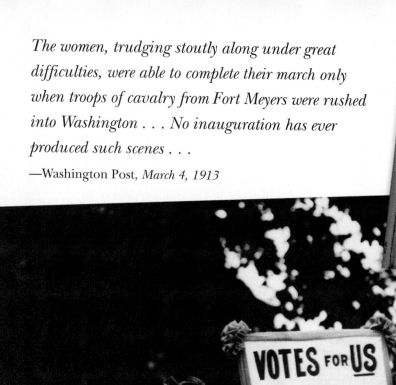

THE JUNGLE

UPTON SINCLAIR

VOTES FOR US WHEN ... ARE WOMEN

VOTES FOR WOMEN

Suffragettes display signs and American flags, while piled into a festooned car.

21

URBAN AMERICA AND THE PROGRESSIVE ERA
1900–1917

WHAT WERE the social and intellectual roots of progressive reform?

TO WHAT extent did progressives redefine the role of the state in American politics?

HOW DID tensions between social justice and social control divide progressives?

HOW DID the impact of new immigration transform American cities?

WHAT NEW forms of activism emerged among the working class, women, and African Americans?

WHAT ROLE did Theodore Roosevelt envision the federal government playing in the national economy?

AMERICAN COMMUNITIES

The Henry Street Settlement House: Women Settlement House Workers Create a Community of Reform

A SHY AND FRIGHTENED YOUNG GIRL APPEARED IN THE DOORWAY OF A weekly home-nursing class for women on Manhattan's Lower East Side. The teacher beckoned her to come forward. Tugging on the teacher's skirt, the girl pleaded in broken English for the teacher to come home with her. "Mother," "baby," "blood," she kept repeating. The teacher gathered up the sheets that were part of the interrupted lesson in bed making. The two hurried through narrow, garbage-strewn, foul-smelling streets, then groped their way up a pitch-dark, rickety staircase. They reached a cramped, two-room apartment, home to an immigrant family of seven and several boarders. There, in a vermin-infested bed, encrusted with dried blood, lay a mother and her newborn baby. The mother had been abandoned by a doctor because she could not afford his fee.

The teacher, Lillian Wald, had enjoyed a comfortable upbringing in a middle-class German Jewish family in Rochester. Despite her parents' objections, she had moved to New York City to become a professional nurse. Resentful of the disdainful treatment nurses received from doctors, and horrified by the inhumane conditions at a juvenile asylum she worked in, Wald determined to find a way of caring for the sick in their neighborhoods and homes. With nursing school classmate Mary Brewster, Wald rented a fifth-floor walk-up apartment on the Lower East Side and established a visiting nurse service. In 1895, philanthropist Jacob Schiff generously donated a red brick Georgian house on Henry Street as a new base of operation.

The Henry Street Settlement stood in the center of perhaps the most overcrowded neighborhood in the world, New York's Lower East Side. Roughly 500,000 people were packed into an area only as large as a midsized Kansas farm. Population density was about 500 per acre, roughly four times the figure for the rest of New York City, and far more concentrated than even the worst slums of London or Calcutta. A single city block might have as many as 3,000 residents. Home for most Lower East Siders was a small tenement apartment that might include paying boarders squeezed in alongside the immediate family. Residents were mostly recent immigrants from southern and eastern Europe: Jews, Italians, Germans, Greeks, Hungarians, Slavs. Men, women, and children toiled in the garment shops, small factories, retail stores, breweries, and warehouses to be found on nearly every street.

The Henry Street Settlement became a model for a new kind of reform community composed essentially of college-educated women who encouraged and supported one another in a wide variety of humanitarian, civic, and political activities. These included support for organized labor, campaigns for better sanitation and more parks, lobbying state legislatures for tougher laws regulating tenement construction and factory safety, and pushing for women's right to vote. Settlement house living arrangements closely resembled those in the dormitories of such new women's colleges as Smith, Wellesley, and Vassar. Like these colleges, the settlement house was an "experiment," but one designed, in settlement house pioneer Jane Addams's words, "to aid in the solution of the social and industrial problems which are engendered by the modern conditions of urban life." Unlike earlier moral reformers, who tried to impose their ideas from outside, settlement house residents lived in poor communities and worked for immediate improvements in the health and welfare of those communities. Yet, as Addams and others repeatedly stressed, the college-educated women were beneficiaries as well. The settlement house allowed them to preserve a collegial spirit, satisfy the desire for service, and apply their academic training.

With its combined moral and social appeal, the settlement house movement attracted many educated young women and grew rapidly. Few women made settlement work a career, but those who did typically chose not to marry, and most lived together with female companions. As the movement flourished, settlement house residents called attention to the plight of the poor and fostered respect for different cultural heritages in countless articles and lectures. Leaders of the movement, including Jane Addams, Lillian Wald, and Florence Kelley, emerged as influential political figures during the progressive era.

During the first two decades of the twentieth century, millions of Americans identified themselves as "progressives" and most, like Lillian Wald, were first drawn to causes and campaigns rooted in their local communities. But many soon saw that confronting the grim realities of an urban and industrial society required national and even global strategies for pursuing reform. It was no cliché for Wald to say, as she did on many occasions, "The whole world is my neighborhood." By the time America entered World War I in 1917, despite its contradictions, the progressive movement had reshaped the political and social landscape of the entire nation.

New York City

THE ORIGINS OF PROGRESSIVISM

etween the 1890s and World War I, a large and diverse number of Americans claimed the political label "progressive." Progressives could be found in all classes, regions, and races. They shared a fundamental belief that America needed a new social consciousness to cope with the problems brought on by the enormous rush of economic and social change in the post–Civil War decades. The devastating depression of the 1890s, the often bloody labor conflicts of that decade, and the Populist revolt caused many Americans to look for a stronger government response to economic and social ills. Yet **progressivism** was no unified movement with a single set of principles. It is best understood as a varied collection of reform communities, often fleeting, uniting citizens in a host of political, professional, and religious organizations, some of which were national in scope.

UNIFYING THEMES

Three basic attitudes underlay the various progressive crusades and movements. The first was anger over the excesses of industrial capitalism and urban growth. Unlike Populist era reformers, who were largely rural and small-town oriented, progressives focused their energies on the social and political ills experienced by Americans in factories or mines and in dreary city tenements or filthy streets. At the same time, progressives shared an essential optimism about the ability of citizens to improve social and economic conditions. They were reformers, not revolutionaries, who believed in using the democratic institutions available to them—the vote, the courts, the legislature—to address social problems. Second, progressives emphasized social cohesion and common bonds as a way of understanding how modern society and economics actually worked. They largely rejected the ideal of individualism that had informed nineteenth-century economic and political theory. For progressives, poverty and success hinged on more than simply individual character; the economy was more than merely a sum of individual calculations. Society's problems, in this view, were structural rather than simply the result of individual failures. Third, progressives believed in the need for citizens to intervene actively, both politically and morally, to improve social conditions. They looked to convert personal outrage into civic activism and to mobilize public opinion in new ways. Progressives thus called for expansion of the legislative and regulatory powers of the state. They moved away from the nineteenth-century celebration of minimal government as the surest way to allow all Americans to thrive.

Progressive rhetoric and methods drew on two distinct sources of inspiration. One was evangelical Protestantism, particularly the late nineteenth-century social gospel movement. Social gospelers rejected the idea of original sin as the cause of human suffering. They emphasized both the capacity and the duty of Christians to purge the world of poverty, inequality, and economic greed. Many progressive activists with roots in the evangelical tradition adapted the old emphasis on individual salvation into a new social activism more focused on finding the common good. A second strain of progressive thought looked to natural and social scientists to develop rational measures for improving the human condition. They believed that experts trained in statistical analysis, engineering, and the sciences could make government and industry more efficient and set new standards for personal behavior. Progressivism thus offered an uneasy combination of social justice and social control, a tension that would characterize American reform for the rest of the twentieth century.

WHAT WERE the social and intellectual roots of progressive reform?

Review Summary

21–12
Herbert Croly, *Progressive Democracy* (1914)

IMAGE KEY

for pages 556–557

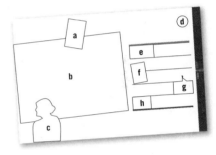

a. Cover, featuring a factory, of "The Jungle" by Upton Sinclair.
b. Suffragettes display signs and American flags, while piled into a festooned car.
c. Suffragette Dorothy Newell has "Votes for Women" written on her back.
d. Bull Moose Party campaign paraphernalia.
e. The Flanner House Baby Clinic, about 1918.
f. Publicity poster for 1913 pageant organized by John Reed and other Greenwich Village radicals supporting the striking silk workers in Paterson, New Jersey.
g. Detail of photo of Women's suffrage parade in Washington, D.C. in 1913.
h. Cartoon showing President Theodore Roosevelt slaying bad trusts and restraining good trusts.

Progressivism A national movement focused on a variety of reform initiatives, including ending corruption, a more business like approach to government, and legislative responses to industrial excess.

NEW JOURNALISM: MUCKRAKING

Changes in journalism helped fuel a new reform consciousness by drawing the attention of millions to urban poverty, political corruption, the plight of industrial workers, and immoral business practices. As early as 1890, journalist Jacob Riis had shocked the nation with his landmark book *How the Other Half Lives,* a portrait of New York City's poor. Riis's book included a remarkable series of photographs he had taken in tenements, lodging houses, sweatshops, and saloons. These striking pictures, combined with Riis's analysis of slum housing patterns, had a powerful impact on a whole generation of urban reformers (see Seeing History).

Within a few years, magazine journalists had turned to uncovering the seamier side of American life. The key innovator was S. S. McClure, a young midwestern editor who in 1893 started America's first large-circulation magazine, *McClure's.* Charging only a dime for his monthly, McClure effectively combined popular fiction with articles on science, technology, travel, and recent history. He attracted a new readership among the urban middle class through aggressive subscription and promotional campaigns, as well as newsstand sales.

18–11
Lincoln Steffens, from *The Shame of the Cities* (1904)

In 1902, McClure began hiring talented reporters to write detailed accounts of the nation's social problems. *McClure's* and other magazines discovered that "exposure journalism" paid off handsomely in terms of increased circulation. The middle-class public responded to this new combination of factual reporting and moral exhortation. Between 1902 and 1908, magazines were full of articles exposing insurance scandals, patent medicine frauds, and stock market swindles.

Muckraking crusades could take many forms. In the 1890s the young African American newspaper editor Ida B. Wells set out to investigate an upsurge in lynchings around the city of Memphis. She paid special attention to the common white defense of lynching—that it was a necessary response to attempts by black men to rape white women. Her 1895 pamphlet *A Red Record* showed that the vast majority of black lynching victims had not even been accused of sexual transgression. Instead, Wells found that lynching was primarily a brutal device to eliminate African Americans who competed with white businesses or who had become too prosperous or powerful (see Chapter 20).

In 1906, David Graham Phillips, in a series for *Cosmopolitan* called "The Treason of the Senate," argued that many conservative U.S. senators were no more than mouthpieces for big business. President Theodore Roosevelt, upset by Phillips's attack on several of his friends and supporters, coined a new term when he angrily denounced Phillips and his colleagues as "muckrakers" who "raked the mud of society and never looked up." Partly due to Roosevelt's outburst, the muckraking vogue began to wane. But muckraking had demonstrated the potential for mobilizing public opinion on a national scale.

INTELLECTUAL TRENDS PROMOTING REFORM

On a deeper level than muckraking, early twentieth-century thinkers challenged several of the core ideas in American intellectual life. Their new theories of education, law, economics, and society provided effective tools for reformers. The emergent fields of the social sciences—sociology, psychology, anthropology, and economics—emphasized observation of how people actually lived and behaved in their communities. Progressive reformers linked the systematic analysis of society and the individual characteristic of these new fields of inquiry to the project of improving the material conditions of Americans. Significantly, many of these intellectual currents transcended national boundaries. American progressives engaged in running dialogues with European counterparts who also contended with crafting effective and rational responses to the needs of overcrowded cities,

Muckraking Journalism exposing economic, social, and political evils, so named by Theodore Roosevelt for its "raking the muck" of American society.

Photographing Poverty in the Slums of New York

"Five Cents a Spot: Lodgers in a Bayard Street Tenement". c. 1899. Museum of the City of New York, Jacob A. Riis Collection.

J acob A. Riis was a twenty-year-old Danish immigrant when he arrived in New York City in 1870. After several years wandering the country as a casual laborer, he returned to New York and began a career as a reporter covering the police beat. By the early 1880s Riis found himself drawn to report on the deteriorating conditions of tenement house life. Riis's reports on the tenement districts reflected a keen outrage and new sense of purpose. "It was upon my midnight trips with the sanitary police," he recalled, "that the wish kept cropping up in me that there were some way of putting before the people what I saw there."

In 1888 Riis taught himself the rudiments of photography. He shot many of these photographs in the dead of the night, taking his subjects by surprise. Other photographs were carefully staged to ensure maximum emotional impact. He spent two years touring the country, presenting an illustrated lecture called "The Other Half: How It Lives and Dies in New York." The use of photography would become a key element for reform crusades in the progressive era and beyond. ■

HERE ARE two Riis photographs, "Five Cents a Spot" and "Home of an Italian Ragpicker." What visual information does each communicate about tenement life? How do they differ in their depiction of New York City's immigrant poor? How do you imagine Riis set up the scene for each of these photographs?

The Jacob A. Riis Collection 157, Museum of the City of New York.

561

Lewis Hine, one of the pioneers of social documentary photography, made this evocative 1908 portrait of "Mamie," a typical young spinner working at a cotton mill in Lancaster, South Carolina. The National Child Labor Committee hired Hine to help document, publicize, and curb the widespread employment of children in industrial occupations. "These pictures," Hine wrote, "speak for themselves and prove that the law is being violated."

Lewis Hine (American, 1874–1940), "A Carolina Spinner," 1908. Gelatin silver print, 4 3/4 × 7 in. Milwaukee Art Museum, Gift of the Sheldon M. Barnett Family. M1973.83.

Social Darwinism   The application of Charles Darwin's theory of biological evolution to society, holding that the fittest and wealthiest survive, the weak and the poor perish, and government action is unable to alter this "natural" process.

impoverished industrial workers, and unresponsive political systems. Jane Addams's original inspiration for the Hull House settlement in Chicago had come when she visited Toynbee Hall in London. Housing reformers in Glasgow and Manchester, as well as workmen's compensation reformers in Berlin, and old age insurance experts in Copenhagen provided important international forums for progressives here and around the world. Despite their national differences, progressives around the world searched for new ways to reinforce social bonds in the modern era.

Sociologist Lester Frank Ward, in his pioneering work *Dynamic Sociology* (1883), offered an important critique of **social Darwinism**, the orthodox theory that attributed social inequality to natural selection and the "survival of the fittest." Ward argued that the conservative social theorists responsible for social Darwinism, such as Herbert Spencer and William Graham Sumner, had wrongly applied evolutionary theory to human affairs. They had confused organic evolution with social evolution. Nature's method was genetic: unplanned, involuntary, automatic, and mechanical. By contrast, civilization had been built on successful human intervention in the natural processes of organic evolution.

Philosopher John Dewey criticized the excessively rigid and formal approach to education found in most American schools. Dewey advocated developing what he called "creative intelligence" in students, which could then be put to use in improving society. Schools ought to be "embryonic communities," miniatures of society, where children were encouraged to participate actively in different types of experiences. By cultivating imagination and openness to new experiences, schools could develop creativity and the habits required for systematic inquiry. Dewey's belief that education was the "fundamental method of social progress and reform" inspired generations of progressive educators.

At the University of Wisconsin, John R. Commons founded the new field of industrial relations and organized a state industrial commission that became a model for other states. Working closely with Governor Robert M. La Follette, Commons and his students helped draft pioneering laws in worker compensation and public utility regulation. Another Wisconsin faculty member, economist Richard Ely, argued that the state was "an educational and ethical agency whose positive aim is an indispensable condition of human progress." Ely believed the state must intervene directly to help solve public problems. He rejected the doctrine of laissez-faire as merely "a tool in the hands of the greedy." Like Commons, Ely worked with Wisconsin lawmakers to apply his expertise in economics to reforming the state's labor laws.

Progressive legal theorists began challenging the conservative view of constitutional law that had dominated American courts. Since the 1870s, the Supreme Court had interpreted the Fourteenth Amendment (1868) as a guarantee of broad rights for corporations. That amendment, which prevented states from depriving "any person of life, liberty, or property, without due process of law," had been designed to protect the civil rights of African Americans against violations by the states. But the Court, led by Justice Stephen J. Field, used the due process clause to strike down state laws regulating business and labor conditions. The Supreme Court and state courts had thus made the Fourteenth Amendment a bulwark for big business and a foe of social welfare measures.

The most important dissenter from this view was Oliver Wendell Holmes Jr. A scholar and Massachusetts judge, Holmes believed the law had to take into account changing social conditions. And courts should take care not to invalidate social legislation enacted democratically. Before the late 1930s, Holmes's pragmatic views of the law seldom convinced a majority of the Court. But his views influenced a generation of lawyers who began practicing what came to be called sociological jurisprudence. In *Muller* v. *Oregon* (1908), the Court upheld an Oregon law limiting the maximum hours for working women, finding that the liberty of contract "is not absolute." Noting that "woman's physical structure and the performance of maternal functions place her at a disadvantage," the Court found that "the physical well-being of woman becomes an object of public interest and care." Louis Brandeis, the state's attorney, amassed statistical, sociological, and economic data, rather than traditional legal arguments, to support his arguments. The "Brandeis Brief" became a common strategy for lawyers defending the constitutionality of progressive legislation.

THE FEMALE DOMINION

In the 1890s, the settlement house movement had begun to provide an alternative to traditional concepts of private charity and humanitarian reform. Settlement workers found they could not transform their neighborhoods without confronting a host of broad social questions: chronic poverty, overcrowded tenement houses, child labor, industrial accidents, public health. They soon discovered the need to engage the political and cultural life of the larger community. As on Henry Street, college-educated, middle-class women were a key vanguard in the crusade for social justice.

21–6
Jane Addams, *Twenty Years at Hull House* (1910)

Jane Addams founded one of the first settlement houses, Hull House, in Chicago in 1889, after years of struggling to find work and a social identity equal to her talents. A member of one of the first generations of American women to attend college, Addams was a graduate of Rockford College. Many educated women were dissatisfied with the life choices conventionally available to them: early marriage or the traditional female professions of teaching, nursing, and library work. Settlement work provided an attractive alternative. Addams often spoke of the "subjective necessity" of settlement houses. By this she meant that they gave young, educated women a way to satisfy their powerful desire to connect with the real world. "There is nothing after disease, indigence and guilt," she wrote, "so fatal to life itself as the want of a proper outlet for active faculties."

Lillian Wald and her allies convinced the New York Board of Health to assign a nurse to every public school in the city. They lobbied the board of education to create the first school lunch programs. They persuaded the city to set up municipal milk stations to ensure the purity of milk. Henry Street also pioneered tuberculosis treatment and prevention. Its leaders became powerful advocates for playground construction, improved street cleaning, and tougher housing inspection. Lillian Wald became a national figure—an outspoken advocate of child labor legislation and woman suffrage and a vigorous opponent of American involvement in World War I.

A portrait of the young Jane Addams, probably taken around the time she founded Hull House in Chicago, in 1889.

OVERVIEW | Currents of Progressivism

	Key Figures	Issues
Local Communities	Jane Addams, Lillian Wald, Florence Kelley, Frederic C. Howe, Samuel Jones	• Improving health, education, welfare in urban immigrant neighborhoods • Child labor, eight-hour day • Celebrating immigrant cultures • Reforming urban politics • Municipal ownership/regulation of utilities
State	Robert M. La Follette, Hiram Johnson, Al Smith	• Limiting power of railroads, other corporations • Improving civil service • Direct democracy • Applying academic scholarship to human needs
National	James K. Vardaman, Hoke Smith, Theodore Roosevelt, Woodrow Wilson	• Disfranchisement of African Americans • Trust-busting • Conservation and western development • National regulation of corporate and financial excesses • Reform of national banking
Intellectual/Cultural	Jacob Riis, Lincoln Steffens, Ida Tarbell, Upton Sinclair, S. S. McClure	• Muckraking
	John Dewey, Louis Brandeis, Edwin A. Ross	• Education reform • Sociological jurisprudence • Empowering "ethical elite"

myhistorylab

Overview: *Currents of Progressivism*

19–11
John Spargo, *The Bitter Cry of Children* (1906)

She offered Henry Street as a meeting place to the National Negro Conference in 1909, out of which emerged the National Association for the Advancement of Colored People.

Social reformer Florence Kelley helped direct the support of the settlement house movement behind groundbreaking state and federal labor legislation. In 1893, she wrote a report detailing the dismal conditions in sweatshops and the effects of long hours on the women and children who worked in them. This report became the basis for landmark legislation in Illinois that limited women to an eight-hour workday, barred children under fourteen from working, and abolished tenement labor. Illinois governor John Peter Altgeld appointed Kelley as chief inspector for the new law. In 1895, Kelley published *Hull House Maps and Papers*, the first scientific study of urban poverty in America. Moving to the Henry Street Settlement in 1898, Kelley served as general secretary of the new National Consumers' League. With Lillian Wald, she established the New York Child Labor Committee and pushed for the creation of the U.S. Children's Bureau, established in 1912. Its director, the first woman to head a federal bureau, was Julia Lathrop, another alumna of Hull House.

New female-dominated occupations, such as social work, public health nursing, and home economics, allowed women to combine professional aspirations with the older traditions of moral reform, especially those centered on child welfare. The new professionalism, in turn, sustained reform commitments and a female dominion that simultaneously expanded the social welfare function of the state and increased women's public authority and influence.

Kelley, Addams, Wald, Lathrop, and their circle consciously used their power as women to reshape politics in the progressive era. Electoral politics and the state were historically male preserves, but female social progressives turned their gender into an advantage. Activists like Kelley used their influence in civil society to create new state powers in the service of social justice. "Women's place is Home," wrote reformer Rheta Childe Dorr, "but Home is not contained within the four walls of an individual home. Home is the community."

PROGRESSIVE POLITICS IN CITIES AND STATES

Progressive reformers poured much of their zeal and energy into local political battles. In cities and states across the nation, progressive politicians became a powerful force, often balancing the practical need for partisan support with nonpartisan appeals to the larger citizenry. Although their motives and achievements were mixed, progressives were united in their attacks on corruption in government, the need to reign in corporate power, and calls for more activist city and state governments.

THE URBAN MACHINE

By the turn of the century, Democratic Party machines, usually dominated by first- and second-generation Irish, controlled the political life of most large American cities. The keys to machine strength were disciplined organization and the delivery of essential services to both immigrant communities and business elites. The successful machine politician viewed his work as a business, and he accumulated his capital by serving people who needed assistance. In exchange for votes, machine politicians offered their constituents a variety of services. These included municipal jobs in the police and fire departments, work at city construction sites, intervention with legal problems, and food and coal during hard times. In exchange for valuable franchises and city contracts, businessmen routinely bribed machine politicians and contributed liberally to their campaign funds.

The machines usually had close ties to organized prostitution and gambling, as well as more legitimate commercial entertainments. Vaudeville and burlesque theater, boxing, horse racing, and professional baseball were other urban enterprises with economic and political links to machines. Entertainment and spectacle made up a central element in the machine political style as well. Constituents looked forward to the colorful torchlight parades, free summer picnics, and riverboat excursions regularly sponsored by the machines.

In the early twentieth century, to expand their base of support, political machines in the Northeast began concentrating more on passing welfare legislation beneficial to working-class and immigrant constituencies. In this way, machine politicians often allied themselves with progressive reformers in state legislatures. In New York, for example,

TO WHAT extent did progressives redefine the role of the state in American politics?

myhistorylab
Review Summary

21–8
Helen M. Todd, *Getting Out the Vote* (1911)

Timothy D. "Big Tim" Sullivan, the popular and influential Democratic Party machine boss of the Bowery and Lower East Side districts of New York City, ca. 1901.

19–10
William T. Riordon, *Plunkitt of Tammany Hall* (1905)

21–9
Walker Percy, *Birmingham under the Commission Plan* (1911)

QUICK REVIEW

Municipal Reform

◆ Urban reformers sought to break alliances between city bosses and business leaders.

◆ Urban reformers developed the concept of the city commission and the city manager.

◆ Business groups often promoted these reforms.

Referendum   Submission of a law, proposed or already in effect, to a direct popular vote for approval or rejection.

Tammany Hall figures such as Robert Wagner, Al Smith, and Big Tim Sullivan worked with middle-class progressive groups to pass child labor laws, factory safety regulations, worker compensation plans, and other efforts to make government more responsive to social needs. As Jewish and Catholic immigrants expanded in number and proportion in the city population, urban machines also began to champion cultural pluralism, opposing prohibition and immigration restrictions and defending the contributions made by new ethnic groups in the cities.

PROGRESSIVES AND URBAN REFORM

Political progressivism originated in the cities. It was both a challenge to the power of machine politics and a response to deteriorating urban conditions. Reformers placed much of the blame for urban ills on the machines and looked for ways to restructure city government. The "good government" movement, led by the National Municipal League, fought to make city management a nonpartisan, even nonpolitical, process by bringing the administrative techniques of large corporations to cities. Reformers revised city charters in favor of stronger mayoral power and expanded use of appointed administrators and career civil servants. They drew up blueprints for model charters, ordinances, and zoning plans designed by experts trained in public administration.

Progressive politicians who focused on the human problems of the industrial city championed a different kind of reform, one based on changing policies rather than the political structure. In Cleveland, for example, wealthy businessman Thomas L. Johnson served as mayor from 1901 to 1909. He emphasized both efficiency and social welfare. His popular program included lower streetcar fares, public baths, milk and meat inspection, and an expanded park and playground system.

STATEHOUSE PROGRESSIVES

On the state level progressives focused on two major reform themes that sometimes coexisted uneasily. On the one hand they looked to make politics more open and accessible by pushing through procedural reforms. The *direct primary*, for example, promised to take the selection of electoral candidates out of the smoke-filled backrooms of party bosses and into the hands of party voters. In 1902 Oregon was the first state to adopt two other reforms: the *initiative*, the popular power to initiate legislation, and the *referendum*, the right to a popular vote on proposed legislation. Several states also adopted a related reform, the "Australian," or secret ballot, which took the mechanics of ballot printing and distribution from the parties and made it the responsibility of the government. California and other states also established the *recall*: the power to remove elected officials from office. And in 1913 the states and Congress ratified the Seventeenth Amendment, shifting the selection of U.S. senators from the state legislatures to direct election by voters. On the other hand, progressive activists sought to remove some decisions from the electoral process entirely. They believed that judgments about railroad regulations, improving a city's sewer system, or establishing tax rates might best be made by informed, unbiased experts appointed to boards and commissions charged with setting policy. Many progressive states became political laboratories for testing both more democratic procedures and a greater reliance on professional expertise.

In Wisconsin, Republican dissident Robert M. La Follette forged a coalition of angry farmers, small businessmen, and workers with his fiery attacks on railroads and other large corporations. Leader of the progressive faction of the state Republicans, "Fighting Bob" won three terms as governor (1900–06), then served as a

U.S. senator until his death in 1925. As governor, he pushed through tougher corporate tax rates, a direct primary, an improved civil service code, and a railroad commission designed to regulate freight charges. La Follette used faculty experts at the University of Wisconsin to help research and write his bills. Other states began copying the "Wisconsin Idea," the application of academic scholarship and theory to the needs of the people.

In New York Theodore Roosevelt won the governor's race in 1898, propelled by his fame as a Spanish-American War hero. Although supported by the Republican Party machine, Roosevelt embraced the progressive view that the people's interest ought to be above partisan politics, and he used his personal popularity with voters to assert independence from party leaders. As governor he held frequent press conferences to communicate more directly with voters and gain support for progressive legislation. Roosevelt's administration strengthened the state's civil service system, set wage and hour standards for state employees, raised teachers' salaries, and placed a franchise tax on corporations controlling public utilities. Roosevelt also championed progressive conservation measures by expanding New York's forest preserves and reforming the fish and game service, thus anticipating his strong support of environmental regulation as president.

Western progressives targeted railroads, mining and timber companies, and public utilities for reform. Large corporations such as Pacific Gas and Electric and the Southern Pacific Railroad had amassed enormous wealth and political influence. They were able to corrupt state legislatures and charge consumers exorbitant rates. An alliance between middle-class progressives and working-class voters reflected growing disillusionment with the ideology of individualism that had helped pave the way for the rise of the big corporation. Between 1905 and 1909, nearly every southern state moved to regulate railroads by mandating lower passenger and freight rates.

Southern progressives also directed their energies at the related problems of child labor and educational reform. In 1900, at least one-quarter of all southern cotton mill workers were between the ages of ten and sixteen, and many worked over sixty hours per week. Led by reform-minded ministers Edgar Gardner Murphy and Alexander McKelway and drawing on the activism of white club women, reformers attacked child labor by focusing on the welfare of children and their mothers and emphasizing the degradation of "Anglo Saxons." In 1903, Alabama and North Carolina enacted the first state child labor laws, setting twelve as a minimum age for employment. But the laws were weakened by many exemptions and no provisions for enforcement, as lawmakers also heard the loud complaints from parents and mill owners who resented the efforts of reformers to limit their choices.

But southern progressivism was for white people only. Indeed, southern progressives believed that the disenfranchisement of black voters and the creation of a legally segregated public sphere were necessary preconditions for political and social reform. With African Americans removed from political life, white southern progressives argued, the direct primary system of nominating candidates would give white voters more influence. Between 1890 and 1910, southern states passed a welter of statutes specifying poll taxes, literacy tests, and property qualifications with the explicit goal of preventing voting by blacks. This systematic disenfranchisement of African American voters stripped black communities of any political power.

Southern progressives also supported the push toward a fully segregated public sphere. Between 1900 and 1910, southern states strengthened Jim Crow laws requiring separation of races in restaurants, streetcars, beaches, and theaters.

The legacy of southern progressivism was thus closely linked to the strengthening of the legal and institutional guarantees of white supremacy.

Contradictions in the progressive approach to political reform were not limited to the South. Undermining party control of voting and elections may have also weakened politicians' incentives to get out the vote. Greater reliance on city commissions and other experts meant less in the way of promised favors for voters, which may have also made voters less interested in elections. Tightening up on residency requirements and voter registration rules in the cities cut into turnout in immigrant and ethnic neighborhoods. The effort to make politics more open, nonpartisan, and voter friendly also led, ironically, to a decline in voter participation and interest around the country. Whereas in the 1890s voter participation in national elections was routinely close to 90 percent, by World War I that figure had fallen to barely 60 percent, where it would stay for most of the rest of the century.

SOCIAL CONTROL AND ITS LIMITS

HOW DID tensions between social justice and social control divide progressives?

myhistorylab

Review Summary

Many middle- and upper-class Protestant progressives feared that immigrants and large cities threatened the stability of American democracy. Progressives often believed they had a mission to frame laws and regulations for the "benefit" of immigrants, industrial workers, and African Americans. These efforts at social control usually required some form of coercion. This was the moralistic and frequently xenophobic side of progressivism, and it provided a powerful source of support for the regulation of drinking, prostitution, leisure activities, and schooling.

THE PROHIBITION MOVEMENT

During the last two decades of the nineteenth century, the Woman's Christian Temperance Union (WCTU) had grown into a powerful mass organization. The WCTU appealed especially to women angered by men who used alcohol and then abused their wives and children. It directed most of its work toward ending the production, sale, and consumption of alcohol. But local WCTU chapters put their energy into nontemperance activities as well, including homeless shelters, Sunday schools, prison reform, child nurseries, and woman suffrage. The WCTU thus provided women with a political forum in which they could fuse their traditional moral posture as guardians of the home with broader public concerns. By 1911, the WCTU, with a quarter million members, was the largest women's organization in American history.

Other **temperance groups** had a narrower focus. The Anti-Saloon League, founded in 1893, began by organizing local-option campaigns in which rural counties and small towns banned liquor within their geographical limits. It drew much of its financial support from local businessmen, who saw a link between closing a community's saloons and increasing the productivity of workers. The league was a one-issue pressure group that played effectively on anti-urban and anti-immigrant prejudice. League lobbyists hammered away at the close connections among saloon culture, liquor dealers, brewers, and big-city political machines.

The battle to ban alcohol revealed deep ethnic and cultural divides within America's urban communities. Opponents of alcohol were generally "pietists," who viewed the world from a position of moral absolutism. These included native-born, middle-class Protestants associated with evangelical churches, along with some old-stock Protestant immigrant denominations. Opponents of prohibition

Prohibition A ban on the production, sale, and consumption of liquor, achieved temporarily through state laws and the Eighteenth Amendment.

Temperance groups Groups dedicated to reducing the sale and consumption of alcohol.

were generally "ritualists" with less arbitrary notions of personal morality. These were largely new-stock, working-class Catholic and Jewish immigrants, along with some Protestants, such as German Lutherans.

THE SOCIAL EVIL

Many of the same reformers who battled the saloon and drinking also engaged in efforts to eradicate prostitution. Crusades against "the social evil" had appeared at intervals throughout the nineteenth century, but they reached a new level of intensity between 1895 and 1920. Antiprostitution campaigns epitomized the diverse makeup and mixed motives of so much progressive reform. Male business and civic leaders joined forces with feminists, social workers, and clergy to eradicate "commercialized vice."

Between 1908 and 1914, exposés of the "white slave traffic" became a national sensation. Dozens of books, articles, and motion pictures alleged an international conspiracy to seduce and sell girls into prostitution. Most of these materials exaggerated the practices they attacked. They also made foreigners, especially Jews and southern Europeans, scapegoats for the sexual anxieties of native-born whites.

Reformers had trouble believing that any woman would freely choose to be a prostitute; such a choice was antithetical to conventional notions of female purity and sexuality. But for wage-earning women, prostitution was a rational choice in a world of limited opportunities. The antivice crusades succeeded in closing down many urban red-light districts and larger brothels, but these were replaced by the streetwalker and call girl, who were more vulnerable to harassment and control by policemen and pimps. Rather than eliminating prostitution, reform efforts transformed the organization of the sex trade.

THE REDEMPTION OF LEISURE

Progressives faced a thorny issue in the growing popularity of commercial entertainment. For large numbers of working-class adults and children, leisure meant time and money spent at vaudeville and burlesque theaters, amusement parks, dance halls, and motion picture houses. These competed with municipal parks, libraries, museums, YMCAs, and school recreation centers. "Commercialized leisure," warned Frederic C. Howe in 1914, "must be controlled by the community, if it is to become an agency of civilization rather than the reverse."

By 1908, movies had become the most popular form of cheap entertainment in America. As the films themselves became more sophisticated and as "movie palaces" began to replace cheap storefront theaters, the new medium attracted a large middle-class clientele as well. Progressive reformers seized the chance to help regulate the new medium as a way of improving the commercial recreation of the urban poor. In 1909, New York City movie producers and exhibitors joined with the reform-minded People's Institute to establish the voluntary National Board of Censorship (NBC). A revolving group of civic activists reviewed new movies, passing them, suggesting changes, or condemning them. Local censoring committees all over the nation subscribed to the board's weekly bulletin. They aimed at achieving what John Collier of the NBC called "the redemption of leisure." By 1914, the NBC was reviewing 95 percent of the nation's film output.

STANDARDIZING EDUCATION

The most important educational trends in these years were the expansion and bureaucratization of the nation's public school systems. In most cities, centralization served to consolidate the power of older urban elites who felt threatened by

Movies, **by John Sloan,** 1913, the most talented artist among the so-called Ashcan realist school of painting. Active in socialist and bohemian circles, Sloan served as art editor for *The Masses* magazine for several years. His work celebrated the vitality and diversity of urban working-class life and leisure, including the new commercial culture represented by the motion picture.

John Sloan, "Movies," 1913. Oil painting. The Toledo Museum of Art.

the large influx of immigrants. Children began school earlier and stayed there longer. Kindergartens spread rapidly in large cities. They presented, as one writer put it in 1903, "the earliest opportunity to catch the little Russian, the little Italian, the little German, Pole, Syrian, and the rest and begin to make good American citizens of them." By 1918, every state had some form of compulsory school attendance. High schools also multiplied, extending the school's influence beyond the traditional grammar school curriculum.

High schools reflected a growing belief that schools should be comprehensive, multifunctional institutions. In 1918, the National Education Association offered a report defining Cardinal Principles of Secondary Education. These included instruction in health, family life, citizenship, and ethical character. Academic programs prepared a small number of students for college. Vocational programs trained boys and girls for a niche in the new industrial order. Boys took shop courses in metal trades, carpentry, and machine tools. Girls learned typing, bookkeeping, sewing, cooking, and home economics. The Smith-Hughes Act of 1917 provided federal grants to support these programs and set up a Federal Board for Vocational Education.

CHALLENGES TO PROGRESSIVISM

While most progressive reformers had roots in Protestantism and the middle-class professions, other Americans vigorously challenged their political vision. Organized workers often invoked progressive rhetoric and ideals but for quite different, sometimes radical, ends.

All these industrial workers shared the need to sell their labor for wages in order to survive. At the same time, differences in skill, ethnicity, and race proved powerful barriers to efforts at organizing trade unions that could bargain for improved wages and working conditions. So, too, did the economic and political power of the large corporations that dominated much of American industry. Yet there were also small, closely knit groups of skilled workers, such as printers and brewers, who exercised real control over their lives and labors. And these years saw many labor struggles that created effective trade unions or laid the groundwork for others. Industrial workers also became a force in local and national politics, adding a chorus of insistent voices to the calls for social justice.

THE NEW GLOBAL IMMIGRATION

On the eve of World War I, close to 60 percent of the industrial labor force was foreign-born. Most of these workers were among the roughly 9 million new immigrants from southern and eastern Europe who arrived in the United States between

HOW DID the impact of new immigration transform American cities?

Review Summary

19–12
Mary Antin, *The Promised Land* (1912)

Newly landed European immigrant families on the dock at Ellis Island in New York harbor, 1900. Originally a black-and-white photograph, this image was later color tinted for reproduction as a postcard or book illustration.

1900 and 1914. Nearly all the new Italian, Polish, Hungarian, Jewish, and Greek immigrants lacked industrial skills. They thus entered the bottom ranks of factories, mines, mills, and sweatshops.

These new immigrants had been driven from their European farms and towns by several forces, including the undermining of subsistence farming by commercial agriculture; a falling death rate that brought a shortage of land; and religious and political persecution. American corporations also sent agents to recruit cheap labor. Except for Jewish immigrants, a majority of whom fled virulent anti-Semitism in Russia and Russian Poland, most newcomers planned on earning a stake and then returning home (see Map 21.1).

The decision to migrate usually occurred through social networks—people linked by kinship, personal acquaintance, and work experience. These "chains," extending from places of origin to specific destinations in the United States, helped migrants cope with the considerable risks entailed by the long and difficult journey. A study conducted by the U.S. Immigration Commission in 1909 found that about 60 percent of the new immigrants had their passage arranged by immigrants already in America.

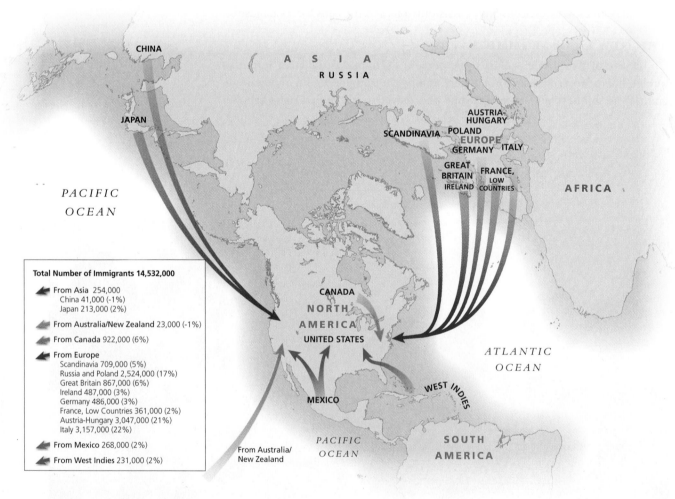

Total Number of Immigrants 14,532,000

From Asia 254,000
  China 41,000 (-1%)
  Japan 213,000 (2%)

From Australia/New Zealand 23,000 (-1%)

From Canada 922,000 (6%)

From Europe
  Scandinavia 709,000 (5%)
  Russia and Poland 2,524,000 (17%)
  Great Britain 867,000 (6%)
  Ireland 487,000 (3%)
  Germany 486,000 (3%)
  France, Low Countries 361,000 (2%)
  Austria-Hungary 3,047,000 (21%)
  Italy 3,157,000 (22%)

From Mexico 268,000 (2%)

From West Indies 231,000 (2%)

MAP 21.1
Immigration to the United States, 1901–20

WHAT FORCES propelled so many people to emigrate from European countries?

The low-paid, backbreaking work in basic industry became nearly the exclusive preserve of the new immigrants. In 1907, of the 14,359 common laborers employed at Pittsburgh's U.S. Steel mills, 11,694 were eastern Europeans. One-third of the immigrant steelworkers were single, and among married men who had been in the country less than five years, about two-thirds reported that their wives were still in Europe. Workers with families generally supplemented their incomes by taking in single men as boarders.

Not all of the new immigrants came from Europe, as hemispheric migration increased sharply as well. Over 300,000 French Canadians arrived in the United States between 1900 and 1930, settling mostly in New England. But the maturing continental railroad system had widened the choice of destinations to communities in upstate New York and Detroit, which had the largest number of French Canadian migrants outside of New England. The pull of jobs in New England's textile industry, along with its physical proximity, attracted male farmers and laborers unable to make a living in the rural districts of Quebec. Roughly one-third of female migrants were domestic servants looking for the higher pay and greater independence associated with factory labor.

Mexican immigration also grew in these years, providing a critical source of labor for the West's farms, railroads, and mines. Between 1900 and 1914, the number of people of Mexican descent living and working in the United States tripled, from roughly 100,000 to 300,000. Economic and political crises spurred tens of thousands of Mexico's rural and urban poor to emigrate north. Large numbers of seasonal agricultural workers regularly came up from Mexico to work in the expanding sugar beet industry and then returned. But a number of substantial resident Mexican communities also emerged in the early twentieth century. Throughout Texas, California, New Mexico, Arizona, and Colorado, western cities developed *barrios*, distinct communities of Mexicans.

Between 1898 and 1907, more than 80,000 Japanese entered the United States. The vast majority were young men working as contract laborers in the West, mainly in California. American law prevented Japanese immigrants (the *Issei*) from obtaining American citizenship because they were not white. This legal discrimination, along with informal exclusion from many occupations, forced the Japanese to create niches for themselves within local economies. Most Japanese settled near Los Angeles, where they established small communities centered around fishing, truck farming, and the flower and nursery business.

URBAN GHETTOS

In large cities, new immigrant communities took the form of densely packed ghettos. The sheer size and dynamism of these cities made the immigrant experience more complex than in smaller cities and more isolated communities. Workers in the urban garment trades toiled for low wages and suffered layoffs, unemployment, and poor health. But conditions in the small, labor-intensive shops of the clothing industry differed significantly from those in the large-scale, capital-intensive industries like steel.

New York City had become the center of both Jewish immigration and America's huge ready-to-wear clothing industry. Most of the industry operated on the grueling piece-rate, or task, system, in which manufacturers and subcontractors paid individuals or teams of workers to complete a certain quota of labor within a specific time.

The garment industry was highly seasonal. A typical workweek was sixty hours with seventy common during the busy season. But there were long stretches of unemployment in slack times. Often forced to work in cramped, dirty, and badly

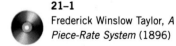

21-1
Frederick Winslow Taylor, *A Piece-Rate System* (1896)

New York City police set up this makeshift morgue to help identify victims of the disastrous Triangle Shirtwaist Company fire, March 25, 1911. Unable to open the locked doors of the sweatshop and desperate to escape from smoke and flames, many of the 146 who died had leaped eight stories to their death.

QUICK REVIEW

Triangle Shirtwaist Fire

- 1911: fire kills 146 workers.
- Managers had locked the exits.
- Tragedy led to the enactment of new industrial safety laws.

---

lit rooms, garment workers strained under a system in which time equaled money.

In November 1909, two New York garment manufacturers responded to strikes by unskilled women workers by hiring thugs and prostitutes to beat up pickets. The strikers won the support of the Women's Trade Union League, a group of sympathetic female reformers that included Lillian Wald, Mary Dreier, and prominent society figures. The Uprising of the 20,000, as it became known, swept through the city's garment district. The strikers demanded union recognition, better wages, and safer and more sanitary conditions. They drew support from thousands of suffragists, trade unionists, and sympathetic middle-class women as well. Hundreds of strikers were arrested, and many were beaten by police. After three cold months on the picket line, the strikers returned to work without union recognition. But the International Ladies Garment Workers Union (ILGWU), founded in 1900, did gain strength and negotiated contracts with some of the city's shirtwaist makers. The strike was an important breakthrough in the drive to organize unskilled workers into industrial unions.

On March 25, 1911, the issues raised by the strike took on new urgency when a fire raced through three floors of the Triangle Shirtwaist Company. As the flames spread, workers found themselves trapped by exit doors that had been locked from the outside. Fire escapes were too narrow and too weak to withstand the heat. Within half an hour, 146 people, mostly young Jewish women, had been killed by smoke or had leaped to their deaths. In the bitter aftermath, women progressives led by Florence Kelley and Frances Perkins of the National Consumers' League joined with Tammany Hall leaders Al Smith, Robert Wagner, and Big Tim Sullivan to create a New York State Factory Investigation Commission. Under Perkins's vigorous leadership, the commission conducted an unprecedented round of public hearings and on-site inspections, leading to a series of state laws that dramatically improved safety conditions and limited the hours for working women and children.

COMPANY TOWNS

Immigrant industrial workers and their families often established their communities in a company town, where a single large corporation was dominant. Cities such as Lawrence, Massachusetts; Gary, Indiana; and Butte, Montana, revolved around the industrial enterprises of Pacific Woolen, U.S. Steel, and Anaconda Copper. Workers had little or no influence over the economic and political institutions of these cities. In the more isolated company towns, residents often had no alternative but to buy their food, clothing, and supplies at company stores, usually for exorbitantly high prices. But they did maintain some community control in other ways. Family and kin networks, ethnic lodges, saloons, benefit societies, churches and synagogues, and musical groups affirmed traditional forms of community in a setting governed by individualism and private capital.

On the job, modern machinery and industrial discipline meant high rates of injury and death. A 1910 study of work accidents revealed that nearly a fourth of all new steelworkers were killed or injured each year. Mutual aid associations, organized around ethnic groups, offered some protection through cheap insurance and death benefits.

In steel and coal towns, women not only maintained the household and raised the children, but they also boosted the family income by taking in boarders, sewing, and laundry. Many women also tended gardens and raised chickens, rabbits, and goats. Their produce and income helped reduce dependence on the company store. Working class women felt the burdens of housework more heavily than their middle-class sisters. Pump water, indoor plumbing, and sewage disposal were often available only on a pay-as-you-go basis. Many women struggled with the effects of their husbands' excessive drinking and faced early widowhood.

The power of large corporations in the life of company towns was most evident among the mining communities of the West, as was violent labor conflict. The Colorado Fuel and Iron Company (CFI) employed roughly half of the 8,000 coal miners who labored in that state's mines. In mining towns such as Ludlow and Trinidad, the CFI thoroughly dominated the lives of miners and their families. By the early twentieth century, new immigrants, such as Italians, Greeks, Slavs, and Mexicans, composed a majority of the population in these western mining communities.

In September 1913, the United Mine Workers led a strike in the Colorado coalfields, calling for improved safety, higher wages, and recognition of the union. Thousands of miners' families moved out of company housing and into makeshift tent colonies provided by the union. In October, Governor Elias Ammons ordered the Colorado National Guard into the tense strike region to keep order. The troops, supposedly neutral, proceeded to ally themselves with the mine operators. By spring, the strike had bankrupted the state, forcing the governor to remove most of the troops. The coal companies then brought in large numbers of private mine guards who were extremely hostile toward the strikers. On April 20, 1914, a combination of guardsmen and private guards surrounded the largest of the tent colonies at Ludlow, where more than a thousand mine families lived. A shot rang out (each side accused the other of firing), and a pitched battle ensued that lasted until the poorly armed miners ran out of ammunition. At dusk, the troops burned the tent village to the ground, routing the families and killing fourteen, eleven of them children. Enraged strikers attacked mines throughout southern Colorado in an armed rebellion that lasted ten days, until President Woodrow Wilson ordered the U.S. Army into the region. News of the Ludlow Massacre shocked millions and aroused widespread protests and demonstrations against the policies of Colorado Fuel and Iron and its owner, John D. Rockefeller Jr.

THE AFL: "UNIONS, PURE AND SIMPLE"

Following the depression of the 1890s, the American Federation of Labor (AFL) emerged as the strongest and most stable organization of workers. Samuel Gompers's strategy of recruiting skilled labor into unions organized by craft had paid off. Union membership climbed from under 500,000 in 1897 to 1.7 million by 1904.

But the strength of craft organization also gave rise to weakness. In 1905, Gompers told a union gathering in Minneapolis that "caucasians" would not "let their standard of living be destroyed by negroes, Chinamen, Japs, or any others." Those "others" included the new immigrants from eastern and southern Europe, men and women, who labored in the steel mills and garment trades. Each trade looked mainly to the welfare of its own. Many explicitly barred women and African Americans from membership.

AFL unions had a difficult time holding on to their gains. Economic slumps, technological changes, and aggressive counterattacks by employer organizations could be devastating. Trade associations using management-controlled efficiency drives fought union efforts to regulate output and shop practices. The National

Association of Manufacturers (NAM), a group of smaller industrialists founded in 1903, launched an "open shop" campaign to eradicate unions altogether. "Open shop" was simply a new name for a workplace where unions were not allowed. Unfriendly judicial decisions also hurt organizing efforts. Not until the 1930s and New Deal legislation would unions be able to count on legislative and legal protections for collective bargaining and the right to strike.

THE IWW: "ONE BIG UNION"

Some workers developed more radical visions of labor organizing. The Western Federation of Miners (WFM) had gained strength in the metal mining regions of the West by leading several strikes marred by violence. In 1899, during a strike in the silver mining district of Coeur d'Alene, Idaho, the Bunker Hill and Sullivan Mining Company had enraged the miners by hiring armed detectives and firing all union members. Desperate miners retaliated by destroying a company mill with dynamite. Idaho's governor declared martial law and obtained federal troops to enforce it. In a pattern that would become familiar in western labor relations, the soldiers served as strikebreakers, rounding up hundreds of miners and imprisoning them for months in makeshift bullpens.

In response to the brutal realities of labor organizing in the West, most WFM leaders embraced socialism and industrial unionism. In 1905, leaders of the WFM, the Socialist Party, and various radical groups gathered in Chicago to found the Industrial Workers of the World (IWW). The IWW charter proclaimed bluntly, "The working class and the employing class have nothing in common. . . . Between these two classes a struggle must go on until the workers of the world unite as a class, take possession of the earth and the machinery of production, and abolish the wage system."

William D. "Big Bill" Haywood, an imposing, one-eyed, hard-rock miner, emerged as the most influential and flamboyant spokesman for the IWW, or **Wobblies**, as they were called. Haywood, a charismatic speaker and effective organizer, regularly denounced the AFL for its conservative emphasis on organizing skilled workers by trade. He insisted that the IWW would exclude no one from its ranks. The Wobblies concentrated their efforts on miners, lumberjacks, sailors, "harvest stiffs," and other casual laborers.

The IWW briefly became a force among eastern industrial workers, tapping the rage and growing militance of the immigrants and unskilled. Wobbly leaders such as Haywood, Elizabeth Gurley Flynn, and Joseph Ettor used class-conscious rhetoric and multilingual appeals to forge unity among the ethnically diverse Lawrence workforce of 25,000.

The IWW failed to establish permanent organizations in the eastern cities, but it remained a force in the lumber camps, mines, and wheat fields of the West. In spite of its militant rhetoric, the IWW concerned itself with practical gains. "The final aim is revolution," said one Wobbly organizer, "but for the present let's see if we can get a bed to sleep in, water enough to take a bath in and decent food to eat." But when the United States entered World War I, the Justice Department used the IWW's anticapitalist rhetoric and antiwar stance to crush it.

REBELS IN BOHEMIA

During the 1910s, a small but influential community of painters, journalists, poets, social workers, lawyers, and political activists coalesced in the New York City neighborhood of Greenwich Village. These cultural radicals, nearly all of middle-class background and hailing from provincial American towns, shared a deep sympa-

Wobblies Popular name for the members of the Industrial Workers of the World (IWW).

thy toward the struggles of labor, a passion for modern art, and an openness to socialism and anarchism.

The term **"bohemian"** referred to anyone who had artistic or intellectual aspirations and who lived with disregard for conventional rules of behavior. Other American cities, notably Chicago at the turn of the century, had supported bohemian communities. But the Village scene was unique, if fleeting. The worldview of the Village's bohemian community found expression in *The Masses*, a monthly magazine founded in 1911 by socialist critic Max Eastman, who was also its editor. "The broad purpose of *The Masses*," wrote John Reed, one of its leading writers, "is a social one—to everlastingly attack old systems, old morals, old prejudices—the whole weight of outworn thought that dead men have saddled upon us."

For some, Greenwich Village offered a chance to experiment with sexual relationships or work arrangements. For others, it was an escape from small-town conformity, or a haven for like-minded artists and activists. Yet the Village bohemians were united in their search for a new sense of community. Intellectuals and artists, as well as workers, feeling alienated from the rest of society, sought shelter in the collective life and close-knit social relations of the Village community.

The Village bohemia lasted only a few years, a flame snuffed out by the chill political winds accompanying America's entry into World War I. Yet for decades, Greenwich Village remained a mecca for young men and women searching for alternatives to conventional ways of living.

Publicity poster for the 1913 pageant, organized by John Reed and other Greenwich Village radicals, supporting the cause of striking silk workers in Paterson, New Jersey. This poster drew on aesthetic styles associated with the Industrial Workers of the World, typically including a heroic, larger-than-life image of a factory laborer.

WOMEN'S MOVEMENTS AND BLACK ACTIVISM

Like working-class radicals, politically engaged women and African American activists often found themselves at odds with more moderate and mainstream progressive reformers. They contested both gender and racial assumptions inherited from the nineteenth century. Some progressives supported the challenges in one or both of these spheres. They helped shape an agenda for social justice that would echo throughout the rest of the twentieth century.

In fighting racial discrimination, African Americans had a more difficult task. As racism gained ground in the political and cultural spheres, black progressives fought defensively to prevent the rights they had secured during Reconstruction from being further undermined. Still, they managed to produce leaders, ideas, and organizations that would have a long-range impact on American race relations.

THE NEW WOMAN

The settlement house movement discussed in the opening of this chapter was just one of the new avenues of opportunity opened to progressive-era women. A steady proliferation of women's organizations attracted growing numbers of educated, middle-class women. With more men working in offices, more children attending school, and family size declining, the middle-class home was emptier. At the same time, more middle-class women were graduating from high school and college.

WHAT NEW forms of activism emerged among the working class, women, and African Americans?

myhistorylab

Review Summary

Bohemian   Artistic individual who lives with disregard for the conventional rules of behavior.

Single-sex clubs brought middle-class women into the public sphere by celebrating the distinctive strengths associated with women's culture: cooperation, uplift, service. The women's club movement combined an earlier focus on self-improvement and intellectual pursuits with newer benevolent efforts on behalf of working women and children. The Buffalo Union, for example, sponsored art lectures for housewives and classes in typing, stenography, and bookkeeping for young working women. It also maintained a library, set up a "noon rest" downtown where women could eat lunch, and ran a school for training domestics.

For many middle-class women, the club movement provided a new kind of female-centered community. Club activity often led members to participate in other civic ventures, particularly "child-saving" reforms, such as child labor laws and mothers' pensions. Some took up the cause of working-class women, fighting for protective legislation and offering aid to trade unions. As wives and daughters of influential and well-off men in their communities, club women had access to funds and could generate support for projects they undertook.

Other women's associations made even more explicit efforts to bridge class lines between middle-class homemakers and working-class women. The National Consumers' League (NCL), started in 1898 by Maud Nathan and Josephine Lowell, sponsored a "white label" campaign in which manufacturers who met safety and sanitary standards could put NCL labels on their food and clothing. Under the dynamic leadership of Florence Kelley, the NCL took an even more aggressive stance by publicizing labor abuses in department stores and lobbying for maximum-hour and minimum-wage laws in state legislatures. In its efforts to protect home and housewife, worker and consumer, the NCL embodied the ideal of "social housekeeping."

BIRTH CONTROL

The phrase "birth control," coined by Margaret Sanger around 1913, described her campaign to provide contraceptive information and devices for women. Sanger had seen her own mother die at age forty-nine after bearing eleven children. In 1910, Sanger was a thirty-year-old nurse and housewife living with her husband and three children in a New York City suburb. Excited by a socialist lecture she had

A supportive crowd surrounds birth control pioneer Margaret Sanger and her sister, Ethel Byrne, as they leave the Court of Special Services in New York City in 1917. Police had recently closed Sanger's first birth control clinic in the immigrant neighborhood of Brownsville, New York, and Sanger herself had spent a month in jail.

attended, she convinced her husband to move to the city, where she threw herself into the bohemian milieu. She became an organizer for the IWW, and in 1912, she wrote a series of articles on female sexuality for a socialist newspaper.

When postal officials confiscated the paper for violating obscenity laws, Sanger left for Europe to learn more about contraception. She returned to New York determined to challenge the obscenity statutes with her own magazine, the *Woman Rebel*. When she distributed her pamphlet *Family Limitation*, postal inspectors confiscated copies and she found herself facing forty-five years in prison. In October 1914, she fled to Europe again. In her absence, anarchist agitator Emma Goldman and many women in the Socialist Party took up the cause.

An older generation of feminists had advocated "voluntary motherhood," or the right to say no to a husband's sexual demands. The new birth control advocates embraced contraception as a way of advancing sexual freedom for middle-class women, as well as responding to the misery of those working-class women who bore numerous children while living in poverty. Sanger returned to the United States in October 1915. After the government dropped the obscenity charges, she embarked on a national speaking tour. In 1916, she again defied the law by opening a birth control clinic in a working-class neighborhood in Brooklyn and offering birth control information without a physician present. Arrested and jailed, she gained more publicity for her crusade. Within a few years, birth control leagues and clinics could be found in every major city and most large towns in the country.

RACISM AND ACCOMMODATION

At the turn of the century, four-fifths of the nation's 10 million African Americans still lived in the South, where most eked out a living working in agriculture. In the cities, most blacks were relegated to menial jobs, but a small African American middle class of entrepreneurs and professionals gained a foothold by selling services and products to the black community. They all confronted a racism that was growing in both intensity and influence in American politics and culture. White racism came in many variants and had evolved significantly since slavery days. The more virulent strains, influenced by Darwin's evolutionary theory, held that blacks were a "degenerate" race, genetically predisposed to vice, crime, and disease and destined to lose the struggle for existence with whites.

African Americans also endured a deeply racist popular culture that made hateful stereotypes of black people a normal feature of political debate and everyday life. Benjamin Tillman, a U.S. senator from South Carolina, denounced the African American as "a fiend, a wild beast, seeking whom he may devour." In northern cities "coon songs," based on gross caricatures of black life, were extremely popular in theaters and as sheet music.

Southern progressives articulated a more moderate racial philosophy. They also assumed the innate inferiority of blacks, but they believed that black progress was necessary to achieve the economic and political progress associated with a vision of the New South. Their solution to the "race problem" stressed paternalist uplift.

Amid this political and cultural climate, Booker T. Washington won recognition as the most influential black leader of the day. Born a slave in 1856, Washington was educated at Hampton Institute in Virginia, one of the first freedmen's schools devoted to industrial education. In 1881, he founded Tuskegee Institute, a black school in Alabama devoted to industrial and moral education. He became the leading spokesman for racial accommodation, urging blacks to focus on economic improvement and self-reliance, as opposed to political and civil rights. In an 1895 speech delivered at the Cotton States Exposition in Atlanta, Washington outlined the key themes of accommodationist philosophy. "Cast down your buckets

18–9
Booker T. Washington, *Atlanta Exposition Address* (1895)

In July 1905, a group of African American leaders met in Niagara Falls, Ontario, to protest legal segregation and the denial of civil rights to the nation's black population. This portrait was taken against a studio backdrop of the falls. In 1909, the leader of the Niagara movement, W. E. B. Du Bois (second from right, middle row) founded and edited *The Crisis*, the influential monthly journal of the National Association for the Advancement of Colored People.

Photographs and Prints Division, Schomburg Center for Research in Black Culture, The New York Public Library, Astor, Lenox and Tilden Foundations.

17–11
W. E. B. Du Bois, *Of Mr. Booker T. Washington and Others* (1903)

21–4
Platform Adopted by the National Negro Committee (1909)

Niagara movement   African American group organized in 1905 to promote racial integration, civil and political rights, and equal access to economic opportunity.

National Association for the Advancement of Colored People   Interracial organization co-founded by W. E. B. Du Bois in 1910 dedicated to restoring African American political and social rights.

where you are," Washington told black people, meaning they should focus on improving their vocational skills as industrial workers and farmers. "In all things that are purely social," he told attentive whites, "we can be as separate as the fingers, yet one as the hand in all things essential to mutual progress."

Washington's message won him the financial backing of leading white philanthropists and the respect of progressive whites. But Washington also gained a large following among African Americans, especially those who aspired to business success. With the help of Andrew Carnegie, he founded the National Negro Business League to preach the virtue of black business development in black communities.

Washington also had a decisive influence on the flow of private funds to black schools in the South. Publicly he insisted that "agitation of questions of social equality is the extremest folly." But privately, Washington also spent money and worked behind the scenes trying to halt disfranchisement and segregation. He offered secret financial support, for example, for court cases that challenged Louisiana's grandfather clause, the exclusion of blacks from Alabama juries, and railroad segregation in Tennessee and Georgia.

RACIAL JUSTICE, THE NAACP, AND BLACK WOMEN'S ACTIVISM

In the early 1900s, scholar and activist W. E. B. Du Bois created a significant alternative to Washington's leadership. A product of the black middle class, Du Bois had been educated at Fisk University and Harvard, where in 1895, he became the first African American to receive a Ph.D. In *The Souls of Black Folk* (1903), Du Bois declared prophetically that "the problem of the twentieth century is the problem of the color line." Through essays on black history, culture, education, and politics, Du Bois explored the concept of "double consciousness." Black people, he argued, would always feel the tension between an African heritage and their desire to assimilate as Americans. *Souls* represented the first effort to embrace African American culture as a source of collective black strength and something worth preserving.

Du Bois criticized Booker T. Washington's philosophy for its acceptance of "the alleged inferiority of the Negro." The black community, he argued, must fight for the right to vote, for civic equality, and for higher education for the "talented tenth" of their youth. In 1905, Du Bois and editor William Monroe Trotter brought together a group of educated black men to oppose Washington's conciliatory views. Discrimination they encountered in Buffalo, New York, prompted the men to move their meeting to Niagara Falls, Ontario. The **Niagara movement** protested legal segregation, the exclusion of blacks from labor unions, and the curtailment of voting and other civil rights.

The Niagara movement failed to generate much change. But in 1909, many of its members, led by Du Bois, attended a National Negro Conference held at the Henry Street Settlement in New York. The group included a number of white progressives sympathetic to the idea of challenging Washington's philosophy. A new interracial organization emerged from this conference, the **National Association for the Advancement of Colored People**. Du Bois, the only black officer of the original NAACP, founded and edited *The Crisis*, the influential NAACP monthly journal. For the next several decades, the NAACP would lead struggles to overturn legal and economic barriers to equal opportunity.

The disenfranchisement of black voters in the South severely curtailed African American political influence. In response, African American women created new strategies to challenge white supremacy and improve life in their communities. Founded in 1900, the Women's Convention of the National Baptist Convention, the largest black denomination in the United States, offered African American women a new public space to pursue reform work and "racial uplift." They organized settlement houses and built playgrounds; they created daycare facilities and kindergartens; they campaigned for women's suffrage, temperance, and advances in public health. In effect, they transformed church missionary societies into quasi–social service agencies.

NATIONAL PROGRESSIVISM

On the presidential level, both Republican Theodore Roosevelt and Democrat Woodrow Wilson laid claim to the progressive mantle—a good example of how on the national level, progressivism animated many perspectives. In their pursuit of reform agendas, both significantly reshaped the office of the president. As progressivism moved to Washington, nationally organized interest groups and public opinion began to rival the influence of the old political parties in shaping the political landscape.

THEODORE ROOSEVELT AND PRESIDENTIAL ACTIVISM

The assassination of William McKinley in 1901 made forty-two-year-old Theodore Roosevelt the youngest man to ever hold the office of president. Roosevelt viewed the presidency as a "bully pulpit"—a platform from which he could exhort Americans to reform their society—and he aimed to make the most of it.

Roosevelt was a uniquely colorful figure, a shrewd publicist, and a creative politician. His three-year stint as a rancher in the Dakota Territory; his fondness for hunting and nature study; his passion for scholarship, which resulted in ten books before he became president—all these set "T. R." apart from most of his upper-class peers. Roosevelt preached the virtues of "the strenuous life," and he believed that educated and wealthy Americans had a special responsibility to serve, guide, and inspire those less fortunate. But he believed the nation was at a crossroads that required the national state to play a more active role in curbing the power of wealthy industrialists.

Roosevelt made key contributions to national progressivism and to changing the office of the president. He knew how to inspire and guide public opinion. In 1902, Roosevelt demonstrated his unique style of activism when he personally intervened in a bitter dispute in the anthracite coal industry. Using public calls for conciliation, a series of White House meetings, and private pressure on the mine owners, Roosevelt secured an arbitrated settlement that won better pay and working conditions for the miners but without recognition of their union. Roosevelt also pushed for efficient government as the solution to social problems. Administrative agencies run by experts, he believed, could find rational solutions that would satisfy everyone.

TRUST-BUSTING AND REGULATION

One of the first issues Roosevelt faced was growing public concern with the rapid business consolidations taking place in the American economy. In 1902, he directed

WHAT ROLE did Theodore Roosevelt envision the federal government playing in the national economy?

myhistorylab
Review Summary

   21-7
Theodore Roosevelt, *The New Nationalism* (1910)

This 1909 cartoon by Clifton Berryman depicts President Theodore Roosevelt slaying those trusts he considered "bad" for the public interest while restraining those whose business practices he considered "good" for the economy. The image also plays on T. R.'s well-publicized fondness for big-game hunting.

Sherman Antitrust Act The first federal antitrust measure, passed in 1890; sought to promote economic competition by prohibiting business combinations in restraint of trade or commerce.

Hepburn Act Act that strengthened the Interstate Commerce Commission (ICC) by authorizing it to set maximum railroad rates and inspect financial records.

Pure Food and Drug Act Act that established the Food and Drug Administration (FDA), which tested and approved drugs before they went on the market.

the Justice Department to begin a series of prosecutions under the **Sherman Antitrust Act**. The first target was the Northern Securities Company, a huge merger of transcontinental railroads. The Justice Department fought the case all the way through a hearing before the Supreme Court. In *Northern Securities* v. *United States* (1904), the Court held that the stock transactions involved in the merger constituted an illegal combination in restraint of interstate commerce.

This case established Roosevelt's reputation as a "trust-buster." During his two terms, the Justice Department filed forty-three cases under the Sherman Antitrust Act to restrain or dissolve business monopolies. Roosevelt viewed these suits as necessary to publicize the issue and assert the federal government's ultimate authority over big business. But he did not really believe in the need to break up large corporations. "Trust-busting" might be good politics, but unlike many progressives, who were nostalgic for smaller companies and freer competition, Roosevelt accepted centralization as a fact of modern economic life. Indeed many of the legal cases against trusts were dropped after business executives met privately with Roosevelt in the White House. What was most important, in T. R.'s view, was to insist on the right and power of the federal government to reign in excessive corporate behavior.

After easily defeating Democrat Alton B. Parker in the 1904 election, Roosevelt felt more secure in pushing for regulatory legislation. In 1906, Roosevelt responded to public pressure for greater government intervention and, overcoming objections from a conservative Congress, signed three important measures into law. The **Hepburn Act** strengthened the Interstate Commerce Commission (ICC) by authorizing it to set maximum railroad rates and inspect financial records.

Two other laws passed in 1906 also expanded the regulatory power of the federal government. The battles surrounding these reforms demonstrate how progressive measures often attracted supporters with competing motives. The **Pure Food and Drug Act** established the Food and Drug Administration (FDA), which tested and approved drugs before they went on the market. The Meat Inspection Act empowered the Department of Agriculture to inspect and label meat products. In both cases, supporters hailed the new laws as providing consumer protection against adulterated or fraudulently labeled food and drugs.

But regulatory legislation found advocates among American big business as well. Large meatpackers such as Swift and Armour strongly supported stricter federal regulation as a way to drive out smaller companies that could not meet tougher standards. The new laws also helped American packers compete more profitably in the European export market by giving their meat the official seal of federal inspectors. Large pharmaceutical manufacturers similarly supported new regulations that would eliminate competitors and patent medicine suppliers.

THE BIRTH OF ENVIRONMENTALISM

As a naturalist and outdoorsman, Theodore Roosevelt also believed in the need for government regulation of the natural environment. The conservation of forest and water resources, he argued, was a national problem of vital import. In 1905, he created the U.S. Forest Service and named conservationist Gifford Pinchot to head it. Pinchot recruited a force of forest rangers to manage the reserves. By 1909, total timber and forest reserves had increased from 45 to 195 million acres, and more than 80 million acres of mineral lands had been withdrawn from public sale.

On the broad issue of managing America's natural resources, the Roosevelt administration took the middle ground between preservation and unrestricted commercial development. But other voices championed a more radical vision of conservation, emphasizing the preservation of wilderness lands against the encroachment of commercial exploitation. The most influential and committed of these was John Muir, an essayist and founder of the modern environmentalist movement. Muir made a passionate and spiritual defense of the inherent value of the American wilderness. He served as first president of the Sierra Club, founded in 1892 to preserve and protect the mountain regions of the West Coast as well as Yellowstone National Park in Wyoming, Montana, and Idaho.

A bitter, drawn-out struggle over new water sources for San Francisco revealed the deep conflicts between conservationists, represented by Pinchot, and preservationists, represented by Muir. After a devastating earthquake in 1906, San Francisco sought federal approval to dam and flood the spectacular Hetch Hetchy Valley, located 150 miles from the city in Yosemite National Park. Conservationists and their urban progressive allies argued that developing Hetch Hetchy would be a victory for the public good over greedy private developers, since the plan called for municipal control of the water supply. To John Muir and the Sierra Club, Hetch Hetchy was a "temple" threatened with destruction by the "devotees of ravaging commercialism." Although, in the end, they lost the battle for Hetch Hetchy, the preservationists gained much ground in the larger campaign of alerting the nation to the dangers of a vanishing wilderness. They began to use their own utilitarian rationales, arguing that national parks would encourage economic growth through tourism and provide Americans with a healthy escape from urban and industrial areas. In 1916, the preservationists obtained their own bureaucracy in Washington with the creation of the National Park Service.

myhistorylab

Exploring America: *Hetchy Hetchy*

REPUBLICAN SPLIT

In 1908, Roosevelt kept his promise to retire after a second term. He chose Secretary of War William Howard Taft as his successor. Taft easily defeated Democrat William Jennings Bryan in the 1908 election. During Taft's presidency, the gulf between "insurgent" progressives and the "stand pat" wing split the Republican Party wide open. To some degree, the battles were as much over style as substance. Compared with Roosevelt, the reflective and judicious Taft brought a much more restrained concept of the presidency to the White House. He supported some progressive measures, including the constitutional amendment legalizing a graduated income tax (ratified in 1913), safety codes for mines and railroads, and the creation of a federal Children's Bureau (1912). But in a series of bitter political fights involving tariff, antitrust, and conservation policies, Taft alienated Roosevelt and many other progressives.

After returning from an African safari and a triumphant European tour in 1910, Roosevelt threw himself back into national politics. He directly challenged Taft for the Republican Party leadership. Although Roosevelt won most of the state primaries, the old guard still controlled the national convention, and renominated Taft in June 1912. Roosevelt's supporters stormed out, and in August, the new Progressive Party nominated Roosevelt and Hiram Johnson of California as its presidential ticket. Roosevelt's "New Nationalism" presented a vision of a strong federal

New Freedom Woodrow Wilson's 1912 program for limited government intervention in the economy to restore competition by curtailing the restrictive influences of trusts and protective tariffs, thereby providing opportunities for individual achievement.

21–11
Woodrow Wilson, *The New Freedom* (1913)

21–3
Eugene V. Debs, *The Outlook for Socialism in the United States* (1900)

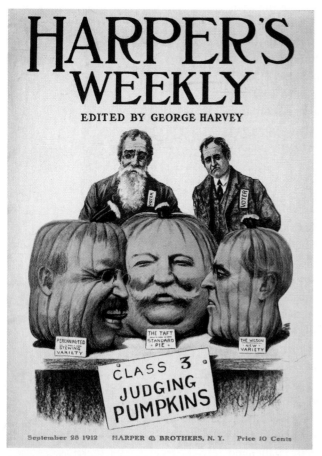

This political cartoon, drawn by Charles Jay Budd, appeared on the cover of *Harper's Weekly,* September 28, 1912. It employed the imagery of autumn county fairs to depict voters as unhappy with their three choices for president. Note that the artist did not include the fourth candidate, Socialist Eugene V. Debs, who was often ignored by more conservative publications such as *Harper's*.

government, led by an activist president, regulating and protecting the various interests in American society. The platform called for woman suffrage, the eight-hour day, prohibition of child labor, minimum-wage standards for working women, and stricter regulation of large corporations.

THE ELECTION OF 1912: A FOUR-WAY RACE

With the Republicans so badly divided, the Democrats sensed a chance for their first presidential victory in twenty years. They chose Governor Woodrow Wilson of New Jersey as their candidate. Although not nearly as well known nationally as Taft and Roosevelt, Wilson had built a strong reputation as a reformer. After teaching history and political science at several schools, he became president of Princeton University in 1902. In 1910, he won election as New Jersey's governor, running against the state Democratic machine. He won the Democratic nomination for president with the support of many of the party's progressives, including William Jennings Bryan.

Wilson declared himself and the Democratic Party to be the true progressives. Viewing Roosevelt rather than Taft as his main rival, Wilson contrasted his **New Freedom** campaign with Roosevelt's New Nationalism. Crafted largely by progressive lawyer Louis Brandeis, Wilson's platform was far more ambiguous than Roosevelt's. The New Freedom emphasized restoring conditions of free competition and equality of economic opportunity. Wilson did favor a variety of progressive reforms for workers, farmers, and consumers. But in sounding older, nineteenth-century Democratic themes of states' rights and small government, Wilson argued against allowing the federal government to become as large and paternalistic as Roosevelt advocated. Socialist Party nominee Eugene V. Debs offered the fourth and most radical choice to voters. The party's 1912 platform called for collective ownership of all large-scale industry and all means of transportation and communication. It demanded shorter working hours, an end to child labor, and the vote for women.

An inspiring orator who drew large and sympathetic crowds wherever he spoke, Debs proved especially popular in areas with strong labor movements and populist traditions. He wrapped his socialist message in an apocalyptic vision. Socialists would "abolish this monstrous system and the misery and crime which flow from it." Debs and the Socialists also took credit for pushing both Roosevelt and Wilson further toward the left. Both the Democratic and Progressive Party platforms contained proposals that had been considered extremely radical only ten years earlier.

In the end, the divisions in the Republican Party gave the election to Wilson (see Map 21.2). In several respects, the election of 1912 was the first "modern" presidential race. It featured the first direct primaries, challenges to traditional party loyalties, an issue-oriented campaign, and a high degree of interest-group activity.

WOODROW WILSON'S FIRST TERM

As president, Wilson followed Roosevelt's lead in expanding the activist dimensions of the office. He became more responsive to pressure for a greater federal role in regulat-

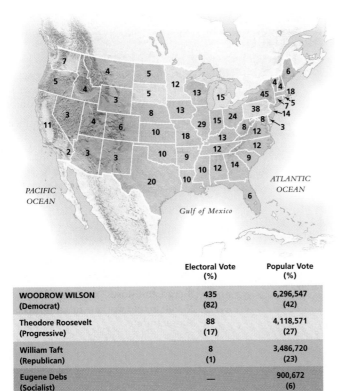

	Electoral Vote (%)	Popular Vote (%)
WOODROW WILSON (Democrat)	435 (82)	6,296,547 (42)
Theodore Roosevelt (Progressive)	88 (17)	4,118,571 (27)
William Taft (Republican)	8 (1)	3,486,720 (23)
Eugene Debs (Socialist)	—	900,672 (6)

MAP 21.2

The Election of 1912 The split within the Republican Party allowed Woodrow Wilson to become only the second Democrat since the Civil War to be elected president. Eugene Debs's vote was the highest ever polled by a Socialist candidate.

WHAT CAUSED the split in the Republican Party?

ing business and the economy. This increase in direct lobbying—from hundreds of local and national reform groups, Washington-based organizations, and the new Progressive Party—was itself a new and defining feature of the era's political life. With the help of a Democratic-controlled Congress, Wilson pushed through a significant battery of reform proposals.

The **Underwood-Simmons Act of 1913** substantially reduced tariff duties on a variety of raw materials and manufactured goods, including wool, sugar, agricultural machinery, shoes, iron, and steel. Taking advantage of the newly ratified **Sixteenth Amendment**, which gave Congress the power to levy taxes on income, it also imposed the first graduated tax (up to 6 percent) on personal incomes. The **Federal Reserve Act** that same year restructured the nation's banking and currency system. It created twelve Federal Reserve Banks, regulated by a central board in Washington. Member banks were required to keep a portion of their cash reserves in the Federal Reserve Bank of their district.

Wilson also supported the **Clayton Antitrust Act** of 1914, which replaced the old Sherman Act of 1890 as the nation's basic antitrust law. The Clayton Act reflected the growing political clout of the American Federation of Labor. It exempted unions from being construed as illegal combinations in restraint of trade, and it forbade federal courts from issuing injunctions against strikers. But Wilson adopted the view that permanent federal regulation was necessary for checking the abuses of big business. The **Federal Trade Commission (FTC)**, established in 1914, sought to give

QUICK REVIEW

Democratic Victory in 1912

♦ Republicans split between Taft and Roosevelt.

♦ Democrats put themselves forward as the "true progressives."

♦ Wilson won with only 42 percent of the popular vote.

Underwood-Simmons Act of 1913 Reform law that lowered tariff rates and levied the first regular federal income tax.

Sixteenth Amendment Authorized a federal income tax.

Federal Reserve Act The 1913 law that revised banking and currency by extending limited government regulation through the creation of the Federal Reserve System.

CHRONOLOGY

1889   Jane Addams founds Hull House in Chicago

1890   Jacob Riis publishes *How the Other Half Lives*

1895   Booker T. Washington addresses Cotton States Exposition in Atlanta, emphasizing an accommodationist philosophy

Lillian Wald establishes Henry Street Settlement in New York

1898   Florence Kelley becomes general secretary of the new National Consumers' League

1900   Robert M. La Follette is elected governor of Wisconsin

1901   Theodore Roosevelt succeeds the assassinated William McKinley as president

1903   Lincoln Steffens publishes *The Shame of the Cities*

1905   President Roosevelt creates U.S. Forest Service and names Gifford Pinchot head

Industrial Workers of the World is founded in Chicago

1906   Upton Sinclair's *The Jungle* exposes conditions in the meatpacking industry

Congress passes Pure Food and Drug Act and Meat Inspection Act and establishes Food and Drug Administration

1908   In *Muller* v. *Oregon* the Supreme Court upholds a state law limiting maximum hours for working women

1909   Uprising of 20,000 garment workers in New York City's garment industries helps organize unskilled workers into unions

National Association for the Advancement of Colored People (NAACP) is founded

1911   Triangle Shirtwaist Company fire kills 146 garment workers in New York City

Socialist critic Max Eastman begins publishing *The Masses*

1912   Democrat Woodrow Wilson wins presidency, defeating Republican William H. Taft, Progressive Theodore Roosevelt, and Socialist Eugene V. Debs

"Bread and Roses" strike involves 25,000 textile workers in Lawrence, Massachusetts

Margaret Sanger begins writing and speaking in support of birth control for women

1913   Sixteenth Amendment, legalizing a graduated income tax, is ratified.

Seventeenth Amendment, shifting the selection of U.S. senators to direct election by voters

1914   Clayton Antitrust Act exempts unions from being construed as illegal combinations in restraint of trade

Federal Trade Commission is established

Ludlow Massacre occurs

1916   National Park Service is established

Clayton Antitrust Act   Replaced the old Sherman Act of 1890 as the nation's basic antitrust law. It exempted unions from being construed as illegal combinations in restraint of trade, and it forbade federal courts from issuing injunctions against strikers.

Federal Trade Commission (FTC)   Government agency established in 1914 to provide regulatory oversight of business activity.

the federal government the same sort of regulatory control over corporations that the ICC had over railroads.

On social issues, Wilson proved more cautious in his first two years. His initial failure to support federal child labor legislation and rural credits to farmers angered many progressives. A Southerner, Wilson also issued an executive order that instituted legal segregation in federal employment, requiring African Americans to work separately from white employees in government offices around Washington, DC. As the reelection campaign of 1916 approached, Wilson worried about defections from the labor and social justice wings of his party. He proceeded to support a rural credits act providing government capital to federal farm banks, as well as federal aid to agricultural extension programs in schools. He also came out in favor of a worker compensation bill for federal employees, and he signed the landmark Keating-Owen Act, which banned children under fourteen from working in enterprises engaged in interstate commerce. But by 1916, the dark cloud of war in Europe had already begun to cast its long shadow over progressive reform.

CONCLUSION

In her memoirs Lillian Wald summarized the growth of the Henry Street Settlement she had founded in 1895 as a home health and visiting nurse service on New York's Lower East Side. "Our experience in one small East Side section," she recalled in 1934, "a block perhaps, has led to a next contact, and a next, in widening circles, until our community relationships have come to include the city, the state, the national government, and the world at large." Much the same could be said of the progressive movement. What had begun as a series of interlocking, sometimes contradictory, reform initiatives had come to redefine Americans' relationship to government itself. Cities and state legislatures now routinely made active interventions to improve the lives of their citizens. Real advances had been made through a range of social legislation covering working conditions, child labor, minimum wages, and worker compensation. Social progressives, too, had discovered the power of organizing into extraparty lobbying groups, such as the National Consumers' League and the National American Woman Suffrage Association. But the national government had now become the focus of political power and reform energy. The president was now expected to provide leadership in policymaking, and new federal bureaucracies exerted more influence over the day-to-day lives of Americans.

Yet many progressive reforms had uneven or unintended consequences. The tensions between fighting for social justice and the urge toward social control remained unresolved. The emphasis on efficiency, uplift, and rational administration often collided with humane impulses to aid the poor, the immigrant, the slum dweller. The large majority of African Americans, blue-collar workers, and urban poor remained untouched by federal assistance programs. The drive for a more open and democratic political process, in particular, had the effect of excluding some people from voting while including others. For African Americans, progressivism largely meant disenfranchisement from voting altogether. Stricter election laws made it more difficult for third parties to get on the ballot. Voting itself steadily declined after 1916. Overall, party voting became a less important form of political participation. Interest-group activity, congressional and statehouse lobbying, and direct appeals to public opinion gained currency as ways of influencing government. Business groups and individual trade associations were among the most active groups pressing their demands on government. Political action often shifted from legislatures to the new administrative agencies and commissions created to deal with social and economic problems. Popular magazines and journals grew significantly in both number and circulation, becoming more influential in shaping and appealing to national public opinion. America's entry into World War I effectively drained the energy out of progressive reform. But the progessive movement, with all its contradictions and internal tensions, had profoundly changed the landscape of American political and social life.

REVIEW QUESTIONS

1. Discuss the tensions within progressivism between the ideals of social justice and the urge for social control. What concrete achievements are associated with each wing of the movement? What were the driving forces behind them?

2. Describe the different manifestations of progressivism at the local, state, and national levels.

3. How did workers use their own values and communities to restrain the power of large corporations during the progressive era?

4. How did the era's new immigration reshape America's cities and workplaces? What connections can you draw between the new immigrant experience and progressive era politics?

5. Analyze the progressive era from the perspective of African Americans. What political and social developments were most crucial, and what legacies did they leave?

6. How do the goals, methods, and language of progressives still find voice in contemporary America?

myhistorylab

Flashcard Review

KEY TERMS

Bohemian (p. 577)
Clayton Antitrust Act (p. 586)
Federal Reserve Act (p. 585)
Federal Trade Commission (FTC)
   (p. 586)
Hepburn Act (p. 582)
Muckraking (p. 560)
National Association for the
   Advancement of Colored People
   (p. 580)
New Freedom (p. 584)
Niagara movement (p. 580)

Progressivism (p. 559)
Prohibition (p. 568)
Pure Food and Drug Act (p. 582)
Referendum (p. 566)
Sherman Antitrust Act (p. 582)
Sixteenth Amendment (p. 585)
Social Darwinism (p. 562)
Temperance groups (p. 568)
Underwood-Simmons Act of 1913
   (p. 585)
Wobblies (p. 576)

RECOMMENDED READING

James Chace, *1912: Wilson, Roosevelt, Taft & Debs—The Election That Changed the Country* (2004). Narrative account of this pivotal presidential election that revolved around competing visions of progressivism.

Alan Dawley, *Struggles for Justice: Social Responsibility and the Liberal State* (1991). Offers an important interpretation of progressivism that focuses on how the working class and women pushed the state toward a more activist role in confronting social problems.

David von Drehle, *Triangle: The Fire That Changed America* (2003). Superb, deeply researched narrative of the disastrous Triangle Fire that re-creates the world of the victims and the reform movement that ensued.

Maureen Flanagan, *America Reformed: Progressives and Progressivisms, 1890s–1920s* (2007). An excellent new overview of progressive era achievements, including fine analysis of the contradictions within the movement.

Louise W. Knight, *Citizen: Jane Addams and the Struggle for Democracy* (2005). Beautifully written new biography of this key progressive figure, focusing on Addams's early life and the evolution of her political thought.

Michael McGerr, *A Fierce Discontent: The Rise and Fall of the Progressive Movement in America, 1870–1920* (2003). A new synthesis arguing that the heart of progressivism lay in the efforts of the urban middle class to reshape the behavior of both the poor and the wealthy.

Michael Perman, *Struggle for Mastery: Disfranchisement in the South, 1888–1908* (2001). A comprehensive, state-by-state overview of the campaigns to remove African Americans from the electoral process.

Daniel T. Rodgers, *Atlantic Crossings: Social Politics in a Progressive Age* (1998). A magisterial work of comparative history focusing on the transnational conversations that deeply influenced American progressive thinkers and reformers.

Christine Stansell, *American Moderns: Bohemian New York and the Creation of a New Century* (2000). Vividly written account that places radical politics and "New Women" at the center of the shaping of modernism.

For study resources for this chapter, go to **www.myhistorylab.com** and choose *Out of Many, Teaching and Learning Classroom Edition.* You will find a wealth of study and review material for this chapter, including pretests and posttests, customized study plan, key-term review flash cards, interactive map and document activities, and documents for analysis.

On the other hand, if there is little enthusiasm, the people everywhere are taking the war as a grim necessity, feeling that they have been forced into it by events beyond their control . . .

—Ray Stannard Baker, June 17, 1917

Female workers build a vehicle in an engineering shop in 1917.

22

A GLOBAL POWER
THE UNITED STATES IN
THE ERA OF THE GREAT WAR
1901–1920

HOW DID Theodore Roosevelt use force as component of U.S. foreign policy?

WHY DID most Americans oppose U.S. involvement in World War I in 1914?

HOW DID the federal government try to change public opinion about U.S. involvement in World War I?

WHAT WERE the domestic effects in the United States of World War I?

WHAT STEPS did the federal government take to suppress the antiwar movement?

HOW CAN we explain Woodrow Wilson's failure to win the peace?

AMERICAN COMMUNITIES
The American Expeditionary Force in France

AT 5:30 A.M. ON SEPTEMBER 26, 1918, SOME 600,000 SOLDIERS OF the American Expeditionary Force (AEF) pulled themselves out of the mud and headed into the dense grey fog on a twenty-mile front between the Meuse River and the Argonne Forest in northern France. The biggest and costliest American operation of World War I had begun. In sheer size and scale, the Meuse-Argonne offensive dwarfed anything an American army had ever attempted. American commander General John J. Pershing aimed to overwhelm the undermanned and dispirited German lines with massive numbers and swift movement and thereby force a German surrender. Pershing hoped to put a distinctively American stamp on ending the war with the Meuse-Argonne offensive.

But the individual infantryman had little time or use for grand strategy. Each man carried a rifle and bayonet, steel helmet, and gas mask, along with 250 rounds of ammunition. His two days of "iron rations" consisted of two cans of corned beef, six boxes of hard crackers, and a quart canteen of water. The American thrust quickly stalled as the Germans put up fierce resistance with well-placed machine gun nests and artillery batteries, spread out amidst a ghostly landscape littered with abandoned trenches, tangled barbed wire fences, water-filled craters, and dead and mangled bodies everywhere. The scene was nothing like the storybooks of war, recalled Lieutenant Maury Maverick. "There were no bugles, no flags, no drums, and as far as we knew, no heroes. . . . I have never read in any military history a description of the high explosives that break overhead. There is a great swishing scream, a smash-bang, and it seems to tear everything loose from you. The intensity of it simply enters your heart and brain and tears every nerve to pieces."

As members of the AEF shipped off for the front, they carried with them vague and often romantic notions of what to expect on the battlefield. By the summer of 1918, when most American soldiers traveled to France, the carnage across Europe was no secret. Nor was the grim reality of death associated with machine guns, tanks, and trench warfare. But the blizzard of posters, films, war bond drives, and other propaganda activities coordinated by the Committee on Public Information (CPI) mostly avoided this side of war. Instead it emphasized appeals to patriotism, manhood, heroism, and the fight for democracy. And many doughboys carried to France images of war shaped by their grandfathers' stories about the Civil War or romantic accounts of medieval knights.

Their experiences in the Meuse-Argonne offensive brought them face-to-face with the very different reality of mass mechanized killing. Rather than the swift victory General Pershing had hoped for, the campaign turned into a slow, sometimes chaotic slog. American combat units measured their gains in yards as they found their advances blunted by tough German defenders. Between September 25 and the Armistice ending the fighting on November 11, each day claimed an average of over 550 Americans dead, with a total of 26,000 Americans killed in the campaign.

In early 1919, encouraged by some senior officers, a group of AEF veterans founded the American Legion, "to preserve the memories and incidents of our association in the great war . . . to consecrate and sanctify our comradeship." American Legion halls soon became a familiar sight in communities across America. But the Legion had a political mission as well, one that would play out during the postwar "Red Scare." Legion leaders saw it as a way to counter radical ideas that might "infect" returning veterans, especially those who suffered from unemployment or had trouble readjusting to civilian life. It would commemorate the war, celebrate sacrifice, and honor the dead, all in the name of promoting "100 percent Americanism" and fighting against "dangerous" socialists and other radical groups. As much a political lobby as a veterans' organization, the American Legion would extend the memory and life of the AEF community well into the twentieth century.

Verdun

BECOMING A WORLD POWER

In the first years of the new century, the United States pursued a more vigorous and aggressive foreign policy than it had in the past. In addition to its newfound imperial presence in Asia, the United States marked out the Western Hemisphere—especially the Caribbean, Mexico, and Central America—as a site for establishing American hegemony. Presidents Theodore Roosevelt, William Howard Taft, and Woodrow Wilson all contributed to "progressive diplomacy," in which commercial expansion was backed by a growing military presence in the hemisphere. This policy reflected a view of world affairs that stressed the links between ensuring American commercial expansion and a foreign policy couched in terms of moralism, order, and a special, even God-given, role for the United States. By 1917, when the United States entered the Great War, the nation was just as complicit in building empire as were the European states and Japan.

ROOSEVELT: THE BIG STICK

Theodore Roosevelt left a strong imprint on the nation's foreign policy. Like many of his class and background, "T.R." took for granted the superiority of Protestant Anglo-American culture and the goal of spreading its values and influence. He believed that to maintain and increase its economic and political stature, America must be militarily strong. In 1900, Roosevelt summarized his activist views, declaring, "I have always been fond of the West African proverb, 'Speak softly and carry a big stick, you will go far.'"

Roosevelt brought the "big stick" approach to disputes in the Caribbean region. Since the 1880s, several British, French, and American companies had pursued plans for building a canal across the Isthmus of Panama, thereby connecting the Atlantic and Pacific Oceans. The canal was a top priority for Roosevelt, and he tried to negotiate a leasing agreement with Colombia, of which Panama was a province. But when the Colombian Senate rejected a final American offer in the fall of 1903, Roosevelt invented a new strategy. A combination of native forces and foreign promoters associated with the canal project plotted a revolt against Colombia. Roosevelt kept in touch with at least one leader of the revolt, Philippe Bunau-Varilla, an engineer and agent for the New Panama Canal Company, and the president let him know that U.S. warships were steaming toward Panama.

On November 3, 1903, just as the USS *Nashville* arrived in Colón harbor, the province of Panama declared itself independent of Colombia. The United States immediately recognized the new Republic of Panama. Less than two weeks later, Bunau-Varilla, serving as a minister from Panama, signed a treaty granting the United States full sovereignty in perpetuity over a ten-mile-wide canal zone.

"The inevitable effect of our building the Canal," wrote Secretary of State Elihu Root in 1905, "must be to require us to police the surrounding premises." Roosevelt agreed. He was especially concerned that European powers might step in if America did not. In 1903, Great Britain, Germany, and Italy had imposed a blockade on Venezuela in a dispute over debt payments owed to private investors. To prevent armed intervention by the Europeans, in 1904 Roosevelt proclaimed what became known as the **Roosevelt Corollary** to the **Monroe Doctrine**. "Chronic wrongdoing, or an impotence which results in a general loosening of the ties of civilized society," the statement read, justified "the exercise of an international police power" anywhere in the hemisphere. Roosevelt and later presidents cited the corollary to justify armed intervention in the internal affairs of the Dominican Republic, Cuba, Haiti, Nicaragua, and Mexico.

HOW DID Theodore Roosevelt use force as component of U.S. foreign policy?

Review Summary

IMAGE KEY
for pages 590–591

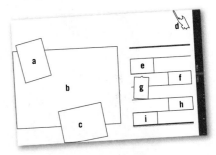

a. British Prime Minister Lloyd George, French Prime Minister George Clemenceau, and U.S. President Woodrow Wilson in Versailles, France in 1919.
b. Women war workers working in an engineering shop, 1917.
c. The *New York Times:* the sinking of the *Lusitania* in 1915.
d. A British World War I biplane being shot down.
e. A 1905 cartoon from *Judge* magazine.
f. President Woodrow Wilson reading his war message to Congress, April, 1917.
g. An American World War I Liberty Loan poster.
h. Women draft protesters at New York's City Hall June 1917.
i. A portrait of Woodrow Wilson (1856–1924).

Roosevelt Corollary   President Theodore Roosevelt's policy asserting U.S. authority to intervene in the affairs of Latin American nations; an expansion of the Monroe Doctrine.

Monroe Doctrine   In December 1823, Monroe declared to Congress that Americans "are henceforth not to be considered as subjects for future colonization by any European power."

THE WORLD'S CONSTABLE.

This 1905 cartoon portraying President Theodore Roosevelt, "The World's Constable," appeared in *Judge* magazine. In depicting the president as a strong but benevolent policeman bringing order in a contentious world, the artist Louis Dalrymple drew on familiar imagery from Roosevelt's earlier days as a New York City police commissioner.

With the outbreak of the Russo-Japanese War in 1904, Roosevelt worried about the future of the **Open Door** policy in Asia. (See Chapter 20.) A total victory by Russia or Japan could upset the balance of power in East Asia and threaten American business enterprises there. He became especially concerned after the Japanese scored a series of military victories over Russia and began to loom as a dominant power in East Asia. Roosevelt mediated a settlement of the Russo-Japanese War at Portsmouth, New Hampshire, in 1905 (for which he was awarded the 1906 Nobel Peace Prize). In this settlement, Japan won recognition of its dominant position in Korea and consolidated its economic control over Manchuria. Yet repeated incidents of anti-Japanese racism in California kept American–Japanese relations strained. In 1907, in the so-called Gentlemen's Agreement, Japan agreed not to issue passports to Japanese male laborers looking to emigrate to the United States, and Roosevelt promised to fight anti-Japanese discrimination.

But Roosevelt did not want these conciliatory moves to be interpreted as weakness. He thus built up American naval strength in the Pacific, and in 1908, he sent battleships to visit Japan in a muscle-flexing display of sea power. In that same year, the two burgeoning Pacific powers reached a reconciliation. The Root-Takahira Agreement affirmed the "existing status quo" in Asia, mutual respect for territorial possessions in the Pacific, and the Open Door trade policy in China.

Open Door   American policy of seeking equal trade and investment opportunities in foreign nations or regions.

TAFT: DOLLAR DIPLOMACY

Roosevelt's successor, William Howard Taft, believed he could replace the militarism of the big stick with the more subtle and effective weapon of business investment. Taft and his secretary of state, corporate lawyer Philander C. Knox, followed a strategy (called "dollar diplomacy" by critics) in which they assumed that political influence would follow increased U.S. trade and investment. As Taft explained in 1910, he advocated "active intervention to secure for our merchandise and our capitalists opportunity for profitable investment."

Overall American investment in Central America grew rapidly, from $41 million in 1908 to $93 million by 1914. Most of this money went into railroad construction, mining, and plantations. The United Fruit Company alone owned about 160,000 acres of land in the Caribbean by 1913. But dollar diplomacy ended up requiring military support. The Taft administration sent the navy and the marines to intervene in political disputes in Honduras and Nicaragua, propping up factions pledged to protect American business interests. A contingent of U.S. Marines remained in Nicaragua until 1933. The economic and political structures of Honduras and Nicaragua were controlled by both the dollar and the bullet (see Map 22.1).

In China, Taft and Knox pressed for a greater share of the pie for U.S. investors. They gained a place for U.S. bankers in the European consortium, building the massive new Hu-kuang Railway in southern and central China. But Knox blundered by attempting to "neutralize" the existing railroads in China. He tried to secure a huge international loan for the Chinese government that would allow it to buy up all the foreign railways and develop new ones. Both Russia and Japan, which had fought wars over their railroad interests in Manchuria, resisted this plan as a threat to the arrangements hammered out at Portsmouth with the help of Theodore Roosevelt. Knox's "neutralization" scheme, combined with U.S. support for the Chinese Nationalists in their 1911 revolt against the ruling Manchu dynasty, prompted Japan to sign a new friendship treaty with Russia. The Open Door to China was now effectively closed, and American relations with Japan began a slow deterioration that ended in war thirty years later.

WILSON: MORALISM AND INTERVENTION IN MEXICO

Wilson, like most corporate and political leaders of the day, emphasized foreign investments and industrial exports as the keys to the nation's prosperity. He believed that the United States, with its superior industrial efficiency, could achieve supremacy in world commerce if artificial barriers to free trade were removed. Wilson often couched his vision of a dynamic, expansive American capitalism in terms of a moral crusade. As he put it in a speech to a congress of salesmen, "[Since] you are Americans and are meant to carry liberty and justice and the principles of humanity wherever you go, go out and sell goods that will make the world more comfortable and more happy, and convert them to the principles of America." Yet he quickly found that the complex realities of power politics could interfere with moral vision.

Wilson's policies toward Mexico, which foreshadowed the problems he would encounter in World War I, best illustrate his difficulties. The 1911 Mexican Revolution had overthrown the brutally corrupt dictatorship of Porfirio Díaz, and popular leader Francisco Madero had won wide support by promising democracy and economic reform for millions of landless peasants. But the U.S. business community was nervous about the future of its investments which, in the previous generation, had come to dominate the Mexican economy.

Wilson at first gave his blessing to the revolutionary movement, expressed regret over the Mexican-American War of 1846–48, and disavowed any interest in

▶ MAP EXPLORATION

To explore an interactive version of this map, go to **http://www.prenhall.com/faraghertlc/map22.1**

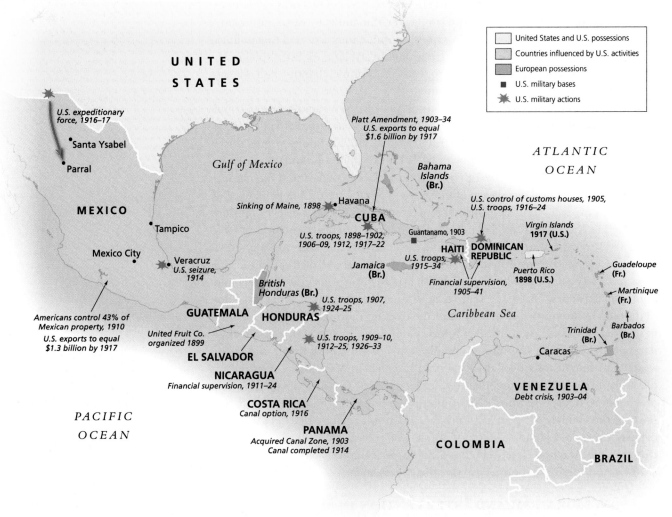

United States and U.S. possessions
Countries influenced by U.S. activities
European possessions
■ U.S. military bases
✴ U.S. military actions

UNITED STATES

U.S. expeditionary force, 1916–17
•Santa Ysabel
•Parral

Gulf of Mexico

ATLANTIC OCEAN

Platt Amendment, 1903–34 U.S. exports to equal $1.6 billion by 1917

Bahama Islands (Br.)

MEXICO

•Tampico

Mexico City•

•Veracruz, *U.S. seizure, 1914*

Sinking of Maine, 1898 •Havana

CUBA

U.S. troops, 1898–1902, 1906–09, 1912, 1917–22

Guantanamo, 1903

Jamaica (Br.)

HAITI
U.S. troops 1915–34

DOMINICAN REPUBLIC

U.S. control of customs houses, 1905, U.S. troops, 1916–24

Virgin Islands 1917 (U.S.)

Puerto Rico 1898 (U.S.)

Financial supervision, 1905–41

Guadeloupe (Fr.)

Martinique (Fr.)

Americans control 43% of Mexican property, 1910 U.S. exports to equal $1.3 billion by 1917

GUATEMALA

British Honduras (Br.)

HONDURAS

U.S. troops, 1907, 1924–25

Caribbean Sea

Trinidad (Br.)

Barbados (Br.)

United Fruit Co. organized 1899

EL SALVADOR

NICARAGUA
Financial supervision, 1911–24

U.S. troops, 1909–10, 1912–25, 1926–33

•Caracas

VENEZUELA
Debt crisis, 1903–04

PACIFIC OCEAN

COSTA RICA
Canal option, 1916

PANAMA
Acquired Canal Zone, 1903 Canal completed 1914

COLOMBIA

BRAZIL

MAP 22.1
The United States in the Caribbean, 1865–1933   An overview of U.S. economic and military involvement in the Caribbean during the late nineteenth and early twentieth centuries. Victory in the Spanish-American War, the Panama Canal project, and rapid economic investment in Mexico and Cuba all contributed to a permanent and growing U.S. military presence in the region.

WHAT WERE the arguments for and against the repeated United States intervention in the Caribbean?

another war. But right before he took office, Wilson was stunned by the ousting and murder of Madero by his chief lieutenant, General Victoriano Huerta. Other nations, including Great Britain and Japan, recognized the Huerta regime, but Wilson refused. He announced that the United States would support only governments that rested on the rule of law. An armed faction opposed to Huerta, known as the Constitutionalists and led by Venustiano Carranza, emerged in northern Mexico. Both sides rejected an effort by Wilson to broker a compromise between them. Carranza, an ardent nationalist, pressed for the right to buy U.S. arms, which he won in 1914. Wilson also isolated Huerta diplomatically by persuading the British to withdraw their support in exchange for American guarantees of English property interests in Mexico.

But Huerta stubbornly remained in power. In April 1914, Wilson used a minor insult to U.S. sailors in Tampico as an excuse to invade. American naval forces bombarded and then occupied Veracruz, the main port through which Huerta received arms shipments. Nineteen Americans and 126 Mexicans died in the battle, which brought the United States and Mexico close to war, and provoked anti-American demonstrations in Mexico and throughout Latin America. Wilson accepted the offer of the ABC Powers—Argentina, Brazil, and Chile—to mediate the dispute. Huerta rejected a plan for him to step aside in favor of a provisional government. But then in August, Carranza managed to overthrow Huerta. Playing to nationalist sentiment, Carranza too denounced Wilson for his intervention.

As war loomed in Europe, Mexico's revolutionary politics continued to frustrate Wilson. For a brief period, Wilson threw his support behind Francisco "Pancho" Villa, Carranza's former ally, who now led a rebel army of his own in northern Mexico. But Carranza's forces dealt Villa a major setback in April 1915. In October, its attention focused on the war in Europe, the Wilson administration recognized Carranza as Mexico's de facto president. Meanwhile, Pancho Villa, feeling betrayed, turned on the United States and tried to provoke a crisis that might draw the United States into war with Mexico.

In March 1916, enraged by Villa's defiance, Wilson dispatched General John J. Pershing and an army that eventually numbered 15,000 to capture him. For a year, Pershing's troops chased Villa in vain, penetrating 300 miles into Mexico. The invasion made Villa a symbol of national resistance in Mexico, and his army grew from 500 men to 10,000 by the end of 1916.

Skirmishes between American forces and Carranza's army brought the two nations to the brink of war again in June 1916. Although Wilson prepared a message to Congress asking permission for American troops to occupy all of northern Mexico, he never delivered it. There was fierce opposition to war with Mexico throughout the country. Perhaps more important, mounting tensions with Germany caused Wilson to hesitate. Wilson thus accepted negotiations by a face-saving international commission.

Wilson's attempt to guide the course of Mexico's revolution and protect U.S. interests left a bitter legacy of suspicion and distrust in Mexico. It also suggested the limits of a foreign policy tied to a moral vision rooted in the idea of American exceptionalism. **Militarism** and **imperialism**, Wilson had believed, were hallmarks of the old European way. American liberal values—rooted in capitalist development, democracy, and free trade—were the wave of the future. Wilson believed the United States could lead the world in establishing a new international system based on peaceful commerce and political stability. In both the 1914 invasion and the 1916 punitive expedition, Wilson declared that he had no desire to interfere with Mexican sovereignty. But in both cases, that is exactly what he did. The United States, he argued, must actively use its enormous moral and material power to create the new order. That principle would soon engage America in Europe's bloodiest war and its most momentous revolution.

This **1914 political** cartoon comments approvingly on the interventionist role adopted by the United States in Latin American countries. By depicting President Woodrow Wilson as a schoolteacher giving lessons to children, the image captures the paternalistic views that American policy makers held toward nations like Mexico, Venezuela, and Nicaragua.

QUICK REVIEW

Wilson and Mexico

◆ Wilson refused to recognize the regime of General Victoriano Huerta.

◆ 1914: Wilson used the excuse of a minor event to attack Veracruz.

◆ Wilson's efforts to control events in Mexico led to the brink of war.

◆ Policies resulted in enduring distrust of the United States in Mexico.

Militarism The tendency to see military might as the most important and best tool for the expansion of a nation's power and prestige.

Imperialism The policy and practice of exploiting nations and peoples for the benefit of an imperial power either directly through military occupation and colonial rule or indirectly through economic domination of resources and markets.

The Great War

WHY DID most Americans oppose U.S. involvement in World War I in 1914?

Review Summary

22–1
The Great War (1914)

W orld War I, or the Great War, as it was originally called, took an enormous human toll on an entire generation of Europeans. At the war's start in August 1914, both sides had confidently predicted a quick victory. Instead, the killing dragged on for more than four years, and in the end, transformed the old power relations and political map of Europe.

The Guns of August

Only a complex and fragile system of alliances had kept the European powers at peace with each other since 1871. Two great competing camps had evolved by 1907: the Triple Alliance (also known as the Central Powers), which included Germany, Austria-Hungary, and Italy; and the Triple Entente (also known as the **Allies**), which included Great Britain, France, and Russia. The alliance system managed to keep small conflicts from escalating into larger ones for most of the late nineteenth and early twentieth centuries. But its inclusiveness was also its weakness: the alliance system threatened to entangle many nations in any war that did erupt. On June 28, 1914, Archduke Franz Ferdinand, heir to the throne of the unstable Austro-Hungarian Empire, was assassinated in Sarajevo, Bosnia. The archduke's killer was a Serbian nationalist who believed the Austro-Hungarian province of Bosnia ought to be annexed to neighboring Serbia. Germany gave Austria-Hungary a blank check to stamp out the Serbian threat, and the Serbians in turn asked Russia for help.

That summer both sides began mobilizing their armies, and by early August they had exchanged declarations of war. Germany invaded Belgium and prepared to move across the French border. At the beginning, most Europeans supported the war effort, believing there would be quick and glorious victories. But after the German armies were stopped at the River Marne in September, the war settled into a long, bloody stalemate.

QUICK REVIEW

The Outbreak of War
- June 28, 1914: Archduke Franz Ferdinand assassinated.
- July 28, 1914: Austria declares war on Serbia with German support.
- Chain reaction draws all European powers into the war.

American Neutrality

The outbreak of war in Europe shocked Americans. President Wilson issued a formal proclamation of neutrality and urged citizens to be "impartial in thought as well as in action." In practice, powerful cultural, political, and economic factors made the impartiality advocated by Wilson impossible. The U.S. population included many ethnic groups with close emotional ties to the Old World. Out of a total population of 92 million in 1914, about one-third were "hyphenated" Americans, either foreign-born or having one or both parents who were immigrants. Strong support for the Central Powers could be found among the 8 million German-Americans, as well as the 4 million Irish-Americans, who shared their ancestral homeland's historical hatred of English rule. On the other side, many Americans were at least mildly pro-Allies due to cultural and language bonds with Great Britain and the tradition of Franco-American friendship.

Economic ties between the United States and the Allies were perhaps the greatest barrier to true neutrality. Early in the war, Britain imposed a blockade on all shipping to Germany. The United States, as a neutral country, might have insisted on the right of nonbelligerents to trade with both sides, as required by international law. But in practice, although Wilson protested the blockade, he wanted to avoid antagonizing Britain and disrupting trade between the United States and the Allies. Trade with Germany all but ended while trade with the Allies increased

Allies In World War I, Britain, France, Russia, and other belligerent nations fighting against the Central Powers but not including the United States.

dramatically. As America's annual export trade jumped from $2 billion in 1913 to nearly $6 billion in 1916, the nation enjoyed a great economic boom and the United States became neutral in name only.

PREPAREDNESS AND PEACE

In February 1915, Germany declared the waters around the British Isles to be a war zone, a policy that it would enforce with unrestricted submarine warfare. All enemy shipping, despite the requirements of international law to the contrary, would be subject to surprise submarine attack. Neutral powers were warned that the problems of identification at sea put their ships at risk. The United States issued a sharp protest to this policy, calling it "an indefensible violation of neutral rights," and threatened to hold Germany accountable.

Patriotic marchers carry on over-sized American flag past spectators, as part of a "preparedness parade" in downtown Mobile Alabama, before American entry into World War I.

University of South Alabama Archives.

On May 7, 1915, a German U-boat sank the British liner *Lusitania* off the coast of Ireland. Among the 1,198 people who died were 128 American citizens. The *Lusitania* was, in fact, secretly carrying war materials, and passengers had been warned about a possible attack. Wilson nevertheless denounced the sinking as illegal and inhuman, and the American press loudly condemned the act as barbaric.

Tensions heated up again in March 1916 when a German U-boat torpedoed the *Sussex*, an unarmed French passenger ship, injuring four Americans. President Wilson threatened to break off diplomatic relations with Germany unless it abandoned its submarine warfare. He won a temporary diplomatic victory when Germany promised that all vessels would be visited prior to attack. But the crisis also prompted Wilson to begin preparing for war. The National Security League, active in large eastern cities and bankrolled by conservative banking and commercial interests, helped push for a bigger army and navy and, most important, a system of universal military training. In June 1916, Congress passed the National Defense Act, which more than doubled the size of the regular army to 220,000 and integrated the state National Guards under federal control. In August, Congress passed a bill that dramatically increased spending for new battleships, cruisers, and destroyers.

Not all Americans supported these preparations for battle, and opposition to military buildup found expression in scores of American communities. As early as August 29, 1914, 1,500 women clad in black had marched down New York's Fifth Avenue in the Woman's Peace Parade. Out of this gathering evolved the American Union against Militarism, which lobbied against the **preparedness** campaign and against intervention in Mexico. Antiwar feeling was especially strong in the South and Midwest.

A group of thirty to fifty House Democrats, led by majority leader Claude Kitchin of North Carolina, stubbornly opposed Wilson's military buildup. Jane Addams, Lillian D. Wald, and many other prominent progressive reformers spoke out for peace.

Wilson acknowledged the active opposition to involvement in the war by adopting the winning slogan "He Kept Us Out of War" in the 1916 presidential campaign. He made a point of appealing to progressives of all kinds, stressing his support for the eight-hour day and his administration's efforts on behalf of farmers. The war-induced prosperity no doubt helped him to defeat conservative Republican Charles Evans.

Preparedness   Military buildup in preparation for possible U.S. participation in World War I.

THE NAVY NEEDS YOU! DON'T READ AMERICAN HISTORY – MAKE IT !

U·S·NAVY RECRUITING STATION
34 EAST 23rd ST., NEW YORK

James Montgomery Flagg's Navy recruiting poster from 1918 combined appeals to patriotism, the opportunity to "make history," and traditional images depicting liberty as a woman.

22–2
Boy Scouts of America, *Boy Scouts Support the War Effort* (1917)

SAFE FOR DEMOCRACY

By the end of January 1917, Germany's leaders had decided against a negotiated peace settlement, placing their hopes instead in a final decisive offensive against the Allies. On February 1, 1917, with the aim of breaking the British blockade, Germany declared unlimited submarine warfare, with no warnings, against all neutral and belligerent shipping. This strategy went far beyond the earlier, more limited use of the U-boat. The decision was made with full knowledge that it might bring America into the conflict. In effect, German leaders were gambling that they could destroy the ability of the Allies to fight before the United States would be able to effectively mobilize manpower and resources.

Wilson was indignant and disappointed. He still hoped for peace, but Germany had made it impossible for him to preserve his twin goals of U.S. neutrality and freedom of the seas. Reluctantly, Wilson broke off diplomatic relations with Germany and called on Congress to approve the arming of U.S. merchant ships. On March 1, the White House shocked the country when it made public a recently intercepted coded message, sent by German foreign secretary Arthur Zimmermann to the German ambassador in Mexico. The Zimmermann note proposed that an alliance be made between Germany and Mexico if the United States entered the war. Zimmermann suggested that Mexico take up arms against the United States and receive in return the "lost territory in New Mexico, Texas, and Arizona." The specter of a German-Mexican alliance helped turn the tide of public opinion in the Southwest, where opposition to U.S. involvement in the war had been strong.

Revelation of the Zimmermann note stiffened Wilson's resolve. He issued an executive order in mid-March, authorizing the arming of all merchant ships and allowing them to shoot at submarines. In that month, German U-boats sank seven U.S. merchant ships, with a heavy death toll. Anti-German feeling increased, and thousands took part in prowar demonstrations in New York, Boston, Philadelphia, and other cities. Wilson finally called a special session of Congress to ask for a declaration of war.

On April 2, on a rainy night, before a packed and very quiet assembly, Wilson made his case. He reviewed the escalation of submarine warfare, which he called "warfare against mankind," and said that neutrality was no longer feasible or desirable. But the conflict was not merely about U.S. shipping rights, Wilson argued. He employed highly idealistic language to make the case for war, reflecting his deeply held belief that America had a special mission as the world's most enlightened and advanced nation. In effect, Wilson wrapped together American commercial and diplomatic interests in the language of universal principles like freedom of the seas and neutral rights. He expressed the realist ambition of making America a world power in terms of an absolute moral imperative. The Senate adopted the war resolution 82 to 6, the House 373 to 50. Wilson's eloquent speech won over not only the Congress, but also most of the press, and even his bitterest political critics, such as Theodore Roosevelt. Upper-class conservatives supported the language emphasizing national interest, while most progressives responded to the appeal of an idealistic mission. On April 6, President Wilson signed the declaration of war. All that remained was to win over the American public.

AMERICAN MOBILIZATION

The overall public response to Wilson's war message was enthusiastic. Most newspapers, religious leaders, state legislatures, and prominent public figures endorsed the call to arms. But the Wilson administration was less certain about the feelings of ordinary Americans and their willingness to fight in Europe. It therefore took immediate steps to win over public support for the war effort, to place a legal muzzle on antiwar dissenters, and to establish a universal military draft. War mobilization was, above all, a campaign to unify the country.

SELLING THE WAR

Just a week after signing the war declaration, Wilson created the **Committee on Public Information (CPI)** to organize public opinion. It was dominated by its civilian chairman, the journalist and reformer George Creel. He had become a personal friend of Wilson's while handling publicity for the 1916 Democratic campaign. Creel quickly transformed the CPI from its original function as coordinator of government news into a sophisticated and aggressive agency for promoting the war. To sell the war, Creel adapted techniques from the emerging field of public relations. He enlisted more than 150,000 people to work on a score of CPI committees. They produced more than 100 million pieces of literature—pamphlets, articles, books—that explained the causes and meaning of the war. Across the nation, a volunteer army of 75,000 "Four Minute Men" gave brief patriotic speeches before stage and movie shows. The CPI also created posters, slides, newspaper advertising, and films to promote the war. It called upon movie stars such as Charlie Chaplin, Mary Pickford, and Douglas Fairbanks to help sell war bonds at huge rallies. Famous journalists like the muckraker Ida Tarbell and well-known artists like Charles Dana Gibson were recruited. Many popular entertainers injected patriotic themes into their work as well, as when Broadway composer George M. Cohan wrote the rousing prowar anthem "Over There," sung by the great opera tenor Enrico Caruso (see Seeing History).

The CPI led an aggressively negative campaign against all things German. Posters and advertisements depicted the Germans as Huns, bestial monsters outside the civilized world. German music and literature, indeed the German language itself, were suspect and were banished from the concert halls, schools, and libraries of many communities. Many restaurants now offered "liberty cabbage" and "liberty steaks" instead of sauerkraut and hamburgers. The CPI also urged ethnic Americans to abandon their Old World ties, to become "unhyphenated Americans." The CPI's push for conformity would soon encourage thousands of local, sometimes violent, campaigns of harassment against German-Americans, radicals, and peace activists.

FADING OPPOSITION TO WAR

By defining the call to war as a great moral crusade, President Wilson was able to win over many Americans who had been reluctant to go to war. In particular, many liberals and progressives were attracted to the possibilities of war as a positive force for social change. Although some progressives—notably Senator Robert M. La Follette of Wisconsin—continued to oppose the war, many more identified with President Wilson's definition of the war as an idealistic crusade to defend democracy, spread liberal principles, and redeem European decadence and militarism.

HOW DID the federal government try to change public opinion about U.S. involvement in World War I?

myhistorylab
Review Summary

22–6
Newton B. Baker, *The Treatment of German-Americans* (1918)

Committee on Public Information (CPI) Government agency during World War I that sought to shape public opinion in support of the war effort through newspapers, pamphlets, speeches, films, and other media.

African American officers of the 367th Infantry Regiment, 77th Division, pose with a girl in France, 1918. Nicknamed the "Buffalos" a reference to the black "buffalo soldiers" who had served in the U.S. Army during the late nineteenth century campaigns against Indians, this was one of only two army units that commissioned African American officers.

QUICK REVIEW

African American Soldiers

♦ 200,000 African Americans served in France.

♦ One in five saw combat.

♦ African American combat units served with distinction in the French army.

Selective Service Act The law establishing the military draft for World War I.

The Woman's Peace Party, founded in 1915 by feminists opposed to the preparedness campaign, dissolved. Most of its leading lights—Florence Kelley, Lillian D. Wald, and Carrie Chapman Catt—threw themselves into volunteer war work. Catt, leader of the huge National American Woman Suffrage Association (NAWSA), believed that supporting the war might help women win the right to vote. She joined the Women's Committee of the Council of National Defense and encouraged suffragists to mobilize women for war service of various kinds. A few lonely feminist voices, such as Jane Addams, continued steadfastly to oppose the war effort. But war work proved very popular among activist middle-class women. It gave them a leading role in their communities—selling bonds, coordinating food conservation drives, and working for hospitals and the Red Cross.

"YOU'RE IN THE ARMY NOW"

The central military issue facing the administration was how to raise and deploy U.S. armed forces. When war was declared, there were only about 200,000 men in the army. Traditionally, the United States had relied on volunteer forces organized at the state level. But volunteer rates after April 6 were less than they had been for the Civil War or the Spanish-American War, reflecting the softness of prowar sentiment. The administration thus introduced the **Selective Service Act**, which provided for the registration and classification for military service of all men between ages twenty-one and thirty-five.

The vast, polyglot army posed unprecedented challenges of organization and control. But progressive elements within the administration also saw opportunities for pressing reform measures, especially for the one-fifth of U.S. soldiers born in another country. Army psychologists gave the new Stanford-Binet intelligence test to all recruits and were shocked to find illiteracy rates as high as 25 percent. The low test scores among recent immigrants and rural African Americans undoubtedly reflected the cultural biases embedded in the tests and a lack of proficiency in English for many test takers. After the war, intelligence testing became a standard feature of America's educational system.

RACISM IN THE MILITARY

African Americans who served found severe limitations in the U.S. military. They were organized into totally segregated units, barred entirely from the marines and the Coast Guard, and largely relegated to working as cooks, laundrymen, stevedores, and the like in the army and navy. Thousands of black soldiers endured humiliating, sometimes violent treatment, particularly from southern white officers. African American servicemen faced hostility from white civilians as well, North and South. The ugliest incident occurred in Houston, Texas, in August 1917. Black infantrymen, incensed over continual insults and harassment by local whites, seized weapons from an armory and killed seventeen civilians. The army executed thirty black soldiers and imprisoned forty-one others for life, denying any of them a chance for appeal.

Selling War

The world War I posters generally defined the war as a clear struggle between good and evil, in which American democracy and freedom opposed German militarism and despotism. Yet artists used a wide range of visual themes to illustrate these stark contrasts. World War I posters drew upon traditional ideas about gender differences (men as soldiers, women as nurturers), but they also illustrated the new wartime expectations of women working outside the home in support of the war effort. Appeals to American patriotism cutting across lines of ethnic and religious difference were common, as was the demonizing of the German enemy. And just as the wartime economy blurred the boundaries between public and private enterprises, businesses adapted patriotic appeals to their own advertising.

Creel aptly titled the memoir of his war experience *How We Advertised America*. These three images illustrate the range of World War I propaganda posters. ■

HOW WOULD you contrast the different kind of patriotic appeals made by "Pershing's Crusaders," "Americans All," and "And They Thought We Couldn't Fight"? Which of these posters do you think makes the most compelling case for supporting the war? How do the artists portray gender differences as part of a visual strategy for winning the war?

http://www.firstworldwar.com/posters/images

More than 200,000 African Americans eventually served in France, but only about one in five saw combat, as opposed to two out of three white soldiers. Black combat units served with distinction in various divisions of the French army. The French government awarded the Croix de Guerre to the all-black 369th U.S. Infantry regiment, and 171 officers and enlisted men were cited individually for exceptional bravery in action. African American soldiers by and large enjoyed a friendly reception from French civilians as well. The contrast with their treatment at home would remain a sore point with these troops upon their return to the United States.

AMERICANS IN BATTLE

22–4
American Troops in the Trenches (1918)

President Wilson appointed General John J. Pershing, recently returned from pursuing Pancho Villa in Mexico, as commander of the American Expeditionary Force (AEF). Pershing insisted that the AEF maintain its own identity, distinct from that of the French and British armies. He was also reluctant to send American troops into battle before they had received at least six months' training. The AEF's combat role would be brief but intense: not until early 1918 did AEF units reach the front in large numbers; eight months later, the war was over (see Map 22.2).

22–7
An Official Report (1917)

By the time the guns went silent on November 11, some 2 million men had served in the AEF. Overall 60,000 Americans had died in battle with 206,000 wounded. Another 60,000 died from diseases, mainly influenza. These figures paled in comparison to the millions lost by the European nations. Yet the American contribution to winning the war was substantial, and both the Allies and the Germans attested to the bravery and enthusiasm that American soldiers displayed on the front. Still, the American impact in the Meuse-Argonne campaign was best understood not in terms of individual heroism or tactical brilliance. Rather, it was the prospect of facing seemingly unlimited quantities of American men and supplies that convinced the exhausted German army to surrender.

THE RUSSIAN REVOLUTION, THE FOURTEEN POINTS, AND ALLIED VICTORY

Since early 1917, the turmoil of the Russian Revolution had changed the climate of both foreign affairs and domestic politics. The repressive and corrupt regime of Czar Nicholas II had been overthrown in March 1917 by a coalition of forces demanding change. The new provisional government vowed to keep Russia in the fight against Germany. But the war had taken a terrible toll on Russian soldiers and civilians and had become very unpopular. The radical **Bolsheviks**, led by V. I. Lenin, gained a large following by promising "peace, land, and bread," and they began plotting to seize power. The Bolsheviks followed the teachings of German revolutionary Karl Marx, emphasizing the inevitability of class struggle and the replacement of capitalism by communism. In November 1917, the Bolsheviks took control of the Russian government.

22–8
Woodrow Wilson, *The Fourteen Points* (1918)

Although sympathetic to the March revolution overthrowing the czar, President Wilson refused to recognize the authority of the Bolshevik regime. Bolshevism represented a threat to the liberal-capitalist values that Wilson believed to be the foundation of America's moral and material power. Thus, in January 1918 Wilson outlined American war aims, known as the **Fourteen Points**, in a speech before Congress. He wanted to counter a fierce Bolshevik campaign to discredit the war as a purely imperialist venture, their sensational publication of secret treaties that the czar had signed with the Allies, and their revelations about annexationist plans across Europe. In effect, Wilson's response to the Bolsheviks was the opening shot of the Soviet-American Cold War that would dominate so much of American domestic politics and foreign affairs for the remainder of the century.

Bolsheviks   Members of the Communist movement in Russia that established the Soviet government after the 1917 Russian Revolution.

Fourteen Points   Goals outlined by Woodrow Wilson for war.

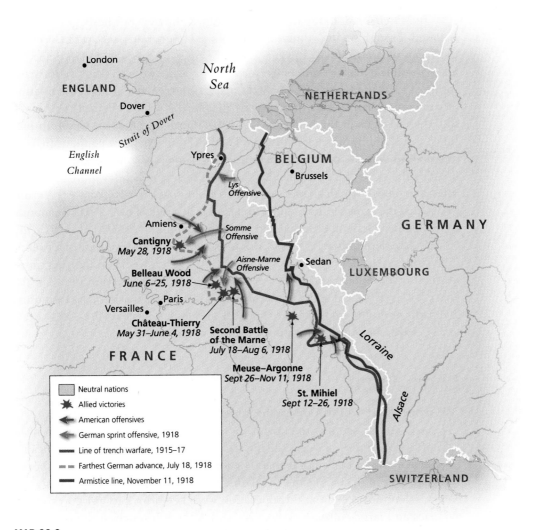

MAP 22.2

The Western Front, 1918   American units saw their first substantial action in late May, helping to stop the German offensive at the Battle of Cantigny. By September, more than 1 million American troops were fighting in a counteroffensive campaign at St. Mihiel, the largest single American engagement of the war.

HOW DID the entrance of the United States help turn the tide of World War I?

As a blueprint for peace, the Fourteen Points contained three main elements. First, Wilson offered a series of specific proposals for setting postwar boundaries in Europe and creating new countries out of the collapsed Austro-Hungarian and Ottoman empires. The key idea here was the right of all peoples to "national self-determination." Second, Wilson listed general principles for governing international conduct, including freedom of the seas, free trade, open covenants instead of secret treaties, reduced armaments, and mediation for competing colonial claims. Third, and most important, Wilson called for a **League of Nations** to help implement these principles and resolve future disputes. The Fourteen Points offered a plan for world order deeply rooted in the liberal progressivism long associated with Wilson. The plan reflected a faith in efficient government and the rule of law as means for solving international problems. It advocated a dynamic democratic capitalism as a middle ground between Old World autocracy and revolutionary socialism.

League of Nations   International organization created by the Versailles Treaty after World War I to ensure world stability.

22–5
Eugene Kennedy, A "Doughboy" Describes the Fighting Front (1918)

WHAT WERE the domestic effects in the United States of World War I?

myhistorylab

Review Summary

In March 1918, to the dismay of the Allies, the new Bolshevik government followed through on its promise and negotiated a separate peace with Germany, the Treaty of Brest-Litovsk. Russia was now lost as a military ally, and its defection made possible a massive shift of German troops to the western front. In the early spring of 1918, the Germans launched a major offensive that brought them within fifty miles of Paris. In early June, about 70,000 AEF soldiers helped the French stop the Germans in the battles of Château-Thierry and Belleau Wood. In July, Allied forces led by Marshal Ferdinand Foch of France began a counteroffensive designed to defeat Germany once and for all. American reinforcements began flooding the ports of Liverpool in England and Brest and Saint-Nazaire in France. The **"doughboys"** (a nickname for soldiers dating back to Civil War–era recruits who joined the army for the money) streamed in at a rate of over 250,000 a month. By September, General Pershing had more than a million Americans in his army.

In late September 1918, the AEF took over the southern part of a twenty-mile front in the Meuse-Argonne offensive. In seven weeks of fighting, most through terrible mud and rain, U.S. soldiers used more ammunition than the entire Union army had in the four years of the Civil War. The Germans, exhausted and badly outnumbered, began to fall back and look for a cease-fire. On November 11, 1918, the war ended with the signing of an armistice.

OVER HERE

In one sense, World War I can be understood as the ultimate progressive crusade: an opportunity to expand the powers of the federal government in order to win the war. Nearly all the reform energy of the previous two decades now turned toward that central goal. The federal government would play a larger role than ever in managing and regulating the wartime economy. Planning, efficiency, scientific analysis, and cooperation were key principles for government agencies and large volunteer organizations. Although much of the regulatory spirit was temporary, the war experience started some important and lasting organizational trends in American life.

ORGANIZING THE ECONOMY

In the summer of 1917, President Wilson established the **War Industries Board (WIB)** as a clearinghouse for industrial mobilization to support the war effort. Led by the successful Wall Street speculator Bernard M. Baruch, the WIB proved a major innovation in expanding the regulatory power of the federal government. Given broad authority over the conversion of industrial plants to wartime needs and the manufacture of war materials, the WIB had to balance price controls against war profits. Only by ensuring a fair rate of return on investment could it encourage stepped-up production.

In August 1917, Congress passed the Food and Fuel Act, authorizing the president to regulate the production and distribution of the food and fuel necessary for the war effort. To lead the Food Administration (FA), Wilson appointed Herbert Hoover. He became one of the best-known figures of the war administration. Hoover imposed price controls on certain agricultural commodities, such as sugar, pork, and wheat. These were purchased by the government and then sold to the public through licensed dealers. The FA also raised the purchase price of grain, so that farmers would increase production. But Hoover stopped short of imposing mandatory food rationing, preferring to rely on persuasion, high prices, and voluntary controls.

Doughboys Nickname for soldiers during the Civil War era who joined the army for money.

War Industries Board (WIB) The federal agency that reorganized industry for maximum efficiency and productivity during World War I.

Hoover's success, like George Creel's at the CPI, depended on motivating hundreds of thousands of volunteers in thousands of American communities. These efforts resulted in a sharp cut-back in the consumption of sugar and wheat as well as a boost in the supply of livestock. The resultant increase in food exports helped sustain the Allied war effort.

The enormous cost of fighting the war, about $33 billion, required unprecedentedly large expenditures for the federal government. The tax structure shifted dramatically as a result. Taxes on incomes and profits replaced excise and customs levies as the major source of revenue. The bulk of war financing came from government borrowing, especially in the form of the pop-ular **Liberty Bonds** sold to the American public. Bond drives became highly organized patriotic campaigns that ultimately raised a total of $23 billion for the war effort. The administra-tion also used the new Federal Reserve Banks to expand the money supply, making borrowing easier. The federal debt jumped from $1 billion in 1915 to $20 billion in 1920.

THE GOVERNMENT–BUSINESS PARTNERSHIP

Overall, the war meant expansion and high profits for Amer-ican business. Total capital expenditure in U.S. manufactur-ing jumped from $600 million in 1915 to $2.5 billion in 1918. Corporate profits as a whole nearly tripled between 1914 and 1919, and many large businesses did much better than that. The total value of farm produce rose from $9.8 billion in 1914 to $21.3 billion by 1918. Expanded farm acreage and increased investment in farm machinery led to a jump of 20 to 30 per-cent in overall farm production.

The most important and long-lasting economic legacy of the war was the organizational shift toward corporatism in American business. The wartime need for efficient management, manufacturing, and distribution could be met only by a greater reliance on the productive and marketing power of large corporations. Never before had business and the federal government cooperated so closely. Under war administrators like Baruch and Hoover, entire industries (such as radio manufacturing) and economic sectors (such as agriculture and energy) were orga-nized, regulated, and subsidized. War agencies used both public and private power—legal authority and voluntarism—to hammer out and enforce agreements. Here was the genesis of the modern bureaucratic state.

Some Americans worried about the wartime trend toward a greater federal pres-ence in their lives. As *The Saturday Evening Post* noted, "All this government activity will be called to account and reexamined in due time." Although many aspects of the government–business partnership proved temporary, some institutions and practices grew stronger in the postwar years. Among these were the Federal Reserve Board, the income tax system, the Chamber of Commerce, the Farm Bureau, and the growing horde of lobbying groups that pressed Washington for special interest legislation.

LABOR AND THE WAR

Organized labor's power and prestige, though by no means equal to those of busi-ness or government, clearly grew during the war. The expansion of the economy, combined with army mobilization and a decline in immigration from Europe, caused

FOOD WILL WIN THE WAR
You came here seeking Freedom
You must now help to preserve it
WHEAT is needed for the allies
Waste nothing

A Food Administration poster blended a call for conservation of wheat with an imaginative patriotic appeal for recent immigrants to support the war effort.

Liberty Bonds   Interest-bearing certificates sold by the U.S. government to finance the American World War I effort.

a growing wartime labor shortage. As the demand for workers intensified, the federal government was forced to recognize that labor, like any other resource or commodity, would have to be more carefully tended to than in peacetime. For the war's duration, working people generally enjoyed higher wages and a better standard of living. Trade unions, especially those affiliated with the American Federation of Labor (AFL), experienced a sharp rise in membership. In effect, the government took in labor as a junior partner in the mobilization of the economy.

Samuel Gompers, president of the ALF, pledged the organization's support for the war effort, and in April 1918, President Wilson appointed him to the National War Labor Board (NWLB). During 1917, the nation had seen thousands of strikes involving more than a million workers. Wages were usually at issue, reflecting workers' concerns with spiraling inflation and higher prices. The NWLB, cochaired by labor attorney Frank Walsh and former president William H. Taft, acted as a kind of supreme court for labor, arbitrating disputes and working to prevent disruptions in production. The great majority of these interventions resulted in improved wages and reduced hours of work. Most important, the NWLB supported the right of workers to organize unions and furthered the acceptance of the eight-hour day for war workers—central aims of the labor movement.

Yet the war also brought widespread use of federal troops under the War Department's new "public utilities" doctrine, under which any private business remotely connected to war production was defined as a public utility. An influx of federal troops poured into lumber camps, coal districts, mining towns, and rail junctions across the nation, as employers requested help in guarding against threatened strikes or alleged "sabotage" by militant workers. Wartime conditions often meant severe disruptions and discomfort for America's workers as well. Overcrowding, rapid workforce turnover, and high inflation rates were typical in war-boom communities.

In the Southwest, the demand for wartime labor temporarily eased restrictions against the movement of Mexicans into the United States. The Immigration Act of 1917, requiring a literacy test and an $8 head tax, had cut Mexican immigration nearly in half, down to about 25,000 per year. But employers complained of severe shortages of workers.

Responding to these protests, in June 1917, the Department of Labor suspended the immigration law for the duration of the war and negotiated an agreement with the Mexican government permitting some 35,000 Mexican contract laborers to enter the United States. Mexicans let in through this program had to demonstrate they had a job waiting before they could cross the border. They received identification cards and transportation to their place of work from American labor contractors. Pressure from southwestern employers kept the exemptions in force until 1921, well after the end of the war, demonstrating the growing importance of cheap Mexican labor to the region's economy.

If the war boosted the fortunes of the AFL, it also spelled the end for more radical elements of the U.S. labor movement. The Industrial Workers of the World (IWW), unlike the AFL, had concentrated on organizing unskilled workers into all-inclusive industrial unions. The Wobblies denounced capitalism as an unreformable system based on exploitation, and they opposed U.S. entry into the war. In September 1917 the Wilson administration responded to appeals from western business leaders for a crackdown on the Wobblies. Justice Department agents, acting under the broad authority of the recently passed **Espionage Act**, swooped down on IWW offices in more than sixty towns and cities, arresting more than 300 people and confiscating files. The mass trials and convictions that followed broke the back of America's radical labor movement and marked the beginning of a powerful wave of political repression.

Espionage Act Law whose vague prohibition against obstructing the nation's war effort was used to crush dissent and criticism during World War I.

Women workers at the Midvale Steel and Ordnance Company in Pennsylvania, 1918. Wartime labor shortages created new opportunities for over 1 million women to take high-wage manufacturing jobs like the women shown here. The opportunities proved temporary, however, and with the war's end, nearly all of these women lost their jobs. By 1920, the number of women employed in manufacturing was lower than it had been in 1910.

WOMEN AT WORK

For many of the 8 million women already in the labor force, the war meant a chance to switch from low-paying jobs, such as domestic service, to higher-paying industrial employment. About a million women workers joined the labor force for the first time. Of the estimated 9.4 million workers directly engaged in war work, some 2.25 million were women. World War I also marked the first time that women were mobilized directly into the armed forces. Over 16,000 women served overseas with the AEF in France, where most worked as nurses, clerical workers, telephone operators, and canteen operators. Another 12,000 women served stateside in the navy and U.S. Marine Corps, and tens of thousands of civilian women were employed in army offices and hospitals. But the war's impact on women was greatest in the broader civilian economy.

In response to the widened range of female employment, the Labor Department created the Women in Industry Service (WIS). Directed by Mary Van Kleeck, the service advised employers on using female labor and formulated general standards for the treatment of women workers. The WIS represented the first attempt by the federal government to take a practical stand on improving working conditions for women.

At war's end, women lost nearly all their defense-related jobs. But the war accelerated female employment in fields already dominated by women. By 1920, more women who worked outside the home did so in white-collar occupations—as telephone operators, secretaries, and clerks, for example—than in manufacturing or domestic service. The new awareness of women's work led Congress to create the Women's Bureau in the Labor Department, which continued the WIS wartime program of education and investigation through the postwar years.

MAP EXPLORATION

To explore this interactive map, go to **http://www.prenhall.com/faraghertlc/map22.3**

Legislation passed:
- 1869–1900
- 1901–1919
- 1920, 19th Amendment
- Partial suffrage 1917–19
- Never ratified 19th Amendment

MAP 22.3

Woman Suffrage by State, 1869–1919 Dates for the enactment of woman suffrage in the individual states. Years before ratification of the Nineteenth Amendment in 1920, a number of western states had legislated full or partial voting rights for women. In 1917, Montana suffragist Jeannette Rankin became the first woman elected to Congress.

Barbara G. Shortridge, *Atlas of American Women* (New York: Macmillan, 1987).

WHAT WERE the reasons behind the regional differences in support of woman suffrage?

WOMAN SUFFRAGE

Until World War I, the fight for woman suffrage had been waged largely within individual states. Western states and territories had led the way. Various forms of woman suffrage had become law in Wyoming in 1869, followed by Utah (1870), Colorado (1893), and Idaho (1896). Rocky Mountain and Pacific Coast states did not have the sharp ethnocultural divisions between Catholics and Protestants that hindered suffrage efforts in the East. For example, the close identification in the East between the suffrage and prohibition movements led many Catholic immigrants and German Lutherans to oppose the vote for women, because they feared it would lead to prohibition (see Map 22.3).

The U.S. entry into the war provided a unique opportunity for suffrage groups to shift their strategy to a national campaign for a constitutional amendment granting the vote to women. The most important of these groups was the National American Woman Suffrage Association (NAWSA). Before 1917, most American suffragists had opposed the war. Under the leadership of Carrie Chapman Catt, the NAWSA threw its support behind the war effort and doubled its membership to 2 million. Catt gambled that a strong show of patriotism would help clinch the century-old fight to win the vote for women.

At the same time, more militant suffragists, led by the young Quaker activist Alice Paul, injected new energy and more radical tactics into the movement. Dissatisfied with the NAWSA's conservative strategy of quiet lobbying and orderly demonstrations, Paul left the organization in 1916. She joined forces with western women voters to form the National Woman's Party. Borrowing from English suffragists, this party pursued a more aggressive and dramatic strategy of agitation. In one demonstration, they chained themselves to the White House fence, and after their arrest, went on a hunger strike in jail. The militants generated a great deal of publicity and sympathy.

Although some in the NAWSA objected to these tactics, Paul's radical approach helped make the NAWSA position more acceptable to Wilson. In 1917, the president urged Congress to pass a woman suffrage amendment as "vital to the winning of the war." The House did so in January 1918 and a more reluctant Senate approved it in June 1919. Another year of hard work was spent convincing the state legislatures. In August 1920, Tennessee gave the final vote needed to ratify the Nineteenth Amendment to the Constitution, finally making woman suffrage legal nationwide.

PROHIBITION

Another reform effort closely associated with women's groups triumphed at the same time. The movement to eliminate alcohol from American life had attracted many Americans, especially women, since before the Civil War. Temperance advocates saw drinking as the source of many of the worst problems faced by the working class, including family violence, unemployment, and poverty. By the early twentieth century, the Woman's Christian Temperance Union, with a quarter-million members, had become the single largest women's organization in American history.

The moral fervor that accompanied America's entry into the war provided a crucial boost to the cause. In 1917, a coalition of progressives and rural fundamentalists in Congress pushed through a constitutional amendment providing for a national ban on alcoholic drinks. The Eighteenth Amendment was ratified by the states in January 1919 and became the law of the land one year later. Although Prohibition would create a host of problems in the postwar years, especially as a stimulus for the growth of organized crime, many Americans, particularly native Protestants, considered it a worthy moral reform.

PUBLIC HEALTH AND THE INFLUENZA PANDEMIC

Wartime mobilization brought deeper government involvement with public health issues, especially in the realm of sex hygiene, child welfare, and disease prevention. The rate of venereal disease among draftees was as high as 6 percent in some states, presenting a potential manpower problem for the army. In April 1917, the War Department mounted a vigorous campaign against venereal disease, which attracted the energies of progressive-era sex reformers—social hygienists and antivice crusaders.

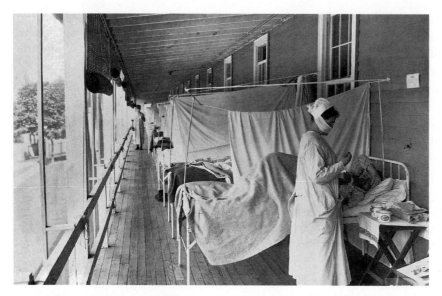

A nurse takes a patient's pulse in the influenza ward at Walter Reed Hospital, Washington, DC, November 1, 1918. Intensified by the crowded conditions on the battlefield, in training camps, and on troop ships, the influenza pandemic killed over half a million Americans and some 21 million people worldwide.

The wartime boost to government health work continued into the postwar years. The Children's Bureau, created in 1912 as a part of the Labor Department, undertook a series of reports on special problems growing out of the war: the increase in employment of married women, the finding of day care for children of working mothers, and the growth of both child labor and delinquency. Julia C. Lathrop, chief of the bureau, proposed a plan to institutionalize federal aid to the states for protection of mothers and children. Congress finally passed the Maternity and Infancy Act in 1921, appropriating over $1 million a year to be administered to the states by the Children's Bureau. In the postwar years, clinics for prenatal and obstetrical care grew out of these efforts and greatly reduced the rate of infant and maternal mortality and disease.

The disastrous influenza pandemic of 1918–19 offered the most serious challenge to national public health during the war years. It was part of a global scourge that originated in South China, then spread to the Philippines and moved across the United States, over to Europe, and then back with returning troops. Wartime conditions—large concentrations of people in military camps, on transport ships, and at the front—made its impact especially devastating. With no cure for the lethal combination of the "flu" and respiratory complications (mainly pneumonia), the pandemic killed over 21 million people worldwide. Few Americans paid attention to the disease until it swept through military camps and eastern cities in September 1918 and killed roughly 550,000 Americans in ten months. Most victims were young adults between the ages of twenty and forty. Much of the care for the sick and dying came from Red Cross nurses and volunteers working in local communities across the nation. With a war on, and the nation focused on reports from the battlefront, even a public health crisis of this magnitude went relatively unnoticed.

REPRESSION AND REACTION

World War I exposed and intensified many of the deepest social tensions in American life. On the local level, vigilantes increasingly took the law into their own hands to punish those suspected of disloyalty. The push for national unity led the federal government to crack down on a wide spectrum of dissenters. The war inflamed racial hatred, and the worst race riots in the nation's history exploded in several cities. At war's end, a newly militant labor movement briefly asserted itself in mass strikes around the nation. Over all these developments loomed the 1917 Bolshevik Revolution in Russia. From 1918 through 1920, the federal government directed a repressive antiradical campaign that had crucial implications for the nation's future.

WHAT STEPS did the federal government take to suppress the antiwar movement?

myhistorylab
Review Summary

MUZZLING DISSENT: THE ESPIONAGE AND SEDITION ACTS

The Espionage Act of June 1917 became the government's key tool for the suppression of antiwar sentiment. It set severe penalties (up to twenty years' imprisonment and a $10,000 fine) for anyone found guilty of aiding the enemy, obstructing recruitment, or causing insubordination in the armed forces. The act also empowered the postmaster general to exclude from the mails any newspapers or magazines he thought treasonous. Within a year, the mailing rights of forty-five newspapers had been revoked.

To enforce the Espionage Act, the government had to increase its overall police and surveillance machinery. Civilian intelligence was coordinated by the newly created Bureau of Investigation in the Justice Department. In May 1918, the **Sedition Act**, an amendment to the Espionage Act, outlawed "any disloyal, profane, scurrilous, or abusive language intended to cause contempt, scorn, contumely, or disrepute" to the government, Constitution, or flag.

These acts became a convenient vehicle for striking out at socialists, pacifists, radical labor activists, and others who resisted the patriotic tide. The Supreme Court upheld the constitutionality of the acts in several 1919 decisions.

In many western communities local vigilantes used the superpatriotic mood to settle scores with labor organizers and radicals. In July 1917, for example, 2,000 armed vigilantes swept through the mining town of Bisbee, Arizona, acting on behalf of the Phelps-Dodge mining company and local businessmen. They wanted to break an IWW-led bitter strike that had crippled Bisbee's booming copper industry. The vigilantes seized miners in their homes, on the street, and in restaurants and stores, delivering an ultimatum that any miner who refused to return to work would be deported. Some 1,400 miners refused to end their walkout; they were forced at gunpoint onto a freight train, which took them to Columbus, New Mexico, where they were dumped in the desert.

In thousands of other instances government repression and local vigilantes reinforced each other. The American Protective League, founded with the blessing of the Justice Department, mobilized 250,000 self-appointed "operatives" in more than 600 towns and cities. Members of the league, mostly businessmen, bankers, and former policemen, spied on their neighbors and staged a series of well-publicized "slacker" raids on antiwar protesters and draft evaders. Many communities, inspired by Committee on Public Information campaigns, sought to ban the teaching of the German language in their schools or the performance of German music in concert halls.

THE GREAT MIGRATION AND RACIAL TENSIONS

Economic opportunity brought on by war prosperity triggered a massive migration of rural black Southerners to northern cities. From 1914 to 1920, between 300,000 and 500,000 African Americans left the rural South for the North. Acute labor shortages led northern factory managers to recruit black migrants to the expanding industrial centers. Black workers eagerly left low-paying jobs as field hands and domestic servants for the chance at relatively high-paying work in meatpacking plants, shipyards, and steel mills (see Table 22.1).

Kinship and community networks were crucial in shaping what came to be called the **Great Migration**. They spread news about job openings, urban residential districts, and boardinghouses in northern cities. Black clubs, churches, and fraternal lodges in southern communities frequently sponsored the migration of their members, as well as return trips to the South. Single African American women often made the trip first, because they could more easily obtain steady work as maids, cooks, and laundresses. Relatively few African American men actually secured high-paying skilled jobs in industry or manufacturing. Most had to settle for such low-paying occupations as construction laborers, teamsters, janitors, or porters.

22–3
Letters from the Great Migration (1917)

Sedition Act Broad law restricting criticism of America's involvement in World War I or its government, flag, military, taxes, or officials.

Great Migration The mass movement of African Americans from the rural South to the urban North, spurred especially by new job opportunities during World War I and the 1920s.

TABLE 22.1

The Great Migration: Black Population Growth in Selected Northern Cities, 1910–20

Northern Cities	1910		1920		Percent Increase
	No.	Percent	No.	Percent	
New York	91,709	1.9%	152,467	2.7%	66.3%
Chicago	44,103	2.0	109,458	4.1	148.2
Philadelphia	84,459	5.5	134,229	7.4	58.9
Detroit	5,741	1.2	40,838	4.1	611.3
St. Louis	43,960	6.4	69,854	9.0	58.9
Cleveland	8,448	1.5	34,451	4.3	307.8
Pittsburgh	25,623	4.8	37,725	6.4	47.2
Cincinnati	19,739	5.4	30,079	7.5	53.2

U.S. Department of Commerce.

But rigid residential segregation of African Americans laid the foundation for the sprawling segregated ghettoes characteristic of twentieth-century northern cities. Shut out of white neighborhoods by a combination of custom and law (such as restrictive covenants forbidding homeowners to sell to non-whites), African American migrants found themselves forced to squeeze into less desirable and all-black neighborhoods. In 1920, for example, approximately 85 percent of Chicago's 110,000 black citizens lived within a narrow strip roughly three miles long and a quarter mile wide. The city's South Side ghetto—surrounded on all sides by railroad tracks—had been born.

The persistence of lynching and other racial violence in the South no doubt contributed to the Great Migration. But racial violence was not limited to the South. Two of the worst race riots in American history occurred as a result of tensions brought on by wartime migration. On July 2, 1917, in East St. Louis, Illinois, a ferocious mob of whites attacked African Americans, killing at least 200. Before this riot, some of the city's manufacturers had been steadily recruiting black labor as a way to keep local union demands down. Unions had refused to allow black workers as members, and politicians had cynically exploited white racism in appealing for votes. In Chicago, on July 27, 1919, antiblack rioting broke out on a Lake Michigan beach. For two weeks, white gangs hunted African Americans in the streets and burned hundreds out of their homes. Twenty-three African Americans and fifteen whites died, and more than 500 were injured. Yet in both East St. Louis and Chicago, local authorities held African Americans responsible for the violence.

African Americans had supported the war effort as faithfully as any group. In 1917, despite a segregated army and discrimination in defense industries, most African Americans thought the war might improve their lot. But black disillusionment with the war grew quickly, as did a newly militant spirit. A heightened sense of race consciousness and activism was evident among black veterans and the growing black communities of northern cities. Taking the lead in the fight against bigotry and injustice, the NAACP held a national conference in 1919 on lynching. It pledged to defend persecuted African Americans, publicize the horrors of lynch law, and seek federal legislation against "Judge Lynch."

LABOR STRIFE

The relative labor peace of 1917 and 1918 dissolved after the armistice. In 1919 alone more than 4 million American workers were involved in some 3,600 strikes. This unprecedented strike wave had several causes. Most of the modest wartime wage gains were wiped out by spiraling inflation and high prices for food, fuel, and housing. With the end of government controls on industry, many employers withdrew their recognition of unions. Difficult working conditions, such as the twelve-hour day in steel mills, were still routine in some industries.

Several of the postwar strikes received widespread national attention. They seemed to be more than simple economic conflicts, and they provoked deep fears about the larger social order. In February 1919, a strike in the shipyards of Seattle, Washington, over wages escalated into a general citywide strike involving 60,000 workers. The local press and Mayor Ole Hanson denounced the strikers as revolutionaries. Hanson effectively ended the strike by requesting federal troops to occupy the city. In September, Boston policemen went out on strike when the police commissioner rejected a citizens' commission study that recommended a pay raise. Massachusetts governor Calvin Coolidge called in the National Guard to restore order and won a national reputation by crushing the strike. The entire police force was fired.

The biggest strike took place in the steel industry and involved some 350,000 steelworkers. Centered in several midwestern cities, this epic struggle lasted from September 1919 to January 1920. The AFL had hoped to build on wartime gains in an industry that had successfully resisted unionization before the war. The steel companies used black strikebreakers and armed guards to keep the mills running. Elbert Gary, president of U.S. Steel, directed a sophisticated propaganda campaign that branded the strikers as revolutionaries. Public opinion turned against the strike and condoned the use of state and federal troops to break it. The failed steel strike proved to be the era's most bitter and devastating defeat for organized labor.

This southern African American family is shown arriving in Chicago around 1910. Black migrants to northern cities often faced overcrowding, inferior housing, and a high death rate from disease. But the chance to earn daily wages of $6 to $8 (the equivalent of a week's wages in much of the South), as well as the desire to escape persistent racial violence, kept the migrants coming.

QUICK REVIEW

Strikes

- 1919: American workers involved in 3,600 strikes.
- Large strikes received national attention.
- Breaking of 1919–1920 steel strike was a bitter defeat for organized labor.

AN UNEASY PEACE

The armistice of November 1918 ended the fighting on the battlefield, but the war continued at the peace conference. In the old royal palace of Versailles near Paris, delegates from twenty-seven countries spent five months hammering out a settlement. Yet neither Germany nor Russia was represented. The proceedings were dominated by leaders of the "Big Four": David Lloyd George (Great Britain), Georges Clemenceau (France), Vittorio Orlando (Italy), and Woodrow Wilson (United States).

HOW CAN we explain Woodrow Wilson's failure to win the peace?

Review Summary

Woodrow Wilson, Georges Clemenceau, and David Lloyd George are among the central figures depicted in John Christen Johansen's *Signing of the Treaty of Versailles.* But all the gathered statesmen appear dwarfed by their surroundings.

John Christen Johansen (1876–1964), "Signing of the Treaty of Versailles," 1919, oil on canvas, 249 cm × 224.5 cm (98-1/16 × 88-3/8"). Gift of an anonymous donor through Mrs. Elizabeth Rogerson, 1926. National Portrait Gallery, Smithsonian Institution, Washington, DC/Art Resource, New York.

Self-determination   The right of a people or a nation to decide on its own political allegiance or form of government without external influence.

Central Powers   Germany and its World War I allies in Austria, Italy, Turkey, and Bulgaria.

PEACEMAKING AND THE SPECTER OF BOLSHEVISM

Even before November 1918, the Allies struggled with how to respond to the revolutionary developments in Russia. British and French leaders wanted to help counterrevolutionary forces overthrow the new Bolshevik regime. President Wilson refused to recognize the authority of the Bolshevik regime. Bolshevism represented a threat to the liberal-capitalist values that Wilson believed to be the foundation of America's moral and material power, and that provided the basis for the Fourteen Points. At the same time, however, Wilson at first resisted British and French pressure to intervene in Russia, citing his commitment to national self-determination and noninterference in other countries' internal affairs.

By August 1918, as the Russian political and military situation became increasingly chaotic, Wilson agreed to British and French plans for sending troops to Siberia and northern Russia. Meanwhile, Japan poured troops into Siberia and northern Manchuria in a bid to control the commercially important Chinese Eastern and Trans-Siberian railways. After the Wilson administration negotiated an agreement that placed these strategic railways under international control, the restoration and protection of the railways became the primary concern of American military forces in Russia.

The Allied armed intervention widened the gulf between Russia and the West. In March 1919, Russian Communists established the Third International, or Comintern. Their call for a worldwide revolution deepened Allied mistrust, and the Paris Peace Conference essentially ignored the new political reality posed by the Russian Revolution.

WILSON IN PARIS

Wilson arrived in Paris with the United States delegation in January 1919. He believed the Great War revealed the bankruptcy of diplomacy based on alliances and the "balance of power." He believed that peacemaking, based on the framework put forward in his Fourteen Points, meant an opportunity for America to lead the rest of the world toward a new vision of international relations. The most controversial element, both at home and abroad, would prove to be the League of Nations.

Despite Wilson's devotion to "open covenants," much of the negotiating in Paris was in fact done in secret among the Big Four. The ideal of **self-determination** found limited expression. The independent states of Austria, Hungary, Poland, Yugoslavia, and Czechoslovakia were carved out of the homelands of the defeated **Central Powers**. But the Allies resisted Wilson's call for independence for the colonies of the defeated nations. A compromise mandate system of protectorates gave the French and British control of parts of the old German and Turkish empires in Africa and western Asia. Japan won control of former German colonies in China. Among those trying, but failing, to influence the treaty negotiations were the sixty-odd delegates to the first Pan African Congress, held in Paris at the same time as the peace talks. The group included Americans W. E. B. Du Bois and William Monroe Trotter as well as representatives from Africa and the West Indies. All were disappointed with the failure of the peace conference to grant self-determination to thousands of Africans living in former German colonies.

Another disappointment for Wilson came with the issue of war guilt. He had strongly opposed the extraction of harsh economic reparations from the Central Powers. But the French and British, with their awful war losses fresh in mind, insisted on making Germany pay. The final treaty contained a clause attributing the war to "the aggression of Germany," and a commission later set German war reparations at $33 billion. Bitter resentment in Germany over the punitive treaty helped sow the seeds for the Nazi rise to power in the 1930s.

The final treaty was signed on June 28, 1919, in the Hall of Mirrors at the Versailles palace. The Germans had no choice but to accept its harsh terms. President Wilson had been disappointed by the secret deals and the endless compromising of his ideals. He had nonetheless won a commitment to the League of Nations, the centerpiece of his plan, and he was confident that the American people would accept the treaty.

THE TREATY FIGHT

Preoccupied with peace conference politics in Paris, Wilson had neglected politics at home. His troubles had actually started earlier. Republicans had captured both the House and the Senate in the 1918 elections. Wilson had then made a tactical error by including no prominent Republicans in the U.S. peace delegation. He therefore faced a variety of tough opponents to the treaty he brought home.

Wilson's most extreme enemies in the Senate were a group of about sixteen **"irreconcilables"** who were opposed to a treaty in any form. The less dogmatic, but more influential, opponents were led by Republican Henry Cabot Lodge of Massachusetts, powerful majority leader of the Senate. They had strong reservations about the League of Nations, especially the provisions for collective security in the event of a member nation's being attacked. Lodge argued that this provision impinged on congressional authority to declare war and placed unacceptable restraints on the nation's ability to pursue an independent foreign policy. Lodge proposed a series of amendments that would have weakened the League. But Wilson refused to compromise, motivated in part by the long-standing hatred he and Lodge felt toward each other.

In September, Wilson set out on a speaking tour across the country to drum up support for the League and the treaty. The crowds were large and responsive, but they did not change any votes in the Senate. The strain took its toll. On September 25, after speaking in Pueblo, Colorado, the sixty-three-year-old Wilson collapsed from exhaustion. A week later, back in Washington, the president suffered a stroke that left him partially paralyzed. With Wilson badly incapacitated, his wife and his doctor exercised significant decision-making authority, and they reinforced his refusal to agree to any amendments on the Treaty and the League Covenant. In November, Lodge brought the treaty out of committee for a vote, having appended to it fourteen reservations—that is, recommended changes. A bedridden Wilson stubbornly refused to compromise and instructed Democrats to vote against the Lodge version of the treaty. On November 19, Democrats joined with the "irreconcilables" to defeat the amended treaty, 39 to 55.

Wilson refused to budge. In January, he urged Democrats to either stand by the original treaty or vote it down. The 1920 election, he warned, would be "a great and solemn referendum" on the whole issue. In the final vote, on March 19, 1920, twenty-one Democrats broke with the president and voted for the Lodge version, giving it a majority of 49 to 35. But this was seven votes short of the two-thirds needed for ratification. As a result, the United States never signed

---

QUICK REVIEW

Defeat of the Treaty

♦ Most Democrats favored the treaty.

♦ Republicans led by Henry Cabot Lodge wanted amendments.

♦ Wilson's refusal to compromise doomed the treaty.

Irreconcilables Group of U.S. senators adamantly opposed to ratification of the Treaty of Versailles after World War I.

the **Versailles Treaty**, nor did it join the League of Nations. The absence of the United States weakened the League and made it more difficult for the organization to realize Wilson's dream of a peaceful community of nations.

THE RED SCARE

The revolutionary changes taking place in Russia became an important backdrop for domestic politics. In the United States, it became common to blame socialism, the IWW, trade unionism in general, and even racial disturbances on foreign radicals and alien ideologies. The accusation of Bolshevism became a powerful weapon for turning public opinion against strikers and political dissenters of all kinds. In the spring of 1919, a few extremists mailed bombs to prominent business and political leaders. That June, simultaneous bombings in eight cities killed two people and damaged the residence of Attorney General A. Mitchell Palmer. With public alarm growing, state and federal officials began a coordinated campaign to root out subversives and their alleged Russian connections.

Palmer used the broad authority of the 1918 Alien Act, which enabled the government to deport any immigrant found to be a member of a revolutionary organization prior to or after coming to the United States. In a series of raids in late 1919, Justice Department agents in eleven cities arrested and roughed up several hundred members of the IWW and the Union of Russian Workers. Little evidence of revolutionary intent was found, but 249 people were deported, including prominent anarchists Emma Goldman and Alexander Berkman. In early 1920, some 6,000 people in thirty-three cities, including many U.S. citizens and non-Communists, were arrested and herded into prisons and bullpens. Again, no evidence of a grand plot was found, but another 600 aliens were deported.

Palmer's popularity had waned by the spring of 1920, when it became clear that his predictions of revolutionary uprisings were wildly exaggerated. A report prepared by a group of distinguished lawyers questioned the legality of the attorney general's tactics. As part of the resistance to Palmer's policies, a group of progressive activists formed the American Civil Liberties Union (ACLU) in 1920. Its founders included Clarence Darrow, Felix Frankfurter, Jane Addams, Helen Keller, and John Dewey. For progressives dispirited by the wartime political repression, the ACLU offered a new political front stressing the militant defense of civil liberties just when they seemed most fragile.

The **Red Scare** left an ugly legacy: wholesale violations of constitutional rights, deportations of hundreds of innocent people, fuel for the fires of nativism and intolerance. The Red Scare took its toll on the women's movement as well. Before the war, many suffragists and feminists had maintained ties and shared platforms with socialist and labor groups. The suffrage movement in particular had brought together women from very different class backgrounds and political perspectives. But the calls for "100 percent Americanism" during and after the war destroyed the fragile alliances that had made a group such as the National American Woman Suffrage Association so powerful. Hostility to radicalism marked the political climate of the 1920s, and this atmosphere narrowed the political spectrum for women activists.

THE ELECTION OF 1920

Woodrow Wilson had wanted the 1920 election to be a "solemn referendum" on the League of Nations and his conduct of the war. Ill and exhausted, Wilson did not run for reelection. A badly divided Democratic Party compromised on Governor James M. Cox of Ohio as its candidate.

Versailles Treaty   The treaty ending World War I and creating the League of Nations.

Red Scare   Post–World War I public hysteria over Bolshevik influence in the United States directed against labor activism, radical dissenters, and some ethnic groups.

CHRONOLOGY

1903	United States obtains Panama Canal rights
1905	President Theodore Roosevelt mediates peace treaty between Japan and Russia at Portsmouth Conference
1908	Root-Takahira Agreement with Japan affirms status quo in Asia and Open Door policy in China
1911	Mexican Revolution begins
1914	U.S. forces invade Mexico
	Panama Canal opens
	World War I begins in Europe
	President Woodrow Wilson issues proclamation of neutrality
1915	Germany declares war zone around Great Britain
	German U-boat sinks *Lusitania*
1916	Pancho Villa raids New Mexico and is pursued by General Pershing
	Wilson is reelected
	National Defense Act establishes preparedness program
1917	February: Germany resumes unrestricted submarine warfare
	March: Zimmermann note, suggesting a German-Mexican alliance, shocks Americans
	April: United States declares war on the Central Powers

	May: Selective Service Act is passed
	June: Espionage Act is passed
	November: Bolshevik Revolution begins in Russia
1918	January: Wilson unveils Fourteen Points
	May: Sedition Act is passed
	June: U.S. troops begin to see action in France
	September: Influenza outbreaks among AEF troops in France
	November: Armistice ends war
1919	January: Eighteenth Amendment (Prohibition) is ratified
	Wilson serves as chief U.S. negotiator at Paris Peace Conference
	June: Versailles Treaty is signed in Paris
	July: Race riot breaks out in Chicago
	Steel strike begins in several midwestern cities
	November: Palmer raids begin
1920	March: Senate finally votes down Versailles Treaty and League of Nations
	August: Nineteenth Amendment (woman suffrage) is ratified
	November: Warren G. Harding is elected president

The Republicans nominated Senator Warren G. Harding of Ohio. A political hack, the handsome and genial Harding had virtually no qualifications to be president, except that he looked like one. Harding's campaign was vague and ambiguous about the Versailles Treaty and almost everything else. "America's present need," he said, "is not heroics but healing; not nostrums but normalcy; not revolution but restoration."

The notion of a "return to normalcy" proved very attractive to voters exhausted by the war, inflation, big government, and social dislocation. Harding won the greatest landslide in history to that date, carrying every state outside the South and taking the popular vote by 16 million to 9 million. Republicans retained their majorities in the House and Senate as well. The overall vote repudiated Wilson and the progressive movement. Americans seemed eager to pull back from moralism in public and international controversies. Yet many of the economic, social, and cultural changes wrought by the war would accelerate during the 1920s. In truth, there could never be a "return to normalcy."

22–9
Warren G. Harding, *Campaign Speech at Boston* (1920)

CONCLUSION

The global impact of the Great War, including the United States' place in relation to the rest of the world, was profound. The war created economic, social, and political dislocations that helped reshape American life long after Armistice Day. The ability to raise and deploy the massive American Expeditionary Force overseas so quickly had proved decisive to ending the fighting. The government's direct intervention in every aspect of the wartime economy was unprecedented, and wartime production needs contributed to a "second industrial revolution" that transformed the economy in the decade following the war. Republican administrations invoked the wartime partnership between government and industry to justify an aggressive peacetime policy fostering cooperation between the state and business. Although the United States would not join the League of Nations, the war turned the United States into a major global force: the world's new leading creditor nation would now also take its place as a powerful commercial and industrial engine in the global economy.

Patriotic fervor and the exaggerated threat of Bolshevism were used to repress radicalism, organized labor, feminism, and the entire legacy of progressive reform. The wartime measure of national prohibition evolved into perhaps the most contentious social issue of peacetime. Sophisticated use of sales techniques, psychology, and propaganda during the war helped define the newly powerful advertising and public relations industries of the 1920s. The growing visibility of immigrants and African Americans, especially in the nation's cities, provoked a xenophobic and racist backlash in the politics of the 1920s. More than anything else, the desire for "normalcy" reflected the deep anxieties evoked by America's wartime experience.

REVIEW QUESTIONS

1. What central issues drew the United States deeper into international politics in the early years of the century? How did American presidents justify a more expansive role? What diplomatic and military policies did they exploit for these ends?

2. Compare the arguments for and against American participation in the Great War. Which Americans were most likely to support entry? Which were more likely to oppose it?

3. How did mobilizing for war change the economy and its relationship to government? Which of these changes, if any, spilled over to the postwar years?

4. How did the war affect political life in the United States? What techniques were used to stifle dissent? What was the war's political legacy?

5. Analyze the impact of the war on American workers. How did the conflict affect the lives of African Americans and women?

6. What principles guided Woodrow Wilson's Fourteen Points? How would you explain the United States' failure to ratify the Treaty of Versailles?

KEY TERMS

myhistorylab

Flashcard Review

Allies (p. 598)

Bolsheviks (p. 604)

Central Powers (p. 616)

Committee on Public Information (CPI) (p. 601)

Doughboys (p. 606)

Espionage Act (p. 608)

Fourteen Points (p. 604)

Great Migration (p. 613)

Imperialism (p. 597)

Irreconcilables (p. 617)
League of Nations (p. 605)
Liberty Bonds (p. 607)
Militarism (p. 597)
Monroe Doctrine (p. 593)
Open Door (p. 594)
Preparedness (p. 599)

Red Scare (p. 618)
Roosevelt Corollary (p. 593)
Sedition Act (p. 613)
Selective Service Act (p. 602)
Self-determination (p. 616)
Versailles Treaty (p. 618)
War Industries Board (WIB) (p. 606)

RECOMMENDED READING

Alan Dawley, *Changing the World: American Progressives in War and Revolution* (2003). Thoughtful analysis that traces the interplay between progressive politics and America's involvement in the Great War.

James H. Hallas, *Doughboy War: The American Expeditionary Force in World War I* (2000). Excellent and wide-ranging account of the AEF told entirely from first-person accounts—letters, diaries, and interviews—of the doughboys themselves.

Robert Hannigan, *The New World Power: American Foreign Policy, 1898–1917* (2002). An ambitious analysis of how the American policy-making elite sought to impose political and economic order around the globe.

Paul L. Murphy, *World War I and the Origin of Civil Liberties* (1979). A good overview of the various civil liberties issues raised by the war and government efforts to suppress dissent.

Ronald Schaffer, *America in the Great War: The Rise of the War Welfare State* (1991). Excellent material on how the war transformed the relationship between business and government and spurred improved conditions for industrial workers.

Richard Slotkin, *Lost Battalions: The Great War and the Crisis of Nationality* (2006). A beautifully written and imaginative account of two AEF units: the African American 369th Infantry (the "Harlem Hellfighters") and the 77th Division (the "Melting Pot"). Slotkin explores the tensions inherent in the wartime mobilization that included large groups of citizens—in these cases blacks and immigrants—who were deemed inferior yet also promised the benefits of full citizenship rights.

Joe William Trotter Jr., ed., *The Great Migration in Historical Perspective* (1991). An excellent collection of essays examining the Great Migration, with special attention to issues of class and gender within the African American community.

Susan Zeiger, *In Uncle Sam's Service: Women Workers with the American Expeditionary Force, 1917–1919* (1999). The first in-depth study of American women's experiences with the armed forces overseas.

Robert H. Zieger, *America's Great War: World War I and the American Experience* (2000). The best recent one-volume synthesis on how the war transformed the United States and its role in the world.

For study resources for this chapter, go to **www.myhistorylab.com** and choose *Out of Many, Teaching and Learning Classroom Edition.* You will find a wealth of study and review material for this chapter, including pretests and posttests, customized study plan, key-term review flash cards, interactive map and document activities, and documents for analysis.

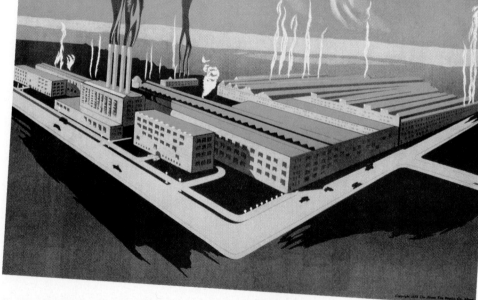

Happy times were here again.

—*Upton Sinclair, from* The Flivver King

Toward a Modern America: The 1920s. "More than a car. FORD:
A National Institution" poster, 1923.

23

THE TWENTIES
1920–1929

HOW DID the widespread use of automobiles change American society in the 1920s?

HOW AND why did the Republican Party dominate 1920s' politics?

HOW DID the new mass media reshape American culture?

WHAT POLITICAL and cultural movements opposed modern cultural trends?

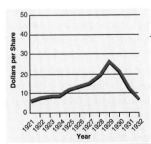

WHICH AMERICANS were less likely to share in postwar prosperity and why?

AMERICAN COMMUNITIES
The Movie Audience and Hollywood:
Mass Culture Creates a New National Community

INSIDE MIDTOWN MANHATTAN'S MAGNIFICENT NEW ROXY THEATER, A sellout crowd eagerly settled in for opening night. Outside, thousands of fans cheered wildly at the arrival of movie stars such as Charlie Chaplin, Gloria Swanson, and Harold Lloyd. A squadron of smartly uniformed ushers guided patrons under a five-story-tall rotunda to some 6,200 velvet-covered seats. The audience marveled at the huge gold and rose-colored murals, classical statuary, plush carpeting, and Gothic-style windows. It was easy to believe newspaper reports that the theater had cost $10 million to build. Suddenly, light flooded the orchestra pit and 110 musicians began playing "The Star Spangled Banner." A troupe of 100 performers took the stage, dancing ballet numbers and singing old southern melodies such as "My Old Kentucky Home" and "Swanee River." Congratulatory telegrams from President Calvin Coolidge and other dignitaries flashed on the screen. Finally, the evening's feature presentation, *The Love of Sunya*, starring Gloria Swanson, began. Samuel L. "Roxy" Rothapfel, the theater's designer, had realized his grand dream—to build "the cathedral of the motion picture."

When Roxy's opened in March 1927, nearly 60 million Americans "worshiped" each week at movie theaters across the nation. The "movie palaces" of the 1920s were designed to transport patrons to exotic places and different times. As film pioneer Marcus Loew put it, "We sell tickets to theaters, not movies." Every large community boasted at least one opulent movie theater. Houston's Majestic was built to represent an ancient Italian garden; it had a ceiling made to look like an open sky, complete with stars and cloud formations. The Tivoli in Chicago featured French Renaissance decor; Grauman's Egyptian in Los Angeles recreated the look of a pharaoh's tomb; and Albuquerque's Kimo drew inspiration from Navajo art and religion.

Hollywood's emergence might be thought of as part of a broader "second industrial revolution" that modernized industrial production and greatly expanded the availability of consumer goods in the postwar years. The studios concentrated on producing big-budget feature films designed for mass audiences, with the "star system" providing the industry's version of product branding. Movie stars like Charlie Chaplin, Mary Pickford, Rudolph Valentino, Gloria Swanson, and Douglas Fairbanks became popular idols as much for their highly publicized private lives as for their roles on screen. Many accumulated great wealth, becoming the nation's experts on how to live well. Americans embraced the culture of celebrity, voraciously consuming fan magazines, gossip columns, and news of the stars. Indeed during the 1920s there was a tight connection between celebrity and the rapid growth of new networks of mass culture—movies, radio, advertising, musical recordings, and big-time sports.

Ordinary Americans found it easy to identify with movie stars despite their wealth and status. Unlike industrialists or politicians, stars had no social authority over large groups of employees or voters. They, too, had to answer to a boss, and most had risen from humble beginnings. But above all, Hollywood, like the movies it churned out, represented for millions of Americans new possibilities: freedom, material success, upward mobility, and the chance to remake one's very identity.

By the end of the decade, the Hollywood "dream factory" had helped forge a national community whose collective aspirations and desires were increasingly defined by those possibilities, even if relatively few Americans realized them during the 1920s.

Of course, Hollywood films offered nothing near an accurate reflection of the complexities of American society. As American culture became increasingly defined by an urban-based mass media that claimed the entire nation for its audience, resentment toward and resistance against the new popular culture was widespread. Movies celebrated prosperity, new technologies, and expanded consumerism, but these were by no means shared equally among Americans in the decade following World War I. And while Hollywood films touted the promise of the modern, and the potential for people to remake themselves, tenacious belief in the old-fashioned verities of prewar America fueled some of the strongest political and cultural currents of the decade.

Hollywood

POSTWAR PROSPERITY AND ITS PRICE

Republican Warren G. Harding won the presidency in 1920, largely thanks to his nostalgic call for a "return to normalcy." But in the decade following the end of World War I, the American economy underwent profound structural changes that guaranteed life would never be "normal" again.

THE SECOND INDUSTRIAL REVOLUTION

The prosperity of the 1920s rested on what historians have called the "second industrial revolution" in American manufacturing, in which technological innovations made it possible to increase industrial output without expanding the labor force. Electricity replaced steam as the main power source for industry in these years, making possible the replacement of older machinery with more efficient and flexible electric machinery.

Much of the newer, automatic machinery could be operated by unskilled and semiskilled workers, and it boosted the overall efficiency of American industry. Thus, in 1929, the average worker in manufacturing produced roughly three-quarters more per hour than he or she had in 1919.

During the late nineteenth century, heavy industries such as machine tools, railroads, iron, and steel had pioneered mass-production techniques. These industries manufactured what economists call producer-durable goods. In the 1920s, modern mass-production techniques were increasingly applied to newer consumer-durable goods—automobiles, radios, washing machines, and telephones—permitting firms to make large profits while keeping prices affordable. With more efficient management, greater mechanization, intensive product research, and ingenious sales and advertising methods, the consumer-based industries helped to nearly double industrial production in the 1920s.

The watchword for all this was efficiency, a virtue that progressives had emphasized in their prewar efforts to improve urban life and the mechanics of government itself. But efficiency was now an obsession for American businessmen, who thought it defined modernity as well. American success in mechanization and the mass production of consumer goods evoked admiration and envy in much of the industrialized (and industrializing) world.

THE MODERN CORPORATION

In the late nineteenth century, individual entrepreneurs such as John D. Rockefeller in oil and Andrew Carnegie in steel had provided a model for success. They maintained both corporate control (ownership) and business leadership (management) in their enterprises. In the 1920s, a managerial revolution increasingly divorced ownership of corporate stock from the everyday control of businesses (see Figure 23.1). A growing class of salaried executives, plant managers, and engineers formed a new elite, who made corporate policy without themselves having a controlling interest in the companies they worked for. They stressed scientific management and the latest theories of behavioral psychology in their effort to make their workplaces

HOW DID the widespread use of automobiles change American society in the 1920s?

myhistorylab
Review Summary

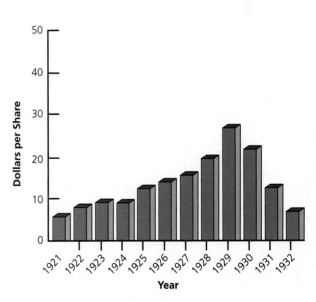

Figure 23.1 Stock Market Prices, 1921–32
Common stock prices rose steeply during the 1920s. Although only about 4 million Americans owned stocks during the period, "stock watching" became something of a national sport.

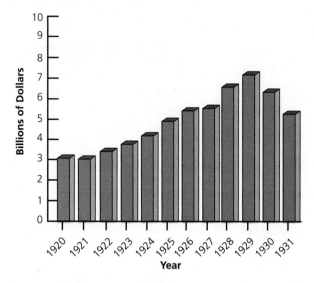

Figure 23.2 Consumer Debt, 1920–31
The expansion of consumer borrowing was a key component of the era's prosperity. These figures do not include mortgages or money borrowed to purchase stocks. They reveal the great increase in "installment buying" for such consumer durable goods as automobiles and household appliances.

more productive, stable, and profitable (see Figure 23.2). Modern managers also brought a more sophisticated understanding of global markets to their management. Exploiting overseas markets, especially in Europe, became a key element in corporate strategy, especially for car manufacturers, chemical companies, and businesses engaged in the new world of modern mass media. During the 1920s, the most successful corporations were those that led in three key areas: the integration of production and distribution, product diversification, and the expansion of industrial research.

By 1929, the 200 largest corporations owned nearly half the nation's corporate wealth—that is, physical plant, stock, and property. Half the total industrial income—revenue from sales of goods—was concentrated in 100 corporations. Oligopoly—the control of a market by a few large producers—became the norm. Four companies packed almost three-quarters of all American meat. Another four rolled nine out of every ten cigarettes. National chain grocery stores, clothing shops, and pharmacies began squeezing out local neighborhood businesses. These changes meant that Americans were increasingly members of national consumer communities, buying the same brands all over the country, as opposed to locally produced goods.

WELFARE CAPITALISM

The wartime gains made by organized labor, and the active sympathy shown to trade unions by government agencies such as the National War Labor Board (NWLB), troubled most corporate leaders. Shortly after the war's end, largely as a result of pressure from business leaders, the Wilson administration dismantled the NWLB and other mechanisms aimed at mediation of labor disputes. To challenge the power and appeal of trade unions and collective bargaining, large employers aggressively promoted a variety of new programs designed to improve worker well-being and morale while also fending off unionization. These schemes, collectively known as **welfare capitalism**, became a key part of corporate strategy in the 1920s.

Large corporations mounted an effective antiunion campaign in the early 1920s called "the American plan" as an alternative to trade unionism and the class antagonism associated with European labor relations. Backed by powerful business lobbies such as the National Association of Manufacturers and the Chamber of Commerce, campaign leaders called for the **open shop**, in which no employee would be compelled to join a union. In effect, an "open shop" meant that no known union member would be hired. If a union existed, nonmembers would still get whatever wages and rights the union had won—a policy that put organizers at a disadvantage in signing up new members.

The open shop undercut the gains won in a union shop, where new employees had to join an existing union, or a closed shop, where employers agreed to hire only union members. As alternatives, large employers such as U.S. Steel and International Harvester began setting up company unions. Their intent was to substitute largely symbolic employee representation in management conferences for the more confrontational process of collective bargaining. These management strategies contributed to a sharp decline in the ranks of organized labor. Total union membership dropped from about 5 million in 1920 to 3.5 million in 1926. A large proportion of the remaining union members were concentrated in the skilled crafts of the building and printing trades.

Welfare capitalism A paternalistic system of labor relations emphasizing management responsibility for employee well-being.

Open shop Factory of business employing workers whether or not they are union members; in practice, such a business usually refuses to hire union members and follows antiunion policies.

The A&P grocery chain expanded from 400 stores in 1912 to more than 15,000 by the end of the 1920s, making it a familiar sight in communities across America. A&P advertisements, like this one from 1927, emphasized cleanliness, order, and the availability of name-brand goods at discount prices.

Another approach encouraged workers to acquire property through stock-purchase plans or, less frequently, home-ownership plans. By 1927, 800,000 employees had more than $1 billion invested in more than 300 companies. Other programs offered workers insurance policies covering accidents, illness, old age, and death. By 1928, some 6 million workers had group insurance coverage valued at $7.5 billion. Many plant managers and personnel departments consciously worked to improve safety conditions, provide medical services, and establish sports and recreation programs for workers. Employers hoped such measures would encourage workers to identify personally with the company and discourage complaints on the job. To some extent they succeeded. But welfare capitalism could not solve the chronic problems faced by industrial workers: seasonal unemployment, low wages, long hours, and unhealthy factory conditions. Indeed corporate policy reinforced economic insecurity for millions of workers and advanced growing income inequality. The failure of the 1920s' economy to distribute gains in productivity more equally would help set the stage for the Great Depression of the 1930s.

THE AUTO AGE

The auto industry offered the clearest example of the rise to prominence of consumer durables. During the 1920s, America made approximately 85 percent of all the world's passenger cars. By 1929, the motor vehicle industry was the most productive in the United States in terms of value. In that year, the industry added 4.8 million new cars to the more than 26 million—roughly one for every five people—already on American roads.

IMAGE KEY

for pages 622–623

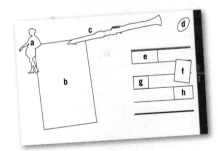

a. Silent film star Gertrude Olmstead wears a ruffled flapper dress with a striped hat in 1925.
b. "More than a car. FORD: A National Institution" poster, 1923.
c. A clarinet like those used during "the Jazz Age" of the 1920s.
d. An old football symbolizes the exuberance of the times.
e. Men are shown piecing together automobiles on an assembly line in the Rouge plant of the Ford Motor Company.
f. Campbell's Tomato Soup advertisement.
g. The price of stocks through the 1920s and early 1930s.
h. Women dressed in the white robes and hoods of the Ku Klux Klan in 1924.

Finished automobiles roll off the moving assembly line at the Ford Motor Company, Highland Park, Michigan, ca. 1920. During the 1920s, Henry Ford achieved the status of folk hero, as his name became synonymous with the techniques of mass production. Ford cultivated a public image of himself as the heroic genius of the auto industry, greatly exaggerating his personal achievements.

QUICK REVIEW

The Automobile Industry

◆ 1920s: America made 85 percent of the world's passenger cars.

◆ By 1925, Ford's assembly line produced one new car every ten seconds.

◆ Auto industry provided a market for steel, rubber, glass, and petroleum products.

This extraordinary new industry had mushroomed in less than a generation. Its great pioneer, Henry Ford, had shown how the use of a continuous assembly line could drastically reduce the number of worker hours required to produce a single vehicle. In 1913, it took thirteen hours to produce one automobile. In 1914, at his sprawling new Highland Park assembly plant just outside Detroit, Ford's system finished one car every ninety minutes. By 1925, cars were rolling off his assembly line at the rate of one every ten seconds.

In 1914, Ford startled American industry by inaugurating a new wage scale: $5 for an eight-hour day. This was roughly double the going pay rate for industrial labor, along with a shorter workday as well. But in defying the conventional economic wisdom of the day, Ford acted less out of benevolence than out of shrewdness. He understood that workers were consumers as well as producers, and the new wage scale helped boost sales of Ford cars. It also reduced the high turnover rate in his labor force and increased worker efficiency. Roughly two-thirds of the labor force at Ford consisted of immigrants from southern and eastern Europe. By the early 1920s Ford also employed about 5,000 African Americans, more than any other large American corporation. Ford's mass-production system and economies of scale permitted him to progressively reduce the price of his cars, bringing them within the reach of millions of Americans.

By 1927, Ford had produced 15 million Model Ts. But by then, the company faced stiff competition from General Motors (GM), which had developed an effective new marketing strategy. Under the guidance of Alfred P. Sloan, GM organized into separate divisions, each of which appealed to a different market segment. The GM business structure, along with its attempts to match production with demand through sophisticated market research and sales forecasting, became a widely copied model for other large American corporations. Both Ford and GM also pushed the idea of purchasing cars on credit, thus helping to make "installment buying" an underpinning of the new consumer culture.

The auto industry provided a large market for makers of steel, rubber, glass, and petroleum products. It stimulated public spending for good roads and extended the housing boom to new suburbs. Showrooms, repair shops, and gas stations appeared in thousands of communities. New small enterprises, from motels to billboard advertising to roadside diners, sprang up as motorists took to the highway. Automobiles widened the experience of millions of Americans. They made the exploration of the world outside the local community easier and more attractive. For some, the car merely reinforced old social patterns, making it easier for them to get to church on Sunday, for example, or visit neighbors. Others used their cars to go to new places, shop in nearby cities, or take vacations. The automobile made leisure, in the sense of getting away from the routines of work and school, a more regular part of everyday life. It undoubtedly also changed the courtship practices of America's youth. Young people took advantage of the car to gain privacy and distance from their parents, and many had their first sexual experiences in automobiles.

CITIES AND SUBURBS

Cars also promoted urban and suburban growth. The federal census for 1920 was the first in American history in which the proportion of the population that lived in urban places (those with 2,500 or more people) exceeded the proportion of the population living in rural areas. More revealing of urban growth was the steady increase in the number of big cities. In 1910, there were sixty cities with more than 100,000 inhabitants; in 1920, there were sixty-eight; and by 1930, there were ninety-two.

Cities promised business opportunity, good jobs, cultural richness, and personal freedom. They attracted millions of Americans, white and black, from small towns and farms, as well as immigrants from abroad. Immigrants were drawn to cities by the presence there of family and people of like background in already

Until 1924, Henry Ford had disdained national advertising for his cars. But as General Motors gained a competitive edge by making yearly changes in style and technology, Ford was forced to pay more attention to advertising. This ad was directed at "Mrs. Consumer," combining appeals to female independence and motherly duties.

established ethnic communities. In a continuation of the Great Migration that began during World War I, roughly 1.5 million African Americans from the rural South migrated to cities in search of economic opportunities during the 1920s, doubling the black populations of New York, Chicago, Detroit, and Houston.

Houston offers a good example of how the automobile shaped an urban community. In 1910, it was a sleepy railroad town with a population of about 75,000 that served the Texas Gulf coast and interior. The enormous demand for gasoline and other petroleum products helped transform the city into a busy center for oil refining. Its population soared to 300,000 by the end of the 1920s. Abundant cheap land and the absence of zoning ordinances, combined with the availability of the automobile, pushed Houston to expand horizontally rather than vertically. It became the archetypal decentralized, low-density city, sprawling miles in each direction from downtown and thoroughly dependent upon automobiles and roads for its sense of community. Suburban communities grew at twice the rate of their core cities, also thanks largely to the automobile boom. Undeveloped land on the fringes of cities became valuable real estate. All the new "automobile suburbs" differed in important ways from earlier suburbs built along mass transit lines. The car allowed for a larger average lot size and, in turn, lower residential density.

The State, the Economy, and Business

HOW AND why did the Republican Party dominate 1920s' politics?

myhistorylab
Review Summary

Throughout the 1920s, a confident Republican Party dominated national politics, certain that it had ushered in a "new era" in American life. A new and closer relationship between the federal government and American business became the hallmark of Republican policy in both domestic and foreign affairs during the administrations of three successive Republican presidents: Warren Harding (1921–23), Calvin Coolidge (1923–29), and Herbert Hoover (1929–33).

Harding and Coolidge

Handsome, genial, and well-spoken, Warren Harding may have looked the part of a president—but acting like one was another matter. Harding was a product of small-town Marion, Ohio, and the machine politics in his native state. Republican Party officials had made a point of keeping Senator Harding, a compromise choice, as removed from the public eye as possible in the 1920 election. They correctly saw that active campaigning could only hurt their candidate by exposing his shallowness and intellectual weakness.

Harding surrounded himself with a close circle of friends, the "Ohio gang," delegating to them a great deal of administrative power. In the summer of 1923, Harding began to get wind of the scandals for which his administration is best remembered.

Soon after Harding's death from a heart attack in 1923, a series of congressional investigations revealed a deep pattern of corruption. The worst affair was the Teapot Dome scandal involving Interior Secretary Albert Fall. Fall received hundreds of thousands of dollars in payoffs when he secretly leased navy oil reserves in Teapot Dome, Wyoming, and Elk Hills, California, to two private oil developers. He eventually became the first cabinet officer ever to go to jail.

But the Harding administration's legacy was not all scandal. Andrew Mellon, an influential Pittsburgh banker, served as secretary of the treasury under all three Republican presidents of the 1920s. Mellon believed government ought to be run on the same conservative principles as a corporation. He was a leading voice for trimming the federal budget and cutting taxes on incomes, corporate profits, and inheritances. Mellon's program sharply cut taxes for both higher-income brackets and for businesses. By 1926, a person with an income of a million a year paid less than a third of the income tax he or she had paid in 1921.

When Calvin Coolidge succeeded to the presidency, he seemed to most people the temperamental opposite of Harding. Taciturn, genteel, and completely honest, Coolidge believed in the least amount of government possible. He spent only four hours a day at the office. His famous aphorism, "The business of America is business," perfectly captured the core philosophy of the Republican new era.

Coolidge easily won election on his own in 1924. He benefited from the general prosperity and the contrast he provided with the disgraced Harding. Coolidge defeated little-known Democrat John W. Davis, the compromise choice of a party badly divided between its rural and urban wings. Also running was Progressive Party candidate Robert M. La Follette of Wisconsin, who mounted a reform campaign that attacked economic monopolies and called for government ownership of utilities. In his full term, Coolidge showed most interest in reducing federal spending, lowering taxes, and blocking congressional initiatives. He saw his primary function as clearing the way for American businessmen. They, after all, were the agents of the era's unprecedented prosperity.

HERBERT HOOVER AND THE "ASSOCIATIVE STATE"

The most influential figure of the Republican new era was Herbert Hoover, who as secretary of commerce dominated the cabinets of Harding and Coolidge before becoming president himself in 1929. A successful engineer, administrator, and politician, Hoover had earned an enviable reputation as wartime head of the U.S. Food Administration and director general of relief for Europe. He effectively embodied the belief that enlightened business, encouraged and informed by the government, would act in the public interest. In this sense Hoover maintained an essentially progressive outlook. But in the modern industrial age, Hoover believed, the government needed only to advise private citizens' groups about what national or international polices to pursue.

Hoover thus fused a faith in old-fashioned individualism with a strong commitment to the progressive possibilities offered by efficiency and rationality. Unlike an earlier generation of Republicans, Hoover wanted not just to create a favorable climate for business but also to actively assist the business community. He spoke of creating an "associative state," in which the government would encourage voluntary cooperation among corporations, consumers, workers, farmers, and small businessmen. This became the central occupation of the Department of Commerce under Hoover's leadership. The Bureau of Standards became one of the nation's leading research centers, setting engineering standards for key American industries such as machine tools and automobiles. The bureau also helped standardize the styles, sizes, and designs of many consumer products, such as canned goods and refrigerators.

Hoover actively encouraged the creation and expansion of national trade associations. By 1929, there were about 2,000 of them. At industrial conferences called by the Commerce Department, government officials explained the advantages of mutual cooperation in figuring prices and costs and then publishing the information. The idea was to improve efficiency by reducing competition. To some, this practice violated the spirit of antitrust laws, but in the 1920s, the Justice Department's Antitrust Division took a very lax view of its responsibility. In addition, the

QUICK REVIEW

The Teapot Dome Scandal

♦ Corruption and scandals plagued the Harding administration.

♦ Albert Fall, the secretary of the interior, leased petroleum reserves in exchange for cash.

♦ As a result of his part in the Teapot Dome scandal, Fall went to prison.

Supreme Court consistently upheld the legality of trade associations. The government thus provided an ideal climate for the concentration of corporate wealth and power.

WAR DEBTS, REPARATIONS, KEEPING THE PEACE

Rejection of the Treaty of Versailles and the League of Nations did not mean disengagement from the rest of the globe. The United States emerged from World War I as the strongest economic power in the world. The war transformed it from the world's leading debtor nation to its most important creditor. New York replaced London as the center of international finance and capital markets. Yet America's postwar policies included a great contradiction: protectionism. The rest of the world owed the United States billions of dollars, but high tariffs on both farm products and manufactured goods made it much more difficult for debtor nations to repay by selling exports.

During the 1920s, war debts and reparations were the single most divisive issue in international economics. In France and Great Britain, which both owed the United States large amounts in war loans, many concluded that the Uncle Sam who had offered assistance during wartime was really a loan shark in disguise. In turn, many Americans viewed Europeans as ungrateful debtors. In 1922, the U.S. Foreign Debt Commission negotiated an agreement with the debtor nations that called for them to repay $11.5 billion over a sixty-two-year period. But by the late 1920s, the European financial situation had become so desperate that the United States agreed to cancel a large part of these debts. Continued insistence by the United States that the Europeans pay at least a portion of the debt fed anti-American feeling in Europe and isolationism at home.

The Germans believed that war reparations, set at $33 billion by the Treaty of Versailles, not only unfairly punished the losers of the conflict but, by saddling their civilian economies with such massive debt, also deprived them of the very means to repay. In 1924, Herbert Hoover and Chicago banker Charles Dawes worked out a plan to aid the recovery of the German economy. The Dawes Plan reduced Germany's debt, stretched out the repayment period, and arranged for American bankers to lend funds to Germany. These measures helped stabilize Germany's currency and allowed it to make reparations payments to France and Great Britain. The Allies, in turn, were better able to pay their war debts to the United States.

In addition to the Dawes Plan and the American role in naval disarmament, the United States joined the league-sponsored World Court in 1926 and was represented at numerous league conferences. In 1928, with great fanfare, the United States and sixty-two other nations signed the Pact of Paris (better known as the Kellogg-Briand Pact), which grandly and naively renounced war in principle. Peace groups, such as the Woman's Peace Party and the Quaker-based Fellowship of Reconciliation, hailed the pact for formally outlawing war. But critics charged that the Kellogg-Briand Pact was essentially meaningless, since it lacked powers of enforcement and relied solely on the moral force of world opinion.

GLOBAL COMMERCE AND U.S. FOREIGN POLICY

Throughout the 1920s, Secretary of State Charles Evans Hughes and other Republican leaders pursued policies designed to expand American economic activity abroad. They understood that capitalist economies must be dynamic; they must expand their markets if they were to thrive. The focus must be on friendly nations and investments that would help foreign citizens to buy American goods. Toward this end, Republican leaders urged close cooperation between bankers and the government as a strategy for expanding American investment and economic influence abroad.

The strategy of maximum freedom for private enterprise, backed by limited government advice and assistance, significantly boosted the power and profits of American overseas investors. But in Central and Latin America, in particular, aggressive U.S. investment also fostered chronically underdeveloped economies, dependent on a few staple crops (sugar, coffee, cocoa, bananas) grown for export. American investments in Latin America more than doubled between 1924 and 1929, from $1.5 billion to over $3.5 billion. A large part of this money went to taking over vital mineral resources, such as Chile's copper and Venezuela's oil. The growing wealth and power of U.S. companies made it more difficult for these nations to grow their own food or diversify their economies. U.S. economic dominance in the hemisphere also hampered the growth of democratic politics by favoring autocratic, military regimes that could be counted on to protect U.S. investments.

WEAKENED AGRICULTURE, AILING INDUSTRIES

Amid prosperity and progress, there were large pockets of the country that lagged behind. Advances in real income and improvements in the standard of living for workers and farmers were uneven at best. In 1920, some 32 million Americans still lived on farms, out of a total population of 106 million. Yet during the 1920s the farm sector failed to share in the general prosperity. The years 1914–19 had been a kind of golden age for the nation's farmers. But with the war's end, American farmers began to suffer from a chronic worldwide surplus of such farm staples as cotton, hogs, and corn.

In the South, farmers' dependency on "King Cotton" deepened, as the region lagged farther behind the rest of the nation in both agricultural diversity and standard of living. Cotton acreage expanded, as large and heavily mechanized farms opened up new land in Oklahoma, west Texas, and the Mississippi-Yazoo delta. But in most of the South, from North Carolina to east Texas, small one- and two-mule cotton farms, most under 50 acres, still dominated the countryside. With few large urban centers and inadequate transportation, even those southern farmers who had access to capital found it extremely difficult to find reliable markets for vegetables, fruit, poultry, or dairy products. Some 700,000 southern farmers, roughly half white and half black, still labored as sharecroppers. Modern conveniences such as electricity, indoor plumbing, automobiles, and phonographs remained far beyond the reach of the great majority of southern farmers. Widespread rural poverty, poor diet, little access to capital—the world of southern agriculture had changed very little since the days of the Populist revolt in the 1890s.

The most important initiatives for federal farm relief were the McNary-Haugen bills, a series of complicated measures designed to prop up and stabilize farm prices. The basic idea, borrowed from the old Populist proposals of the 1890s, was for the government to purchase farm surpluses and either store them until prices rose or sell them on the world market. But President Calvin Coolidge viewed these measures as unwarranted federal interference in the economy and vetoed the McNary-Haugen Farm Relief bill of 1927 when it finally passed

23–2
H. L. Mencken, *The Sahara of the Bozart* (1920)

Congress. American farmers hoping to export produce abroad also suffered from the high tariffs imposed by European countries trying to protect their own devastated economies.

To be sure, some farmers thrived. Improved transportation and chain supermarkets allowed for a wider and more regular distribution of such foods as oranges, lemons, and fresh green vegetables. Citrus, dairy, and truck farmers in particular profited from the growing importance of national markets. Wheat production jumped more than 300 percent during the 1920s. Across the plains of Kansas, Nebraska, Colorado, Oklahoma, and Texas, wheat farmers brought the methods of industrial capitalism to the land. They hitched disc plows and combined harvester-threshers to gasoline-powered tractors, tearing up millions of acres of grassland to create a vast wheat factory. With prices averaging above $1 per bushel over the decade, mechanized farming created a new class of large-scale wheat entrepreneurs on the plains.

Overall, per capita farm income remained well below what it had been in 1919, and the gap between farm and nonfarm income widened. By 1929, the average income per person on farms was $223, compared with $870 for nonfarm workers. By the end of the decade, hundreds of thousands had quit farming altogether for jobs in mills and factories. And fewer farmers owned their land. In 1930, 42 percent of all farmers were tenants, compared with 37 percent in 1919.

Large sectors of American industry also failed to share in the decade's general prosperity. As oil and natural gas gained in importance, America's coal mines became a less important source of energy. A combination of shrinking demand, new mining technology, and a series of losing strikes reduced the coal labor force by one-quarter. The United Mine Workers, perhaps the strongest AFL union in 1920, with 500,000 members, had shrunk to 75,000 by 1928. Economic hardship was widespread in many mining communities dependent on coal, particularly Appalachia and the southern Midwest. And those miners who did work earned lower hourly wages.

In textiles, shrinking demand and overcapacity (too many factories) were chronic problems. To improve profit margins, textile manufacturers in New England and other parts of the Northeast began a long-range shift of operations to the South, where nonunion shops and substandard wages became the rule. Older New England manufacturing centers such as Lawrence, Lowell, Nashua, Manchester, and Fall River were hard hit by this shift. The center of the American textile industry shifted permanently to the Piedmont region of North and South Carolina. By 1933, factories there employed nearly 70 percent of the workers in the industry.

THE NEW MASS CULTURE

New communications media reshaped American culture in the 1920s, and much of the new mass culture was exported to the rest of the economically developed world. The phrase "Roaring Twenties" captures the explosion of image- and sound-making machinery that came to dominate so much of American life.

MOVIE-MADE AMERICA

The early movie industry, centered in New York and a few other big cities, had made moviegoing a regular habit for millions of Americans, especially immigrants and

HOW DID the new mass media reshape American culture?

Review Summary

the working class. They flocked to cheap, storefront theaters, called nickelodeons, to watch short Westerns, slapstick comedies, melodramas, and travelogues. By 1914, there were about 18,000 "movie houses" showing motion pictures, with more than 7 million daily admissions and $300 million in annual receipts. With the shift of the industry westward to Hollywood, movies entered a new phase of business expansion. Large studios such as Paramount, Fox, Metro-Goldwyn-Mayer (MGM), Universal, and Warner Brothers dominated the business with longer and more expensively produced movies—feature films. Each studio combined the three functions of production, distribution, and exhibition, and each controlled hundreds of movie theaters around the country.

The era of silent films ended when Warner Brothers scored a huge hit in 1927 with *The Jazz Singer*, starring Al Jolson, which successfully introduced sound. New genres—musicals, gangster films, and screwball comedies—soon became popular. To maintain their hold on European markets, the major studios established production facilities abroad that used foreign actors for the "dubbing" of American films into other languages. The higher costs associated with "talkies" also increased the studios' reliance on Wall Street investors and banks for working capital.

At the heart of Hollywood's success was the star system and the accompanying cult of celebrity, both of which help define American popular culture to this day (see Seeing History). Stars became vital to the fantasy lives of millions of fans. For many in the audience, there was only a vague line separating the on-screen and off-screen adventures of the stars. Studio publicity, fan magazines, and gossip columns reinforced this ambiguity. Film idols, with their mansions, cars, parties, and private escapades, became the national experts on leisure and consumption. Their movies generally emphasized sexual themes and celebrated youth, athleticism, and the liberating power of consumer goods. Young Americans in particular looked to movies to learn how to dress, wear their hair, talk, or kiss.

But many Americans, particularly in rural areas and small towns, worried about Hollywood's impact on traditional sexual morality. They attacked the permissiveness associated with Hollywood life, and many states created censorship boards to screen movies before allowing them to be shown in theaters. To counter growing calls for government censorship, Hollywood's studios came up with a plan to censor themselves. In 1922, they hired Will Hays to head the Motion Picture Producers and Distributors of America. As the movie industry's czar, Hays lobbied against censorship laws, wrote pamphlets defending the movie business, and began setting guidelines for what could and could not be depicted on the screen. He insisted that movies be treated like any other industrial enterprise, for he understood the relationship between Hollywood's success and the growth of the nation's consumer culture.

RADIO BROADCASTING

In the fall of 1920, Westinghouse executive Harry P. Davis noticed that amateur broadcasts from the garage of an employee had attracted attention in the local Pittsburgh press. A department store advertised radio sets capable of picking up these "wireless concerts." Davis converted this amateur station to a stronger one at the Westinghouse main plant. Beginning with the presidential election returns that November, station KDKA offered regular nightly broadcasts that were probably heard by only a few hundred people. Radio broadcasting, begun

23–11
Motion Picture Diaries (1920s)

as a service for selling cheap radio sets left over from World War I, would soon sweep the nation.

Before KDKA, wireless technology had been of interest only to the military, the telephone industry, and a few thousand "ham" (amateur) operators who enjoyed communicating with each other. The "radio mania" of the early 1920s was a response to the new possibilities offered by broadcasting. By 1923, nearly 600 stations had been licensed by the Department of Commerce, and about 600,000 Americans had bought radios. For millions of Americans, especially in rural areas and small towns, radio provided a new and exciting link to the larger national community of consumption.

Who would pay for radio programs? In the early 1920s, owners and operators of radio stations included radio equipment manufacturers, newspapers, department stores, state universities, cities, ethnic societies, labor unions, and churches. But by the end of the decade, commercial (or "toll") broadcasting emerged as the answer. The dominant corporations in the industry—General Electric, Westinghouse, Radio Corporation of America (RCA), and American Telephone and Telegraph (AT&T)—settled on the idea that advertisers would foot the bill for radio. Millions of listeners might be the consumers of radio shows, but sponsors were to be the customers. AT&T leased its nationwide system of telephone wires to allow the linking of many stations into powerful radio networks, such as the National Broadcasting Company (NBC) in 1926 and the Columbia Broadcasting System (CBS) in 1928. The rise of network radio squeezed out many of the stations and programs aimed at ethnic communities or broadcast in languages other than English, thus promoting a more homogenized culture.

NBC and CBS led the way in creating popular radio programs that relied heavily on older cultural forms. The variety show, hosted by vaudeville comedians, became network radio's first important format. Radio's first truly national hit, *The Amos 'n' Andy Show* (1928), was a direct descendant of nineteenth-century "blackface" minstrel entertainment. Radio did more than any previous medium to publicize and commercialize once isolated forms of American music such as country-and-western, blues, and jazz. Broadcasts of baseball and college football games proved especially popular. In 1930, some 600 stations were broadcasting to more than 12 million homes with radios, or roughly 40 percent of American families. By that time, all the elements that characterize the present American system of broadcasting—regular daily programming paid for and produced by commercial advertisers, national networks carrying shows across the nation, and mass ownership of receiver sets in American homes—were in place.

Radio broadcasting created a national community of listeners, just as motion pictures created one of viewers. And like movies it also transcended national boundaries. Broadcasting had a powerful hemispheric impact. In both Canada and Mexico, governments established national broadcasting systems to bolster cultural and political nationalism. Yet American shows—and advertising—continued to dominate Canadian airwaves. Large private Mexican radio stations were often started in partnership with American corporations such as RCA, as a way to create demand for receiving sets. Language barriers limited the direct impact of U.S. broadcasts, but American advertisers became the backbone of commercial radio in Mexico. Radio broadcasting thus significantly amplified the influence of American commercialism throughout the hemisphere.

QUICK REVIEW

Radio

♦ 1920: Westinghouse's KDKA offered regular nightly broadcasts.

♦ 1923: 600 stations licensed by the Department of Commerce.

♦ Advertisers paid the cost of production and broadcast of programs.

Creating Celebrity

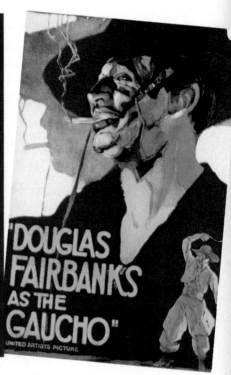

A common definition for "celebrity" is one who is famous for being famous. Although politics, the arts, science, and the military have produced famous people for centuries, the celebrity is a twentieth-century phenomenon, one closely linked to the emergence of modern forms of mass media. In the 1920s Hollywood's "star system," along with tabloid newspapers and the new profession of public relations, created the modern celebrity. Film producers were at first wary of identifying screen actors by name, but they soon discovered that promoting popular leading actors would boost the box office for their movies. The use of "close-ups" in movies and the fact that screen images were literally larger than life distinguished the images of film actors from, say, stage performers or opera singers.

Fans identified with their favorites in contradictory ways. Stars like Charlie Chaplin and Mary Pickford were like royalty. Audiences were also curious about the stars' private lives. Film studios took advantage of this curiosity by carefully controlling the public image of their stars through press releases, planted stories in newspapers, and carefully managed interviews and public appearances. By the 1920s film stars were essentially studio owned and operated commodities, requiring enormous capital investment. ■

WHAT VISUAL themes strike you as most powerful in the accompanying images? How do they compare to celebrity images of today? Why do you think male stars such as Valentino and Fairbanks were so often portrayed as exotic foreigners?

New Forms of Journalism

A new kind of newspaper, the tabloid, became popular in the postwar years. The *New York Daily News*, founded in 1919 by Joseph M. Patterson, was the first to develop the tabloid style. Its folded-in-half page size made it convenient to read on buses or subways. The *Daily News* devoted much of its space to photographs and other illustrations. With a terse, lively reporting style that emphasized sex, scandal, and sports, *Daily News* circulation reached 400,000 in 1922 and 1.3 million by 1929.

This success spawned a host of imitators in New York and elsewhere. The circulation of existing dailies was little affected. Tabloids had instead discovered an audience of millions who had never read newspapers before. Most of these new readers were poorly educated working-class city dwellers, many of whom were immigrants or children of immigrants.

The tabloid's most popular new feature was the gossip column, invented by Walter Winchell, an obscure former vaudevillian who began writing his column "Your Broadway and Mine" for the *New York Daily Graphic* in 1924. Winchell described the secret lives of public figures with a distinctive, rapid-fire, slangy style that made the reader feel like an insider. He chronicled the connections among high society, show business stars, powerful politicians, and the underworld. By the end of the decade, scores of newspapers "syndicated" Winchell's column, making him the most widely read—and imitated—journalist in America.

Journalism followed the larger economic trend toward consolidation and merger. Newspaper chains like Hearst, Gannett, and Scripps-Howard flourished during the 1920s. There was a sizable increase in the number of these chains and in the percentage of total daily circulation that was chain-owned. By the early 1930s, the Hearst organization alone controlled twenty-six dailies in eighteen cities, accounting for 14 percent of the nation's newspaper circulation. One of every four Sunday papers sold in America was owned by the Hearst group.

Advertising Modernity

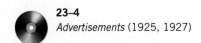

23–4
Advertisements (1925, 1927)

A thriving advertising industry both reflected and encouraged the growing importance of consumer goods in American life. Previously, advertising had been confined mostly to staid newspapers and magazines and offered little more than basic product information. The most creative advertising was usually for dubious products, such as patent medicines. The successful efforts of the government's Committee on Public Information, set up to "sell" World War I to Americans, suggested that new techniques using modern communication media could convince people to buy a wide range of goods and services. As a profession, advertising reached a higher level of respectability, sophistication, and economic power in American life during the 1920s.

The larger ad agencies moved toward a more scientific approach by sponsoring market research and welcoming the language of psychology to their profession. Indeed psychology's growing prestige as a field in the 1920s was reflected throughout the world of mass culture. Advertisers began focusing on the needs, desires, and anxieties of the consumer, rather than on the qualities of the product. "There are certain things that most people believe," noted one ad agency executive in 1927. "The moment your copy is linked to one of those beliefs, more than half your battle is won."

Ad agencies and their clients invested extraordinary amounts of time, energy, and money trying to discover and, to some extent, shape those beliefs. Leading agencies such as Lord and Thomas in Chicago and J. Walter Thompson in New

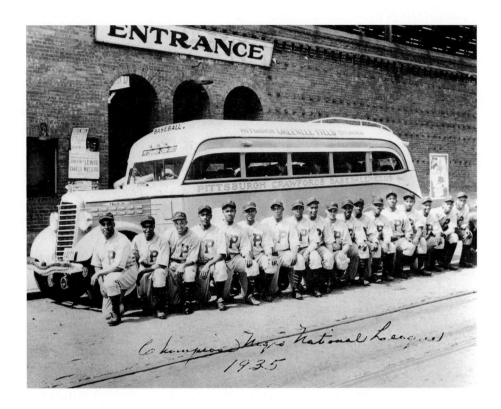

The Pittsburgh Crawfords, one of the most popular and successful baseball teams in the Negro National League, organized in 1920. Excluded from major league baseball by a "whites only" policy, black ballplayers played to enthusiastic crowds of African Americans from the 1920s through the1940s. The "Negro leagues" declined after major league baseball finally integrated in 1947.

York combined knowledge gained from market research and consumer surveys with carefully prepared ad copy and graphics to sell their clients' wares. High-powered ad campaigns made new products like Fleischmann's Yeast, Kleenex, and Listerine household words across the country. Above all, advertising celebrated consumption itself as a positive good. In this sense, the new advertising ethic was a therapeutic one, promising that products would contribute to the buyer's physical, psychic, or emotional well-being.

THE PHONOGRAPH AND THE RECORDING INDUSTRY

Like radio and movies, the phonograph came into its own in the 1920s as a popular entertainment medium. Dance crazes such as the fox trot, tango, and grizzly bear, done to complex ragtime and Latin rhythms, boosted the record business tremendously. Dixieland jazz, which recorded well, also captured the public's fancy in the early 1920s, and records provided the music for new popular dances like the Charleston and the black bottom. In 1921, more than 200 companies produced some 2 million records, and annual record sales exceeded $100 million.

Record sales declined toward the end of the decade, due to competition from radio. But in a broader cultural sense, records continued to transform American popular culture. Record companies discovered lucrative regional and ethnic markets for country music, which appealed primarily to white Southerners, and blues and jazz, which appealed primarily to African Americans. Country musicians like the Carter Family and Jimmie Rodgers, and blues singers like Blind Lemon Jefferson and Ma Rainey and Bessie Smith, had their performances put on records for the first time. Their records sold mainly in specialized "hillbilly" and "race" markets. Yet they were also played over the radio, and millions of Americans began to hear musical styles and performers who had previously been isolated from the general population. Jazz records by such African American artists as Louis Armstrong and Duke Ellington found a wide audience overseas as well, and jazz emerged as a uniquely American cultural form with broad appeal around the globe. The combination of records and radio started an extraordinary cross-fertilization of American musical styles that continues to this day.

SPORTS AND CELEBRITY

During the 1920s, spectator sports enjoyed an unprecedented growth in popularity and profitability. As radio, newspapers, magazines, and newsreels exhaustively documented their exploits, athletes took their place alongside movie stars in defining a new culture of celebrity. Big-time sports, like the movies, entered a new corporate phase. Yet it was the athletes themselves, performing extraordinary feats on the field and transcending their often humble origins, who attracted millions of new fans. The image of the modern athlete—rich, famous, glamorous, and often a rebel against social convention—came into its own during the decade.

Major league baseball had more fans than any other sport, and its greatest star, George Herman "Babe" Ruth, embodied the new celebrity athlete. Aided by the new "live ball," Ruth's prodigious home run hitting completely changed baseball strategy and attracted legions of new fans to the sport. Ruth was a larger-than-life character off the field as well. In New York, media capital of the nation, newspapers and magazines chronicled his enormous appetites—for food, whiskey, expensive cars, and big-city nightlife. He hobnobbed with politicians, movie stars, and gangsters, and he regularly visited sick children in hospitals. Ruth became the first athlete avidly sought after by manufacturers for celebrity endorsement of their products.

Baseball attendance exploded during the 1920s, reaching a one-year total of 10 million in 1929. The attendance boom prompted urban newspapers to increase their baseball coverage, and the larger dailies featured separate sports sections. The best sportswriters, such as Grantland Rice, Heywood Broun, and Ring Lardner, brought a poetic sensibility to descriptions of the games and their stars. William K. Wrigley, owner of the Chicago Cubs, discovered that by letting local radio stations broadcast his team's games, the club could win new fans, especially among housewives.

Babe Ruth, baseball's biggest star, shakes hands with President Warren G. Harding at the Opening Day of the brand new Yankee Stadium, Bronx, New York, April 4, 1923. The new celebrity culture of the 1920s routinely brought together public figures from the worlds of politics, sports, show business, and even organized crime.

Among those excluded from major league baseball were African Americans, who had been banned from the game by an 1890s "gentleman's agreement" among owners. During the 1920s, black baseball players and entrepreneurs developed a world of their own, with several professional and semi-professional leagues catering to expanding African American communities in cities. The largest of these was the Negro National League, organized in 1920 by Andrew "Rube" Foster. Black ballclubs also played exhibitions against, and frequently defeated, teams of white major leaguers. African Americans had their own baseball heroes, such as Josh Gibson and Satchel Paige, who no doubt would have been stars in the major leagues if not for racial exclusion.

The new media configuration of the 1920s created heroes in other sports as well. Radio broadcasts and increased journalistic coverage made college football a big-time sport. The center of college football shifted from the old elite schools of the Ivy League to the big universities of the Midwest and Pacific Coast, where most of the players were now second-generation Irish, Italians, and Slavs. Athletes like boxers Jack Dempsey and Gene Tunney, tennis players Bill Tilden and Helen Wills, golfer Bobby Jones, and swimmers Gertrude Ederle and Johnny Weissmuller became household names who brought legions of new fans to their sports.

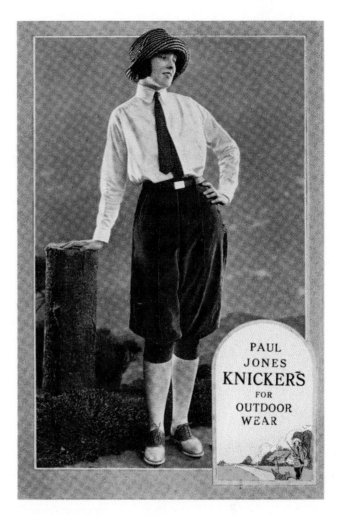

A woman in a man's shirt and necktie wears a pair of Paul Jones knickers in this 1922 advertisement. Her boyish, almost androgynous look reflects one way that notions of the "new woman" intersected with the worlds of fashion and advertising.

A NEW MORALITY?

Movie stars, radio personalities, sports heroes, and popular musicians became the elite figures in a new culture of celebrity defined by the mass media. They were the model for achievement in the new age. Great events and abstract issues were made real through movie close-ups, radio interviews, and tabloid photos. The new media relentlessly created and disseminated images that are still familiar today: Babe Ruth trotting around the bases after hitting a home run; the wild celebrations that greeted Charles Lindbergh after he completed the first solo transatlantic airplane flight in 1927; the smiling gangster Al Capone, bantering with reporters who transformed his criminal exploits into important news events.

But images do not tell the whole story. Consider one of the most enduring images of the "Roaring Twenties," the flapper. She was usually portrayed on screen, in novels, and in the press as a young, sexually aggressive woman with bobbed hair, rouged cheeks, and short skirt. She loved to dance to jazz music, enjoyed smoking cigarettes, and drank bootleg liquor in cabarets and dance halls. She could also be competitive, assertive, and a good pal. As writer Zelda Fitzgerald put it in 1924: "I think a woman gets more happiness out of being gay, light-hearted, unconventional, mistress of her own fate. . . . I want [my daughter] to be a flapper, because flappers are brave and gay and beautiful."

Was the flapper a genuine representative of the 1920s? Did she embody the "new morality" that was so widely discussed and chronicled in the media of the day? The flapper certainly did exist, but she was neither as new nor as widespread a phenomenon as the image would suggest. The delight in sensuality, personal pleasure, and rhythmically complex dance and music had long been key elements of subcultures on the fringes of middle-class society. In the 1920s, these activities

23-5
Margaret Sanger, *Family Planning* (1926)

23-9
Eleanor Wembridge, *Petting and Necking* (1925)

became normative for a growing number of white middle-class Americans, including women. Jazz, sexual experimentation, heavy makeup, and cigarette smoking spread to college campuses.

Several sources, most of them rooted in earlier years, can be found for the increased sexual openness of the 1920s. Troops in the armed forces during World War I had been exposed to government-sponsored sex education. New psychological and social theories like those of Havelock Ellis, Ellen Key, and Sigmund Freud stressed the central role of sexuality in human experience, maintaining that sex is a positive, healthy impulse that, if repressed, could damage mental and emotional health. The pioneering efforts of Margaret Sanger in educating women about birth control had begun before World War I (see Chapter 21). In the 1920s, Sanger campaigned vigorously—through her journal *Birth Control Review*, in books, and on speaking tours—to make contraception freely available to all women.

Sociological surveys also suggested that genuine changes in sexual behavior began in the prewar years among both married and single women. A 1938 survey of 777 middle-class females found that among those born between 1890 and 1900, 74 percent were virgins before marriage; for those born after 1910, the figure dropped to 32 percent. Women born after the turn of the century were twice as likely to have had premarital sex as those born before 1900. The critical change took place in the generation that came of age in the late teens and early twenties. By the 1920s, male and female "morals" were becoming more alike.

The emergence of homosexual subcultures also reflected the newly permissive atmosphere of the postwar years. Although such subcultures had been a part of big city life since at least the 1890s, they had been largely confined to working-class saloons associated with the urban underworld. By the 1920s, the word "homosexual" had gained currency as a scientific term for describing romantic love between women or between men, and middle-class enclaves of self-identified homosexuals took root in cities like New York, Chicago, and San Francisco. But if these enclaves provided some sense of community and safety for homosexuals, the repressive shadow of the larger culture was never far away. Psychologists of the era, with Freud in the lead, condemned "perversion" as a mental illness and counseled the need for a "cure."

MODERNITY AND TRADITIONALISM

One measure of the profound cultural changes of the 1920s was the hostility and opposition expressed toward them by large sectors of the American public. Deep and persistent tensions, with ethnic, racial, and geographical overtones, characterized much of the decade's politics.

PROHIBITION

The Eighteenth Amendment, banning the manufacture, sale, and transportation of alcoholic beverages, took effect in January 1920. Prohibition was the culmination of a long campaign that associated drinking with the degradation of working-class family life and the worst evils of urban politics. Supporters, a coalition of women's temperance groups, middle-class progressives, and rural Protestants, hailed the new law as "a noble experiment." But it became clear rather quickly that enforcing the new law would be extremely difficult. The **Volstead Act** of 1920 established a federal Prohibition Bureau to enforce the Eighteenth Amendment. Yet the bureau was severely understaffed with only about 1,500 agents to police the entire country.

WHAT POLITICAL and cultural movements opposed modern cultural trends?

myhistorylab
Review Summary

Volstead Act   The 1920 law defining the liquor forbidden under the Eighteenth Amendment and giving enforcement responsibilities to the Prohibition Bureau of the Department of the Treasury.

The public demand for alcohol, especially in the big cities, led to widespread lawbreaking. Drinking was such a routine part of life for so many Americans that bootlegging quickly became a big business. Nearly every town and city had at least one "speakeasy," where people could drink and enjoy music and other entertainment. Local law enforcement personnel, especially in the cities, were easily bribed to overlook these illegal establishments. By the early 1920s, many eastern states no longer made even a token effort at enforcing the law.

But because liquor continued to be illegal, Prohibition gave an enormous boost to violent organized crime. The profits to be made in the illegal liquor trade dwarfed the traditional sources of criminal income—gambling, prostitution, and robbery. The pattern of organized crime in the 1920s closely resembled the larger trends in American business: smaller operations gave way to larger and more complex combinations. Successful organized crime figures, like Chicago's Al "Scarface" Capone, became celebrities in their own right and received heavy coverage in the mass media. Capone himself shrewdly used the rhetoric of the Republican new era to defend himself: "Everybody calls me a racketeer. I call myself a businessman. When I sell liquor it's bootlegging. When my patrons serve it on a silver tray on Lake Shore Drive, it's hospitality."

Organized crime, based on its huge profits from liquor, also made significant inroads into legitimate businesses, labor unions, and city government, especially in large cities. By the time Congress and the states ratified the Twenty-First Amendment in 1933, repealing Prohibition, organized crime was a permanent feature of American life.

IMMIGRATION RESTRICTION

Sentiment for restricting immigration, growing since the late nineteenth century, reached its peak immediately after World War I. Barriers against Asian immigrants were already in place with the Chinese Exclusion Act of 1882 and the so-called Gentleman's Agreement with Japan in 1907. The movement to curb European immigration reflected the growing preponderance after 1890 of "new immigrants"—those from southern and eastern Europe—over the immigrants from northern and western Europe, who had predominated before 1890. Between 1891 and 1920, roughly 10.5 million immigrants arrived from southern and eastern Europe. This was nearly twice as many as arrived during the same years from northern and western Europe (see Figure 23.3).

The "new immigrants" were mostly Catholic and Jewish, and they were darker-skinned than the "old immigrants." To many old-stock Americans, they seemed more exotic, more foreign, and less willing and able to assimilate the nation's political and cultural values. They were also relatively poorer, more physically isolated in the nation's cities, and less politically strong than earlier immigrants. In the 1890s, the anti-Catholic American Protective Association called for a curb on immigration, and by exploiting the economic depression of that decade, it reached a membership of 2.5 million. In 1894, a group of prominent Harvard graduates, including Senator Henry Cabot Lodge (Rep., Massachusetts) and John Fiske, founded the Immigration Restriction League, providing an influential forum for the fears of the nation's elite. The league used newer scientific arguments, based on a flawed application of Darwinian evolutionary theory and genetics, to support its call for immigration restriction. The new immigration, Lodge argued, "is bringing to the country people whom it is very difficult to assimilate and who do not promise well for the standard of civilization in the United States."

Theories of scientific racism, which had become more popular in the early 1900s, reinforced anti-immigrant bias. Eugenicists, who enjoyed considerable

QUICK REVIEW

Restrictions on Immigration

- Immigration Act of 1921 reduced immigration and established quotas for nationalities.
- Immigration Act of 1924 restricted immigration on the basis of national origins.
- New laws became a permanent feature of national policy.

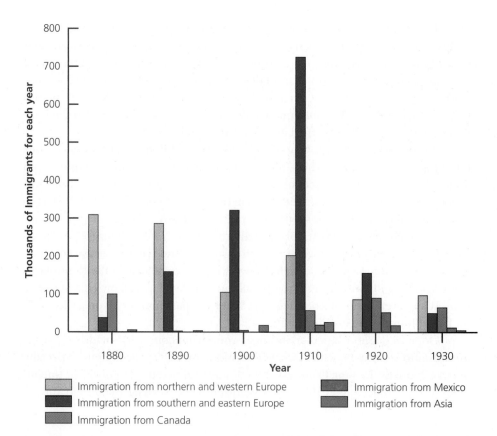

Figure 23.3 Immigration trends to the United States by contingent/region 1880–1930.

Adapted from Historical Statistics of the United States, Millenial Edition (NY: Cambridge University Press, 2006).

vogue in those years, held that heredity determined almost all of a person's capacities and that genetic inferiority predisposed people to crime and poverty. Such pseudoscientific thinking sought to explain historical and social development solely as a function of "racial" differences.

Against this background, the war and its aftermath provided the final push for the restriction of European immigration. The "100 percent American" fervor of the war years fueled nativist passions. So did the Red Scare of 1919–20, which linked foreigners with Bolshevism and radicalism of all kinds in the popular mind. The postwar depression coincided with the resumption of massive immigration, bringing much hostile comment on the relationship between rising unemployment and the new influx of foreigners. The American Federation of Labor proposed stopping all immigration for two years. Sensational press coverage of organized crime figures, many of them Italian or Jewish, also played a part.

In 1921, Congress passed the **Immigration Act**, setting a maximum of 357,000 new immigrants each year. Quotas limited annual immigration from any European country to 3 percent of the number of its natives counted in the 1910 U.S. census. But restrictionists complained that the new law still allowed too many southern and eastern Europeans in, especially since the northern and western Europeans did not fill their quotas. The Reed-Johnson National Origins Act of 1924 revised the quotas to 2 percent of the number of foreign-born counted for each nationality in the census for 1890, when far fewer southern or eastern Europeans were present in the United States. The maximum total allowed each year was also cut to 164,000. A *Los Angeles Times* headline expressed both the fundamental premise and flawed science of the new law: "Nordic Victory Is Seen in Drastic Restrictions."

The 1924 National Origins Act in effect limited immigration to white Europeans eligible for immigration by country of origin (nationality), while it divided

23–3
National Origins Quota Act (1924)

23–12
US Congress, *Debating Immigration Restriction* (1921)

Immigration Act   1921 act setting a maximum of 357,000 new immigrants each year.

Women members of the Ku Klux Klan in New Castle, Indiana, August 1, 1923. The revived Klan was a powerful presence in scores of American communities during the early 1920s, especially among native-born white Protestants, who feared cultural and political change. In addition to preaching "100 percent Americanism," local Klan chapters also served a social function for members and their families.

the rest of the world into "five colored races" (black, mulatto, Chinese, and Indian) who were ineligible for immigration. These new restrictions dovetailed with two recent Supreme Court decisions, *Ozawa* v. *U.S.* (1922) and *U.S.* v. *Thind* (1923), in which the Court held that Japanese and Asian Indians were unassimilable aliens and racially ineligible for U.S. citizenship. By the 1920s, American law had thus created the peculiar new racial category of "Asian" and codified the principle of racial exclusion in immigration and naturalization law.

THE KU KLUX KLAN

If immigration restriction was resurgent nativism's most significant legislative expression, a revived Ku Klux Klan (KKK) was its most effective mass movement. The original Klan had been formed in the Reconstruction South as an instrument of white racial terror against newly freed slaves (see Chapter 17). It had died out in the 1870s. The new Klan, born in Stone Mountain, Georgia, in 1915, was inspired by D. W. Griffith's racist spectacle *The Birth of a Nation*, a film released in that year depicting the original KKK as a heroic organization. The new Klan patterned itself on the secret rituals and antiblack hostility of its predecessor and, until 1920, it was limited to a few local chapters in Georgia and Alabama.

When Hiram W. Evans, a dentist from Dallas, became imperial wizard of the Klan in 1922, he transformed the organization. Evans hired professional fundraisers and publicists and directed an effective recruiting scheme that paid a commission to sponsors of new members. The Klan advocated "100 percent Americanism" and "the faithful maintenance of White Supremacy." It staunchly supported the enforcement of Prohibition, and it attacked birth control and Darwinism. The new Klan made a special target of the Roman Catholic Church, labeling it a hostile and dangerous alien power.

The new Klan presented itself as the righteous defender of the embattled tra-ditional values of small-town Protestant America. But ironically, to build its mem-bership rolls, it relied heavily on the publicity, public relations, and business techniques associated with modern urban culture. By 1924, the new Klan counted more than 3 million members across the country. "Native, White, Protestant Supremacy," proved especially attractive in the Midwest and South, including many cities. Klansmen boycotted businesses, threatened families, and sometimes resorted to violence—public whippings, arson, and lynching—against their chosen ene-mies. The Klan's targets sometimes included white Protestants accused of sexual promiscuity, blasphemy, or drunkenness, but most victims were African Ameri-cans, Catholics, and Jews. Support for Prohibition enforcement probably united Klansmen more than any single issue.

On another level, the Klan was a popular social movement, a defensive bas-tion against forces of modernity. Perhaps a half million women joined the Women of the Ku Klux Klan, and women constituted nearly half of the Klan membership in some states. Klanswomen drew on family and community traditions, such as church suppers, kin reunions, and gossip campaigns, to defend themselves and their families against what they saw as corruption and immorality. The Klan's power was strong in many communities precisely because it fit so comfortably into the everyday life of white Protestants.

At its height, the Klan also became a powerful force in Democratic Party politics, and it had a strong presence among delegates to the 1924 Democratic National Convention. The Klan began to fade in 1925, when its Indiana leader, Grand Dragon David C. Stephenson, became involved in a sordid personal affair. With one of its most famous leaders disgraced and in jail, the new Klan began to lose members and influence.

FUNDAMENTALISM IN RELIGION

Paralleling political nativism in the 1920s was the growth of religious fundamen-talism. In many eastern Protestant churches, congregations focused less on reli-gious practice and worship than on progressive social and reform activities in the larger community. By the early 1920s, a fundamentalist revival had developed in reaction to these tendencies, particularly in the South and Midwest. The funda-mentalists emphasized a literal reading of the Bible, and they rejected the tenets of modern science as inconsistent with the revealed word of God. Fundamental-ist publications and Bible colleges flourished, particularly among southern Baptists.

One special target of the fundamentalists was the theory of evolution, first set forth by Charles Darwin in his landmark work *The Origin of Species* (1859). By 1925, five southern state legislatures had passed laws restricting the teaching of evolution.

A young biology teacher, John T. Scopes, deliberately broke the Tennessee law prohibiting the teaching of Darwinism in 1925, in order to challenge it in court. The resulting trial that summer in Dayton, a small town near Chattanooga, drew international attention to the controversy. Scopes's defense team included attorneys from the American Civil Liberties Union and Clarence Darrow, the most famous trial lawyer in America. The prosecution was led by William Jennings Bryan, the old Democratic standard-bearer who had thrown himself into the fun-damentalist and antievolutionist cause. Held in a circus atmosphere in sweltering heat, the trial attracted thousands of reporters and partisans to Dayton and was broadcast across the nation by the radio.

The Scopes "monkey trial"—so called because fundamentalists trivialized Darwin's theory into a claim that humans were descended from monkeys—became one of the most publicized and definitive moments of the decade. Scopes's guilt was never in question. The jury convicted him quickly, although the verdict was later thrown out on a technicality. The struggle over the teaching of evolution continued in an uneasy stalemate; state statutes were not repealed, but prosecutions for teaching evolution ceased. Fundamentalism, a religious creed and a cultural defense against the uncertainties of modern life, continued to have a strong appeal for millions of Americans.

PROMISES POSTPONED

The prosperity of the 1920s was unevenly distributed and enjoyed across America. Older progressive reform movements that had pointed out inequities faltered in the conservative political climate. But the new era did inspire a range of critics deeply troubled by unfulfilled promises in American life.

FEMINISM IN TRANSITION

The achievement of the suffrage removed the central issue that had given cohesion to the disparate forces of female reform activism. In addition, female activists of all persuasions found themselves swimming against a national tide of hostility to political idealism. During the 1920s, the women's movement split into two main wings over a fundamental disagreement about female identity. Should activists stress women's differences from men—their vulnerability and the double burden of work and family—and continue to press for protective legislation, such as laws that limited the length of the workweek for women? Or should they emphasize the ways that women were like men—sharing similar aspirations—and push for full legal and civil equality?

In 1920, the National American Woman Suffrage Association reorganized itself as the **League of Women Voters**. The league represented the historical mainstream of the suffrage movement, those who believed that the vote for women would bring a nurturing sensibility and a reform vision to American politics. This view was rooted in politicized domesticity, the notion that women had a special role to play in bettering society: improving conditions for working women, abolishing child labor, humanizing prisons and mental hospitals, and serving the urban poor. Most league members continued working in a variety of reform organizations, and the league itself concentrated on educating the new female electorate, encouraging women to run for office, and supporting laws for the protection of women and children.

A newer, smaller, and more militant group was the National Woman's Party (NWP), founded in 1916 by militant suffragist Alice Paul. The NWP downplayed the significance of suffrage and argued that women were still subordinate to men in every facet of life. The NWP opposed protective legislation for women, claiming that such laws reinforced sex stereotyping and prevented women from competing with men in many fields. Largely representing the interests of professional and business women, the NWP focused on passage of a brief Equal Rights Amendment (ERA) to the Constitution, introduced in Congress in 1923: "Men and women shall have equal rights throughout the United States and every place subject to its jurisdiction." Many of the older generation of women reformers opposed the ERA as elitist, arguing that far more women benefited from protective laws than were injured by them. ERA supporters countered that maximum-hours laws or laws prohibiting women from night work prevented women from getting many lucrative jobs.

WHICH AMERICANS were less likely to share in postwar prosperity and why?

myhistorylab
Review Summary

League of Women Voters   League formed in 1920 advocating for women's rights, among them the right for women to serve on juries and equal pay laws.

Sheppard-Towner Act The first federal social welfare law, passed in 1921, providing federal funds for infant and maternity care.

But most women's groups did not think there was a "fair field." Positions solidified. The League of Women Voters, the National Consumers' League, and the Women's Trade Union League opposed the ERA. ERA supporters generally stressed individualism, competition, and the abstract language of "equality" and "rights." ERA opponents emphasized the grim reality of industrial exploitation and the concentration of women workers in low-paying jobs in which they did not compete directly with men. ERA advocates dreamed of the labor market as it might be, one in which women might have the widest opportunity. Anti-ERA forces looked at the labor market as it was, insisting it was more important to protect women from existing exploitation. The NWP campaign failed to get the ERA passed by Congress, but the debates it sparked would be echoed during the feminist movement of the 1970s, when the ERA became a central political goal of a resurgent feminism.

The most significant, if limited, victory for feminist reformers was the 1921 **Sheppard-Towner Act**, which established the first federally funded health care program, providing matching funds for states to set up prenatal and child health care centers. These centers also provided public health nurses for house calls. Although hailed as a genuine reform breakthrough, especially for women in rural and isolated communities, the act aroused much opposition. Many Republicans, including President Harding, had supported it as a way to curry favor with newly enfranchised women voters. But their support faded when it became clear that there was little "gender gap" in voting patterns. The NWP disliked Sheppard-Towner for its assumption that all women were mothers. Birth control advocates such as Margaret Sanger complained that contraception was not part of the program. The American Medical Association (AMA) objected to government-sponsored health care and to nurses who functioned outside the supervision of physicians. By 1929, largely as a result of intense AMA lobbying, Congress cut off funds for the program.

MEXICAN IMMIGRATION

While immigration restriction sharply cut the flow of new arrivals from Europe, the 1920s also brought a dramatic influx of Mexicans to the United States. Mexican immigration, which was not included in the immigration laws of 1921 and 1924, had picked up substantially after the outbreak of the Mexican Revolution in 1911, when politically inspired violence and economic hardships provided incentives to cross the border to *El Norte* (see Figure 23.4).

The primary pull was the tremendous agricultural expansion occurring in the American Southwest. Irrigation and large-scale agribusiness had begun transforming California's Imperial and San Joaquin Valleys from arid desert into lucrative fruit and vegetable fields. Cotton pickers were needed in the vast plantations of Lower Rio Grande Valley in Texas and the Salt River Valley in Arizona. The sugar beet fields of Michigan, Minnesota, and Colorado attracted many Mexican farm workers. American industry had also begun recruiting Mexican workers, first to fill wartime needs and later to fill the gap left by the decline in European immigration.

The new Mexican immigration appeared more permanent than previous waves—that is, more and more newcomers stayed—and, like other immigrants, settled in cities. This was partly the unintended consequence of new policies designed to make immigration

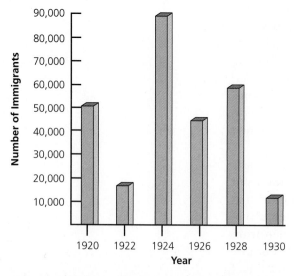

Figure 23.4 Mexican Immigration to the United States in the 1920s Many Mexican migrants avoided official border crossing stations so they would not have to pay visa fees. Thus, these official figures probably underestimated the true size of the decade's Mexican migration. As the economy contracted with the onset of the Great Depression, immigration from Mexico dropped off sharply.

Mexican workers gathered outside a San Antonio labor bureau in 1924. These employment agencies contracted Mexicans to work for Texas farmers, railroads, and construction companies. Note the three Anglo men in front (wearing suits and ties), who probably owned and operated this agency. During the 1920s, San Antonio's Mexican population doubled from roughly 40,000 to over 80,000, making it the second largest *colonia* in *El Norte* after Los Angeles.

more difficult. As the Border Patrol (established in 1924) made border crossing more difficult (through head taxes, visa fees, literacy tests, and document checks), what had once been a two-way process for many Mexicans became a one-way migration. Permanent communities of Mexicans in the United States grew rapidly. Many of the immigrants alternated between agricultural and factory jobs, depending on the seasonal availability of work. Mexican women often worked in the fields alongside their husbands. They also had jobs as domestics and seamstresses, or took in laundry and boarders.

Racism and local patterns of residential segregation confined most Mexicans to barrios. Housing conditions were generally poor, particularly for recent arrivals, who were forced to live in rude shacks without running water or electricity. Disease and infant mortality rates were much higher than average, and most Mexicans worked at low-paying, unskilled jobs and received inadequate health care. Legal restrictions passed by states and cities made it difficult for Mexicans to enter teaching, legal, and other professions. Mexicans were routinely banned from local public works projects as well. Many felt a deep ambivalence about applying for American citizenship. Loyalty to the Old Country was strong, and many cherished dreams of returning to live out their days in Mexico.

Nativist efforts to limit Mexican immigration were thwarted by the lobbying of powerful agribusiness interests. The Los Angeles Chamber of Commerce typically employed racist stereotyping in arguing to keep the borders open. Mexicans, it claimed, were naturally suited for agriculture, "due to their crouching and bending habits, . . . while the white is physically unable to adapt himself to them."

Mutual aid societies—*mutualistas*—became key social and political institutions in the Mexican communities of the Southwest and Midwest. They provided death benefits and widows' pensions for members and also served as centers of resistance to civil rights violations and discrimination. In 1928, the Federation of Mexican Workers Unions formed in response to a large farm labor strike in the Imperial Valley of California. A group of middle-class Mexican professionals in Texas organized the League of United Latin American Citizens (LULAC) in 1929. The founding of these organizations marked only the beginnings of a long struggle to bring economic, social, and racial equality to Mexican Americans.

THE "NEW NEGRO"

The Great Migration spurred by World War I showed no signs of letting up during the 1920s, and African American communities in northern cities grew rapidly. By far the largest and most influential of these communities was New York City's Harlem. Previously a residential suburb, Harlem began attracting middle-class African Americans in the prewar years. After the war, heavy black migration from the South and the Caribbean encouraged real estate speculators and landlords to remake Harlem as an exclusively black neighborhood (see Map 23.1).

 MAP EXPLORATION

To explore an interactive version of this map, go to **http://www.prenhall.com/faraghertlc/map23.1**

MAP 23.1
Black Population, 1920 Although the Great Migration had drawn hundreds of thousands of African Americans to the urban North, the southern states of the former Confederacy still remained the center of the African American population in 1920.

WHY WERE African Americans drawn to Northern cities?

Harlem emerged as the demographic and cultural capital of black America, but its appeal transcended national borders, as mass migration from the Caribbean helped reshape the community. Between 1900 and 1930, some 300,000 West Indians emigrated to the United States, roughly half of whom settled in New York City. Some of the leading cultural, business, and political figures of the era—poet Claude McKay, newspaper publisher P. M. H. Savory, labor organizer Hubert Harrison, black nationalist Marcus Garvey—had roots in the West Indies. Most black Caribbean migrants came from societies where class differences mattered more than racial ones, and many refused to accept racial bigotry without protest. A large number also carried with them entrepreneurial experience that contributed to their success in running small businesses. Intraracial tensions and resentment between American-born blacks and an increasingly visible West Indian population were reflections of Harlem's transformation into a hemispheric center for black people.

Harlem was also headquarters to Marcus Garvey's Universal Negro Improvement Association. An ambitious Jamaican immigrant who had moved to Harlem in 1916, Garvey created a mass movement that stressed black economic self-determination and unity among the black communities of the United States, the Caribbean, and Africa. With colorful parades and rallies and a central message affirming pride in black identity, Garvey attracted as many as a million members worldwide. Garvey's best-publicized project was the Black Star Line, a black-owned and -operated fleet of ships that would link people of African descent around the world. But insufficient capital and serious financial mismanagement resulted in the spectacular failure of the enterprise. In 1923, Garvey was found guilty of mail fraud in his fundraising efforts; he later went to jail and was subsequently deported to England. Despite the disgrace, Harlem's largest newspaper, the *Amsterdam News*, explained Garvey's continuing appeal to African Americans: "In a world where black is despised, he taught them that black is beautiful. He taught them to admire and praise black things and black people."

The demand for housing in this restricted geographical area led to skyrocketing rents, but most Harlemites held low-wage jobs. This combination produced extremely overcrowded apartments, unsanitary conditions, and the rapid deterioration of housing stock. Disease and death rates were abnormally high. Harlem was well on its way to becoming a slum. Yet Harlem also boasted a large middle-class population and supported a wide array of churches, theaters, newspapers and journals, and black-owned businesses. It became a mecca, as poet and essayist James Weldon Johnson wrote, for "the curious, the adventurous, the enterprising, the ambitious, and the talented of the entire Negro world."

Harlem became the political and intellectual center for what writer Alain Locke called the "New Negro." Locke was referring to a new spirit in the work of black writers and intellectuals, an optimistic faith that encouraged African Americans to develop and celebrate their distinctive culture, firmly rooted in the history, folk culture, and experiences of African American people. This faith was the common denominator uniting the disparate figures associated with the **Harlem Renaissance**. The assertion of cultural independence resonated in the poetry of Langston Hughes and Claude McKay, the novels of Zora Neale Hurston and Jessie Fauset, the essays of Countee Cullen and James Weldon Johnson, the acting of Paul Robeson, and the blues singing of Bessie Smith.

There was a political side to the "New Negro" as well. The newly militant spirit that black veterans had brought home from World War I matured and found a variety of expressions in the Harlem of the 1920s. New leaders and movements began to appear alongside established organizations like the National Association

Exploring America: *Harlem Renaissance*

23–14
Charles S. Johnson, *The City Negro* (1925)

Harlem Renaissance   A new African American cultural awareness that flourished in literature, art, and music in the 1920s.

for the Advancement of Colored People. A. Philip Randolph began a long career as a labor leader, socialist, and civil rights activist in these years, editing the *Messenger* and organizing the Brotherhood of Sleeping Car Porters.

Through the new mass media of radio and phonograph records, millions of Americans now listened and danced to a distinctively African American music, as jazz began to enter the cultural mainstream. Jazz found wildly enthusiastic fans in European capitals like Berlin and Paris, and noted classical composers such as Maurice Ravel and Igor Stravinsky treated it as a serious art form. The best jazz bands of the day, led by artists such as Duke Ellington, Fletcher Henderson, Cab Calloway, and Louis Armstrong, often had their performances broadcast live from such Harlem venues as the Cotton Club and Small's Paradise. Yet these clubs themselves were rigidly segregated. Black dancers, singers, and musicians provided the entertainment, but no African Americans were allowed in the audience. Chronicled in novels and newspapers, Harlem became a potent symbol to white America of the ultimate good time. Yet the average Harlemite never saw the inside of a nightclub. For the vast majority of Harlem residents, working menial jobs for low wages and forced to pay high rents, the day-to-day reality was depressingly different.

ALIENATED INTELLECTUALS

War, Prohibition, growing corporate power, and the deep currents of cultural intolerance troubled many intellectuals in the 1920s. Some felt so alienated from the United States that they left to live abroad. In the early 1920s, Gertrude Stein, an American expatriate writer living in Paris, told the young novelist Ernest Hemingway: "All of you young people who served in the war, you are a lost generation." The phrase "a lost generation" was widely adopted as a label for American writers, artists, and intellectuals of the postwar era. Yet it is difficult to generalize about so diverse a community. For one thing, living abroad attracted only a handful of American writers. Alienation and disillusion with American life were prominent subjects in the literature and thought of the 1920s, but artists and thinkers developed these themes in very different ways.

The mass slaughter of World War I provoked revulsion and a deep cynicism about the heroic and moralistic portrayal of war so popular in the nineteenth century. Novelists Ernest Hemingway and John Dos Passos, who both served at the front as ambulance drivers, depicted the war and its aftermath in world-weary and unsentimental tones. The search for personal moral codes that would allow one to endure life with dignity and authenticity was at the center of Hemingway's fiction. In the taut, spare language of *The Sun Also Rises* (1926) and *A Farewell to Arms* (1929), he questioned idealism, abstractions, and large meanings.

Hemingway and F. Scott Fitzgerald were the most influential novelists of the era. Fitzgerald joined the army during World War I but did not serve overseas. His work celebrated the youthful vitality of the "Jazz Age" (a phrase he coined) but was also deeply distrustful of the promises of American prosperity and politics. Fitzgerald's finest work, *The Great Gatsby* (1925), written in the south of France, depicted the glamorous parties of the wealthy, while evoking the tragic limits of material success.

At home, many American writers engaged in sharp attacks on small-town America and what they viewed as its provincial values. Essayist H. L. Mencken, caustic editor of the *American Mercury*, heaped scorn on fundamentalists, Prohibition, and nativists, while ridiculing what he called the "American booboisie."

The most popular and acclaimed writer of the time was novelist Sinclair Lewis. In a series of novels satirizing small-town life, such as *Main Street* (1920) and

23–15
Sinclair Lewis, *Our Ideal Citizen* (1922)

especially *Babbitt* (1922), Lewis affectionately mocked his characters. His treatment of the central character in *Babbitt*—George Babbitt of Zenith—also had a strong element of self-mockery, for Lewis could offer no alternative set of values to Babbitt's crass self-promotion, hunger for success, and craving for social acceptance. In 1930, Lewis became the first American author to win the Nobel Prize for literature.

In the aftermath of the postwar Red Scare, American radicalism found itself on the defensive throughout the 1920s. But one *cause célèbre* did attract a great deal of support from intellectuals. In 1921, two Italian American immigrants, Nicola Sacco and Bartolomeo Vanzetti, were tried and convicted for murder in the course of robbing a shoe factory in South Braintree, Massachusetts. Neither Sacco, a shoemaker, nor Vanzetti, a fish peddler, had criminal records, but both had long been active in militant anarchist circles, labor organizing, and antiwar agitation. Their trial took place amidst an intense atmosphere of nativist and antiradical feeling, and both the judge and prosecuting attorney engaged in clearly prejudicial conduct toward the defendants. A six-year struggle to save Sacco and Vanzetti following the trial failed, despite attracting support from a broad range of liberal intellectuals, including Harvard law professor and future Supreme Court justice Felix Frankfurter. The two men were finally executed in 1927, and for many years, their case would remain a powerful symbol of how the criminal justice system could be tainted by political bias and anti-immigrant fervor.

Another side of intellectual alienation was expressed by writers critical of industrial progress and the new mass culture. The most important of these was a group of poets and scholars centered in Vanderbilt University in Nashville, Tennessee, collectively known as the Fugitives. They included Allen Tate, John Crowe Ransom, Donald Davidson, and Robert Penn Warren, all of whom invoked traditional authority, respect for the past, and older agrarian ways as ideals to live by.

THE ELECTION OF 1928

The presidential election of 1928 served as a kind of national referendum on the Republican new era. It also revealed just how important ethnic and cultural differences had become in defining American politics. The contest reflected many of the deepest tensions and conflicts in American society in the 1920s: native-born versus immigrant; Protestant versus Catholic; Prohibition versus legal drinking; small-town life versus the cosmopolitan city; fundamentalism versus modernism; traditional sources of culture versus the new mass media (see Map 23.2).

The 1928 campaign featured two politicians who represented profoundly different sides of American life. Al Smith, the Democratic nominee for president, was a pure product of New York City's Lower East Side. Smith came from a background that included Irish, German, and Italian ancestry, and he was raised as a Roman Catholic. He rose through the political ranks of New York's Tammany Hall machine. A personable man with a deep sympathy for poor and working-class people, Smith served four terms as governor of New York, pushing through an array of laws

	Electoral Vote (%)	Popular Vote (%)
HERBERT HOOVER (Republican)	**444** **(82)**	**21,391,993** **(58.2)**
Alfred E. Smith (Democrat)	87 (17)	15,016,169 (40.9)
Norman Thomas (Socialist)	—	267,835 (0.7)
Other parties (Socialist Labor, Prohibition)	—	62,890 (0.2)

MAP 23.2
The Election of 1928 Although Al Smith managed to carry the nation's twelve largest cities, Herbert Hoover's victory in 1928 was one of the largest popular and electoral landslides in the nation's history.

WHAT VALUES did Hoover claim to stand for in the election of 1928?

CHRONOLOGY

1920 Prohibition takes effect

Warren G. Harding is elected president

Station KDKA in Pittsburgh goes on the air

Census reports that urban population is greater than rural population for the first time

1921 First immigration quotas are established by Congress

Sheppard-Towner Act establishes first federally funded health care program

1923 Equal Rights Amendment is first introduced in Congress

Harding dies in office; Calvin Coolidge becomes president

1924 Ku Klux Klan is at height of its influence

Dawes Plan for war reparations stabilizes European economies

Reed-Johnson Immigration Act tightens quotas established in 1921

1925 Scopes trial pits religious fundamentalism against modernity

F. Scott Fitzgerald publishes *The Great Gatsby*

1926 National Broadcasting Company establishes first national radio network

1927 McNary-Haugen Farm Relief bill finally passed by Congress but is vetoed by President Coolidge as unwarranted federal interference in the economy

Warner Brothers produces *The Jazz Singer*, the first feature-length motion picture with sound

Charles Lindbergh makes first solo flight across the Atlantic Ocean

1928 Kellogg-Briand Pact renounces war

Herbert Hoover defeats Al Smith for the presidency

1929 Robert and Helen Lynd publish their classic community study, *Middletown*

---

reforming factory conditions, housing, and welfare programs. Two of his closest advisers were the progressives Frances Perkins and Belle Moskowitz. Smith thus fused older-style machine politics with the newer reform emphasis on state intervention to solve social problems.

Herbert Hoover easily won the Republican nomination after Calvin Coolidge announced he would not run for reelection. Hoover epitomized the successful and forward-looking American. An engineer and self-made millionaire, he offered a unique combination of experience in humanitarian war relief, administrative efficiency, and probusiness policies. Above all, Hoover stood for a commitment to voluntarism and individualism as the best method for advancing the public welfare. He was one of the best-known men in America and promised to continue the Republican control of national politics.

Smith himself quickly became the central issue of the campaign. His sharp New York accent, jarring to many Americans who heard it over the radio, marked him clearly as a man of the city. So did his brown derby and fashionable suits, as well as his promise to work for the repeal of Prohibition. As the first Roman Catholic nominee of a major party, Smith also drew a torrent of anti-Catholic bigotry, especially in the South and Midwest. For his part, Smith ran a largely conservative race. He appointed John Raskob, a Republican vice president of General Motors, to manage his campaign and tried to outdo Hoover in his praise for business. Democrats remained regionally divided over Prohibition, Smith's religion, and the widening split between rural and urban values. Hoover did not have to do much, other than take credit for the continued prosperity.

Hoover polled 21 million votes to Smith's 15 million, and swept the electoral college 444 to 87, including New York State. Even the Solid South, reliably

Democratic since the Civil War, gave five states to Hoover—a clear reflection of the ethnocultural split in the party. Yet the election offered important clues to the future of the Democrats. Smith ran better in the big cities of the North and East than any Democrat in modern times. He outpolled Hoover in the aggregate vote of the nation's twelve largest cities and carried six of them, thus pointing the way to the Democrats' future dominance with urban, northeastern, and ethnic voters.

CONCLUSION

America's big cities, if not dominant politically, now defined the nation's cultural and economic life as never before. With Hollywood movies leading the way, the new mass media brought cosmopolitan entertainment and values to the remotest small communities. The culture of celebrity knew no geographic boundaries. New consumer durable goods associated with mass-production techniques—automobiles, radios, telephones, household appliances—were manufactured largely in cities. The advertising and public relations companies that sang their praises were also distinctly urban enterprises. Even with the curtailing of European immigration, big cities attracted a kaleidoscopic variety of migrants: white people from small towns and farms, African Americans from the rural South, Mexicans from across the border, and intellectuals and professionals looking to make their mark.

Many Americans, of course, remained deeply suspicious of postwar cultural and economic trends. Yet the partisans of Prohibition, members of the Ku Klux Klan, and religious fundamentalists usually found themselves on the defensive against what they viewed as alien cultural and economic forces centered in the cities. Large sectors of the population did not share in the era's prosperity. But the large numbers who did—or at least had a taste of good times—ensured Republican political dominance throughout the decade. Thus, America in the 1920s balanced dizzying change in the cultural and economic realms with conservative politics. The reform crusades that attracted millions during the progressive era were a distant memory. Political activism was no match for the new pleasures promised by technology and prosperity.

REVIEW QUESTIONS

1. Describe the impact of the "second industrial revolution" on American business, workers, and consumers. Which technological and economic changes had the biggest impact on American society?

2. Analyze the uneven distribution of the 1920s' economic prosperity. Which Americans gained the most, and which were largely left out?

3. How did an expanding mass culture change the contours of everyday life in the decade following World War I? What role did new technologies of mass communication play in shaping these changes? What connections can you draw between the "culture of consumption" then and today?

4. What were the key policies and goals articulated by Republican political leaders of the 1920s? How did they apply these to both domestic and foreign affairs?

5. How did some Americans resist the rapid changes taking place in the post–World War I world? What cultural and political strategies did they employ?

6. Discuss the 1928 election as a mirror of the divisions in American society.

myhistorylab

Flashcard Review

KEY TERMS

Harlem Renaissance (p. 651)
Immigration Act (p. 644)
League of Women Voters (p. 647)
Open shop (p. 626)
Sheppard-Towner Act (p. 648)
Volstead Act (p. 642)
Welfare capitalism (p. 626)

RECOMMENDED READING

Roger Daniels, *Guarding the Golden Door: American Immigration Policy and Immigrants Since 1882* (2002). A comprehensive overview by a pioneering scholar in the field, with special emphasis on how racism and ethnocentrism have shaped American immigration policy.

Victoria De Grazia, *Irresistible Empire: America's Advance through Twentieth Century Europe* (2005). A sophisticated analysis of how and why American commercial culture made such strong inroads into postwar Europe.

Lynn Dumenil, *The Modern Temper: America in the 1920s* (1995). An excellent synthesis of recent scholarship, which emphasizes the ambivalence that many Americans felt toward the emergence of modern society.

David J. Goldberg, *Discontented America: The United States in the 1920s* (1999). Focuses on Americans' continuing discomfort with racial, ethnic, religious, and class differences during the decade.

Desmond King, *Making Americans: Immigration, Race, and the Origins of Diverse Democracy* (2000). Fine analysis of the shift of U.S. immigration policies in the 1920s, with special attention to the influence of eugenics, and the long-term consequences of the new restrictive legislation.

Charles L. Ponce de Leon, *Self Exposure: Human Interest Journalism and the Emergence of Celebrity in America, 1890–1940* (2002). A thoughtful cultural history that explores the intersection of new mass media, journalism, and the American fascination with celebrity.

Susan Smulyan, *Selling Radio: The Commercialization of American Broadcasting, 1920–1934* (1994). The best analysis of the rise of commercial radio broadcasting in the 1920s.

Joshua Zeitz, *Flapper* (2006). A lively and well-researched new account of "the flapper" phenomenon, with emphasis on how a wide variety of women contributed to new cultural images for females.

For study resources for this chapter, go to **www.myhistorylab.com** and choose *Out of Many, Teaching and Learning Classroom Edition*. You will find a wealth of study and review material for this chapter, including pretests and posttests, customized study plan, key-term review flash cards, interactive map and document activities, and documents for analysis.

The Scopes Monkey Trial as a Harbinger of Change

The Roaring '20's was a decade of turmoil and change in the United States on many levels. All this insecurity unsettled American traditionalists, especially religious fundamentalists. In rural states fundamentalists possessed a majority and control of the state legislature. John Washington Butler, a part time preacher and full time farmer served in the Tennessee legislature, had never read anything about evolution, but heard it denied the teachings of the Bible. He formulated a bill to forbid the teaching of evolution in the schools of Tennessee titled "AN ACT prohibiting the teaching of the Evolution Theory in all the Universities, Normals and all other public schools of Tennessee..."

The Butler Act immediately provoked a reaction from the American Civil Liberties Union. To challenge the law, John T. Scopes, part time biology teacher from Dayton, Tennessee, agreed to be arrested and placed on trial. The Scopes Monkey Trial, as it soon came to be known, became the first trial ever broadcast live on national radio. William Jennings Bryan, a prominent fundamentalist Christian, was seeking the Democratic presidential nomination again for the 1928 election and saw this trial as a vehicle to promote his candidacy. Clarence Darrow, nationally famous criminal lawyer, liberal, and agnostic, took the role of the defense. A circus of a trial followed.

EXAMINE THE history and impact of Tennessee's Butler Act (1925) and the trial of John T. Scopes that followed. Would contemporary observers have considered the jury decision to be the final decision on the issue of teaching evolution in the public schools of America-or did they have an inkling of the future of this issue?

John T. Scopes was found guilty and fined. The sentence was appealed to the Tennessee Supreme Court, which upheld the Dayton sentence, but set the sentence aside on a legal technicality that the jury had not set the fine levied against Scopes. The Butler Act would not be repealed by the Tennessee state legislature until 1967. The U.S. Supreme Court would declare similar laws to be unconstitutional in an Arkansas case in 1968.■

Scopes trial in Tennessee in 1925. Clarence Darrow (standing) and John T. Scopes (seated behind Darrow, in a white shirt staring straight ahead).

Butler Act, 1925

THAT IS shall be unlawful for any teacher in any of the Universities, Normals and all other public schools of the State which are supported in whole or in part by the public school funds of the State, to teach any theory that denies the story of the Divine Creation of man as taught in the Bible, and to teach instead that man has descended from a lower order of animals.

In the national media Clarence Darrow and William Jennings Bryan were the chief protagonists of the trial. Darrow, the famous criminal lawyer, agnostic, and liberal stood for the defense. William Jennings Bryan volunteered for the prosecution and was given the honorary title of "colonel." During the trial a famous confrontation between Darrow and Bryan occurred when Bryan offered to testify as a biblical expert. Darrow demolished Bryan's arguments and even forced him to contradict the fundamentalist literal interpretation of Genesis as a seven-day creation event.■

H. L. Mencken, Aftermath (of the Scopes Trial), *Baltimore Evening Sun*, September 14, 1925

TRUE ENOUGH, even a superstitious man has certain inalienable rights. He has a right to harbor and indulge his imbecilities as long as he pleases, provided only he does not try to inflict them upon other men by force. He has a right to argue for them as eloquently as he can, in season and out of season. He has a right to teach them to his children. But certainly he has no right to be protected against the free criticism of those who do not hold them. He has no right to demand that they be treated as sacred. He has no right to preach them without challenge....

The meaning of religious freedom, I fear, is sometimes greatly misapprehended. It is taken to be a sort of immunity, not merely from governmental control but also from public opinion. A dunderhead gets himself a long-tailed coat, rises behind the sacred desk, and emits such bilge as would gag a Hottentot. Is it to pass unchallenged? If so, then what we have is not religious freedom at all, but the most intolerable and outrageous variety of religious despotism. Any fool, once he is admitted to holy orders, becomes infallible. Any half-wit, by the simple device of ascribing his delusions to revelation, takes on an authority that is denied to all the rest of us.■

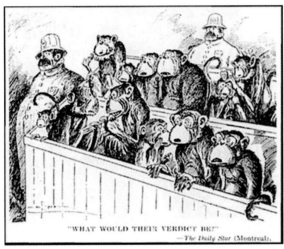

"WHAT WOULD THEIR VERDICT BE?"
— *The Daily Star* (Montreal).

What Would Their Verdict Be? *The Daily Star* (Montreal), reprinted in the *Literary Digest,* July 25, 1925

Epperson V. Arkansas, 393 U.S. 97 (1968)

IN THE present case, there can be no doubt that Arkansas has sought to prevent its teachers from discussing the theory of evolution because it is contrary to the belief of some that the Book of Genesis must be the exclusive source of doctrine as to the origin of man. No suggestion has been made that Arkansas' law may be justified by considerations of state policy other than the religious views of some of its citizens. It is clear that fundamentalist sectarian conviction was and is the law's reason for existence. Its antecedent, Tennessee's "monkey law," candidly stated its purpose: to make it unlawful "to teach any theory that denies the story of the Divine Creation of man as taught in the Bible, and to teach instead that man has descended from a lower order of animals." Perhaps the sensational publicity attendant upon the Scopes trial induced Arkansas to adopt less explicit language. It eliminated Tennessee's reference to "the story of the Divine Creation of man" as taught in the Bible, but there is no doubt that the motivation for the law was the same: to suppress the teaching of a theory which, it was thought, "denied" the divine creation of man.

Arkansas' law cannot be defended as an act of religious neutrality. Arkansas did not seek to excise from the curricula of its schools and universities all discussion of the origin of man. The law's effort was confined to an attempt to blot out a particular theory because of its supposed conflict with the Biblical account, literally read. Plainly, the law is contrary to the mandate of the First, and in violation of the Fourteenth, Amendment to the Constitution.

The judgment of the Supreme Court of Arkansas is Reversed.■

THE DECLARATION OF INDEPENDENCE

When in the course of human events it becomes necessary for one people to dissolve the political bands which have connected them with another and to assume, among the powers of the earth, the separate and equal station to which the laws of nature and of nature's God entitle them, a decent respect to the opinions of mankind requires that they should declare the causes which impel them to the separation.

We hold these truths to be self-evident, that all men are created equal; that they are endowed by their Creator with certain unalienable rights; that among these are life, liberty, and the pursuit of happiness. That, to secure these rights, governments are instituted among men, deriving their just powers from the consent of the governed; that, whenever any form of government becomes destructive of these ends, it is the right of the people to alter or to abolish it, and to institute a new government, laying its foundation on such principles, and organizing its powers in such form, as to them shall seem most likely to effect their safety and happiness. Prudence, indeed, will dictate that governments long established should not be changed for light and transient causes; and, accordingly, all experience hath shown that mankind are more disposed to suffer, while evils are sufferable, than to right themselves by abolishing the forms to which they are accustomed. But when a long train of abuses and usurpations, pursuing invariably the same object, evinces a design to reduce them under absolute despotism, it is their right, it is their duty, to throw off such government and to provide new guards for their future security. Such has been the patient sufferance of these colonies, and such is now the necessity which constrains them to alter their former systems of government. The history of the present King of Great Britain is a history of repeated injuries and usurpations, all having, in direct object, the establishment of an absolute tyranny over these States. To prove this, let facts be submitted to a candid world:

He has refused his assent to laws the most wholesome and necessary for the public good.

He has forbidden his governors to pass laws of immediate and pressing importance, unless suspended in their operation till his assent should be obtained; and, when so suspended, he has utterly neglected to attend to them.

He has refused to pass other laws for the accommodation of large districts of people, unless those people would relinquish the right of representation in the legislature, a right inestimable to them and formidable to tyrants only.

He has called together legislative bodies at places unusual, uncomfortable, and distant from the depository of their public records, for the sole purpose of fatiguing them into compliance with his measures.

He has dissolved representative houses, repeatedly for opposing, with manly firmness, his invasions on the rights of the people.

He has refused, for a long time after such dissolutions, to cause others to be elected; whereby the legislative powers, incapable of annihilation, have returned to the people at large for their exercise; the state remaining, in the meantime, exposed to all the danger of invasion from without and convulsions within.

He has endeavored to prevent the population of these States; for that purpose, obstructing the laws for naturalization of foreigners, refusing to pass others to encourage their migration hither, and raising the conditions of new appropriations of lands.

He has obstructed the administration of justice by refusing his assent to laws for establishing judiciary powers.

He has made judges dependent on his will alone for the tenure of their offices and the amount and payment of their salaries.

He has erected a multitude of new offices and sent hither swarms of officers to harass our people and eat out their substance.

He has kept among us, in time of peace, standing armies, without the consent of our legislatures.

He has affected to render the military independent of, and superior to, the civil power.

He has combined with others to subject us to a jurisdiction foreign to our Constitution and unacknowledged by our laws, giving his assent to their acts of pretended legislation—

For quartering large bodies of armed troops among us;

For protecting them by mock trial, from punishment for any murders which they should commit on the inhabitants of these States;

For cutting off our trade with all parts of the world;

For imposing taxes on us without our consent;

For depriving us, in many cases, of the benefit of trial by jury;

For transporting us beyond seas to be tried for pretended offences;

For abolishing the free system of English laws in a neighboring province, establishing therein an arbitrary government, and enlarging its boundaries, so as to render it at once an example and fit instrument for introducing the same absolute rule into these colonies;

For taking away our charters, abolishing our most valuable laws, and altering, fundamentally, the powers of our governments.

For suspending our own legislatures and declaring themselves invested with power to legislate for us in all cases whatsoever.

He has abdicated government here by declaring us out of his protection and waging war against us.

He has plundered our seas, ravaged our coasts, burnt our towns, and destroyed the lives of our people.

He is, at this time, transporting large armies of foreign mercenaries to complete the works of death, desolation, and tyranny already begun with circumstances of cruelty and perfidy scarcely paralleled in the most barbarous ages, and totally unworthy the head of a civilized nation.

He has constrained our fellow citizens, taken captive on the high seas, to bear arms against their country, to become the executioners of their friends and brethren, or to fall themselves by their hands.

He has excited domestic insurrections amongst us and has endeavored to bring on the inhabitants of our frontiers, the merciless Indian savages, whose known rule of warfare is an undistinguished destruction of all ages, sexes, and conditions.

In every stage of these oppressions, we have petitioned for redress in the most humble terms; our repeated petitions have been answered only by repeated injury. A prince whose character is thus marked by every act which may define a tyrant is unfit to be the ruler of a free people.

Nor have we been wanting in attention to our British brethren. We have warned them, from time to time, of attempts made by their legislature to extend an unwarrantable jurisdiction over us. We have reminded them of the circumstances of our emigration and settlement here. We have appealed to their native justice and magnanimity, and we have conjured them, by the ties of our common kindred, to disavow these usurpations, which would inevitably interrupt our connections and correspondence. They, too, have been deaf to the voice of justice and consanguinity.

We must, therefore, acquiesce in the necessity which denounces our separation, and hold them, as we hold the rest of mankind, enemies in war, in peace, friends.

We, therefore, the representatives of the United States of America, in general Congress assembled, appealing to the Supreme Judge of the world for the rectitude of our intentions, do, in the name and by the authority of the good people of these colonies, solemnly publish and declare, that these united colonies are, and of right ought to be, free and independent states: that they are absolved from all allegiance to the British Crown, and that all political connection between them and the state of Great Britain is, and ought to be, totally dissolved; and that, as free and independent states, they have full power to levy war, conclude peace, contract alliances, establish commerce, and to do all other acts and things which independent states may of right do. And, for the support of this declaration, with a firm reliance on the protection of Divine Providence, we mutually pledge to each other our lives, our fortunes, and our sacred honor.

THE CONSTITUTION OF THE UNITED STATES OF AMERICA

We the people of the United States, in order to form a more perfect union, establish justice, insure domestic tranquillity, provide for the common defense, promote the general welfare, and secure the blessings of liberty to ourselves and our posterity, do ordain and establish this Constitution for the United States of America.

ARTICLE I

SECTION 1.   All legislative powers herein granted shall be vested in a Congress of the United States, which shall consist of a Senate and House of Representatives.

SECTION 2.   1. The House of Representatives shall be composed of members chosen every second year by the people of the several States, and the electors in each State shall have the qualifications requisite for electors of the most numerous branch of the State legislature.

2. No person shall be a representative who shall not have attained to the age of twenty-five years, and been seven years a citizen of the United States, and who shall not, when elected, be an inhabitant of that State in which he shall be chosen.

3. Representatives and direct taxes[1] shall be apportioned among the several States which may be included within this Union, according to their respective numbers, which shall be determined by adding to the whole number of free persons, including those bound to service for a term of years, and excluding Indians not taxed, three fifths of all other persons.[2] The actual enumeration shall be made within three years after the first meeting of the Congress of the United States, and within every subsequent term of ten years, in such manner as they shall by law direct. The num-

ber of representatives shall not exceed one for every thirty thousand, but each State shall have at least one representative; and until such enumeration shall be made, the State of New Hampshire shall be entitled to choose three, Massachusetts eight, Rhode Island and Providence Plantations one, Connecticut five, New York six, New Jersey four, Pennsylvania eight, Delaware one, Maryland six, Virginia ten, North Carolina five, South Carolina five, and Georgia three.

4. When vacancies happen in the representation from any State, the executive authority thereof shall issue writs of election to fill such vacancies.

5. The House of Representatives shall choose their speaker and other officers; and shall have the sole power of impeachment.

SECTION 3.   1. The Senate of the United States shall be composed of two senators from each State, chosen by the legislature thereof,[3] for six years; and each senator shall have one vote.

2. Immediately after they shall be assembled in consequence of the first election, they shall be divided as equally as may be into three classes. The seats of the senators of the first class shall be vacated at the expiration of the second year, of the second class at the expiration of the fourth year, and of the third class at the expiration of the sixth year, so that one third may be chosen every second year; and if vacancies happen by resignation, or otherwise, during the recess of the legislature of any State, the executive thereof may make temporary appointments until the next meeting of the legislature, which shall then fill such vacancies.[4]

3. No person shall be a senator who shall not have attained to the age of thirty years, and been nine years a cit-

---

[1]See the Sixteenth Amendment.
[2]See the Fourteenth Amendment.

[3]See the Seventeenth Amendment.
[4]See the Seventeenth Amendment.

izen of the United States, and who shall not, when elected, be an inhabitant of that State for which he shall be chosen.

4. The Vice President of the United States shall be President of the Senate, but shall have no vote, unless they be equally divided.

5. The Senate shall choose their other officers, and also a president pro tempore, in the absence of the Vice President, or when he shall exercise the office of the President of the United States.

6. The Senate shall have the sole power to try all impeachments. When sitting for that purpose, they shall be on oath or affirmation. When the President of the United States is tried, the chief justice shall preside: and no person shall be convicted without the concurrence of two thirds of the members present.

7. Judgment in cases of impeachment shall not extend further than to removal from office, and disqualification to hold and enjoy any office of honor, trust or profit under the United States: but the party convicted shall nevertheless be liable and subject to indictment, trial, judgment and punishment, according to law.

SECTION 4. 1. The times, places, and manner of holding elections for senators and representatives, shall be prescribed in each State by the legislature thereof; but the Congress may at any time by law make or alter such regulations, except as to the places of choosing senators.

2. The Congress shall assemble at least once in every year, and such meeting shall be on the first Monday in December, unless they shall by law appoint a different day.

SECTION 5. 1. Each House shall be the judge of the elections, returns and qualifications of its own members, and a majority of each shall constitute a quorum to do business; but a smaller number may adjourn from day to day, and may be authorized to compel the attendance of absent members, in such manner, and under such penalties as each House may provide.

2. Each House may determine the rules of its proceedings, punish its members for disorderly behavior, and, with the concurrence of two thirds, expel a member.

3. Each House shall keep a journal of its proceedings, and from time to time publish the same, excepting such parts as may in their judgment require secrecy; and the yeas and nays of the members of either House on any question shall, at the desire of one fifth of those present, be entered on the journal.

4. Neither House, during the session of Congress, shall, without the consent of the other, adjourn for more than three days, nor to any other place than that in which the two Houses shall be sitting.

SECTION 6. 1. The senators and representatives shall receive a compensation for their services, to be ascertained by law, and paid out of the Treasury of the United States. They shall in all cases, except treason, felony, and breach of the peace, be privileged from arrest during their attendance at the session of their respective Houses, and in going to and returning from the same; and for any speech or debate in either House, they shall not be questioned in any other place.

2. No senator or representative shall, during the time for which he was elected, be appointed to any civil office under the authority of the United States, which shall have been created, or the emoluments whereof shall have been increased, during such time; and no person holding any office under the United States shall be a member of either House during his continuance in office.

SECTION 7. 1. All bills for raising revenue shall originate in the House of Representatives; but the Senate may propose or concur with amendments as on other bills.

2. Every bill which shall have passed the House of Representatives and the Senate, shall, before it become a law, be presented to the President of the United States; If he approves he shall sign it, but if not he shall return it, with his objections, to that House in which it shall have originated, who shall enter the objections at large on their journal, and proceed to reconsider it. If after such reconsideration two thirds of that House shall agree to pass the bill, it shall be sent, together with the objections, to the other House, by which it shall likewise be reconsidered, and if approved by two thirds of that House, it shall become a law. But in all such cases the votes of both Houses shall be determined by yeas and nays, and the names of the persons voting for and against the bill shall be entered on the journal of each House respectively. If any bill shall not be returned by the President within ten days (Sundays excepted) after it shall have been presented to him, the same shall be a law, in like manner as if he had signed it, unless the Congress by their adjournment prevent its return, in which case it shall not be a law.

3. Every order, resolution, or vote to which the concurrence of the Senate and the House of Representatives may be necessary (except on a question of adjournment) shall be presented to the President of the United States; and before the same shall take effect, shall be approved by him, or being disapproved by him, shall be repassed by two thirds of the Senate and House of Representatives, according to the rules and limitations prescribed in the case of a bill.

SECTION 8. 1. The Congress shall have the power

1. To lay and collect taxes, duties, imposts, and excises, to pay the debts and provide for the common defense and general welfare of the United States; but all duties, imposts, and excises shall be uniform throughout the United States.

2. To borrow money on the credit of the United States;

3. To regulate commerce with foreign nations, and among the several States, and with the Indian tribes;

4. To establish a uniform rule of naturalization, and uniform laws on the subject of bankruptcies throughout the United States;

5. To coin money, regulate the value thereof, and of foreign coin, and fix the standard of weights and measures;

6. To provide for the punishment of counterfeiting the securities and current coin of the United States;

7. To establish post offices and post roads;

8. To promote the progress of science and useful arts, by securing for limited times to authors and inventors the exclusive right to their respective writings and discoveries;

9. To constitute tribunals inferior to the Supreme Court;

10. To define and punish piracies and felonies committed on the high seas, and offenses against the law of nations;

11. To declare war, grant letters of marque and reprisal, and make rules concerning captures on land and water;

12. To raise and support armies, but no appropriation of money to that use shall be for a longer term than two years;

13. To provide and maintain a navy;

14. To make rules for the government and regulation of the land and naval forces;

15. To provide for calling forth the militia to execute the laws of the Union, suppress insurrections and repel invasions;

16. To provide for organizing, arming, and disciplining the militia, and for governing such part of them as may be employed in the service of the United States, reserving to the States respectively, the appointment of the officers, and the authority of training the militia according to the discipline prescribed by Congress;

17. To exercise exclusive legislation in all cases whatsoever, over such district (not exceeding ten miles square) as may, by cession of particular States, and the acceptance of Congress, become the seat of the government of the United States, and to exercise like authority over all places purchased by the consent of the legislature of the State in which the same shall be, for the erection of forts, magazines, arsenals, dockyards, and other needful buildings; and

18. To make all laws which shall be necessary and proper for carrying into execution the foregoing powers, and all other powers vested by this Constitution in the government of the United States, or any department or officer thereof.

SECTION 9.   1. The migration or importation of such persons as any of the States now existing shall think proper to admit, shall not be prohibited by the Congress prior to the year one thousand eight hundred and eight, but a tax or duty may be imposed on such importation, not exceeding ten dollars for each person.

2. The privilege of the writ of habeas corpus shall not be suspended, unless when in cases of rebellion or invasion the public safety may require it.

3. No bill of attainder or ex post facto law shall be passed.

4. No capitation, or other direct, tax shall be laid, unless in proportion to the census or enumeration hereinbefore directed to be taken.[5]

5. No tax or duty shall be laid on articles exported from any State.

6. No preference shall be given by any regulation of commerce or revenue to the ports of one State over those of another: nor shall vessels bound to, or from, one State be obliged to enter, clear, or pay duties in another.

7. No money shall be drawn from the treasury, but in consequence of appropriations made by law; and a regular statement and account of the receipts and expenditures of all public money shall be published from time to time.

8. No title of nobility shall be granted by the United States: and no person holding any office of profit or trust under them, shall, without the consent of the Congress, accept of any present, emolument, office, or title, of any kind whatever, from any king, prince, or foreign State.

SECTION 10.   1. No State shall enter into any treaty, alliance, or confederation; grant letters of marque and reprisal; coin money; emit bills of credit; make any thing but gold and silver coin a tender in payment of debts; pass any bill of attainder, ex post facto law, or law impairing the obligation of contracts, or grant, any title of nobility.

2. No State shall, without the consent of the Congress, lay any imposts or duties on imports or exports, except what may be absolutely necessary for executing its inspection laws: and the net produce of all duties and imposts laid by any State on imports or exports, shall be for the use of the treasury of the United States; and all such laws shall be subject to the revision and control of the Congress.

3. No State shall, without the consent of the Congress, lay any duty of tonnage, keep troops, or ships of war in time of peace, enter into any agreement or compact with another State, or with a foreign power, or engage in war, unless actually invaded, or in such imminent danger as will not admit of delay.

ARTICLE II

SECTION 1.   1. The executive power shall be vested in a President of the United States of America. He shall hold his office during the term of four years, and, together with the Vice President, chosen for the same term, be elected, as follows:

2. Each State shall appoint, in such manner as the legislature thereof may direct, a number of electors, equal to the whole number of senators and representatives to which the State may be entitled in the Congress: but no senator or representative, or person holding any office of trust or profit under the United States, shall be appointed an elector.

The electors shall meet in their respective States, and vote by ballot for two persons, of whom one at least shall not be an inhabitant of the same State with themselves. And they shall make a list of all the persons voted for, and of the number of votes for each; which list they shall sign and certify, and transmit sealed to the seat of the government of the United States, directed to the president of the Senate. The president of the Senate shall, in the presence of the Senate and House of Representatives, open all the certificates, and the votes shall then be counted. The person having the greatest number of votes shall be the President, if such number be a majority of the whole number of electors appointed; and if there be more than one who have such majority, and have an equal number of votes, then the House of Representatives shall immediately choose by ballot one of them for President; and if no person have a majority, then from the five highest on the list the said House shall in like manner choose the President. But in choosing the President, the votes shall be taken by

---

[5]See the Sixteenth Amendment.

States, the representation from each State having one vote; a quorum for this purpose shall consist of a member or members from two thirds of the States, and a majority of all the States shall be necessary to a choice. In every case after the choice of the President, the person having the greatest number of votes of the electors shall be the Vice President. But if there should remain two or more who have equal votes, the Senate shall choose from them by ballot the Vice President.[6]

3. The Congress may determine the time of choosing the electors, and the day on which they shall give their votes; which day shall be the same throughout the United States.

4. No person except a natural born citizen, or a citizen of the United States, at the time of the adoption of this Constitution, shall be eligible to the office of President; neither shall any person be eligible to the office who shall not have attained to the age of thirty-five years, and been fourteen years a resident within the United States.

5. In case of the removal of the President from office, or of his death, resignation, or inability to discharge the powers and duties of the said office, the same shall devolve on the Vice President, and the congress may by law provide for the case of removal, death, resignation or inability, both of the President and Vice President, declaring what officer shall then act as President, and such officer shall act accordingly until the disability be removed, or a President shall be elected.

6. The President shall, at stated times, receive for his services a compensation which shall neither be increased nor diminished during the period for which he shall have been elected, and he shall not receive within that period any other emolument from the United States, or any of them.

7. Before he enter on the execution of his office, he shall take the following oath or affirmation:—"I do solemnly swear (or affirm) that I will faithfully execute the office of President of the United States, and will to the best of my ability, preserve, protect and defend the Constitution of the United States."

SECTION 2.   1. The President shall be commander in chief of the army and navy of the United States, and of the militia of the several States, when called into the actual service of the United States; he may require the opinion in writing, of the principal officer in each of the executive departments, upon any subject relating to the duties of their respective offices, and he shall have power to grant reprieves and pardons for offenses against the United States, except in cases of impeachment.

2. He shall have power, by and with the advice and consent of the Senate, to make treaties, provided two thirds of the senators present concur; and he shall nominate, and by and with the advice and consent of the Senate, shall appoint ambassadors, other public ministers and consuls, judges of the Supreme Court, and all other officers of the United States, whose appointments are not herein otherwise provided for, and which shall be established by law; but the Congress may by law vest the appointment of such infe-

rior officers, as they think proper, in the President alone, in the courts of laws, or in the heads of departments.

3. The President shall have power to fill up all vacancies that may happen during the recess of the Senate, by granting commissions which shall expire at the end of their next session.

SECTION 3.   He shall from time to time give to the Congress information of the state of the Union, and recommend to their consideration such measures as he shall judge necessary and expedient; he may, on extraordinary occasions, convene both Houses, or either of them, and in case of disagreement between them with respect to the time of adjournment, he may adjourn them to such time as he shall think proper; he shall receive ambassadors and other public ministers; he shall take care that the laws be faithfully executed, and shall commission all the officers of the United States.

SECTION 4.   The President, Vice President, and all civil officers of the United States, shall be removed from office on impeachment for, and conviction of, treason, bribery, or other high crimes and misdemeanors.

ARTICLE III

SECTION 1. The judicial power of the United States shall be vested in one Supreme Court, and in such inferior courts as the Congress may from time to time ordain and establish. The judges, both of the Supreme and inferior courts, shall hold their offices during good behavior, and shall, at stated times, receive for their services, a compensation, which shall not be diminished during their continuance in office.

SECTION 2.   1. The judicial power shall extend to all cases, in law and equity, arising under this Constitution, the laws of the United States, and treaties made, or which shall be made, under their authority;—to all cases of admiralty and maritime jurisdiction;—to controversies to which the United States shall be a party;[7]—to controversies between two or more States;—between a State and citizens of another State;—between citizens of different States;—between citizens of the same State claiming lands under grants of different States, and between a State, or the citizens thereof, and foreign States, citizens or subjects.

2. In all cases affecting ambassadors, other public ministers and consuls, and those in which a State shall be party, the Supreme Court shall have original jurisdiction. In all the other cases before mentioned, the Supreme Court shall have appellate jurisdiction, both as to law and fact, with such exceptions, and under such regulations as the Congress shall make.

3. The trial of all crimes, except in cases of impeachment, shall be by jury; and such trial shall be held in the State where the said crimes shall have been committed; but when not committed within any State, the trial shall be such place or places as the congress may by law have directed.

---

[6]Superseded by the Twelfth Amendment.

[7]See the Eleventh Amendment.

SECTION 3.   1. Treason against the United States shall consist only in levying war against them, or in adhering to their enemies, giving them aid and comfort. No person shall be convicted of treason unless on the testimony of two witnesses to the same overt act, or on confession in open court.

2. The Congress shall have power to declare the punishment of treason, but no attainder of treason shall work corruption of blood, or forfeiture except during the life of the person attained.

ARTICLE IV

SECTION 1. Full faith and credit shall be given in each State to the public acts, records, and judicial proceedings of every other State. And the Congress may by general laws prescribe the manner in which such acts, records and proceedings shall be proved, and the effect thereof.

SECTION 2.   1. The citizens of each State shall be entitled to all privileges and immunities of citizens in the several States.[8]

2. A person charged in any State with treason, felony, or other crime, who shall flee from justice, and be found in another State, shall on demand of the executive authority of the State from which he fled, be delivered up to be removed to the State having jurisdiction of the crime.

3. No person held to service or labor in one State under the laws thereof, escaping into another, shall, in consequence of any law or regulation therein, be discharged from such service or labor, but shall be delivered up on claim of the party to whom such service or labor may be due.[9]

SECTION 3.   1. New States may be admitted by the Congress into this Union; but no new State shall be formed or erected within the jurisdiction of any other State, nor any State be formed by the junction of two or more States, or parts of States, without the consent of the legislatures of the States concerned as well as of the Congress.

2. The Congress shall have power to dispose of and make all needful rules and regulations respecting the territory or other property belonging to the United States; and nothing in this Constitution shall be so construed as to prejudice any claims of the United States, or of any particular State.

SECTION 4.   The United States shall guarantee to every State in this Union a republican form of government, and shall protect each of them against invasion; and on application of the legislature, or of the executive (when the legislature cannot be convened) against domestic violence.

ARTICLE V

The Congress, whenever two thirds of both Houses shall deem it necessary, shall propose amendments to this Constitution, or, on the application of the legislatures of two thirds of the several States, shall call a convention for proposing amendments, which in either case shall be valid

to all intents and purposes, as part of this Constitution, when ratified by the legislatures of three fourths of the several States, or by conventions in three fourths thereof, as the one or the other mode of ratification may be proposed by the Congress; Provided that no amendment which may be made prior to the year one thousand eight hundred and eight shall in any manner affect the first and fourth clauses in the ninth section of the first article; and that no State, without its consent, shall be deprived of its equal suffrage in the Senate.

ARTICLE VI

1. All debts contracted and engagements entered into, before the adoption of this Constitution, shall be as valid against the United States under this Constitution, as under the Confederation.[10]

2. This Constitution, and the laws of the United States which shall be made in pursuance thereof; and all treaties made, or which shall be made, under the authority of the United States, shall be the supreme law of the land; and the judges in every State shall be bound thereby, any thing in the Constitution or laws of any State to the contrary notwithstanding.

3. The senators and representatives before mentioned, and the members of the several State legislatures, and all executive and judicial officers, both of the United States and of the several States, shall be bound by oath or affirmation to support this Constitution; but no religious test shall ever be required as a qualification to any office or public trust under the United States.

ARTICLE VII

The ratification of the conventions of nine States shall be sufficient for the establishment of this Constitution between the States so ratifying the same.

Done in Convention by the unanimous consent of the States present the seventeenth day of September in the year of our Lord one thousand seven hundred and eighty-seven, and of the independence of the United States of America the twelfth. In witness whereof we have hereunto subscribed our names.

[Signatories' names omitted]

Articles in addition to, and amendment of, the Constitution of the United States of America, proposed by Congress, and ratified by the legislatures of the several States, pursuant to the fifth article of the original Constitution.

Amendment I
[First ten amendments ratified December 15, 1791]
Congress shall make no law respecting an establishment of religion, or prohibiting the free exercise thereof; or abridging the freedom of speech, or of the press; or the right of the people peaceably to assemble, and to petition the government for a redress of grievances.

---

[8]See the Fourteenth Amendment, Sec. 1.

[9]See the Thirteenth Amendment.

[10]See the Fourteenth Amendment, Sec. 4.

Amendment II

A well regulated militia, being necessary to the security of a free State, the right of the people to keep and bear arms, shall not be infringed.

Amendment III

No soldier shall, in time of peace be quartered in any house, without the consent of the owner, nor in time of war, but in a manner to be prescribed by law.

Amendment IV

The right of the people to be secure in their persons, houses, papers, and effects, against unreasonable searches and seizures, shall not be violated, and no warrants shall issue, but upon probable cause, supported by oath or affirmation, and particularly describing the place to be searched, and the persons or things to be seized.

Amendment V

No person shall be held to answer for a capital or otherwise infamous crime, unless on a presentment or indictment of a grand jury, except in cases arising in the land or naval forces, or in the militia, when in actual service in time of war or public danger; nor shall any person be subject for the same offense to be twice put in jeopardy of life or limb; nor shall be compelled in any criminal case to be a witness against himself, nor be deprived of life, liberty, or property, without due process of law; nor shall private property be taken for public use, without just compensation.

Amendment VI

In all criminal prosecutions, the accused shall enjoy the right to a speedy and public trial, by an impartial jury of the State and district wherein the crime shall have been committed, which district shall have been previously ascertained by law, and to be informed of the nature and cause of the accusation; to be confronted with the witnesses against him; to have compulsory process for obtaining witnesses in his favor, and to have the assistance of counsel for his defense.

Amendment VII

In suits at common law, where the value in controversy shall exceed twenty dollars, the right of trial by jury shall be preserved, and no fact tried by a jury shall be otherwise reexamined in any court of the United States, than according to the rules of the common law.

Amendment VIII

Excessive bail shall not be required, nor excessive fines imposed, nor cruel and unusual punishments inflicted.

Amendment IX

The enumeration in the Constitution of certain rights shall not be construed to deny or disparage others retained by the people.

Amendment X

The powers not delegated to the United States by the Constitution, nor prohibited by it to the States, are reserved to the States respectively, or to the people.

Amendment XI [January 8, 1798]

The judicial power of the United States shall not be construed to extend to any suit in law or equity, commended or prosecuted against one of the United States by citizens of another State, or by citizens or subjects of any foreign State.

Amendment XII [September 25, 1804]

The electors shall meet in their respective States, and vote by ballot for President and Vice President, one of whom, at least, shall not be an inhabitant of the same State with themselves; they shall name in their ballots the person voted for as President, and in distinct ballots, the person voted for as Vice President, and they shall make distinct lists of all persons voted for as President and of all persons voted for as Vice President, and of the number of votes for each, which lists they shall sign and certify, and transmit sealed to the seat of the government of the United States, directed to the President of the Senate;—The President of the Senate shall, in the presence of the Senate and House of Representatives, open all the certificates and the votes shall then be counted;—The person having the greatest number of votes for President, shall be the President, if such number be a majority of the whole number of electors appointed; and if no person have such majority, then from the persons having the highest numbers not exceeding three on the list of those voted for as President, the House of Representatives shall choose immediately, by ballot, the President. But in choosing the President, the votes shall be taken by States, the representation from each State having one vote; a quorum for this purpose shall consist of a member or members from two thirds of the States, and a majority of all the States shall be necessary to a choice. And if the House of Representatives shall not choose a President whenever the right of choice shall devolve upon them, before the fourth day of March next following, then the Vice President shall act as President, as in the case of the death or other constitutional disability of the President. The person having the greatest number of votes as Vice President shall be the Vice President, if such number be a majority of the whole number of electors appointed, and if no person have a majority, then from the two highest numbers on the list, the Senate shall choose the Vice President; a quorum for the purpose shall consist of two thirds of the whole number of Senators, and a majority of the whole number shall be necessary to a choice. But no person constitutionally ineligible to the office of President shall be eligible to that of Vice President of the United States.

Amendment XIII [December 18, 1865]

SECTION 1. Neither slavery nor involuntary servitude, except as a punishment for crime whereof the party shall have been duly convicted, shall exist within the United States, or any place subject to their jurisdiction.

SECTION 2.   Congress shall have power to enforce this article by appropriate legislation.

Amendment XIV [July 28, 1868]

SECTION 1.   All persons born or naturalized in the United States, and subject to the jurisdiction thereof, are citizens of the United States and of the State wherein they reside. No State shall make or enforce any law which shall abridge the privileges or immunities of citizens of the United States; nor shall any State deprive any person of life, liberty, or property, without due process of law; nor deny to any person within its jurisdiction the equal protection of the laws.

SECTION 2.   Representatives shall be apportioned among the several States according to their respective numbers, counting the whole number of persons in each State, excluding Indians not taxed. But when the right to vote at any election for the choice of electors for President and Vice President of the United States, representatives in Congress, the executive and judicial officers of a State, or the members of the legislature thereof, is denied to any of the male inhabitants of such State, being twenty-one years of age, and citizens of the United States, or in any way abridged, except for participating in rebellion, or other crime, the basis of representation there shall be reduced in the proportion which the number of such male citizens shall bear to the whole number of male citizens twenty-one years of age in such State.

SECTION 3.   No person shall be a senator or representative in Congress, or elector of President and Vice President, or hold any office, civil or military, under the United States, or under any State, who having previously taken an oath, as a member of Congress, or as an officer of the United States, or as a member of any State legislature, or as an executive or judicial officer of any State, to support the Constitution of the United States, shall have engaged in insurrection or rebellion against the same, or given aid or comfort to the enemies thereof. But Congress may by a vote of two thirds of each House, remove such disability.

SECTION 4.   The validity of the public debt of the United States, authorized by law, including debts incurred for payment of pensions and bounties for services in suppressing insurrection or rebellion; shall not be questioned. But neither the United States nor any State shall assume or pay any debt or obligation incurred in aid of insurrection or rebellion against the United States, or any claim for the loss or emancipation of any slave; but all such debts, obligations, and claims shall be held illegal and void.

SECTION 5.   The Congress shall have the power to enforce, by appropriate legislation, the provisions of this article.

Amendment XV [March 30, 1870]

SECTION 1. The right of citizens of the United States to vote shall not be denied or abridged by the United States or by any State on account of race, color, or previous condition of servitude.

SECTION 2. The Congress shall have power to enforce this article by appropriate legislation.

Amendment XVI [February 25, 1913]

The Congress shall have power to lay and collect taxes on incomes, from whatever source derived, without apportionment among the several States, and without regard to any census or enumeration.

Amendment XVII [May 31, 1913]

The Senate of the United States shall be composed of two senators from each State, elected by the people thereof, for six years; and each senator shall have one vote. The electors in each State shall have the qualifications requisite for electors of the most numerous branch of the State legislature.

When vacancies happen in the representation of any State in the Senate, the executive authority of such State shall issue writs of election to fill such vacancies: Provided, That the legislature of any State may empower the executive thereof to make temporary appointments until the people fill the vacancies by election as the legislature may direct.

This amendment shall not be so construed as to affect the election or term of any senator chosen before it becomes valid as part of the Constitution.

Amendment XVIII [11] [January 29, 1919]

After one year from the ratification of this article, the manufacture, sale, or transportation of intoxicating liquors within, the importation thereof into, or the exportation thereof from the United States and all territory subject to the jurisdiction thereof for beverage purposes is thereby prohibited.

The Congress and the several States shall have concurrent power to enforce this article by appropriate legislation.

This article shall be inoperative unless it shall have been ratified as an amendment to the Constitution by the legislatures of the several States, as provided in the constitution, within seven years from the date of the submission hereof to the States by Congress.

Amendment XIX [August 26, 1920]

The right of citizens of the United States to vote shall not be denied or abridged by the United States or by any State on account of sex.

Congress shall have the power to enforce this article by appropriate legislation.

Amendment XX [January 23, 1933]

SECTION 1.   The terms of the President and Vice President shall end at noon on the 20th day of January and the terms of Senators and Representatives at noon on the 3d day of January, of the years in which such terms would have ended if this article had not been ratified; and the terms of their successors shall then begin.

SECTION 2.   The Congress shall assemble at least once in every year, and such meeting shall begin at noon on the 3d day of January, unless they shall by law appoint a different day.

---

[11]Repealed by the Twenty-first Amendment.

SECTION 3. If, at the time fixed for the beginning of the term of President, the President-elect shall have died, the Vice President-elect shall become President. If a President shall not have been chosen before the time fixed for the beginning of his term, or if the President-elect shall have failed to qualify, then the Vice President-elect shall act as President until a President shall have qualified; and the Congress may by law provide for the case wherein neither a President-elect nor a Vice President-elect shall have qualified, declaring who shall then act as President, or the manner in which one who is to act shall be selected, and such person shall act accordingly until a President or Vice President shall have qualified.

SECTION 4. The Congress may by law provide for the case of the death of any of the persons from whom, the House of Representatives may choose a President whenever the right of choice shall have devolved upon them, and for the case of the death of any of the persons from whom the Senate may choose a Vice President whenever the right of choice shall have devolved upon them.

SECTION 5. Sections 1 and 2 shall take effect on the 15th day of October following the ratification of this article.

SECTION 6. This article shall be inoperative unless it shall have been ratified as an amendment to the Constitution by the legislatures of three-fourths of the several States within seven years from the date of its submission.

Amendment XXI [December 5, 1933]

SECTION 1. The Eighteenth Article of amendment to the Constitution of the United States is hereby repealed.

SECTION 2. The transportation or importation into any State, Territory, or possession of the United States for delivery or use therein of intoxicating liquors in violation of the laws thereof, is hereby prohibited.

SECTION 3. This article shall be inoperative unless it shall have been ratified as an amendment to the Constitution by conventions in the several States, as provided in the Constitution, within seven years from the date of the submission thereof to the States by the Congress.

Amendment XXII [March 1, 1951]

No person shall be elected to the office of the President more than twice, and no person who has held the office of President, or acted as President, for more than two years of a term to which some other person was elected President shall be elected to the office of the President more than once.

But this article shall not apply to any person holding the office of President when this article was proposed by the Congress, and shall not prevent any person who may be holding the office of President, or acting as President, during the term within which this article becomes operative from holding the office of President or acting as President during the remainder of such term.

This article shall be inoperative unless it shall have been ratified as an amendment to the Constitution by the legislatures of three-fourths of the several States within seven years from the date of its submission to the States by the Congress.

Amendment XXIII [March 29, 1961]

SECTION 1. The District constituting the seat of Government of the United States shall appoint in such manner as the Congress may direct.

A number of electors of President and Vice President equal to the whole number of Senators and Representatives in Congress to which the District would be entitled if it were a State, but in no event more than the least populous State; they shall be in addition to those appointed by the States, but they shall be considered, for the purposes of the election of President and Vice President, to be electors appointed by a State; and they shall meet in the District and perform such duties as provided by the twelfth article of amendment.

SECTION 2. The Congress shall have power to enforce this article by appropriate legislation.

Amendment XXIV [January 23, 1964]

SECTION 1. The right of citizens of the United States to vote in any primary or other election for President or Vice President, for electors for President or Vice President, or for Senator or Representative in Congress, shall not be denied or abridged by the United States or any State by reason of failure to pay any poll tax or other tax.

SECTION 2. The Congress shall have power to enforce this article by appropriate legislation.

Amendment XXV [February 10, 1967]

SECTION 1. In case of the removal of the President from office or of his death or resignation, the Vice President shall become President.

SECTION 2. Whenever there is a vacancy in the office of the Vice President, the President shall nominate a Vice President who shall take office upon confirmation by a majority of both Houses of Congress.

SECTION 3. Whenever the President transmits to the President pro tempore of the Senate and the Speaker of the House of Representatives his written declaration that he is unable to discharge the powers and duties of his office, and until he transmits to them a written declaration to the contrary, such powers and duties shall be discharged by the Vice President as Acting President.

SECTION 4. Whenever the Vice President and a majority of either the principal officers of the executive departments or of such other body as Congress may by law provide, transmit to the President pro tempore of the Senate and the Speaker of the House of Representatives their written declaration that the President is unable to discharge the powers and duties of his office, the Vice President shall immediately assume the powers and duties of the office as Acting President.

Thereafter, when the President transmits to the President pro tempore of the Senate and the Speaker of the House of Representatives his written declaration that no inability exists, he shall resume the powers and duties of his office unless the Vice President and a majority of either the principal officers of the executive departments or of such other body as Congress may by law provide, transmit within four days to the President pro tempore of the Senate and the Speaker of the House of Representatives their written declaration that the President is unable to discharge the powers and duties of his office. Thereupon Congress shall decide the issue, assembling within forty-eight hours for that purpose if not in session. If the Congress, within twenty-one days after receipt of the latter written declaration, or, if Congress is not in session, within twenty-one days after Congress is required to assemble, determines by two-thirds vote of both Houses that the President is unable to discharge the powers and duties of his office, the Vice President shall continue to discharge the same as Acting President; otherwise, the President shall resume the powers and duties of his office.

Amendment XXVI [June 30, 1971]

SECTION 1.   The right of citizens of the United States who are eighteen years of age or older to vote shall not be denied or abridged by the United States or by any State on account of age.

SECTION 2.   The Congress shall have power to enforce this article by appropriate legislation.

Amendment XXVII[12] [May 7, 1992]

No law, varying the compensation for services of the Senators and Representatives, shall take effect until an election of Representatives shall have intervened.

---

[12]James Madison proposed this amendment in 1789 together with the ten amendments that were adopted as the Bill of Rights, but it failed to win ratification at the time. Congress, however, had set no deadline for its ratification, and over the years—particularly in the 1980s and 1990s—many states voted to add it to the Constitution. With the ratification of Michigan in 1992 it passed the threshold of 3/4ths of the states required for adoption, but because the process took more than 200 years, its validity remains in doubt.

PRESIDENT AND VICE PRESIDENT

1. George Washington (1789)
   John Adams (1789)

2. John Adams (1797)
   Thomas Jefferson (1797)

3. Thomas Jefferson (1801)
   Aaron Burr (1801)
   George Clinton (1805)

4. James Madison (1809)
   George Clinton (1809)
   Elbridge Gerry (1813)

5. James Monroe (1817)
   Daniel D. Thompkins (1817)

6. John Quincy Adams (1825)
   John C. Calhoun (1825)

7. Andrew Jackson (1829)
   John C. Calhoun (1829)
   Martin Van Buren (1833)

8. Martin Van Buren (1837)
   Richard M. Johnson (1837)

9. William H. Harrison (1841)
   John Tyler (1841)

10. John Tyler (1841)

11. James K. Polk (1845)
    George M. Dallas (1845)

12. Zachary Taylor (1849)
    Millard Fillmore (1849)

13. Millard Fillmore (1850)

14. Franklin Pierce (1853)
    William R. King (1853)

15. James Buchanan (1857)
    John C. Breckinridge (1857)

16. Abraham Lincoln (1861)
    Hannibal Hamlin (1861)
    Andrew Johnson (1865)

17. Andrew Johnson (1865)

18. Ulysses S. Grant (1869)
    Schuyler Colfax (1869)
    Henry Wilson (1873)

19. Rutherford B. Hayes (1877)
    William A. Wheeler (1877)

20. James A. Garfield (1881)
    Chester A. Arthur (1881)

21. Chester A. Arthur (1881)

22. Grover Cleveland (1885)
    T. A. Hendricks (1885)

23. Benjamin Harrison (1889)
    Levi P. Morgan (1889)

24. Grover Cleveland (1893)
    Adlai E. Stevenson (1893)

25. William McKinley (1897)
    Garret A. Hobart (1897)
    Theodore Roosevelt (1901)

26. Theodore Roosevelt (1901)
    Charles Fairbanks (1905)

27. William H. Taft (1909)
    James S. Sherman (1909)

28. Woodrow Wilson (1913)
    Thomas R. Marshall (1913)

29. Warren G. Harding (1921)
    Calvin Coolidge (1921)

30. Calvin Coolidge (1923)
    Charles G. Dawes (1925)

31. Herbert C. Hoover (1929)
    Charles Curtis (1929)

32. Franklin D. Roosevelt (1933)
    John Nance Garner (1933)
    Henry A. Wallace (1941)
    Harry S. Truman (1945)

33. Harry S. Truman (1945)
    Alben W. Barkley (1949)

34. Dwight D. Eisenhower (1953)
    Richard M. Nixon (1953)

35. John F. Kennedy (1961)
    Lyndon B. Johnson (1961)

36. Lyndon B. Johnson (1963)
    Hubert H. Humphrey (1965)

37. Richard M. Nixon (1969)
    Spiro T. Agnew (1969)
    Gerald R. Ford (1973)

38. Gerald R. Ford (1974)
    Nelson A. Rockefeller (1974)

39. James E. Carter Jr. (1977)
    Walter F. Mondale (1977)

40. Ronald W. Reagan (1981)
    George H. Bush (1981)

41. George H. Bush (1989)
    James D. Quayle III (1989)

42. William J. Clinton (1993)
    Albert Gore (1993)

43. George W. Bush (2001)
    Richard Cheney (2001)

PRESIDENTIAL ELECTIONS

Year	Number of States	Candidates	Party	Popular Vote*	Electoral Vote[†]	Percentage of Popular Vote
1789	11	GEORGE WASHINGTON	No party designations		69	
		John Adams			34	
		Other Candidates			35	
1792	15	GEORGE WASHINGTON	No party designations		132	
		John Adams			77	
		George Clinton			50	
		Other Candidates			5	
1796	16	JOHN ADAMS	Federalist		71	
		Thomas Jefferson	Democratic-Republican		68	
		Thomas Pinckney	Federalist		59	
		Aaron Burr	Democratic-Republican		30	
		Other Candidates			48	
1800	16	THOMAS JEFFERSON	Democratic-Republican		73	
		Aaron Burr	Democratic-Republican		73	
		John Adams	Federalist		65	
		Charles C. Pinckney	Federalist		64	
		John Jay	Federalist		1	
1804	17	THOMAS JEFFERSON	Democratic-Republican		162	
		Charles C. Pinckney	Federalist		14	
1808	17	JAMES MADISON	Democratic-Republican		122	
		Charles C. Pinckney	Federalist		47	
		George Clinton	Democratic-Republican		6	
1812	18	JAMES MADISON	Democratic-Republican		128	
		DeWitt Clinton	Federalist		89	
1816	19	JAMES MONROE	Democratic-Republican		183	
		Rufus King	Federalist		34	
1820	24	JAMES MONROE	Democratic-Republican		231	
		John Quincy Adams	Independent-Republican		1	
1824	24	JOHN QUINCY ADAMS	Democratic-Republican	108,740	84	30.5
		Andrew Jackson	Democratic-Republican	153,544	99	43.1
		William H. Crawford	Democratic-Republican	46,618	41	13.1
		Henry Clay	Democratic-Republican	47,136	37	13.2
1828	24	ANDREW JACKSON	Democrat	647,286	178	56.0
		John Quincy Adams	National Republican	508,064	83	44.0
1832	24	ANDREW JACKSON	Democrat	687,502	219	55.0
		Henry Clay	National Republican	530,189	49	42.4
		William Wirt	Anti-Masonic	} 33,108	7	
		John Floyd	National Republican		11	2.6

* Percentage of popular vote given for any election year may not total 100 percent because candidates receiving less than 1 percent of the popular vote have been omitted.

[†] Prior to the passage of the Twelfth Amendment in 1904, the electoral college voted for two presidential candidates; the runner-up became Vice-President. Data from Historical Statistics of the United States, Colonial Times to 1957 (1961), pp. 682–683, and The World Almanac.

PRESIDENTIAL ELECTIONS (CONTINUED)

Year	Number of States	Candidates	Party	Popular Vote	Electoral Vote	Percentage of Popular Vote
1836	26	MARTIN VAN BUREN	Democrat	765,483	170	50.9
		William H. Harrison	Whig		73	
		Hugh L. White	Whig		26	
		Daniel Webster	Whig	739,795	14	49.1
		W. P. Mangum	Whig		11	
1840	26	WILLIAM H. HARRISON	Whig	1,274,624	234	53.1
		Martin Van Buren	Democrat	1,127,781	60	46.9
1844	26	JAMES K. POLK	Democrat	1,338,464	170	49.6
		Henry Clay	Whig	1,300,097	105	48.1
		James G. Birney	Liberty	62,300		2.3
1848	30	ZACHARY TAYLOR	Whig	1,360,967	163	47.4
		Lewis Cass	Democrat	1,222,342	127	42.5
		Martin Van Buren	Free Soil	291,263		10.1
1852	31	FRANKLIN PIERCE	Democrat	1,601,117	254	50.9
		Winfield Scott	Whig	1,385,453	42	44.1
		John P. Hale	Free Soil	155,825		5.0
1856	31	JAMES BUCHANAN	Democrat	1,832,955	174	45.3
		John C. Frémont	Republican	1,339,932	114	33.1
		Millard Fillmore	American ("Know Nothing")	871,731	8	21.6
1860	33	ABRAHAM LINCOLN	Republican	1,865,593	180	39.8
		Stephen A. Douglas	Democrat	1,382,713	12	29.5
		John C. Breckinridge	Democrat	848,356	72	18.1
		John Bell	Constitutional Union	592,906	39	12.6
1864	36	ABRAHAM LINCOLN	Republican	2,206,938	212	55.0
		George B. McClellan	Democrat	1,803,787	21	45.0
1868	37	ULYSSES S. GRANT	Republican	3,013,421	214	52.7
		Horatio Seymour	Democrat	2,706,829	80	47.3
1872	37	ULYSSES S. GRANT	Republican	3,596,745	286	55.6
		Horace Greeley	Democrat	2,843,446	*	43.9
1876	38	RUTHERFORD B. HAYES	Republican	4,036,572	185	48.0
		Samuel J. Tilden	Democrat	4,284,020	184	51.0
1880	38	JAMES A. GARFIELD	Republican	4,453,295	214	48.5
		Winfield S. Hancock	Democrat	4,414,082	155	48.1
		James B. Weaver	Greenback-Labor	308,578		3.4
1884	38	GROVER CLEVELAND	Democrat	4,879,507	219	48.5
		James G. Blaine	Republican	4,850,293	182	48.2
		Benjamin F. Butler	Greenback-Labor	175,370		1.8
		John P. St. John	Prohibition	150,369		1.5
1888	38	BENJAMIN HARRISON	Republican	5,447,129	233	47.9
		Grover Cleveland	Democrat	5,537,857	168	48.6
		Clinton B. Fisk	Prohibition	249,506		2.2
		Anson J. Streeter	Union Labor	146,935		1.3

* *Because of the death of Greeley, Democratic electors scattered their votes.*

PRESIDENTIAL ELECTIONS   (CONTINUED)

Year	Number of States	Candidates	Party	Popular Vote	Electoral Vote	Percentage of Popular Vote
1892	44	GROVER CLEVELAND	Democrat	5,555,426	277	46.1
		Benjamin Harrison	Republican	5,182,690	145	43.0
		James B. Weaver	People's	1,029,846	22	8.5
		John Bidwell	Prohibition	264,133		2.2
1896	45	WILLIAM MCKINLEY	Republican	7,102,246	271	51.1
		William J. Bryan	Democrat	6,492,559	176	47.7
1900	45	WILLIAM MCKINLEY	Republican	7,218,491	292	51.7
		William J. Bryan	Democrat; Populist	6,356,734	155	45.5
		John C. Woolley	Prohibition	208,914		1.5
1904	45	THEODORE ROOSEVELT	Republican	7,628,461	336	57.4
		Alton B. Parker	Democrat	5,084,223	140	37.6
		Eugene V. Debs	Socialist	402,283		3.0
		Silas C. Swallow	Prohibition	258,536		1.9
1908	46	WILLIAM H. TAFT	Republican	7,675,320	321	51.6
		William J. Bryan	Democrat	6,412,294	162	43.1
		Eugene V. Debs	Socialist	420,793		2.8
		Eugene W. Chafin	Prohibition	253,840		1.7
1912	48	WOODROW WILSON	Democrat	6,296,547	435	41.9
		Theodore Roosevelt	Progressive	4,118,571	88	27.4
		William H. Taft	Republican	3,486,720	8	23.2
		Eugene V. Debs	Socialist	900,672		6.0
		Eugene W. Chafin	Prohibition	206,275		1.4
1916	48	WOODROW WILSON	Democrat	9,127,695	277	49.4
		Charles E. Hughes	Republican	8,533,507	254	46.2
		A. L. Benson	Socialist	585,113		3.2
		J. Frank Hanly	Prohibition	220,506		1.2
1920	48	WARREN G. HARDING	Republican	16,143,407	404	60.4
		James M. Cox	Democrat	9,130,328	127	34.2
		Eugene V. Debs	Socialist	919,799		3.4
		P. P. Christensen	Farmer-Labor	265,411		1.0
1924	48	CALVIN COOLIDGE	Republican	15,718,211	382	54.0
		John W. Davis	Democrat	8,385,283	136	28.8
		Robert M. La Follette	Progressive	4,831,289	13	16.6
1928	48	HERBERT C. HOOVER	Republican	21,391,993	444	58.2
		Alfred E. Smith	Democrat	15,016,169	87	40.9
1932	48	FRANKLIN D. ROOSEVELT	Democrat	22,809,638	472	57.4
		Herbert C. Hoover	Republican	15,758,901	59	39.7
		Norman Thomas	Socialist	881,951		2.2
1936	48	FRANKLIN D. ROOSEVELT	Democrat	27,752,869	523	60.8
		Alfred M. Landon	Republican	16,674,665	8	36.5
		William Lemke	Union	882,479		1.9
1940	48	FRANKLIN D. ROOSEVELT	Democrat	27,307,819	449	54.8
		Wendell L. Willkie	Republican	22,321,018	82	44.8

PRESIDENTIAL ELECTIONS   (CONTINUED)

Year	Number of States	Candidates	Party	Popular Vote	Electoral Vote	Percentage of Popular Vote
1944	48	FRANKLIN D. ROOSEVELT	Democrat	25,606,585	432	53.5
		Thomas E. Dewey	Republican	22,014,745	99	46.0
1948	48	HARRY S. TRUMAN	Democrat	24,105,812	303	49.5
		Thomas E. Dewey	Republican	21,970,065	189	45.1
		J. Strom Thurmond	States' Rights	1,169,063	39	2.4
		Henry A. Wallace	Progressive	1,157,172		2.4
1952	48	DWIGHT D. EISENHOWER	Republican	33,936,234	442	55.1
		Adlai E. Stevenson	Democrat	27,314,992	89	44.4
1956	48	DWIGHT D. EISENHOWER	Republican	35,590,472	457*	57.6
		Adlai E. Stevenson	Democrat	26,022,752	73	42.1
1960	50	JOHN F. KENNEDY	Democrat	34,227,096	303†	49.9
		Richard M. Nixon	Republican	34,108,546	219	49.6
1964	50	LYNDON B. JOHNSON	Democrat	42,676,220	486	61.3
		Barry M. Goldwater	Republican	26,860,314	52	38.5
1968	50	RICHARD M. NIXON	Republican	31,785,480	301	43.4
		Hubert H. Humphrey	Democrat	31,275,165	191	42.7
		George C. Wallace	American Independent	9,906,473	46	13.5
1972	50	RICHARD M. NIXON‡	Republican	47,165,234	520	60.6
		George S. McGovern	Democrat	29,168,110	17	37.5
1976	50	JIMMY CARTER	Democrat	40,828,929	297	50.1
		Gerald R. Ford	Republican	39,148,940	240	47.9
		Eugene McCarthy	Independent	739,256		
1980	50	RONALD REAGAN	Republican	43,201,220	489	50.9
		Jimmy Carter	Democrat	34,913,332	49	41.2
		John B. Anderson	Independent	5,581,379		
1984	50	RONALD REAGAN	Republican	53,428,357	525	59.0
		Walter F. Mondale	Democrat	36,930,923	13	41.0
1988	50	GEORGE BUSH	Republican	48,901,046	426	53.4
		Michael Dukakis	Democrat	41,809,030	111	45.6
1992	50	BILL CLINTON	Democrat	43,728,275	370	43.2
		George Bush	Republican	38,167,416	168	37.7
		H. Ross Perot	United We Stand, America	19,237,247		19.0
1996	50	BILL CLINTON	Democrat	45,590,703	379	49.0
		Robert Dole	Republican	37,816,307	159	41.0
		H. Ross Perot	Reform	7,866,284		8.0
2000	50	GEORGE W. BUSH	Republican	50,459,624	271	47.9
		Albert Gore, Jr.	Democrat	51,003,328	266	49.4
		Ralph Nader	Green	2,882,985	0	2.7
2004	50	GEORGE W. BUSH	Republican	59,117,523	286	51.1
		John Kerry	Democrat	55,557,584	252	48.0
		Ralph Nader	Green	405,623	0	0.3

* *Walter B. Jones received 1 electoral vote.*

† *Harry F. Byrd received 15 electoral votes.*

‡ *Resigned August 9, 1974: Vice President Gerald R. Ford became President.*

ADMISSION OF STATES INTO THE UNION

State	Date of Admission	State	Date of Admission
1. Delaware	December 7, 1787	26. Michigan	January 26, 1837
2. Pennsylvania	December 12, 1787	27. Florida	March 3, 1845
3. New Jersey	December 18, 1787	28. Texas	December 29, 1845
4. Georgia	January 2, 1788	29. Iowa	December 28, 1846
5. Connecticut	January 9, 1788	30. Wisconsin	May 29, 1848
6. Massachusetts	February 6, 1788	31. California	September 9, 1850
7. Maryland	April 28, 1788	32. Minnesota	May 11, 1858
8. South Carolina	May 23, 1788	33. Oregon	February 14, 1859
9. New Hampshire	June 21, 1788	34. Kansas	January 29, 1861
10. Virginia	June 25, 1788	35. West Virginia	June 20, 1863
11. New York	July 26, 1788	36. Nevada	October 31, 1864
12. North Carolina	November 21, 1789	37. Nebraska	March 1, 1867
13. Rhode Island	May 29, 1790	38. Colorado	August 1, 1876
14. Vermont	March 4, 1791	39. North Dakota	November 2, 1889
15. Kentucky	June 1, 1792	40. South Dakota	November 2, 1889
16. Tennessee	June 1, 1796	41. Montana	November 8, 1889
17. Ohio	March 1, 1803	42. Washington	November 11, 1889
18. Louisiana	April 30, 1812	43. Idaho	July 3, 1890
19. Indiana	December 11, 1816	44. Wyoming	July 10, 1890
20. Mississippi	December 10, 1817	45. Utah	January 4, 1896
21. Illinois	December 3, 1818	46. Oklahoma	November 16, 1907
22. Alabama	December 14, 1819	47. New Mexico	January 6, 1912
23. Maine	March 15, 1820	48. Arizona	February 14, 1912
24. Missouri	August 10, 1821	49. Alaska	January 3, 1959
25. Arkansas	June 15, 1836	50. Hawaii	August 21, 1959

DEMOGRAPHICS OF THE UNITED STATES

POPULATION GROWTH

Year	Population	Percent Increase
1630	4,600	
1640	26,600	478.3
1650	50,400	90.8
1660	75,100	49.0
1670	111,900	49.0
1680	151,500	35.4
1690	210,400	38.9
1700	250,900	19.2
1710	331,700	32.2
1720	466,200	40.5
1730	629,400	35.0
1740	905,600	43.9
1750	1,170,800	29.3
1760	1,593,600	36.1
1770	2,148,100	34.8
1780	2,780,400	29.4
1790	3,929,214	41.3
1800	5,308,483	35.1
1810	7,239,881	36.4
1820	9,638,453	33.1
1830	12,866,020	33.5
1840	17,069,453	32.7
1850	23,191,876	35.9
1860	31,443,321	35.6
1870	39,818,449	26.6
1880	50,155,783	26.0
1890	62,947,714	25.5
1900	75,994,575	20.7
1910	91,972,266	21.0
1920	105,710,620	14.9
1930	122,775,046	16.1
1940	131,669,275	7.2
1950	151,325,798	14.5
1960	179,323,175	18.5
1970	203,302,031	13.4
1980	226,542,199	11.4
1990	248,718,301	9.8
2000	281,421,906	13.1

Source: *Historical Statistics of the United States* (1975);
Statistical Abstract by the United States (2001).
Note: Figures for 1630–1780 include British colonies within
limits of present United States only; Native American
population included only in 1930 and thereafter.

WORK FORCE

Year	Total Number Workers (1000s)	Farmers as % of Total	Women as % of Total	% Workers in Unions
1810	2,330	84	(NA)	(NA)
1840	5,660	75	(NA)	(NA)
1860	11,110	53	(NA)	(NA)
1870	12,506	53	15	(NA)
1880	17,392	52	15	(NA)
1890	23,318	43	17	(NA)
1900	29,073	40	18	3
1910	38,167	31	21	6
1920	41,614	26	21	12
1930	48,830	22	22	7
1940	53,011	17	24	27
1950	59,643	12	28	25
1960	69,877	8	32	26
1970	82,049	4	37	25
1980	106,940	3	43	23
1990	125,840	3	45	16
2000	140,863	2	47	12

Source: *Historical Statistics of the United States* (1975); *Statistical Abstract of the United States* (2001).

VITAL STATISTICS (IN THOUSANDS)

Year	Births	Deaths	Marriages	Divorces
1800	55	(NA)	(NA)	(NA)
1810	54.3	(NA)	(NA)	(NA)
1820	55.2	(NA)	(NA)	(NA)
1830	51.4	(NA)	(NA)	(NA)
1840	51.8	(NA)	(NA)	(NA)
1850	43.3	(NA)	(NA)	(NA)
1860	44.3	(NA)	(NA)	(NA)
1870	38.3	(NA)	9.6 (1867)	0.3 (1867)
1880	39.8	(NA)	9.1 (1875)	0.3 (1875)
1890	31.5	(NA)	9.0	0.5
1900	32.3	17.2	9.3	0.7
1910	30.1	14.7	10.3	0.9
1920	27.7	13.0	12.0	1.6
1930	21.3	11.3	9.2	1.6
1940	19.4	10.8	12.1	2.0
1950	24.1	9.6	11.1	2.6
1960	23.7	9.5	8.5	2.2
1970	18.4	9.5	10.6	3.5
1980	15.9	8.8	10.6	5.2
1990	16.7	8.6	9.8	4.7
1997	14.6	8.6	8.9	4.3

Source: *Historical Statistics of the United States* (1975); *Statistical Abstract of the United States* (1999).

RACIAL COMPOSITION OF THE POPULATION

(IN THOUSANDS)

Year	White	Black	Indian	Hispanic	Asian/Pacific Islander
1790	3,172	757	(NA)	(NA)	(NA)
1800	4,306	1,002	(NA)	(NA)	(NA)
1820	7,867	1,772	(NA)	(NA)	(NA)
1840	14,196	2,874	(NA)	(NA)	(NA)
1860	26,923	4,442	(NA)	(NA)	(NA)
1880	43,403	6,581	(NA)	(NA)	(NA)
1900	66,809	8,834	(NA)	(NA)	(NA)
1910	81,732	9,828	(NA)	(NA)	(NA)
1920	94,821	10,463	(NA)	(NA)	(NA)
1930	110,287	11,891	(NA)	(NA)	(NA)
1940	118,215	12,866	(NA)	(NA)	(NA)
1950	134,942	15,042	(NA)	(NA)	(NA)
1960	158,832	18,872	(NA)	(NA)	(NA)
1970	178,098	22,581	(NA)	(NA)	(NA)
1980	194,713	26,683	1,420	14,609	3,729
1990	208,727	30,511	2,065	22,372	2,462
2000	211,461	34,658	2,476	35,306	10,642

Source: U.S. Bureau of the Census, U.S. *Census of Population: 1940,* vol. II, part 1, and vol. IV, part 1; *1950,* vol. II, part 1; *1960,* vol. I, part 1; *1970,* vol. I, part B; and *Current Population Reports,* P25-1095 and P25-1104; *Statistical Abstract of the United States* (2001).

IMMIGRATION BY THE ORIGIN

(IN THOUSANDS)

Period	Europe	Americas	Asia
1820–30	106	12	—
1831–40	496	33	—
1841–50	1,597	62	—
1851–60	2,453	75	42
1861–70	2,065	167	65
1871–80	2,272	404	70
1881–90	4,735	427	70
1891–1900	3,555	39	75
1901–10	8,065	362	324
1911–20	4,322	1,144	247
1921–30	2,463	1,517	112
1931–40	348	160	16
1941–50	621	355	32
1951–60	1,326	997	150
1961–70	1,123	1,716	590
1971–80	800	1,983	1,588
1981–90	762	3,616	2,738
1991–2000	1,100	3,800	2,200

Source: Historical Statistics of the United States (1975); *Statistical Abstract of the United States* (1991); Population Estimates Program, Population Division, U.S. Census Bureau, April 2001.

Acquired Immune Deficiency Syndrome (AIDS) A complex of deadly pathologies resulting from infection with the human immunodeficiency virus (HIV).

Act of Toleration Act passed in 1661 by King Charles II ordering a stop to religious persecution in Massachusetts.

Affirmative action A set of policies to open opportunities in business and education for members of minority groups and women by allowing race and sex to be factors included in decisions to hire, award contracts, or admit students to higher education programs.

Alamo Franciscan mission at San Antonio, Texas that was the site in 1836 of a siege and massacre of Texans by Mexican troops.

Albany Conference A 1754 meeting, held in Albany, NY, between the British and leaders of the Iroquois Confederacy.

Albany Movement Coalition formed in 1961 in Albany, a small city in southwest Georgia, of activists from SNCC, the NAACP, and other local groups.

Alien Act Act passed by Congress in 1798 that authorized the president to imprison or deport suspected aliens during wartime.

Alliance for Progress Program of economic aid to Latin America during the Kennedy administration.

Allies In World War I, Britain, France, Russia, and other belligerent nations fighting against the Central Powers but not including the United States.

Almanac A combination calendar, astrological guide, and sourcebook of medical advice and farming tips.

American Colonization Society Organization founded in 1817 by antislavery reformers, that called for gradual emancipation and the removal of freed blacks to Africa.

American Federation of Labor (AFL) Union formed in 1886 that organized skilled workers along craft lines and emphasized a few workplace issues rather than a broad social program.

American Indian Movement (AIM) Group of Native-American political activists who used confrontations with the federal government to publicize their case for Indian rights.

American Society for the Promotion of Temperance Largest reform organization of its time dedicated to ending the sale and consumption of alcoholic beverages.

American System The program of government subsidies favored by Henry Clay and his followers to promote American economic growth and protect domestic manufacturers from foreign competition.

Americans with Disabilities Act An act that required employers to provide access to their facilities for qualified employees with disabilities.

Annapolis Convention Conference of state delegates at Annapolis, Maryland, that issued a call in September 1786 for a convention to meet at Philadelphia to consider fundamental changes.

Anti-Federalists Opponents of the Constitution in the debate over its ratification.

Archaic period The period roughly 10,000 to 2,500 years ago marked by the retreat of glaciers.

Articles of Confederation Written document setting up the loose confederation of states that comprised the first national government of the United States.

Athapascan A people that began to settle the forests in the northwestern area of North America around 5000 B.C.E.

Atlantic Charter Statement of common principles and war aims developed by President Franklin Roosevelt and British Prime Minister Winston Churchill at a meeting in August 1941.

Axis powers The opponents of the United States and its allies in World War II.

Aztecs A warrior people who dominated the Valley of Mexico from 1100–1521.

Bank War The political struggle between President Andrew Jackson and the supporters of the Second Bank of the United States.

Battle of the Bulge German offensive in December 1944 that penetrated deep into Belgium (creating a "bulge"). Allied forces, while outnumbered, attacked from the north and south. By January, 1945, the German forces were destroyed or routed, but not without some 77,000 Allied casualities.

Bay of Pigs Site in Cuba of an unsuccessful landing by fourteen hundred anti-Castro Cuban refugees in April 1961.

Beatnik Term used to designate members of the Beats.

Beats A group of writers from the 50s whose writings challenged American culture.

Beaver Wars Series of bloody conflicts, occurring between 1640s and 1680s, during which the Iroquois fought the French for control of the fur trade in the east and the Great Lakes region.

Beringia A subcontinent bridging Asia and North America, named after the Bering Straits.

Berlin blockade Three-hundred-day Soviet blockade of land access to United States, British, and French occupation zones in Berlin, 1948–1949.

Bill for Establishing Religious Freedom A bill authored by Thomas Jefferson establishing religious freedom in Virginia.

Bill of Rights A written summary of inalienable rights and liberties.

Black codes Laws passed by states and municipalities denying many rights of citizenship to free black people before the Civil War.

Black Panther Party Political and social movement among black Americans, founded in Oakland, California, in 1966 and emphasizing black economic and political power.

Black Power Philosophy emerging after 1965 that real economic and political gains for African Americans could come only through self-help, self-determination, and organizing for direct political influence.

Bleeding Kansas Violence between pro- and antislavery forces in Kansas Territory after the passage of the Kansas-Nebraska Act in 1854.

Blitzkrieg German war tactic in World War II ("lightning war") involving the concentration of air and armored firepower to punch and exploit holes in opposing defensive lines.

Bohemian Artistic individual who lives with disregard for the conventional rules of behavior.

Bolsheviks   Members of the Communist movement in Russia that established the Soviet government after the 1917 Russian Revolution.

Bonus Army   Unemployed veterans of World War I gathering in Washington in 1932 demanding payment of service bonuses not due until 1945.

Bosnia   A nation in southeast Europe that split off from Yugoslavia and became the site of bitter civil and religious war, requiring NATO and U.S. intervention in the 1990s.

Boston Massacre   After months of increasing friction between townspeople and the British troops stationed in the city, on March 5, 1770, British troops fired on American civilians in Boston.

Boston Tea Party   Incident that occurred on December 16, 1773, in which Bostonians, disguised as Indians, destroyed £18,000 worth of tea belonging to the British East India Company in order to prevent payment of the duty on it.

Brown v. Board of Education   Supreme Court decision in 1954 that declared that "separate but equal" schools for children of different races violated the Constitution.

Cahokia   One of the largest urban centers created by Mississippian peoples, containing 30,000 residents in 1250.

Californios   Californians of Spanish descent.

Calvinist theology of election   Belief that salvation was the result of God's sovereign decree and that few people would receive God's grace.

Caminetti Act   1893 act giving the state the power to regulate the mines.

Camp David Accords   Agreement signed by Israel and Egypt in 1978 that set the formal terms for peace in the Middle East.

Carpetbaggers   Northern transplants to the South, many of whom were Union soldiers who stayed in the South after the war.

Central Intelligence Agency (CIA)   Agency established in 1947 that coordinates the gathering and evaluation of military and economic information on other nations.

Central Powers   Germany and its World War I allies in Austria, Italy, Turkey, and Bulgaria.

Chinese Exclusion Act   Act which suspended Chinese immigration, limited the civil rights of resident Chinese, and forbade their naturalization.

Civil Rights Act of 1964   Federal legislation that outlawed discrimination in public accommodations and employment on the basis of race, skin color, sex, religion, or national origin.

Civil Rights Bill   1866 act that gave full citizenship to African Americans.

Clayton Antitrust Act   Replaced the old Sherman Act of 1890 as the nation's basic antitrust law. It exempted unions from being construed as illegal combinations in restraint of trade, and it forbade federal courts from issuing injunctions against strikers.

Coercive Acts   Legislation passed by Parliament in 1774; included the Boston Port Act, the Massachusetts Government Act, the Administration of Justice Act, and the Quartering Act of 1774.

Cold war   The political and economic confrontation between the Soviet Union and the United States that dominated world affairs from 1946 to 1989.

Committee on Public Information (CPI)   Government agency during World War I that sought to shape public opinion in support of the war effort through newspapers, pamphlets, speeches, films, and other media.

Compromise of 1850   The four-step compromise which admitted California as a free state, allowed the residents of the New Mexico and Utah territories to decide the slavery issue for themselves, ended the slave trade in the District of Columbia, and passed a new fugitive slave law to enforce the constitutional provision stating that a slave escaping into a free state shall be delivered back to the owner.

Compromise of 1877   The Congressional settling of the 1876 election which installed Republican Rutherford B. Hayes in the White House and gave Democrats control of all state governments in the South.

Confederate States of America   Nation proclaimed in Montgomery, Alabama, in February 1861, after the seven states of the Lower South seceded from the United States.

Congress of Industrial Organizations   An alliance of industrial unions that spurred the 1930s organizational drive among the mass-production industries.

Congress of Racial Equality (CORE)   Civil rights group formed in 1942 and committed to nonviolent civil disobedience.

Congressional Reconstruction   Name given to the period 1867–1870 when the Republican-dominated Congress controlled Reconstruction-era policy.

Conspicuous consumption   Highly visible displays of wealth and consumption.

Constitution   The written document providing for a new central government of the United States.

Constitutional Convention   Convention of delegates from the colonies that first met to organize resistance to the Intolerable Acts.

Constitutional Union Party   National party formed in 1860, mainly by former Whigs, that emphasized allegiance to the Union and strict enforcement of all national legislation.

Continental Army   The regular or professional army authorized by the Second Continental Congress and commanded by General George Washington during the Revolutionary War.

Contract with America   Platform proposing a sweeping reduction in the role and activities of the federal government on which many Republican candidates ran for Congress in 1994.

Contras   Nicaraguan exiles armed and organized by the CIA to fight the Sandinista government of Nicaragua.

Copperheads   A term Republicans applied to Northern war dissenters and those suspected of aiding the Confederate cause during the Civil War.

Council of Economic Advisers   Board of three professional economists established in 1946 to advise the president on economic policy.

Counterculture   Various alternatives to mainstream values and behaviors that became popular in the 1960s, including experimentation with psychedelic drugs, communal living, a return to the land, Asian religions, and experimental art.

Coureurs de bois   French for "woods runner," an independent fur trader in New France.

Covenant Chain An alliance between the Iroquois Confederacy and the colony of New York which sought to establish Iroquois dominance over all other tribes.

Coxey's Army A protest march of unemployed workers, led by Populist businessman Jacob Coxey, demanding inflation and a public works program during the depression of the 1890s.

Cuban missile crisis Crisis between the Soviet Union and the United States over the placement of Soviet nuclear missiles in Cuba.

Culpeper's Rebellion The overthrow of the established government in the Albermarle region of North Carolina by backcountry men in 1677.

Dawes Severalty Act An 1887 law terminating tribal ownership of land and allotting some parcels of land to individual Indians with the remainder opened for white settlement.

Declaration of Sentiments The resolutions passed at the Seneca Falls Convention in 1848 calling for full female equality, including the right to vote.

D-Day June 6, 1944, the day of the first paratroop drops and amphibious landings on the coast of Normandy, France, in the first stage of Operation Overlord during World War II.

Declaratory Act Law passed in 1776 to accompany repeal of the Stamp Act that stated that Parliament had the authority to legislate for the colonies "in all cases whatsoever."

Democrats Political party formed in the 1820s under the leadership of Andrew Jackson; favored states' rights and a limited role for the federal government.

Denmark Vesey's conspiracy The most carefully devised slave revolt in which rebels planned to seize control of Charleston in 1822 and escape to freedom in Haiti, a free black republic, but they were betrayed by other slaves, and seventy-five conspirators were executed.

Department of Homeland Security (DHS) Cabinet-level department created by George Bush to manage U.S. security.

Deregulation Reduction or removal of government regulations and encouragement of direct competition in many important industries and economic sectors.

Desert culture A way of life based on hunting small game and the foraging of plant foods.

Détente (French for "easing of tension") Used to describe the new U.S. relations with China and the Soviet Union in 1972.

Dixiecrat States' Rights Democrats.

Doughboys Nickname for soldiers during the Civil War era who joined the army for money.

Dred Scott decision Supreme Court ruling, in a lawsuit brought by Dred Scott, a slave demanding his freedom based on his residence in a free state, that slaves could not be U.S. citizens and that Congress had no jurisdiction over slavery in the territories.

Economic Recovery Tax Act of 1981 A major revision of the federal income tax system.

Edmunds Act 1882 act that effectively disenfranchised those who believed in or practiced polygamy and threatened them with fines and imprisonment.

Edmunds-Tucker Act 1887 act which destroyed the temporal power of the Mormon Church by confiscating all assets over $50,000 and establishing a federal commission to oversee all elections in the Utah territory.

Emancipation Proclamation Decree announced by President Abraham Lincoln in September 1862 and formally issued on January 1, 1863, freeing slaves in all Confederate states still in rebellion.

Embargo Act Act passed by Congress in 1807 prohibiting American ships from leaving for any foreign port.

Emergency Banking Act 1933 act which gave the president broad discretionary powers over all banking transactions and foreign exchange.

Empresarios Agents who received a land grant from the Spanish or Mexican government in return for organizing settlements.

Enclave Self-contained community.

Encomienda In the Spanish colonies, the grant to a Spanish settler of a certain number of Indian subjects, who would pay him tribute in goods and labor.

Engagés Catholic immigrants to New France.

Enlightenment Intellectual movement stressing the importance of reason and the existence of discoverable natural laws.

Enumerated goods Items produced in the colonies and enumerated in acts of Parliament that could be legally shipped from the colony of origin only to specified locations.

Environmental Protection Agency (EPA) Federal agency created in 1970 to oversee environmental monitoring and cleanup programs.

Equal Pay Act of 1963 Act that made it illegal for employers to pay men and women different wages for the same job.

Era of Good Feelings The period from 1817 to 1823 in which the disappearance of the Federalists enabled the Republicans to govern in a spirit of seemingly nonpartisan harmony.

Espionage Act Law whose vague prohibition against obstructing the nation's war effort was used to crush dissent and criticism during World War I.

Executive Order 9835 Signed by Harry Truman in 1947 to establish a loyalty program requiring federal employees to sign loyalty oaths and undergo security checks.

Federal Emergency Management Agency (FEMA) Agency charged with providing assistance to communities hit by natural disasters.

Federal Reserve Act The 1913 law that revised banking and currency by extending limited government regulation through the creation of the Federal Reserve System.

Federal Trade Commission (FTC) Government agency established in 1914 to provide regulatory oversight of business activity.

Federalists Supporters of the Constitution who favored its ratification.

Female Moral Reform Society Antiprostitution group founded by evangelical women in New York in 1834.

Field Order 15 Order by General William T. Sherman in January 1865 to set aside abandoned land along the southern Atlantic coast for forty-acre grants to freedmen; rescinded by President Andrew Johnson later that year.

Fifteenth Amendment Passed by Congress in 1869, guaranteed the right of American men to vote, regardless of race.

Fireside chat Speeches broadcast nationally over the radio in which President Franklin D. Roosevelt explained complex issues and programs in plain language, as though his listeners were gathered around the fireside with him.

First Continental Congress Meeting of delegates from most of the colonies held in 1774 in response to the Coercive Acts.

First Reconstruction Act 1877 act that divided the South into five military districts subject to martial law.

Forest Efficiency Creation of a comfortable life through the development of a sophisticated knowledge of available resources.

Forest Management Act 1897 act which, along with the National Reclamation Act, set the federal government on the path of large-scale regulatory activities.

Fourteen Points Goals outlined by Woodrow Wilson for war.

Frame of Government William Penn's constitution for Pennsylvania which included a provision allowing for religious freedom.

Free silver Philosophy that the government should expand the money supply by purchasing and coining all the silver offered to it.

Free speech movement Student movement at the University of California, Berkeley, formed in 1964 to protest limitations on political activities on campus.

Freedmen's Bureau Agency established by Congress in March 1865 to provide social, educational, and economic services, advice, and protection to former slaves and destitute whites; lasted seven years.

Freedom Summer Voter registration effort in rural Mississippi organized by black and white civil rights workers in 1964.

French and Indian War The last of the Anglo-French colonial wars (1754–1763) and the first in which fighting began in North America. The war ended with France's defeat. Also known as the **Seven Years' War**.

Fugitive Slave Law Part of the Compromise of 1850 that required the authorities in the North to assist Southern slave catchers and return runaway slaves to their owners.

Gang System The organization and supervision of slave field hands into working teams on Southern plantations.

General Land Revision Act of 1891 Act which gave the president the power to establish forest reserves to protect watersheds against the threats posed by lumbering, overgrazing, and forest fires.

G.I. Bill Legislation in June 1944 that eased the return of veterans into American society by providing educational and employment benefits.

Gilded Age Term applied to late nineteenth-century America that refers to the shallow display and worship of wealth characteristic of that period.

Gospel of wealth Thesis that hard work and perseverance lead to wealth, implying that poverty is a character flaw.

Grandfather clauses Rules that required potential voters to demonstrate that their grandfathers had been eligible to vote; used in some Southern states after 1890 to limit the black electorate.

Grange The National Grange of the Patrons of Husbandry, a national organization of farm owners formed after the Civil War.

Granger laws State laws enacted in the Midwest in the 1870s that regulated rates charged by railroads, grain elevator operators, and other middlemen.

Great Awakening Tremendous religious revival in colonial America striking first in the Middle Colonies and New England in the 1740s and then spreading to the southern colonies.

Great Compromise Plan proposed at the 1787 Constitutional Convention for creating a national bicameral legislature in which all states would be equally represented in the Senate and proportionally represented in the House.

Great Depression The nation's worst economic crisis, extending through the 1930s, producing unprecedented bank failures, unemployment, and industrial and agricultural collapse.

Great Migration The mass movement of African Americans from the rural South to the urban North, spurred especially by new job opportunities during World War I and the 1920s.

Great Sioux War From 1865 to 1867 the Oglala Sioux warrior Red Cloud waged war against the U.S. Army, forcing the U.S. to abandon its forts built on land relinquished to the government by the Sioux.

Great Society Theme of Lyndon Johnson's administration, focusing on poverty, education, and civil rights.

Great Uprising of 1877 Unsuccessful railroad strike to protest wage cuts and the use of federal troops against strikers; the first nationwide work stoppage in American history.

Gulf of Tonkin resolution Request to Congress from President Lyndon Johnson in response to North Vietnamese torpedo boat attacks in which he sought authorization for "all necessary measures" to protect American forces and stop further aggression.

Harlem Renaissance A new African American cultural awareness that flourished in literature, art, and music in the 1920s.

Hepburn Act Act that strengthened the Interstate Commerce Commission (ICC) by authorizing it to set maximum railroad rates and inspect financial records.

Hispanic-American Alliance Organization formed to protect and fight for the rights of Spanish Americans.

Holocaust The systematic murder of millions of European Jews and others deemed undesirable by Nazi Germany.

Homestead Act Law passed by Congress in May 1862 providing homesteads with 160 acres of free land in exchange for improving the land within five years of the grant.

Homestead Act of 1862 1862 act which granted a quarter section (160 acres) of the public domain free to any settler who lived on the land for at least five years and improved it.

Horizontal combination The merger of competitors in the same industry.

House Concurrent Resolution 108 Resolution passed in 1953 that allowed Congress to pass legislation to terminate a specific tribe as a political entity.

House of Burgesses The legislature of colonial Virginia. First organized in 1619, it was the first institution of representative government in the English colonies.

House Un-American Activities Committee (HUAC) Originally intended to ferret out pro-Fascists, it later investigated "un-American propaganda" that attacked constitutional government.

Huguenots French Protestant religious dissenters who planted the first French colonies in North America.

Immigration Act 1921 act setting a maximum of 357,000 new immigrants each year.

Immigration and Nationality Act Act passed in 1965 that abolished national origin quotas and established overall hemisphere quotas.

Imperialism The policy and practice of exploiting nations and peoples for the benefit of an imperial power either directly through military occupation and colonial rule or indirectly through economic domination of resources and markets.

Indentured Servants Individuals who contracted to serve a master for a period of four to seven years in return for payment of the servant's passage to America.

Indian Removal Act President Andrew Jackson's measure that allowed state officials to override federal protection of Native Americans.

Indios Name first used by Christopher Columbus for the Taino people of the Caribbean.

Industrial Revolution Revolution in the means and organization of production.

Intercourse Act Passed in 1790, this law regulated trade and intercourse with the Indian tribes and declared public treaties between the U.S. and Indian nations the only means of obtaining Indian lands.

International Monetary Fund (IMF) International organization established in 1945 to assist nations in maintaining stable currencies.

Internet The system of interconnected computers and servers that allows the exchange of email, posting of Web sites, and other means of instant communication.

Interstate Commerce Commission (ICC) The 1887 law that expanded federal power over business by prohibiting pooling and discriminatory rates by railroads and establishing the first federal regulatory agency, the Interstate Commerce Commission.

Intolerable Acts American term for the Coercive Acts and the Quebec Act.

Irreconcilables Group of U.S. senators adamantly opposed to ratification of the Treaty of Versailles after World War I.

Island-hop The Pacific campaigns of 1944 that were the American naval versions of the Blitzkrieg.

Jay's Treaty Treaty with Britain negotiated in 1794 in which the United States made major concessions to avert a war over the British seizure of American ships.

Jim Crow laws Segregation laws that became widespread in the South during the 1890s.

Judicial review A power implied in the Constitution that gives federal courts the right to review and determine the constitutionality of acts passed by Congress and state legislatures.

Judiciary Act of 1789 Act of Congress that implemented the judiciary clause of the Constitution by establishing the Supreme Court and a system of lower federal courts.

Kansas-Nebraska Act Law passed in 1854 creating the Kansas and Nebraska Territories but leaving the question of slavery open to residents, thereby repealing the Missouri Compromise.

King George's War The third Anglo-French war in North America (1744–1748), part of the European conflict known as the War of the Austrian Succession.

King Philip's War Conflict in New England (1675–1676) between Wampanoags, Narragansetts, and other Indian peoples against English settlers; sparked by English encroachments on native lands.

King William's War The first of a series of colonial struggles between England and France, these conflicts occur principally on the frontiers of northern New England and New York between 1689 and 1697.

Knights of Labor Labor union founded in 1869 that included skilled and unskilled workers irrespective of race or gender.

Know-Nothings Name given to the antiimmigrant party formed from the wreckage of the Whig Party and some disaffected Northern Democrats in 1854.

Kosovo Province of Yugoslavia where the United States and NATO intervened militarily in 1999 to protect ethnic Albanians from expulsion.

Ku Klux Klan Perhaps the most prominent of the vigilante groups that terrorized black people in the South during Reconstruction era, founded by the Confederate veterans in 1866.

Land Ordinance of 1785 Act passed by Congress under the Articles of Confederation that created the grid system of surveys by which all subsequent public land was made available for sale.

Landrum-Griffin Act 1959 act that widened government control over union affairs and further restricted union use of picketing and secondary boycotts during strikes.

League of Nations International organization created by the Versailles Treaty after World War I to ensure world stability.

League of Women Voters League formed in 1920 advocating for women's rights, among them the right for women to serve on juries and equal pay laws.

Lecompton constitution Proslavery draft written in 1857 by Kansas territorial delegates elected under questionable circumstances; it was rejected by two governors, supported by President Buchanan, and decisively defeated by Congress.

Legal Tender Act Act creating a national currency in February 1862.

Lend-Lease Act An arrangement for the transfer of war supplies, including food, machinery, and services to nations whose defense was considered vital to the defense of the United States in Word War II.

Liberal Republicans Disaffected Republicans that emphasized the doctrines of classical economics.

Liberty Bonds Interest-bearing certificates sold by the U.S. government to finance the American World War I effort.

Liberty Party The first antislavery political party, formed in 1840.

Limited Nuclear Test-Ban Treaty Treaty, signed by the United States, Britain, and the Soviet Union, outlawing nuclear testing in the atmosphere, in outer space, and under water.

Lincoln-Douglas debates   Series of debates in the 1858 Illinois senatorial campaign during which Douglas and Lincoln staked out their differing opinions on the issue of slavery.

Loyalists   British colonists who opposed independence from Britain.

Manhattan Project   Scientific research project during World War II specifically devoted to developing the atomic bomb.

Manifest Destiny   Doctrine, first expressed in 1845, that the expansion of white Americans across the continent was inevitable and ordained by God.

Manumission   The freeing of a slave.

Marbury v. *Madison*   Supreme Court decision of 1803 that created the precedent of judicial review by ruling as unconstitutional part of the Judiciary Act of 1789.

March on Washington   Historic gathering of over 250,000 people in Washington D.C. in 1963 marching for jobs and freedom.

Market revolution   The outcome of three interrelated developments: rapid improvements in transportation, commercialization, and industrialization.

Marshall Plan   Secretary of State George C. Marshall's European Recovery Plan of June 5, 1947, committing the United States to help in the rebuilding of post–World War II Europe.

Massachusetts Bay Company   A group of wealthy Puritans who were granted a royal charter in 1629 to settle in Massachusetts Bay.

Mayflower Compact   The first document of self-government in North America.

McCarthyism   Anti-Communist attitudes and actions associated with Senator Joe McCarthy in the early 1950s, including smear tactics and innuendo.

Medicare   Basic medical insurance for the elderly, financed through the federal government; program created in 1965.

Mercantilism   Economic system whereby the government intervenes in the economy for the purpose of increasing national wealth.

Mesoamerica   The region stretching from central Mexico to Central America.

Mexican-American War   War fought between Mexico and the United States between 1846 and 1848 over control of territory in southwest North America.

Middle Passage   The voyage between West Africa and the New World slave colonies.

Militarism   The tendency to see military might as the most important and best tool for the expansion of a nation's power and prestige.

Missouri Compromise   Sectional compromise in Congress in 1820 that admitted Missouri to the Union as a slave state and Maine as a free state and prohibited slavery in the northern Louisiana Purchase territory.

Monroe Doctrine   Declaration by President James Monroe in 1823 that the Western Hemisphere was to be closed off to further European colonization and that the United States would not interfere in the internal affairs of European nations.

Mormonism   The doctrines based on the Book of Mormon, taught by Joseph Smith and the succeeding prophets and leaders of the Church.

Morrill Act of 1862   Act by which "land-grant" colleges acquired space for campuses in return for promising to institute agricultural programs. Also known as Morrill Land Grant Act.

Morrill Land Grant Act   Law passed by Congress in July 1862 awarding proceeds from the sale of public lands to the states for the establishment of agricultural and mechanical colleges.

Morrill Tariff Act   Act that raised tariffs to more than double their prewar rate.

Muckraking   Journalism exposing economic, social, and political evils, so named by Theodore Roosevelt for its "raking the muck" of American society.

Multiculturalism   Movement that emphasized the unique attributes and achievements of formerly marginal groups and recent immigrants.

My Lai Massacre   Killing of twenty-two Vietnamese civilians by U.S. forces during a 1968 search-and-destroy mission.

Nat Turner's Revolt   Uprising of slaves in Southampton County, Virginia, in the summer of 1831 led by Nat Turner that resulted in the death of fifty-five white people.

National Aeronautics and Space Administration (NASA)   Federal agency created in 1958 to manage American space flights and exploration.

National American Woman Suffrage Association (NAWSA)   The organization, formed in 1890, that coordinated the ultimately successful campaign to achieve women's right to vote.

National Association for the Advancement of Colored People   Interracial organization co-founded by W. E. B. Du Bois in 1910 dedicated to restoring African American political and social rights.

National Bank Act   Act prohibiting state banks from issuing their own notes and forcing them to apply for federal charters.

National Industrial Recovery Act   1933 act which was meant to be a systematic plan for economic recovery.

National Labor Relations Act   Act establishing Federal guarantee of right to organize trade unions and collective bargaining.

National Organization for Women (NOW)   Organization founded to campaign for the enforcement of laws related to women's issues.

National Reclamation Act   1902 act which added 1 million acres of irrigated land to the United States.

National Security Council (NSC)   The formal policymaking body for national defense and foreign relations, created in 1947 and consisting of the president, the secretary of defense, the secretary of state, and others appointed by the president.

National Security Council Paper 68 (NSC-68)   Policy statement that committed the United States to a military approach to the Cold War.

Nation of Islam (NOI)   Religious movement among black Americans that emphasizes self-sufficiency, self-help, and separation from white society.

Nativism   Favoring the interests and culture of native-born inhabitants over those of immigrants.

Neutrality Act of 1939   Permitted the sale of arms to Britain, France, and China.

New Deal The economic and political policies of the Roosevelt administration in the 1930s.

New Deal coalition Coalition that included traditional-minded white Southern Democrats, big-city political machines, industrial workers of all races, trade unionists, and many Depression-hit farmers.

New Freedom Woodrow Wilson's 1912 program for limited government intervention in the economy to restore competition by curtailing the restrictive influences of trusts and protective tariffs, thereby providing opportunities for individual achievement.

New Frontier John F. Kennedy's domestic and foreign policy initiatives, designed to reinvigorate sense of national purpose and energy.

New Jersey Plan Proposal of the New Jersey delegation for a strengthened national government in which all states would have an equal representation in a unicameral legislature.

New Lights People who experienced conversion during the revivals of the Great Awakening.

Niagara movement African American group organized in 1905 to promote racial integration, civil and political rights, and equal access to economic opportunity.

Nisei U.S. citizens born of immigrant Japanese parents.

Nonimportation movement A tactical means of putting economic pressure on Britain by refusing to buy its exports to the colonies.

North American Free Trade Agreement (NAFTA) Agreement reached in 1993 by Canada, Mexico, and the United States to substantially reduce barriers to trade.

North Atlantic Treaty Organization (NATO) Organization of ten European countries, Canada, and the United States whom together formed a mutual defense pact in April 1949.

Northwest Ordinance of 1787 Legislation that prohibited slavery in the Northwest Territories and provided the model for the incorporation of future territories into the union as co-equal states.

Nullification A constitutional doctrine holding that a state has a legal right to declare a national law null and void within its borders.

Nullification Crisis Sectional crisis in the early 1830s in which a states' rights party in South Carolina attempted to nullify federal law.

Office of Economic Opportunity (OEO) Federal agency that coordinated many programs of the War on Poverty between 1964 and 1975.

Old Lights Religious faction that condemned emotional enthusiasm as part of the heresy of believing in a personal and direct relationship with God outside the order of the church.

Omaha Act of 1882 Act which allowed the establishment of individual title to tribal lands.

Open Door American policy of seeking equal trade and investment opportunities in foreign nations or regions.

Open shop Factory of business employing workers whether or not they are union members; in practice, such a business usually refuses to hire union members and follows antiunion policies.

Operation Desert Storm U.S. military campaign to force Iraqi forces out of Kuwait.

Operation Overlord United States and British invasion of France in June 1944 during World War II.

Operation Torch The Allied invasion of Axis-held North Africa in 1942.

Oregon Trail Overland trail of more than two thousand miles that carried American settlers from the Midwest to new settlements in Oregon, California, and Utah.

Organization of Petroleum Exporting Countries (OPEC) Cartel of oil-producing nations in Asia, Africa, and Latin America that gained substantial power over the world economy in the mid- to late- 1970s by controlling the production and price of oil.

Panic of 1857 Banking crisis that caused a credit crunch in the North; it was less severe in the South, where high cotton prices spurred a quick recovery.

Pan-Indian military resistance movement Movement calling for the political and cultural unification of Indian tribes in the late eighteenth and early nineteenth centuries.

Patriots British colonists who favored independence from Britain.

Pendleton Civil Service Reform Act A law of 1883 that reformed the spoils system by prohibiting government workers from making political contributions and creating the Civil Service Commission to oversee their appointment on the basis of merit rather than politics.

Peninsular campaign Union offensive led by McClellan with the objective of capturing Richmond.

Pentagon Papers Classified Defense Department documents on the history of the United States' involvement in Vietnam, prepared in 1968 and leaked to the press in 1971.

Pequot War Conflict between English settlers and Pequot Indians over control of land and trade in eastern Connecticut.

Persian Gulf War War initiated by President Bush in response to Iraq's invasion of Kuwait.

Pilgrims Settlers of Plymouth Colony, who viewed themselves as spiritual wanderers.

Plan of Union Plan put forward by Benjamin Franklin in 1754 calling for an intercolonial union to manage defense and Indian affairs. The plan was rejected by participants at the Albany Congress.

Plessy* v. *Ferguson Supreme Court decision holding that Louisiana's railroad segregation law did not violate the Constitution as long as the railroads or the state provided equal accommodations.

Popular sovereignty A solution to the slavery crisis suggested by Michigan senator Lewis Cass by which territorial residents, not Congress, would decide slavery's fate.

Populism A mass movement of the 1890s formed on the basis of the Southern Farmers' Alliance and other reform organizations.

Powhatan Confederacy A village of communities of the Chesapeake united under Chief Wahunsonacook, who was called King Powhatan by the colonists.

Preparedness Military buildup in preparation for possible U.S. participation in World War I.

Progressivism A national movement focused on a variety of reform initiatives, including ending corruption, a more business like approach to government, and legislative responses to industrial excess.

Prohibition   A ban on the production, sale, and consumption of liquor, achieved temporarily through state laws and the Eighteenth Amendment.

Proposition 187   California legislation adopted by popular vote in California in 1994, which cuts off state-funded health and education benefits to undocumented or illegal immigrants.

Proprietary colony   A colony created when the English monarch granted a huge tract of land to an individual or group of individuals, who became "lords proprietor."

Protective association   Organizations formed by mine owners in response to the formation of labor unions.

Protestant Reformation   Martin Luther's challenge to the Catholic Church, initiated in 1517, calling for a return to what he understood to be the purer practices and beliefs of the early church.

Protestants   All European supporters of religious reform under Charles V's Holy Roman Empire.

Pueblo Revolt   Rebellion in 1680 of Pueblo Indians in New Mexico against their Spanish overlords.

Pure Food and Drug Act   Act that established the Food and Drug Administration (FDA), which tested and approved drugs before they went on the market.

Puritanism   Movement to purify and reform the English Church.

Puritans   Individuals who believed that Queen Elizabeth's reforms of the Church of England had not gone far enough in improving the church. Puritans led the settlement of Massachusetts Bay Colony.

Putting-out system   Production of goods in private homes under the supervision of a merchant who "put out" the raw materials, paid a certain sum per finished piece, and sold the completed item to a distant market.

Quakers   Members of the Society of Friends, a radical religious group that arose in the mid-seventeenth century. Quakers rejected formal theology, focusing instead on the Holy Spirit that dwelt within them.

Quartering Act   Acts of Parliament requiring colonial legislatures to provide supplies and quarters for the troops stationed in America.

Quasi-War   Undeclared naval war of 1797 to 1800 between the United States and France.

Quebec Act   Law passed by Parliament in 1774 that provided an appointed government for Canada, enlarged the boundaries of Quebec, and confirmed the privileges of the Catholic Church.

Queen Anne's War   American phase (1702–1713) of Europe's War of the Spanish Succession.

Radical Republicans   A shifting group of Republican congressmen, usually a substantial minority, who favored the abolition of slavery from the beginning of the Civil War and later advocated harsh treatment of the defeated South.

Rancherias   Dispersed settlements of Indian farmers in the Southwest.

Reconquista   The long struggle (ending in 1492) during which Spanish Christians reconquered the Iberian peninsula from Muslim occupiers.

Red Power   Term for pan-Indian identity.

Red Scare   Post–World War I public hysteria over Bolshevik influence in the United States directed against labor activism, radical dissenters, and some ethnic groups.

Referendum   Submission of a law, proposed or already in effect, to a direct popular vote for approval or rejection.

Renaissance   The intellectual and artistic flowering in Europe during the fourteenth, fifteenth, and sixteenth centuries sparked by a revival of interest in classical antiquity.

Republican Party   Party that emerged in the 1850s in the aftermath of the bitter controversy over the Kansas-Nebraska Act, consisting of former Whigs, some Northern Democrats, and many Know-Nothings.

Republicanism   A complex, changing body of ideas, values, and assumptions that influenced American political behavior during the eighteenth and nineteenth centuries.

Roe v. Wade   U.S. Supreme Court decision (1973) that disallowed state laws prohibiting abortion during the first three months (trimester) of pregnancy and established guidelines for abortion in the second and third trimesters.

Roosevelt Corollary   President Theodore Roosevelt's policy asserting U.S. authority to intervene in the affairs of Latin American nations; an expansion of the Monroe Doctrine.

Royal Proclamation of 1763   Royal proclamation declaring the trans-Appalachian region to be "Indian Country."

Rush-Bagot Treaty of 1817   Treaty between the United States and Britain that effectively demilitarized the Great Lakes by sharply limiting the number of ships each power could station on them.

Sabbatarianism   Reform movement that aimed to prevent business on Sundays.

Sand Creek Massacre   The near annihilation in 1864 of Black Kettle's Cheyenne band by Colorado troops under Colonel John Chivington's orders to "kill and scalp all, big and little."

Santa Fé Trail   The 900-mile trail opened by American merchants for trading purposes following Mexico's liberalization of the formerly restrictive trading policies of Spain.

Scalawags   Southern whites, mainly small landowning farmers and well-off merchants and planters, who supported the Southern Republican party during Reconstruction.

Second American Party System   The basic pattern of American politics of two parties, each with appeal among voters of all social voters and in all sections of the country.

Second Great Awakening   Religious revival among black and white Southerners in the 1790s.

Sedition Act   An act passed by Congress in 1798 that provided fines for anyone convicted writing, publishing, or speaking out against the government or its officers.

Segregation   A system of racial control that separated the races, initially by custom but increasingly by law during and after Reconstruction.

Selective Service Act   The law establishing the military draft for World War I.

Self-determination   The right of a people or a nation to decide on its own political allegiance or form of government without external influence.

Seneca Falls Convention   The first convention for women's equality in legal rights, held in upstate New York in 1848.

Separatists   Members of an offshoot branch of Puritanism. Separatists believed that the Church of England was too corrupt to be reformed and hence were convinced they must "separate" from it to save their souls.

Seven Years' War   War fought in Europe, North America, and India between 1756 and 1753, pitting France and its allies against Great Britain and its allies.

Shakers   The followers of Mother Ann Lee, who preached a religion of strict celibacy and communal living.

Sharecropping   Labor system that evolved during and after Reconstruction whereby landowners furnished laborers with a house, farm animals, and tools and advanced credit in exchange for a share of the laborers' crop.

Sheppard-Towner Act   The first federal social welfare law, passed in 1921, providing federal funds for infant and maternity care.

Sherman Antitrust Act   The first federal antitrust measure, passed in 1890; sought to promote economic competition by prohibiting business combinations in restraint of trade or commerce.

Sherman Silver Purchase Act   1890 act which directed the Treasury to increase the amount of currency coined from silver mined in the West and also permitted the U.S. government to print paper currency backed by the silver.

Silicon Valley   The region of California including San Jose and San Francisco that holds the nation's greatest concentration of electronics firms.

Sixteenth Amendment   Authorized a federal income tax.

Slaughterhouse cases   Group of cases resulting in one sweeping decision by the U.S. Supreme Court in 1873 that contradicted the intent of the Fourteenth Amendment by decreeing that most citizenship rights remained under state, not federal, control.

Slave codes   A series of laws passed mainly in the Southern colonies in the late seventeenth and early eighteenth centuries to defend the status of slaves and codify the denial of basic civil rights to them.

Social Darwinism   The application of Charles Darwin's theory of biological evolution to society, holding that the fittest and wealthiest survive, the weak and the poor perish, and government action is unable to alter this "natural" process.

Social Security Act of 1935   Act establishing federal old-age pensions and unemployment insurance.

Sons of Liberty   Secret organizations in the colonies formed to oppose the Stamp Act.

Southern Christian Leadership Conference (SCLC)   Black civil rights organization founded in 1957 by Martin Luther King Jr., and other clergy.

Southern Farmers' Alliance   The largest of several organizations that formed in the post-Reconstruction South to advance the interests of beleaguered small farmers.

Southern Manifesto   A document signed by 101 members of Congress from Southern states in 1956 that argued that the Supreme Court's decision in *Brown* v. *Board of Education of Topeka* itself contradicted the Constitution.

Specie Circular   Proclamation issued by President Andrew Jackson in 1836 stipulating that only gold or silver could be used as payment for public land.

Stamp Act   Law passed by Parliament in 1765 to raise revenue in America by requiring taxed, stamped paper for legal documents, publications, and playing cards.

States' Rights   Favoring the rights of individual states over rights claimed by the national government.

Stono Rebellion   One of the largest and most violent slave uprisings during the Colonial Period that occurred in Stono, South Carolina.

Strategic Arms Limitation Treaty   Treaty signed in 1972 by the United States and the Soviet Union to slow the nuclear arms race.

Strategic Defense Initiative (SDI)   President Reagan's program, announced in 1983, to defend the United States against nuclear missile attack with untested weapons systems and sophisticated technologies.

Student Nonviolent Coordinating Committee (SNCC)   Black civil rights organization founded in 1960 and drawing heavily on younger activists and college students.

Students for a Democratic Society (SDS)   The leading student organization of the New Left of the early and mid-1960s.

Suffrage   The right to vote in a political election.

Sugar Act   Law passed in 1764 to raise revenue in the American colonies. It lowered the duty from 6 pence to 3 pence per gallon on foreign molasses imported into the colonies and increased the restrictions on colonial commerce.

Sunbelt   The states of the American South and Southwest.

Taft-Hartley Act   Federal legislation of 1947 that substantially limited the tools available to labor unions in labor-management disputes.

Tammany Society   A fraternal organization of artisans begun in the 1780s that evolved into a key organization of the new mass politics in New York City.

Tariff of 1816   A tax imposed by Congress on imported goods.

Tea Act   Act of Parliament that permitted the East India Company to sell through agents in America without paying the duty customarily collected in Britain, thus reducing the retail price.

Tejanos   Persons of Spanish or Mexican descent born in Texas.

Temperance   Reform movement originating in the 1820s that sought to eliminate the consumption of alcohol.

Temperance groups   Groups dedicated to reducing the sale and consumption of alcohol.

Tenements   Four- to six-story residential dwellings, once common in New York, built on tiny lots without regard to providing ventilation or light.

Tennessee Valley Authority (TVA)   Federal regional planning agency established to promote conservation, produce electric power, and encourage economic development in seven Southern states.

Tenure of Office Act   Act stipulating that any officeholder appointed by the president with the Senate's advice and consent could not be removed until the Senate had approved a successor.

Thirteenth Amendment   Constitutional amendment ratified in 1865 that freed all slaves throughout the United States.

Tories   A derisive term applied to Loyalists in America who supported the king and Parliament just before and during the American Revolution.

Townshend Revenue Acts   Act of Parliament, passed in 1767, imposing duties on colonial tea, lead, paint, paper, and glass.

Trail of Broken Treaties   1972 event staged by the American Indian Movement (AIM) that culminated in a week-long occupation of the Bureau of Indian Affairs in Washington, D.C.

Trail of Tears   The forced march in 1838 of the Cherokee Indians from their homelands in Georgia to the Indian Territory in the West.

Treaty of Fort Laramie   The treaty acknowledging U.S. defeat in the Great Sioux War in 1868 and supposedly guaranteeing the Sioux perpetual land and hunting rights in South Dakota, Wyoming, and Montana.

Treaty of Ghent   Treaty signed in December 1814 between the United States and Britain that ended the War of 1812.

Treaty of Greenville   Treaty of 1795 in which Native Americans in the Old Northwest were forced to cede most of the present state of Ohio to the United States.

Treaty of Paris   The formal end to British hostilities against France and Spain in February 1763.

Truman Doctrine   President Harry Truman's statement in 1947 that the United States should assist other nations that were facing external pressure or internal revolution.

Underwood-Simmons Act of 1913   Reform law that lowered tariff rates and levied the first regular federal income tax.

Union League   Republican party organizations in Northern cities that became an important organizing device among freedmen in Southern cities after 1865.

USA Patriot Act   Federal legislation adopted in 2001 in response to the terrorist attacks on September 11 to facilitate anti-terror actions by federal law enforcement and intelligence agencies.

Versailles Treaty   The treaty ending World War I and creating the League of Nations.

Vertical integration   The consolidation of numerous production functions, from the extraction of the raw materials to the distribution and marketing of the finished products, under the direction of one firm.

Virginia Company   A group of London investors who sent ships to Chesapeake Bay in 1607.

Virginia Plan   Proposal calling for a national legislature in which the states would be represented according to population.

Virtual representation   The notion that parliamentary members represented the interests of the nation as a whole, not those of the particular district that elected them.

Volstead Act   The 1920 law defining the liquor forbidden under the Eighteenth Amendment and giving enforcement responsibilities to the Prohibition Bureau of the Department of the Treasury.

Voting Rights Act   Legislation in 1965 that overturned a variety of practices by which states systematically denied voter registration to minorities.

War Democrats   Those from the North and the border states who broke with the Democratic Party and supported the Abraham Lincoln's military policies during the Civil War.

War Hawks   Members of Congress, predominantly from the South and West, who aggressively pushed for a war against Britain after their election in 1810.

War Industries Board (WIB)   The federal agency that reorganized industry for maximum efficiency and productivity during World War I.

War of 1812   War fought between the United States and Britain from June 1812 to January 1815 largely over British restrictions on American shipping.

War on Drugs   A paramilitary operation to halt drug trafficking in the United States.

War on Poverty   Set of programs introduced by Lyndon Johnson between 1963 and 1966 designed to break the cycle of poverty by providing funds for job training, community development, nutrition, and supplementary education.

War Powers Act   Gave the U.S. president the power to reorganize the federal government and create new agencies; to establish programs censoring news, information, and abridging civil liberties; to seize foreign-owned property; and award government contracts without bidding.

Watergate   A complex scandal involving attempts to cover up illegal actions taken by administration officials and leading to the resignation of President Richard Nixon in 1974.

Welfare capitalism   A paternalistic system of labor relations emphasizing management responsibility for employee well-being.

Welfare Reform Act   Act passed by Congress in 1996 that abolished the Aids to Families with Dependent Children (AFDC) welfare program.

Whigs   The name used by advocates of colonial resistance to British measures during the 1760s and 1770s.

Whiskey Rebellion   Armed uprising in 1794 by farmers in western Pennsylvania who attempted to prevent the collection of the excise tax on whiskey.

Wilmot Proviso   The amendment offered by Pennsylvania Democrat David Wilmot in 1846 which stipulated that "as an express and fundamental condition to the acquisition of any territory from the Republic of Mexico ... neither slavery nor involuntary servitude shall ever exist in any part of said territory."

Wobblies   Popular name for the members of the Industrial Workers of the World (IWW).

Woman's Christian Temperance Union (WCTU)   Women's organization whose members visited schools to educate children about the evils of alcohol, addressed prisoners, and blanketed men's meetings with literature.

Women's Educational and Industrial Union   Boston organization offering classes to wage-earning women.

World Trade Organization (WTO)   International organization that sets standards and practices for global trade, and the focus of international protests over world economic policy in the late 1990s.

XYZ Affair   Diplomatic incident in 1798 in which Americans were outraged by the demand of the French for a bribe as a condition for negotiating with American diplomats.

Yalta Conference   Meeting of U.S. President Franklin Roosevelt, British Prime Minister Winston Churchill, and Soviet Premier Joseph Stalin held in February 1945 to plan the final stages of World War II and postwar arrangements.

Yeoman   Independent farmers of the South, most of whom lived on family-sized farms.

Text, Tables, Maps and Figures

Chapter 4 Figure 4.1: Reproduced from *The American Colonies: From Settlement to Independence.* Copyright © R.C. Simmons 1976 by permission of PFD (www.pfd.co.uk) on behalf of Professor Richard Simmons. **Figure 4.2:** from TIME ON THE CROSS: THE ECONOMICS OF AMERICAN NEGRO SLAVERY by Robert William Fogel and Stanley L. Engerman. Copyright © 1974 by Robert William Fogel and Stanley L. Engerman. Used by permission of W.W. Norton & Company, Inc.

Chapter 8 Figure 8.1: Used by permission of American Antiquarian Society.

Chapter 9 Figure 9.2: from AMERICA MOVES WEST 5/E by Riegel R. 1971. Reprinted with permission of Wadsworth, a division of Thomson Learning: www.thomsonrights.com. Fax 800 730-2215.

Chapter 11 Figure 11.1: From RIGHT TO VOTE by ALEXANDER KEYSSAR. Reprinted by permission of BASIC BOOKS, a member of Perseus Books Group.

Chapter 12 Figure 12.1: Reprinted from Thomas Dublin: *Transforming Women's Work: New England Lives in the Industrial Revolution.* Copyright © 1994 by Thomas Dublin. Used by permission of the publisher, Cornell University Press.

Chapter 13 Figure 13.1: Reprinted by permission of the estate of Robert Ernst. **Figure 13.2:** From THE ALCOHOLIC REPUBLIC: AN AMERICAN TRADITION by W.J. Rarabaugh, copyright © 1979 by Oxford University Press, Inc. Used by permission of Oxford University Press, Inc. **Map 13.2:** Reprinted from Whitney R. Cross, *The Burned-Over District: The Social and Intellectual History of Enthusiastic Religion in Western New York 1800–1850.* Copyright © 1950 by Cornell University. Used with permission of the publisher, Cornell University Press.

Chapter 14 Figure 14.1: From *The Plains Across: The Overland Emigrants and the Trans-Mississippi West, 1840–60.* Copyright 1979 by the Board of Trustees of the University of Illinois. Used

with permission of the University of Illinois Press. **Map 14.7:** From *Historical Atlas of California,* by Warren A. Beck and Ynez D. Haase. Copyright © 1974 by The University of Oklahoma Press, Norman. Reprinted by permission of the publisher. All rights reserved.

Chapter 18 Map 18.1: From *Historical Atlas of Oklahoma, 3rd edition,* by John W. Morris, Charles R. Goins and Edwin C. McReynolds. Copyright © 1965, 1976, 1986 by the University of Oklahoma Press, Norman. Reprinted by permission of the publisher. All rights reserved. **Map 18.4:** "The Geography of the American West, 1847–1964", Donald W. Meinig from *ANNA: Annals of the Association of American Geographers,* vol. 55, issue 2. Reprinted by permission of Blackwell Publishers. www.blackwell-synergy.com

Chapter 19 Table 19.1: From THE GILDED AGE edited by Charles W. Calhown. © 1996. Reprinted by permission of Rowman & Littlefield. **Map 19.2:** From *Historical Atlas of the United States,* 1st edition by LORD. © 1962. Reprinted with permission of Wadsworth, a division of Thomson Learning: www.thomsonrights.com. Fax: 800 730-2215.

Chapter 22 Map 22.3: From *ATLAS OF AMERICAN WOMEN,* by Barbara C. Shortridge. © 1987. Reprinted by permission of Thomson Learning: www.thomsonrights.com. Fax 800 730-2215.

Chapter 28 Page 821: Reprinted by arrangement with the Estate of Martin Luther King Jr., c/o Writers House for the proprietor New York, NY. *Copyright 1963 Martin Luther King, Jr., copyright renewed 1991 Coretta Scott King.*

Chapter 29 Figure 29.4: From THE GALLUP POLL, 1835–1971 by George Gallup, Copyright © 1972 by the American Institute of Public Opinion. Used by permission of Random House.

Chapter 1 Image Key: **Page xlviii:** A. Cahokia Mounds State Historic Site, painting by Michael Hampshire; **Page 1:** B. Service Historique de la Marine, Vincennes, France/Lauros/Giraudon/Bridgeman Art Library; C. Service Historique de la Marine, Vincennes, France/ Lauros/Giraudon/Bridgeman Art Library; D. Courtesy of the Denver Museum of Nature and Science; E. David Hiser/David Hiser Photography; F. Rota/Neg. No. 324281, Photographed by Rota, Engraving by DeBry. American Museum of Natural History Library; **Page xlviii:** G. © Warren Morgan/CORBIS; **Page 3:** James Chatters/ James Chatters/Agence France Presse/Getty Images; **Page 5:** © Warren Morgan/CORBIS; **Page 11:** David Muench/CORBIS-NY; **Page 12:** Tony Linck/SuperStock, Inc.; **Page 15:** Bayerische Staatsbibliothek Munchen. Rar. 5k.

Chapter 2 Image Key: **Page 24:** A. © Hulton-Deutsch Collection/ CORBIS; Image in lower left; Stapleton Collection/© Stapleton Collection/CORBIS; **Page 25:** C. Robert Frerck/© Robert Frerck/ Odyssey/Chicago; D. Getty Images Inc. - Hulton Archive Photos; E. Library of Congress; F. The Granger Collection; Image in lower right; Stapleton Collection/© Stapleton Collection/CORBIS; **Page 28:** October, from Tres Riches Heures du Duc de Berry. Musee Conde, Chantilly/Bridgeman-Giraudon, Art Resource, NY; **Page 31:** Beinecke Rare Book and Manuscript Library, Yale University; **Page 33:** Photo Courtesy of the Edward E. Ayer Collection, The Newberry Library, Chicago; **Page 34:** The Granger Collection; **Page 41:** John White (1570–93), "Woman and Child of Pomeiooc." Watercolor. British Museum, London. The Bridgeman Art Library International Ltd.

Chapter 3 Image Key: **Page 46:** A. Dorling Kindersley/© Dorling Kindersley; B. Beinecke Rare Book and Manuscript Library, Yale University; C. Getty Images, Inc. - Photodisc; **Page 47:** D. Bettmann/ © Bettmann/CORBIS; E. Courtesy of Pilgrim Hall Museum, Plymouth, Massachusetts; F. © Bettmann/CORBIS; G. Jonathan Carver, A TREATISE ON THE CULTURE OF THE TOBACCO PLANT (London, 1779), Manuscripts and Rare Book Division, Swem Library, College of William and Mary; H. Courtesy, American Antiquarian Society; I. New Amsterdam, 1650-53. The Hague Facsimile. Museum of the City of New York. The J. Clarence Davies Collection 34.100.29; J. Courtesy of the John Carter Brown Library at Brown University; **Page 49:** Kevin Fleming/Corbis/Bettmann; **Page 51:** Courtesy of the Library of Congress; **Page 52:** From Samuel de Champlain, Les Voyages, Paris, 1613. Illustration opp. pg. 232. Rare Books Division, The New York Public Library, Astor Lenox and Tilden Foundations. The New York Public Library/Art Resource, NY; **Page 53:** Getty Images Inc. - Hulton Archive Photos; **Page 55:** The Granger Collection; **Page 58:** Courtesy, American Antiquarian Society; **Page 60:** Courtesy of The John Carter Brown Library, at Brown University; **Page 63:** Courtesy of The Historical Society of Pennsylvania Collection, Atwater Kent Museum of Philadelphia; **Page 65:** Courtesy of the John Carter Brown Library at Brown University; **Page 70:** Courtesy of the Pilgrim Hall Museum, Plymouth, Massachusetts; **Page 71:** Eliot Elisofon/Getty Images/Time Life Pictures.

Chapter 4 Image Key: **Page 72:** A. Courtesy of The John Carter Brown Library, at Brown University; B. Courtesy of the Library of Congress; **Page 73:** C. Dorling Kindersley/© Dorling Kindersley, Courtesy of the Wilberforce House Museum, Hull; D. British Library; E. Courtesy, American Antiquarian Society; F. John F. Watson, "Annals of Philadelphia," being a collection of memoirs, anecdotes, & incidents of Philadelphia. The London Coffee House. The Library Company of Philadelphia; G. Abby Aldrich Rockefeller Folk Art Museum, Colonial Williamsburg Foundation, VA; H. Samuel Scott (c. 1702–1772) "Old East India Wharf at London Bridge" (CT2825) © Victoria & Albert Museum, London/Art Resource, NY; **Page 75:** Library of Congress; **Page 76:** Beinecke Rare Book and Manuscript Library, Yale University; **Page 80:** Bibliotheque de L'Arsenal, Paris, France/The Bridgeman Art Library; **Page 81:** (top left) The Granger Collection, New York;

(bottom right) The Granger Collection, New York; **Page 87:** Courtesy of the Massachusetts Historical Society, Boston. **Page 97:** Virginia Historical Society, Richmond, Virginia.

Chapter 5 Image Key: **Page 100:** A. Liz McAulay/Liz McAulay © Dorling Kindersley, Courtesy of the Worthing Museum and Art Gallery; B. MARK SEXTON/The Granger Collection; C. David Murray/David Murray © Dorling Kindersley; D. Frank Greenaway/Frank Greenaway © Dorling Kindersley, Courtesy of the Natural History Museum, London; E. © Judith Miller/Dorling Kindersley/Sara Covelli; **Page 101:** G. © National Maritime Museum, London; H. Library of Congress; I. North Wind Picture Archives; J. John Wollaston, "George Whitefield," ca. 1770. National Portrait Gallery, London; **Page 106:** Laurie Platt Winfrey, Inc.; **Page 107:** Jack W. Dykinga/Jack Dykinga Photography; **Page 109:** EROS Data Center, U.S. Geological Survey; **Page 111:** Beinecke Rare Book and Manuscript Library, Yale University; **Page 114:** (left) The Granger Collection; (right) The Granger Collection; **Page 118:** "Human Races (Las Castas)", 18th century, oil on canvas, 1.04 × 1.48 m. Museo Nacional del Virreinato, Tepotzotlan, Mexico. Schalkwijk/Art Resource, NY.

Chapter 6 Image Key: **Page 126:** A. (top/bottom left) Getty Images, Inc.; B. Steve Gorton/Steve Gorton © Dorling Kindersley; **Page 127:** A. (top/bottom right) Dave King/Dave King © Dorling Kindersley; C. The Granger Collection, New York; **Page 127:** D. Colonial Williamsburg Foundation; E. © Judith Miller/Dorling Kindersley/ Sloan's; F. Library of Congress; G. © Christie's Images Inc. 2004; H. © Bettmann/CORBIS; I. Joseph Sohm/© Joseph Sohm; Visions of America/CORBIS; **Page 134:** National Museum of the American Indian/Smithsonian Institution; **Page 136:** Art Resource/The New York Public Library; **Page 141:** Library of Congress; **Page 143:** © Christie's Images Inc. 2004; **Page 145:** National Archives and Records Administration; **Page 147:** The New York Public Library, Prints Division, Stokes Collection; **Page 149:** The Granger Collection; **Page 150:** The Granger Collection.

Chapter 7 Image Key: **Page 154:** A. Courtesy of the Library of Congress; B. Getty Images Inc. - Hulton Archive Photos; C. © COR-BIS; **Page 155:** D. DAVID BOHL/Photograph courtesy of the Concord Museum, Concord, MA and the archives of the Lexington Historical Society, Lexington, MA Photograph by David Bohl; E. Anne S.K. Brown Military Collection, John Hay Library, Brown University; F. Benjamin West, 1783 "American Commissioners of Preliminary Negotiations". Courtesy, Winterthur Museum; G. Corbis/Bettmann; **Page 154:** H. Art Resource/Yale University Art Gallery/John Trumbull (American 1756–1843), "The Surrender of Lord Cornwallis at Yorktown, 19 October 1781", 1787-c. 1828. Oil on canvas, 53.3 × 77.8 × 1.9 cm (21 × 30 5/8 × 3/4 in.) Art Resource; **Page 157:** Anne S.K. Brown Military Collection, John Hay Library, Brown University; **Page 158:** The Granger Collection; **Page 162:** Gilbert Stuart, "The Mohawk Chief Joseph Brant," 1786. Oil on canvas, 30 × 25 in. Fenimore Art Museum, Cooperstown, New York; **Page 167:** The Granger Collection, New York; **Page 169:** Library of Congress; **Page 172:** © CORBIS; **Page 176:** Corbis/Bettmann; **Page 177:** © Bettmann/CORBIS.

Chapter 8 Image Key: **Page 180:** A. Library of Congress; B. Courtesy of The Historical Society of Pennsylvania Collection, Atwater Kent Museum of Philadelphia; C. © Bettmann/CORBIS; **Page 181:** D. Gallery of the Republic; E. Getty Images Inc. - Hulton Archive Photos; F. Francis Kemmelmeyer, "General George Washington Reviewing the Western Army at Fort Cumberland the 18th of October 1794," after 1794. Oil on paper backed with linen, 18 1/8 × 23 1/8. Courtesy of Winterthur Museum; G. "White House Historical Association (White House Collection)" (25); H. The Library Company of Philadelphia; **Page 185:** Print and Picture Collection, The Free Library of Philadelphia; **Page 189:** (left) Smithsonian Institution, NNC, Douglas Mudd; (right) Smithsonian Institution, NNC, Douglas

Mudd; **Page 190:** John Trumbull (1756–1843), "Portrait of Alexander Hamilton" (1755/57– 1804), statesman, 1806, oil on canvas, 76.2 × 61 cm (20 × 24 in). Gift of Henry Cabot Lodge. National Portrait Gallery, Smithsonian Institution, Washington, DC/Art Resource, NY; **Page 195:** Beinecke Rare Book and Manuscript Library, Yale University; **Page 199:** The Granger Collection.

Chapter 9 Image Key: **Page 206:** A. Collection of The New-York Historical Society; B. From the collection of Mac G. and Janelle C. Morris; C. Getty Images Inc. - Hulton Archive Photos; **Page 207:** D. National Museum of American History, Smithsonian Institution; E. © Museum of the City of New York/CORBIS; F. Library of Congress; G. John Wesley Jarvis, "Black Hawk and His Son Whirling Thunder," 1833. Oil on canvas, 23 1/2 × 30 in. (60.3 × 76 cm.) Gilcrease Museum, Tulsa, Oklahoma. 0126.1007; H. Bettmann/© Bettmann/CORBIS; I. Getty Images Inc. - Hulton Archive Photos; **Page 211:** Illustration by Kittlitz, F. H. v. (Friedrich Heinrich von) in Litke, F. P. (Fedor Petrovich),Voyage autour du monde, exécuté par ordre de Sa Majesté l'empereur Nicolas 1er, sur la corvette le Séniavine, dans les années 1826, 1827, 1828. [Rare Book C0024] Alaska and Polar Regions Collections, Elmer E. Rasmuson Library, University of Alaska Fairbanks. **Page 213:** National Museum of American History, Smithsonian Institution, - Photo No. 73–11287; **Page 215:** (left) Courtesy of the Library of Congress; (right) Library of Congress; **Page 221:** (left) The Granger Collection, New York; **Page 226:** Courtesy of the Bostonian Society/Old State House; **Page 230:** (top) Courtesy of the Library of Congress; (bottom) Courtesy of the Library of Congress.

Chapter 10 Image Key: **Page 238:** A: Tina Chambers, Dorling Kindersley Media Library; B. Corbis/Bettmann; C. The Granger Collection; D. Dorling Kindersley/Wilberforce House © Hull Museums; E. Library of Congress; **Page 239:** F. Dorling Kindersley/© Dorling Kindersley; G. "Returning from the Cotton Fields in South Carolina", ca. 1860, stereograph by Barbard, negative number 47843. © Collection of The New-York Historical Society; H. Library of Congress; I. Corbis/Bettmann; J. Carl G. von Iwonski, Block House, New Braunfels. Daughters of the Republic of Texas Library. Yanaguana Society Collection; K. James Cameron (1817–1882), "Colonel and Mrs. James A. Whiteside, Son Charles and Servants", oil on canvas; c. 1858–1859. Hunter Museum of Art, Chattanooga, Tennessee, Gift of Mr. and Mrs. Thomas B. Whiteside. Hunter Museum of American Art, Chattanooga, Tennessee; L. Courtesy of the Library of Congress; **Page 243:** Copyright © The Granger Collection, New York/The Granger Collection; **Page 246:** Culver Pictures, Inc.; **Page 252:** (top) The Granger Collection; (bottom) Library of Congress; **Page 253:** (left) American Numismatic Society of New York; (right) American Numismatic Society of New York; **Page 254:** Carl G. von Iwonski, Block House, New Braunfels. Daughters of the Republic of Texas Library. Yanaguana Society Collection; **Page 259:** Courtesy of the Library of Congress.

Chapter 11 Image Key: **Page 266:** A. National Numismatic Collection/Smithsonian Institution; B. © Bettmann/CORBIS; C. Courtesy, American Antiquarian Society; **Page 267:** D. C Squared Studios/Getty Images, Inc. - Photodisc; E. Thomas Sully, "General Andrew Jackson," 1845, Oil on Canvas. The Corcoran Gallery of Art, Washington, DC, Gift of William Wilson Corcoran. 69.49; F. Courtesy of the Library of Congress; G. Courtesy of the Library of Congress; H. National Museum of American History, Smithsonian Institution; **Page 275:** Courtesy of the Library of Congress; **Page 277:** Robert Cruikshank. "The President's Levee, or all Creation going to the White House." Courtesy of the Library of Congress; **Page 278:** (left) The Granger Collection, New York; (right) The Granger Collection; **Page 283:** Courtesy of the Library of Congress; **Page 285:** Library of Congress; **Page 288:** Collection of the Boston Athenaeum; **Page 292:** Courtesy of the Library of Congress; **Page 293:** The Granger Collection, New York.

Chapter 12 Image Key: **Page 294:** A. Courtesy of the Library of Congress; C. Art Resource/The New York Public Library, Research Libraries; **Page 295:** D. Rob Huntley/ Museum of American Textile History/Rob Huntley/Lightstream; E. The Granger Collection; F. Lowell Historical Society; G. Chicago Historical Museum; H. RON CHAPPLE/Getty Images, Inc. - Taxi; **Page 299:** The Granger Collection; **Page 302:** Library of Congress; **Page 305:** Chicago Historical Society; **Page 307:** Lee Snider/ Corbis/Bettmann; **Page 309:** (left) James L. Amos/National Geographic Image Collection; (right) Joseph H. Bailey/National Geographic Image Collection; **Page 311:** Courtesy American Antiquarian Society; **Page 312:** Baker Library, Harvard Business School; **Page 317:** Library of Congress; **Page 320:** Library of Congress; **Page 321:** (top) From the Collection of the New Bedford Whaling Museum; (center) Getty Images Inc. - Hulton Archive Photos; (bottom) Courtesy of the Library of Congress.

Chapter 13 Image Key: **Page 322:** A. Map of Proposed route of Erie Canal, 1811 Negative Number 420757, © Collection of the New-York Historical Society, New York City; B. The Granger Collection, New York; C. The Granger Collection; **Page 323:** D. © Bettmann/CORBIS; E. The Granger Collection; F. "Seabury Champlin's June 3, 1791 Certificate of Membership in NY Mechanic Society", Abraham Godwin, print. Courtesy, Winterthur Museum; G. Getty Images Inc. - Hulton Archive Photos; H. Frederick Douglass (1817?–95). Oil on canvas, c1844, attr. to E. Hammond. The Granger Collection; **Page 328:** Chicago Historical Society; **Page 330:** The Granger Collection; **Page 332:** The Bridgeman Art Library International; **Page 333:** "Irish Emigrant" in "Diogenes, Hys Lantern," August 23, 1852, p. 158. **Page 335:** Frank and Marie-Therese Wood Print Collections, The Picture Bank; **Page 340:** Library of Congress; **Page 344:** (left) Courtesy of the Library of Congress; (right) Library of Congress; **Page 345:** The Granger Collection; **Page 347:** Lynn Museum.

Chapter 14 Image Key: **Page 350:** A. Geoff Brightling/Geoff Brightling © Dorling Kindersley; B. Getty Images Inc. - Hulton Archive Photos; D. Peter Anderson/Peter Anderson © Dorling Kindersley; **Page 351:** E. Lynton Gardiner/Lynton Gardiner © Dorling Kindersley, Courtesy of The American Museum of Natural History; F. © Christie's Images Inc. 2004; G. Alfred Jacob Miller, "The Interior of Fort Laramie," 1858-60. The Walters Art Museum, Baltimore; H. Nathaniel Currier, "General Winfield Scott at the Siege of Vera Cruz, March 1847," 1847. Lithograph. The Granger Collection; I. Frank Marryat, "The Bar of a Gambling Saloon," published 1855. Lithograph. Collection of The New-York Historical Society, New York City; **Page 359:** Scotts Bluff National Monument; **Page 361:** "Fort Vancouver," artist unknown, ca. 1845–1848. Paul Kane Collection. WA MSS 278. Yale Collection of Western Americana, Beinecke Rare Book and Manuscript Library; **Page 362:** Smithsonian American Art Museum, Washington, D.C./Art Resource, NY; **Page 366:** Courtesy of the Library of Congress; **Page 371:** Courtesy of the California History Room, California State Library, Sacramento, California; **Page 374:** The Granger Collection, New York.

Chapter 15 Image Key: **Page 378:** A. © CORBIS; B. Courtesy of the Library of Congress; C. © CORBIS; **Page 379:** D. Bettmann/© Bettmann/CORBIS; E. Bettmann/© Bettmann/CORBIS; F. Abraham Lincoln Presidential Library & Museum (ALPLM); G. The Granger Collection, New York; H. Getty Images, Inc. - Photodisc; **Page 383:** © Bettmann/CORBIS; **Page 386:** Getty Images Inc.-Hulton Archive Photos; **Page 387:** (left) Getty Images, Inc. - Liaison; (right) Courtesy of the Library of Congress; **Page 390:** The Granger Collection; **Page 392:** Getty Images Inc. - Hulton Archive Photos; **Page 393:** The Granger Collection; **Page 394:** © CORBIS; **Page 397:** The Granger Collection; **Page 399:** Getty Images Inc. - Hulton Archive Photos.

Chapter 16 Image Key: **Page 404:** A. United States Department of the Interior; B. National Archives and Records Administration; C. Dave King/Dave King/Dorling Kindersley © Confederate Memorial Hall,

New Orleans; **Page 405:** D. Dave King/Dave King/Dorling Kindersley © Confederate Memorial Hall, New Orleans; E. Dave King/Dave King/Dorling Kindersley © Confederate Memorial Hall, New Orleans; F. The Granger Collection, New York; G. William Washington, "Stonewall Jackson Entering the City of Winchester, Virginia." Oil painting. Valentine Museum Library, Richmond, Virginia; H. © CORBIS; I. Getty Images Inc. - Hulton Archive Photos; J. The New-York Historical Society; **Page 407:** The Granger Collection, New York; **Page 410:** Corbis/Bettmann; **Page 413:** Library of Congress; **Page 414:** Courtesy of the Library of Congress. J. B. Elliott, Cincinnati, 1861; **Page 421:** Center of Military History, U.S. Army; **Page 426:** Culver Pictures, Inc.; **Page 427:** Courtesy of the Library of Congress.

Chapter 17 Image Key: **Page 432:** A. Library of Congress/Courtesy of the Library of Congress; B. Library of Congress/Courtesy of the Library of Congress; D. © CORBIS; E. Musselman Library/Courtesy of Special Collections, Musselman Library, Gettysburg College, Gettysburg, PA; **Page 433:** F. Thomas C. Roche/Courtesy of the Library of Congress; G. The Granger Collection, New York; H. Library of Congress; I. The Picture Bank, Frank & Marie Therese Wood Print Collection; **Page 435:** The Granger Collection, New York; **Page 436:** Corbis/Bettmann; **Page 438:** Library of Congress; Courtesy of the Library of Congress; **Page 441:** Courtesy of Schlesinger Library, Radcliffe Institute, Harvard University; **Page 444:** The Granger Collection, New York; **Page 445:** The Granger Collection, New York. **Page 447:** (bottom left) Library of Congress; (top right) Courtesy of the Library of Congress; **Page 449:** (left) From The Henry Clay Warmoth Papers #752, Southern Historical Collection, Wilson Library, University of North Carolina at Chapel Hill; (right) Rutherford B. Hayes Presidential Center; **Page 454:** The Denver Public Library, Western History Collection, Photographer J. B. Silvis, Call Number X-22221. **Page 456:** The Picture Bank, Frank & Marie Therese Wood Print Collection; **Page 462:** Collection of The New-York Historical Society, [negative and/or accession number]; **Page 463:** (top) John Vachon/Courtesy of the Library of Congress; (bottom) Dorothea Lange/Library of Congress.

Chapter 18 Image Key: **Page 464:** A. Lynton Gardiner/Lynton Gardiner © Dorling Kindersley, Courtesy of The American Museum of Natural History; B. The Granger Collection, New York; C. Dave King/Dave King/Dorling Kindersley © Confederate Memorial Hall, New Orleans; **Page 465:** D. © Dorling Kindersley; E. © Judith Miller/Dorling Kindersley/Cowan's Historic Americana Auctions; F. Chinese mining laborers, Idaho, 76-119.2/A, Idaho State Historical Society; G. Library of Congress; H. Nebraska State Historical Society, Solomon D. Butcher Collection; I. Library of Congress; **Page 471:** National Anthropological Archives, Smithsonian Institution (3238E); **Page 474:** Jackson, William Henry. American (1843–1942) John, The Cook, baking slapjacks. 1874. Albumen print 9.7 × 8.8 cm. Museum purchase 74:0041:0212; **Page 479:** The Granger Collection; **Page 478:** Denver Public Library; **Page 481:** Nebraska State Historical Society, Solomon D. Butcher Collection; **Page 483:** Library of Congress; **Page 487:** Courtesy of the Library of Congress; **Page 490:** Granger/The Granger Collection.

Chapter 19 Image Key: **Page 498:** A. © Rykoff Collection/CORBIS; B. Lewis W. Hine/George Eastman House; **Page 499:** C. © Schenectady Museum; Hall of Electrical/CORBIS; D. "The Two Philanthropists." Color lithograph by J. Keppler from "Puck," February 23, 1881, neg. #48872. Collection of The New-York Historical Society, New York City; E. The Granger Collection, New York; F. U.S. Department of the Interior, National Park Service, Edison National Historic Site; G. Mark Rykoff/© Rykoff Collection/CORBIS; **Page 503:** Andrew Leyerle © Dorling Kindersley. Courtesy of Marshall Field and Company; **Page 505:** Courtesy of the Library of Congress; **Page 506:** The Granger Collection, New York; **Page 507:** North Wind Picture Archives; **Page 508:** © Bettmann/CORBIS. **Page 510:** Cook Collection, Valentine Richmond History Center; **Page 514:** "The Bowery at Night," 1885. Watercolor. Museum of the City of New York; **Page 516:** Courtesy of the Library of

Congress; **Page 517:** The Granger Collection; **Page 520:** The Granger Collection, New York; **Page 521:** Courtesy of the Library of Congress.

Chapter 20 Image Key: **Page 524:** A. Picture Research Consultants/Picture Research Consultants & Archives; B. Courtesy of the Library of Congress; C. ICHi-08428; Destruction of the battleship Maine in Havana harbor; in the Spanish-American war; Havana (Cuba) 1898 Feb. 15; Creator-Kurz & Allison/Chicago Historical Society; D. © Bettmann/CORBIS; E. © Bettmann/CORBIS; **Page 525:** F. © Bettmann/CORBIS; G. The Granger Collection, New York; H. Library of Congress; I. Courtesy of the Library of Congress; J. Culver Pictures; K. By permission of the Houghton Library, Harvard University; L. The Granger Collection, New York; **Page 524:** M. © Bettmann/CORBIS; **Page 525:** N. Courtesy of the Library of Congress; **Page 529:** The Granger Collection, New York; **Page 530:** Library of Congress; **Page 533:** The Granger Collection, New York; **Page 534:** Courtesy of the Library of Congress; **Page 535:** Courtesy of the Library of Congress; **Page 536:** North Wind Picture Archives; **Page 539:** The Granger Collection, New York; **Page 543:** Courtesy of the Divinity School, Yale University; **Page 545:** North Wind Picture Archives; **Page 548:** The Granger Collection; **Page 550:** Library of Congress; **Page 554:** The Granger Collection, New York; **Page 555:** Courtesy of the Library of Congress.

Chapter 21 Image Key: **Page 556:** A. © Bettmann/CORBIS; B. Library of Congress; C. Corbis/Bettmann; **Page 557:** D. © Bettmann/CORBIS; E. Indiana Historical Society, A70; F. The original Paterson Pageant Program, on which this drawing appeared, is part of the collection of the American Labor Museum/Botto House National Landmark. The poster is a copy of the program cover; G. © Bettmann/CORBIS; H. The Granger Collection, New York; **Page 561:** The Jacob A. Riis Collection 157, Museum of the City of New York; **Page 563:** Wallace Kirkland/Time Life Pictures/Getty Images/Time Life Pictures; **Page 565:** Daniel J. Czitrom; **Page 571:** The Granger Collection, New York; **Page 574:** UPI/Corbis/Bettmann; **Page 577:** The original Paterson Pageant Program, on which this drawing appeared, is part of the collection of the American Labor Museum/Botto House National Landmark. The poster is a copy of the program cover. **Page 578:** CORBIS-NY; **Page 582:** The Granger Collection, New York. **Page 584:** Theodore Roosevelt Collection, Harvard College Library.

Chapter 22 Image Key: **Page 590:** A. © Bettmann/CORBIS; B. Getty Images Inc. - Hulton Archive Photos; C. Bettmann/© Bettmann/CORBIS; **Page 591:** D. Richard Ward © Dorling Kindersley; E. The Granger Collection; F. Library of Congress; G. The Granger Collection, New York; H. National Archives and Records Administration; I. The Granger Collection, New York; **Page 594:** The Granger Collection; **Page 597:** The Granger Collection, New York; **Page 600:** Courtesy of the Library of Congress; **Page 602:** Getty Images Inc.-Hulton Archive Photos; **Page 603:** (bottom left) © CORBIS All Rights Reserved; (bottom right) Courtesy of the Library of Congress; (top center) Courtesy of the Library of Congress; **Page 607:** Russ Lappa/Prentice Hall School Division; **Page 609:** National Archives and Records Administration; **Page 612:** © Harris & Ewing, Inc./CORBIS All Rights Reserved; **Page 615:** © Stock Montage.

Chapter 23 Image Key: **Page 622:** A. Getty Images Inc. - Hulton Archive Photos; B. Swim Ink/© Swim Ink/CORBIS; C. EyeWire Collection/Getty Images - Photodisc; **Page 623:** D. C Squared Studios/Getty Images, Inc. - Photodisc; E. Wisconsin Historical Society/WHi-5020; F. By permission of Campbell Soup Company; G. Courtesy W. A. Swift Photograph Collection, Archives and Special Collections, Ball State University; H. Courtesy W. A. Swift Photograph Collection, Archives and Special Collections, Ball State University; **Page 627:** A&P Food Stores LTD; **Page 628:** Brown Brothers; **Page 629:** Ford Motor Company; **Page 637:** (left) Picture Desk, Inc./Kobal Collection; (middle) Everett Collection; (right) Everett Collection; **Page 639:** National Baseball Hall of Fame Library, Cooperstown, N.Y.; **Page 640:** Corbis/Bettmann; **Page 641:** Corbis/Bettmann;